PSYCHOLOGY AND ITS CITIES

Within the social and political upheaval of American cities in the decades surrounding the turn of the 20th century, a new scientific discipline, psychology, strove to carve out a place for itself. In this new history of early American psychology, Christopher D. Green highlights the urban contexts in which much of early American psychology developed and tells the stories of well-known early psychologists, including William James, G. Stanley Hall, John Dewey, and James McKeen Cattell, detailing how early psychologists attempted to alleviate the turmoil around them. American psychologists sought out the daunting intellectual, emotional, and social challenges that were threatening to destabilize the nation's burgeoning urban areas and proposed novel solutions, sometimes to positive and sometimes to negative effect. Their contributions helped develop our modern ideas about the mind, person, and society. This book is ideal for scholars and students interested in the history of psychology.

Christopher D. Green is Professor of Psychology, York University, Canada. He is former President of the Society for the History of Psychology and former editor of the *Journal of the History of the Behavioral Sciences*.

PSYCHOLOGY AND ITS CITIES

A New History of Early American Psychology

Christopher D. Green

Routledge
Taylor & Francis Group

NEW YORK AND LONDON

First published 2019
by Routledge
711 Third Avenue, New York, NY 10017

and by Routledge
2 Park Square, Milton Park, Abingdon, Oxon, OX14 4RN

Routledge is an imprint of the Taylor & Francis Group, an informa business

© 2019 Taylor & Francis

Library of Congress Cataloging-in-Publication Data
Names: Green, Christopher D., author.
Title: Psychology and its cities : a new history of early American
   psychology / Christopher D. Green.
Description: New York, NY : Routledge, 2018. | Includes bibliographical
   references.
Identifiers: LCCN 2018008802 | ISBN 9781138059429 (hardback : alk.
   paper) | ISBN 9781138059436 (pbk. : alk. paper) | ISBN 9781315163581
   (ebook)
Subjects: LCSH: Psychology—United States—History.
Classification: LCC BF108.U5 G74 2018 | DDC 150.973—dc23
LC record available at https://lccn.loc.gov/2018008802

ISBN: 978-1-138-05942-9 (hbk)
ISBN: 978-1-138-05943-6 (pbk)
ISBN: 978-1-315-16358-1 (ebk)

Typeset in Bembo
by Apex CoVantage, LLC

I have had some terrific teachers over the years. I dedicate this book to my formal supervisors and my informal mentors: Anton De Man and Stuart McKelvie of Bishop's University; Bernie Lyman of Simon Fraser University; John Kennedy, André Kukla, and Doug Creelman of the University of Toronto; Ray Fancher of York University; Andrew Winston of the University of Guelph; Ludy Benjamin of Texas A&M University; and Michael Sokal of Worcester Polytechnic Institute. I would never have made it this far into the academic life without their wisdom, support, and assistance.

BRIEF CONTENTS

CONTENTS

ACKNOWLEDGEMENTS

History of psychology is a remarkable collegial area of academia. Virtually everyone I know is positively happy to share their expertise for the mere asking. I cannot adequately express my gratitude to all of the people who generously assisted me when I came calling with my questions. I name as many as I can below. I beg the forgiveness of anyone I may have accidentally left out. I could not have done it without you.

Bilal Afsin, York University, ON, Canada
David Baker, Cummings Center for the History of Psychology, University of Akron, OH, USA
Nicole Barenbaum, University of the South, TN, USA
Lizzette Royer Barton, Cummings Center for the History of Psychology, University of Akron, OH, USA
Jennifer Bazar, York University, ON, Canada
Ludy T. Benjamin, Jr., Texas A&M University, TX, USA
Jeremy Blatter, Harvard University, MA, USA
Geoffrey Blowers, University of Hong Kong, PRC
Jeremy Burman, York University, ON, Canada
James Capshew, Indiana University, IN, USA
John Carson, University of Michigan, MI, USA
Eric Charles, American University, Washington, DC, USA
Ian Davidson, York University, ON, Canada
Elaine D. Engst, Cornell University Archives, NY, USA
Rand Evans, University of East Carolina, NC, USA
Raymond Fancher, York University, ON, USA
Ingrid Farreras, Hood College, MD, USA
Cathy Faye, Center for the History of Psychology, University of Akron, OH, USA

Alfred Fuchs, Bowdoin College, ME, USA
Julia Gardner, Special Collection Center, University of Chicago, IL, USA
Kevin Gruenfeld, Philadelphia, PA, USA
Dan Hanlon, American Psychological Association Archives, Washington, DC, USA
Tyler Hnatuk, York University, ON, Canada
John Hogan, St. John's University, NY, USA
Amy James, Baltimore City Archives, MD, USA
Ann Johnson, University of St. Thomas, MN, USA
Deborah Johnson, University of Southern Maine, ME, USA
Patrick Kerwin, Library of Congress, Washington, DC, USA
Russell Kosits, Redeemer College, ON, Canada
Susan Lamb, McGill University, QC, Canada
David Leary, University of Richmond, VA, USA
Donald Lesure, Ashfield Museum, MA, USA
Helmet Lück, Fern University, Hagen, Germany
Katharine Milar, Earlham College, IN, USA
Susannah Mulvale, York University, ON, Canada
Michael Palij, New York University, NY, USA
James Pate, Georgia State University, GA, USA
Trevor Pearce, University of North Carolina, Charlotte, NC, USA
Michael Pettit, York University, ON, Canada
Alexandra Rutherford, York University, ON, Canada
Elizabeth Scarborough, Indiana University, South Bend, IN, USA
Laura Shieb, Rauner Special Collections Library, Dartmouth College, NH, USA
Douglas Skeen, Enoch Pratt Free Library, Baltimore, MD, USA
Michael Sokal, Worcester Polytechnic Institute, MA, USA
Lothar Spillman, University of Freiburg, Germany
Jordan Steele, Johns Hopkins University Archives, MD, USA
Jim Stimpert, Johns Hopkins University Archives, MD, USA
Damon Talbot, Maryland Historical Society, MD, USA
Adam Taves, York University, ON, Canada
Eugene Taylor, Harvard and Saybrook Universities, MA, USA
Thomas Teo, York University, ON, Canada
Roger Thomas, University of Georgia, GA, USA
Dejan Todorovic, University of Belgrade, Serbia
Elizabeth Valentine, Royal Holloway, University of London, UK
Hendrika Vande Kemp, Annandale, VA, USA
Kelli Vaughn-Johnson, York University, ON, Canada
Fordyce Williams, Clark University Archives, MA, USA
Andrew S. Winston, University of Guelph, ON, Canada
Robert Wozniak, Bryn Mawr College, PA, USA
Jacy Young, York University, ON, Canada

INTRODUCTION

Cities are the engines of innovation in modern society. Although raw materials and innovative ideas may come from the countryside, it is mainly in cities—with their concentration of capital, their intensive industry, and their abundance of talent—that the great transformations of society are wrought.

This is not merely the prejudice of hindsight, from an era in which cities not only dominate the economy but also hold the bulk of the population. As one writer at the turn of the 20th century put it:

> The city is the spectroscope of society; it analyses and shifts the population, separating and classifying the diverse elements. The entire progress of civilization is a process of differentiation, and the city is the greatest differentiator. The mediocrity of the country is transformed by the city into the highest talent or the lowest criminal. Genius is often born in the country, but it is brought to light and developed by the city [just as] the boy thief of the village becomes the daring bank robber of the metropolis.[1]

Even at the time of the country's birth, when cities claimed a relatively modest hold over the nation's population and economy, the bitter debate between Thomas Jefferson and Alexander Hamilton could be seen as a nostalgic vision of a nation of yeoman farmers set against a more forward-looking view of the leading roles that urban capital, labor, and industry would play in the most successful countries of the 19th century. From one vantage point, the Civil War was a conflict over the terrible lengths to which a rural agrarian society must go in order to compete even tolerably well with a modern industrial and, ultimately, urban one. Even then, it is a competition that is not sustainable over the long term.

These generalizations were as true for the intellectual world as they were for industrial. Anyone might have a novel thought anywhere, but it is in the cauldron of the city that new ideas are best supported, challenged, tested, improved, and pitted against competing visions. Cities drive those who might otherwise indulge in comfortable convention to question, doubt, reject, rethink, rework, and start anew.

Psychology was no exception to these dynamics. American psychology was born and grew to maturity in the midst of some of the most troubled times the nation has ever experienced. The country was still absorbing the cataclysmic effects of the Civil War—over 600,000 killed in a country of just over 30 million. Then came the failed attempt at reconciliation between the regions that had been such bitter opponents—the Reconstruction—in which widespread corruption undermined whatever small chance there had been of reintegrating Southerners into the country they had fought so desperately to escape.

How the nearly four million recently freed slaves would be integrated into a free society—what land they would own, what jobs they would hold, what homes they would have, what schools they would attend, what enterprises they would lead, what political power they would attain—were by no means settled questions. Many former slaves remained in the South to farm—the only life most had ever known. Early promises of "40 acres and a mule" were rescinded during Reconstruction, and Black farmers were mostly forced into sharecropping: working land owned by White landholders, retaining only a portion of their harvest (often less than half) to pay off their farming debts and to support their families. It was often a miserable, virtually feudal existence. In search of a better fate, many other freed slaves fled to Northern cities to find a new way of life far from the sites of their old bondage. There they found sprawling, congested cities seemingly full of new opportunities, but also teeming with masses of impoverished immigrants who had arrived before the war, and with whom they now had to compete, sometimes bitterly, for poorly paid, precarious, and sometimes dangerous jobs in manufacturing, construction, transportation, and domestic service. As a result, racial tensions, rather than being resolved by the war, continued to run high, in both North and South.

As if the intense racial conflict that beset America wasn't enough to contend with, by the mid-1870s the effects of rapid industrialization, which had been accelerated by the war, began to tear even further at the fabric of the nation. Enormous fortunes, never before been seen in the Republic, were accumulated by industrialists like Cornelius Vanderbilt, Andrew Carnegie, and John D. Rockefeller. Governments were uncertain whether they should regulate and restrain such avaricious companies as they increasingly sought total control over their domains and, if so, how they might actually manage to do so. Capital was growing more powerful than even government. Periodic economic "panics" and "crashes" added to the uncertainty, leading large swaths of the population to feel that they had become mere pawns in a game played by tycoons. None of the traditional virtues they had been taught would lead to a good life—honesty, thrift, hard work—seemed now to have much impact on their ultimate fate.

Indeed, the question of the relation between capital and labor was brought to a head in 1877, when the first of what would be several violent railway strikes spread from the east coast to a number of the nation's cities. The chaos lasted for weeks. Protesters burned company buildings to the ground. Police and private security shot protesters. Strikers retaliated with whatever weapons they had. About a hundred people were killed, hundreds more were wounded, and millions of dollars in property was destroyed. A population that had, just a little over a decade before, lived through a catastrophic Civil War over slavery now began to fear that that a second civil war was at hand, this one over the increasing power of capital and the role of labor in the economy, in government, and in society at large.

It was on this anvil of uncertainty that a few young men began to explore a new "scientific" way of examining human thought, feeling, and conduct at a few of the country's more progressive colleges. Science itself was a relative newcomer to American higher education. Many schools still disdained it as being intellectually inferior to the classics, philosophy, and denominational theology that dominated most curricula at the time. A speculative form of "psychology" sometimes made an appearance in those lessons—often under the traditional English titles of "mental philosophy" or "mental science"—but the idea of psychology being pursued as an empirical scientific endeavor struck many as misguided, bizarre or plain impossible.[2] The mind, it was obvious to most, had a divine origin, not a natural one, and its thoughts were guided, at least ideally, by the eternal principles of logic, not by the kind of natural laws that governed mere matter. Feeling, even more so, lay entirely outside of the brute realm of nature.

Nevertheless, a few schools—Harvard, most notably—began to teach a form of "experimental" psychology that was then being developed in Germany by a few physiologists. The Americans, though, combined this German "physiological psychology" with Charles Darwin's radical new theory of evolution by natural selection, which had recently come to the US. In addition, a new form of higher education—advanced research-based training for students who had already earned their undergraduate degrees—began to appear not only in some of the older schools, like Harvard, but also in a few entirely new universities. Johns Hopkins in Baltimore was the first of these, soon to be followed by Clark University in Worcester, and a little later, the University of Chicago. Laboratories—the very icon of this "new psychology," as it was sometimes called—soon began popping up in schools across the country. The names of many of those who founded the early laboratories are familiar to anyone who has looked at American psychology's history: William James, G. Stanley Hall, James McKeen Cattell, Joseph Jastrow, Edmund C. Sanford, J. Mark Baldwin, etc.

Strangely, however, this well-known story of the development of the "new psychology" in America has rarely been connected to the context of immense urban upheaval in which it took place. It is as though the intellectual development was sealed off from socioeconomic and political conditions in which it arose. Yet, many of the founders and early builders of American psychology taught at colleges and universities situated in the very cities where the turmoil was most intense: New York, Boston, Baltimore, and especially Chicago. The original reason for this odd state of affairs is simple enough to trace: when psychologists started writing about the history of their field—as with the medical history written in the same era—the primary goal was to celebrate the "heroes" and the intellectual achievements of the (still relatively new) discipline. Edwin Boring's 1929 classic textbook, *A History of Experimental Psychology*, was aimed at establishing that scientific psychology was already an academic institution worthy of celebrating in so ostentatious a way.[3] For these writers, the biographical and the intellectual took precedence over the socioeconomic and the political. Psychology came into existence through the leadership of a few "great men" (and sometimes the pull of a vague "Frontier" or the push of an even vaguer "*Zeitgeist*"). It was not seen as importantly connected to the "great events" then unfolding outside the college walls. Indeed, these events were, if anything, a distraction to the "deep thoughts" unfolding within. Psychology was driven forward by the genius of its leaders and by its own inexorable momentum.

Surely, Boring would have said, the destitute immigrants, former slaves, lowly laborers, and their uneducated children had contributed little to this latest achievement of the Western intellectual tradition. Even the industrial titans of the age had contributed only the lucre that was required to build and operate the universities. Grateful as we might be for their generosity, the credit for having actually created the new psychology lay with a different sort of people: the scholars, scientists, and other intellectuals. Other historical accounts of psychology were written at about the same time as Boring's, each with its own separate intellectual agenda, but the idea that psychology was autonomous—both from other disciplines and from "outside" events—was mostly an unquestioned underlying assumption.[4]

By the 1970s and 1980s, many writers of the history of psychology had started to become more sophisticated in their historiographic practices. They gradually recognized, as historians of many other domains already had, the impact that "external" events had exerted on the course of psychology's development, and they increasingly included these insights in their writings. By that time, though, there were decades more of psychological history to study, and the events of the founding decades had been "covered" so thoroughly that most historians moved on to newer and more fertile ground, the better to explore the whole of the discipline's past and to display their own scholarly originality.

New biographies of American psychology's "founders" were written with some of the newer historiographic sensibilities in mind—many of William James and John Dewey, of course, along with important new contributions to the understanding of Hall, Cattell, Thorndike, and others. But there were few attempts to re-examine the early decades of American psychology within the urban contexts where it first came into being.

That is the aim of this book: to understand the rapid development of American psychology from academic novelty to popular industry as an effect of the colossal urban upheaval in which it appeared. My original plan was to discover how the psychologies of various major metropolises—New York, Boston, Baltimore, Chicago—had differed from each other in their responses to major events that had occurred in each of those places. What I soon found, however, was that they had all faced essentially the same set of crises: a population explosion caused by massive and continuous immigration, an inability (and sometimes unwillingness) to create and maintain public services that were adequate to serve the needs of the ever-growing, diversifying citizenry. These included, of course, housing, water, policing, transportation, communication, and eventually electrical power. Most difficult and contentious of all, though, was the effort to create a universal education system that would produce the sophisticated kinds of adults who could successfully navigate through and thrive in the increasingly intricate urban environment. And all of this had to be done while nearly every major industry was undergoing the most rapid, most revolutionary technological transformations the world had ever seen. It was, in retrospect, a virtually impossible balancing act and, as we shall see, often enough American cities failed to negotiate it successfully. The results of those failures were often fatal for citizens and for the police, and occasionally even for the politicians who led them.

There were different "flavors" to the ways in which various cities handled this suite of challenges, but the suite itself was more or less common to all. So, the theme of this book, rather than focusing on how psychologists in different cities dealt with their different local problems, became how the challenges posed in nearly every city in America in the decades surrounding the turn of the 20th century affected the development of psychology across the country. It is important to note at the outset that not all of the most influential psychologists lived in major cities at the time because not all colleges and universities were located in large urban areas. Columbia, for instance, was in tumult of New York City, and Johns Hopkins was in midst of busy Baltimore. University of Chicago, from its start, had to deal with the trials of being in that ever-fractious metropolis. By contrast, though, Yale, Princeton, and Cornell were more or less removed from the mounting urban anxieties, nestled in towns that had grown up around them. As we shall see, the style of psychology that tended to take root in urban institutions, even when the psychologists themselves refused to reside in the city, often had a somewhat different character than the psychology developed at schools in more pastoral settings. Different factors seem to have been at play. Harvard had, perhaps, the most interesting position of all, being separated from Boston by not much more than the Charles River. Nevertheless, life in cozy, clubby Cambridge always seemed more socially and spiritually removed from the metropolis than it was geographically.

Because of the importance that cities play in my story, I treat them more or less as characters in their own rights, alongside of the human figures. Cities have their own births, their own upbringings, so to speak, and those histories have had an impact on the ways in which they have responded to threats, opportunities, crises, and successes. Their geography has affected their development—ocean harbor, river port, rail hub, etc. They have had long-standing relationships with their neighbors—New York with Boston, Chicago with St. Louis, Baltimore with Washington, DC—which have also played a role in the characters they have developed. In short, they have "personalities" and, if I have written more than the reader expects about the histories of the cities featured in my narrative, I did so in order to reveal more about their personalities and how they interacted with the human characters who lived and worked within them.

In order to introduce the context in which psychology arose, I begin my story long before the discipline itself took root. I start with a sensational case of (apparent) murder that was riling the residents of New York City, where William James was born in 1842. In Chapter 1, I follow the James family and the New York in which they lived until they permanently left the city, in the wake of a huge wave of immigration from Ireland and Germany, when William was 13 years of age.

In Chapter 2, I trace the early life of G. Stanley Hall, beginning with his birth in the farmland of western Massachusetts in 1844. I follow his separate discovery of New York City as a graduate student in the late 1860s, then on into Germany, and finally to his first teaching position in Ohio in the 1870s. Chapter 3 picks up the trail of the James family again, returning to the US from a sojourn in Europe, and settling in Newport, Rhode Island. Teenaged William oscillated between art and science as possible vocations. As the Civil War broke out, William's father bought him out of the draft, and he enrolled in the science school at Harvard. Dissatisfied, he soon switched to medicine. The family was not spared the horrors of the war though; one of William's younger brothers was grievously wounded and recuperated over a period of months in the family home. William traveled widely, joining a naturalist expedition to Brazil in 1865, and taking regular jaunts to Europe to discover his "true" vocation. Despite his privileged life, in the late 1860s he fell into a terrible melancholy from which he would not completely recover for several years. The agonizing experience would mark his work in various ways for decades to come.

Chapter 4 focuses on the meeting of James and Hall at Harvard in 1876. There is a sense in which their work and their experiences, together and separate, set the stage for psychology in America. Hall earned a PhD in a kind of physiological-philosophical psychology under James' nominal supervision but, in reality, they discovered the topic together. It was during this period that the first great railway strike broke out in America, bringing with it mass violence the likes of which had rarely before seen. James and Hall were not directly affected, but all of America was put on notice that things would not continue on in the future as they had in the past. What form they would take exactly was by no means clear, but the social, political, and economic life of the country was undergoing some kind of profound transformation. Hall would leave the country for a time to work in the great physiology laboratories of Germany, and in Wilhelm Wundt's brand new psychology laboratory in Leipzig.

Chapter 5 sees Hall return home to America to find few academic openings for a person with his unconventional kinds of expertise. Pedagogy, however—a topic he had more or less picked up "on the side" while in Europe—found a ready audience in cities like Boston and Baltimore, which were struggling to create universal public school systems. Hall's public lectures on what he called "Child Study" turned him into an overnight sensation in educational circles. He was soon offered a professorship at the recently opened Johns Hopkins. It was here he created his first laboratory, and launched the nation's first experimental psychology journal. Soon he was offered an even more remarkable position, though: the founding presidency of a new university in Worcester, Massachusetts called Clark.

The scene in Chapters 6 and 7 shifts to Chicago, which was then both a very young and an immensely vast city (founded in 1833, the second-largest city in the US by 1890). It was raw and crude but revolutionary in its capacity to overthrow old industrial systems for new ones. It was also ever balanced on the edge of political chaos and mass violence. If the dreaded second civil war was going to come, it would probably start here, and nearly everyone knew it. Another new university, this one created from small portion of the vast fortune of John D. Rockefeller, had opened there in 1892, and its administrators were searching for a philosophy professor. They somewhat reluctantly chose a rather obscure man then at the University of Michigan named John Dewey. With his move to Chicago, Dewey became increasingly captured by the seemingly intractable problems of modern urban life and, rather than defensively burying himself in the academy, he decided to make the entire city his classroom. He taught philosophy to impoverished immigrant laborers at Jane Addams' famous settlement house. He gradually developed an entirely new approach to schooling, premised on the idea that it is far more important, in the modern world, to help children learn to cooperate with people of different backgrounds and attitudes than it is to teach them ancient Biblical passages and arcane mathematical puzzles.

At the same time, Dewey and his younger colleagues revolutionized important aspects of psychology, arguing that the fundamental idea of the "reflex" is not essentially physiological in nature, as has been assumed since the time of Descartes, but is, instead, a kind of practical fiction. "Stimulus" and "response" are not physical but, rather, "function factors."[5] It does not matter that one has not traced the underlying neurology of a particular response to a given stimulus. What matters is that we understand what roles those terms play in advancing (and constraining) our comprehension of the situation. Some 650 miles to east, at Cornell, psychologist Edward Bradford Titchener objected strenuously: one must understand the fundamental "structures" of psychology—pure sensations, images, and feelings—before one can even begin to understand their functions. To do as Dewey suggested would be like trying to study the physiology of an organism before one knew the basic arrangement of its body parts. Thus opened a major fault line in American psychology—that between the cautious, abstract, immaculate musings of Titchener, sequestered in the relative wilderness of central New York state—and the ready, immediate, practical approach of Dewey, caught in the pressing, menacing metropolis of Chicago.

Chapter 8 returns to New York and Boston in the 1890s. The country was then deep in the throes of a second colossal wave of immigration, this time mostly from eastern and southern Europe—Poles, Russians, Jews, Italians, and Greeks. As before, when the Irish and Germans came in the 1850s, every municipal system was stressed beyond capacity. Moral panic spread as established American communities braced themselves against the influx of often-destitute newcomers. James McKeen Cattell, having earned a doctorate in Leipzig and briefly held a psychology professorship in his native Pennsylvania, arrived to take up a new post at Columbia University. He brought with him a new psychological tool: the "mental test." He did not recognize it himself, but he was carrying the seeds of a new technology that would ultimately prove invaluable to the public schools systems of America. Although his particular form of the test failed, Cattell became what might be termed the leading "manager" of psychology, and of other sciences as well. He founded, owned, and edited many journals; he served on the executive committees of multiple scientific societies; he created a company to publish books and tests and various other psychological products. Cattell became a kind of scientific entrepreneur, in the original sense; he was a go-between who greased the gears of the great scientific "machine" that was gradually being assembled in America. He became quite wealthy doing it, too.

Meanwhile, back at Harvard, William James published his long-awaited textbook, *Principles of Psychology* in 1890. Then he gradually rose to become one of America's leading public intellectuals. He gave many public lectures. His philosophical writings were couched in a style that was accessible, even enjoyable, to a wide array of readers. He wrote on topics that interested many—e.g., religion, spiritualism, humanity's place in the universe. As academic journals grew in both number and abstruseness, James continued to write for a range of high-brow popular magazines. He recognized, however, that for Harvard to remain a leader in the new psychology, it had to have a top-flight laboratory, and he also saw that he personally had neither the time nor the interest to do it correctly. So he brought in a rising star from Germany to restore Harvard's prestige in the topic: Hugo Münsterberg. Münsterberg would court controversy nearly everywhere he went, but he would soon become one of the most visible psychologists on the American scene.

Although the "new" psychologists up to this time had been intent on establishing the discipline's scientific credentials, in ever-pragmatic America, there had always been lurking in the background the sense that psychology had something wider to offer the nation; services that not only schools, but also businesses, industries, governments, courts, hospitals, even the general public might be willing to pay for if only some psychologist could figure out what it was and how to provide it. Accordingly, Chapter 9 describes the early rise of applied psychology: 1) The development of psychotherapy in Boston out of a curious alliance between medical neurologists and church ministers (and, of course, William James); 2) The arrival of psychoanalysis in the US when Hall invited both Sigmund Freud and Carl Jung to give a series of lectures at his Clark University in Worcester; 3) The development, in Philadelphia, of a new kind of "clinic" specialized in diagnosing and treating the peculiar learning difficulties presented by some students in the burgeoning public school system; 4) The elaboration, by Hall, of a newly recognized stage of human development—"adolescence"—which required special consideration by those who were advancing the new idea of universal public high school in America's cities; 5) The rise to prominence of a number of female psychological researchers who began to successfully challenge, through scientific research, many of the traditional myths and fabrications that had long been used to justify the subjugation of women; and 6) The effort, especially by Münsterberg, to insert psychological understanding into the process of criminal justice. Finally, Chapter 9 examines William James' final philosophical explorations, in which he questioned the validity of psychology's central concept, consciousness, and sought to replace it with a non-dualistic alternative that he called "experience."

One early reviewer remarked that, beginning in Chapter 9, the book seemed to take on the character of multiple short stories instead of a single coherent narrative. I think that is, in part, because psychology itself split along many different paths at about that time. It was not coherent as a discipline. It developed a kind of "ragged" character as psychologists struck out many different directions, testing the old boundaries, looking for new professional opportunities, seeing what work the still-young discipline could do in the increasingly complex and fractious world around them.

In the final chapter we see psychology, over the first two decades of the 20th century, gradually change from a discipline that had been more or less defined by the individual research projects of professors at their several schools into a more collective, corporate, and national project. A number of individuals—notably Frank and Lillian Gilbreth, Walter Dill Scott, Harry Hollingworth, and Walter Binghman—began to market their psychological expertise to business and industry for the purposes of increasing efficiency, improving personnel selection, and enhancing the effectiveness of advertising. Psychological "consulting," thus, became a new way in which a person could make a living, if one could attract enough paying clients. We also see, here, that the never-ending growth of public education continued to outstrip the resources that cities could devote to it. William Wirt, a disciple of Dewey, developed a system to make the more elaborate equipment and other resources required by modern educational available to more students by rotating them through different specialized spaces over the course of the school day. Wirt's system—known as the Gary Plan—became a political football in the most massive school system of them all—New York, and the conflict resulted in weeks of rioting that ultimately brought down the city's mayor.

This was also the era in which Alfred Binet's intelligence test was brought across the Atlantic by Henry Goddard and used to differentiate among different categories of "feeble-minded" children. Goddard became particularly concerned with those he labeled "morons"—people who appeared "normal" but who were subtly intellectually inferior and, as he and many others feared, might gradually undermine the entire American gene pool unless drastic measures were taken against them. On the other side of the continent, Lewis Terman would revise Binet's test to better suit the American context, and then begin a decades-long research project on children who were possessed of "gifted" intellectual abilities.

The second decade of the 20th century was also the time in which psychological research with animals gradually gained respectability. As though in answer to James' doubts about the validity of consciousness, animal researchers developed an approach in which mental states need not be imputed to animals at all, but their behavior could be understood entirely on the basis of the stimuli to which they had been previously exposed and the responses they had made. The program erupted on to the wider psychological scene when John B. Watson dubbed it "behaviorism" and declared it to be the only legitimate form of scientific psychology, whether one was studying "lower" animals or the "highest" animal of all—human beings.

Finally, World War I served to fundamentally change the character of psychology's disciplinary structure. The transformation began when Robert M. Yerkes, president of the American Psychological Association in 1917, energetically advanced a plan to conduct intelligence tests on every single man recruited into the US Army. Ostensibly, the test would determine which men were fit for service and, if so, what more complex duties they might be suited to. Yerkes brought psychologists into the program from all over the country, making it, in effect, the first truly national research project in American psychology's history. The resulting collection of data was massive by any measure: more than 1.7 million recruits were tested. Yerkes' rival at Northwestern, Walter Dill Scott, rejected Yerkes' exclusive focus on intelligence, though, embarking on a multifaceted testing program of his own in another branch of the army. Although the success of both endeavors was debated within the army itself, they both lent the very idea of psychological testing such widespread visibility and legitimacy that, by the 1920s, psychology was finally being recognized by the general public as a trustworthy source of scientific knowledge and authority.

It was here, in about 1920, in the wake of World War I, that a new era in the history of psychology began to open and, thus, that my account of American psychology's beginnings comes to an end.

Notes

1 Adna F. Webber, *The Growth of the Cities in the Nineteenth Century* (New York, NY: Mac-Millan, 1899), 442.

2 The word "psychology" (or its Latin cognate, *psychologia*, dates back to at least the 16th century, but it was popularized in German by the early 18th-century philosopher Christian Wolff. Wolff's distinction between "rational" and "empirical" psychology was picked up by Frenchmen Denis Diderot and Jean Le Rond d'Alembert in their landmark *Encyclopédie* of the late 18th century. Still, English philosophers rarely used the term until after 1860 (see Google Ngram). One of the most influential early users of the term in English was Herbert Spencer, who published the first volume of his *Principles of Psychology* in 1870.

3 Edwin G. Boring, *A History of Experimental Psychology* (New York, NY: Century, 1929).

4 e.g., Gardner Murphy, *Historical Introduction to Modern Psychology* (New York, NY: Harcourt, Brace, 1929); Walter B. Pillsbury, *The History of Psychology* (New York, NY: W. W. Norton, 1929); Edna Heidbredder, *Seven Psychologies* (New York, NY: Century, 1933). There had been earlier histories of psychology, but they had focused mainly on the philosophical precursors of the new form of the discipline: George Sidney Brett, *A History of Psychology*, 3 vols. (London, UK: Allen & Unwin, 1912–1921); James Mark Baldwin, *History of Psychology: A Sketch and an Interpretation*, 2 vols. (New York, NY: G. P. Putnam, 1913).

5 John Dewey, "The Reflex Arc Concept in Psychology," *Psychological Review* 3 (1896): 358.

1

NEW YORK CITY, BIRTHPLACE OF WILLIAM JAMES

1. New York City, 1842

Mary Cecilia Rogers did not return home the evening of Sunday, July 25, 1841. That morning, she had gone out for a walk. She left the home where she lived with her widowed mother, Phoebe, at 126 Nassau St.[1] It was in the lower east side of New York City, just a block south of City Hall Park (see Figure 1.1). She said that she would return that evening.[2] But she did not.

According to some initial reports, she was seen meeting a young man at Theater Alley, just a block west of her home. The two of them then headed toward Barclay St., the western end of which was known as the dock for the ferry to Hoboken, NJ. According to the report of her fiancé, Daniel C. Payne, however, she had arrived at the room he rented four blocks south of her home, at 47 Johns St., at about 10 a.m. She told him that she was to meet her cousin, a Mrs. Downing, who lived on Greenwich St.[3]

By Monday, some of Mary Rogers' friends arranged to have a notice of her disappearance placed in the Tuesday newspapers. It was on Wednesday that her body was discovered floating in the Hudson River just off of Castle Point in Hoboken, NJ (today the home of Stevens Institute of Technology). "It was evident," the nascent *New York Tribune* reported, "that she had been horribly outraged and murdered." The article went on to note that Miss Rogers "was a young woman of good character, and was soon to have been married to a worthy young man of this City."[4]

It was the *New York Herald* (then in its sixth year of publication), however, that took the lead in publicizing the story. On 4 August it declared:

> How utterly ridiculous is all this! It is not nearly a week since the dead body
> of this beautiful and unfortunate girl has been discovered, and yet no other

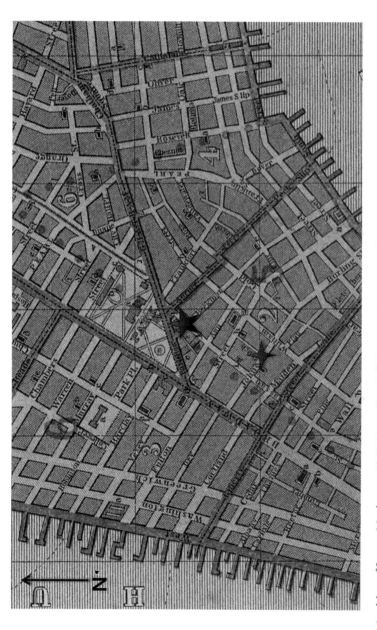

FIGURE 1.1 Map of Lower Manhattan, 1842. Note City Hall Park near the center of the image. Mary Rogers lived near the corner of Nassau and Beekman (5-pointed star). One report said she met a man at Theatre Alley (the narrow unlabeled street just above the star that runs from Beekman to Ann between Nassau and the park), and then the two of them crossed the southern tip of the Park (upwards on the map) to Barclay St., heading toward the Hoboken Ferry dock, another four blocks west. Her fiancé, Daniel Payne lived 3 blocks south and 1 block east, on John St. near Dutch St. (4-pointed star).

Credit: Image from Morse, Sidney E. & Breese, Samuel. *Morse's North American Atlas.* New York, NY: Harper & Brothers, 1845.

steps have been taken by the judicial authorities, than a brief and inefficient inquest by [Hoboken coroner] Gilbert Merritt. One of the most heartless and atrocious murders that was ever perpetrated in New York, is allowed to sleep the sleep of death—to be buried in the deep bosom of the Hudson.[5]

The newspapers made the story of Mary Rogers' murder a sensation for the people of New York. Until the 1830s, newspapers had been rather elite affairs with titles like the *Courier and Enquirer*, and the *Journal of Commerce*.[6] These publications had small circulations, typically less than 2,000, and they were aimed primarily at the business community: they covered mostly shipping, markets, and national political affairs. They also cost six cents a copy, which put them out of the reach of most working New Yorkers. A few politically radical workers' papers had come and gone, but they had not earned the loyalty of ordinary New Yorkers. Then, in September of 1833, a printer named Benjamin Day, who had worked on one of the radical papers, the *Daily Sentinel*, conceived and launched an entirely new kind of newspaper that focused on local news—especially scandal, crime, the police, and the courts. Following the example of the wildly successful *Penny Magazine* in the UK, he set the price of his new paper at one cent. He called it the *New York Sun*, which proclaimed on its front page: "It shines for all." Unlike the radical papers and the business sheets, the *Sun* did not take an official partisan stand. It did not reflexively denounce prominent members of the "opposing" party. Although the *Sun* tended Democratic, its stance was as defender of the city and its people. To circulate the new paper, Day had "newsboys," often drawn from the local orphanages, sell most of the papers on the streets of New York, offering them in bundles of 100 copies for 67¢. Any newsboy who sold all his papers would earn himself 33¢ a day.

The *Sun* was wildly successful. Within just a few months, it had the highest circulation in the city, at over 4,000. By 1835 its circulation was 15,000. Soon, others began to copy Day's formula. One of these was the *New York Herald*, launched in 1835 by a Scottish immigrant named James Gordon Bennett. Looking for a niche outside of the *Sun*'s sphere, the *Herald* was pitched at a slightly elevated tone. Unlike the *Sun*, the *Herald* included business news, though of a different cast than in the old commerce papers. It became known for its exposés of crookedness and incompetence among New York's mostly unregulated companies and markets. The paper also displayed Bennett's own anti-Catholic and anti-abolitionist streaks, tending toward support for the "Know-Nothings" politically, though it was not as extreme as they in its view of immigration (Bennett being an immigrant himself). When the market crash of 1837 threw many of the city's residents out of work, sometimes out of their homes, the *Herald* played to the crowd by running scolding accounts of the lavish parties that New York's rich were still throwing for themselves while the rest of the city suffered. The result was an organized boycott of the paper by the city's "high society" which damaged Bennett's *Herald*, but did not break it.[7]

The boycott did, however, open a niche in the city's journalistic ecology for a "respectable" Whig paper that focused on news of the city, but was rather more respectful of municipal powerbrokers. That niche was filled, from April of 1841, by Horace Greely's *New York Tribune*. The *Tribune* did not kowtow to the city's elites, but neither did it go out of its way to tweak them. It covered crime, but not in the salacious tones of the *Sun*.

The murder of Mary Rogers rapidly became a *cause célèbre* for New York's papers, especially for the *Herald*. For a woman just 21 years of age, Rogers was already well known in the city as the "beautiful cigar girl" (or 'segar' as some had it). She held a job at a fashionable tobacco shop, owned by one John Anderson, located on Broadway. It was a popular hangout of many Tammany Hall politicians and other Democratic Party figures (which may well have played a role in the Know-Nothing *Herald*'s decision to take the lead in demanding that more be done to find the killer). The proximity of Anderson's cigar shop to City Hall and to "Publisher's Row" made Rogers a familiar figure to many New York politicians and journalists.[8]

Nearly three years before Rogers' death, in October of 1838, she had become the object of city-wide attention when the *Sun* reported that she had disappeared from home, leaving a suicide note behind. Two weeks after her disappearance, however, another newspaper found that she had only visited a friend in Brooklyn, and it accused the *Sun* of authoring a hoax for the sake of publicity, a stunt that would not have been entirely out of character. In 1835, just two years after its launch, the *Sun* ran a piece claiming that the great English astronomer, John Herschel, had discovered of a range of fantastic beings living on the moon. The article was, of course, a transparent bid for attention that came to be known as the Great Moon Hoax (see Figure 1.2).

Despite the explanation that Rogers had simply gone to Brooklyn for few days, rumors persisted that Rogers had eloped with a sailor,[9] so the insistence by the *Tribune* (cited above) that she was a "young woman of good character" was aimed at making a specific point with readers who recalled the earlier incident. By the time Rogers disappeared again in July of 1841, her acquaintance with many newspapermen and politicians may have garnered her story much more attention than it might have received otherwise. The mayors of the day—Isaac Varian and his successor Robert Morris, both Democrats—personally took part in the interrogations of various suspects and witnesses. Murder was a relatively rare event in the New York City of 1841.[10] In the first six months of 1841, for instance, there had been four convictions for "manslaughter," and two more for "assault and battery with intent to kill" but none for murder.[11] Murder of a "respectable" young woman was rarer still.

Soon after the discovery of Rogers' body, a string of suspects and witnesses were hauled in for interrogation. Two men were arrested on August 4, along with a sailor. All were soon discharged, however.[12] Another sailor was questioned on August 5, also discharged.[13] One suspect was pursued as far away as Worcester,

FIGURE 1.2 Engraving that accompanied the *New York Sun*'s "Great Moon Hoax" article of August 25, 1835.

Massachusetts and brought back to New York to face investigation. Although it was true that he knew Rogers from the cigar shop, and that he had recently been seen with a young woman on Staten Island, he turned out to have no connection to the Rogers murder.[14] The story received an additional salacious boost when it was revealed that Rogers had a former fiancé, a lawyer named Alfred Cromeline, whom she had recently left for Daniel Payne. Two days before her disappearance, Rogers had written to Cromeline asking him to visit her at home. He had declined to do so, saying he had been "coldly received"[15] at the Rogers' home on an earlier visit since their breakup. The next day her name "was written on Cromeline's slate"[16] (presumably at the door of his residence) and a rose was placed in his keyhole. The possibility that the murder was a result of a love triangle began to circulate.

As early as August 9, just over two weeks after the murder, the supposition that a gang of men might have been responsible started to take hold. The *Herald* reported an unrelated story of a Baltimore woman being snatched from the company of a "gentleman" by "eight or ten young men & ruffians." It then asked rhetorically,

> Can this outrage throw any light on the murder of Mary Rogers? . . . We hear of no clue arrived at, and but very little exertion made for the discovery

and punishment of the brutal ravishers and murderers. Let a public meeting be set a foot, a subscription raised in order to offer a reward for the murderers [note the presumed plural] of Mary Rogers. We will give FIFTY DOLLARS; and we doubt not that in less than 24 hours a thousand dollars may be raised, to be paid into the hands of the Mayor of New York, for the purpose of stimulating the energetic and indefatigable police.[17]

The solicitation of money for a police investigation was hardly incidental. In 1841, New York did not yet have a modern professional police force. On the streets, there were just two elected, unpaid constables per ward to watch over the city during the day. At night there were dozens of poorly paid watchmen ("leatherheads," as they were often called) who were political appointees. The inducement for corruption could hardly have been greater. Neither the constables nor watchmen were trained full-time policemen. They mostly did their law enforcement "on the side," and both groups tended to pay attention to investigations that came with the promise of a reward. Sometimes not willing to wait for an offer, they were known to exact "fees" from crime victims. As an amateur force, they were easily overwhelmed, and the city had, of late, been increasingly forced to call upon the militia to help preserve the peace. There was also a hierarchy of police officers who kept the system running and who relayed orders downwards from the mayor or the city council.

There had been gangs in New York back to the 18th century, but things became increasingly unruly in the mid-1830s as White Protestant New Yorkers began to feel they were losing control of the city to waves of foreigners.[18] In July 1834, a mob ransacked the house of a prominent abolitionist named Lewis Tappan.[19] That same year also saw Samuel Morse (best known today for having invented the telegraph and the code that bears his name) publish a series of articles in the staunchly Presbyterian *New York Observer* in which he claimed that the Austrian government and Pope Gregory XVI were using Jesuit agents to undermine freedom and democracy in the US.[20] Many went so far as to argue that Irish Catholics were not "White" and, on that basis, should be denied the possibility of American citizenship.[21] In 1835, a group of virulently anti-immigration, anti-Catholic New Yorkers led by Morse formed the Native American Democratic Association (NADA) to challenge the political power of Tammany Hall, which catered to New York's large immigrant populations. NADA won 40% of the vote in the New York state elections of 1835. Emboldened by the surprisingly positive result, Morse ran for mayor in 1836, but was badly defeated by the Democratic incumbent, Cornelius Van Wyck Lawrence. Still, the group's initial success in New York rapidly spread to other jurisdictions where White Protestants felt themselves to be under threat. In 1842, the movement went national under the name The American Republican Party. Horace Greely of the *Tribune* immediately dubbed them the "Know-Nothings," the moniker by which they are best known today.

Although the ethnic tensions of the mid-1830s had made gang violence a rising issue in the city, matters were greatly exacerbated by the market crash of 1837. As one pair of New York historians put the matter,

> if being a waged employee diminished one's sense of autonomy and control, being fired devastated it. Security and self-esteem were best pursued elsewhere. [A young man could] don colorful gang regalia, rendezvous with his comrades, and regain at least the illusion of being in control of his life, of being a man among men.[22]

In short, the gangs went from being a means-to-an-end to being a source of personal identity.

Irish Gangs dominated the notorious Five Points slum, and they operated in the neighboring Bowery district, both less than a half-mile north of where Mary Rogers lived. Charles Dickens visited the Five Points in 1842, though only under the protection of two police officers. He walked the narrow alleys, surveyed the busy taverns, and even strolled into the unlocked rooms of sleeping residents. He described it as "reeking everywhere with dirt and filth," and noted that its residents had their "counterparts at home [in London] and all the wide world over." "Debauchery has made the very houses prematurely old," the novelist continued. "See how the rotten beams are tumbling down, and how the patched and broken windows seem to scowl dimly, like eyes that have been hurt in drunken frays."[23]

The area's gangs went by names like the Forty Thieves, the Dead Rabbits, and the O'Connell Guards. Protestant gangs, of course, immediately sprung up to oppose them, with names like the American Guard and the Bowery Boys. Most despised of all were the African American gangs. As one New Yorker wrote about them, "those black devils have always been a nuisance, but now 'a respectable white man' can hardly walk down Broadway of a Sunday afternoon without being jostled off the sidewalk by their desperate gangs."[24]

Some gangs attached themselves to political parties or to other political institutions, such as Tammany Hall. Others took control of the volunteer fire companies that were ostensibly responsible for protecting the city. The weapons of choice when gangs did battle had traditionally been sticks and bricks. Increasingly, however, there were deadly incidents involving knives and guns, and the public was increasingly fearful of being caught in the crossfire.[25] Something had to be done, but there was strong opposition to the establishment of a professional police force, modeled on Robert Peel's "Bobbies" in London. Publicly, the objection was that a "civic army" did not become a democratic republic like the US. Not far beneath the surface, however, were the vested interests of political and ethnic control of particular neighborhoods, and the nefarious financial rewards that flowed from such influence. Despite those misgivings, the Rogers murder re-ignited the debate over a professional police force, and Bennett's suggestions, first, that gangs were behind the killing and, second, that the police would be unlikely to do much about it unless offered a reward, fanned the flames of distrust.

In this context, the *Herald*'s suggestion that a gang had been responsible for the mysterious murder of Mary Rogers cast the incident in a new and more menacing light. If it marked a new level of threat posed by urban violence, then it shifted the significance of the event from being merely an engaging, if sorrowful, tale of the downfall of an unlucky girl, to one that might have real significance for New York residents.

As if not wanting to be scooped by the *Herald*, the day immediately after the "gangs" editorial was published, the *Tribune* published a report that Rogers had been seen the night she died in Hoboken with as many as eight "young men."[26] The city was now so hungry for news of the incident, the *Herald* felt the need to announce that, "nothing has transpired at the Police office worth detailing to our readers on this melancholy subject."[27] On August 12, the *Herald* published a searing editorial on the state of justice in the city, accusing the judges of indifference and police of complicity. The condemnation closed with the words:

> New York is disgraced and dishonored in the eyes of the Christian and civilized world unless one great, one big, one strong, moral movement be made to reform and reinvigorate the administration of criminal justice, and to protect the lives and property of its inhabitants from public violence and public robbery.[28]

The same issue contained letters from possible witnesses (including one who wrote anonymously for fear of retaliation by unnamed gangs), and a report of a public meeting at which contributions for the reward fund were collected.

In the absence of further information, but needing to keep up the drumbeat against the gangs, a few days later the *Herald* speculated that the killing:

> was done in this city by some of the soaplocks [Bowery Boys] or fire rowdies, and who either by force or fraud got her into some of the Engine Houses adjacent to the north river, kept her there all day, and at night, during the pelting of that pitiless storm, they consigned her body to the North River—either alive or dead.[29]

Both the *Herald* and the *Tribune* ran nearly daily reports, many of them focusing on the presumed involvement of the city's gangs, until the end of August. In September, coverage began to fall off until, late in the month, the *Herald* ran a short series of illustrated articles on where Rogers was last seen alive and where, in the editor's opinion, she had probably been murdered. On October 9 it was reported that Rogers' fiancé, Daniel Payne, had been found dead of an apparent suicide, near the presumed murder site in Hoboken.[30]

The case was never definitively concluded. In the end, the best the *Herald* and the *Tribune* could do was to quarrel with each other: A year later, in early November of 1842, the woman proprietor of the Hoboken tavern at which Mary Rogers was reported to have been last seen alive, one Frederica Loss, was accidentally shot by one of her sons and died a few days later.[31] In the wake of this event, on November 18, the *Tribune* published an article declaring that the mystery of Mary Rogers' murder was solved. Mrs. Loss, it was said, had confessed on her deathbed to Judge Merritt (the Hoboken coroner) that Mary Rogers had come to her house with a physician who had attempted to perform an abortion. The procedure had killed Rogers and Mrs. Loss had instructed her sons to dump the body in the river.[32] The next day the *Herald*, which, it appeared, had been embarrassingly scooped by its rival, declared the *Tribune*'s story to be "all falsehood, and absolute fabrication," and published a letter from Merritt saying he had not received such testimony from Mrs. Loss.[33] The *Tribune* replied that it had received the story from two unnamed "Magistrates" and that it had erred in attributing the story to Merritt.[34] The *Herald* twice demanded to know the Magistrates' names.[35] The *Tribune* sneered back "Our envious neighbors may as well forbear their snarling. They only set the public laughing at their ludicrous misery."[36] The *Tribune* demanded a reward from the Mayor for cracking the case.[37]

The *Herald* mysteriously dropped its call for the names of the magistrates, and the *Tribune* never volunteered them. The papers moved on to other news stories and the Rogers case was transformed into a kind of civic legend: a fictionalized version of it written by Edgar Allan Poe, titled *The Mystery of Marie Rogêt*, started a serialized run in a magazine called *Snowden's Ladies' Companion*.

Whether Mary Rogers was actually murdered or died of a botched abortion, the political wheels that her traumatic death set in motion carried on far into the future. New York State Governor William Seward (later Abraham Lincoln's Secretary of State) made specific reference to the Rogers case in calling for police reform in 1842.[38] He designed a New York Municipal Police Act, providing for a professional and full-time, though still neighborhood-controlled, force, in 1844. By that time, however, the "Know-Nothings" had defeated both the Democrats and Whigs to take New York mayoralty. The city's new chief executive was John Harper, the man who had published a sensational book titled *The Awful Disclosures of Maria Monk* in 1836 during the great anti-Catholic outburst that had been led by Samuel Morse that year. The book purported to tell the story of a former nun from Montréal who "revealed" that religious sisters were forced to submit sexually to priests, with the children of such unions being murdered. Monk got wrong basic details about the order to which she had supposedly belonged, and even her mother discounted the tales as products of insanity,[39] but the book was wildly popular among those caught up in the rising anti-Catholic tide.

Mayor Harper would have nothing to do with Governor Seward's vision of a professional police force. Instead, he bulked up to the old system with 200 additional policemen, all appointed at his own discretion (which meant, in practice, that they had to be White, American-born Protestants who professed to being non-drinkers). He ordered them to wear dark blue uniforms and star-shaped copper badges (thus "cops"), the descendants of which remain with us today. Harper also attempted to ban most alcohol sales, to fire "foreign" municipal workers, and to banish unlicensed vendors (many of them immigrants) from city streets.

Policing was far from the only municipal issue that provoked tension between the established Protestants and the Catholic newcomers. Public education was also a frequent political flash point. New York City's public schools, such as they were, had traditionally been openly and strictly Protestant in their outlook. Bible readings—*King James* Bible readings—were a mainstay of the curriculum. The Public School Society refused even to operate schools in the predominantly Catholic Five Points slum. The Catholic Bishop of New York, John Hughes, himself an 1817 immigrant from Ireland, demanded public funding from the government for Catholic schools. Governor Seward knew this to be a political impossibility, but he tried to work out a compromise that would enable Catholics to participate in the public system. In 1842, the basic structure of a non-denominational public school system was passed by the New York assembly, but neither side would accept the outcome. Protestant mobs attacked Bishop Hughes' home. The just-created New York Board of Education tendentiously declared the King James Bible not to be a sectarian document; classroom readings from it continued. Hughes finally gave up his attempts to reform the public schooling system, turning his attention instead to establishing a network of private Catholic schools in New York.

New Yorkers' flirtation with John Harper and his obstinate Know-Nothing movement began to cool, however, as citizens came to understand the level of conflict what the nativists' heated rhetoric would mean in practice: In May 1844 came the report that 3000 nativists in Philadelphia had marched into the Irish ward of that city, ransacking houses and beating residents. The cause had been the local Bishop's request that Catholic students in the city's school be permitted to use the Catholic Douay translation of the Bible during daily religious readings instead of the Protestant King James version. Anti-Catholic agitators maliciously declared that the Irish were trying to "take the Bible out of school," and then used the allegation as a pretext for mass intimidation and violence. After a relatively quiet June, the mobs returned during the July 4 weekend, burning down two Catholic churches, destroying hundreds of Catholic homes, and killing over 30 people. The disorder came to be known as the Philadelphia Bible Riots. However, when particularly zealous nativists in New York called for a rally of their own in solidarity with the riots in the City of Brotherly Love, electoral support for Harper and his party collapsed in New York.

The Democrats took back the city in the elections of 1845 and implemented Seward's plan for a professional police force. The battles over immigration and religion had hardly even begun, though, either in New York City or elsewhere in the country. In just a few years time, the Irish Potato Famine and a failed revolution in the German states would send millions more Catholic immigrants streaming into America's port cities, New York most of all.

2. William James Comes Into the World

This was the fractious city into which William James was born on the 11th of January 1842. His father, Henry, was 30 years of age, and his mother, Mary, was 31.[40] The standard account is that William came into the world in the magnificent Astor House hotel, on the west side of Broadway between Vesey and Barclay Streets (see Figure 1.1). The hotel was only about 300 yards from City Hall and about 200 yards west of Mary Rogers' home. It was virtually across the street from P. T. Barnum's American Museum, which had opened just a year earlier (see Figure 1.3).

Barnum's Museum may have been the most visited attraction in America at the time. Over the course of its life it housed an incredibly diverse array of objects from the zoological to the historical to the fantastical: paintings, dioramas, weapons said to have been used by John Brown in his (in)famous raid at Harper's Ferry, a hat worn by Ulysses S. Grant, a wide variety of wax sculptures depicting

FIGURE 1.3   The street on which William James was born. The Astor House hotel is to the right. The south end of City Hall Park is to the left. Barnum's American Museum is beyond that, bearing the large American flag. The spire of Trinity Church can be seen in the distance.

Credit: August Köllner. Broad-Way, New York, 1850. Lithograph, lithographer after Isidore-Laurent Deroy, printed by Cattier, Paris, published by Goupil & Co., New York. The Metropolitan Museum of Art, Bequest of Susan Dwight Bliss, 1966 (67.630.36).

various historical and present-day scenes, the trunk of a tree under which Jesus' disciples allegedly sat, and, perhaps most notoriously of all, the mummified body of the "Fejee Mermaid," to name but a few. There were live animals as well: a "flea circus," exotic snakes, a dog that ran a loom, seals that performed tricks, dancing bears, beluga whales, even hippopotami and elephants. A "doctor" of phrenology sat prepared to assess the shapes of visitors' skulls and comment on their characters. There were even human exhibits: displayed in the 3,000-seat theater that Barnum called "The Lyceum," there were presented midgets such as "General" Tom Thumb, "giants" such as Anna Swan, "Esquimaux" and other "exotic" ethnic individuals, even the original "Siamese twins" Chang and Eng. Phineas Gage, whose famous 1848 injury is still recounted in textbooks of psychology and neurology today, appeared at Barnum's Museum for a time, bearing the tamping rod that had been blown through his head.

The story of William James' birth in the Astor House hotel is made somewhat curious by the fact that his parents had already rented a house at 5 Washington Place, uptown near the University of the City of New York,[41] then just 10 years old. What is more, just three days before William's birth, his father had purchased a house at 21 Washington Place from one of his brothers.[42]

New York was a very different city in the early 1840s than the one we know today. First, it consisted only of Manhattan, and it was truly an island. There were no bridges to Brooklyn, then a separate city, or tunnels to New Jersey. The only ways off the island were to take a ferry boat or to ride the full, rugged 13 miles to the north end of the island and cross the Bronx River onto the American mainland. Few of the city's buildings rose higher than four stories, save church spires. (The Astor House and Barnum Museum were exceptions, at five stories.) There was no Central Park. Indeed, hardly anyone lived that far up island. Contemporary maps of the city often stopped at around 30th street. Much of northern Manhattan was still farmland. Gas streetlights, introduced less than 20 years before,[43] were dim and few. There was, of course, no electricity, no telegraph, and no form of transportation or even communication faster than a horse. Even reliable access to clean drinking water was a serious problem for New Yorkers of the early 19th century: In 1822, thousands of New Yorkers had died in a Yellow Fever epidemic. In 1832, cholera had killed 3,500—one in every 65 New Yorkers.[44] A reliable source of fresh water for the city was only secured in October 1842, nine months *after* William James' birth, with the completion of the Croton Aqueduct. Its opening was considered so significant that it prompted huge civic celebrations around the new commemorative water fountain that was built in City Hall Park, across the street from William's birthplace. So powerful a symbol was the aqueduct that, even 14 years later, the teenage "Willy" James, then residing in Switzerland, would write to a friend, about Lake Geneva, that it was "as pure and clear as filtered Croton water."[45]

Henry James Sr.'s intellectual development was, in 1842, still a work in progress. A serious burn had resulted in the amputation of one of his legs at the age of 13. After a long, painful recovery, he had rebelled against his father's conventional Presbyterian strictures, becoming an erratic, often-drunken young man. He spent a tumultuous time at Union College in Schenectady NY, where his status was protected mainly by the fact that his father was the school's most important patron. Henry's father (also named William) had once even stepped in with his own money to bail the school out of a looming bankruptcy.[46] After the senior William's death in 1832, Henry had attended Princeton Seminary between 1835 and 1837, in the midst of a period of great strife for the Presbyterian Church. With the widespread religious revival that came to be known as the Second Great Awakening sweeping the northeastern US, Presbyterians were split between the staid and restrained Old School, and a rising New School that demanded spontaneous public displays of pious enthusiasm. Although Henry James briefly flirted with the new practices, rather than side with either faction, he became a follower of an 18th-century radically egalitarian, anti-clerical critic of the Scottish Presbyterian Church named Robert Sandeman. Henry James came to believe that the clergy served no good purpose, that good works and other religious practices—whether reserved or ardent—played no role in true Christianity, and that only through simple, direct belief could one achieve salvation.

This, of course, implied that most so-called Christians of the day were deluded about their status with Christ, and Henry was not particularly shy about voicing this conclusion, both in print and in person.[47] One of his colleagues in this extreme religious program was a fellow former-Princetonian, Hugh Walsh, whose two sisters, Mary and Catherine, had become Sandemanian converts as well. This caused no small degree of strain between the Walsh children and their Old School Presbyterian mother. Nevertheless, Henry James would marry Mary Walsh in 1840. Because clergy were regarded by both Henry and Mary as the pointless agents of a corrupt church, the wedding ceremony was a civil one, led by no less a personage than the Mayor of New York, Isaac Varian.[48] Mary Walsh's sister, Catherine, would never marry but often lived with or near Henry and Mary throughout their lives, becoming the beloved "Aunt Kate" of William James' childhood.

As Henry James' religious fire began to gradually smolder, he turned his attention to the work of the one-time Unitarian minister, Ralph Waldo Emerson, who was a core member of the group of thinkers and writers in Concord, Massachusetts known as the "Transcendentalists." Emerson's small 1836 book *Nature* is often regarded as a founding document of the movement, and his 1837 lecture "The American Scholar" is sometimes said to have started a uniquely American form of public philosophy.[49] In 1840, the Transcendentalists founded an influential (if short-lived) journal called *The Dial*. Remarkably for the era, it was edited by a woman, the redoubtable Margaret Fuller, who was one of America's earliest public feminists, and who would later go on to write and edit for Horace Greely's *New York Tribune*.[50] In 1841, several of them experimented with communal living at the Brook Farm just outside of Boston. In March 1842, Henry James saw Emerson's first lectures in New York City and was so impressed that he immediately wrote to him. The letter was quickly followed by a series of personal meetings.

Although James, with his strong religious impulses, could not accept Emerson's "naturalism," the two men struck up a complicated lifelong friendship. Also in 1842, Henry James discovered the work of Emanuel Swedenborg, the Swedish scientist-turned-spiritual-philosopher who would come to dominate his thinking in later years.

Despite all the vicissitudes of Henry James' early religious life, one thing that remained constant, as it did for many Protestant Americans of the time, was his distrust of Catholicism. One of James' ministers in Albany in the early 1830s, Rev. John N. Campbell, had identified the sizeable immigration of Catholics to America with the Great Apostasy foretold in the Biblical Book of Daniel (and this was well before the truly massive immigration of Irish and German Catholics that began in the late 1840s). Although James was not among those extremists who believed that Catholics should be prohibited from becoming citizens, he did not believe they could remain loyal either to the nation or to the principles on which the republic was founded. "Catholicism would always horrify him," is how Henry James' major biographer described his blunt feelings on the matter.[51]

Henry James was able to devote such energy to the intellectual and spiritual aspects of his life because he had inherited great wealth from his father's vast estate, after the latter's death in 1832.[52] The family had then been based up the Hudson River in the state capital of Albany. Henry's father, William, had emigrated from County Cavan in Northern Ireland around 1789.[53] William of Albany, as he is often called,[54] made his initial fortune in real estate. He became friends with the prominent politician, DeWitt Clinton.[55] Clinton was the driving political force behind the building of the Erie Canal. So closely identified did he become with the project that its opponents derogatorily referred to the canal as "Clinton's Ditch." William of Albany was an eager investor in the canal, and he made millions from this investment, at one point becoming New York State's second wealthiest man.[56]

As is well known, the Erie Canal revolutionized the economic structure of the US as soon as it opened in 1825. The great American geographical challenge, nearly from the time of the first colonies, was how to transport goods and people into and out of the massive continent's interior. The Appalachian Mountains, running all the way from Maine to Alabama, posed a formidable obstacle in the age of the ox cart. Only two major waterways led to the interior of the country. The first, from the north, was the St. Lawrence River, then controlled by the British with whom the US had been at war as recently as 1815. The second, far to the south, was the Mississippi River, the gateway of which was the city of New Orleans, which was the site of the bloodiest battle in the War of 1812. Another path to the interior was sorely needed. New York City was set on an attractive harbor, but the major river leading from it, the Hudson, went north to Albany, not west into the interior.

The Erie Canal changed all of this by paralleling the (non-navigable) Mohawk River, which flows into the Hudson from the west through a gap between the Adirondacks Mountains and the Alleghany Plateau.[57] The canal then cut clear through western New York all the way to Lake Erie (see Figure 1.4). From there,

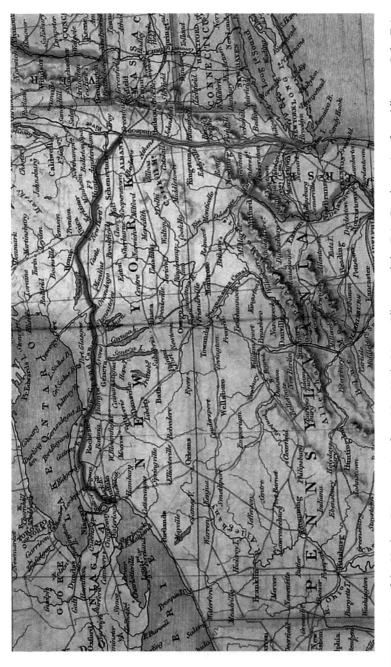

FIGURE 1.4 Map of the Hudson River running from New York City to Albany, and the Erie Canal, running from Albany to Lake Erie.

Credit: Original map published in *Betts's Family Atlas*, 1838, pp. 54–55.

ships could travel west to (what would later become) Chicago, and beyond. The Canal cut the cost for shipping a ton of goods from New York City to Buffalo from $100 to just $9.[58] In the process, it changed New York itself from a large but fairly ordinary American city, into the commercial dynamo of North America. Further, the opportunities that this transformation created drew migrants—both foreign and domestic—in numbers that had never before been seen. From 1820 to 1830, the city's population increased by nearly two-thirds, from 124,000 to 203,000. Over the next decade it would add nearly its entire 1820 population again, rising to 313,000 by 1840.

William of Albany's shrewd investment in the greatest venture of the age insured that generations of his descendants would live in comfort and leisure. For his son Henry, who, recall, had lost a leg to fire as a young teen, the inheritance freed him from his probable occupational course—becoming a minister—and enabled him to spend his life thinking independently, even radically, about the spiritual issues that gripped his interest. Money was never to be taken entirely for granted, however, in the erratic political and economic atmosphere of early 19th-century America. President Andrew Jackson's risky and self-serving fiscal policies[59] had led to the Panic of 1837, which caused a severe economic depression that lasted through 1843, just after the younger William James' birth.

3. The First European Excursion, and Back Again

Within weeks of the William's birth in January 1842, the family moved up from the hurly burly of downtown to the genteel confines of Washington Place. In January of 1843 Henry gave a series of public lectures on Christianity. They seem to have been something less than an unalloyed success. Initial turnout was respectable, but dropped off markedly as the series proceeded.[60] Henry renewed his acquaintance with Emerson, however, and met others of the Transcendentalist circle later that year. In April 1843, William's first brother, Henry Jr., was born. Before the year was out, however, Henry Sr. had decided that he must leave New York in order to find the cosmic answers he sought. The stresses of the bustling, growing, sometimes chaotic New York often drove James to seek more tranquil environs. He considered moving to rural Massachusetts to be closer to Emerson, who shared Henry's suspicion of and distaste for urban life. The Concord philosopher once wrote, "I always seem to suffer some loss of faith on entering cities. They are great conspiracies; the parties are all maskers who have taken mutual oaths of silence not to betray each other's secret."[61] New York, in particular, he told Henry, made him "shudder as he approached."[62] Henry, however, received little encouragement from Emerson to join him in the New England countryside, so he set his sights on Europe instead. In October 1843, he sold the family home on Washington Place and sailed, with his young family, for England.

Almost immediately upon his arrival, Henry set about meeting the popular Scottish essayist, Thomas Carlyle, whose works he admired, and the influential

English philosopher, John Stuart Mill, whose empiricism did not impress him so greatly. Although Henry stayed briefly in London, the family soon escaped city life, renting a country cottage in Windsor, west of London, nearly in the shadow of the great castle there. Once settled in, he set himself to the task of converting his New York lectures on Christianity into a book. In May 1844, however, he experienced a sudden emotional collapse that left him spiritually shaken to his core. It has become customary to quote James' vivid description of the event:

> To all appearance it was a perfectly insane and abject terror, without ostensible cause, and only to be accounted for, to my perplexed imagination, by some damnèd shape squatting invisible to me within the precincts of the room, and raying out from his fetid personality influence fatal to life.[63]

This account, however, was written some 35 years after the events—long after it had taken on a particular meaning in the long arc of his life. It is, thus, perhaps wise to interpret it with some caution.

Unable to recover his composure, James traveled back toward London to Richmond, to take a "water cure" that was then fashionable. The treatment had little effect but while there he met a wealthy supporter of various radical causes, most especially the socialism espoused by Charles Fourier.[64] Her name was Sophia Chichester. Upon hearing James' description of his affliction, she announced that he had experienced what the Swedish religious visionary Emanuel Swedenborg[65] called a "vastation"; the final sloughing off of sinful "waste" just prior to spiritual regeneration. James seized upon this interpretation and was soon in London again, purchasing as much of Swedenborg's quite sizeable oeuvre as he could lay his hands on. He also introduced himself to London's leading Swedenborgian, James John Garth Wilkinson, with whom he would maintain a lifelong correspondence. Swedenborg had been known to James before this—American Presbyterians mostly regarded him as having been mad[66]—but now Henry began a close study of Swedenborg's spiritual thought; especially his mystical verse-by-verse interpretation of the Bible.

In October 1844, almost exactly a year after he had fled to England, James and his family returned to New York. His older son, William, was now closing in on three years of age, and his younger son, Henry Jr., was 18 months old. They returned to the exclusive uptown neighborhood where they had lived before, residing with Mary's mother at first. While away, the Jameses had missed the worst excesses of the Know-Nothings' administration of the city. The extremes of nativism had begun to be discredited by the time he returned, and the Democrats were on the verge of a return to power, but suspicion of immigrants was still widespread.

After about a year of living at his mother-in-law's house, Henry James and his family left the city again, moving up the Hudson to Albany, taking a family house across the street from his own mother's. He returned to writing up his 1843 lectures on Christianity, and he worked on his Swedenborg studies. Rarely one to compromise with institutional authority, James bickered with the Swedenborgian "New Jerusalem Church" that was centered in Boston. He gave two lectures at an Albany club on social and religious themes, publishing one of them. He also took up Charles Fourier's brand of socialism and pursued various plans to start a periodical, none of which came to fruition. Two more sons were born—Garth Wilkinson (Wilky) in 1845, named after his Swedenborgian friend in London, and Robertson (Bob) in 1846.

In 1847 James moved his family back to New York City, this time to Fifth Avenue, between Eighth and Ninth streets—a little further north than their former home near Washington Square. The following year he moved even further from downtown, up to Fourteenth Street (see Figure 1.5). Henry took up company with a loose network of New York journalists and became deeply involved with the Fourierist magazine, *Harbinger*. This periodical had originally been published at the Transcendentalists' Brook Farm, outside of Boston but, after a fire had destroyed a new building project there, it had moved to an office in New York City. The magazine advanced the cause of utopian socialism but, as one reader observed, "while the *principles* to which the paper is professedly devoted are distinguished for favoring the common people, the *tone* of the paper itself seems to us quite aristocratic."[67]

Henry regularly contributed funds to support *Harbinger*, as well as his time. Throughout 1848 he had a desk of his own in the magazine's office, where he wrote columns and letters under the pen name "Y.S." His topics were often only tangentially related to the aims of the magazine: at one point, he was moved to defend a clairvoyant Mesmerist who had become popular in the city. He carried on bitter and lengthy disputes, in print, with some of the magazine's correspondents and critics. In one astonishing essay, James seemed to argue that the wealthy and powerful, by having disentangled themselves from physical wants, become godlike. This divine status was then used to justify the exertion of control over those who are weaker and poorer. He extended this logic to the case of one business driving competitors out of the market—monopolistic capitalism as a sign of divinity? He even went so far as to defend certain types of murder in these terms.[68] This seems very nearly the opposite of the utopian socialist vision of Fourier, yet the magazine's editor appears to have done little to rein James in, perhaps fearing the loss of his patronage.

In 1848 James launched into a passionate, if ill-advised, public defense of Fourier's radical views on marriage and sexual relations. Essentially, Fourier had argued that the institution of marriage turns people into the "property" of their spouses and that, instead, people should be free to follow their "passionate attractions." Because these views conflicted so starkly with conventional Christian morality, even the most committed American Fourierists usually evaded the widespread disrepute that would befall their hero by refraining from openly discussing these ideas. If forced to comment, they usually put some distance between themselves

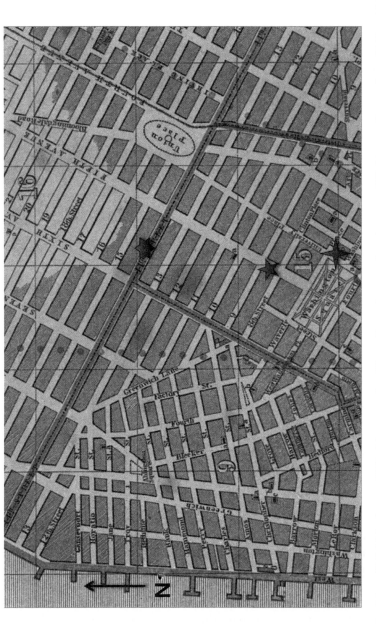

FIGURE 1.5 Map of Mid-Manhattan, 1842. After marrying, Henry James Sr. moved to the area of Washington Square from 1842 to 1845, apart from his year-long trip to England. After more than a year in Albany, he returned to New York City in 1847, moving his family north of Washington Square (4-pointed star) to Fifth Ave. between 8th and 9th Streets (5-pointed star). In 1848, they moved again, still further north, to a house on 14th Street between Fifth and Sixth Avenues (6-pointed star). This last residence is what William and Henry Jr. thought of as their boyhood home, and where they were raised until the family left the city for good in 1855.

Credit: Image from Morse, Sidney E. & Breese, Samuel. *Morse's North American Atlas.* New York, NY: Harper & Brothers, 1845.

and Fourier on this issue, redirecting attention to the political arrangements that the French theorist advanced. James would brook no such compromise and published multiple columns enunciating and vociferously defending Fourier's view on sexuality, even against other Fourierists. When the *Harbinger* folded in 1849, James continued to publish in other New York periodicals. Although his actions invited criticism—not least from the Presbyterian owner-editor of the *New York Observer* Samuel Irenæus Prime, and from the prominent Unitarian clergyman William Henry Channing[69]—they also brought him a degree of literary celebrity.

In 1849 James was invited to speak on the topic of socialism at Boston's eminently respectable Town & Country Club (in no small part due to the influence of Emerson).[70] The lectures were soon repeated in New York, and were notable enough to be cited three decades later in his obituary as having "attracted great attention."[71] In 1850 he began writing regularly, if usually anonymously, for Horace Greely's *New York Tribune*. It is easy to see this as the period of Henry James' greatest intellectual ascendancy. But even as Greely gave James the most public forum he had ever had, he simultaneously published counterarguments of his own, calling into question the seriousness with which James' ideas should be taken. All this suggests that Greely saw James more as a controversial voice whose eccentric views would sell papers, rather than as a serious thinker whose views deserved sober public consideration.[72]

Henry James' chief biographer, Alfred Habegger, recounted James' writings and debates of this period with all seriousness, if rather unsympathetically. By contrast, one of his eldest son's most eminent biographers dismissed it all as "small storms of heated rhetoric."[73] Another of William's biographers described Henry Sr. as "mystical, astonishingly impractical, and absorbed by abstractions."[74] To be sure, Henry James was treated with respect, if not actual importance, by a small circle of New England and Mid-Atlantic social and religious thinkers. Even among them, however, patience with his bombastic style could wear thin. Bronson Alcott, a leader among the Concord Transcendentalists, once described James as "damaged goods."[75]

If Henry James had hoped to be the answer to Emerson's 1837 call for an "American scholar," he certainly was not. His thought was far too bound up with European traditions, even if they were dissident lines of thought. An interesting comparison with James is his near contemporary, the poet Walt Whitman. Whitman was born on Long Island, raised in Brooklyn, and lived much of his adult life in and around New York City. Like James, Whitman was drawn to the transcendentalist view of the relationship between man, nature, and society. Indeed, Whitman's first book of poetry, *Leaves of Grass*, published in 1855, was an explicit response to Emerson's "call," not, in his case, for the "American scholar" but, rather, for the emergence of a new, uniquely American kind of poet.[76] But Whitman's style was not entirely commensurate with Emerson's vision. Whitman's "nature" was more gritty, immediate, material—in a word, more natural—than Emerson's idealized, quasi-Romantic vision of the cosmos. Indeed, Whitman is not generally regarded as having been a transcendentalist poet. He is more often characterized as a transitional figure between transcendentalism and realism. Although Emerson heartily praised the first edition of *Leaves of Grass*,[77] as the controversy over Whitman's sexual (especially homosexual) themes grew, Emerson urged the poet to curb the explicitness of his imagery, and then publicly distanced himself from Whitman.[78]

In any case, it was not so much the approach to sexuality that distinguished Whitman's success in establishing a uniquely American voice from James' failure to do so. It is, instead, in Whitman's celebration of the new American city—especially New York—with its bustling, diverse, sometimes-violent, but always energetic throngs. This represented a development in Whitman's lifelong moral journey. Back in 1842—the year that his now-forgotten temperance novel, *Franklin Evans*, was published—Whitman was the editor of a minor paper called the *Aurora* which denounced the "Irish rabble" and their "villainous priests," and endorsed the mob attack on Bishop's Hughes' house.[79] More than a decade later, though, Whitman rejoiced what he called "America's busy, teeming, intricate whirl . . ."[80] In that first 1855 edition of *Leaves of Grass*, Whitman proclaimed himself to be:

> Of every hue and trade and rank, of every caste and religion,
> Not merely of the New World but of Africa Europe or Asia . . . a
> wandering savage,
> A farmer, mechanic, or artist . . . a gentleman, sailor, lover or quaker,
> Prisoner, fancy-man, rowdy, lawyer, physician, or priest.[81]

By the 1860 edition he could write:

> American mouth-songs!
> Those of mechanics—each one singing, his, as it should be blithe and
> strong,
> The carpenter singing his, as he measures his plank or beam,
> The mason singing his, as he makes ready for work, or leaves off work,
> The boatman singing what belongs to him in his boat—the deckhand
> singing on the steamboat deck,
> The shoemaker singing as he sits on his bench—the hatter singing as he
> stands,
> The wood-cutter's song—the ploughboy's on his way in the morning, or
> at the noon intermission, or at sundown;
> The delicious singing of the mother—or of the young wife at work—or
> of the girl sewing or washing—Each singing what belongs to him or her
> and to none else,
> The day what belongs to the day—At night the party of young fellows,
> robust, friendly, clean-blooded, singing with melodious voices, melodious
> thoughts.

Come! some of you! still be flooding The States with hundreds and
thousands of mouth-songs fit for The States only.[82]

By contrast, Henry James' eccentric philosophy seems to have been hardly
influenced by the momentous events that were besieging New York at the time
he lived there. From the evidence of his writings, he seems to have been almost
completely aloof, in a way that only his independent wealth could make possible.
His steady moves northward out the city's core give some hint of his discomfort
with what Henry Jr. would later dub, in the novel set in his old neighborhood,
the "long, shrill city."[83]

By the time Henry James' two oldest boys, William and Henry Jr., were school-
age, their father, decisive as he may have been in other realms, could not settle
on an educational plan for them. He shuffled them around from school to school
nearly every year. Some schools focused on language training, others on classics
and the arts, still others on business skills.[84] He seems to have been torn between
his respect for classical education and his horror at the corruption, as he saw it,
of the "old ways." The ragtag "common" schools, of course, were not regarded as
a serious option for a man of Henry James' social standing. Even with his choice
of the city's private schools, he complained that his young boys had "import[ed]
shocking bad-manners from the street."[85] He was clearly aware of and reacting
against the social revolution that was unfolding in the rapidly swelling metropolis.
Despite his outward radicalism, Henry James' voice was still an old one steeped in
European sensibility, not a fresh, new American one.

4. A Flood of Newcomers, the Agony of Slavery, and the Failure of Politics

Whatever Henry James' misgivings about New York's cosmopolitanism were, it
is certain that he was not prepared for the deluge to come. In 1847 alone, over
50,000 Irish Catholics landed in New York, then a city just over 350,000. They
were, of course, refugees of the potato famine then spreading across the Emerald
Isle.[86] By 1850—just three years later—the city's population had swelled by 45%
to over 500,000.[87] It has been estimated that over the course of the famine years,
as many as 650,000 new Irish arrived in New York City.[88] By the mid-1850s, New
York had more Irish than Dublin. Most of those who came were not from the
Irish capital, however. They had been subsistence tenant farmers from the western
portion of the country. They had no experience of cities and possessed few skills
that would enable them to successfully navigate a massive metropolis like New
York. As a result, the bulk of the new arrivals crowded into the rapidly expanding
tenement slums of the city, especially the notorious Five Points (just 1 ½ miles
southeast of the Jameses' Fifth Avenue home of 1847).

If fear and suspicion of Catholic immigration had been a strong current in
American politics in the mid-1840s, by the mid-1850s it exploded. New York's
old "Know-Nothing" American Republican Party went national as the Native

American Party. It nearly swept the Massachusetts legislature in 1854. Know-Nothing candidates also took mayoralties in Boston, Philadelphia, Washington, DC, Chicago, and San Francisco (where the key issue was Chinese immigration rather than Irish). In New York, however, where Know-Nothingism had already had its turn, its mayoral candidate finished in third with about a quarter of the vote.

It wasn't only refugees who came sailing into New York harbor. In 1849, 3000 ships loaded with goods of every kind sailed into the harbor from 150 ports around the world: Europe, California, China, Japan.[89] Thus, New York was not only the immigration capital of North America. It had become the undisputed commercial capital as well.

As important a challenge as immigration was, it was far from the only topic on the American political agenda of the early 1850s. Slavery was rapidly becoming a critical issue as well. The Compromise of 1850 delayed the secession of Southern states for another decade, but only at the price of a strengthened Fugitive Slave Act that was unacceptable to the growing contingent of Northern abolitionists. The Act did not resolve, but merely forestalled the question of slavery in the expanding West. The publication, in 1852, of Harriet Beecher Stowe's novel, *Uncle Tom's Cabin*, helped to transform the abolition of slavery from a "radical" position—one which had been opposed not 20 years before even by Stowe's father, Lyman Beecher[90]—into a mainstream current of Northern politics. Just two years later, Democratic Illinois senator Stephen Douglas would design the Kansas-Nebraska Act, which not only created the two territories, but also empowered the settlers within them to determine for themselves whether to embrace slavery. Southerners sprang at the opportunity to expand their regional practice to new sectors of the rapidly growing country and, thereby build what they anticipated would be an impregnable political fortress around it. At the same time, a former Whig congressman from Illinois by the name of Abraham Lincoln would start to make a national name for himself by vocally opposing the Kansas-Nebraska Act (though he would deny being an abolitionist) and, in the process, begin a rivalry with Douglas that would grow to historical proportions over the next several years. The passage of the Act persuaded the radical abolitionist John Brown that only violent action could bring slavery to an end. His "Pottawatomie Massacre" of 1856 was a major event in the violent clashes between 1854 and 1858 that collectively came to be known as "Bleeding Kansas." National attention was also focused on the story of a young family who escaped from their enslavement in Kentucky in January 1856, crossing the rarely-frozen Ohio River to Cincinnati. When southern bounty hunters and US Marshals caught up with them, the young mother of the family, Margaret Garner, killed one of her four children and attempted to kill the other three, rather than have them returned to bondage. At her subsequent trial, the *defense* argued that the murder charge in Ohio should take precedence over the claims of the Fugitive Slave Act. The judge disagreed, and sent Garner back to Kentucky along with her husband.[91] The following year, 1857, saw the momentous Dred Scot decision, in which the Supreme Court declared that no person of African ancestry could claim US citizenship. Two years later, John Brown returned to national prominence with his failed raid on the arsenal at Harper's Ferry, Virginia in 1859.

What Henry James thought of all this is something of a mystery. Most of his published writings betray little concrete recognition of the *hoi polloi*, apart from a condescending presumption that they would be better served by a Fourierist-Swedenborgian social-religious order. Although the early 1850s were among Henry James' most productive literary years, they were mostly occupied by various spiritual and religious wars of his own making: *Moralism and Christianity* was published in 1850, *Lectures and Miscellanies* in 1852, *The Church of Christ, Not an Ecclesiasticism* in 1854, and *The Nature of Evil* in 1855. In one of his best-known essays, "Democracy and Its Issues," he promoted an anarchic ideal of democracy which, he said, "explodes the old conceptions of government" and in which people would spontaneously exercise the "exclusive right to govern themselves" without benefit of elections, assemblies, legislation, or other institutions by which democracies typically operate. Henry James dismissed all of this civic machinery as the product of societies being "imperfectly evolved."[92] Apart from a rather generic observation that the so-called "dangerous classes" were only so because of systemic injustices which must be resolved,[93] he gave little indication of how the fractious city in which he lived—with its often-violent ethnic, religious, and economic clashes—might eventually attain his utopian vision beyond declaring, rather enigmatically, that the removal of "those factitious restraints which keep appetite and passion on the perpetual look out for escape," would "instantly" result in the brotherhood of humankind.[94]

James' neighborhood, of course, was well out of the urban ruckus. Its residents were mostly businessmen, lawyers, and other professionals. His household, however, employed a steady stream of servants, mostly young Irish Catholic women. His youngest child, Alice (born in 1848), remarked much later in her life that, "we are quite wrong in thinking that our servants lie because they are Catholics."[95] This may give the most honest indication of the feeling her family had toward the new immigrants. Henry Jr. would put the matter more delicately in his novel, *Washington Square*, in which a character opines that "Irish immigrants . . . alight, with large appetites, in the New World."[96] Politically speaking, Henry James, Sr. was generally a moderate Whig. He had little patience for Democrats of the day who tended towards populism nationally, and pandered to working-class immigrants in New York. Surprisingly, however, he publicly supported the (sporadic) efforts of the Tammany Hall Democratic mayor Fernando Wood to clean up vice in the city. It may be that James had become, as his biographer claims, "increasingly alienated by New York's filth, disorder, and corruption."[97] More personally, however, it may have been that James became passionate specifically about the topic of gambling because one of his younger brothers, John Barber James, had fallen victim to professional gamblers and Henry had been involved in cleaning up the ensuing mess.[98]

Whatever disruption of the old order was caused by the country's new arrivals, even more was caused by the emergence of new technologies. The 1850s marked the ascendance of steam powered trains in New York City. By 1851, Albany was connected to Buffalo via the New York & Erie railway, making virtually redundant the Canal that had once been celebrated as one of the greatest engineering feats in all of human history. Later that same year, steam engines began regularly rumbling directly into the city.[99] Terminating up at 32nd street (for fear that a locomotive might explode in the midst of the crowded metropolis), passengers and cargo would then be loaded onto old horse-drawn rail cars and driven down along 10th avenue, stopping at the end of James' own 14th street, about four long blocks from his house. They would then continue down the western side of the island before cutting slightly inland to Hudson, and finally down to Chambers street (where a subway station sits today).[100]

The 1850s was also a decade of major political realignment nationally. The presidential election of 1848 had seen the victory of the Mexican-American war hero Zachary Taylor who, although a Virginia slave owner, had opposed the expansion of slavery into the newly acquired, formerly Mexican territories in the west. Whatever his intentions might have been, "Old Rough and Ready," as Taylor was known, died just sixteen months into his term. He was succeeded by his Vice President, Millard Fillmore, a New Yorker who favored the expansion of slavery. In addition, in the wake of the California gold rush, Fillmore oversaw the transformation of that distant, wild, western territory into a major economic engine for the country as a whole. Thousands of people made the three-month ship voyage from the east around Cape Horn, in a desperate stab at treasure. Some, such as Cornelius Vanderbilt, made millions, engineering passages across Central America, cutting a few days off the trip. Thousands more attempted the more even dangerous voyage across the vast plains and mountain ranges by means of ox cart. Some of the greatest fortunes were made by those who shipped eastern goods to the west coast, selling them to those who hoped to dig riches out of the ground or pan it out of the rivers. A man might or might not find gold, but he would always need food, clothing, tools, and furniture.[101] Perhaps the most famous of these opportunistic entrepreneurs today were the three Jewish tailors, all brothers, who had just immigrated to New York from Bavaria: Jonas, Louis, and Levi Strauss. Their tough canvas, and later denim, trousers, characteristically died indigo, became the blue jeans worn by millions today.

President Fillmore was forced to admit California as a "free" state, but the future of slavery in the west remained the most pressing political issue of the day. Making merely unsettled matters into positively unstable ones, Fillmore, as a sitting president, failed to win the presidential nomination of his own party at the 1852 Whig convention. The party selected, instead, a military man, General Winfield Scott.[102] During the Whig nomination process, Henry James complained in a letter to Emerson that the "votaries of Mars" would give Scott the Whig nomination.[103] In the general election of 1852, however, James supported Scott for president. With the Whigs in disarray after the nomination debacle, the Democratic nominee, Franklin Pierce, easily defeated Scott for the presidency, carrying 27 of 31 states. The Whig Party immediately began to disintegrate over the issue of slavery. Anti-slavery Whigs joined with "Free-Soil" Democrats under the banner of the new "Republican Party" in 1854. Whigs who were not moved by the slavery issue aligned themselves with the Native American Party, which had been re-energized by a string of state and municipal victories in 1854, and then adopted the simplified name, the "American Party." Henry James does not seem to have joined this group officially, but did echo the commonly heard fear that the Pope's agents were swarming the country, plotting to overthrow the government.[104] The American Party and the remaining Whigs both nominated Fillmore in the 1856 presidential election. But Fillmore carried only Maryland, finishing not only behind the victor, Democrat James Buchanan, but also behind the abolitionist Republican nominee, John C. Frémont of California.[105] The debacle effectively crushed the last vestiges of Whiggism in the US, and set the country on an inexorable course toward civil war.

More than a year prior to Buchanan's election, however, Henry James decided to flee with his family to Europe once again. Whether and to what degree this latest departure was due to the increasing clatter and chaos of the city, or a result of the dire political posture of the nation more broadly, or in deference to another idiosyncratic spasm of Henry's eccentric philosophical spirit, it is hard to say. They set sail across the Atlantic on June 27, 1855 and, although they would ultimately return to the US, they would never again live in New York City.

New York, of course, would continue on.

Notes

1 "A Horrible Murder," *New York Tribune*, August 2, 1841, 2.
2 "The Case of Mary C. Rogers," *New York Tribune*, August 12, 1841, 2.
3 "The Late Murder of a Young Girl at Hoboken," *New York Herald*, August 3, 1841, 2nd edition, 2.
4 "A Horrible Murder," 2.
5 "Editorial with No Title," *New York Herald*, August 4, 1841, 2nd edition.
6 Founded, interestingly, by the abolitionist brothers, Arthur and Lewis Tappan, and the rabidly anti-immigrant Samuel Morse.
7 For more detail, see Edwin G. Burrows and Mike Wallace, *Gotham: A History of New York City to 1898* (New York, NY: Oxford University Press, 1999), 522–27.
8 It is often said that Anderson had hired her to work the counter expressly with the aim of attracting male customers to his store. Apparently the novelty of an attractive young woman selling tobacco drew enough attention that she became a minor municipal celebrity, as city leaders looked for distractions from the effects of the brutal market crash of 1837.
9 "The Late Murder of a Young Girl at Hoboken."
10 The US census of 1840 put the population of New York City (which included only Manhattan at that time) at 313,000 residents.
11 "Criminal Statistics of the City," *New York Tribune*, July 9, 1841, 1. In September of 1841, a New York printer named Samuel Adams would be murdered by John Colt,

brother of the repeating gun's inventor, Samuel Colt. The trial gripped the city and resulted in Colt's being sentenced to hang, though he committed suicide in jail hours before his scheduled execution.

12 "Arrests on Suspicion of Murder," *New York Tribune*, August 5, 1841, 2.

13 Ibid., August 6, 1841, 2.

14 A succession of stories appeared on this "promising" suspect in the *New York Tribune*, every day, August 17–21, 1841.

15 "The Murder of Miss Rogers," *New York Tribune*, August 13, 1841, 2.

16 Ibid.

17 "The Outrage on Mary Rogers, and Similar Attacks in Other Places—A Public Meeting," *New York Herald*, August 9, 1841, 2nd edition.

18 The feeling was not unique to New York. In August 1834, in Boston, a crowd charged across the river to Charlestown and set fire to a Catholic convent soon after listening to an anti-Catholic tirade by the Presbyterian firebrand Lyman Beecher (probably a portion of his anti-Catholic treatise, *A Plea for the West* (New York, NY: Leavitt, Lord, & Co., 1835) which would be published the following year). It is noteworthy that the first Catholic church in Boston, Saint Mary's, had opened earlier that same year, in the predominantly Irish North End. In 1835, a sensational book by Rebecca Reed titled *Six Months in a Convent* (Boston, MA: Russell, Odiome, & Metcalf, 1835) reported, to a Protestant readership eager for sordid details, horrifying tales of the prison-like conditions that prevailed in the convent (though the stories were entirely fictional, as it turned out).

19 Tappan would later serve as attorney for the survivors of the *Amistad*, the ship of abducted Africans who had fought and defeated the crew that was taking them to the American slave market. The ship was found floating off the Long Island coast in 1839 and the court case over what to do with those on board gripped the nation.

20 Samuel Morse, *Foreign Conspiracy Against the Liberties of the United States* (serialized in *The New York Observer*, 1834).

21 Matthew Frye Jacobson, *Whiteness of a Different Color: European Immigrants and the Alchemy of Race* (Cambridge, MA: Harvard University Press, 1998).

22 Burrows and Wallace, *Gotham*, 634.

23 Charles Dickens, *American Notes for General Circulation* (New York, NY: Harper & Brothers, 1842), 35.

24 Cited in Burrows and Wallace, *Gotham*, 634.

25 See esp. Ibid., 633–35.

26 "The Murder of Miss Rogers," August 10, 1841, 2.

27 "City Intelligence," *New York Herald*, August 10, 1841.

28 "The Administration of Criminal Justice in New York," *New York Herald*, August 12, 1841.

29 "The Mary Rogers Mystery," *New York Herald*, August 14, 1841; and "The Murder of Mary Rogers—The Inquest on Daniel C. Payne, Her Lover," *New York Herald*, October 11, 1841.

30 "More Mystery—Extraordinary Circumstance—Suicide of the Lover of Mary Rogers," *New York Herald*, October 9, 1841.

31 Mrs. Loss' three sons were interrogated about the Rogers affair on 19 November, though little new came of the questioning. The verbatim report was published in "The Mary C. Rogers Mystery—Examination of Mrs. Loss' Boys Yesterday at Jersey City," *New York Herald*, November 20, 1841.

32 "The Mary Rogers Mystery Explained," *New York Tribune*, November 18, 1842, 2.

33 "The Mary Rogers' [Sic] Mystery," *New York Herald*, November 20, 1842.

34 "The Mary Rogers Mystery," November 21, 1842, 2.

35 Ibid., November 22, 1842. Untitled, *New York Herald*, November 24, 1842.

36 Untitled, *New York Tribune*, November 22, 1842.

37 Ibid., November 28, 1842.

38 Cited in Burrows and Wallace, *Gotham*, 637.

39 It has even been suggested that Monk was brain damaged from a childhood accident.

40 Coincidentally, Charles Dickens would arrive in New York Harbor for his first tour of America just 11 days later, on January 22, 1842. The trip became the basis of his travelogue, *American Notes for General Circulation*, published in October of the same year.

41 Renamed New York University in 1896.

42 Alfred Habegger, *The Father: A Life of Henry James, Sr.* (New York, NY: Farrar, Strauss, and Giroux, 1994), 187–89.

43 In 1823. Ric Burns, *New York: A Documentary Film* (Steeplechase Films, 1999), episode 2, 3:20.

44 John Thorn, "Baseball's Unchanging Past: A Necessary Illusion" (24th Annual Cooperstown Symposium on Baseball and American Culture, Cooperstown, NY, 2012).

45 Letter to Edgar Beach Van Winkle, July 1, 1856, Ignas K. Skrupskelis and Elizabeth M. Berkeley, eds., *The Correspondence of William James* (Charlottesville, VA and London, UK: University of Virginia Press, 1992), vol. 4, 16.

46 Daniel W. Bjork, *William James: The Center of His Vision* (Washington, DC: American Psychological Association, 1997), 3.

47 In July 1838 Henry James published, at his own expense, a new edition of Sandeman's *Letters on Theron and Aspasio* (originally published in 1757), including an inflammatory preface of his own. Later in 1838, James went to great lengths to visit the most prominent, yet still secretive, Sandemanian in the world: the English physicist Michael Faraday. Presumably, he did not gain the insight into the relationship between the spiritual and material worlds for which he had been hoping because he never recounted what had occurred during their meeting. See Habegger, *Henry James Sr.*, 157, 176–78.

48 Varian was a Tammany Hall Democrat, forced from office by the "Glentworth scandal" of 1840 in which large numbers of Pennsylvania laborers were sent to New York, ostensibly to work for the city, but who were actually paid to vote for the Whig presidential candidate, William Henry Harrison. Varian and fellow-Democrat Robert Morris, then New York's Recorder of Deeds, illegally seized documents crucial to the case which they feared would be destroyed by the Whigs before being entered into evidence at court. Governor William Seward (a Whig) dismissed Morris from his post, but could do nothing about the duly elected Mayor Varian. Varian did not run for re-election in 1841, but Morris became the Democratic candidate and succeeded Varian as mayor. Varian went on to become a State Senator. The Varian family farm now houses the Museum of Bronx History.

49 It has become common among scholars of William James to assert that he came to personally embody the kind of uniquely American scholar for whom Emerson had called for in the book. Douglas Anderson, however, has advanced a plausible claim for it having been, instead, Charles Sanders Peirce (Douglas Anderson, "Peirce and Pragmatism," in *The Oxford Handbook of American Philosophy*, ed. Cheryl Misak (Oxford, UK: Oxford University Press, 2008), 38–59. Much more is said about Peirce and his relationship to James later.

50 Fuller (1810–1850) was from Cambridge, MA. Her father, Timothy Fuller, was a congressman and orator. Through her brother, Arthur, she was also the great aunt of the architect, Buckminster Fuller. Early in her life, she was a teacher at the Temple School in Boston, which had been founded by the leading Transcendentalist, Bronson Alcott. Perhaps more prominently, she was a convener of public meetings about women's education. When Emerson was looking to hire an editor for *The Dial*, Fuller agreed to the job where several others had declined. In 1843, she wrote a series of influential feminist essays collectively titled "The Great Lawsuit." These were initially published in *The Dial*, but they were republished in book form as *Woman in the Nineteenth Century* (New York, NY: Greeley & McElrath, 1845). In 1844, Fuller left *The Dial* to write for

the *Tribune*, where she reviewed literature and offered social commentary. In 1846 she became the *Tribune*'s European correspondent, the first woman in the US to hold such a post. While across the Atlantic, she became romantically involved with a prominent Italian revolutionary, Giovanni Ossoli. After returning to New York, Fuller, Ossoli, and their two-year old son died in a shipwreck near Fire Island, New York on July 19, 1850.

51 Habegger, *Henry James Sr.*, 127.

52 Henry's father, William James of Albany, attempted to punish Henry for his profligate youth by willing him an annuity that was smaller than those given to several of his siblings, in the hope that this would force him to become productive. The will was challenged in court and, according to one biographer, Henry eventually received holdings that brought him about $10,000 per year (Katherine Weissbourd, *Growing Up in the James Family: Henry James Sr., as Son and Father* (Ann Arbor, MI: UMI Research Press, 1978), 28). This is the modern equivalent of $230,000 per year (using inflation calculator at www.westegg.com/inflation/infl.cgi, January 22, 2015). Although Weissbourd's slim volume includes many interesting facts, it is unfortunately marred by its neo-psychoanalytic (specifically, Eriksonian) speculations about Henry's relationship to his father and the impact that this might have had on his dealings with the church and with conventional Protestant theology more broadly. The account in Habegger's *Henry James Sr.* is not tendentious in this way, and is much more extensive. See also Austin Warren, *The Elder Henry James* (New York, NY: Palgrave Macmillan, 1934).

53 The exact date has never been firmly fixed. If 1789 is correct, it would mean that William James arrived the very year that Washington was inaugurated the first president of the US.

54 It has become conventional to designate him thus in order to distinguish him both from Henry's brother, Rev. William James of Rochester, and from Henry's eldest son, William James, the famous Harvard professor of psychology and philosophy.

55 Clinton started out as a Democratic-Republican, the party of Presidents Thomas Jefferson, James Madison, and James Monroe. He served as US Senator (1802–03) and as Mayor of New York City (most of 1803–1815). In 1812, however, he ran for US President as a candidate for the Federalist Party, the Democratic-Republicans' chief rival. He lost to the incumbent, Madison, but fell short by less than 8,000 in the popular vote. Clinton became head of the Erie Canal Commission in 1816 and, the next year, won the Governorship of New York State, which he held for 8 of the next 11 years (1817–1822, 1825–1828).

56 Behind only New York City real estate magnate Jacob Astor. Toll receipts from the Canal topped a half-million dollars in the first year alone. Burrows and Wallace, *Gotham*, 431.

57 Two major segments of the northeastern Appalachians.

58 Burrows and Wallace, *Gotham*, 431.

59 The country's central financial institution at the time was the Second Bank of the United States. The Second Bank's charter was due for renewal in 1836, but Jackson, fearing that it would be used by the opposition Whigs against his Democratic Party in the presidential election to be held later that same year, vetoed the bill renewing its charter. This left the country without a central bank, so Jackson had the control of the currency dispersed to private, local banks that were sympathetic to Jackson's cause— "pet" banks, as they were called. The pet banks, interested only in their own private gain and not in the general national interest, initiated a rapid and massive increase of the money supply which, predictably, led to high inflation, a rapid deterioration in wage-earners' real incomes, and a land speculation bubble, all of which prompted the greatest financial crash the US had ever seen the following year, 1837.

60 Habegger, *Henry James Sr.*, 199.

61 Letter to Thomas Carlyle, 1840, cited in Morton White and Lucia White, *The Intellectual Versus the City: From Thomas Jefferson to Frank Lloyd Wright* (Cambridge, MA: Harvard University Press, 1962), 39.

62 Ibid., 42.

63 Henry James, *Society the Redeemed Form of Man, and the Earnest of God's Omnipotence in Human Nature, Affirmed in Letters to a Friend* (Boston, MA: Houghton, Osgood, 1879).

64 Charles Fourier (1772–1837) was a French socialist thinker who laid out a vision for a utopian community. More than two dozen communities were started in the US that followed his principles, among them the Transcendentalists' Brook Farm in West Roxbury, Massachusetts. Fourier's ideas also influenced the leaders of the failed German revolution of 1848 and the Paris Commune of 1871.

65 Emanuel Swedenborg (1688–1772) was a Swedish scientist. In his 50s, he started having religious visions that he believed led him to the "True Christianity" which had become clouded by hundreds of years of theology, via mystical interpretations of Biblical Scripture. He wrote 18 theological works in the last 30 years of his life, most notably the eight-volume *Arcana Cœlestia, or Heavenly Secrets*, (1749–1756). He was anti-Trinitarian and believed that faith must be accompanied by charity in order for one to attain salvation. He was tried for heresy at the age of 80 and, as a result, the court declared that his system should not be taught.

66 Habegger, *Henry James Sr.*, 228–29.

67 Cited in Ibid., 268. The comment appeared in a short-lived (1844–1846) Putney, Vermont newspaper called *The Perfectionist, and the Theocratic Watchman* (vol. 5, p. 79). Habegger tentatively attributed it to John Humphrey Noyes, another Christian utopian who founded a commune in Oneida, NY in 1848, and who is said to have coined the term "free love."

68 Ibid., 273–75.

69 Nephew of the eminent theologian William Ellery Channing, who had died seven years before.

70 Letter from Ralph Waldo Emerson to Henry James, August 28, 1849. William James Papers bMS Am 1092.9 C 3990. Houghton Library, Harvard University.

71 *New York Post*, December 19, 1882, cited in Habegger, *Henry James Sr.*, 296.

72 Greely liked provocative writers in his paper. From 1852 to 1862 he hired an obscure but often inflammatory German philosopher by the name of Karl Marx to write dozens of columns per year (see www.marxists.org/archive/marx/works/subject/newspapers/new-york-tribune.htm).

73 Robert D. Richardson, *William James: In the Maelstrom of Modernity* (Boston, MA: Houghton-Mifflin, 2006), 32.

74 Bjork, *William James*, 1.

75 Fields, Annie. Journals. July 28, 1864. Annie Adams Fields Papers. Massachusetts Historical Society. Boston. Cited in Habegger, *Henry James Sr.*, 305; and in Richardson, *William James*, 32.

76 Ralph Waldo Emerson, "The Poet," in *Essays: Second Series* (Boston, MA: J. Munroe, 1844).

77 Miller James E., Jr., *Walt Whitman* (New York, NY: Twayne Publishers, 1962), 27.

78 Letter cited in David S. Reynolds, *Walt Whitman's America: A Cultural Biography* (New York, NY: Vintage Books, 1995), 194, 343.

79 Burrows and Wallace, *Gotham*, 631.

80 In the poem later titled "Eidolons" from "Book I. Inscriptions" of *Leaves of Grass*, 1855.

81 Walt Whitman, *Leaves of Grass* (Brooklyn, NY, 1855). The poem begins "I celebrate myself." This passage appears on p. 24. A better-known version of this passage first appeared in section 16 of the 1867 edition of the poem, which had been titled "Song of Myself":

Of every hue and caste am I, of every rank and religion;
A farmer, mechanic, artist, gentleman, sailor, quaker;
A prisoner, fancy-man, rowdy, lawyer, physician, priest.

82 *Leaves of Grass* (1860 edition) "Chants Democratic. 20." A better-known version of this poem, first appearing in the 1867 edition, begins with "I hear America singing," but does not include the crucial final stanza.

83 Henry James, *Washington Square* (New York: Harper & Bros., 1880). This quote from p. 16 of the 1964 Signet Classic edition.

84 See Habegger, *Henry James Sr.*, 312–16.

85 Letter to Emerson August 31,1849. William was once reported to have rejected Henry Jr. with the retort that "I play with boys who curse and swear." Both cited in Habegger, *Henry James, Sr.*, 287, 288.

86 It wasn't only the Irish who were landing: 50,000 Germans, also mostly Catholic, arrived in New York in 1847 as well.

87 Boston was receiving, proportionally, even larger numbers of Irish: 37,000 in 1847 to a city of just 115,000. Philadelphia and Baltimore experienced major influxes as well. But nowhere were the raw numbers as large as in New York.

88 See www.historyplace.com/worldhistory/famine/america.htm (Accessed 4 August 2010).

89 Burrows and Wallace, *Gotham*, 653.

90 In his capacity as president of Lane Theological Seminary in Cincinnati.

91 The tracing of Margaret Garner's ultimate fate is fraught with difficulty, but it is clear that she was subsequently sold multiple times, in part to thwart Northern officers' efforts to return her to Ohio to try her on the outstanding murder charge. She appears to have lived in Arkansas, New Orleans, and finally Mississippi, where she succumbed to Typhoid fever in 1858. A fictionalized version of Garner's story was popularized in Toni Morrison's novel *Beloved* (New York, NY: Alfred Knopf, 1987), later adapted to film.

92 Originally presented as a lecture in New York in 1850. Published in Henry James, Sr., *Lectures and Miscellanies* (New York, NY: Redfield, 1852). Quoted passages from pp. 2–3.

93 Ibid., 22.

94 Ibid., 48.

95 The remark was recorded in the February 13, 1890 entry of her journal, published as Leon Edel, ed., *The Diary of Alice James* (New York, NY: Dodd, Mead, 1964), 85. She went on to remark that all of her servants lied, whether Catholic or not.

96 James, *Washington Square* (originally published 1880). This quote is from p. 80 of the 1964 Signet Classic edition.

97 Habegger, *Henry James Sr.*, 343.

98 Suggested in Ibid., 354–57.

99 Actually, the first "rail boom" in New York had been in the 1830s, in the wake of the launch of the fabled Baltimore & Ohio. Indeed, the New York & Erie had been chartered back in 1832, but had taken nearly two decades to build. The immediate impact on New York City had been small, however. The little New York & Harlem railway ran up and down the island beginning the 1830s, using a small steam engine down to 27th Street, and then horses from that point to its terminus at City Hall. Despite that early foray, it was only in the 1850s that trains became an important part of New York City's commercial scene.

100 Burrows and Wallace, *Gotham*, 655.

101 A barrel of flour that sold for six dollars in New York could be sold for as much as $200 in California. Some companies could pay for a clipper ship of the fastest new design with the profits of a single shipment west. See Ibid., 651.

102 Scott had been a leader of US troops during Mexican-American War of 1846–1848, and in two earlier Indian wars. There is no indication that he proposed to launch new military ventures, though the possibility of invading Cuba was in the air. Slavery was the primary issue of the day. Scott was opposed to expanding it to the newly acquired

western territories, but much of his party was in favor. It is not clear who, if anyone, Henry James supported for the Whig nomination. The sitting president, Millard
Fillmore, although from New York, was mostly favored by southern delegates. The
New England delegates rallied round the 70-year-old Daniel Webster, locking up the
convention for 53 ballots until Scott emerged (barely) victorious. Webster died just
weeks later.

103 March 8, 1852, William James Papers, bMS Am 1902.9D, 4107, Houghton Library,
Harvard University.

104 Habegger, *Henry James Sr.*, 354.

105 The 14-year-old William James "supposed" in one letter that his older correspondent
would vote for Frémont because "he seems to have the best chance." (Letter to Edgar
Beach Van Winkle, July 1, 1856, *Correspondence of William James*, vols. 4, 4.

2

GRANVILLE STANLEY HALL

The Farmboy Goes to Gotham

1. Rural Massachusetts

On February 1, 1844, just over two years after the birth of William James, a first child was born to a young married couple in Ashfield, Massachusetts: Granville Bascom Hall and Abigail Beals Hall.[1] They named their new son Granville after his father, but his middle name, Stanley, was what he would be called all his life. It was a signal year in the modernization of America. In May, Samuel Morse officially opened the telegraph wire he had strung from the Capitol Building in Washington, DC to Mount Clare train station in Baltimore, the first of its kind in the US. The year before he had persuaded Congress to subsidize the project to the tune of $30,000 (about $700,000 today). Also in May (and later July), the Philadelphia Bible riots (described in the last chapter) unfolded, rocking urban America's relationship with its rapidly growing immigrant communities.

Few childhoods could have been as different from William James' as Stanley Hall's was. Hall's birthplace of Ashfield was in rural Franklin County, situated in the northwestern region of Massachusetts. Its distance psychologically from both the technological marvels and religious clashes of the 1840s was, perhaps, even greater than its geographical distance. Urbanization and industrialization were distant concerns for the old stock community of Hall's childhood. Indeed, it was said that only one household in all of Ashfield was not Anglo-Saxon Protestant, an Irish family.[2] The town of Ashfield was over 100 miles from Boston—two or three long days' ride with a horse and wagon—and it was nearly as far, too, from the emerging factory towns of Lowell and Worcester. The primary occupation of Franklin country was farming—mostly corn, potatoes, oats, wheat, dairy, and wool.[3] The county seat of Greenfield sat about 20 miles to Ashfield's northeast, along the Connecticut River. The river was a major transport corridor, providing ready access south to Long Island Sound and, thence, to New York City. The river also served as a convenient boundary between the rapid, sometimes radical developments—both political and industrial—in the eastern part of the state, and the more traditional and conservative western region. Thirty miles to Ashfield's west lay Pittsfield, the only sizeable city of western Massachusetts, just a few miles from the New York state border (see Figure 2.1).[4]

Hall described himself as being of "sturdy, old, New England, Puritan stock."[5] Both of his parents could trace their ancestry to the arrival of *The Mayflower* in 1620: His mother was a descendant of John Alden, who is traditionally claimed to have been the first *Mayflower* passenger to set foot on Plymouth Rock. Alden was a signer of the Mayflower Compact, the original governing document of the Plymouth Colony. Stanley's father was descended from the *Mayflower* preacher and early Plymouth Colony leader, Elder William Brewster.[6]

Hall's ancestors had moved west from the Cape three generations before. The land was hilly, but still afforded better tillage than the rocky land near the coast,

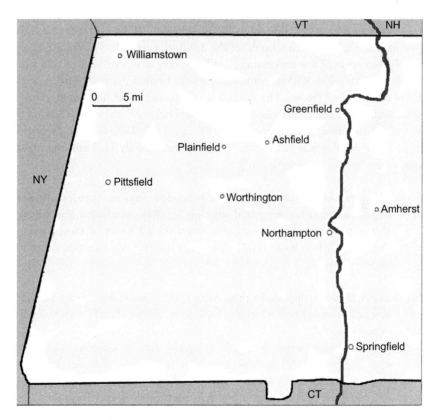

FIGURE 2.1 Map of western Massachusetts, including several towns relevant to G. Stanley Hall's early life.

and it was inexpensive. Hall's father had tried to move even farther west, purchasing 320 acres of government land in Wisconsin (in present-day Milwaukee), but he was unable to make a go of it and returned to Ashfield shortly after Stanley's birth. The family then purchased a hundred-acre farm in nearby Worthington to which it moved in 1846, when Stanley was just two years old. Although the move was less than 20 miles, it placed the Hall family in a different county, Hampshire, which was centered on the town of Northampton, also on the Connecticut River. Stanley's younger brother Robert was born in 1846. A sister, Julina, was born in 1847.

True to its Puritan roots, the Hall family was strictly Congregationalist. Stanley's father was described as a Calvinist of the old school,[7] and his mother was religiously conservative as well. Despite the traditional suspicion of higher education among "old school" American Protestants,[8] however, Abigail Beals had attended a "Female Seminary" in Albany, NY (which was considerably closer to her hometown of Plainfield, MA[9] than was Boston). She applied to attend Mt. Holyoke College, just 35 miles southeast of Plainfield, but was refused admission, reportedly on the grounds that there was no room at the school that year.[10] Stanley's father paid for some additional schooling for himself beyond that which was provided by the "common schools" of the day. Both parents had served as teachers briefly. As a result of this uncommon, if still not very advanced, level of education, Stanley was raised in a home with many books beyond the traditional two: the Bible and *Pilgrim's Progress*. His mother is said to have read her children stories from William Shakespeare, Walter Scott, Charles Dickens,[11] and the *Arabian Nights*, as well as from that literary sensation of the age, *Uncle Tom's Cabin*, published in 1852 when Stanley was just eight.[12] Of his father's family, Hall said that it was marked by "extreme conservatism":

> They had little sympathy with new-fangled ways or even labor-saving devices for it rather suggested shirking. . . . My grandfather, for instance, always preferred the slow-moving oxen for all kinds of farm work to horses, and when his sons introduced the latter he was reluctant to see the improvement.[13]

Hall's father, however, displayed a progressive spirit in some aspects of his life: He "kept abreast of innovations in farming techniques and machinery, even inventing some of his own."[14]

The elder Hall, however, had little sympathy for the Catholic immigrants who were beginning to fill up America's cities. In 1855, he won election to the Massachusetts Legislature under the banner of the anti-Catholic, anti-immigrant Know-Nothing Party. This was just one year after the party had swept state elections and was at the very height of its popularity. In apparent contrast with his adamant opposition to Catholic immigrants, Hall's father was also opposed to slavery (though such a split in sympathies was not uncommon at the time). He was supporter of Charles Sumner, the abolitionist US senator from Massachusetts[15] who, in May 1856, was beaten into unconsciousness on the Senate floor by a South Carolina congressman, Preston Brooks, in retribution for a speech in which he had denounced the Kansas-Nebraska Act and ridiculed the southern politicians who had been behind it (one of whom was related to Brooks). Sumner became a great hero and martyr in the north, being re-elected to the Senate in November of the same year despite not being able to return to his seat in the Senate for three years due to the injuries he had suffered.[16] The attack on Sumner was so notorious that it was memorialized in waxworks at Barnum's American Museum in New York.[17] It also served to galvanize the fledgling Republican party, which finished second in the 1856 presidential election. The Know-Nothings were done and Hall did not run for office again. Still, the Hall family remained devoted to Sumner and his cause: Stanley reported in his autobiography that, at the age of fifteen, he walked the 18 miles to Greenfield to hear Sumner speak, describing the senator as "a god-man with a head and voice like Jove."[18] When war came, the elder Hall,

> made war speeches at prayer meetings and in public, imploring the blessing of Heaven upon Lincoln and the northern army, refused to meet a slaveholder who spent summers in Ashfield, and later grew almost bitter toward Lincoln because he so long delayed to free the slaves and finally did so as a war measure.[19]

As fiercely as he opposed slavery, however, even more fiercely he protected his son from having to fight in the war, using a minor knee injury that Stanley had sustained to obtain a certificate of exemption from military service, and later purchasing a "substitute." These were measures that drew censure from some of his neighbors—those whose sons had fought, some of whom had died—and it was a source of shame to Stanley to the end of his days.[20]

Hall describes a great deal of his early childhood in terms of the animals he encountered—the cows and sheep he was responsible for herding, the horses he bridled and harnessed, the mother sow that attacked him, and especially the wild animals that he killed. Raised on tales of Daniel Boone, and given both an old shotgun by his father and a new pistol by his uncle at age 11,[21] the young Hall wreaked terror on the small critters of the surrounding countryside (though probably no more than many other boys of his time and place). He regaled readers of his autobiography with stories of his having hunted and trapped rats, chipmunks, squirrels, muskrats, woodchucks, skunks, and raccoons, among others. From many of these he took skins and tails, carefully preserving them in order to later display them as trophies to his friends. He reported that he was "very cruel" to frogs, without elaborating further.[22] From out of the air he shot crows and hawks and passenger pigeons. Of these last, he wrote wistfully (if somewhat disingenuously):

> I well remember, too, the vast flocks of passenger pigeons that flew in my earliest boyhood, sometimes almost clouding the sun and alighting in rows

as thick as they could stand on the beech and other trees in the forest. These I used to shoot in great numbers, sometimes getting an alignment of a row of them and bringing down a number at a shot. . . . Now one of the mysteries of natural history is the complete disappearance of these birds from this country . . ."[23]

He suggested that this childhood fascination with animals might have "laid the foundations" for the interest he would take in animal and comparative psychology in his adulthood.[24] This was a penchant that would forever separate him intellectually from one of his strongest professional allies, the English-born Cornell

FIGURE 2.2 Granville Stanley Hall, age six, and his parents.

Credit: Hall, *Life and Confessions of a Psychologist.* New York: D. Appleton, 1924.

FIGURE 2.2 (continued)

psychologist Edward Bradford Titchener. It aligned him, instead, with those whom Titchener implied, with his dismissive epithet "Functionalist," were not to be taken wholly seriously as scientists (though Hall would never use that term explicitly to describe his own position within the field).

Hall's local elementary schooling involved Bible study, reading, geography, arithmetic, grammar, writing, and history. In higher grades he was also taught algebra, Latin, Greek, and literature (Milton and Pope), which, Hall said, "gave us a sense of esoteric superiority because here our parents were not able to help us and we felt we had entered upon an education that was really 'higher.'"[25] Hall wrote many stories and orations as a young teenager, rarely read by anyone other than himself. Writing held a special import for Hall because, a natural left-hander, he had been forced to switch to the right side as a teen, which had a profoundly negative impact on the legibility of his script.[26] For a time he thought he would become a historian, but this idea, "entirely died out soon after I entered college and was supplanted by other aims."[27] A portion of his autobiography reads like a tour through the "old yellow chest, which my mother long made the receptacle of everything we children wrote,"[28] and which Hall apparently kept in his possession until old age.

Music played a large role in Hall's early life. In addition to singing in a number of choirs, he learned to play a variety of musical instruments—violin, piano, accordion; with the last of these he "surreptitiously officiated as musician at dances at neighbors' houses, although my parents strongly disapproved." With some of his friends he formed a band of "jew's harp, harmonica, and 'bones.'" They learned to clog dance; "A group of us taught each other "steps copied from the strolling negro minstrels."[29] Although he would only play privately later in life, he confessed to falling into reveries even as an adult in which he was a "great performer playing either at a concert to admiring and applauding crowds, or surprising a little circle or perhaps some individual friend by suddenly coming forward and displaying wonderful capacity as a performer." It seems that music always had a hold on Hall's imagination.

At the age of sixteen, Hall became certified as a teacher and worked for a year at various schools in the area surrounding Ashfield. He was often billeted at the homes of his students, some of whom were older than he was. He would come home to his parents on weekends, weather permitting. The following year, however, with his parents' assistance, he traveled to Williston Academy, a private secondary school at which he prepared in earnest to enter college. Although only 24 miles from home, Hall entered, at Williston, an entirely new society of young men (and women) who had some experience of the wider world and the ambition to make their mark in it. The Williston curriculum was mostly classical, and the standards of achievement were set for those who aspired to go to Harvard and Yale. Hall did not graduate because his progress in mathematics lagged somewhat. Nevertheless, upon sitting an oral examination at Williams College, in the extreme northwest of the state, Hall was admitted to start college in the fall of 1863.

2. Off to College

Far to the south of Hall's home, the Civil War raged on. In January of 1863, President Lincoln proclaimed the freedom of all American slaves. In the first week of July, some 370 miles away in Gettysburg, Pennsylvania, the course of the war and of the country began to turn, purchased at the nearly inconceivable price of 50,000 casualties. In mid-July, hundreds of New Yorkers were killed and thousands more wounded as poor, desperate Irish and German immigrants turned against the poor, desperate, and mostly defenseless Black residents of the city. Their outrage was provoked by the shocking realization that by becoming US citizens, which enabled them to vote for the Tammany Hall politicians who protected them, they had also become eligible to be drafted into a war which they saw primarily as emancipating southern slaves who would come to New York to compete with them for the few miserable jobs that were now available to them. So great was their fury that one of their targets was an asylum for Black orphans. The mob was especially enraged by the provision of the draft act that allowed the wealthy to buy their way out of the mayhem. Thousands of federal troops, armed with bayonets and artillery, were required to restore what normally passed for order in New York after three days of violent chaos. Similar "Draft Riots"—echoes of the tumult in Gotham—were soon seen in Boston and other cities.

Protected from the draft by the exemption his father had purchased, Hall went to college rather than to war. Hall's school, Williams College, operated under the presidency of a man named Mark Hopkins, as it had for almost the previous three decades. Although Hopkins is almost forgotten today, at the time he was widely regarded as one of the great minds of New England. Physician, philosopher, and theologian, Hopkins' intellectual orientation followed in the tradition of William Hamilton (1788–1856), the Edinburgh philosopher who had folded a dose of Kantian Idealism into the Scottish common sense tradition. That tradition was dear to the President of Williams. As Hall once put it, for Hopkins "there were no open questions but only further details to be filled in."[30]

Hall recorded that "the Hopkins cult has been intense at Williams," but it was not without its dissenters. John A. Bascom, later president of the University of Wisconsin, was among Hall's teachers at Williams. Bascom gently guided Hall away from Hamilton, nudging him instead in the direction of the empiricist and associationist philosophy of John Stuart Mill. Hall took the bait, later calling Mill his "first love and hero in philosophy."[31]

Apart from Hopkins and Bascom, Hall found the general intellectual caliber of the Williams faculty to be below that at his prep school, Williston. Latin and Greek were no harder than they had been before. Little natural science was taught. The lack of challenge, however, gave Hall much time for elective reading. He joined a literature club that read and discussed Ralph Waldo Emerson, Thomas Carlyle, and Samuel Taylor Coleridge, among others. Emerson—the radical Concord sage who had befriended Henry James Sr.—came to town to speak once, leading to what Hall called an "Emerson craze"[32] among the students, though the faculty ignored him, distrustful of his "ultra-Unitarianism."[33] Hall even went to visit the great man afterwards, but could later recall little of the encounter except being overawed by his mere presence.

At the end of his sophomore year, Hall was pressured by some seniors to become a more active, more evangelical Christian. He sometimes referred to this as his "conversion," though usually in scare quotes. He attended prayer meetings and taught a Bible class to "mature ladies" in a nearby town. His parents were very pleased by this apparent change in their son, but he later suggested that he was just going through the motions, writing of the experience: "I cannot think that it made any great change in my life."[34]

Perhaps the main effect of Williams on Hall was to bring him into contact with men who would go on to significant academic careers of their own, some even attaining college presidencies, as would Hall. Also, while Hall was at Williams, the renowned author, progressive reformer, and Harvard art professor Charles Eliot Norton purchased a summer house in Hall's hometown of Ashfield. It has been said that Norton was regarded as "the most cultivated man in United States."[35] Norton's mere presence seems to have changed the character of the town, somewhat. As Hall remembers it:

> Norton organized his famous dinners for the benefit of the Academy where for twenty-five years the people of the town, and the many who came from a distance as these festivals grew in fame, heard perhaps for two hours after the banquet the most distinguished speakers—Mark Twain, who once came up from Hartford; [novelist] George Cable from Northampton; [journalist] Parke Godwin from Cummington; Rudyard Kipling (although I am not certain that he ever spoke there); Mathew Arnold; [poet and ambassador to England] James Russell Lowell . . .; Presidents [Charles W.] Eliot of Harvard and [Franklin] Carter of Williams; ex-ambassador [to Germany and Austria-Hungary, William Walter] Phelps; Senator G. F. Hoar, and others.[36]

The young Hall himself was invited, where he was displayed as a promising local product to the various luminaries in attendance.[37]

The end of the war, the assassination of Lincoln, the botched "Reconstruction" of the South, the impeachment of Johnson—none of these events find any place in Hall's autobiography, and they apparently had little memorable impact on his then still-young life.

3. New York City

After graduation from Williams in 1867, Hall was not certain what to do with himself, but desired still more education. Although he did not feel terribly devout, he held out the promise of his becoming a clergyman to persuade his parents

FIGURE 2.3   G. Stanley Hall, 1866, age 22.

Credit: Hall, *Life and Confessions of a Psychologist*. New York: D. Appleton, 1924.

to help fund his way through Union Theological Seminary in New York City. Union had been founded during the great schism between the Old School and New School Presbyterians in the mid-1830s, mentioned in the last chapter. In particular, when the New School Presbyterians of the Princeton Seminary found that they could no longer operate alongside those of the Old School, who dominated the Princeton faculty, the New Schoolers departed and joined with others to found their own seminary in New York City. Union was the result.[38] By the time Hall arrived some thirty years later, Union was ecumenically accepting students from various Protestant denominations, though it was still predominantly Presbyterian and Congregationalist.[39]

Despite its reputation for excellence, Hall found "a distinct let-down of tone and standard" moving from Williams to Union.[40] Hall, once again, created his own educational experience: He joined a positivism club that read the works of Auguste Comte and Herbert Spencer. He also read leading scientific figures such as Charles Darwin and John Tyndall. In short, he gave himself an education in modern secularism while ostensibly studying for the ministry.

Hall had never been to a city of any size—not even Albany or Springfield, he said. But now he was in the largest city in America, and did not miss the opportunity to seek out things he could find almost nowhere else. He went to lectures, theater, concerts, and opera. He saw Charles Dickens speak. He had his head "read" at Fowler and Wells' famous phrenology "emporium." He consulted spiritualist mediums who would later be revealed as frauds. He attended police court, a prison, a morgue, and a home for "foundlings." He saw P.T. Barnum's American Museum—the one that had been virtually across the street from William James' birthplace—burn to the ground with many of its display animals still inside; often described as one of the most spectacular fires the city had ever seen.[41]

Working for the City Missionary Society, Hall visited tenements, inviting the residents to religious meetings, and witnessing "scenes of intense pathos." He would "invite street-walkers to the midnight mission for them nearby."[42] He explored the notorious Five Points slum and the neighboring Bowery district. He saw the leading preachers of his day, including Henry Ward Beecher (son of Lyman Beecher and brother of Harriet Beecher Stowe). He attended the religious services not only of other Protestant denominations, but also Catholic, Eastern Orthodox, and even Jewish rites.

Although Hall was in New York for just three years,[43] it had a profound impact on his outlook. He was introduced to a wider, more variegated world than he had ever dreamt possible during his perambulations around the towns of western Massachusetts. It was also during this time that philosophy started to become the focus of his scholarly interests, and that he began to conceive the possibility of becoming a professor.

A more senior student at Union, George Sylvester Morris, returned from a study trip to Germany during Hall's time there. Hall was impressed by Morris' worldliness—a model of the kind of scholar Hall himself would like to become. Morris arrived back in New York with a direct knowledge of the approach to biblical studies known as the "Higher Criticism," which was then prominent in German theological scholarship. He also had an understanding and appreciation of Hegelian philosophy that was relatively rare in America at the time.[44] Hall came to believe, probably correctly, that to become a scholar like Morris, he would have to follow Morris' footsteps to Germany for a period of intense study. Unlike Morris, however, Hall did not have the money to pursue such a path, and his parents, he knew without asking, would disapprove of such a venture, fearing that it might lead to the condition American Protestants dreaded most: skepticism.

Through a friend of his at Union identified only as "Mann," Hall became personally acquainted with Henry Ward Beecher. Beecher had once asked Hall whether theological training had made him more or less devout. Hall frankly answered that it had made him less so. Months later, when Hall was acting as student-minister to a community in rural Pennsylvania—learning first hand just how little he was going to enjoy such a career—he received a kind of summons from Beecher to meet him in New York. When Hall arrived, Beecher inquired about his desire to study in Germany, an aspiration to which Hall quickly confessed. Beecher gave him an envelope addressed to Henry Sage, a man who had made a fortune in the lumber trade, and who would later use it to endow the school of philosophy at Cornell University. Hall obeyed, presenting the letter at Sage's New York City office. According to Hall, Sage met him personally, read the letter, grumbled about the liberties Beecher took with his purse, but wrote Hall a check for $500 on the spot, a loan, and told him to sail for Germany the next day.[45] Hall did as he was told and, in a flash, was the American scholar studying abroad that he had thought he never could be.[46]

4. Germany

Hall left for Germany in June of 1869,[47] arriving first at Bonn, where he enrolled in courses with the Biblical scholar Johann Peter Lange, whom Hall said was "held in great reverence at Union."[48] Lange was an elderly man, a follower of F. D. E. Schleiermacher's school of biblical interpretation (hermeneutics), and he had long been a central figure in the Modern Liberal Theology movement (in which many of Union's professors participated as well). Hall won an invitation to Lange's house for supper, along with the professor's middle-aged daughters, where he witnessed what he called, "the charming life and disposition of Westpahlians."[49]

After about six months, Hall moved from Bonn to Berlin, where he took courses not only in theology, but also in physiology, with famed neuro-muscular researcher Emil Du Bois-Reymond.[50] In addition, he attended the clinics of the neurologist who directed the department of nervous and mental diseases at Charité Hospital, Carl Westphal, as well as the surgical demonstrations of Bernhard van Langenbeck.[51] These contacts were Hall's first direct exposure to topics closely related to psychology in a natural-scientific mode. Such a discipline had not yet fully come into existence but it would later serve as the launch pad of Hall's professional career. Still, at this time, Hall's primary focus—at least officially—was the theology courses of Issak August Dorner[52] and, especially the philosophy of Friedrich Adolf Trendelenberg. The latter was a renowned scholar of Aristotle's work and, at first, Hall found that his own knowledge of ancient Greek lagged behind that of other members of the seminar. He persevered, however, and continued on in Trendelenberg's course on Greek philosophy the following year. Despite his Classical focus, Trendelenberg had a reputation for being a forward-looking philosopher, fully alive to the profound transformation of traditional religious belief systems then underway; a realignment of religion in response to (sometimes in opposition to) developments in historical criticism and natural science. Where psychology would ultimately reside—theology, philosophy, or science—when these massive epistemological shifts were complete was an important and controversial question at the time, and it is said that Trendelenberg was at work on a book about psychology when he died at the age of 69, just two years after Hall's encounter with him. Hall later recalled that had been,

> greatly impressed by his [Trendelenberg's] conception of motion or movement as the prime category, in which he differed from Hegel by placing it first and holding that the ideas of both being and nothing were evolved from it. This conception I much later tried to develop in several articles.[53]

Indeed, Hall's subsequent doctoral dissertation at Harvard would be on muscular movement and there can be little doubt his prior exposure to Trendelenberg, Westphal, and Du Bois-Reymond played their parts in raising the salience of movement as a research question for Hall.

In July of 1870, a year after Hall had arrived in Germany, the Franco-Prussian War broke out. The Prussian universities closed as students enlisted in the army, but Hall and several other Americans recast themselves as *ad hoc* war correspondents under the guidance of a "Dr. Jacobi" who was said to be passing their reports on to various New York newspapers.[54] Hall came within a few miles of the front at the Battle of Sedan (September 1, 1870). After a few weeks, Hall was replaced by more experienced reporters, and he returned to Berlin for the duration of the war. The Prussian victory the following year brought about great changes in German society. Most obviously, it precipitated the final unification of the German states. More subtly, according to Hall, the country,

> received a new soul, and the great transition from culture to *Kultur*, which has since brought her to grief [a reference to the outcome of WWI], if not then actually begun was accelerated greatly. . . . Every Prussian seemed to stand more erect, was less *gemütlich* [warm, congenial], and less respectful to foreigners, as one noted even in asking the way upon the street.[55]

It wasn't all courses and wars for Hall in Germany, however. One of the new pastimes he learned while in Europe was ballroom dancing. His Congregationalist parents were, of course, aghast when he foolishly reported this to them in a letter. His father, slightly misquoting the poet Alexander Pope, warned him: "Vice is a monster of so hideous mien!" Hall reassured his father that his moral character was intact, suggested that the Christian "law of love" did not permit him to offend his hosts by refusing, and he continued to dance.[56] On another occasion, during his second summer there, Hall and a young German acquaintance set out on a walking trip from Bonn to Switzerland (about 500 km). Their resolve quickly broke down, however, and they soon resorted to taking boats and trains much of the way. They made it well into the Alps, climbing one day on to what Hall described as a "spur" of the Wetterhorn (the summit of which had only been reached for the first time some 15 years earlier). They spent the night there in the home of a local "peasant."[57]

5. New York Again, and Then Out West

Hall returned to the US in the fall of 1870.[58] He believed that he had lined up a college professorship at the University of Minnesota,[59] but his German education actually brought suspicion down upon him, the president writing him that his beliefs would "unsettle men and teach them to hold no opinions."[60] Disappointed, Hall returned to New York and worked quickly toward the completion of his degree at Union. His attention was no longer on theology, if it ever really had been. He joined a number of "radical" discussion groups—his old positivist circle, as well as groups of evolutionists, social reformers, and utopians. Among the people he met was John Fiske, a vocal American advocate of Herbert Spencer's philosophy and a man who, unbeknownst to Hall, was closely involved with the people who would make up the cerebral salon known as the "Metaphysical Club" in Cambridge, Massachusetts: Chauncey Wright, Charles Sanders Peirce, Oliver Wendell Holmes, Jr., and William James, among others. From the discussions of the Metaphysical Club would emerge the characteristically American philosophy of pragmatism and an evolutionary approach to psychology that would inform the school of thought known as Functionalism.

Needing money, as always, Hall took over a job from his departing friend, George S. Morris.[61] The position was tutoring the sons of one of the most prominent Jewish bankers in New York, Jesse Seligman. The Seligmans virtually made Hall a part of their family. From his post with Seligman, Hall made the acquaintance of a wide range of prominent individuals in the city, Jewish and Gentile. Among these was the radical Jewish activist, later a Columbia University professor of ethics, Felix Adler.

After Hall had been working in the Seligman house for more than year, he was visited there by a biographer and historian named James K. Hosmer whom he had first met in Germany.[62] Hosmer was the son of the president of Antioch College in Yellow Springs, Ohio. He arrived to offer Hall a position teaching rhetoric and literature at the notoriously radical college: Antioch was fully under the administration of the Unitarian Church, a denomination that had become so liberal that some Protestants did not consider it to be truly Christian. Although far to the west, Antioch was, no doubt, already well known to Hall: Its first president had been Horace Mann, the prominent educational reformer in Massachusetts—often described as the "Father" of the Common School Movement—who had headed into the relative wilderness of western Ohio after losing a bid to become governor of the Bay State. Antioch was famous—some would say infamous—for being co-educational at a time when such an arrangement was extremely rare and controversial in the US. The co-educational character of the school was not limited to the students alone: One of Mann's nieces, Rebecca Pennell, was among its original faculty members and may have been the first female professor in the US to hold the same rank and receive the same pay as her male colleagues.[63] Antioch was also open to African American students; the Trustees passed a by-law to this effect in 1863. It is not clear whether any African American students were actually admitted, but even the commitment to do so was considered provocative in the shadow of the Civil War.[64]

Although Hall found, at Antioch, the freedom to read and teach controversial topics such as the ideas of Comte, Mill, Darwin, and Spencer, he also found that his professional duties there never seemed to end. During his first year, he taught English, French, and German language and literature, as well as serving as the college librarian. He was the leader of the choir, sometimes the church organist, and he also took turns leading Sunday church services. In addition, he held "rhetorical exercises" in the evenings. In his second year, he managed to focus most of his efforts on teaching philosophy, but there was still little time for personal study.

Despite the pressures Antioch placed on his time, several times he made the 400-mile trip west to St. Louis to participate in the discussions of the Hegelian circle that had gathered there around William Torrey Harris, the founder of the *Journal of Speculative Philosophy*.[65] Hall even published some of his earliest work in Harris' journal.[66] Like many ambitious young scholars in America at the time, Hall was drawn equally to the rationalist philosophical views of Hegel, on the one hand, and to the empiricist views of English philosophers and scientists, on the other. Both had an exciting, dynamic quality that had been lacking in the static Protestant theologies of their upbringings. However, whereas the English view, best exemplified perhaps by Darwin, appeared to offer a wildly disorganized, even chaotic view of historical change—a view that seemed to lead to nowhere in particular—the Hegelian view of historical development was ordered, logical, and tended toward a definable, morally elevated, endpoint. As a result, the young Hall and many others of his generation embraced a curious amalgam of Darwin and Hegel; a kind of safe, teleological Darwinism in which evolution surely occurs, but perhaps not as haphazardly as Darwin envisioned; not under the constant threat, as it seemed to them, of spinning perversely out of control towards disorder, destruction, and ultimately evil. Instead, it is a view of history that steadily progresses toward some vaguely but acceptably Christian and uplifting goal—such as, "God coming to consciousness in man."[67] As Hall's biographer put the matter, "Hall saw Darwinian evolution as the scientific analogue of Hegelian development."[68]

Although Antioch was legendary for its freedom from any particular religious dogma, such was not the case in the surrounding county of Greene. While teaching at the nearby "colored" college, Wilberforce, Hall's class was once invaded by what he called "an interesting outbreak of religious frenzy when an active revival was in progress."[69] Even at home in Yellow Springs, there was a women's temperance group that would post representatives outside of all the establishments that sold "demon liquor," marking down the name of every man who entered (giving one some idea of just how small and intimate a town it was). The town was not without its share of violence as well. Hall reported that he was once involved in catching and extracting confessions from a number of students who had bought essays they were supposed to have written themselves for courses. The papers had been purchased from a local group of Antioch alumni who had set up shop in town. By publishing the names of the confessors, Hall and his colleagues managed to put an end to what he called this "traffic in brains."[70] The leader of the essay-writing outfit, apparently unhappy with this turn of events, took a potshot at Hall with a revolver on the street a few days later. The bullet missed its mark, landing in a nearby post. Another shot was fired at the window of his home a few nights after. Later still, he reported, a small bottle of acid was thrown through a window while he was conducting his rhetorical exercises. The bottle broke and the contents spilled on his clothes, ruining them, but not harming Hall's person. Hall wrote about these events, nearly 50 years later, with perfect detachment, but one wonders whether these terrifying attacks had something to do with his departure from Antioch.

In any case, in 1874, Hall purchased and read a German textbook by a relatively obscure professor then teaching at the University of Zürich. The book had the rather extraordinary title of *Grundzüge der physiologischen Psychologie* (*Principles of Physiological Psychology*). Its author, Wilhelm Wundt, was a former assistant to the great Hermann Helmholtz and had published a series of lectures on the mind in the 1860s. The *Grundzüge* was unlike anything Hall had been seen before. It contained a program for recasting large portions of psychology, which until then had been regarded as a branch of philosophy, as an experimental discipline instead. The scheme followed along the same lines that had led to stunning advances in physiology during the previous few decades (such as discovering that nerves signaled each other by means of electricity, and even measuring the speed at which these signals were transmitted along the nerves). Wundt had taken the very equipment that was central to the success of laboratory physiology—the kymograph, the chronograph and chronoscope, etc.—and used it to apparently subtract away the time required for sensation and for motor reaction, leaving behind just the time required for "apperception"—the mental act of holding an idea or image in the central focus of consciousness.[71]

Hall was electrified by the possibilities raised by a wholly experimental psychology, and he decided to go study under Wundt. He resigned his Antioch position. The school persuaded him to stay one additional year but, in 1876, by which time Wundt had moved to a new professorship at Leipzig, Hall started his long journey toward becoming a thing which, as yet, barely existed, and which did not yet exist in the US at all: an experimental psychologist.

Notes

1 The details of Hall's upbringing are drawn primarily from G. Stanley Hall, *Life and Confessions of a Psychologist* (New York, NY: Appleton, 1923); from Dorothy Ross, *G. Stanley Hall: The Psychologist as Prophet* (Chicago, IL: University of Chicago Press, 1972); and from Louis N. G. Wilson, *Stanley Hall: A Sketch* (New York, NY: G. E. Stechert, 1914) (note that Wilson mistakenly gives 1846 as the year of Hall's birth). Edward L. Thorndike, "Biographical Memoir of G. Stanley Hall: 1846–1924," *National Academy of Sciences, Biographical Memoirs* 7, no. 5 (1925) drew from Wilson for biographical material on Hall (including the incorrect year of birth). Ross (pp. 5–6, n. 10) said the confusion arose from Hall himself having reported 1845 and then 1846 as the year of his birth, late in his life. Ross argued that the date of 1844 is confirmed in Hall's earliest writings on the subject, and in a letter his sister wrote to Wilson (who had published the wrong date 11 years earlier), which is recounted in a 1925 letter from Wilson to E. B. Titichener (of whom Wilson was once a student). See also the very sympathetic account of Hall's life and career in Lorine Pruette, *G. Stanley Hall: A Biography of a Mind* (Freeport, NY: Books for Libraries, 1926/1970).
2 Ross, *G. Stanley Hall*, 8.
3 Wilson, *Stanley Hall*, 11 (n. 1).
4 According to the US Census, the population of Pittsfield was 3,747 in 1840 and 5,872 in 1850.
5 Hall, *Life and Confessions*, 81.
6 By coincidence, famed Yale philosopher and psychologist George Trumbull Ladd (1842–1921) was also a descendant of William Brewster. See Emma C. Brewster Jones, *The Brewster Genealogy, 1566–1907: A Record of the Descendants of William Brewster of the "Mayflower," Ruling Elder of the Pilgrim Church Which Founded Plymouth Colony in 1620* (New York, NY: Grafton Press, 1908), 274, 620, 621.
7 The characterization comes from the noted Cambridge, Massachusetts intellectual, Charles Eliot Norton, who spent summers in Ashfield, in a letter addressed to the president of Johns Hopkins University, Daniel Coit Gilman, dated April 14, 1881. Cited in Ross, *G. Stanley Hall*, 5 (n. 8). Hall himself, however, said that the extended Hall family had a "general belief in religion, but always with moderation. No Hall was ever a pietist," (Hall, *Life and Confessions*, 58.).
8 See, e.g., Richard Hofstadter, *Anti-Intellectualism in American Life* (New York, NY: Random House, 1962), esp. chapter 4. Congregationalists and Presbyterians, among the various evangelical Protestant denominations, were not as adamantly opposed to education as the Methodists and the Baptists (see esp. p. 102). There were even some Congregationalist academies (and, of course, several prominent Presbyterian colleges: e.g., Yale, Princeton). Outside of New England, Congregationalism and Presbyterianism were so closely allied that the former partially lost its separate identity (see p. 90). Hofstadter reports what he calls a "bit of Protestant folklore": "A Methodist, it is said, is a Baptist who wears shoes; a Presbyterian is a Methodist who has gone to college; and an Episcopalian is a Presbyterian who lives off his investments" (p. 90, n. 9).
9 Plainfield, MA is 10 miles west of Ashfield, MA.
10 Hall, *Life and Confessions*, 32.
11 Coincidentally, Dickens' first trip to America had come just two years before Stanley's birth, in the first half of 1842, and his travelogue was published in October of the same year: Charles Dickens, *American Notes for General Circulation* (New York, NY: Harper & Brothers, 1842).
12 Hall, *Life and Confessions*, 45.
13 Ibid., 56–57. Richard Hofstadter also noted that American farmers of the era were notoriously hostile to technological advance (Hofstadter, *Anti-Intellectualism in American Life*, 275–77).

14 Ross, *G. Stanley Hall*, 6. See also the senior Hall's 1860 lecture praising famers who "produce fruits of the earth as the result of theory applied to practice," reprinted in Hall, *Life and Confessions*, 65–72. The lecture continues: "These [farmers] prove theories, discarding the false ones and practicing the true. Combining virtue and intelligence with physical and moral strength … none deserve more respect" (p. 67).

15 Hall, *Life and Confessions*, 63.

16 Stanley Hall reports in his autobiography (Ibid., 97–98) that, as a 12-year-old child, he made effigies of "Bully" Brooks, Stephen Douglas (the Illinois senator who supported slavery and ran as the Democratic candidate for president against Abraham Lincoln), and other "local characters whom we were taught to execrate." The young Hall then shot these effigies with his own gun "in a kind of mimic murder on the principle of savage magic."

17 See http://lostmuseum.cuny.edu/archive/search/sumner/

18 Hall, *Life and Confessions*, 118.

19 Ibid., 149–50.

20 Ibid., 148–49.

21 Ibid., 91, 97, respectively.

22 Ibid., 97.

23 Ibid., 94.

24 Ibid., 95.

25 Ibid., 122.

26 Ibid.

27 Ibid., 124.

28 Ibid., 121.

29 Ibid., 116.

30 Ibid., 168.

31 Ibid., 162. Interestingly, Bascom, would later author a textbook titled *Principles of Psychology* (New York, NY: G. P. Putnam, 1869), among others, but Bascom's work in psychology does not seem to have been the impetus for Hall's eventual interest in the topic.

32 Hall, *Life and Confessions*, 163.

33 Ibid.

34 Ibid.

35 Linda Dowling, *Charles Eliot Norton: The Art of Reform in Nineteenth-Century America* (Durham, NH: University of New Hampshire Press, 2007).

36 Hall, *Life and Confessions*, 170–71.

37 It cannot have hurt matters, when Hall arrived at Harvard several years later, that Charles Eliot Norton was a first cousin of the Cambridge College's president, Charles William Eliot.

38 Alfred Habegger, *The Father: A Life of Henry James, Sr.* (New York, NY: Farrar, Strauss and Giroux, 1994), 133–34.

39 For an account of how the Congregationalists virtually merged with the Presbyterian Church in America, outside of New England, see Hofstadter, *Anti-Intellectualism in American Life*, 90.

40 Hall, *Life and Confessions*, 177.

41 Although never proven, there has long been speculation that the fire was the results of arson. Stoking this suggestion is the fact that when Barnum began work on a second museum in 1868, that building mysteriously burned down as well, before the attraction ever opened. It was after that disaster that Barnum moved into the business for which he is best remembered today, the circus.

42 Hall, *Life and Confessions*, 179.

43 Hall said in his autobiography that he was in New York for a "single year" (Ibid., 178), but Ross (*G. Stanley Hall*) has shown that he was at Union for nearly two years before going to Germany, and for somewhat more than one additional year after his return.

44 In that same year, 1867, the first philosophical periodical in America was launched by William Torrey Harris of St. Louis, Missouri. Titled the *Journal of Speculative Philosophy*, it aimed to educate Americans about the importance of Hegel by way of original articles and translations of relevant German works, mostly related to the Hegelian tradition. In just the second volume, 1868, the Cambridge, Massachusetts polymath Charles Sanders Peirce published three of his earliest articles, "Questions Concerning Certain Faculties Claimed for Man," "Some Consequences of Four Incapacities," and "Grounds of Validity and the Laws of Logic." Some regard these as the founding documents of semiotics—the study of signs. *JSP* became an early testing ground for a number of rising American philosophers, including William James, Josiah Royce, John Dewey, and even Stanley Hall himself.

45 Hall claimed in his autobiography that it was $1000 (Hall, *Life and Confessions*, 182), but Ross (*G. Stanley Hall*, 34–35) found the letter and it was for $500.

46 Hall, *Life and Confessions*, 182–83.

47 Hall claimed in his autobiography that is was summer of 1868, but Ross cites letters that persuasively show that it was nearly a year later.

48 Hall, *Life and Confessions*, 187.

49 Ibid.

50 Wilhelm Wundt had studied with Du Bois-Reymond and his mentor, Johannes Müller, in Berlin in 1856 before returning to Heidelberg to become Hermann Helmholtz's assistant. In 1874 Wundt left Helmholtz's laboratory to take up his first professorship at Zürich. The following year he would be called to Leipzig, where he would open the Psychological Institute that led to his often being described the "founder" of experimental psychology.

51 Ross, *G. Stanley Hall*, 40.

52 Dorner had been the mentor of Hall's (and Morris') primary theology professor at Union, Henry B. Smith (see Ross, *G. Stanley Hall*, 37). One of Hall's earliest journal articles was a multipart summary of Dorner's theological system (G. Stanley Hall, "Outlines of Dr. J. A. Dorner's System of Theology," *Presbyterian Quarterly and Princeton Review* n.s. 1 (1872): 720–47; n.s. 2 (1873): 60–93, 261–73). Dorner himself apparently objected, saying that it was not "on the whole, a correct view" and that it was "inaccurate in several particulars" (cited in Ross, *G. Stanley Hall*, 37, n. 25).

53 Hall, *Life and Confessions*, 191.

54 This was almost certainly the German-Jewish physician Abraham Jacobi (1830–1919) who pioneered the field of pediatrics. His revolutionary activities in the early 1850s led to his being convicted of treason and imprisoned in 1851. Released in 1853, he fled first to the UK, then to the US, where he worked as a physician in New York. From 1861 he was a professor of medicine, variously, at New York College of Medicine, City University of New York, and Columbia University. He eventually served as president of the New York Academy of Medicine and as co-editor of the *American Journal of Obstetrics and Diseases of Women and Children*. Perhaps most interesting to the present account, Jacobi was an uncle (by marriage) of the anthropologist, Franz Boas: the sister (Sophie Meyer) of Jacobi's first wife (Fanny Meyer) was Boas' mother. Hall would later recruit Boas into the professorship of anthropology at Clark University. Boas would leave for Columbia University during the Clark "crisis" of 1892 (detailed later), where he would come to be known as the "Father" of American anthropology. Jacobi later married Mary Putnam, the daughter of George Palmer Putnam, the founder of the prominent New York publishing house.

55 Hall, *Life and Confessions*, 195. Given, however, that he did not actually stay in Germany until the end of the war, one wonders whether this statement was speculation, or an observation about the behavior of Germans during the war itself.

56 Letter from G. Bascom Hall to G. Stanley Hall, April 7, 1870; letter from G. Stanley Hall to parents, [April, 1870]. Both from G. Stanley Hall Papers, Box B1–1–2, folder

"Germany, 1869–1870," Clark University Archives. Cited by Ross, *G. Stanley Hall*, 36–37.

57 Hall, *Life and Confessions*, 195.

58 Hall (*Life and Confessions*, 196) claimed in his autobiography that he departed in 1871, but Ross (*G. Stanley Hall*, 41) cites letters showing conclusively that it was late 1870. Any one of these misstatements by Hall—about the date of his departure, the amount of money Sage loaned him, or the date of his return—might be, on their own, dismissed as simple misremembering. However, collectively, they provide "evidence" for the false claim that he perpetrated from shortly after his return until the end of his life that his first study tour of Germany had been a "triennium"; three years in duration. In truth it had been somewhat less than a year-and-a-half. What profit Hall, especially late in his life, believed he gained by perpetuating the myth of a three-year trip is anyone's guess. Perhaps he thought it would make him seem more worldly early in his career and, once made, the claim could not be retracted without dishonor.

59 Ross, *G. Stanley Hall*, 48. Hall says in his autobiography only that it was a "large midwestern state university" (Hall, *Life and Confessions*, 196).

60 Hall, *Life and Confessions*, 196.

61 Morris was leaving to take up an instructorship at the University of Michigan. He and Hall would meet again under more competitive circumstances, in the early 1880s.

62 Ross, *G. Stanley Hall*, 49.

63 In fact, she had originally been offered only half the salary of her male colleagues, but complained about the discrepancy and won parity. See John Rury and Glenn Harper, "The Trouble With Coeducation: Mann and Women at Antioch, 1853–1860," *History of Education Quarterly* 26 (1986): 481–502.

64 The Fifteenth Amendment to the US constitution, allowing Black men to vote in elections, would not be ratified until 1870. The Civil Rights Act of 1875, providing for equal treatment in "public accommodations," would not come into force for more than a decade. Interestingly, the Civil Rights Act would be proposed by none other than Massachusetts Senator Charles Sumner, the hero of Hall's father. The Supreme Court struck it down as being unconstitutional in 1883, setting the stage for the long Jim Crow era, formally started with the 1896 Supreme Court ruling on *Plessy v. Ferguson*, permitting "separate but equal" accommodations for Blacks and Whites. The Jim Crow era officially lasted until the Civil Rights Act of 1964.

65 As noted above, *JSP* was the first serious philosophical periodical in America. Harris originally came from Connecticut River valley, like Hall, but moved to St. Louis to become a school teacher in 1857, after two undistinguished years at Yale. Harris rose quickly through the ranks of St. Louis educators, becoming the superintendent of schools there in 1868, a position he held until 1880. While in St. Louis, he came under the influence of a Prussian-born mechanic, self-taught in Hegelian philosophy, named Henry Conrad Brokmeyer. (His name is sometimes spelled "Brockmeyer," and his middle name is occasionally given as "Clay.") Brokmeyer worked at various manual trades and land speculation. After serving in the Civil War, he experienced a meteoric political career, rising to Lieutenant Governor of Missouri, 1877–1881. (See Denys P. Leighton, "Brokmeyer, Henry Conrad (1826–1906)," ed. Lawrence O. Christensen et al., *Dictionary of Missouri Biography* (Columbia, MO: University of Missouri Press, 1999); John Kaag, "America's Hands-on Hegelian," *The Chronicle of Higher Education*, March 20, 2016, http://chronicle.com/article/Americas-Hands-On-Hegelian/235720; see also Brokmeyer's posthumously-published semi-autobiographical novella, *A Mechanic's Diary* (Washington, DC: E. C. Brokmeyer, 1910)). Hegel's writings filled Harris with a philosophical purpose; he became a fervent advocate of the German Idealist. In 1866, Harris submitted a Hegelian critique of Herbert Spencer to Charles Eliot Norton's *North American Review*. Norton asked Chauncey Wright for his opinion of the essay, who scoffed that it was "the mere dry husk of Hegelianism." Wright's friend, Harvard

Latin professor Ephraim W. Gurney, dismissed it as "a howling wilderness" (letter from Wright to Norton, July 24, 1866, reprinted in *Letters of Chauncey Wright; With Some Account of His Life*, ed. James Bradley Thayer (Cambridge, MA: John Wilson and Son, 1878), 87). Harris launched *JSP* the following year, 1867, in which the very first article was his piece on Spencer. Harris also attempted to bring the modern pedagogical teachings of the Swiss Romantic Johann Heinrich Pestalozzi and his German student, Friedrich Fröbel, to America. Following Fröbel, Harris was involved in founding the first permanent, public kindergarten in the US In 1880, Harris left St. Louis to join the New England Transcendentalists, where he received a mixed reception. In 1889, he was appointed US Commissioner of Education, a position he would hold under successive presidential administrations until his retirement in 1906.

66 G. Stanley Hall, "Anti-Materialism," *Journal of Speculative Philosophy* 6 (1872): 216–22; G. Stanley Hall, "Hegel as the National Philosophy of Germany," *Journal of Speculative Philosophy* 6 (1872): 53–82, 97–129, 258–79, 340–50; 7 (1873): 17–25, 44–59, 57–74; 8 (1874): 1–13 (a translation of Karl Rosenkranz, *Hegel Als Deutscher National-Philosoph* (Leipzig: Duncker & Humblot, 1870), with commentary).

67 Hall, *Life and Confessions*, 358.

68 Ross, *G. Stanley Hall*, 47.

69 Hall, *Life and Confessions*, 201.

70 Ibid., 202.

71 The simplest studies of this sort had been conducted by the Dutch ophthalmologist, Franz Donders, in Utrecht a few years before, but Wundt elaborated Donders' basic design into an extensive program for research into the fundamental nature of the mind. Wundt actually believed that there were five stages: sensation and perception, followed by apperception, followed by will and motor action. See David K. Robinson, "Reaction Time Experiments in Wundt's Institute and beyond," in *Wilhelm Wundt in History: The Making of a Scientific Psychology*, ed. Robert W. Rieber and David K. Robinson (New York, NY: Kluwer, 2001), 161–97.

3

WILLIAM JAMES COMES TO HARVARD

1. A Second (and Third) European Sojourn; Then to Newport

Henry James Sr. and his family arrived in Switzerland in July of 1855. He had high expectations for the "progressiveness" of the private schools that he had picked out for his sons in Geneva, but his hopes were dashed almost the instant they enrolled. He quit the schools by September and the family removed to Paris, then to London, all by October. After less than two years in London, they moved again, this time to Boulogne. Henry Jr. contracted typhus there and took several months to recover.

William, now a teenager, took strongly to the study of art while in Europe. He was especially drawn to the revolutionary work of Eugène Delacroix. One psychoanalytic biographer has attributed young William's keen interest in the theme of ferocious animals attacks, which is found in some of Delacroix's paintings, to an unconscious murderous rage against his father,[1] but it seems more parsimonious to note simply that violent scenes excite the attention of many adolescent boys, and William was no exception. As he matured, William also developed an interest in mathematics and science, about which he wrote much to his New York friend, Ed Van Winkle. Van Winkle was entering Union College in engineering, an exciting prospect that sparked the interest of young William. By March of 1858, however, William had concluded that he was not "cut out for an engineer"; that he would rather "get a microscope and go out . . . into the woods and fields and ponds . . . to make as many discoveries as possible."[2] His father, delighted with William's growing interest in science, bought him a microscope for Christmas that year. Henry Sr.'s own relationship with natural science had been a fraught one since his youth. He was largely ignorant of the topic but nevertheless fascinated by it. He urgently wanted to find a principle of unification among the "bewildering heap of facts" under what he presumed would be "laws exclusively spiritual"; such disparate phenomena as one finds in the natural world can only be, he presumed, "the material expression of spiritual truth." He then quoted Scripture (*Hebrews*, 11.3) as support.[3] His former science teacher at Albany Academy, Joseph Henry, replied only that science was not merely a "heap of facts" but, instead, a systematic search for overarching laws.

Five years before this exchange, when Henry Sr. was meeting with Faraday, he may have thought that the great physicist, armed with his Sandemanian faith, had unlocked the secret to the unification of spirit and science, and that he might be willing to share it with his young American visitor. On the contrary, though, Henry Sr. found that Faraday kept his religion and his science in distinct mental compartments.[4] Now, a generation after the encounter with Faraday, it is possible that Henry Sr. expected his intelligent oldest son, William, whom he had carefully raised in his stew of unorthodox theologies, would uncover the answer to Henry Sr.'s questions about the spiritual foundations of science, if only he grew up to be a scientist.[5]

Although, with historical hindsight, we have come to see William James as a highly cosmopolitan figure, the teenage "Willy" was a parochial American through and through. Living in Europe for the first time since he was a toddler, he came to despise Paris, comparing both it and London unfavorably to his native New York in terms of physical beauty. Parisians he found to be dishonest and rude. Londoners, by contrast, he thought too polite.[6] The level of privilege to which he had become accustom—and the vast but unrecognized gulf that existed between his standard of living and that of most people—is revealed in the same letter, where he described residing in even a rather luxurious Paris *appartement* as "a queer way of living, this, all huddled up together on one floor." Two years later, he had come to attribute his early impressions of the French to "miserable prejudice" that he was "heartily ashamed of." "I like the French more and more every day," he confessed.[7] Trying out a youthful, optimistic socialism on his old friend, he now opined that if food and shelter were assured everyone . . . even "a common laborer who digs a canal" might be able to "find out something new."[8] In his view, the aim of everyone's life should be discovery.

The Jameses returned to US in July of 1858, but Henry Sr. could not bring himself to live once again in the hurly burly of New York. After a brief stay in Albany, the family set up, instead, amidst the genteel charms of little Newport, Rhode Island. William had fully expected to join his friend Ed Van Winkle at Union College, but Henry Sr. forbade it, declaring colleges to be "hotbeds of corruption"[9] (probably recalling his own wild years at Union).

Newport was probably the least cosmopolitan environment in which the James children had ever lived. William described his summer as "a very pleasant but a very idle one. . . . But that's the drawback of living as such a place as Newport, where Nature offers such irresistible temptations."[10] Both William's and Henry Jr.'s interest in art began to intensify. They took lessons from the well-known

American painter, William Morris Hunt, who was then living in Newport as well. They became acquainted with another of Hunt's students, the multi-talented John LaFarge, who was just then beginning his long and successful career as a painter, illustrator, and worker in stained glass (see Plates 1 and 2 in the color plate section). LaFarge—from New York City, like the James boys—was Catholic, having attended St. John's College (now Fordham University). This fact may have "horrified" Henry Sr. just as much as the emerging artistic inclinations of his two eldest sons.

Mere months after settling into Newport, the perennially discontented Henry Sr. insisted that the family return to Europe. Plans were made to leave in late September. Then plans were changed: Henry Sr. went alone, leaving the family behind. The family was supposed to follow in the spring. In fact, they did not leave Newport until October of the following year, 1859. A few weeks later, they were back in Geneva in search of educational opportunities not only for William and Henry Jr., but also for the two younger sons, Wilky and Bob. (Education for the fifth child and lone daughter, Alice, did not concern her father much.) The plan was to stay on the Continent for at least three years. Whatever Henry Sr.'s hopes might have been for the renewed European adventure, though, it did not lessen William's love of painting. In August of 1860, he declared art to be his "vocation."[11] Then, from Bonn, where he was expected to learn German, William wrote to his father, then living in Paris, inquiring in the most serious intellectual tone he could muster about Henry Sr.'s ideas with respect to the nature of art.[12] The family returned to the US a month later.

Although the Jameses could not have been unaware of the increasing American tension over the issue of slavery, little could have prepared them for the political turmoil that greeted them in the fall of 1860. The Democratic Party had split in two, the northern segment nominating Illinois Senator Stephen Douglas for president; the southern faction having separately nominated President Buchanan's vice president, former Kentucky senator John C. Breckinridge, who was not yet 40 years of age. The old Whig party had dissolved entirely. Those former Whigs who were inclined to limit the spread of slavery in the new western territories had joined the new Republican party, which nominated former Illinois congressman Abraham Lincoln. Southern Whigs, who hoped to continue the decades-long effort to ignore and finesse the slavery issue, joined with former Know-Nothings of the north to form the Constitutional Union Party, led by former Tennessee senator John Bell. In the November election, Breckinridge, the southern Democrat, won almost all of the South, including Maryland and Delaware. Bell of the Constitutional Union Party won the border states of Virginia and Kentucky, plus his home state of Tennessee. Douglas and the northern Democrats were nearly shut out, winning just Missouri and a minority portion of New Jersey's electoral votes. Lincoln won the nearly all of the northern states plus the far western states of California and Oregon. This gave him a landslide in the electoral college, his 180 votes being more than twice the total of his closest competitor, Breckinridge.

FIGURE 3.1 William James on the Agassiz Expedition to Brazil, 1865.

Credit: William James Papers, Houghton Library, Harvard University.

But Lincoln had received the endorsement of less than 40% of the voting populace. Immediately, southerners declared Lincoln's victory illegitimate and, within
six weeks, states started seceding from the Union, beginning with South Carolina.
Four months later, the country would enter upon the bloodiest war in its history.

The national crisis did not exactly launch the James family into action. The two
younger sons, Wilky and Bob, still underage, were sent to a school in Concord,
run by a personal friend of Emerson's and Thoreau's: Frank Sanborn. Sanborn was
a "progressive" educator and a defender of the radical abolitionist, John Brown.

Whether the senior James had become a fervent advocate of the abolitionist cause remains uncertain. William restarted his art lessons with Hunt on a nearly daily basis until April. Then he abruptly quit, apparently having changed his mind about a career in art. At the outbreak of war, William signed up for a ninety-day stint with the local militia, but opted not (or, perhaps, was forbidden by his father) to enlist for the three-year term the War Department imposed in May. Instead, he decided to attend the Lawrence Scientific School at Harvard University, starting in the fall of 1861.

2. Boston and New York

The story of Boston's origin and development was radically different from that of New York, where James had grown up. The religious Dissenters (from the Church of England) who founded the old Massachusetts Bay Colony in the 1620s had been hardened by religious persecution in England. They were furiously puritanical in spirit and demanded a strict conformity from their fellow citizens.[13] When they noisily campaigned for religious freedom, what they meant was the freedom to practice *their* specific form of faith. As soon as they acquired some measure of power over their own situation, they ruthlessly persecuted and excluded not only the hated Anglicans, but also Quakers, Baptists, and anyone else who departed from their particular variety of Dissent.

Even the various groups of Puritans who came to Massachusetts did not get along well, quarreling one with another over minor doctrinal details. The Plymouth and Massachusetts Bay Colonies—so similar to each other that they are hardly distinguishable in the minds of many today—remained distinct and separate entities, both politically and religiously, until 1691 when William and Mary stepped in to unite all the English possessions along the north coast (and, not incidentally, to end the 70 years of theocratic rule that had dominated several of them).[14] As Alexis de Tocqueville so acutely observed, "Puritanism . . . was almost as much a political theory as a religious doctrine. No sooner had they landed on this inhospitable shore . . . than the immigrants turned their attention to the constitution of their society."[15] And a large society it was, drawing some 20,000 colonists over the course of the 1630s alone.

As early as 1624, a plot of land across the river from present-day Boston was first occupied by Europeans. In 1628, the area was formally christened Charlestown (named after the British monarch). Just two years later, though, unable to secure a reliable source of fresh water, the Charlestown residents purchased from one William Blaxton (or Blackstone) a plot of land covering much of what is now the Boston Common and Beacon Hill. They renamed the area "Boston," after a small city in Lincolnshire (central England, near the eastern coast). John Winthrop, a leading figure of the Massachusetts Colony, famously declared Boston to be the Biblical "City upon a Hill." As elsewhere in the colonies around the bay, strict obedience to the church was enforced. Transgressors were vigorously prosecuted.

For instance, in 1635, the theologian Roger Williams was exiled for sedition and heresy. Although Williams is often lauded today as an advocate of religious freedom and of a separation between church and state, he first angered Bostonians by declaring their church to be not wholly "separate" from the Church of England; in other words, they were not "pure" enough. After being banished from Boston, he established a new colony at Providence (only later united with Rhode Island), where he founded the First Baptist Church in America. Just three years after the Williams case, in 1638, Anne Hutchinson was banished from Boston for the heresy of antinomianism (refusal to submit to religious law when the Holy Spirit inwardly instructs the individual otherwise). She and some of her followers were invited by Williams to settle near him at Providence. They did for a time, but she soon moved on to land in present-day Brooklyn. Perhaps most notoriously, in 1660, one of Hutchinson's former followers, Mary Dyer, was hanged along with three others, for violating the ban on Quakers in Boston. The following year, the English government stepped in to legally protect Quakers. Now it was the British King instructing the Dissenters on religious tolerance.[16]

Nevertheless, for all the rigidity of early Boston society (or perhaps because of it), from the very start the city had a near-obsession with education. Just five years after its founding, in 1635, the Boston Latin School was established to educate the young in erudite matters far beyond the farming and trade that was necessary to keep the young colony afloat. The following year, in 1636, New College was created just across the river in a town they dubbed "Cambridge," the first such institution in North America. Two years later, when a local pastor bequeathed his library and half of his fortune to the school, the trustees renamed it after their generous benefactor, John Harvard.

It is worth noting just how markedly the story of the early of New York contrasts with that of Boston: The southern tip of the island that the local indigenous people called "Manahatta" was first occupied by Europeans in 1624. The settlers here were not English religious radicals, like in Boston, but Dutch traders. As such, the guiding objectives of Nieuw Amsterdam, as the outpost was first called, were mercantile rather than spiritual. It was run by the massive Dutch West India Company, and its primary purpose was to funnel beaver and otter pelts back to the Netherlands. Because the focus was nearly exclusively on business, the town was religiously and culturally diverse in ways that would have horrified Bostonians of the era. Many of the first few hundred residents were not even Dutch, but French-speaking Belgian Huguenots who were escaping oppression at home. Unlike their Boston counterparts, their aim was not to establish an exclusively Huguenot society. (Indeed, there wasn't even a church in Nieuw Amsterdam for the first 17 years of its existence.) Their aim was to use their newfound freedom to get rich, and that is just what many of them did.

All was not happy in the first years, however. The new colony struggled to establish itself as the northwesternmost outpost of the international Dutch trading network. Fur, although it could be lucrative, was not as prestigious and attractive a commodity as spices or slaves. In 1643, an incompetent governor tried to tax the local Indians, then launched a war against them that almost brought the colony to ruin. In order to recover its investment, the Company brought in a new governor in 1647, Peter Stuyvesant, who, perhaps ironically, was a Puritan. Stuyvesant started by banning drinking on Sundays and imposing fines for missing church. This was a new order for the unruly colonists, but Stuyvesant also built new roads and canals, improved and expanded the port, and the raised the colony's profile by converting it from being primarily a fur market into a slave market. He also built a wall from the Husdon River straight across the island to the East River, in order to keep out not only Indians but also the hostile English, who had their eye on this potential lynchpin between their Massachusetts and Virginia colonies. Stuyvesant's wall would mark the basic path of the modern Wall Street.

Despite Stuyvesant's own personal Puritanical principles, as a matter of business he let nearly anyone into the colony who was willing to work. By the early 1650s, the population had risen to 3000 people who spoke 18 different languages. By 1654, the Dutch were a minority in their own colony. That same year, 23 Sephardic Jews, fleeing persecution in Brazil, arrived to take up residence. This turn of events exceeded what Stuyvesant's religious conscience could tolerate; he petitioned the Dutch West India Company to bar Jews from living in Nieuw Amsterdam. To his astonishment, the Company Directors refused his request, reminding the governor that the colony was a business venture, not a religious one. The new immigrants were allowed in and, with it, the first Jewish community in North America was established. Perhaps no other single event points up the different characters of early New York and Boston.

Dutch control of the fabulous port was not to last long, however. In August of 1664, just 40 years after it began, the English sailed four warships into the harbor, intent on taking the city. Stuyvesant prepared for battle but the residents, including his own son, petitioned him to give the city up without a fight order to avoid damage to, or even destruction of, their homes and businesses. Stuyvesant reluctantly agreed and the transfer was peacefully made. Apparently national interests were no more relevant than religious ones when this city's residents were faced with a possible disruption of commerce. The former governor, far from being persecuted by his new masters, retired to his lucrative fruit farm north of the city. The main visible change to the city, apart from the Union Jack flying above it, was that it was henceforth known as New York. The next day, business carried on pretty much as usual. The strong commercial character of the city was set during its brief Dutch period, and even a transfer of national possession did little to alter it.

3. William James Arrives at Harvard

By the time James arrived in Boston, the city had, of course, shaken off much of the religious authoritarianism that marked its beginnings in the 17th century. As early as the 1640s, the various religious groups of New England had agreed to a statement called the Cambridge Platform, under which each individual church was independent, not subject to the rule of others or to higher religious authorities. This is often taken to be the founding document of the Congregational church in America. However, the Platform also had the consequence of enabling some churches to gradually liberalize their theologies without having to answer to the more conservative churches. Many adopted a provision call the Half-Way Covenant, which granted membership to those who lived a "Christian life" without demanding that they publicly recount their "regeneration" (being "born again," as we might say today). Less dramatic paths to faith were recognized. In particular, the role that reason can play in the growth of faith was increasingly acknowledged by some sects. The more liberal churches became especially popular in the Boston area, in no small part because they recognized the need of urban businessmen to carry on their affairs—often with people of very different faiths on other continents—with a minimum of intervention from the church.[17]

By the end of the century, a layman named John Leverett and two of his colleagues published a manifesto calling explicitly for a "broad and catholick" church. Far from prompting the kind of dire official reaction that had been seen earlier in the century, the pamphlet led to Leverett's being appointed president of Harvard College in 1708. This was the start of Harvard's long trek from being a Congregationalist institution to being a Unitarian one, though there was another century or so to go before it was complete. Traditional Puritans were horrified at the direction Harvard seemed to be headed. Many of them abandoned the Cambridge college and, in search of a new home, rallied around Connecticut's Collegiate School, which had been founded only in 1701. In 1718, Cotton Mather, scion of one of Massachusetts' leading religious families, persuaded a Welsh businessman with family connections to Connecticut, Elihu Yale, to contribute goods worth £560 to the school and its cause.[18] In exchange, Mather arranged for the school to be renamed after its benefactor, and Yale College was born. Yale became the conservative Congregationalists' bulwark against the suspect liberalism of Harvard. Traces of this ancient antagonism between the two schools can be seen even today.

The 1730s saw the rise of a popular religious movement in the US that has come to be called the Great Awakening. It preached the old Calvinist doctrine of predestination, but embraced a simpler, more emotionally direct, revivalist form of faith. Led by a Yale graduate named Jonathan Edwards, the movement—simultaneously conservative and radical—became widespread in New England. The liberal ministers of Boston, however, were not impressed. Led by one Charles Chauncey, the opponents of revivalism emphasized ever more strongly the critical role that they believed human will and thought to play in the process of salvation. This was precisely the opposite of traditional Calvinist doctrines of sudden conversion and predestination. The liberals were adopting a controversial position known as Arminianism.[19] They also began to question the doctrine of Trinity. Although the New England churches united behind the cause of the American revolution in the 1770s and 1780s, a rift within the old Calvinist consensus on which New England had been built was deepening.

In 1805, the controversy came to a head when Harvard filled their long-vacant Hollis professorship of theology with a well-known liberal named Henry Ware. In response, the remaining Massachusetts conservatives abandoned Harvard utterly and turned to Yale for their general education. They also established their own seminary just west of Boston, Andover, for the training of conservative ministers. What had been, until this time, a growing unease among diverse strains of Calvinism, now flared up into open conflict. In 1815, Harvard was accused by conservative Jedidiah Morse of being Unitarian—a liberal British religious movement until that time—rather than being Congregationalist at all. Morse demanded that the conservative Congregationalist churches separate themselves from the liberal ones. In 1819, the influential liberal minister, William Ellery Channing, responded to Morse's accusation with a widely publicized sermon titled, "Unitarian Christianity." The split became finalized with the founding of the American Unitarian Association in 1825. Boston and eastern Massachusetts became increasingly Unitarian. Western Massachusetts—where Stanley Hall would be born a couple of decades later—remained conservative Congregationalist.

Even if the fierce Purtian leaders of an earlier age had gone extinct in Boston, the city continued to be gently but firmly ruled by a cadre of aristocratic families known as the Boston Brahmins: the Adamses and Cabotts, the Delanos and Emersons, the Lodges and Lowells, the Putnams and Quincys, among others. As a result, the city sported little of the chaotic populism that marked life and politics in New York. Even the arrival of the Irish, who flooded into the Boston by the tens of thousands in the late 1840s, was unable to much disrupt the hierarchical order of things (except, perhaps, indirectly, as the nativist Know-Nothings of the middle and lower class Protestant population were swept into power and then out again in the mid-1850s). As one famous bit of doggerel put matters:

> And this is good old Boston,
> The home of the bean and the cod,
> Where the Lowells talk only to Cabots,
> And the Cabots talk only to God.

Henry Adams was a member of the Brahmin elite: grandson of John Quincy Adams and great-grandson of John Adams, the 6th and 2nd presidents of the United States, respectively. Of Boston religious life during his childhood in the 1850s, he wrote:

> The score of Unitarian clergymen about Boston, who controlled society and Harvard College . . . proclaimed as their merit that they insisted on no doctrine, but taught, or tried to teach, the means of leading a virtuous, useful, unselfish life, which they held to be sufficient for salvation. . . . The boy

[Henry Adams himself] went to church twice every Sunday; he was taught to read his Bible, and he learned religious poetry by heart; he believed in a mild deism; he prayed; he went through all the forms; but neither to him nor to his brothers or sisters was religion real. . . . The religious instinct had vanished, and could not be revived.[20]

It is interesting to note how far a cry this is from the meticulous attention that was paid to the precise character of the spiritual world in the home of Henry James Sr. His oldest son, William, though still young, had already traveled far and wide by the end of the 1850s, and had seen religious observances and practices of many kinds. His religious instinct, had not vanished like Henry Adams'. Although nearly as unorthodox as his father, William James would spend a lifetime exploring, questioning, testing, and refining his religious instinct.

Although Bostonians' attention to the technicalities of conventional religion might have been softening, the city was still known for having a rather stern moral sensibility. Although the phrase "Banned in Boston"—referring to books and pamphlets that were censored in the city because of their supposedly lewd content—did not become popular until later in the 19th century, the sense of the city maintaining a somewhat more prudish outlook than others on account of its Puritan origins was widespread.

The Boston into which William James arrived in the early 1860s looked very different from the city of today. (See Plate 3 in the color plate section.) This was not just a matter of the lack of skyscrapers and cars and other modern technologies. It was physically far smaller. Originally, Boston sat on the Shawmut Peninsula—a blob of land at the end of a terribly slender long neck; it was only about two city blocks wide in places. The present-day West End, North End, and Fort Hill areas were each small but distinct peninsulas extending from the main blob, separated by coves: Mill Cove and Town Cove, respectively. And there was a third cove, the West Cove, between West End and Beacon Hill (see Plate 3). There were originally a number of high hills on the peninsula. All but Beacon Hill were, over the centuries, leveled and used to fill in the coves.

The greatest and most famous of Boston's many land reclamation projects was Back Bay. The original bay lay to the west of the neck, and it included not only the area between Boylston Street and the river (the neighborhood now designated "Back Bay"), but also covered much of the area all the way back to present-day Washington Street. All of this was either river or unusable marshland. To the east of the neck was the South Bay, on the other side of which was another peninsula that is, today, a portion of South Boston. The entire area north of present-day 1st St. and W. Broadway was under water.

The Mill cove was dammed and turned into a pond in the 1630s, but not actually filled in until the 1820s. Present-day Causeway St. marks the position of the old dam. The West End was extended and the West Cove filled in mostly during the second quarter of the 19th century. The Massachusetts General Hospital was built on this reclaimed ground. The original hospital building, opened in 1823, sat approximately in the southeast corner of the MGH's present vast campus and, at that time, it sat hard upon the edge of the Charles River.[21] It was here in 1846 that the dentist, William Morton, first demonstrated the effectiveness of ether as a surgical anesthetic. Harvard built its medical school directly across from the MGH in 1847. When William James arrived in 1861, the filling out of the West End around MGH was still a project very much in progress.[22] Soon after, the flats west of Beacon Hill were expanded as well.

The process of filling in the Back Bay began around 1820, when a dam was built from the Common in the east, along the line that Beacon Street now follows, all the way to present-day Brookline Avenue. Then a second short dam was built from the end of Gravelly Point to the first dam, and the resulting basin between the short dam and the Common was drained. The original intent had not been to fill in the Back Bay, but rather to harness its tidal forces for as many as 81 mills that were to be built on Gravelly Point. The project was expected to bring the city ten thousand new workers and eight million dollars of investment, and making Boston the industrial envy of New York and Philadelphia.[23] As early as the mid-1830s, however, the edges of the old shore began to be extended, creating the ground under the present Public Garden adjoining the Common, and building north to present-day Tremont Street. In addition, railroad lines were built through the basin. It wasn't until the late 1850s, however, that development began in earnest in the Back Bay.[24] Trainload after trainload of gravel was brought from the town of Needham, 12 miles to the southwest, to fill in the more than 600 acres of the Back Bay. The process continued all through the war and was not complete until late in the 1880s. This was the Boston into which William James arrived in 1861; one which was rapidly expanding *physically*—more than doubling, in fact—the land area that the city had originally possessed in the 17th century.

Although Henry Sr. had opposed his oldest son's desire to attend college—that "hotbed of corruption"—the Lawrence Scientific School was considered to be a different kind of institution. For one thing, it was separate from Harvard College, where the education, such as it was, had become encrusted with tradition and convention to the point of near-irrelevancy. Charles Eliot, who would be James' chemistry professor (and later serve as the university's president for 40 years) described Harvard as having "struck bottom" when he graduated less than a decade before, in 1853.[25] "Small and stagnant" is how one of James' biographers described the Harvard of that era.[26] In all fairness, though, the problem was not Harvard's alone. As Laurence Vesey noted in his celebrated history of the American university, the old American college had been becoming increasingly obsolete since the era of Andrew Jackson. The new university, partially based on European models—less overtly religious, with the addition of sciences, original research, and professional schools—would revive American higher education in the coming decades but, in the 1860s, that process had only barely begun.[27]

The opening of the Lawrence School in 1847 was one of the first foundation stones to be laid for the more dynamic institution to come, but it would take time. Henry Adams, who graduated from Harvard in 1858, just three years before James entered, said of the place:

> Any other education would have required a serious effort, but no one took Harvard College seriously. All went there because their friends went there, and the College was their ideal of self-respect. Harvard College, as far as it educated at all, was a mild, liberal school, which sent young men into the world with all they needed to make respectable citizens, and something of what they wanted to make useful ones.[28]

But James' New York friends were not at Harvard. Although he came from an exceedingly wealthy family, he was not of Adams' "Brahmin" circle.[29] James did not "fall" into Harvard by default, as they did. He was a New York boy with extensive experience of Europe who had spent an extended "summer," of sorts, tucked away in Newport. To enroll at Harvard College would have required him to demonstrate proficiency in Latin and Greek. It also would have committed him to four years of a curriculum dominated by Classics. Instead, he went to Lawrence, which had virtually no entry requirements at the time. Lawrence was ruled, as it had been since opening in 1847, by the world famous Swiss zoologist, Louis Agassiz. Agassiz required that all of one's courses be taken in a single department of study; no "dabbling" in other branches of science.

Almost immediately upon James' arrival, he started attending a series of public lectures on natural history that Agassiz was giving in Boston. But natural history was not James' department. James chose to study chemistry. The reasons remain unclear. Perhaps because it was the most exciting natural science at the time, a number of new elements having recently been discovered. The publication of Charles Darwin's *Origin of Species*, less than two years before James' arrival at Harvard, might have made zoology an appealing field as well. Agassiz, however—once a student of the great French naturalist Georges Cuvier, and a staunch fixist about species—was adamantly opposed to Darwin from the time of *Origin*'s publication until his death in 1873. Darwin did have allies at Lawrence, most notably his long-time correspondent Asa Gray, but to study with Gray would have put James in the department of botany. In any case, James' decision to pursue chemistry placed him under the supervision of the school's future president, Charles Eliot, then a mere assistant professor. Thus, while millions of America's young men went off to war, James spent much of the year in the chemistry laboratory and in the merry parlors of leafy Cambridge. Letters home focused mainly on family gossip. One of his cousins, Minnie Temple, cut her hair short, and the entire family was in an uproar thinking she had gone mad, James included.[30]

In addition to chemistry, James attended lectures on comparative vertebrate anatomy with Jeffries Wyman, perhaps best known as the first man to formally describe the gorilla to Euro-American scientific audiences. Wyman was a deeply religious Unitarian who was never able to fully accept Darwin's theory of natural selection, though he did embrace a theistic form of evolution. He had been a student of one of Darwin's most vocal English critics, Richard Owen.[31]

Before the end of his first term at Lawrence, James decided that he would only study chemistry for one year and then, after taking a term off, turn to comparative anatomy with Wyman. After that, he planned to study medicine and then spend several years under the tutelage of Agassiz. It was an eclectic plan, to be sure, but it wasn't too far from what he actually did.[32]

James returned home to Newport for the summer of 1862. When he headed back to Harvard in the fall, his brother Henry came along too, eager to begin law school. William continued in his chemistry courses, despite his earlier plan to stay home and then start working with Wyman. He also attended lectures on physics given at Harvard, along with Aggasiz's public lecture series on geology. That same fall, however, the next brother in line, Wilky, age 17, enlisted in the army, and the structure of William's life began to come unraveled.

4. War Intervenes

William's chemistry teacher, Charles Eliot, completed his five-year appointment at Harvard at the end of 1862 and was not renewed for the following year. William did not re-enroll at Lawrence. Instead, he decided to follow his own "course" of readings: physics, history, philology, theology, ancient philosophy, European literature. At the start of 1863, the Emancipation Proclamation came into force. William and Henry Jr. both applied to teach at a southern school (that was in Northern hands) to educate liberated slaves, but neither ended up going.

In March of 1863 the national military draft went into effect. Just a month later, William's name appeared on the draft list. His father paid the $300 for a "substitute" so that he could continue his studies. At the start of May, one of William's and Henry's cousins who had enlisted, Willy Temple, was killed at Chancellorsville. In mid-May, William's and Henry's youngest brother, Bob, enlisted. A week later, Wilky's regiment shipped out. It was no ordinary outfit: it was the 54th Massachusetts, a regiment of a thousand Black soldiers (and 30 White officers) led by the 25-year-old Colonel Robert Gould Shaw.[33] As they marched through the streets of Boston to cheering throngs, William became intensely self-consciousness of staying behind.[34]

Just six weeks later, in mid-July, discontent with the Draft Act began to spread across cities in the Northeast, especially among the poor, who could not afford to pay for "substitutes." Opposition was particularly strong in Irish communities, which mostly opposed emancipation for fear that freed black slaves would come north and compete for jobs with the already-impoverished Irish. Lying in the background of Irish resistance was the feeling that emancipation was an English initiative (the English had ended slavery in the Empire 30 years earlier), and almost anything seen as English was opposed by the Irish.[35] Desperately poor, they did not have the luxury of taking the long view that discrimination against any racial or ethnic group helped to continue discrimination against them as well.

As described in the previous chapter, the explosion of anti-draft violence was particular brutal and bloody in New York City in July 1863. Related disruptions were seen in Boston as well, but they took on a somewhat different character because of three key differences between New York and Boston. First, although New York had invented and had periodically flirted with Know-Nothingism, the nativist movement had not come to dominate government in New York as it had in Boston and in Massachusetts more broadly in 1855. As a result, the oppression of the Irish had been correspondingly more intense in Boston. Not only had systematic discrimination against the Irish in employment become a central part of the legislative program. In addition, the Know-Nothing state government had passed, in 1855, a law providing for the deportation to England (of all places) all Irish mental patients and paupers in state institutions. It also attempted, but failed, to raise the residency requirement for acquiring US citizenship (and, thereby, the right to voting) from just 5 years to 21 years, a move that would have disenfranchised the Irish for almost another generation. A second important difference between the two cities was that, whereas the Irish were politically powerful in New York, thanks in no small part to the success of Tammany Hall, there was no equivalent organization in Boston and, thus, by contrast with New York, the Irish remained mostly excluded from civic politics until quite late in the century. Third, the Irish and black communities in New York lived side-by-side, sometimes even competing for housing and jobs the same sections of town. Thus there was a great deal of opportunity for friction between them. Their respective gangs fought each other with deadly regularity. In Boston, however, the two neighborhoods were quite separate—the Irish mostly confined to the North End, near the docks, while the black community lived in a small segregated area near Beacon Hill.

The chief result of these three differences was that the Boston Draft Riot of July 14, 1863 was not a race riot, as its equivalent had been in New York. As one historian of Boston put it, it was "a nativist riot in reverse. . . . They vented their wrath upon the symbols of Yankees oppression visible in their own neighborhood. . . . [It was] an insurrection by the Irish poor against what they believed was Yankee tyranny and nativism."[36]

The Irish crowds, in some cases led by women with their children in tow, scuffled with draft marshals who had come to conscript their husbands and sons into the army. When city police were sent in to protect the marshals, they were attacked mostly with thrown stones and other projectiles. Soon the mobs turned to arming themselves more effectively by looting gun shops and even armories.[37] The Republican governor, John Andrew, called in the army to restore order, but the only regiment nearby was the 55th Massachusetts, the second all-Black regiment in the Union army and, as it happens, the very one to which Bob James had been assigned. Governor Andrew's biographer, writing 40 years after the fact, claimed that the governor immediately grasped that such a unit "could not safely be employed to put down a riot of free, White, American citizens."[38] This must be regarded as something of an anachronism, if not an actual whitewash, considering that the people at issue were despised Irish immigrants, not even considered "White" by many,[39] and that the governor in question was a Republican whom they regarded as a key political enemy. Nevertheless, Andrew was astute enough to realize that if there was a way to badly enflame the situation and turn it into a race riot of the kind that New York had seen but a few days earlier, sending in a Black armed force to quash the violence was probably the way to do so.

Instead, he gathered together six companies of (White) state militia, and some other nearby (White) federal troops to quiet the unrest. Bob James and the other White officers of the 55th were among these. They were not a large enough force to gain control of the situation, however. Indeed, Bob James' later recounted a suspenseful tale of being trapped with a few other soldiers in a room above a gun shop that was surrounded by newly-armed looters.[40]

That evening, with the situation in the North End still out of control, Major Stephen Cabot (a member of one of Boston's most prominent Brahmin families) marched into town at the head of a column of one hundred additional troops. They immediately moved to reinforce the guard around a gunhouse at which the only two canon in the city were stored. The mob attacked them, attempting to break into the gunhouse. Against gunfire of the soldiers, the crowd, reportedly including many women and children, continued to batter its way in. Ultimately, Cabot ordered one of the canons turned on the crowd and fired, point blank. Then he had it fired again.

The reported death toll was only between six and eight, but it is said that many bodies were carried away in the dark and buried without being reported to the authorities.[41] The crowd around the gunhouse scattered. Rain came later in the evening and, by the morning, the crowds had dispersed. Within a few days, the protest had ended completely. The question of whether the riot made any difference is an interesting one to consider. Certainly there was no official change in the draft policy. It is notable, however, that although Boston's official draft quota for the next two years was 3,300, only 713 more were drafted.[42]

Of these near-catastrophic events in Boston's history, were hear nothing in William James' correspondence. Indeed, there is a mysterious gap in his letter-writing (or at least in the preservation of his letters) between October 1862 and the fall of 1863. His letters only rarely touched on great events: not the Irish, not slavery, not elections, not the massive land reclamation projects taking place in the city. Even the war only sparked the occasional mention.[43] He mostly wrote of recent visits he had received from or paid to relatives and friends. They were often full of quirky parody, word-play, and even the occasionally humorous doodle. He often wrote in French to his sister Alice. To his mother and father, like many students of all eras, he often wrote of the need for money.

In the same month as the Draft Riot (July, 1863), Henry Jr. was drafted into the army. Because he had injured his back helping to fight a fire in Newport a couple of years before, however, he was deemed physically unable to serve. In the middle of that same month, Wilky's regiment led the attack on Fort Wagner in South Carolina. Nearly half the Union force was killed in the failed assault. Wilky was badly wounded and shipped home to Newport. He spent the summer confined to a bed on the main floor of the house for the rest of the summer. The event changed the war from a distant abstraction to a visible, personal reality; what Oliver Wendell Holmes Jr. later ominously described as "the blue steel edge of actuality."[44]

In the fall of 1863, James returned to Harvard, this time studying primarily anatomy with Jeffries Wyman. He began to take an interest in evolution and in Darwin's theory, at about this time. Along with his growing interest in Darwin was a more general adoption of the language of positivist science, though it is doubtful that James was ever a committed positivist. That would have brought him too directly in conflict with his father's views. It was more of a youthful trying-out of intellectual roles.

He was also feeling the pressure to make a decision about his future profession although, given his father's wealth, it was unlikely he was going to fall into poverty should he delay further. He thought about becoming a naturalist, though he had not yet done any serious collecting in the field. His work thus far had been in museums with specimens acquired by others. He felt, however, probably correctly,

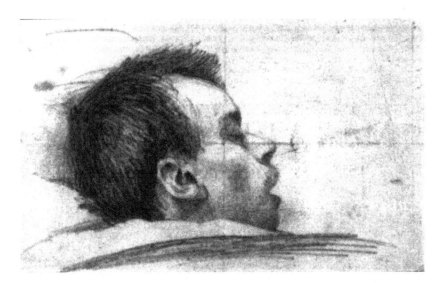

FIGURE 3.2 William James' 1863 drawing of his brother, Wilky, recovering at home in Newport from the wounds he suffered at the attack on Fort Wagner, South Carolina.

Credit: William James Papers, Houghton Library, Harvard University.

that such a choice would not provide many options for income. So, he chose to study medicine which, he told his mother, was halfway between the business he needed to earn a living and the science he felt he needed to have a life.[45]

Becoming a physician at that time did not have the high prestige it does today. Harvard medical school had, essentially, no entrance requirements. One attended a set of lecture courses and took an oral examination at the end. If one meant to practice, one would attempt to catch on as an apprentice with an established physician, often at nearby Massachusetts General Hospital. James began his medical education in earnest in January 1864. He seems to have found it intellectually sterile and occasionally downright distasteful. He found "much humbug therein," but thought that surgery might occasionally do some actual good.[46]

In May, his family left their home in Newport for a new one in Boston. It was in Beacon Hill, then as now, the most exclusive neighborhood in the city. James, who had been living in various rooms around Boston and Cambridge, moved in with his parents, aunt, and sister once again. By the fall of 1864 he had met Charles Eliot Norton, the Boston Brahmin who would soon purchase a country house in Ashfield and discover there the promising local talent named Stanley Hall. Norton was the co-editor (with another "Brahmin," James Russell Lowell) of one of the most influential magazines in the US, the *North American Review*. William's younger brother Henry had published a story there earlier in the year, so William proposed to Norton that he write a review of *Lectures on the Elements of Composition* by Thomas Henry Huxley ("Darwin's bulldog," as he had come to be known since his "debate" with Anglican Bishop Samuel Wilberforce).[47]

Norton accepted William's offer and was apparently pleased enough with the result that he had William write another piece on an article by Alfred Russell Wallace, the co-discoverer of the theory of natural selection. In that article Wallace claimed that evolution no longer applied to humans on an individual scale, but only at the level of whole communities (what would later be called "group selection"). Societies that protected their weakest members did better in the long run than those that allowed only the strongest to thrive. James expressed general approval of Wallace and disapproval of Herbert Spencer's "social Darwinism"— the view, roughly, that the poor should be left to their torment without social or government assistance because they were unable to "compete" in the increasingly ruthless modern capitalist environment. James' article evinced an appreciation of Wallace's effort to show where Spencer and his followers had gone astray.

5. Brazil and Back

Early in 1865, as the war dragged on, an opportunity came to William to assist on a major naturalist expedition to the Amazon River, organized by none other than the renowned Louis Agassiz. He dropped his medical studies to join the exciting trek. Agassiz was the great opponent of Darwin among American scientists, and the aim of the expedition was to show that fish populations in various parts of the

Amazon, and other unconnected river systems, were not related to each other in the ways that Darwin's theory implied. James was not in agreement with Agassiz on this issue, though it hardly mattered what a 23-year-old undergraduate student with no field experience thought about such things.

Agassiz and his team of 16 left New York by ship at the end of March, 1865. Before they landed in Brazil, three weeks later, the South had surrendered, ending the Civil War, and a conspiracy led by a disgruntled southern actor had attacked the leadership of the US Government, killing Lincoln and wounding his Secretary of State, William Seward (the former Governor of New York, see Chapter 1).

At first, James was miserable. He was violently seasick on the passage. Soon after arriving, he contracted varioloid (a weakened type of smallpox), which laid him up for several weeks. He complained about nearly everything from the bugs to Agassiz's dealings with the Brazilian emperor, to the prices vendors charged them, to the very dirt itself. He decided almost immediately that he was not cut out for the naturalist business, after all. By the time the team moved north from Rio to the Amazon River, however, James had begun to settle in and eventually became a trusted member of the team, leading some on his own side-expeditions up tributaries of the great waterway. Just before he left, he had an insight that may have foreshadowed his later interest in pragmatism:

> the idea of people swarming about as they do at home, killing themselves with thinking about things that have no connexion with their merely external circumstances, studying themselves into fevers, going mad about religion, philosophy, love, & sich [sic], . . . seems almost incredible and imaginary.[48]

Of course, James would, in later years, come to study himself into a fever on these very topics but, under the pragmatic approach, he would strive to understand them precisely in their connection to people's external circumstances.

The expedition did not meet its primary goal of disproving Darwin's theory, of course. It did, however, result in the identification of hundreds of new species of fish and, with that, bring forth a new appreciation of the fecundity of freshwater systems. Perhaps more important, James learned something important about the relationship between the accumulation of facts and the broad abstract speculations in which his father typically traded: "No one sees farther into a generalization," he observed, "than his own knowledge of details extends." Although he still considered Agassiz's conclusions "humbug," he now saw what he called "the weight and solidity about the movement of Agassiz's mind, owing to the continual presence of this great background of special facts."[49]

After nine or ten months away—a world away—James arrived back in Boston in January or February of 1866.[50] In May, his family moved out of the city to Swampscott, Massachusetts, but James remained behind, increasingly interested in philosophy, especially Stoicism. He also began to strike up a deeper friendship with Oliver Wendell Holmes Jr. He had known Holmes, the son of a Harvard Medical professor, before the war, but not well. Homes had joined the Union Army, served three years, and been wounded three times. Holmes wanted to go into law rather than follow the path of his father into medicine. James' own medical studies were stalling; he said he was "drudging gloomily on."[51] The two men argued about materialism, determinism, chance, and other philosophical problems. James also attended a series of lectures on the logic of science at the Lowell Institute given by Charles Sanders Peirce, another acquaintance who was the son of the Harvard professor of mathematics and astronomy, Benjamin Peirce.[52] Of one talk, James said he "c[oul]d not understand a word but rather enjoyed the sensation of listening to [it] for an hour."[53] Entertaining as all this was, it did not solve the central problem that James still faced: what to do with his life.

FIGURE 3.3 William James' 1866 self-portrait, when he was a medical student.

Credit: William James Papers, Houghton Library, Harvard University.

Late in the year, James' family moved back, this time taking a house in Cambridge. Everyone in the family seemed to be in crisis: Wilky, now recovered from his war wounds, was spending huge sums on a failing venture to teach emancipated Blacks to farm in Florida; Bob was aimlessly flitting from idea to idea but, more ominously, sinking ever more deeply into the throes of alcoholism; Alice had a mental breakdown, the first of many, and was sent to New York to undergo a fashionable form of Swedish massage then known as the "movement cure." William himself complained of problems with his eyesight, the aftermath of his sickness in Rio, he thought.[54] Then he suffered a painful back episode that left him mostly immobile and, eventually, deeply depressed.

6. The European Cure

In his despair, James turned to an escape that his father had resorted to many times: he booked passage to Europe. He left in April 1867 for France. After a brief pause in Paris, he headed to Dresden where there was a sizeable American enclave. At first, his main activity was reading, interspersed with walks in the park. He read French novels for relaxation, but also perused some German philosophy and literature—especially Hegel and Goethe. He traveled to a resort in Bohemia to "take the waters." He put up a brave face in letters to his mother and sister, saying he was improving. To his father and his friends, however, he confessed that his back was as bad as ever, now joined by intestinal troubles. His despondency had deepened as well, to the point that he sometimes mused about suicide.

It is difficult to know how seriously to take all this. Many of James' biographers have considered this dark period to constitute the cauldron of profound doubt and self-examination in which the original and refreshing intellect we know today as William James was incubated. From another perspective, however, it can seem like a self-conscious literary trope: the specter of a young man upon whom few adult demands have ever been made and, yet, so wealthy that he can afford to indulge in years of aimless emotional turmoil—O! *What* shall I do with myself!—fleeing to an extended European retreat to sort himself out. The young men of America's farms and mines and factories could afford no such luxury.

In some of his letters back home, James began to seriously debate his father on the issues that had excited the senior man's intellect over 30 years—the spiritual versus the natural, the universal versus the subjective, the overarching generalization versus the mass of particular facts. On each point, the son was gradually lining up closer to the side opposite of his father.

In the fall, James moved to Berlin, where he was able to share rooms with an old Newport friend, Tom Perry. Despite his various physical and psychic infirmities, he managed to embark on a rigorous schedule of university lectures in physiology—as many as eleven per week. Among the professors whose courses he attended was the famed Emil DuBois-Reymond, discoverer of the fundamental mode of activity in the nerves: the action potential. Physiology was among the great scientific successes of the age. The topic had been converted, in the hands of a generation of gifted scientists, many of them German, from a speculative appendage of anatomy into a strict, experimental, laboratory-based science in its own right.

Central to that ascendancy had been the invention and use of new laboratory instruments that enabled researchers not only to measure precisely the duration of various events, but also to stretch the records of instantaneous events, or to compress ones that extended over long time frames, in order to be able see and understand, on a scale perceptible to human eyes, just how they unfolded. The kymograph, for instance, invented by Carl Ludwig in the 1840s, consisted of a rotating cylinder around which was spiraled a wobbly line inscribed by a stylus whose side-to-side movements were sensitive to some physiological process. (Today one is most likely to see a similar device recording seismic activity.) The kymograph was, perhaps, best at recording regular cyclical movements such as breathing and pulse. However, by speeding up the rotation of the cylinder, one could record the details of actions that occur so quickly that they are nearly invisible to the naked eye (such as a frog catching a fly with its tongue). By slowing down the cylinder's rotation, one could record movements that occur so slowly they are nearly invisible to the naked eye (such as the daily movements of plants). In its day, the kymograph seemed as revolutionary to physiology as the telescope and the microscope had been to astronomy and anatomy.[55]

Around this time, James first mused vaguely about pursuing physiology, especially its connections to psychology, as his primary field of inquiry. In November he wrote, "some measurements have allready [sic] been made in the region lying between the physical changes in the nerves and the appearance of consciousness—(in the shape of sense perceptions)."[56] Here he first mentioned the possibility of traveling to Heidelberg to study with the great physiologist Hermann Helmholtz, who had first measured the speed of nervous transmission, and with "a man named Wundt." He meant, of course, Wilhelm Wundt, who would go on to found the first Institute for Experimental Psychology, in Leipzig a decade hence.

All of the intellectual stimulation around him in Germany, however, was not sufficient to rid James of his gloom. By the spring of 1868, he felt that he had sunk into a permanent depression. Still, he manage to write a few book reviews for magazines back home, including one of Darwin's *Variation of Animals and Plants Under Domestication*. He returned to Dresden, visited the art museums and read literature, both ancient and modern. He mused about the nature of evil and the meaning of life. In addition to returning twice more to the therapeutic baths of Bohemia, James indulged in various other popular (but mostly ineffective) treatments for his continuing back pain including, at one point, blistering.

Generally, James was supportive of political liberalization.[57] The mixing of different ethnic groups, however, seems to have made him uneasy, particularly in his young adulthood. Ralph Baton Perry, perhaps the most admiring of James'

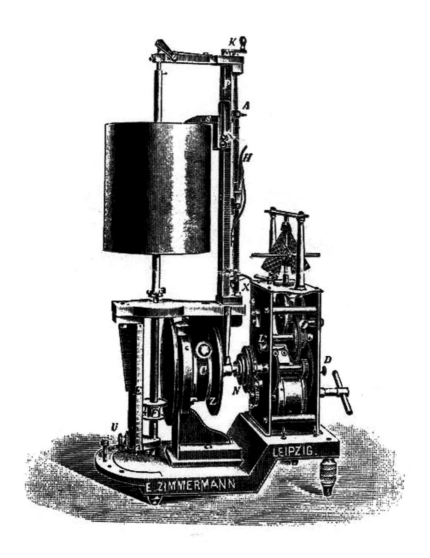

FIGURE 3.4 Kymograph, manufactured by the Zimmermann company of Leipzig.

Credit: Reproduced from Zimmermann, E. (1900). *Psychologische und physiologische Apparate, Mikrotome,* p. 1, figure 3.1.)

many sympathetic biographers, phrased the matter delicately: "When James was in Europe he was always keenly interested in the broader aspect of politics, and above all in national traits."[58] The ethnic mix of Berlin seems to have been beyond James' ability to absorb with equanimity. In October, 1867, he wrote to his sister:

> Jews are more numerous here than any where [*sic*] in Germany and are said to own most of the wealth and edit most of the newspapers. They look

detestable—a real jewish looking jew, with a long robe, a goat's beard, and two little ringlets before the ears, like I saw in Teplitz [Bohemia], is quite a stylish animal, with an harmonious and pronounced expression of his own. But the jews here put on all christian graces, wear nothing but whiskers, and have an unnatural and revolting aspect.[59]

It is easy to over-interpret the words of a historical figure that, though perhaps common in their own time, are exceptional and repugnant today, but James' words here have particular significance in their own context. The Northern German Confederation had constitutionally come into existence only two-and-a-half months before, on July 1, 1867.[60] As one of its government's first acts, on July 3, it had emancipated its Jewish citizens (i.e., granted them land ownership rights, entry into professions, and other civil rights). Although Jews had been emancipated in Prussia, of which Berlin was the capital, decades before (in 1812), the new law guaranteed these rights across northern German states, including some that had been resistant to granting such rights earlier. So, for James to have made this particular remark in this place at this time was, for instance, roughly tantamount to making derogatory comments about the physical appearances of African Americans who had succeeded economically in the immediate wake the US Civil Rights Act of the 1964. It thus appears that, for all his cosmopolitanism, simple ethnic prejudice was still among James sentiments at this time, and that it was not limited to the Irish Catholics of America's cities. That said, it is also important to note that, later in life, James would befriend and support a number of Jewish colleagues and students: Gertrude Stein, Morris Cohen, Boris Sidis, and Horace Kallen, among others. Whether his attitude toward Jews "in general" had changed by that time is not as clear.

One thing that James' experience in Germany gradually taught him was that, in order to be a working scientist, one must actually conduct experiments (reinforcing the lesson of Brazil, that one must collect specimens in order to be a naturalist). In December 1868, he mentioned visiting Helmholtz and Wundt in Heidelberg again. But it wasn't just lectures he was after this time. He hoped to work in their laboratories: "I shall hate myself until till I get doing some special work: this reading leads nowhere."[61] At the end of June 1868, he finally took action, traveling to Heidelberg to gain practical laboratory experience under the tutelage of Helmholtz and Wundt. Helmholtz had a professorship at the university. Wundt, however, who had been an assistant in Helmholtz's laboratory from 1857 to 1865, had resigned his position to establish his own physiology laboratory in his apartment building. For several years this private facility functioned as his home base: he taught his classes there and conducted his own original research.[62] Wundt was, however, still a relatively minor figure at this time, not a "great physiologist," as he is sometimes described. He had not yet won a professorship of his own, though he had published several minor books. These included his *Vorlesungen über die Menschen- und Tierseele* (*Lectures on Human and Animal Psychology*), published in 1863, but it had not been a successes. His most important book had probably been

Beiträge zur Theorie der Sinneswahrnehmung (*Contributions on the Theory of Sensory Perception*), written and published under the supervision of Helmholtz in 1862. His hugely influential psychology textbook, *Grundzüge der physiologischen Psychologie* (*Principles of Physiological Psychology*), was still six years in the future.

A meeting between the younger Wundt and the younger James might have been an interesting event, but it was not to be. For reasons that are not entirely clear, James never made it to Helmholtz's lectures and never came face-to-face with Wundt. One biographer surmised that he had failed to obtain the requisite letters of introduction, and that he may have been overwhelmed by his own sense of inadequacy.[63] This is an understandable inference, given that James himself wrote of being seized by a "blue despair," and so he "fled" the city. But that may have been little more than a melodramatic turn of phrase, because he immediately went on to note that, once in Heidelberg, he found that neither Helmholtz nor Wundt would be lecturing that summer. He then went on to disparage Heidelberg's relative dearth of cultural attractions as a reason for not sticking around until the fall.[64] So, the Heidelberg fiasco may have been more the result of poor timing coupled with some embarrassment at his failure to plan adequately, as much as a reflection of deeper psychological issues.

One important development in (what would come to be known as) "physiological psychology" of which James may not have been aware at the time was the research the Dutch ophthalmologist, Franz Donders was conducting in Utrecht.[65] From 1865, Donders had been attempting to measure the duration of simple decisions by comparing the length of time it took people to react to a single stimulus (e.g., a red card), to the length of time it took them to react to only one of two different possible stimuli (e.g., only to the red card, but not to the blue). The difference between these two times he took to be the time it took the person to decide whether the "correct" stimulus had been presented. Exploring various complications of this sort of experimental scheme was central to Wundt's early work in experimental psychology.

Quitting Heidelberg, James went briefly to Berlin, then back to Dresden. He also seemed to abandon, at least for the moment, his interest in physiology, returning to novels and philosophy. He read Kant's *Critique of Pure Reason* for the first time, as well as a number of commentaries on it. He also came across the work of a lesser philosopher whose ideas would become quite important to him, Charles Renouvier.

By November, James had had enough of Germany. (Stanley Hall would arrive just seven months later.) He returned to the US, high enough in spirits, at least, to feel that he could finally complete his long-delayed medical degree, but wishing that he could somehow make his way into what he called "a scientific life."[66] He planned the thesis that was required for his medical degree, discussing his ideas with his friend and recent medical graduate, Henry Pickering Bowditch.[67] He submitted his finished thesis in May 1869 and took his examination in June.

The final medical examination was an unusual affair, a bit like modern "speed dating" (one of James' sons called it a mad tea party). Nine professors sat at nine desks representing the nine topics on which each candidate was to be examined. Students entered the room nine at a time, each taking a seat before one of the professors. Then, each professor examined the student before him on the assigned topic until, after ten minutes, a bell was rung. At that point, all the students shifted one desk over to be examined on the next topic, for ten minutes, until the bell was rung once again. And so it went for 90 minutes, until all nine students had been examined, albeit briefly, on each of the nine topics. Then the name of each student was read aloud and each of the professors raised a paddle, white for pass, black for fail. Any student who passed at least five of the nine topics, got an MD and a license to practice.[68] James passed his exam, but medicine was not really on his mind. Deeper issues, moral issues—the essence of human nature and of human will, in particular—were gnawing at him, and they would set the stage for a personal crisis that has widely been regarded as the private foundation to James' intellectual career. As he wrote to a friend in March of 1869, just before completing his degree, he had begun to fear,

> that we are Nature through and through, that we are *wholly* conditioned, that not a wiggle of our will happens save as the result of physical laws. . . . [T]he defensive tactics of the French "spiritualists" fighting a steady retreat before materialism will never do anything.[69]

7. Reforming the College, Reforming America

Nearly everyone knew that something was wrong with the way not only Harvard, but American colleges generally, educated young men. The Classical curriculum had become obsolete, having little to do with the modern, technological, entrepreneurial life that graduates would be likely to lead after leaving school. The medical and law schools were moribund. Even the few science schools—Yale, Dartmouth, and Columbia each had one as well as Harvard—were weak. The very year that James graduated, Harvard's Trustees embarked on a bold experiment. Rather than hiring yet another philosopher or theologian to be president of the college, as was the custom, they appointed a scientist with the express intent of building a new model of modern American collegiate education. The man they selected to do it was none other than Charles William Eliot, William James' former chemistry professor at Lawrence. Eliot wasn't just a chemist, though. His father, Samuel Atkins Eliot, had been a member of the Massachusetts House of Representatives in the mid-1830s and mayor of Boston from 1837 to 1839. He had also served in the Massachusetts Senate and, briefly, in the US Congress. Perhaps more important than all of these, from 1842 to 1853 he had been the Treasurer of Harvard College. Although he had died in 1862, just a year before his son Charles' contract was not renewed as a chemistry instructor at the Lawrence Scientific School, Samuel Eliot's legacy undoubtedly smoothed the way for Charles' eventual ascension to the presidency.

Charles Eliot was only 35 at the time he took Harvard's reins, but his appointment was not simply a case nepotism. In the years since he had left Lawrence, back in 1863, he had toured Europe, studying the higher educational systems of several countries there. Early in 1869, Eliot published an article based on his observations titled "The New Education" in *Atlantic Monthly*. He argued against both the traditional Classical curriculum and against a narrow vocational education, as some wanted. In their place, he promoted a broad education centered on modern disciplines, such as natural science, mathematics, political economy, modern languages, and modern history.[70] He also rejected scientific education as it had been practiced at Harvard to that point, in which "a young man who has studied nothing but chemistry, or nothing but engineering, and who is densely ignorant of everything else may obtain the sole degree given by the school,—that of a Bachelor of Science."[71] Instead, Eliot argued, every student, whether in arts or in science, should take courses in a range of topics. Harvard hired Eliot to implement his new model. He added elective courses so that college education would not be so narrow as it had been before. He founded graduate programs. He elevated medicine and law to graduate degrees, so that all students in those schools would have earned a bachelor's degree before entering.

Most of the other old eastern colleges resisted, holding on to the American tradition that college was mainly for disciplining the mind with ancient languages and mathematics, and for inculcating Christian character with moral philosophy and denominational dogmatics, not for training students in recent scholarly developments. Yale, as had been its role on the American collegiate scene since its very inception, led the conservative refusal most steadfastly. Noah Porter, Yale's president from 1871, bolstered Christian foundations, ensured that science stay in "its place" outside of the main college curriculum, and blocked the creation of elective courses. The rigidity of Yale's stance was extraordinary even in its time. In 1880, Eliot wrote to Johns Hopkins president Daniel Coit Gilman that, "The manners and customs of the Yale Faculty are those of a porcupine on the defensive. The other colleges were astonished at first, but now they just laugh."[72] Princeton, led since 1868 by the Scotsman James McCosh, fell somewhere between the two, allowing some electives, attempting to broker a compatibilist accord between Protestantism and evolutionary theory, but still holding that the mission of the college was moral edification more than advanced scholarship.

James was ambivalent about the appointment of Eliot to the Harvard presidency. He wrote to his friend Henry Bowditch that Eliot's "great personal defects, tactlessness, meddlesomeness, and disposition to cherish petty grudges seem pretty universally acknowledged; but his ideas seem good and his economic powers first-rate."[73] Whether one liked Eliot personally or not, his reforms aligned with the new America that was being shaped right before everyone's eyes by an explosion of new technologies.

The year 1869 was also the year that the transcontinental railroad was completed. Trains, and the telegraph lines that accompanied them, were transforming the American economy and the American way of life like nothing seen before. Rail lines had started to roll out across the landscape immediately after the opening of the Erie Canal, as other cities on the Atlantic seaboard scrambled to prevent New York from becoming, effectively, the only international port in the eastern US. As described before, a group of Baltimore businessmen got off to the fastest start, chartering the Baltimore & Ohio Railroad in 1827, and starting construction in 1828. It would take two-and-a-half decades, but the line did eventually reach all the way to the Ohio River. By that time, the Erie Canal had itself been superseded to some degree by the new rail line that ran from New York to Buffalo, presided over by Erastus Corning, which eventually became known as the New York Central. In 1867, it was bought out by "The Commodore," Cornelius Vanderbilt, who had gotten his start in transportation back in 1807, ferrying passengers in his own little periauger[74] across New York Harbor from Manhattan to Staten Island.

The "robber barons" of the major rail companies were primarily interested in carrying commodities in great quantities across the continent—grain, livestock, coal, steel, oil. In short order, though, retailers in a number of urban centers began to realize the potential of rail lines to provide them with something that had never before been possible: a national market. Prior to rail, the so-called "national economy" was more or less the sum total of a number of relatively autonomous local economies, each comprised of a regional urban center and the surrounding farmland and wilderness that supplied it with the raw materials it required to produce a few basic manufactured goods. The country was, as one historian famously put it, "a nation of loosely connected islands."[75] Breaking out of that model, the Chicago merchant Aaron Montgomery Ward produced the first major mail order catalog in 1872. As the web of rail expanded, anyone anywhere in the country could, in principle, buy anything made in any city in the country.

This was a retail revolution. With rapidly increasing consumer demand for commercially made products, shipped by train, manufacturing began to take over from farming as the country's chief economic engine. One business historian has argued that this transformation—the emergence of the first mass consumer culture—drove an increasing preoccupation with personal individuality and subjectivity in late 19th-century America. If so, it may well have also driven the paradoxical twin of self-absorption: anxiety about personal status.[76] It is not very much of a stretch to suggest that this novel socioeconomic landscape provided extremely fertile ground in which the discipline (and practice) of psychology would grow so rapidly over the next few decades into a pervasive aspect of the American cultural scene.

Eighty years earlier Thomas Jefferson and Alexander Hamilton had debated what kind of country the newly-born United States would be. Jefferson saw mostly a gauzy image of his present: slave-powered farms run by a wealthy but (putatively) benevolent landed gentry.[77] Hamilton saw (mainly in his mind's eye) an urban, industrial future that really began to come into being only after the Civil War.

Of course, expanding urban industry required cheap labor nearly as much as the Southern plantations had. Battles over the value and the cost—both monetary and human—of labor did not end with the emancipation of the slaves. With the coming of the factories, these ever-contentious issues simply moved into a new arena.

8. William James Hits Bottom

As he was in so many things, William James was a transitional figure in this revolution. Although he was never really "of" the modern world of technology, mass production, and narrow specialization, because he had been raised in New York City he had experienced its coming into being long before many of his fellow Americans; long before Stanley Hall, for instance.

Immediately after James completed his medical degree, he did little. He spent the summer of 1869 in the Connecticut countryside. He visited and was visited by various cousins. In the fall William moved back into his parents house in Cambridge. Henry Sr.'s latest book had been published, *The Secret of Swedenborg*. William read it and found it mostly impenetrable, though he dutifully acknowledged to Henry Jr., their father's "genius." Charles Sanders Peirce reviewed it anonymously in the *North American Review* and even he, with his polymathic talents, found it "terribly difficult." Years later, the novelist William Dean Howells quipped that Henry James "wrote *The Secret of Swedenborg* and kept it."[78]

Peirce also pinpointed as clearly and concisely as anyone the real problem that Henry James Sr. faced in being taken seriously as a thinker: "Though this book presents some very interesting and impressive religious views, and the spiritual tone of it is in general eminently healthy, it is altogether out of harmony with the spirit of this age."[79] The elder James was still working out problems that had seemed pressing thirty years earlier. In the age of the locomotive and the telegraph, they seemed, at best, quaint and, at worst, simply irrelevant.

In the fall of 1869, William's relationship with one of his cousins, Minnie Temple—the "mad" one who had cut her hair short a few years before—began to change. Minnie had always been unconventional, abrupt, sometimes antic, but also smart and self-possessed. James had found her unpleasant, a "bad thing."[80] In his reviews of books about the position of women in society—John Stuart Mill's radical *The Subjection of Women* and Horace Bushnell's reactionary *Women's Suffrage, the Reform Against Nature*—James had argued gently in favor of the need—men's need—for women to be dependent.[81] Whatever else Minnie was, she was certainly not that. Her uninhibited character had drawn the attention, mostly favorable but also cautious, of several of the young men in James' circle.

Nevertheless, William and Minnie's relationship deepened and became more intimate in late 1869 and early 1870. They discussed life, death, religion, and other matters of profound personal belief. It is difficult to know exactly what transpired between them because the documentary record from this time is fragmentary—some journal entries are missing, some letters are partial. Perhaps that is indicative of something in itself, as some have suggested, or perhaps it is just the luck of the archival draw. Whatever the exact character of their newfound bond was, they were knowingly entering a room from which there was only one exit. Minnie was suffering from tuberculosis, and her condition was deteriorating. James had another "dorsal collapse" in January of 1870, "and a moral one." If humans are "Nature through and through," as he had written to his friend Ward the year before, then what, if anything, is our "moral" aspect? Are all those things that were thought to elevate humanity above the animals—reason, love, determination, compassion, invention, art, and civilization itself—only an illusion? James consoled himself—perhaps distracted himself from Minnie's visible decline—by wrestling with the conflicting demands of fate and free will. It was a painful journey for him. He thought he had "about touched bottom" on February 1. Minnie's condition continued to worsen, though. She died on March 8, 1870. That seems to have been when the "bottom" that James thought he had already "touched," fell out completely.[82]

He tumbled into a devastating personal crisis that bore no small resemblance to the "vastation" his father had suffered 26 years before. He suffered "horrible fear of [his] own existence." He was haunted by,

> the image of an epileptic patient whom I had seen in the asylum, a black-haired youth with greenish skin, entirely idiotic, who used to sit all day on one of the benches, or rather shelves against the wall, with his knees drawn up against his chin, and the coarse gray undershirt. . . . moving nothing but his black eyes and looking absolutely non-human. . . . *That shape am I*, I felt, potentially. Nothing that I possess can defend me against that fate, if the hour for it should strike for me as it struck for him. . . . After this the universe was changed for me altogether.[83]

No act of will, James thought, regardless of how strong or pure, could protect him if a purely materialist determinism governed the world. It wasn't until late April, after nearly two months of suffering this "horrible dread," that he is conventionally said to have found some measure of defense against this bleak fatalism in the writings of the French philosopher, Charles Renouvier, who argued that human freedom lay at the core of Kant's Critical Philosophy. James resolved to believe in free will for one year as a means of extracting himself from his horror.[84]

In no small part because of James' later contributions to the topic of human will, much has been made of his discovery of Renouvier at this critical point in his life. It is important to note, however, that Renouvier's volunteerism did not lift James out of his terrible depression. He would struggle with it for two or three more difficult years before he returned to a more equanimous state of mind. Whether it was Renouvier's philosophy, a gradual distancing from Minnie's terrible death, or just the spontaneous lifting of an acute depressive episode, no one can say with certainty.

Notes

1 Howard M. Feinstein, *Becoming William James* (Ithaca, NY: Cornell University Press, 1984).

2 Letter to Edgar Beach Van Winkle. March 1, 1858. In Ignas K. Skrupskelis and Elizabeth M. Berkeley, eds., *The Correspondence of William James* (Charlottesville, VA and London, UK: University of Virginia Press, 1992), vol. 4, 14.

3 Letter to one of Henry James' early teachers, the prominent physicist Joseph Henry, 9 July 1843, cited in Alfred Habegger, *The Father: A Life of Henry James, Sr.* (New York, NY: Farrar, Strauss and Giroux, 1994), 204. Joseph Henry was professor at the Albany Academy from 1826, and at Princeton from 1832. He was the first man to be named Secretary of the Smithsonian Institution, a position that he held from 1846 until his death in 1878. To be fair to Henry James, in an era when Mesmerism was at the height of its popularity, the idea that science and spirit could illuminate each other was a popular and exciting one. See, e.g., Alison Winter, *Mesmerized: Power of Mind in Victorian Britain* (Chicago, IL: University of Chicago Press, 1998).

4 See, e.g., John Hall Gladstone, *Michael Faraday* (London, UK: Palgrave Macmillan, 1872), 92.

5 See the letter from Henry James Sr. to his mother, 1860(?) cited in Katherine Weissbourd, *Growing Up in the James Family: Henry James Sr., as Son and Father* (Ann Arbor, MI: UMI Research Press, 1978), 45.

6 Letter to Edgar Beach Van Winkle, July 1, 1856. Skrupskelis and Berkeley, *Correspondence of William James*, vol. 4, 3.

7 Letter to Edgar Beach Van Winkle, March 1, 1858. Ibid., vol. 4, 15.

8 Letter to Edgar Beach Van Winkle, March 1, 1858. Ibid., vol. 4, 12–13. The implicit reference to those whose labor helped to generate his grandfather's and, in turn, his own wealth is striking.

9 Letter from William James to Edgar Beach Van Winkle, August 12, 1858. Ibid., vol. 4, 19.

10 Letter from William James to Edgar Beach Van Winkle, September 18, 1858. Ibid., vol. 4, 21.

11 Letter from William James to Thomas Sergeant Perry, August 5, 1860. Ibid., vol. 4, 33.

12 Letter from William James to Henry James Sr., August 19, 1860. Ibid., vol. 4, 36–37.

13 The outline of the story will be well known to American readers. The ship, *Mayflower*, with its 102 religiously separatist "pilgrims" landed in 1620 at the point of land they dubbed Plymouth, some 40 miles south of what is now central Boston. Soon after, Puritan settlements dotted the region.

14 James II had tried something similar with the short-lived Dominion of New England in late 1680s, but it had collapsed soon after the outbreak of the "Glorious Revolution" in 1688.

15 Alexis De Tocqueville, *Democracy in America*, trans. Gerald E. Bevan, vol. 1 (London, UK: Penguin, 1835/2003), 46.

16 It took some time for the rigid character of the colony to change. As late as 1692, of course, twenty members of Salem, just 20 miles up the coast from Boston, were executed for witchcraft.

17 Some of the more conservative early New England churches had gone so far as to regulate prices and control profit in accord with their understanding of the Bible.

18 Cotton Mather's father, Increase Mather, had been rector and president of Harvard from the mid-1680s. In point of fact, he was out of the colony during almost all of his term of office but, a stern defender of orthodoxy, he nevertheless feuded mightily with college faculty, whom he viewed as unacceptably lax, theologically. Mather's opponents forced him out in 1701. At that point, the Mather family turned their hopes toward the school that would soon become Yale. Meanwhile, at Harvard, the noted liberalizer John

Leverett was appointed Harvard's first lay president just seven years after Mather's fiery departure.

19 That is, they were following the controversial teachings of the Dutch theologian Jacobus Arminius (1560–1609) which had been condemned in Switzerland and had led to a profound crisis in Calvinism in Leiden in the early 17th century.

20 Henry Adams, *The Education of Henry Adams* (Boston, MA: Houghton-Mifflin, 1918), loc. 532 of Kindle edition.

21 In calling the long white colonnaded building "original," I am not including the "Bullfinch Pavilion" which was built in the 1820s. See Nancy S. Seasholes, *Gaining Ground: A History of Landmaking in Boston* (Cambridge, MA: MIT Press, 2003), Figure 5.10 on p. 116.

22 See Ibid., Figure 5.13 on p. 120.

23 Ibid., 156–57. It is important to recall that this was exactly the time that the building of the Erie Canal was radically altering the economic geography of North America, and many cities on the eastern seaboard were scrambling to challenge New York's impending supremacy. To the south, in Maryland, the Baltimore and Ohio railroad was being organized in response to the Erie Canal as well.

24 See especially the 1858 photograph of the still-undeveloped Back Bay in Seasholes, *Gaining Ground*, Figure 7.19 on p. 181.

25 Cited in Robert D Richardson, *William James: In the Maelstrom of Modernity* (Boston, MA: Houghton-Mifflin, 2006), 41.

26 Ibid.

27 Laurence R. Veysey, *The Emergence of the American University* (Chicago, IL: University of Chicago Press, 1961), 4. There are many studies of the origins and development of higher education in the US. Veysey's is considered a classic. Another more recent study is John R. Thelin, *A History of American Higher Education*, 2nd ed. (Baltimore, MD: Johns Hopkins University Press, 2011).

28 Adams, *Education*, 54. As an interesting aside, Adams attended Harvard at the same time as a Southern colonel by the name of Robert E. Lee, whom he described as having "liberal Virginian openness towards all he liked [and] . . . the Virginian habit of command. . . . [But] the habit of command was not enough. . . . No one knew how ignorant he was; how childlike; how helpless before the relative complexity of a school. . . . The Southerner, with his slave-owning limitations, was as little fit to succeed in the struggle of modern life as though he were still a maker of stone axes, living in caves."

29 Although the Adams family is often considered to have been of the "Botson Brahmins," the Adams' regarded themselves as being apart, from Qunicy. As Henry Adams once put the matter, "the only distinctive mark of all the Adamses, since old Sam Adams' father a hundred and fifty years before, had been their inherited quarrel with State Street," the symbolic center of Massachusetts' government and finance. Adams, *Education*, third-to-last paragraph of chapter 1.

30 Letter from William James to his cousin (and Minnie's older sister) Katherine Temple Emmet, dated November 1861 by Skrupskelis and Berkeley, eds. of *Correspondence of William James*, vol. 4, 48–50.

31 Owen was responsible for the founding of the Natural History Museum in London, and was the person who coined the term "*Dinosauria*" to describe the massive extinct animals whose fossils were being uncovered by Mary Anning and others in England and elsewhere.

32 Letter from William James to the James Family, dated November 10, 1861 by Skrupskelis and Berkeley, eds. of *Correspondence of William James*, vols. 4, 50–52.

33 The story of the Massachusetts 54th was told in the 1989 film *Glory*.

34 See Richardson, *William James*, 55.

35 Jack Tager, *Boston Riots: Three Centuries of Social Violence* (Boston, MA: Northeastern University Press, 2001), 132.

36 Ibid., 134–35.

37 Thomas H. O'Connor's popular *Bibles, Brahmins, and Bosses: A Short History of Boston*, 3rd ed. (Boston, MA: Boston Public Library, 1991) does not mention the Draft Riot. His later book, *The Boston Irish: A Political History* (Boston, MA: Northeastern University Press, 1995) mentions it briefly, but claims that there was "no looting of shops, no destruction of property" (p. 90). He cites a study by William F. Hanna ("The Boston Draft Riot," *Civil War History* 36 (1990): 262–73) in which it is claimed that "destruction of property was kept to a minimum" (p. 262) but then goes on to describe incidents of lootings in detail. This minimization is hard to believe if one takes seriously Bob James' eyewitness account of the events (though see below some reasons to doubt it). More important still is Tager's more recent, more detailed account of the events that day (*Boston Riots*).

38 Henry G. Pearson, *Life of John A. Andrew, Governor of Massachusetts, 1861–1865* (Boston, MA: Houghton-Mifflin, 1904), cited in Tager, *Boston Riots*, 36.

39 See, e.g., Matthew Frye Jacobson, *Whiteness of a Different Color: European Immigrants and the Alchemy of Race* (Cambridge, MA: Harvard University Press, 1998).

40 Bob James' story was told in a public address that he gave in Concord MA on March 10, 1896 titled "Three Years' Service with the Fifty-Fifth Massachusetts Volunteer Infantry." Although the 45-page transcript is exceedingly rare, the passage pertaining to the Boston Civil War Riot is published in Jane Maher, *Biography of Broken Fortunes: Wilkie and Bob, Brothers of William, Henry, and Alice James* (Hamdon, CT: Arcon, 1986). Skrupskelis and Berkeley, the editors of *The Correspondence of William James* (vol. 11, 128 n.), have questioned the veracity of Bob's story.

41 Tager, *Boston Riots*, 136–37.

42 Ibid., 138.

43 E.g., He alluded, in letters from December 23 and 25, 1861 to his friend Thomas Sergeant Perry, to the *Trent* affair, in which a British ship was caught by the US Navy transporting Confederate envoys (*Correspondence of William James*, vol. 4, 60, 64). The matter nearly brought the US to war with England. See Henry Adams, *Education*, chap. 8 for a detailed description from the perspective of the US ambassador's son and assistant. One exception to James' relative silence is his September 30, 1866 letter to Frederick George Bromberg (then in Mobile, AL), which discusses the actions of Andrew Johnson and the implications of the "New Orleans Massacre" of July 30, 1866 in some detail (*Correspondence of William James*, vol., 143).

44 Letter from Oliver Wendell Holmes to Lewis Einstein dated March 21, 1912. Oliver Wendell Holmes Papers, Harvard Law School Library, Harvard University. Cited in Richardson, *William James*, 77, from Liva Baker, *The Justice from Beacon Hill* (New York, NY: HarperCollins, 1991), 155.

45 Letter from William James to Mary Robertson Walsh James, dated by an archivist November 2, 1863. Skrupskelis and Berkeley, *Correspondence of William James*, vol. 4, 86.

46 Letter from William James to Jeannette Barber Gourlay. Ibid., vol. 4, 90. Correspondence, vol. 4, p. 90.

47 Letter from William James to Charles Eliot Norton dated September 3, 1864. Ibid., vol. 4, 92–93. There are many popular myths pertaining to the exchange between Huxley and Wilberforce. See Ian Hesketh, *Of Apes and Ancestors : Evolution, Christianity, and the Oxford Debate* (Toronto, ON: University of Toronto Press, 2009). One interesting issue that is often overlooked is that Wilberforce was the son of William Wilberforce, the man who had led the English political fight to end slavery in the Empire some 30 years earlier. It was from this connection, as much as from his clerical garments, that Wilberforce drew his substantial cultural credibility.

48 Letter from William James to Mary Robertson Walsh James dated December 9, 1865. Skrupskelis and Berkeley, *Correspondence of William James*, vol. 4, 132.

49 Letter from William James to Henry James, Sr. dated September 12, 1865. Ibid., vol. 4, 122.

50 There is some confusion about when he returned exactly. In a letter of Dec 9, 1865 he told his mother that he was on the verge of returning, which should have gotten him

back in early January (Ibid., vols. 4, 131). In a letter to Frederick George Bromberg, he says that he had gotten home by the 1st of March (Ibid., vols. 4, 142).

51 Letter from William James to Alice James, Dec 12, 1866. *Correspondence of William James*, vol. 4, 148.

52 The Peirce family's presence at Harvard went back one additional generation to Charles' paternal grandfather, Benjamin Sr., who had graduated from the school in 1801 and had later gone on to serve as its librarian. He also wrote a history of the Crimson College. There were politicians in Charles' background as well: Benjamin Sr. had been a Massachusetts State legislator (representing Salem), and Charles' maternal grandfather, Elijah Hunt Mills, a Federalist, had risen to the office of Speaker of the US House of Representatives in 1820, and then served as US Senator from 1820 to 1826. The Peirce family had deep roots in New England. The first of them, weavers from Norwich, had arrived in Watertown, MA in 1634. See Frederick Clifton Pierce, *Peirce Genealogy: Being the Record of the Posterity of John Pers, an Early Inhabitant of Watertown, in New England, Who Came from Norwich, Norfolk County, England; With Notes on the History of Other Families Peirce, Pierce, Pearce, Etc.* (Worcester, MA: Chas. Hamilton, 1880).

53 Letter from William James to Alice James, Nov. 14, 1866. Skrupskelis and Berkeley, *Correspondence of William James*, vol. 4, 144.

54 Letter from William James to Frederick George Bromberg, September 30, 1866. Ibid., vol. 4, 142.

55 See, e.g., Merriley Borell, "Instrumentation and the Rise of Modern Physiology," *Science and Technology Studies* 5 (1987): 53–62, esp. p. 56.

56 Letter from William James to Thomas Wren Ward, November 7, 1867. *Correspondence of William James*, vols. 4, 226.

57 See, e.g., James' letter to Edmund Tweedy of December 18, 1867. Ibid., vols. 4, 242.

58 Ralph Barton Perry, *The Thought and Character of William James.*, vol. 1 (London, UK: Oxford University Press, 1935), 252.

59 Letter from William James to Alice James. October 17, 1867. Skrupskelis and Berkeley, *Correspondence of William James*, vol. 4, 215. It was not James' only intolerant remarks about the Jewish people. He once described Jews in Rome as "squatting along the sides of houses just like maggots in a piece of flesh" (cited in Gordon Lyndall, *A Private Life of Henry James: Two Women and His Art* (New York, NY: Norton, 1998), 92.

60 The Confederation was one of the main outcomes of the Austro-Prussian War, which had concluded less than a year earlier, in August of 1866.

61 Letter from William James to Henry James, Sr. December 26, 1867. *Correspondence of William James*, vols. 4, 243.

62 Wolfgang G. Bringmann, Urslua Boss, and Gustav A. Ungerer, "Wundt's Laboratories," in *A Pictorial History of Psychology*, ed. Wolfgang G. Bringmann et al. (Carol Stream, IL: Quintessence, 1997), 126–32.

63 Richardson, *William James*, 93.

64 Letter from William James to Henry James, Sr., July 3, 1868. *Correspondence of William James*, vols. 4, 327.

65 Donders does not appear in the index of the 1856–1877 volume (vol. 4) of the *Correspondence*.

66 Letter from William James to Thomas Wren Ward. October 9, 1868. Skrupskelis and Berkeley, *Correspondence of William James*, vol. 4, 346.

67 Bowditch would go on to become a professor, and eventually Dean, of Harvard Medical School.

68 The description of the examination process follows that outlined by Richardson, *William James*, 103.

69 Letter from William James to Thomas Wren Ward. March, 1869 [exact date not given]. Skrupskelis and Berkeley, *Correspondence of William James*, vol. 4, 370–71.

70 In September 1870, he appointed Henry Adams to a professorship in history. A number of Eliot's early faculty appointments were "head hunted" from other schools as a result of his substantially increasing Harvard professors' salaries. For instance, F. H. Storer arrived from MIT to take a professorship in Agricultural Chemistry in 1870. Physicist E. C. Pickering also came from MIT, in 1876, to become Director of the Harvard Observatory. Sanskritist C. R. Lanman came from Johns Hopkins in 1880 to head the Department of Indo-Iranian Languages. Classicist F. D. Allen was drawn from Yale in 1880, to become professor of Classical Philology.

71 Charles William Eliot, "The New Education," *Atlantic Monthly*, 1869, quotation from 210.

72 Letter from C. W. Eliot to D. C. Gilman dated March 9, 1880. MS 1, Papers of Daniel Coit Gilman, Series 1, Box 13, Folder 44, Johns Hopkins University. Also cited in Veysey, *The Emergence of the American University*, 50.

73 Letter from William James to Henry Pickering Bowditch, May 22, 1869 (the letter was misdated 1868 by James). *Correspondence of William James*, vol. 4, 379.

74 A two-masted sailing vessel with a shallow draft (often flat bottomed).

75 Robert H. Wiebe, *The Search for Order, 1877–1920* (New York, NY: Hill & Wang, 1967), 4.

76 Charles R. Morris, *Tycoons: How Andrew Carnegie, John D. Rockefeller, Jay Gould, and J. P. Morgan Invented the American Supereconomy* (New York, NY: Henry Holt, 2005), esp. chap. 6.

77 Although Jefferson was resolutely anti-urban in his 1784 *Notes on Virginia,* after the near catastrophe of the War of 1812, Jefferson privately conceded that America could not forever remain dependent on the industrial cities of Europe for its manufactured products. If the US were to survive, it would have to reluctantly admit the modern metropolis into its midst. See esp. Morton White and Lucia White, *The Intellectual versus the City: From Thomas Jefferson to Frank Lloyd Wright* (Cambridge, MA: Harvard University Press, 1962), 24–25.

78 Variants of the story appear everywhere, almost none with citations. The original source is a letter from Charles Eliot Norton to Eliot Norton, dated June 11, 1907, published in Sara Norton and Mark Antony De Wolfe Howe, eds., *The Letters of Charles Eliot Norton*, vol. 2 (Boston, MA: Houhgton Mifflin, 1913), vol. 2, 379. The full passage is: "I [CE Norton] was speaking to him [WD Howells] about Dr. [William] James' new book [presumably *Pragmatism*], and said that it was brilliant but not clear. 'Like his father,' said Mr. Howells, 'who wrote The Secret of Swedenborg and kept it.'" (My thanks to Nicole Barenbaum who located the source of this story.)

79 "Anonymous Review of The Secret of Swedenborg," *North American Review* 110 (1870): 463–68.

80 Cited in Lyndall, *Private Life of Henry James*, 91.

81 Mentioned in Richardson, *William James*, 105 and in chap. 15, n.3.

82 The quoted phrases in this paragraph come from James' diary, and are cited in Ibid., 117.

83 This passage was published by James more than 30 years later in *The Varieties of Religious Experience* (New York, NY: Longmans, Green, 1902), 160. At that time, he attributed it to an anonymous French "sufferer," although he later conceded that he was describing a crisis he had experienced as a young man himself (Letter from James to Frank Abauzit, the French translator of *Varieties,* dated June 1, 1904, reproduced in William James, *The Varieties of Religious Experience* (Cambridge, MA: Harvard University Press, 1985), 508). The dating remains a matter of some debate, although early 1870 is the common conclusion (based in part on diary entries from April 1870 that indicate the easing of a serious personal crisis. It is also in this passage (especially the clause, "That shape am I") that David E. Leary found the crucial evidence that James was framing his experience in terms of a formulation derived from the work of the eminent German philosopher of the will, Arthur Schopenhauer. Leary also discovered that James was voraciously (and apparently secretly) reading Schopenhauer's works at just about the

time of his crisis (see "New Insights into William James's Personal Crisis in the Early 1870s: Part I. Arthur Schopenhauer and the Origin & Nature of the Crisis," *William James Studies* 11 (2015): 7).

84 Barrels of ink have been spilt in the attempt to fully capture and correctly interpret the significance of James' crisis. For a review of this voluminous literature, see Paul J. Croce, "A Mannered Memory and Teachable Moment: William James and the French Correspondent in the Varieties," *William James Studies* 4 (2009): 36–69. Many of James' biographers have cited James' letter to Renouvier (November 2, 1872, *Correspondence of William James*, vols. 4, 430–31), but they have, perhaps, sometimes read a little too much into his simple statement that *"je puis dire que par elle [votre philosophie] je commence à renaître à la vie morale"* [I can say that by it [your philosophy] I am starting to be reborn to the moral life]. In the context of the letter, it seems clear that he means he is taking philosophical questions of morality seriously again, not that he had personally been returned to morality (though to be fair, James was one of those philosophers who tried to "live" philosophy, not just study it in the abstract).

4

JAMES AND HALL MEET

1. James and the McLean

The question of whether William James' melancholy, in the months after Minnie Temple's death, became so severe that he was obliged to take refuge at the McLean Asylum—a nearby private, exclusive, even legendary sanctuary for the "insane"—is one that still cannot be answered with certainty. There is a suggestive gap in James' written output between August and November of 1870—no letters, no journal entries. The family has never commented definitively on the matter. The McLean has steadfastly declined to release any records or other information, regarding all such matters as confidential in perpetuity. Historian Robert J. Richards recorded that he "spoke with someone who had worked in the hospital archives in an official capacity, and she confirmed James' stay as a patient at McLean."[1] Journalist Alex Beam reported that "several doctors and even a former director of the hospital have assured me not only that James stayed at the hospital more than once, but that they saw his name on the patient record list."[2] There are other William Jameses, however, including the psychologist-philosopher's son, who also went through a period of depression, so there may have been a misidentification here. Even if James was a patient at the McLean, he may well have been admitted under a pseudonym. Beam says that historian Linda Simon was allowed to examine anonymous intake logs for 1870–71, and that she found no one matching William James' general characteristics.[3] The prominent historian of psychoanalysis Paul Roazen said in print that James was there,[4] but he told Beam that he was there near the end of his life, not in 1870.[5] James' only surviving grandson, Michael James, has attempted to free the case file, but has been unable to satisfy the McLean's requirement that all surviving relatives agree in writing.[6] In short, it seems not improbable that James spent a short stay at the McLean at the end of 1870, but there is no direct evidence of it.

2. The Metaphysical Club

James spent much of 1871 out of view. Letters were sparse: two to Henry Bowditch, then studying under some of Europe's greatest scientists—Jean-Martin Charcot, Claude Bernard, Carl Ludwig—one in February, and another in April.[7] That same month, Charles Eliot offered Bowditch an assistant professorship in physiology at the Harvard Medical School. In June, Bowditch tried to light a bit of a fire under his perennially despondent but talented friend, writing to James from Leipzig that he expected James to join the laboratory he would be setting up at Harvard in the fall.[8] If there was a reply, it hasn't survived. The next extant letter from James dates from August to his brother Bob, then in Milwaukee. After that, nothing surviving until May of 1872. By then, his journal entries had begun again. As always, he read voraciously. Even his bad back, his poor eyes, and his dark mood did not interfere with his massive reading program: novels, plays, travel books especially by naturalists, Indian religious texts, even Swedenborg.

We know from others that in the winter of 1871–72, James joined an off-campus reading and discussion group that called themselves, "half-ironically, half-defiantly," the Metaphysical Club.[9] It was led by a man in his early forties, a kind of independent Cambridge scholar named Chauncey Wright. Nearly everyone considered Wright to be the smartest man in town, even though he was only intermittently connected with Harvard in any official capacity.[10] Wright had graduated from Harvard in 1852 and had taken up a job as a calculator for a nautical magazine. It was said that he could squeeze a year's worth of computations into three months, leaving him free to pursue his interests the rest of the year. One of his chief interests was running informal intellectual salons. He would invite some of the brightest people he knew (almost never members of the Harvard faculty, though many of his guests went on to be such later),[11] and they would take turns both presenting and ferociously debating essays on the contentious topics of the day. Indeed, Wright's whole being exuded controversy: he was an empiricist, a positivist, and possibly an atheist. He lived in a room he rented from a Black woman who had escaped slavery in the South. During the war, he had been involved in having her children freed and brought north. When Charles Darwin's *Origin of Species* came out in 1859, Wright promptly read it and became a vocal advocate of the new theory. He wrote reviews and articles criticizing some of the leading intellectuals of the day: Harvard philosophy professor Francis Bowen and the president of the College of New Jersey (later Princeton) James McCosh were among his targets. His friend, Charles Eliot Norton, liked to publish Wright's provocative pieces in his *North American Review*.

For the Metaphysical Club of the early 1870s, Wright chose several men who were considerably younger than himself (or perhaps they had chosen him): Charles Peirce, 32 (with whom he probably had the most in common intellectually), Oliver Wendell Holmes, 31 (the future Supreme Court Justice), and John Fiske, 30 (the prominent Spencerian whom Stanley Hall had seen speak in New York). James was also 30. Somewhat older were Francis Ellingwood Abbott, 36 (the Unitarian philosopher who would attempt to turn theology into a science), Nicholas St. John Green, 42 (a lawyer devoted to empiricism, especially to Alexander Bain). Green brought along a much younger legal colleague, Joseph Bangs Warner, 24.

Just before the Club was formed, in 1870, Wright had published a piece criticizing the view of Alfred Russel Wallace—the co-discoverer of the principle of natural selection—that random mutation and selection could not account for the development of the human mind. Wright responded:

> [The] natural limitation of belief by belief, in which consists so large a part of their proper evidence, is so prominent a feature in the beliefs of the rational mind, that philosophers had failed to discover their true nature, as elementary facts, until this was pointed out by the greatest of living psychologists, Professor Alexander Bain. . . . [O]ur knowledges and rational beliefs result, truly and literally, from the survival of the fittest among our original and spontaneous beliefs.[12]

In short, the question was, for Wright, not so much how natural selection, operating at the level of biology, had produced the human brain. It was, rather, how natural selection, operating at the level of thought, produces the contents of the human mind. That is to say, Wright saw that the general process of "natural selection" is no more essentially tied to the origin of biological species than, say, the infinitesimal calculus is essentially tied to physical mechanics. Those are just the scientific contexts in which each happened to be first discovered. Once natural selection is understood as an abstract process—replication with variation, followed by selection according to "fitness"—it can be deployed as an explanatory apparatus in a wide array of scientific domains. Evolutionary psychologists of today would likely find that answer evasive, but Darwin himself saw it as being very much to the point, and cited Wright's article in his 1871 book, *The Descent of Man*. Although Wright could not have known it at the time, by migrating the dynamics of natural selection from the biological realm to the psychological one, he set much of the agenda for American psychology for the next half-century.

In 1871 Wright published another article defending Darwin against an English opponent of his, St. George Mivart.[13] In it, he bemoaned the widespread misunderstanding of Darwin's theory even by his would-be advocates. Citing the widening acceptance in his day of a theory proposed by Jean Baptiste Lamarck some 70 years earlier—i.e., that offspring can inherit characteristics acquired by their parents through effort or accident—Wright complained:

> It would seem, at first sight, that Mr. Darwin has won a victory, not for himself, but for Lamarck. Transmutation, it would seem, has been accepted, but Natural Selection, its explanation, is still rejected by many converts to the general theory, both on religious and scientific grounds.[14]

Darwin was so impressed by this article that he arranged to have it republished as a pamphlet at his own expense and circulated throughout England.

After Wright published a third article defending evolution in 1872,[15] Darwin had his sons, then visiting America, seek Wright out personally. Once they had assured their father that Wright was of good character, Darwin invited Wright to his home in Downe, Kent. Upon meeting the great man, Wright slipped into what he exuberantly described as a "beatific condition."[16] But Darwin's full aim in bringing Wright to England was not accomplished by merely a pleasant social call. He also took the opportunity to commission Wright to author an account of the evolution, by natural selection, of the human mind. Wright immediately agreed, and produced, in 1873, "The Evolution of Self-Consciousness." In that work, perhaps Wright's most important, he wrote:

> The word evolution . . . misleads by suggesting a continuity in the *kinds* of powers and functions in living beings, that is, by suggesting transition by insensible steps from one *kind* to another. . . . The truth is, on the contrary, that according to the theory of evolution, new uses of old powers arise discontinuously both in the bodily and mental natures of the animal.[17]

The effect of Wright's combative posture was to electrify the best young minds of Cambridge, Massachusetts—James, Holmes, Peirce, and the others—and to entice them to hear what they suspected they had been denied in the lecture halls of genteel Harvard. Perhaps the most lasting contribution to come from the Metaphysical Club's deliberations was the development of the philosophical position that would come to be known as "pragmatism." At several of the Club's meetings, Nicholas Green invoked the definition of belief that had been put forward by Bain—A belief is just that upon which a man is prepared to act. The emphasis on action—on ideas doing work, rather than just being static mental contents—caught on with everyone in the group.

Peirce, in particular, developed it into a comprehensive theory of meaning, which he outlined in print in 1878: "Consider what effects, that might conceivably have practical bearings, we conceive the object of our conception to have. Then, our conception of these effects is the whole of our conception of the object."[18] Having a penchant for controversy no weaker than Wright's, Peirce used, as his first example of this maxim, the dispute between Catholic and Protestant Christians over the nature of the transubstantiation. "To talk about something as having all the sensible characters of wine," Peirce prodded, "yet being in reality blood, is senseless jargon." He then declared it "absurd to say that thought has any meaning unrelated to its only function." In case the point was missed, he went on: "It is foolish for Catholics and Protestants to fancy themselves in disagreement about the elements of the sacrament if they agree in regard to all their sensible effects, here or hereafter."[19] Only then, once he had commanded his conventional readers' full attention with a case nearly certain to evoke fury, did Peirce deign to consider blander but intellectually more significant examples from science and logic.

Pragmatism would, of course, be adopted by many in the late 19th century, most notably by William James. Many of its adopters, however, some not fully comprehending Peirce's intent, mangled and distorted his ideas to suit their own (often literary) purposes. Not being one to suffer such imprecision impassively, Peirce eventually changed the name of his position to "pragmaticism," quipping that the new term was "ugly enough to be safe from kidnappers."[20]

The Metaphysical Club did not last long. The young men whom Wright had assembled were all beginning careers and families, and the time they could afford to devote to intellectual recreations of that sort was rapidly dwindling. Holmes began the law practice that would eventually take him to a seat on the Supreme Court. Peirce moved to Washington, DC to work as a geodesist for the US Coast Survey.[21] The position was secured for Peirce by his father, Benjamin, who was on the verge of retiring as the Coast Survey's Superintendent after seven years.

Although geodesy was Peirce's occupation, astronomy was his scientific passion, and these were exciting times for watchers of the skies. In 1874, there was a rare Transit of Venus, which would enable scientists to measure the distance of the sun from the Earth with greater accuracy than ever before. A second one was expected in 1882. In 1877, two tiny moons were discovered to be circling Mars by a US Naval Observatory professor named Asaph Hall. There was also a controversial debate over whether a planet, tentatively named "Vulcan," might be hidden inside the orbit of Mercury.[22] Peirce was young, talented, skilled, and connected—the world, it seemed, could hardly help but be his oyster.

James, by contrast, took up Bowditch's invitation to spend time in his new physiology laboratory. He was finally getting the hands-on bench experience that he had long, though ambivalently, sought. In 1872 Jeffries Wyman decided to retire from teaching comparative anatomy at Harvard. Eliot sought a replacement and Bowditch recommended James. Somewhat tentatively, Eliot offered James an instructorship. James accepted and thereby began his long and legendary professional association with America's paradoxically oldest and most modern college.

3. The Harvard Instructor and Assistant Professor

While James was wiling away the fall of 1872, waiting for his January course to begin, downtown Boston suffered a catastrophic fire, the most destructive in the city's history. In all, 776 buildings spread over 65 acres of the city were destroyed. These included two of the city's largest newspapers, *The Globe* and *The Herald*. The blaze was so large that fire departments traveled from every other state in New England except Vermont to assist. There was over $73 million in damage (over $1.3 billion in today's terms), and it killed at least 20 people. Without doubt, it was the greatest calamity to have befallen Boston since before the Civil War.

One might have expected William James to express some alarm at the tragedy or sympathy for its victims. Yet, what he wrote, from the safe distance of his parents' cozy Cambridge house, was "It was so snug & circumscribed an affair that one had felt no *horror* about it at all. Rich men suffered, but upon the community at large I should say that its effect had been rather exhilarating than otherwise."[23] It was an odd quirk of James' personality that he could summon up colossal indignation about a calamity or injustice taking place thousands of miles away, but he sometimes seemed indifferent or even contemptuous of disasters that struck nearer to home, so long as they did not threaten him personally. In a contrast that might be funny if it were not so bizarre, the following year he published a piece in the *North American Review* in which he vehemently called for a million-dollar "vacation trust" to fund "a month of idleness" for working-class people,[24] but he was unable to summon up much concern when their workplaces (if not homes) burned to the ground.

James' first course as an instructor began in January of 1873. It was the second half of a course on comparative anatomy and physiology. It seems to have gone well. The simple medicine of regular work, something that had never really been required of James before, seemed to attenuate his years of emotional turmoil. He liked the work. He began to think of teaching as a possible career. At the end of term, he asked if he might teach the full course the following year. Eliot agreed. In August, however, James quailed. He told Eliot to find a substitute and he fled, once again, to Europe. There seems to have been no specific aim in sight, just escape: London, Boulogne, Paris, Florence (where his brother Henry was living), Rome, Venice. By the end of it, five months later, he longed to be back at Harvard teaching.[25] He returned in March 1874 and arranged with Eliot to teach the full course the next academic year. He continued to work in Bowditch's laboratory, and he began directing the anatomical museum that Wyman had assembled during his many years at Harvard.[26]

It was about this time that James began developing a serious interest in the relation between drugs and religious mysticism. In November of 1874, the *Atlantic Monthly* anonymously published a review authored by James of a pamphlet that had been written by an obscure self-styled philosopher named Benjamin Paul Blood.[27] Blood, who was a decade older than James, lived in the upstate town of Amsterdam, and most of his writings, ranging over a variety of "grand" topics, had appeared as letters to tiny local newspapers. He was a farmer by trade, but he made his name as a local strongman who also did mathematical tricks like multiplying large numbers in his head.[28] In 1860, Blood was given nitrous oxide for the first time, while in a dentist's chair, and he came away convinced that he had experienced a great religious revelation. He continued to experiment with the curious gas and, in 1874, he composed a short tract about his experiences titled *The Anaesthetic Revelation and the Gist of Philosophy*.

On reading it, James became entranced with the idea that our "normal" state of consciousness is only one of many that we might assume and, more important, that certain forms of knowledge might be available to us only while in certain mental states. He began experimenting himself, publishing his own findings in 1882.[29] He started up a lively correspondence with Blood, and he used his *Atlantic* review to ensure that Blood's views were broadcast well beyond the boundaries of his upstate town. At the end of his long life, Blood would write a book about philosophical pluralism titled *Pluriverse*.[30] James, of course, adopted pluralism late in his life as well, but its seeds may well have been planted here, in 1874, with an obscure pamphlet and an anonymous review.

In July 1875, James' most important publication to date appeared in the *North American Review*. Like nearly all of his early pieces, it was a book review, but this time it was a description and assessment of Wilhelm Wundt's new textbook *Grundzüge der physiologischen Psychologie* (*Principles of Physiological Psychology*, 1874). Wundt had won his first professorship, in Zurich, the year before and, even though his great Leipzig laboratory was still a few years off, his career as the official "founder" (if not actually the originator) of a new experimental psychology was now fully underway. Of the Germans' new "physiological" interest in the mind, James quipped appreciatively, "there is little of the grand style about these new prism, pendulum, and galvanometer philosophers. They mean business, not chivalry."[31]

James began his review by praising the new German physiologists for being able to separate their metaphysical and religious stances from their scientific investigations into psychology, unlike, he noted pointedly, James McCosh, president of the College of New Jersey (later Princeton), and Noah Porter, the even more religiously orthodox president of Yale. Then James cited Wundt as the "paragon" of the new breed.

> The style is extremely concise, dry, and clear, and as the author is as thoroughly at home in the library as in the laboratory, the work is really a cyclopædia of reference . . . we can think of no book (except perhaps the Origin of Species) in the course of which the author propounds so many separate opinions.[32]

Comparing Wundt's work with Helmholtz's epoch-making measurements of the speed of neural transmission, James described Wundt's "complication experiment": reaction times were taken under a variety of different conditions, and the different results were compared and interpreted as reflecting the durations of the mental processes involved. There are mentions of the complexities generated by Wundt's ultimate targets of investigation: attention, consciousness, apperception, and volition.

Then James came to a point that is emblematic of much of his career as a psychologist: Mental experience is a complex mass and is wholly personal. The "pure sensation" is not a natural element of the mind; it is an abstraction that would never enter experience unless one severely circumscribes one's attention with the specific aim of "finding" it. As James put it:

> These acts postulate interests on the part of the subject, interests which, as ends or purposes set by his emotional constitution, keep interfering with the pure flow of impressions and their association, and causing the vast majority of mere sensations to be ignored.[33]

Here James' critique veered away from Wundt. Instead, he abruptly raised the psychology of Herbert Spencer, the popular "social Darwinist," only to reject it for missing this central truth of the matter: sensations are not the natural foundations of mental activity but its artificial constructions. However, he laid the insight—one that is often attributed to James himself—at the feet of Chauncey Wright and his 1873 article, "Evolution of Self-Consciousness."[34]

James then briefly returned to Wundt, lauding his suggestion that consciousness is able to "synthesize" disparate mental contents into new wholes so fully that it seems impossible analyze them back into the original parts again. He quickly assimilated the idea, however, to John Stuart Mill's "mental chemistry," a comparison that would become quite popular, but would also impair the English-language understanding of Wundt for decades to come.[35] Finally, James posed an evolutionary question against Wundt's accomplishment,[36] a question that clearly reflected a view of the mind he had learned from Wright and which prefigured some of his own most important psychological insights in the years to come:

> Taking a purely naturalistic view of the matter, it seems reasonable to suppose that, unless consciousness served some useful purpose, it would not have been superadded to life. Assuming hypothetically that this is so, there results an important problem for psycho-physicists to find out, namely, how consciousness helps an animal, how much complication of machinery may be saved in the nervous centres, for instance, if consciousness accompany their action.[37]

He closed with the opinion that, although the book had many "shortcomings," it was still "indispensable for study and reference."[38]

In the summer of 1875, James went to Wisconsin to visit his two youngest brothers. In September, while James was still away, Chauncey Wright suffered a stroke and died.[39] James published an obituary in *The Nation*. Wright's passing marked, for James, the loss of his most important philosophical mentor (apart, perhaps, from his father). Even though James did not ultimately adopt the path Wright had laid out in its entirety, the mark of the man could be seen in James' thought for decades afterwards.

Starting in the fall of 1875, James taught the anatomy and physiology course at Harvard again. He also taught, for the first time, a small graduate seminar on physiology and psychology. Near the end of term, he proposed a new course: "Physiological Psychology." It is not surprising that he used the phrase found in the title of Wundt's textbook. In a letter to Eliot, James specifically cited Wundt as an example of how the field was developing—a synthesis of medical training, physiological research, and broader philosophical interests.[40] It was a combination that James believed himself to exemplify. Apparently, Eliot did as well. He promoted James to assistant professor of physiology and scheduled the course for the 1876–1877 school year.

Perhaps surprisingly, though, James did not use Wundt's book as the required text for his new course. Instead, for "practical reasons" (probably just the problem of using a German textbook in an American undergraduate course), he used Herbert Spencer's *Principles of Psychology*.[41] Spencer had been a published evolutionist prior to Darwin. His position was not really Darwinian, however (despite his often being called a "social Darwinist"). He drew on the Lamarckian position and on an even older tradition in which the cosmos is thought to be naturally (or perhaps supernaturally) developing, progressing even, toward some predestined endpoint.[42] With the publication of *Origin of Species*, Spencer came to incorporate natural selection into his repertoire of evolutionary causes, but did not seem to fully grasp the import of mutations being random rather than teleological in character. The Darwinians, who were advancing the cause of natural science generally as much as that of natural selection specifically, were always uncomfortable with Spencer's speculative and cosmic approach. They did not really regard him as a fellow scientist.

But James did not select Spencer's book for his new course so that he could promote it. Indeed, he would privately come to call Spencer "an ignoramus as well as a charlatan."[43] Instead, he used Spencer's ideas as a launch pad for his (and Wright's) critique of it from a more strictly Darwinian perspective.[44] Like Wright, James spoke of "spontaneous variations" arising and being selected at the level of thought, not just at the level of the physical organism. This, James believed, made room for his cherished freedom of the will within a scientific framework. Sometime in 1875 or 1876, James set up a demonstration laboratory in the Lawrence School building so that psychological phenomena that had been pioneered elsewhere by others could be repeated for the benefit of instructors and students alike.[45]

4. Stanley Hall at Harvard

Also in 1876, the new Assistant Professor James acquired his first graduate student. It was Stanley Hall, just arrived from Antioch College, still trying to finance a voyage back to Germany to study with Wundt. Although the two men, Hall and James, were only two years apart in age and shared a bevy of similar interests, the circumstances of their births and upbringings could hardly have been more different. Hall was born and raised in an inland rural community; James grew up in the midst of the largest and most cosmopolitan port city in America (when his family wasn't touring the great cities of Europe). Hall's parents were frugal farmers of Puritan English stock, born of a tradition that stretched back nearly to the very beginning of European habitation in North America; James was born into a fabulously wealthy intellectual family whose immigration to America from Ireland had come just two generations before. Hall's family practiced a highly conventional form of Congregationalism. James' father, as we have seen, was a virtual renegade from his own father's Presbyterianism and made it his life's work to assemble an original and eccentric theological framework within which he could subsist. There was one way, however, in which Hall's and James' early lives were markedly similar: when the Civil War came, their fathers had each purchased for them exemptions from the draft.

Three years before, Hall had returned from Germany heavily in debt. He did not have the money for the new trip he aspired to make, either. It is possible that Hall knew William James when he arrived in the fall of 1876. Hall had published several pieces in the *Journal of Speculative Philosophy*, but James was suspicious of the Hegelian mood there, as he was of most grand philosophical systems. James' first article in *JSP* wouldn't appear for two years yet. It is quite possible that Hall was a reader of the *North American Review*, in which a number of James' reviews had appeared (though often anonymously), and it probably would not have been evident from the array of books he had reviewed just where his primary interest lay. Soon after Hall arrived, letters from both he and James appeared in *The Nation*, criticizing the state of philosophical education in the US. It is not clear whether this was a coordinated venture or just a lucky happenstance.[46] It is certain, however, that Hall knew President Eliot. The two had briefly met the summer before, and Eliot was first cousin to the most famous man in Hall's hometown of Ashfield, Charles Eliot Norton.

Knowing Hall's dilemma, Eliot offered him an instructorship in English so that he could save money for his study trip to Germany. Hall noted to himself that Harvard's current professor of philosophy, Francis Bowen, would be retiring soon, and thought that he might be able to position himself for a chance at the professorship in philosophy.[47] So, Hall reluctantly agreed to the delay, and decided to take some courses at the same time, mostly from James. Soon he was registered for the PhD in philosophy that had only recently appeared in Harvard's offerings.

Almost as soon as Hall arrived, however, his younger brother, with whom he was rooming in nearby Cambridgeport, took ill and died, at the age of just 31. After seeing his way through the family tragedy, Hall moved into rooms in Somerville, a little further away from Harvard.

The year demanded a great deal of work from Hall: in addition to teaching the same lecture to three classes each week, he had to mark twelve papers from each of 250 students. He was struck with scarlet fever near the end of the school year and attempted to resign before finishing what he regarded as a burdensome marking load. Eliot replied that he and the students could wait until he recovered. He eventually did, and completed his task, but he was not reappointed for a second year.

Teaching obligations and illness aside, during his first year at Harvard Hall wrote a piece for the *Journal of Speculative Philosophy*, the first article in which he put forward an original thesis of his own.[48] Titled "Notes on Hegel and his Critics," Hall engaged in a searching critique of Hegel's ideas and arguments with respect to "pure thought," "pure being," (and its opposite, "nothing"), and "pure vacuous space." The questions were important elements of the Kantian legacy in philosophy. Mostly Hall rehearsed arguments from other philosophers, but near the end of the article, he brought into focus a thesis first advanced by his German philosophical mentor Trendelenburg:

> Only movement is and is not at the same point and moment . . . and so movement, understood in the most generic sense, common to thoughts and things, and not becoming, is what is motivated here. But motion is an original factor, of a new species. It is, even Trendeleburg admitted, the existing contradiction which formal reasoning easily proves impossible. Thus contradictions *are* overcome, though static logic is powerless to tell us how.[49]

From this highly metaphysical starting point, Hall then turned to psychology. Motion, he claimed, had been shown by the German physiologist Karl von Vierordt and the Austrian psychologist Sigmund Exner to be "the only immediate sensation . . . not founded on unconscious inferences of any kind." Hall then, by way of a hasty claim that thought is nothing but the mental "counterpart" of physical movement quickly concluded that "time is the internal result, space the external condition, of movement."[50] This may seem a rather exotic and abstruse argument to modern eyes, but it is how early experimental psychology often achieved intellectual significance in the context of 19th-century scholarship: by claiming to offer solutions to long-standing, philosophical disputes that seemed irresolvable. If nothing else, physiological psychology was sometimes able to bring forth new phenomena disruptive enough to comfortable old positions that it might reorganize a field by breaking an old impasse.

That same year, 1878, Hall completed his dissertation on a related topic, *The Muscular Perception of Space*. Although Hall had spent a great deal of time working in Bowditch's physiology laboratory, his dissertation was broadly conceptual, if not actually philosophical, in character. Although Bowditch was clearly involved, he was not among the official supervisors of the dissertation.[51] Instead, it was signed off by James, then 36, the devoutly Christian Berkeleyan empiricist Francis Bowen, then 67, and by the venerable Unitarian theologian, Frederic Henry Hedge, then 73. One can only imagine what the two senior members of the committee made of Hall's study, deeply informed by the new experimental physiology, considered as a species of philosophical treatise.

In what must have seemed a coup for Hall, a portion of the dissertation was published in the periodical that had been launched just two years before by Alexander Bain and his protégé, George Croom Robertson, *Mind*. It was the first English-language journal dedicated specifically to psychology, and Hall's article was the first by an American to appear in it.[52] In this rendering of Hall's work, there was less of Hegel and his entourage, but more of Wundt, DuBois-Reymond, Helmholtz, etc. Speculation on pure being and pure thought was largely replaced by descriptions of the classic neuro-muscular experiments that had helped to bring physiology to the forefront of scientific investigation in the previous few decades. The conclusions reached, however, were not unfamiliar:

> Muscular sense is thus absolutely unique in that the incommensurability between the form of external excitation and subjective sensation found in every other sense does not exist here. It is the motion of the limb, the muscle, the nerve-end itself, which responds by the feeling not of heat, light or sound, but of motion again. This sense is not a mere sign of some unknown *Ding an sich* [Kant's noumenal "thing-in-itself"]. Movement, as perceived directly by consciousness, is not even found heterogeneous in quality when perceived indirectly by the special senses of sight and touch. No degree of subjective or objective analysis, though it may simplify and intercalate any number of forms, can change its essential character as motion.[53]

Muscular sense, that is, serves as the long sought-after bridge between the mind, which controls the muscles from within, and the outer, material world, which opposes and resists the muscles from without. It was a grand claim, to be sure, but giddy young sciences (and giddy young scientists) often start with the greatest unsolvable problems of the disciplines from which they have emerged, only later to fully comprehend the complexity of the phenomena they aim to explain, and the limitations that exist for the new science every bit as much as they did for the old.

Interestingly, in his autobiography Hall reduced the number of years he spent at Harvard to one, and he incorrectly recollected that he had completed his doctorate only after spending three more years in Germany.[54] In fact, it was soon *after* completing his doctorate at Harvard in 1878 that he resumed his original plan of traveling to Germany to study the new physiology and psychology.

5. America in the 1870s, Beyond the Boundaries of Cambridge

The 1870s were a turbulent time for America, but little of this comes through in either Hall's or James' personal writings of the period. In the wake of Andrew Johnson's disastrous completion of Lincoln's second term, the nation turned to its greatest war hero, Ulysses S. Grant, electing him president in 1868. Expectations were high that Grant would be able to salvage the situation in the South and in Washington itself. Henry Adams wrote that the populace was implicitly guided by "the parallel they felt between Grant and Washington."[55] But it was all a mirage. As inspiring an army commander as Grant might have been during the war, he was wholly unprepared for the job of presiding over a national government and a national economy. The collapse in confidence was almost immediate upon Grant's taking office. "Grant's [cabinet] nominations," wrote Adams, "had the singular effect of making the hearer ashamed.... [They] betrayed his intent as plainly as they betrayed his incompetence. A great soldier might be a baby politician."[56] Corruption quickly reached new heights in both politics and business, soon followed by widespread public disappointment and disillusionment. In 1869, for instance, the notorious speculators Jay Gould and James Fisk manipulated the monetary policy of the economically-naïve Grant. Using their friendship with Grant's brother-in-law to gain access, they persuaded the President not to sell government gold, ostensibly as a way of assisting western wheat farmers. Meanwhile, they secretly attempted to corner the market in private gold. The scheme ultimately failed, but Grant's belated response to their plot precipitated the financial panic known as "Black Friday." Soon after, Gould began his career as an archetypal railway "robber baron," eventually controlling 15% of the train tracks in America.

Widespread dissatisfaction with Grant's ability to manage the nation's affairs led to a deep division in Republican ranks. The "Liberal Republican" party nominated Horace Greely (founder of the *New York Tribune*) for president in 1872.[57] The Democratic Party, still in disarray in the wake of the Civil War, threw its support behind Greely as well, in a desperate attempt to take advantage of the Republican split. Matters were complicated by the fact that Greely died between voting day and the time the electors gathered to cast their ballots. It made no difference to the final outcome as Grant won the popular vote easily, out-distancing Greely by 12 percentage points. The corruption continued unabated. Grant's Secretary of War, William W. Belknap was impeached by a unanimous vote of the House of Representatives for taking bribes. He resigned in order to avoid prosecution, but the Senate tried him anyway. The vote for conviction fell a few votes short on the strength of Senators who believed they no longer had jurisdiction once Belknap had fled office.

Despite his general administrative ineptitude, Grant was able to oversee successive victories in civil rights for freed slaves and other African Americans during his terms in office. The Fifteenth Amendment to the Constitution, prohibiting states from denying Blacks the right to vote, was ratified in 1870. The Civil Rights Acts of 1871 protected Blacks (at least on paper) from ethnic violence, particularly at the hands of the Ku Klux Klan. The Civil Rights Act of 1875 mandated equal treatment of all people by "public accommodations." It would be struck down in 1883 by the US Supreme Court, which ruled that the constitution does not empower the state to prohibit discrimination by private individuals. The 1883 ruling paved the way for more than a half-century of "Jim Crow" laws, until the Civil Rights Act of 1964.

A few months after Grant started his second term, September of 1873, the largest investment bank in the country—Jay Cooke, based in Philadelphia—declared bankruptcy and closed. Cooke had borrowed heavily to finance the Northern Pacific Railroad, but the post-war boom in track-building had already peaked back in 1871. Falling grain prices had led western farmers to demand, and win, "Granger laws" that regulated the rates rail companies could charge to ship commodities back east.[58] In the face of this uncertainty, investors began to back away from the over-extended railroads. Corruption in Grant's government made subsidies politically unpalatable, and a meeting of New York financiers brought no infusion of cash either. So, Cooke simply closed his doors, precipitating the worst economic crash the US had ever seen: the "Panic of 1873."

Competition among the large rail companies—the Erie, the Baltimore & Ohio, the Pennsylvania, and of course Vanderbilt's New York Central—became ferocious.[59] Prevented from raising rates by the Granger laws (and by the capacity of an economically strapped populace to pay more), cutting wages became the primary means of maintaining profits. Indeed, it was not just the railroad companies that turned to this dark tactic. Many industries used the "Panic" as a pretext for cutting wages; miners, steel workers, factory workers, longshoremen, printers, and government workers were all hit. Unemployment became rampant, perhaps as high as 25% nationally. Protests of thousands, sometimes tens of thousands, were seen in most major cities. The government response was typically to send in police and militia, batons flailing. As the slump deepened, newspapers and governments alike began vilifying the victims with two new terms: "tramps" and "hoodlums." The "tramp evil" had to be stamped out.[60] *The New York World* newspaper declared charity itself to be an "epidemic." One writer in *The Nation* suggested that free soup be prohibited. The American Social Science Association declared that "imposter paupers" were being used by labor as a weapon in the fight for "unnaturally" high wages.

Even as Herbert Spencer's ideas were being criticized and rejected in some intellectually elite circles, like Chauncey Wright's Metaphysical Club, his "social Darwinism" was being taken up in powerful quarters of American society. Edward L. Youmans' magazine, *Popular Science Monthly*, just launched in 1872, had been created primarily to disseminate Spencer's ideas on the western side of the Atlantic.[61] For advocates of Spencer's *Social Statics*, it was only right and natural that those who could not compete should be "selected out." Those who could succeed—the Vanderbilts, the Rockefellers, and the Carnegies—would survive. Those who supported the poor were regarded, at best, as ignorant of these "scientific facts." Some were denounced in the press and by politicians as "unfit" foreigners or, worse still, as communists. Suggestions were increasingly heard that poverty was the result of defective, hereditary traits, rather than of the economic situation.[62] Even the co-founder of the State Charities Aid Association Josephine Shaw Lowell[63] declared "able-bodied paupers" to be the bearers of a new kind of social disease, a moral contagion that could be spread to others if not rooted out and isolated. She prescribed hard labor at work houses until they were "educated morally and mentally."[64] The crisis was incomprehensible to most Americans because the industrial worker, the urban poor, the immigrant slum-dweller, though numerous, did not yet figure in the nation's self-image.[65]

By the same token, the "organizational revolution" that was just taking hold in the industrial workplace was incomprehensible to the laborers: at the heart of movement was the gradually emerging idea that all workers are like cogs in a giant machine that only works with maximum efficiency (i.e., most profitably) when they all do their jobs in very particular ways at very particular speeds. Over the next half-century this understanding would spread from business to government to education and to nearly every other mass institution in America.[66] Indeed, one might argue that this fundamental transformation in institutional structure was the single most significant aspect of the socioeconomic environment in which American psychology took root—it was the sea in which psychology swam.

The Panic of 1873 also enabled corporations to effectively dismantle the limited organized labor movement that had come into existence in the few years since the end of the war. With no laws to prevent owners from simply firing all organized workers, and a steady supply of unemployed men ready to take any job offered at nearly any wage, companies did their best to rid themselves of what they viewed as an illegitimate impediment to their power. In March 1877, for instance, the Reading Railroad announced to its employees that they must either quit the Brotherhood of Locomotive Engineers or lose their jobs. They proposed that those who remained behind could choose to take up a company-run life insurance policy to replace the one offered by the Brotherhood. However, they would lose all their investment should they quit or strike, and there was nothing to prevent the company from altering the terms of the policy should it so choose. In response, the Brotherhood called a strike but, using non-Brotherhood replacements, the Reading was running normally again (though operated by many dangerously inexperienced workers) by mid-summer.[67]

To make the price of challenging industrial ownership chillingly clear, ten coal miners in northeastern Pennsylvania were hanged in June of 1877 for being active in the shadowy group known as the "Molly Maguires." The Mollies were an Irish secret society that was said to have infiltrated America and been responsible for killings and kidnappings of mine officials and strikebreakers over a number of years. Although there was violence in and around the mines, especially during strikes, historians have never been able to establish the actual existence of the group in America. Nevertheless, the miners were convicted largely on the testimony of a single Pinkerton officer who had been hired to break union activity in the mine by Franklin Gowen, owner of both the Philadelphia & Reading Railroad and the Philadelphia & Reading Coal and Iron Co. Many train and mine companies used so-called "police" (security guards they had hired or contracted from private companies such as Pinkerton) as spies to infiltrate and expose union activity. Gowen also personally prosecuted the case against the "Molly" miners. Whether or not the men were "Mollies"—whether or not the "Mollies" actually existed—workers all over the country were put on notice that there were no limits to what Capital would do to protect its investment.

Early in 1877, the largest rail companies then hatched a scheme that would enable them to systematically reduce wages throughout the system: they would "pool" the freight revenue among themselves, granting each company a guaranteed percentage. As each company cut wages and faced labor unrest, the other three would buoy it up by means of the pool. After the Brotherhood had been broken and "peace" restored at one company, then the next one, in turn, would cut its wages while being guaranteed a revenue stream by the pool. This would allow all of them to be victorious in their manufactured serial crises until wages were as low as ownership could get them.[68] At this time, an engineer made about $1000 per year, depending on the company he worked for. Conductors, brakemen, and other trainmen made considerably less.

By July 1877, the rail workers had had enough. After B&O cut wages for the second time in a year, workers in Martinsburg, West Virginia brought all their trains to a stop. The governor sent in state militiamen, but they refused to fire on the strikers. Within days, the strike spread to B&O's station in Cumberland, Maryland. The governor ordered two regiments of the National Guard to put down the strike, but the soldiers met ferocious resistance from the general population of Baltimore, who blocked the way to the trains that were to take them to Cumberland. Troops fired on the crowd, killing at least ten and wounding dozens of others. The recently inaugurated president, Rutherford B. Hayes, sent federal troops to Baltimore to restore order.[69]

Violence then erupted in Pittsburgh where militiamen gunned down at least 20 strikers, but were forced to take refuge from the furious mob in a railway roundhouse. The strikers set the structure on fire, destroying over 100 locomotives and 1,000 rail cars. The militia killed at least 20 more people fighting their way out of the burning building. The strike spread to Philadelphia, where much of the city center was burned, then to Reading, where 16 were killed by troops. In Shamokin, Pennsylvania, the rail workers were joined by coal miners, making the events of 1877 the first *de facto* general strike in US history. President Hayes again sent in federal troops to put down the strike by force.

Still the unrest spread to Chicago, St. Louis, and a number of smaller cities in between. Dozens more were killed and hundreds wounded. There were strikes and other actions across New York State as well—Buffalo, Rochester, Syracuse, Albany. Although the strikers were met by public support in many cities, they were roundly denounced by nearly everyone who had a pulpit from which to be heard. Even Henry Ward Beecher spoke out against the strike. In New York City, instead of a violent rampage, the workers staged a largely peaceful protest of 20,000. William Vanderbilt had pleaded with the mayor to ban it and, although he was officially refused, it was made known that thousands of police and troops would be on alert, and that heavy weaponry would be positioned at various important sites around the city, in case things got out of hand. As the rally ended, after two hours of speeches, police waded into the crowd without apparent provocation, beating with batons anyone who did not disperse quickly enough for their liking.[70]

FIGURE 4.1   Illustration from *Harper's Magazine*, August 11, 1877, of National Guard troops fighting their way into Camden Station, Baltimore, Maryland.

As federal troops moved from city to city, crushing resistance, the most violent, most widespread strike in American history gradually came to an end after a month-and-a-half of massive destruction and explosive violence. Millions upon millions of dollars in damage had been done as mobs attacked and set fire to buildings and equipment related to the massive railroad industry that had come symbolize, to them, the brutal character of the new capitalist order. Some people began to opine that the labor question had now overtaken the race question in national politics. A new civil war, just twelve years after the end of the first one, now seemed a distinct possibility.

6. James and Hall Go Their Separate Ways

Strangely, we see nothing in James' correspondence or in Hall's autobiography on these portentous matters.[71] Starting in September of 1876, James began intently courting a woman named Alice Howe Gibbens.[72] Alice had grown up under difficult circumstances. Born in 1849, she was the oldest child of a Harvard-trained physician, Daniel Gibbens, who, like Henry James Sr., had an interest in Emanuel Swedenborg's spiritual philosophy. Unfortunately, he was also a recurrent alcoholic whose erratic behavior interfered with the process—crucial to a physician—of amassing a steady and trusting clientele. After failing as a town doctor in the family's home outside of Boston, he tried for a fresh start in 1855, leading his young family on a dangerous migration to distant California. After just a few years there, however, the adventure was undermined by legal conflicts over land title, and by his reversion to drink. After a humiliating return the Boston area, Alice's father moved away from the family permanently, though he stayed in touch with his daughters by mail. During the Civil War he took up a position as an administrator for the military governor of New Orleans. His fortunes seemed to improve there, both personally and financially. He even wrote his estranged wife asking her to find a new house for the family. In 1865, however, he was unexpectedly transferred to Mobile, Alabama where things seemed to unravel. Just days before he was to head home, he committed suicide.[73]

In their grief and humiliation, his wife and daughters—Alice was now sixteen—moved away to Europe—Germany and Italy—for five years. They returned to Boston just in time for their small income to be slashed by the financial crash of 1873. The girls, now young adults, were forced to take jobs for income. Alice and one of her sisters took up teaching at a private girls' school in Beacon Hill. Demanding as the work was, it had the side-benefit of bringing the Gibbenses in contact with Boston's "Brahmins." Alice was invited to join the prestigious "Radical Club," where issues from the religious to the scientific were discussed by some of Boston's best minds. It was there that she met figures such as the radical "scientific" theologian Francis Ellingwood Abbot and the Harvard physiologist who was helping James to find his footing as a Harvard instructor, Henry Bowditch. She also met, in early 1876, an older man with a strong commitment to Swedenborg, just like her own family had: none other than Henry James, Sr. According to an oft-repeated family tale, Henry went home after meeting her and announced to the family that he had met William's future wife.[74] By September of that year, William would be in earnest pursuit of Alice Gibbens' hand.

The courtship did not prevent William from pursuing others ambitions, though. In April 1877, he wrote to Daniel Coit Gilman, the young president of a newly founded university in Baltimore, Johns Hopkins, inquiring about a position in philosophy that he had heard about from Hall.[75] Unlike other American schools of the day, Hopkins was focused on original scientific research by faculty members and on graduate education. It did not even have an undergraduate college. Finding a philosopher sympathetic to that mission was proving to be something a problem for Gilman. James had recommended his old friend Charles Peirce to Gilman back in November 1875,[76] but Gilman had decided to hold off on the sensitive appointment.[77] Now, a year-and-a-half later, James was tiring of physiology and had told Harvard president Eliot of his desire to be considered for a philosophical post. Francis Bowen was then 66, but there was no reason for James to expect that Harvard would hire a relative philosophical neophyte like himself to replace Bowen when he retired. He thought he might have chance at Hopkins though; or, at least, that he could bring some pressure to bear on Eliot to retain him if he made a modest display of considering a move to Baltimore. By December of 1877, he had arranged to give a series of lectures the following February on "the connection of mind & body."[78] Still without any substantive publications, James offered to send Gilman book reviews as evidence of his qualification for a philosophical post. Only in 1878 did James publish his first two substantial philosophical statements in the *Journal of Speculative Philosophy*.[79] By the end of the year he had a third article set to be published there, and another in the hands of the editor of the new English journal called *Mind*.[80]

It is interesting to observe that Henry Adams, who had just then finished his seven-year stint as Harvard's professor of medieval history, considered the Crimson College of this era to be "fallacious from beginning to end."[81] In the chapter about this small part of his life, pointedly titled "Failure," he opined that professors "might perhaps be frauds without knowing it," such was their narrowness and insulation from the outside world.[82] Having just fled from the corruption of Washington, DC during Grant's presidency, Adams noted, "American society feared total wreck in the maelstrom of political and corporate administration, but it could not look for help to college dons."[83] Adams had interacted closely with both Congressmen and professors and, despite the pervasive dishonesty of the former, he said he preferred Congressmen. What was worse, Harvard was a bore: "Several score of the best-educated, most agreeable, and personally the most sociable people in America united in Cambridge," he wrote, "to make a social desert that would have starved a polar bear. . . . Society was a faculty-meeting without business."[84] Among this group he explicitly named William James: they "tried their best to break out and be like other men in Cambridge or Boston, but society called them professors, and professors they had to be."[85]

––––––––––

While James settled into his role as a Harvard professor, Hall continued with the plan of action that had brought him back to the east coast in the first place: returning to Germany to study physiology and the new psychology. Before he left America, however, he published a long article on the nature of color perception for the *American Academy of Arts and Sciences*.[86] He also examined the reactions of a celebrated blind and deaf woman, Laura Bridgman, who was living in an institution in South Boston at the time. The following year, the British journal that had published his thesis, *Mind*, also published an article of Hall's about Bridgman.[87]

Money, as always, was an issue for Hall. He had saved some while at Harvard, and he also received an unexpected gift to support his travels from the banker whose children he had tutored in New York, Jesse Seligman.[88] Leaving late in the summer of 1878, Hall first returned to Berlin, where he started working in the physiological laboratory of Emil Du Bois-Reymond. With the great man's assistant, Hugo Kronecker, Hall conducted research on the electrical stimulation of muscles and the spinal cord.[89] Needing to better understand electrical phenomena in order to do this work well, he took courses on the physics and mathematics of electricity. He also attended Helmholtz's lectures on physics. While in Berlin, Hall returned to his interest in psychopathology, befriending the rising neuropathologist Paul Flechsig, whom he would meet again in Leipzig. Hall also returned to the clinic of Karl Westphal at the famous Charité Hospital in order to study living cases of insanity. As it was with James back at Harvard, mental illness was an ongoing interest of Hall's and of many others who did not yet understand what relationship, if any, there would be between the new physiological psychology and (to use the increasingly fashionable German term of the day) psychiatry.

While in Berlin, Hall met a woman he had known back in Antioch, Cornelia Fisher. She had come to Germany to study art. Whether there had been a romance between them before is not clear, but in this place and time, a relationship quickly blossomed and the two were married in September of 1879. Indeed, Hall said that "Germany almost remade me."[90] Its more liberal attitudes toward religion, toward alcohol, toward relations between the sexes, toward the simple joy of passing a Sunday afternoon in outdoor recreations with friends, led him to discard, more fully than even in New York, many of the Puritan imperatives with which he had been raised. Indeed, he came to appreciate more fully the Seligmans, and to regard them as a sort of second, "European" family.[91]

In the fall of 1879, Hall traveled to Leipzig where he went to work in the physiology laboratory of Carl Ludwig.[92] At first he worked on studies of reaction time with Ludwig's assistant, Johannes Von Kries.[93] Later he worked with Ludwig directly on reflexes, though the work resulted in no published articles.[94] For historians of psychology, this is the time when Hall became the first American to work in the newly established laboratory of the "founder" of experimental psychology, Wilhelm Wundt. Hall, however, was disappointed with what he found there. Writing to James in February of 1880, he said that Wundt's studies were "inexact," that he was "sore from criticism & sneers of his fellow physiologists." Worse still, according to Hall, Wundt was "burning with ambition to be a philosopher within a system," and was "a man who has done more speculation & less valuable observing than any man I know who has had such a career. His experiments, which I attend, I think utterly unreliable & defective in method."[95]

It is hard to know precisely what to make of these claims. Were these Hall's observations alone? To what degree did these remarks simply echo what Hall had heard in the physiology labs of Ludwig and others? Perhaps Hall had decided to side with the physiologists, who seemed to him "more scientific," but they had chosen the safer, more established route to scientific respectability whereas Wundt had taken the bolder step of attempting to push the boundaries of natural science outward. Also, Wundt's professorship was in philosophy (where "psychology" traditionally had been), and physiologists may have been dismissive of him on that account alone. Tension between the established top of the academic heap, philosophy, and the rapidly expanding and increasingly prestigious natural sciences was a common dynamic in German universities of that era. This is suggested in Hall's comment that he was himself "considered somewhat of a usurper, not entirely scientific."[96] Later in his life, Hall had mostly good things to say about Wundt: that he was "one of the most popular lecturers" at Leipzig and that he was an "indefatigable worker." He also wrote of his "great admiration" of Wundt.[97]

James married Alice Howe Gibbens in July of 1878, after a two-year-long, tortuously complex, on-again-off-again romance. Upon news of the engagement, James' mentally fragile sister, also named Alice, with whom he had enjoyed a close and playful relationship, fell into her most serious hysterical breakdown yet. She was nearly 30 years old, but fiercely demanded that her aging father sit by her bedside day and night for months lest she commit suicide.[98] Alice, the sister, is a figure of enduring fascination to many. Some have attributed her recurrent fits of madness to the strains caused by the social and intellectual restrictions that were imposed upon talented and ambitious women in her era. Others have found in her little more than a manipulative madwoman. Clearly, periods of intense melancholy, anxiety, and loneliness weighed heavily upon her. She was not well liked by some: Lilla Cabot Perry once described her as being "clever but coldly self-absorbed."[99] She had few friends outside of the family, and she could become intensely jealous when she did not command the full attention of those few she had.[100] She is known to us primarily through a diary she wrote during the last two years of her life, in which she commented sharply, with an outsider's eye,[101] on British manners and politics, as well as on the more profound vicissitudes of existence. Because her older brothers objected to its being made public, the collection of thoughts and observations was not published until 40 years after her death. There are also letters between her and her brothers. These sparse materials have spawned a much larger assemblage of books and articles from those who would have her known as an excellent, but unappreciated mind in her own right, not merely as the little sister of the illustrious Brothers James.[102]

Despite Alice's alarming collapse upon hearing of her brother's engagement, William and his new wife went to the Adirondacks for a rustic 10-week honeymoon.[103] The new husband spent part of his time working on philosophy articles, to bolster his claim with President Eliot that he should be Harvard's next professor of philosophy. In May of 1879, the Jameses had their first child, Henry III. James kept on writing and publishing.

In June of 1880, he travelled alone to Europe and visited Hall. They met in Heidelberg and spent, essentially, three whole days talking to each other. Relations between them could be strained. Although they had similar interests, they were still from different worlds. On this occasion, however, the two men seem to have gotten along well. Hall felt he was done with philosophy, that natural science was the only way forward in psychology. James, by contrast, was attempting to extricate himself from physiology and insert himself into philosophy. Both men were intellectually complex. James was no happier with traditional metaphysics than was Hall. He was just content to use the word "philosophy" for the thing he wanted to do instead. Hall, on the other hand, could not completely drop the teleology that had been so much a part of his early Hegelian training. Hall spoke of evolution, but he meant by that something closer to development—progress toward some pre-ordained endpoint—not just the hurly burly of Darwin's random variation and selection.

Hall latched on to the evolutionary theory of the German embryologist, Ernst Haeckel. Haeckel believed that the physical development of the embryo recapitulates the evolution of the species as a whole. If, for instance, one followed the developmental trajectory of a mammalian fetus, according to Haeckel, one saw it pass through stages similar to those of microbes, fish, and reptiles, before differentiating into fully mammalian form. Hall began to think of mental development in parallel recapitulationist ways.[104] The baby is a kind of mental hominin. But, as it grows, it passes through the stages of various "primitive" human types (in the view of Hall and many others of his time), gradually learning to inhibit a host of primal impulses and to develop a range of "civilized," "adaptive" habits until it emerges as a fully-grown (White, Western) adult. Notice that this entails a pre-Darwinian view of evolution as growth-toward-a-goal, rather than just random variations being selected for or against entirely on the basis of the contingencies of a particular environment.

Toward the end of his second tour of Germany, Hall came to the conclusion that "neither psychology not philosophy would ever make bread and that the most promising line of work would be to study the applications of psychology to education."[105] Thus, before he returned to America, he took pedagogical tours of France and England. He visited the top *lycées* in Paris' and a "pedagogical museum." He consulted with Oxford and Cambridge professors, and he visited the best private schools—Eton, Harrow, Rugby—in order to be able to return to the US not only with prestigious European training in physiology and psychology, but also able to present himself as a specialist in a field that was almost wholly unknown there: pedagogy.

This not only provided Hall with a unique "calling card" on which he might be able to base a successful academic career (it combined the ineffable aura of European scholarship with the hard-headed "practical" knowledge Americans most respected). It also created some intellectual space between himself and the mentor who, as he saw it, was obstructing his way to positions either at Harvard or at Johns Hopkins. Of the many things in which James was interested, mental *development* and practical education did not rank high among them. Hall would always see in James a rival—a man just two years his senior who did not have as advanced a scientific education as he—but who always seemed to be regarded as the top man in the field, regardless of what Hall might do to earn a greater share of respect. And Hall did a great many things.

Notes

1 Robert J Richards, *Darwin and the Emergence of Evolutionary Theories of Mind and Behavior* (Chicago, IL: University of Chicago Press, 1987), 417, n. 21.

2 Alex Beam, *Gracefully Insane: The Rise and Fall of America's Premier Mental Hospital* (New York, NY: Public Affairs, 2001), 45.

3 Ibid., 46.

4 Paul Roazen, *Freud and His Followers* (New York, NY: Knopf, 1975).

5 Beam, *Gracefully Insane*, 46.

6 Personal communication with John J. McDermott, General Editor of the James *Correspondence*, April 2010.

7 In the second letter we find one of James' few forays into the wider world of the social and political. He outlines his hopes and fears for the recently launched Franco-Prussian War.

8 Letter from Henry Pickering Bowdtich to William James, June 11, 1871. Ignas K. Skrupskelis and Elizabeth M. Berkeley, eds., *The Correspondence of William James* (Charlottesville, VA and London, UK: University of Virginia Press, 1992), vol. 4, 419.

9 This was Charles Sanders Peirce's characterization in a 1907 paper titled "Pragmatism" that was not published until Charles Hartshorne, Paul Weiss, and Arthur Burks, eds., *Collected Papers of Charles Sanders Peirce*, vol. 5, sec. 12 (Cambridge, MA: Harvard University Press, 1935). The most extensive discussion of this group and its legacy is in Louis Menand, *The Metaphysical Club: A Story of Ideas in America* (New York, NY: Farrar, Straus and Giroux, 2001).

10 Charles Eliot persuaded him to teach a course in psychology in 1870. He taught mostly the British empiricist, Alexander Bain. The course was not considered a success because, although Wright was known as a brilliant conversationalist, he was apparently a terribly monotonous lecturer. In 1874, the experiment was attempted again, this time with a physics course. The results were much the same. Lecture was not Wright's *métier*; open debate was.

11 In the mid-1860s, the former instructor in chemistry and future president Charles Eliot had been a member.

12 Chauncey Wright, "The Limits of Natural Selection," in *Philosophical Discussions*, ed. Charles E. Norton (New York, NY: Burt Franklin, 1971), 116 (originally published in North American Review 111 (1870): 282–311).

13 Chauncey Wright, "The Genesis of Species," *North American Review* 113 (1871): 63–103 (Reprinted in *Philosophical Discussions*, ed. Charles E. Norton (New York, NY: Burt Franklin, 1971), 126–67.

14 Chauncey Wright, "The Genesis of Species," in *Philosophical Discussions*, ed. Charles E. Norton (New York, NY: Burt Franklin, 1971), 128.

15 Chauncey Wright, "Evolution by Natural Selection," *North American Review* 115 (1872): 1–30 (Reprinted in C. E. Norton (Ed.), *Philosophical Discussions* (New York, NY: Burt Franklin, 1971), 168–98.)

16 Edward H. Madden, *Chauncey Wright and the Foundations of Pragmatism* (Seattle, WA: University of Washington Press, 1963), 28.

17 Quotation from Chauncey Wright, "Evolution of Self-Consciousness," in *Philosophical Discussions*, ed. Charles E. Norton (New York, NY: Burt Franklin, 1971), 199–200 (originally published in *North American Review* 116 (1873): 245–310).

18 Charles Sanders Peirce, "How to Make Our Ideas Clear," *Popular Science Monthly* 12 (1878): 293. See also his slightly earlier article, "The Fixation of Belief," *Popular Science Monthly* 12 (1877): 1–15. These articles were just the first two in a series of six that Peirce published on the logic of science in *Popular Science Monthly*, all in less than a year.

19 Peirce, "How to Make Our Ideas Clear," 293.

20 Charles Sanders Peirce, "What Pragmatism Is," *The Monist* 15 (1905): See also Charles Sanders Peirce, "Prolegomena to an Apology for Pragmaticism," *The Monist* 16 (1906): 492–546. Peirce was careful to exclude James (and the Oxford pragmatist F. C. S. Schiller) from the group who, as he put it, had "abused" the term in a "merciless way," though he did gently note that James' pragmatism bore "a certain difference in the point of view" to his own (p. 165).

21 Geodesy is the study of the size and shape of the Earth. Throughout the 19th century, it was pursued primarily by means of gravimetry—measurement of (the acceleration caused by) the Earth's gravitational field, which involved making extremely precise observations of the period of a special pendulum: being further from the center of Earth, such as on a mountain, slightly weakens the pull of gravity which, in turn, leads to a slightly longer time for the pendulum to swing from side to side. Peirce rapidly became not only a leading expert in taking these measurements, but also a highly innovative one. During the 1870s he redesigned British physicist Henry Kater's classic 1817 "reversible pendulum" in order to cancel out tiny errors caused by air resistance, thereby increasing the accuracy of the measurements.

22 Proposed in 1859 by the French mathematician who had previously predicted the existence of Neptune, Urbain Le Verrier, Vulcan was to have explained a small perturbation observed in the orbit of Mercury. Two prominent American astronomers, James Craig Watson and Lewis Swift, claimed to observe the elusive body during the total solar eclipse of 1878, but their sightings could not be reliably confirmed. In the end, the apparent perturbation of Mercury's orbit was explained by relativistic effects described by Einstein early in the 20th century.

23 Letter from William James to Henry James, Jr. November 24, 1872. *Correspondence of William James*, vol. 1, 178. It is worth noting that the Great Chicago Fire had occurred just the year before, and it had been far more destructive of both lives and property than that in Boston: 2000 acres, 17,500 buildings, 300 dead, 100,000 homeless (1/3 of the city's population). Perhaps James' dismissive attitude toward the Boston conflagration should be understood in that light.

24 William James, "Vacations," *The Nation* 17 (1873): 90–91.

25 Letter from William James to Robertson James. December 8, 1873. *Correspondence of William James*, vol., 465.

26 Jeffries Wyman died in April 1874. Louis Agassiz had died in December 1873.

27 William James, "Review of 'The Anaesthetic Revelation and the Gist of Philosophy,'" *Atlantic Monthly* 33, no. 205 (November 1974): 627–28.

28 See, e.g., Dmitri Tymoczko, "The Nitrous Oxide Philosopher," *Atlantic Monthly*, May 1996.

29 William James, "Subjective Effects of Nitrous Oxide," *Mind* 7 (1882): 186–208. James claimed that he understood Hegel better while under the influence.

30 Benjamin Paul Blood, *Pluriverse; An Essay in the Philosophy of Pluralism* (Boston, MA: Marshall Jones, 1920), Retrieved on January 20, 2015 from http://archive.org/details/cu31924029019003.

31 William James, "Review of *Grundzüge Der Physiologischen Psychologie*," *North American Review* 121 (1875): 196.

32 Ibid., 197.

33 Ibid., 199.

34 Chauncey Wright, "Evolution of Self-Consciousness," *North American Review* 116 (1873): 245–310.

35 See Arthur L. Blumenthal, "A Re-Appraisal of Wilhelm Wundt," *American Psychologist* 30 (1975): 1081–88, esp. 1083. Blumenthal, however, attributed the confusion to the long shadow cast by Edwin G. Boring's *A History of Experimental Psychology* (New York, NY: Century, 1929) rather than to James' 1875 review, which was the inaugural description of Wundt's book in the English language. Whether Boring got it from James's review remains a matter of speculation.

36 Wundt was ambivalent about Darwin's theory. Although his few remarks on the topic were generally favorable in the 1860s, he seems to have learned about it from the unauthorized, unreliable, and distinctly "Lamarkian" German translation of *Origin of Species* produced by Heinrich Bronn in 1860. See Robert J. Richards, "Wundt's Early Theories of Unconscious Inference and Cognitive Evolution in Their Relation to Darwinian Biopsychology," in *Wundt Studies: A Centennial Collection*, ed. Wolfgang G. Bringmann and Ryan D. Tweney (Toronto, ON: C. J. Hogrefe, 1980), 42–70, esp. 56. See also Janet Browne, *Charles Darwin: The Power of Place* (New York, NY: Knopf, 2002), 140–41. As Wundt came, in the late 1860s, to understand the true nature of Darwin's theory, he rejected natural selection as the primary mechanism of evolution (Richards, "Wundt's Early Theories," 58).

37 James, "Review of *Grundzüge*," 201.

38 Ibid.

39 See the letter from Henry James, Sr. to William James, September 12, 1875, apparently written immediately after Wright's death (*Correspondence of William James*, vol. 4, 519).

40 Letter from William James to Charles William Eliot, December 2, 1875. Ibid., vol. 4, 526–28.

41 See Letter from William James to Charles Renouvier, July 29, 1876, Ibid., vol. 4, 541.

42 One can find variants of this perspective in the highly popular and controversial *Vestiges of the Natural History of Creation* (London, UK: John Churchill, 1844) (published anonymously, but later discovered to have been authored by the prominent publisher Robert Chambers), and in the work of Charles Darwin's grandfather, Erasmus Darwin.

43 Letter from William James to Carl Stumpf, February 6, 1887, *Correspondence of William James*, vol. 6, 203. It was in this same letter that James (in)famously complained of Wundt: "Cut him up like a worm, and each fragment crawls, he is no *noeud vital* in his mental medulla oblongata, so that you can't kill him all at once. . . . He isn't a genius, he is a *professor*. . .. He is the finished example of how much mere *education* can do for a man."

44 Richards, *Darwin and the Emergence*, 425–26.

45 James wrote: "I, myself, 'founded' the instruction in experimental psychology at Harvard in 1874–5, or 1876, I forget which." William James, "Letter," *Science* N.S. 2, no. 45

(1895): 626. It could not have been 1874 because he was not teaching a psychology course at that time.

46 Dorothy Ross says that they wrote "in concert" (*G. Stanley Hall: The Psychologist as Prophet* (Chicago, IL: University of Chicago Press, 1972), 62. James said in a letter to Thomas Wren Ward that his letter was simply "a reply to a correspondent" (August 4, 1876, *Correspondence of William James*, vols. 4, 543).

47 It was a frankly wild idea. There was no position currently open and, besides, Hall had published very little on the topic thus far, beyond his translations (now eight) of German Idealism in the *Journal of Speculative Philosophy*. Before leaving Antioch, Hall had written to the president of the newly-opened Johns Hopkins University, Daniel Coit Gilman, inquiring about the philosophy professorship and had been told fairly directly that he was not yet qualified for such a post. But the very idea that Hall might slip into Bowen's post ahead of James tells us something about just how little James was thought of as a *philosopher* at this time.

48 G. Stanley Hall, "Notes on Hegel and His Critics," *Journal of Speculative Philosophy* 12 (1878): 93–103. Interestingly, James first article in the *Journal of Speculative Philosophy*, a critique of Spencer's theory of mind, appeared in the same issue.

49 Ibid., 99.

50 Ibid., 100.

51 It is possible that Bowditch was not on the committee, as has been suggested by Ross (*G. Stanley Hall*, 70, n. 22), because his appointment was to the medical school, not to the department of philosophy, where Hall was a student. Soon after, however, Bowditch and Hall published "Optical Illusions of Motion" in the British-based *Journal of Physiology* (3 (1882): 297–307) for which Bowditch served as the American editor.

52 For the early history of the journal *Mind*, and its conflicted relationship with experimental psychology, see Francis Neary, "A Question of 'Peculiar Importance': George Croom Robertson and the Changing Relationship Between British Psychology and Philosophy," in *Psychology in Britain: Historical Essays and Personal Reflections*, ed. Geoffrey C. Bunn, Alexander D. Lovie, and Graham D. Richards (Leicester, UK: BPS Books, 2001), 54–71; and Christopher D. Green, "The Curious Rise and Fall of Experimental Psychology in Mind," *History of the Human Sciences* 22 (2009): 37–57, doi:10.1177/0952695108099134.

53 G. Stanley Hall, "The Muscular Perception of Space," *Mind* 3 (1878): 442.

54 G. Stanley Hall, *Life and Confessions of a Psychologist* (New York, NY: Appleton, 1923), 219.

55 Henry Adams, *The Education of Henry Adams* (Boston, MA: Houghton-Mifflin, 1918), 225.

56 Ibid., 227.

57 Interestingly, former congressman and ambassador, Charles Francis Adams (son and grandson, respectively, to presidents John Quincy Adams and John Adams, as well as Henry Adams' father) came a close second for the Liberal Republican nomination.

58 Robert V. Bruce, *1877: The Year of Violence* (Indianapolis, IN: Bobbs-Merrill, 1959), 32.

59 Cornelius Vanderbilt, the old "Commodore" died in January 1877, leaving the New York Central, among other holdings, to his eldest son, William. His fortune has been estimated as having been over $100,000,000.

60 Bruce, *1877*, 13, 20. See also Edwin G. Burrows and Mike Wallace, *Gotham: A History of New York City to 1898* (New York, NY: Oxford University Press, 1999), 1030.

61 See M. Pittenger, "Edward Livingston Youmans," in *American National Biography*, ed. J. A. Garraty and M. C. Carnes (New York, NY: Oxford University Press, 1999), 143–44.

62 Examples from *The World, The Nation*, and the *ASSA* all cited in Burrows and Wallace, *Gotham*, 1030–31.

63 Lowell was the sister of the Robert Gould Shaw, the man who died leading the Black soldiers of the 54th Massachusetts (and its White officers, including Wilky James) into battle at Fort Wagner. Her own husband had been killed in that battle as well.

64 See Burrows and Wallace, *Gotham*, 1031–32.

65 See Robert H. Wiebe, *The Search for Order, 1877–1920* (New York, NY: Hill & Wang, 1967).

66 See, e.g., Dorothy Ross, *Origins of American Social Science* (Cambridge, UK: Cambridge University Press, 1991); Dorothy Ross, *Modernist Impulses in the Human Sciences, 1870–1930* (Baltimore, MD: Johns Hopkins University Press, 1994); and, more recently, Maury Klein, *The Genesis of Industrial America, 1870–1920* (New York, NY: Cambridge University Press, 2007); Hunter Heyck, "The Organizational Revolution and the Human Sciences," *Isis* 105 (2014): 1–31.

67 Bruce, *1877*, 37–39.

68 Ibid., 40–41.

69 The elevation (one hesitates to say "election") of Ohio Governor Rutherford B. Hayes to the presidency in 1876 had been a fiasco of the first order. Hayes had lost the popular vote to the Democratic Governor of New York, Samuel Tilden by nearly a quarter-million ballots but, through corruption, electoral violence, and political arm-twisting, he ultimately won the electoral college by a single vote. Inexplicably, three southern states—Florida, Louisiana, and South Carolina, the very three states in which Federal troops remained stationed since the end of the war—came to be represented by Republican electors. Hayes pulled the troops from those states soon after his inauguration. Although Hayes was able to wrench the presidency from Tilden, he had to suffer through the nickname of "Rutherfraud" throughout his term, and did not run for re-election in 1880.

70 Burrows and Wallace, *Gotham*, 1036–37.

71 There are a couple of passing mentions of the Hayes election affair in James' letters. Nothing at all on the widespread riots that rocked the nation in the summer of 1877.

72 See the many letters from William James to Alice Howe Gibbens dating from September 1876 to September 1877. *Correspondence of William James*, vol. 4, 543–86. Much of what follows here derives from Susan E. Gunter, *Alice in Jamesland: The Story of Alice Howe Gibbens James* (Lincoln, NB: University of Nebraska Press, 2009).

73 There are indications that he may have been involved in a widespread scandal involving the skimming of money from the sales of cotton by the federal government. His boss had been indicted and Daniel Gibbens had been subpoenaed to testify and he seems to have feared that he would soon be arrested. He had also returned to his earlier dissolute ways after years apparently on the wagon.

74 The story is repeated in Gunter, *Alice in Jamesland*, 32.

75 Letter from William James to Daniel Coit Gilman, April 23, 1877. *Correspondence of William James*, vol. 4, 557–58.

76 Letter from William James to Daniel Coit Gilman, November 25, 1875. Ibid., 524–26. See also the letter from Charles Sanders Peirce to William James, December 16, 1875. Ibid., vol. 4, 529. Peirce's first wife Melusina ("Zina") Fay, had left him in the fall. They would formally separate in October 1876, but not legally divorce until 1883, a matter that would lead to Peirce's academic downfall. Fay was an early feminist who had published on a plan called "Co-operative Housekeeping": groups of 15 to 20 women would share the domestic tasks with which they were saddled in order to relieve them of some of their daily drudgery and enable them to pursue other interests. See Melusina Fay Peirce, *Co-Operative Housekeeping: How Not to Do It and How to Do It* (Boston, MA: J.R. Osgood, 1884).

77 See Philip J. Pauly, "G. Stanley Hall and His Successors: A History of the First Half-Century of Psychology at Johns Hopkins University," in *One Hundred Years of Psychological Research in America: G. Stanley Hall and the Johns Hopkins Tradition*, ed. Stewart H. Hulse and Bert F. Green (Baltimore, MD: Johns Hopkins University Press, 1986), 21–51.

78 Letter from William James to Daniel Coit Gilman, December 30, 1877. *Correspondence of William James*, 588–89.

79 William James, "Remarks on Spencer's Definition of Mind as Correspondence," *Journal of Speculative Philosophy* 12 (1878): 1–18; "Brute and Human Intellect," *Journal of Speculative Philosophy* 12 (1878): 236–76.

80 William James, "The Spatial Quale," *Journal of Speculative Philosophy* 13 (1879): 64–87; William James, "Are We Automata?" *Mind* 4 (1879): 1–22.

81 Adams, *Education*, 265.

82 Ibid., 266.

83 Ibid., 267. Lest there be any doubt about his views on the character of congressmen, Adams quoted approvingly an unnamed Grant cabinet secretary who once blurted out, "You can't use tact with a Congressman! A Congressman is a hog! You must take a stick and hit him on the snout!" (Ibid., 226). Adams wrote about himself in the third person throughout his own autobiography.

84 Adams, *Education*, 267.

85 Ibid.

86 G. Stanley Hall, "Color Perception," *Proceedings of the American Academy of Arts and Sciences* n.s. 5 (1876): 402–43.

87 *Mind* had already published an anonymous report about Bridgman in only its second issue ("The Education of Laura Bridgman," *Mind* 1 (1876): 263–67). The correspondent has since been identified as J. G. McKendrick, a prominent Scottish physiologist. (My thanks to Henrika Vande Kemp for identifying the author.) McKendrick's report consisted mostly of quotations from S. G. Howe, the physician who had "discovered" Bridgman 30 years before as a six-year-old (Hall says eight) in "a little village in the mountains," and attempted to educate her. Hall's piece ("Laura Bridgman," *Mind* 4 (1879): 149–72), by contrast, was much more extensive and recounted his own personal examinations of Bridgman's abilities, comparing them with then-current theories of sensation, perception, and higher functions such as language and dreaming.

88 Ross, *G. Stanley Hall*, 80.

89 Hugo Kronecker and G. Stanley Hall, "Die Willkürliche Muskelaction," *Archiv Für Anatomie Und Physiologie; Physiologische Abtheilung, Supp.* (1879): 11–47.

90 Hall, *Life and Confessions*, 219.

91 Ibid., 223.

92 Hall reversed the Berlin and Leipzig portions of his trip in his autobiography.

93 Johannes Von Kries and G. Stanley Hall, "Ueber Die Abhängigkeit Der Reactionszeiten Vom Ort Des Reizes," *Archiv Für Anatomie Und Physiologie; Physiologische Abtheilung, Supp.* (1879): 1–10.

94 In *Life and Confessions*, 205, Hall told a story about Ludwig writing up the research that the two of them had worked on together, but then listing only Hall as the author, mentioning himself only a footnote. If the paper indeed existed, it does not seem to have been published.

95 Letter from G. Stanley Hall to William James, February 15, 1880. *Correspondence of William James*, vol. 5, 85–88.

96 Hall, *Life and Confessions*, 208.

97 Ibid.

98 Leon Edel, "Portrait of Alice James," in *The Diary of Alice James* (New York, NY: Dodd, Mead, 1964), 6.

99 Ibid. Unfortunately, Edel gives no specific source for this quotation. Lilla Cabot Perry was a member of one of the most eminent families in Boston and went on to become an impressionist painter in her own right, studying under and befriending Claude Monet.

100 For instance, when her closest companion, Katherine Peabody Loring, ventured to take her own invalid sister on a trip to London in 1884, Alice insisted on accompanying them. Then she refused to leave her cabin for most of the voyage. Alice's brother Henry, then living in England, was forced to rush to Liverpool to collect

her and nurse her back to health over the course of several weeks. Loring's sister would recover, but Alice refused to cross the Atlantic again. She lived out most of her remaining years in London, and Loring remained with her, away from her own home, through those eight difficult years. Alice could not bear Loring to leave her alone for any length of time unless Henry came to attend in her place. Although Alice was beloved by her siblings, one can hear just a trace of exasperation when Henry once wrote to his Aunt Kate of Loring's long devotion to Alice that it was "a gift of providence so rare and little-to-be-looked-for in this hard world that to brush it aside would be almost an act of impiety" (Ibid., 11–13. Again, Edel unfortunately gives no specific source for this quotation.).

101 Perhaps not totally an outsider: her devotion to her Irish heritage played a role in her views of the ongoing Home Rule debate.

102 See especially Jean Strouse, *Alice James: A Biography* (London, UK: Jonathan Cape, 1980); Ruth Bernard Yeazell, *The Death and Letters of Alice James* (Berkeley, CA: University of California Press, 1981). See also the stage play by Susan Sontag, *Alice in Bed* (New York, NY: Farrar, Straus and Giroux, 1993).

103 Robert D. Richardson, *William James: In the Maelstrom of Modernity* (Boston, MA: Houghton-Mifflin, 2006), 190.

104 In fairness, the idea that mental development of the individual reflects the mental evolution of the species could also be found in pedagogical theorists of the Herbartian tradition, such as Tuiskon Ziller and Wilhelm Rein. Herbert Spencer had adopted a similar view as early as the 1860s (*Education: Intellectual, Moral, and Physical* (London, UK: G. Mawaring, 1861), and he claimed they were presaged in the work of Johann Heinrich Pestalozzi, more than a half-century before (see Charles Everett Strickland, "The Child and the Race: The Doctrine of Recapitulation and Culture Epochs in the Rise of the Child-Centered Ideal in American Educational Thought, 1875–1900" (Doctoral dissertation, University of Wisconsin, 1963)). Hall, however, mostly credited his own version of these ideas to Haeckel's "recapitulationism"; see, e.g., Christopher D. Green, "Hall's Developmental Theory and Haeckel's Recapitulationism," *European Journal of Developmental Psychology* 12 (2015): 656–65.

105 Hall, *Life and Confessions*, 215.

5

BALTIMORE AND THE JOHNS HOPKINS UNIVERSITY

1. The Maryland Colony and Baltimore

Whereas Massachusetts was established as a colony dedicated to a fierce religious monism and New York was established as a trading center not much concerned about questions of religion at all, Maryland was founded in 1634 as a colony in which English Catholics could practice their faith without the prejudice that so afflicted them in the home country. It was not, however, established to be exclusively Catholic, a mirror image of Massachusetts. It was created as a place of religious tolerance extraordinary for its day. Religion was not an irrelevancy—a potential interference with trade—as in New York. Religion was very much to the point in Maryland, but tolerance of different forms of Christianity (for their toleration did not extend beyond the boundaries of Christianity) was the atmosphere they explicitly hoped to foster. In time, a government was formed in which representatives elected by the colonists occupied a "lower" house of assembly and nominees of the proprietor occupied an "upper" house.

Of course, idealistic aspirations such as these rarely work out exactly as planned, and such was the case in Maryland. The land around Chesapeake Bay that was granted by Charles I to George Calvert, Lord Baltimore and proprietor of the new colony, overlapped with land that had been already granted to the Virginia and Pennsylvania colonies, both of which were deeply hostile to Catholics. It also covered land that was already being farmed by one William Claiborne, a Virginia Protestant who had "discovered" the area years before. He refused to submit to the rule of George Calvert's son, Cecil, 2nd Lord Baltimore,[1] and, in 1635, defended his farm again Maryland authorities by force of arms. Claiborne was defeated and many of his supporters were arrested, but Claiborne himself escaped.

A decade later, in 1645, Claiborne returned at the head of an insurrection that succeeded in overthrowing Lord Baltimore and his government for a short time. Baltimore was restored to authority the following year but, by then, events in England were starting to cast a shadow that could not be ignored in the North American colonies. Parliament defeated and beheaded Charles I in 1649; Cromwell became Lord Protector of the Realm. Catholics were on the run again, even in the colonies that had been established to protect them. In 1651 a government commission was assembled to administer the colonies around Chesapeake Bay, and it was led by none other than William Claiborne. A sad echo of the English Civil War ensued which the Protestant forces won in 1655. Ten members of the Maryland's Catholic leadership were sentenced to death. Four were actually executed. Religious tolerance was formally rescinded. At the restoration of the monarchy in England, however, Maryland was restored to Lord Baltimore and the policy of toleration was once again renewed. Then, in 1689, when William and Mary ascended to the throne, Protestants again overthrew the Maryland government. Tolerance was quashed and the colony became a royal holding until 1716 when, under George I, the colony was returned to the heir of the Baltimores, and religious tolerance was restored yet again. After nearly a century of instability, this last government of Maryland continued uninterrupted until the American Revolution.

European settlement did not come to the area around what is now the city of Baltimore until the 1660s. The first church did not appear until 1692. It was not formally established as a port by the Maryland Assembly until 1706, and it was not given the official name of "Baltimore" until 1729. The town was formally incorporated in 1745. So, although Maryland became a colony at approximately the same time as Massachusetts and New York, the city of Baltimore is more than a century younger than either Boston or New York City. Around the time of the Revolution, Baltimore was known for trade in tobacco, grain, iron ore, cotton, and it soon became a ship-building hub as well. In 1845, the US founded its Naval Academy just 26 miles south of Baltimore, in the state capital of Annapolis. Being south of the Mason-Dixon line—established in 1760 to end the lingering boundary dispute between Maryland and Pennsylvania—Baltimore considered itself to be the largest Southern US city. Of course, the Civil War brought new meaning to the Mason-Dixon line, and Maryland's non-secession from the Union led to the modern convention by which authors often describe Baltimore as being politically northern but "spiritually" southern. Slavery declined in and around Baltimore after the 1810s and the city gained a reputation as a refuge of free Blacks, having a higher proportion than any other US city. It was in Baltimore that the legendary civil rights leader Frederick Douglass escaped the slavery to which he had been born in Talbot county, on the Chesapeake's eastern shore.

The most heroic episode in the city's history—the moment on which much of its civic pride and identity is based—was the Battle of Baltimore during the War of 1812. In late August 1814, the British navy sailed up the Chesapeake and the British ground troops they were carrying sacked and burned both Washington,

DC and Alexandria, Virginia. They then turned their guns on Baltimore, which they believed to be a significant base of the privateers whose attacks on British merchant ships had started the war two years earlier. The capture of Baltimore would not only have likely forced the US to sue for peace. It may also have thrown into doubt American independence itself, won just 31 years before.

The ensuing battle involved a series of land and maritime engagements, during which the British were prevented from attacking the city directly. Not only was Baltimore saved from destruction but the British officer who had ordered the burning of Washington was killed by an American sniper. On the mid-September morning after the final clash at Fort McHenry, the Americans raised Mary Pickersgill's gigantic 30–by-42-footflag, which famously inspired Francis Scott Key (a lawyer then on board a British ship to negotiate the release of prisoners) to write the poem that would later become the lyrics to the "Star Spangled Banner." Thus was Baltimore's position secured in the popular heroic narrative of American history.

Military glory does not fill stomachs, however, and it was not long after the British had been beaten that the city's economic matters moved to the fore. With the opening of the Erie Canal in New York in the 1820s, eastern seaports like Baltimore were faced with the dilemma of slipping into near-irrelevance compared with Manhattan, or of devising some way of transporting goods and people cheaply into and out of the interior of the continent. In 1827, 25 Baltimore businessmen chartered a company to build a railroad to the Ohio River, from which one could navigate west to the Mississippi. The Baltimore & Ohio Railroad would not only enable the city to compete with New York's Canal; the train would actually be decidedly faster than the Erie barges. The rail line to Wheeling, Virginia (West Virginia after secession), on the Ohio River, was not completed until 1853, by which time trains were beginning to make the Erie Canal redundant even in New York, but the sections of track that opened in the intervening two-and-a-half decades were sufficient to prevent Baltimore from sinking into obscurity.

The 1830s were a harsh time in Baltimore's history. Political tensions increased between the city, under-represented in the Maryland legislature, and the land-owning, slave-holding interests that dominated the largely rural state. Rising calls for abolition in the North, as well as the Nat Turner rebellion of 1831, led to popular violence and legal action against the Black community. Schemes to deport Maryland's entire Black population to Liberia were seriously considered by the legislature.[2] A terrible cholera epidemic in 1832 killed perhaps 1% of the city's population. The economy steadily worsened in the run up to the Panic of 1837. Mills began to close, throwing hundreds out of work. A series of high-profiles arsons in early 1835—including the Courthouse, the Athenaeum, attempts on churches, and even an orphanage—terrorized the city's populace. The squeeze on the poorest members of society led to the usual dreary cycle of rising labor violence and political repression.[3]

A massive influx of Irish and German immigrants in the late 1840s and 1850s further complicated relations between the Black and White communities in

Baltimore, as it did in cities all along the eastern seaboard. During those decades Baltimore was the second-largest city in the US, ranking behind only New York. Competition for unskilled jobs was fierce. Political tension and violence soon followed in patterns we have already seen elsewhere: the rise of Know-Nothing municipal governments, the manipulation of police forces, conflict over education rights, and so forth. By the mid-1840s, however, the B&O Rail investment finally began to pay off. New factories and the jobs that railways typically bring started to spring up. Baltimore became known for the manufacture of furniture, carriages, train cars, pianos, farm tools, and for industrial baking. Its mills processed wool, and, of course, cotton, the backbone of the Southern economy. The boom of the 1840s eased tensions between the various ethnic communities of laborers. Housing construction in the city soared from 600 per year in 1845 to 2,000 per year in 1851.[4] Despite the success, though, there was still civic concern that Baltimore was not growing as fast as Philadelphia and New York. By the mid-1850s, the massive purchasing by the B&O Railroad that had driven the economy over the previous few decades began to slacken after the line to Wheeling was complete. Also, Baltimore merchants were still focused on the rural South as their primary clients, and on trading commodities with Brazil. As a result, it did not experience the synergies of industrial expansion to the same extent as, say, New York. As one historian of the city put it, "Baltimore capitalists were old-fashioned. . . . [T]he city followed a very conservative banking policy, recirculating within a small circle."[5] Despite these anxieties, the city was more prosperous than it had ever been. The boom, naturally, busted again in 1857, its virtually customary 20-year cycle, but Baltimore recovered more rapidly than many other cities.

Everything was changed, however, by the pivotal presidential election of 1860. Marylanders voted for neither Lincoln nor Douglas, but for the southern Democrat and sitting Vice President, John C. Breckenridge, who swept the South and finished second in the electoral vote.[6] As one Southern state after another seceded from the Union in the wake of the election, Maryland remained tenuously with the North and, despite sabotage by pro-Confederate bands, necessitating the imposition of martial law, Baltimore became an important Union military base during the ensuing war.

The end of the great conflict brought a wave of newly-emancipated slaves to Baltimore who were in need of work for themselves, schools for their children, and hospitals for their ill and elderly. The end of the 1860s also saw an enormous influx of German immigrants to Baltimore, rising to as high as 12,000 in 1868 alone.[7] Many of the new arrivals were Catholic (fleeing Bismark's *Kulturkampf*). The integration of these new ethnic communities into the city provoked, here as elsewhere, new rounds of civic conflict over jobs, housing, education, and "correct" public behavior (e.g., drinking). However, the migrants also brought with them new trades, whole new industries, and much-needed jobs. New suburbs were laid out, new mills and factories established, new schools and churches built, and new public transportation lines begun.[8] An eruption of new public buildings changed the look of the downtown: a new city hall, a US courthouse, a central post office, and a palatial YMCA were built.

Still, despite the substantial post-war growth, Baltimore was gradually dropping in significance on the American scene. Other cities were growing faster and Baltimore had fallen to sixth in population by 1870.[9] One of the reasons may have been that, despite their outward activity, Baltimore's industry was not innovative. Instead, many of Baltimore's corporations were focused on winning government decrees entitling them to:

> exclusive, legally defensible rights of some kind that would ensure it a competitive advantage. . . . Baltimore's businessmen were least effective in using patents. Only the canneries and a few foundries generated significant patents or technological advantages; the other industries depended on patents and machinery developed elsewhere.[10]

The rail companies continued to exert a tremendous influence over the city's governance, winning for themselves concessions and favors that drained municipal coffers of much-needed cash. As a result, municipal infrastructure lagged behind that of competing cities. For instance, only a series of catastrophic floods and droughts in the late 1860s and early 1870s forced the city to finally modernize its public waterworks. In the meantime, hundreds had died of water-born disease caused by the antiquated and inadequate water system.

Despite these failings, Baltimoreans retained an enormous sense of civic pride. "If New York is to become another London. . . .," declared the *Sun* newspaper in 1872, then "Baltimore shall become another New York."[11] There was one important amenity, however, enjoyed by the peoples of New York, Boston, Philadelphia, and even St. Louis of which the denizens of Baltimore could not yet boast—a university.[12] This embarrassment could not be borne much longer, so one of the city's wealthiest men leapt in to fill the lacuna with his own personal fortune.

2. The Johns Hopkins University

Johns Hopkins, a prominent Quaker abolitionist who had been a director of the B&O Railroad, passed away in 1873. At the time, Hopkins was not only one of Baltimore's wealthiest men, but one of America's. In his will, he made massive provision for the founding of a large number of public institutions in the city: an asylum for "colored" orphans, a university, a hospital, schools of nursing and medicine, and more. Before his death, he established Boards of Trustees to see that his plans were carried out. Just three years later, the Johns Hopkins University was founded. It was to be built entirely on interest accruing from Hopkins' own B&O Railroad stock, a financial foundation that, in 1873, seemed as firm as any could be.

The man chosen by the university's trustees to lead the school through its early development was Daniel Coit Gilman, a 44-year-old former Yale librarian whose stellar career as a university administrator is sometimes regarded as a key turning point in American higher education. While at Yale, he was deeply involved in the founding of the Sheffield Scientific School in 1861. In 1863 he became a professor of geography, but was called to the presidency of the University of California in 1872. Dogged by political interference on the west coast, he accepted an offer to become president of the newly established Johns Hopkins University in 1876, where he would remain for the next 25 years. It was not, perhaps, the most propitious moment to open such an institution. The following year there was another financial crash—right on "schedule," 20 years after the last one. The crash provoked the Great Strike of 1877 (described in the previous chapter) which, it will be recalled, began in earnest in Baltimore, throwing the city, and eventually the whole country, into crisis. The crash also caused the value of the B&O stocks, on which the new university's funding depended, to collapse. This left the Trustees with little money to develop the school, either in terms of buildings or personnel. The original plan had been to build a complete new campus uptown at Mr. Hopkins' own estate, called Clifton, but that could no longer be achieved on the funds available. Mr. Hopkins' will prevented the Trustees from selling the stocks themselves to exploit what capital remained, so Gilman carried on as best he could. He had the Trustees purchase buildings near downtown Baltimore, centered on one that they re-dubbed "Hopkins Hall," at the corner of Howard St. and "Little" Ross St. (now Druid Hill Ave.)

Like Harvard's President Eliot before him, Gilman toured Europe looking for a new model on which to base advanced education in America. Also like Eliot, he saw the centrality of science and technology to the new economy and, indeed, to the new culture. Unlike Eliot, however, rather than producing a new scheme for the undergraduate college, he envisioned a school that focused on graduate education and faculty research. It is often said that Gilman followed the German model of the university but he denied this, claiming to have taken the best of what he found at various European and American universities.[13] Gilman recruited eminent and promising professors from far and wide, and the school's novel (for the US) emphasis on research succeeded brilliantly and rapidly: in just four years, Hopkins' faculty had published more than all other American scholars combined over the previous generation.[14] Among Gilman's "star" professors was the classicist Basil Lanneau Gildersleeve, who transformed the teaching of Latin and Greek in the US with his textbooks and who founded the *American Journal of Philology*. There was also the historian Herbert Baxter Adams, who founded the American Historical Association and promoted "scientific" methods in historical research. Gilman also hired economist Richard T. Ely, first Secretary of the American Economic Association and an important Progressive who advocated government intervention to curtail the abuse of workers that seemed endemic to late 19th-century industry. As well, there was the Jewish-English mathematician

James Joseph Sylvester who made especially important contributions to matrix theory and combinatorics, and who founded the *American Journal of Mathematics*. In the natural sciences, there was the physiologist H. Newell Martin who had been a collaborator with Thomas Henry Huxley in his native England; there was physicist Henry A. Rowland who was later the first president of the American Physical Society; and there was the chemist Ira Remsen, perhaps best known for having discovered saccharin and who would go on to become Johns Hopkins' second president.

The professorship in philosophy, however, posed a uniquely knotty problem for Gilman. On the one hand, he did not want the kind of traditional Protestant theologian who typically held such positions in American colleges. He wanted a philosopher who was in sympathy with the modern, scientific, research-oriented spirit of the institution. On the other hand, he needed to be careful to select someone who was religiously "safe," who would not provoke conflict with the various, sometimes-fractious religious communities of the surrounding city and state. Unusual for universities of its time, Johns Hopkins had no religious affiliation, a fact that aroused more than a little apprehension in the populace, in whom conventional Christian belief was widespread and deeply felt, even if not quite mandatory. In addition to its large Protestant population, Maryland still retained a sizeable number of Catholics, descendants of the original Maryland colonists and more recent Irish and German communities. Lingering suspicion was kept from boiling over into outrage by the fact that a number of prominent Quakers and Presbyterians occupied seats on the university's Board of Trustees, and they were among its primary benefactors. Religion was, thus, an issue that Gilman had to continuously monitor and, periodically, actively tend to.

It is not clear why Gilman had declined William James' recommendation of Charles Sanders Peirce for the philosophy post just prior to the school's opening. If any philosopher in America was sympathetic to science and research at that time, Peirce was. He may simply have not been accomplished enough at the time—he had published articles in the *Journal of Speculative Philosophy*, but not yet his famous set on pragmatic philosophy in *Popular Science Monthly*. In addition, he was rapidly acquiring a reputation for being hard to deal with. Peirce once described *himself* as being "vain, snobbish, incivil, reckless, lazy, and ill-tempered."[15] As a result, he had begun to accumulate powerful enemies, not least of whom was Simon Newcomb, a former student of Peirce's father who had risen from poverty in Nova Scotia to become a major scientific figure in the US. In 1877 he would become director of the Nautical Almanac Office at the United States Naval Observatory. Some have suggested that Newcomb was jealous of the younger and more talented Peirce; others have said that Newcomb simply despised Peirce's imperious, dismissive attitude toward nearly everyone who did not agree with him.[16] In any case, Newcomb intervened to prevent Peirce's advancement on more than one occasion. But Newcomb was not alone; Harvard's President Eliot disliked Peirce so intensely that he banished him from the Harvard campus. Harvard philosopher

George Herbert Palmer once wrote to another university president urging him *not* to hire Peirce.

As we saw before, in 1877 James inquired about a philosophical position for himself at Johns Hopkins. Gilman, intrigued, invited him to give a series of lectures in 1878 on the topic of the relationship between the mind and the brain. One historian has characterized them as delivering "an extremely powerful evolutionary argument."[17] After having demonstrated his familiarity with the current state of brain physiology—and having acquainted his audience with it as well—James took on Darwin's own "bulldog," Thomas Henry Huxley, who had argued that consciousness is, metaphorically, only so much ephemeral "steam" coming off the real engine of behavior: the purely physical activity of the brain.[18] Consciousness, according to Huxley, does not enter into the actual causal nexus; it is merely epiphenomenal, a causally inert side effect. James, for whom consciousness was the chief matter separating psychology from physiology, objected to this characterization, and he did so employing Huxley's own weapon: evolutionary theory. Consciousness, James reasoned, would not have evolved, nor would it have been retained in the very "highest" animals—humans—if it did not confer some important evolutionary advantage upon those possessing it. Therefore, he continued, conscious cannot be a simple side effect; it must have some essential role to play, at least in the most complex forms of mentality. Speculating on what that role might be, James suggested that the brains of higher animals are so stupendously complex that they are difficult to control; so delicate is the balance that keeps them functioning properly that they are liable to become erratic at the slightest random perturbation. They have "hair-triggers," as James put it. However, he went on, if consciousness were able to "load the dice"—to use its capacity to foresee the probable outcomes of various actions to gently nudge brain activity in a beneficial direction—then the danger posed by its massive complexity could be largely averted. Moreover, James continued, this scheme would make consciousness not merely an interesting but passive phenomenon. It would, instead, make it a powerful "fighter for ends," as he would later say.[19] It would enable the organism to focus on and attain particular *interests*. He even went on to suggest that, with this power to affect the course of brain function, consciousness might be able to guide the course of evolution itself, shortening the time required for natural selection to meet looming environmental challenges.[20]

James' response to Huxley was published the following year, 1879.[21] The fact that it was published in the London-based journal *Mind* was probably no accident. James wanted to ensure that Huxley and his British colleagues saw it. More important, however, was the fact that there were still no journals of psychology or philosophy in the US at the time, but for the *Journal of Speculative Philosophy*. *Mind* was publishing mostly British authors at the time (save a few translations of Wundt, Helmholtz, and the French philosopher Hippolyte Taine). The only American to have appeared in *Mind* was Stanley Hall, with his PhD thesis in 1878. Hall would publish two more articles in *Mind* in 1879. The race between Hall and James to become the *Grandee* of American psychology was on.

James' February 1878 lectures at Johns Hopkins were a great success, so much so that he was invited to essentially repeat them at the Lowell Institute in Boston in the fall of that year. More important, James had begun to subtly change the trajectory of American psychology. Rather than building a scientific psychology by following the established successes of German physiology, as Wundt had done, James had effectively announced that the American form of the discipline would be modeled on the more recent, more exciting (not to mention, more English) achievements of evolutionary science. But they would not follow the English example slavishly, as James' reply to Huxley showed. Chauncey Wright's interpretation of the implications of evolutionary theory for the study of consciousness, though perhaps hidden from most people's view, would guide James and his circle for some time.

James' Hopkins lectures had one other important effect that would not be felt for long while to come: they led the prominent New York publisher Henry Holt, in June of 1878, to contract James to write a new textbook on the topic of physiological psychology. The book would bring a fresh new view of the field to light, displacing the older philosophical textbooks by people like Thomas Upham of Bowdoin and Noah Porter of Yale that then still buttressed most college courses in the topic.[22] Porter was particular disdainful of the new scientific developments in psychology. So far as he was concerned—and he spoke for a broad circle of American college traditionalists in this matter—the Christian soul was the vital force behind the mind and the body. The new psychology had proven itself unable to discover anything about the soul. "So much the worse for science," he scoffed.[23] Herbert Spencer's controversial and eccentric tome, *Principles of Psychology*, was gathering some American followers, but it had nothing to say about the emerging experimental form of the field. It would be twelve more years before James could complete his two-volume masterwork, *Principles of Psychology*, but much of the outlook presented there found its origin here, in the lectures of 1878.

Despite the success of the James' Baltimore lectures, Gilman was not able to persuade James to leave Harvard for Hopkins. Instead, James used Gilman's offer to pressure Eliot to move his Assistant Professorship from physiology to philosophy, which Eilot did. But James was not the only candidate Gilman was wooing for the Hopkins philosophy professorship. In December of 1877, Gilman offered a single course in the history of philosophy to George Sylvester Morris, the very man who the young Stanley Hall had admired for having gone to Germany to study with Friedrich Adolf Trendelenburg back in the 1860s, when they were both students at Union Seminary in New York. Morris had gone on to a chair in Modern Languages and Literature at the University of Michigan, where he had labored since 1870, but he longed for a chair in philosophy instead. He was blocked from the one at Michigan by an older and much-beloved minister who had taken up the philosophy chair just a year before Morris had arrived (so it was unlikely that he would be vacating it very soon).[24] Still, Morris persevered, publishing a translation of Friedrich Ueberweg's *History of Philosophy* in an effort to bolster his philosophical credentials.[25]

Although Morris was better established in philosophy than William James was at the time, he fit uncomfortably into Hopkins' scientific ethos. First, he was ambivalent about the importance of natural science. Second, although devoutly religious, the approach to Christianity he had learned from his German training made him not as "safe" a candidate as Gilman believed he required to keep Baltimore's self-appointed guardians of religious orthodoxy content.[26] Despite all of this, Morris taught the course that Gilman offered him in January of 1878 and was sufficiently successful that he was invited to return the following January to give a second series of lectures, this one on ethics.

Peirce, of course, was watching matters unfold at Johns Hopkins closely. Although psychology had never really been his specialty, in 1877 he published an article in *The American Journal of Science and Arts* that has led one historian of the discipline to declare him to have been "the first American experimental psychologist."[27] Titled "A Note on the Sensation of Color," Peirce called into question the assumption of Gustav Fechner, founder of the field of psychophysics, that the apparent hue of a color remains constant across changing intensities. Peirce found instead that, as intensity increased, hue tended toward the yellow part of the spectrum. He presented empirical data on his own color perception, across many trials, to determine his "photometric probable error" and to confirm his hypothesis. His work was far more rigorous, far more mathematically sophisticated than that of anyone else conducting psychological research in America at the time.

Peirce wrote to Gilman in March 1878, just after James had given his first lecture series, offering to teach logic.[28] Gilman initially offered him a half-lectureship, but later withdrew it after Peirce tangled with Hopkins's highly-valued but testy mathematics professor, James Joseph Sylvester.[29] It seems that Peirce never learned the life lesson that public quarrels, no matter how learned, do not endear you to many people, especially to the administrators who are going to have to clean up the resulting mess.

3. Hall's Return to America

Almost from the moment of its launch in 1876, the journal *Mind* began recruiting correspondents to write about the state of philosophy in various countries. Wundt wrote one about German philosophy in 1877.[30] Having published Hall's thesis in 1878, *Mind*'s editor, George Croom Robertson, naturally turned to Hall to describe the American philosophical scene.[31] Hall probably thought that the resulting article would establish his philosophical reputation. Instead, it was so damning of the general state of philosophy in the US that it likely nixed whatever chance he ever had of being called to a chair anywhere in the country. Even Harvard, one of very few places he did not relegate to the status of backwater, became less likely to ever bring Hall on board.[32] According to Hall, nearly all US colleges were mired in the dogmatics of their particular Protestant denominations, taught by well-meaning but hidebound, unenlightened men who knew little or nothing of recent developments in European philosophy. Even where there was interest in European philosophy— e.g., William Harris' Hegelian circle in St. Louis and the positivist discussion groups in which Hall had participated in New York—they were presided over by amateurs. It is not that Hall was incorrect in these observations; his vision was ruthlessly clear. It is that he would soon return to these people in search of a job, and his pointed public criticism of them would do little to enhance his desirability.

When Hall returned to the US, he had come to see his country and his own upbringing in a new and negative way.

> The narrow, inflexible orthodoxy, the settled lifeless *mores*, the Puritan eviction of the joy that comes from amusements from [sic] life, the provincialism of our interests, our prejudice against continental ways of living and thinking, the crudeness of our school system, the elementary character of the education imparted in our higher institutions of learning. . . . Most of all, we were so smugly complacent with our limitations, so self-satisfied with our material prosperity, and so ignorant of Europe, save as tourists see it. I fairly loathed and hated so much that I saw about me . . .[33]

Regardless of how Hall may have felt, he was back in the US with a wife and two small children to support, living in a small house in Somerville, Massachusetts (outside of Cambridge), in debt, and unemployed. He took the offer of a course in the history of philosophy at his alma mater of Williams College, but his high aspirations of bringing to them the new German philosophy were in open conflict with the desires of his students.[34] While still in Germany, he had written Gilman about the possibility of the Johns Hopkins position more than once. James offered his support, declaring even that Hall's new German training "entirely reverses the positions we held relative to each other 3 years ago. He is a more learned man than I can ever hope to become."[35] Gilman remained unconvinced. Hall then tried to marshal James, Henry Bowditch, and Charles Eliot Norton to nominate him for a Lowell Institute lecture series, like James had given in 1878. Nothing came of it. Finally, he collected together bits and pieces that he had published in *The Nation*, along with some earlier scientific writings and a few new essays. He published this rather motley sheaf as a book called *Aspects of German Culture*.[36] He wrote of the success of natural science, and of the need to reform American religion, but he avoided the strident tone of the earlier *Mind* article on American philosophy that had caused him such grief. Here he attempted to craft a reconciliation between religion and science by way of, on the one hand, recourse to the German "higher criticism" and, on the other hand, an end to scientific radicals' "gross and tasteless" rebukes of religion. The book did not do well, but it reached some important eyes. Charles Eliot Norton, for instance, called it "remarkable." Hall also published a new article in *Mind* on hypnosis.[37]

Late in 1880, when things perhaps appeared to Hall most bleak, President Eliot of Harvard rode up to Hall's house and, without even getting off of his horse (according to Hall's version of the story), offered him a series of lectures on the novel topic of "pedagogy." They would be sponsored by the university, but were to be delivered in Boston so that the city's school teachers could more easily attend them. Hall persuaded Eliot to let him give a course in German philosophy as well. This was, far and away, the best academic offer Hall had ever received. The philosophy course went well enough, but the pedagogy lectures, which began in February of 1881, turned out to be far more significant for his future career than Hall could probably have imagined.

Massachusetts was the American center of gravity for progressive ideas about education. As mentioned before, the Puritans had set up schools almost as soon as they arrived in the early 17th century. The educational vision of the era—well into the 19th century—was of the inculcation of conventional morality enforced by stern physical discipline. Breaking the child's "will" in order to produce meek and obedient Christian subjects was the order of the day. Latin and mathematics were typically part of the curriculum, but more for the purposes of building mental discipline (which, it was then thought, would readily transfer over to other domains of knowledge) than for any particular value their content was thought to have. Learning was mostly by rote. Memorization of Bible passages and other texts with religious themes was standard practice.

In 1837, Horace Mann, a Massachusetts state legislator, became the first head of the state's Board of Education. He began his term by personally touring and examining every school in the state. Dismayed by much of what he found, he began writing annual reports about the condition of education in the state. He promoted far-reaching school reforms. Among these were that education should be universal, and that it should be paid for from the public purse. Schools should accept children of all backgrounds and, thus, the curriculum itself should be non-denominational. The schools should be better equipped and the teachers better trained and better paid. Although Mann promoted a moral education more than an intellectual one, he advocated the discontinuation of corporal punishment in the schools.[38] Although he met fierce resistance from traditionalists, many of Mann's proposals were implemented, first in Massachusetts and, later, in New York and other states beyond.

Mann then inaugurated the "normal school" system in Massachusetts, in which teachers—primarily women, which was a novel phenomenon—were trained for the new "profession" of teaching. He organized conventions at which teachers could exchange ideas and practices, and he founded the *Common School Journal* in which he disseminated "progressive" educational ideas. In 1848, he returned to electoral politics, filling the US congressional seat left vacant by the death of former-president John Quincy Adams. In 1852 he ran for governor of Massachusetts, but was defeated. Only then, as we have already seen, did he move west to take up the presidency of the newly founded Antioch College in Yellow Springs, Ohio.

About a decade after Mann's death in 1859, the head of the nearby Dayton normal school, Francis Wayland Parker, decided to travel to Germany to learn about the educational reforms that were underway there. He became enamored of a system envisioned by Romantic philosophers such as Jean Jacques Rousseau, Friedrich Fröbel, Johann Heinrich Pestalozzi, and Johann Friedrich Herbart. They believed, among other things, that children's natural dispositions should be respected and that their interests should be catered to. This would make learning a more enjoyable and, thus, more productive process. Obviously, this was all in stark contrast to the traditional American Protestant goal of "beating the will" out of the child.

In 1875, Parker returned to his original home of New England and became superintendent of the school system in Quincy, Massachusetts. There he began a grand educational experiment in which schooling was centered on the putative needs of the child, rather than on the demands of the teacher (a Copernican revolution in the classroom, it has been called).[39] Rote memorization, testing, and grading were eliminated. Corporal punishment was banished. Group activities were encouraged, rather than having children sit at desks arranged in rigid rows. Arts and sciences entered the curriculum, displacing some traditional subjects. Physical education was promoted. Children were encouraged, as much as possible, to learn by means of their own experience, not just via the lecture and the textbook. Parker faced stiff opposition, but testing mandated by his opponents showed that Quincy students were better than most others in the state.

In 1880, Parker was invited to bring the Quincy Plan into Boston's public schools. This was the context of excitement and controversy into which G. Stanley Hall was hired by Charles Eliot to give his public lecture series on the topic of pedagogy. It was reported that Eliot, while introducing Hall to his audience, "was hardly able to pronounce the word *pedagogy* without evident distaste."[40] Harvard's public show of skepticism notwithstanding, the turnout for the first lecture, in February of 1881, was large[41] and included a number of prominent personages: There was the Superintendent of Boston Public Schools John Dudley Philbrick who, in the question period after one lecture defied Hall "to find any imperfection in the school system of Boston."[42] (Hall did not record his answer to so provocative a question.) There was Charles Francis Adams, scion of the great Adams dynasty in Massachusetts (Henry Adams' older brother) and a prominent supporter of Francis Parker's Romantic educational reforms in his distinguished family's ancestral home of Quincy. Elizabeth Peabody, often said to be the founder of the first kindergarten in American, based on Fröbel's model, was in attendance as well.[43] In introducing Hall, Eliot challenged the audience to decide whether Hall was right in promoting the new discipline of pedagogy, or whether Harvard would be right to ignore it (which, of course, it wasn't, having sponsored those very lectures).

For the most part, Hall tentatively endorsed the Romantic views of the child and education that were central to progressive educational reform. What made his position unique was that he substantiated these claims not so much with reference to philosophy as by way of the new scientific physiology and psychology that he had just studied so intensively in Germany. Indeed, he argued that much more scientific investigation of children—their abilities, needs, dispositions, proclivities, desires—was needed in order to make education even more child-centered; in order to make certain classroom activities fit the nature of the child as much as the advocates of progressive education insisted.

Hall's pedagogical lectures provided the greatest academic success that he had experienced, and he moved to capitalize on them immediately by publishing two pieces in the somewhat stodgy *Princeton Review*.[44] In the first, Hall brandished in print for the first time his psychologized version of recapitulationism: "The pupil should, and in fact naturally does, repeat the course of the development of the race, and education is simply the expediting and shortening of this course."[45] All in all, though, Hall trod rather softly; he enunciated what his primary biographer called a "timid Romanticism."[46] He acknowledged even the occasional need for corporal punishment. He did not argue with the need to inculcate Christian morality, except to displace traditional, literalist, harsh Protestant belief with the softened, historicized faith he had acquired in Germany.

In 1882 Hall was invited to speak before an audience of school superintendents at the meeting of the National Education Association (NEA). This is where his call for the scientific study of the nature of the child was transformed into the "Child Study Movement," for which Hall deserves a great deal of the credit.[47] He followed the lecture with an article in the *Princeton Review* that was intended to exemplify the process.[48] Titled "The Contents of Children's Minds," it marked Hall's most ambitious attempt thus far to put into practice the sort of research for which he had been calling. The study consisted chiefly of closely questioning children on the state of their knowledge and recording the results in tabular form. Perhaps not surprisingly, Hall found that children have substantial epistemic gaps and are misinformed about many things. As Hall put it himself, what he really conducted was "a study of children's ignorance."[49] Nevertheless, the article created a sensation in the community of teachers and scholars who were enthusiastic about child study. Hall received dozens of inquires about it, and he turned this attention to his advantage by calling upon his correspondents to collect additional data for him. Before long he was overwhelmed with detailed records of children's beliefs.

Hall's biographer noted that he mostly asked questions about topics that would be more familiar to country children than to those who dwelt in cities.[50] Indeed, he wrote explicitly: "As our methods of teaching grow natural we realize that city life is unnatural, and that those who grow up without knowing the country are defrauded of that without which childhood can never be complete or normal. On the whole the material of the city is no doubt inferior in pedagogic value to country experience."[51] It is easy to conclude here that Hall was unthinkingly presuming that his own childhood experience had been the "right" or "normal" experience to have. However, he may have been proposing that, as children develop by recapitulating the experiences of the species, it is more "natural" for them to start the process in a rural environment, where the human race started, rather than in the "unnatural"—for that stage of development—confines of the city:

> We cannot accept without many careful qualifications the evolutionary dictum that the child's mental development should repeat that of the race. Unlike primitive man the child's body is feeble and he is ever influenced

DR. G. STANLEY HALL'S SYSTEM OF EDUCATION.
—Chicago Times-Herald.

FIGURE 5.1   Cartoon critical of Hall's educational theory, *Chicago Times-Herald* (June 3, 1899).

Credit: Reprinted in *The Argue* (Holbrook, AZ), June 3, 1899, p. 6. Retrieved May 10, 2017 from http:// chroniclingamerica.loc.gov/lccn/sn94051341/1899-06-03/ed-1/seq-6/ (I would like to acknowledge to Jacy Young for introducing me to this cartoon.)

by a higher culture about him. Yet from the primeval intimacy with the qualities and habits of plants, with the instincts of animals—so like those of children . . . it is certain that not a few educational elements of great value can be selected [from the country] and systematized for children.[52]

Hall was soon asked to join important committees of the NEA, where he encountered, once again, William Torrey Harris (who would be appointed US Commissioner of Education at the end of the decade). Harris was less than pleased that, as he saw it, issues he had been working on steadily for over a decade were suddenly coming to prominence associated with Hall's name instead of his. Although they largely agreed on the Romantic turn in pedagogy, Harris was still a Hegelian with little use for empirical study; First Principles and Reason alone would, in his view, lead us to the correct conclusions. Hall, by contrast, had made progressive reforms that were especially appealing in the American context by tethering them to "science." It was Hall's trump card.

By late 1881, other opportunities started to draw Hall away from both Boston and Harvard. After years of trying to attract the attention of Johns Hopkins' president, it was not philosophy or physiology that brought President Gilman around to Hall's talents, but the success of the Boston pedagogy lectures. Even before the lectures had run their course, Gilman had heard of their popularity and asked Hall to lecture at Hopkins. Hall agreed, and prepared a set of lectures on psychology for presentation in Baltimore in January 1882.

Although Gilman could not attend Hall's Hopkins lectures himself, a report on the event from one of his faculty members was encouraging enough that, in March 1882, Gilman offered him a 3-year half-lectureship (spring terms, opposite Morris in the fall) in psychology and pedagogics in the department of philosophy. As if to reassure Gilman that he had not made a mistake, Hall formally launched his child study movement at an NEA speech that spring. Later the same year he published an empirical study of optical illusions with Bowditch.[53]

Baltimore was an entirely new environment for Hall. Unlike the intensely moral abolitionism of the Massachusetts in which he had been born and raised, unlike even the unsteady ethnic tolerance of New York with its keen focus on mercantile matters, Baltimore was Southern, if not Confederate precisely. Sympathy for the old landowners and against their former slaves was palpable, even at Johns Hopkins. Although Mr. Hopkins himself had been a Quaker, many of the early Trustees of the university were drawn from a "small group of wealthy men of deeply Southern loyalties and of narrow and largely Methodist and Presbyterian convictions."[54] Hall's response was to bury himself in his work. An opportunity like this had never come his way before, and he was determined not to let it escape.

4. Finding a Philosopher Suited to Johns Hopkins

Gilman, who had opened Hopkins in 1876 with no instructor in philosophy, now had an embarrassment of riches: Morris in history and ethics, Peirce in logic, and Hall in psychology and pedagogy.[55] Although the three lecturers seemed to get along well, each had reason to believe that he alone had the inside track to the professorship. One obvious option—appointing more than one professor in the area—seems not to have appealed to Gilman. The delicate state of Hopkins' finances may well have prevented him from contemplating such a course.[56]

Time was not on Gilman's side, however. In December 1880, not long after the death in September of Peirce's father, the younger Peirce announced that he would be forced to leave Hopkins on account of some travel required by his geodetic work with the US Coast Survey.[57] At that time he sold nearly 300 books from his personal collection to the school, declaring that, "upon leaving the university I shall bid adieu to the study of Logic and Philosophy (except experimental psychology)."[58] By March 1881, a large salary increase had coaxed Peirce back,[59] but it was clear that he was on the hunt for higher-paying work than he had in his combined Hopkins and Coast Survey positions. Peirce attempted to recreate the circumstances that had nurtured his own philosophical maturation in back in Cambridge: he founded a new "Metaphysical Club," and played, to his students, the role that Chauncey Wright had played to him in the early 1870s.[60]

Morris was hunting for more as well. In June 1881, Michigan played the best hand it could muster at the time, given that they already had a professor of philosophy in place: they offered Morris a half-professorship in ethics, the history of philosophy, and logic and they tailored it specifically not to interfere with his Hopkins duties.[61] If Gilman wanted Morris to stay at Hopkins, he would have to fight Michigan for him.

September 1882 saw the arrival of some exceptional graduate students: James McKeen Cattell, who had won an entry fellowship, and John Dewey, who had impressed Morris with an article he had published in the *Journal of Speculative Philosophy*. They joined physiologist Henry Herbert Donaldson, who had come in 1881 and was starting work with Hall on tactile perception, as well as Christine Ladd, who had come in 1878 and, although now known mostly for her work on color vision, was then primarily a student of mathematics and logic.[62] Soon after, Joseph Jastrow would arrive as well to study with Peirce. Cattell, Dewey, Donaldson, Ladd, and Jastrow were all contributors to Peirce's new Metaphysical Club,[63] and all went on to significant careers in their own rights. Cattell, however, was stripped of his fellowship the following May and, furious at Hall's duplicitous behavior in the matter,[64] he barged out of the department and went on to complete his doctorate in Leipzig under the supervision of Wilhelm Wundt.[65]

The year 1883 saw the publication of *Studies in Logic by Members of the Johns Hopkins University*, under the editorship of Peirce.[66] The book contained a number of significant original contributions to the field authored by Peirce and his students over the previous two years.[67] The prominent English logician John Venn (namesake of Venn diagrams) was highly impressed by it, writing that it "seems to me to contain a greater quantity of novel and suggestive matter than any other recent works on the same or allied subject which has happened to come under my notice."[68] Later that year, Peirce began a series of experimental studies with

Joseph Jastrow aimed at demonstrating a critical flaw in the view of perception that underlay Fechner's psychophysical law. They presented their findings at the October 1884 meting of the National Academy of Sciences and published their report in NAS's *Memoirs* the following year.[69]

Hall, determined that control of psychology at Johns Hopkins would be his, not Peirce's, opened an experimental psychology laboratory on his own initiative in February of 1883.[70] It was the first such facility in America dedicated to original research, but was located in a private house adjacent to the Johns Hopkins buildings.[71] The first published research conducted in the laboratory was authored by Hall and the Hopkins gymnasium director, Edward Mussey Hartwell. It appeared in *Mind* in January of 1884.[72] Jastrow later recalled that his experimental work with Peirce, which was carried out in Jastrow's own rooms starting in December 1883, began before any research by Hall or his students at Hopkins.[73] However,

FIGURE 5.2 Western portion of Baltimore, 1876. The location of Johns Hopkins is circled.

Credit: From O.W. Gray, *Gray's Atlas of the United States*, Philadelphia, PA: Steadman, Brown, & Lyon, 1876.

given that Hall and Hartwell's article in *Mind* was published in January 1884, the research that led to it must have begun well before the previous month. The first publication by any of Hall's students, based on work undertaken in the new lab, did not appear until more than two years after the lab had opened.[74]

Part of the problem in founding a psychology laboratory as part of the school proper was Hopkins' lack of a real campus in the early days. As mentioned, unable to afford to build on the late Mr. Hopkins' estate north of the city, Gilman had started to acquire existing buildings. Then, over the strenuous objections of some of his Trustees, he began to erect new structures. Soon, the little cluster of buildings formed a kind of urban "campus" on the street then known as "Little Ross" (now Druid Hill Ave.), just west of Howard St., and across from what was then the western terminus of Centre St.[75] The site was north of downtown, but not nearly as far out of the city as the objecting Trustees thought it should be. To its advantage, the location afforded easy access to the 60,000-volume library of the Peabody Institute (which was not then yet affiliated with Hopkins). It was also close to a large theater called the Academy of Music, and to Baltimore City College (just to the west in the map). But the buildings there were never wholly sufficient to house the new and ever-growing school.

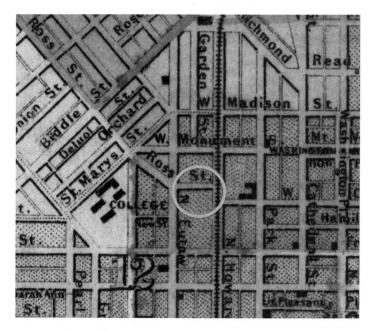

FIGURE 5.3   Detail of Baltimore, 1876, where original Johns Hopkins Campus was located.

Credit: From O.W. Gray, *Gray's Atlas of the United States*, Philadelphia, PA: Steadman, Brown, & Lyon, 1876.

Initially, two older adjoining residences at the southwest corner of Howard and Ross were converted into a single Administration Building. Then, in late 1876, just before the school officially opened, a modest new 3-story edifice called Hopkins Hall was erected just west of the Administration Building, on Ross. A chemistry laboratory for Ira Remsen was added to the west of Hopkins Hall the following year. Other departments occupied nearby houses that had been purchased by the school. By 1882, with space becoming a critical issue, the chemistry building was expanded and a new biology building was added to its west, also on Ross, about block away from Howard, at Eutaw.

Although Hall had started his laboratory in a nearby house early in 1883, he was able to move it to the new biology building by the end of the year. Other pieces fell into place for Hall during 1883 as well. In April, his old friend George Sylvester Morris won the permanent philosophical position at Michigan that he had long sought. When he left Hopkins the following year, he took with him, as an instructor, his just-graduated protégé, John Dewey. That left just Hall and Peirce to compete for the sole philosophy professorship. Peirce was, by far, the more accomplished scholar, but personal matters would intervene to decide the contest.

Peirce had been separated from his wife Melusina "Zina" Fay since 1875.[76] In the early 1880s he took up with a woman of somewhat mysterious background named Juliette. Her family name was sometimes given as Froissy, other times as Portalai. Her exact identity has never been established. As the relationship with Juliette became permanent, Peirce filed for divorce from Fay. Before the marriage was officially dissolved, however, he began living with Juliette as his wife, in New York, far from Johns Hopkins. Simon Newcomb, was just starting as Johns Hopkins' professor of astronomy and mathematics (replacing Sylvester, who had won a long-sought appointment at Oxford). As noted before, Newcomb actively despised Peirce. Upon discovering the untoward facts of Peirce's love life, he reported them to one of the more devout Quakers among the Johns Hopkins Trustees, James Carey Thomas.[77] Thomas, in turn, demanded swift and decisive action against Peirce from President Gilman.

From the start, there had been tension between Hopkins and the population of Baltimore. The first strain was regional: there were few Southerners on faculty, apart from the Classicist, Basil Gildersleeve, who had been wounded while fighting for the Confederacy. Even most of the students were Northerners, so many residents of the city saw the university as a "Yankee" or even a despised "carpetbagger" institution.[78] The second conflict was religious: although there were sizeable communities of Catholics, Quakers, and Methodists in Baltimore, a particularly conservative form of Presbyterianism had taken for itself the role of civic moral arbiter. When controversy erupted, as it did from time to time—over a professor teaching evolution, or materialism, or pantheism—Gilman would quickly point to several of his faculty who were actively engaged with local churches, and to the Hopkins departments that were engaged in some of the finest Biblical studies in the country. He would even personally request his faculty to attend church regularly in order to further the goal of appearing religiously unexceptionable to wary Baltimoreans. G. Stanley Hall was among those who, although no longer much of a believer, attended church for the sake of peace between the school and the city.[79]

Potential conflicts with the citizenry, like that now posed by Peirce's unortho-dox marital behavior, were matters that Gilman strove to avoid at all cost, even if it meant losing one of the best minds the country had to offer. Firing Peirce outright, however, would have attracted unwanted attention and risked public scandal. So the Board of Trustees decided, instead, to implement a policy of that would limit all instructors' contracts to just one year in length. This, of course, included Peirce. When Peirce's contract came due in April 1884, they quietly declined to renew it. That same month, Hall, being the last man standing in the philosophy department, was offered the sole professorship in the topic (though it was officially called "Psychology & Pedagogy"). Peirce, on the other hand, would never hold an academic position again. His professional decline was rapid and permanent. By the early 1890s, his published writings had become "rambling and diffuse."[80] Christine Ladd-Franklin, who continued to see him regularly, later confided to the mathematician Edwin Bidwell Wilson that Peirce was "beginning to lose his mind early in the nineties," and specifically cited his 1892 article "Man's Glassy Essence" as "very definite" evidence.[81] Wilson confirmed Ladd-Franklin's evaluation: having seen Peirce lecture in 1905, followed by a long discussion, he pronounced Peirce "unintelligible" and "not coherent," even to a mathematician of Wilson's caliber. Wilson softened the condemnation, however, saying that Peirce had just lost the "bite of his mind."[82] On the other hand, it was in the 1900s that Peirce did most of what many now consider to be his most brilliant work on a topic that he virtually invented: semiotics, the theory of signs.

As the years drew on, Peirce was only able to find work writing dictionary entries and book reviews. He and his wife gradually withdrew nearly completely to their house in rural Milford, Pennsylvania, where they endured increasingly abject poverty. Peirce's older brother James occasionally paid down Charles' debts, but he died in 1906. Charles' old friend William James occasionally arranged for paid lectures by Peirce in the Boston area, and James eventually solicited contri-butions for a private pension fund, of sorts. Peirce would die, nearly destitute and nearly forgotten, in April of 1914.

5. Hall the Professor, the Editor, the (Self-)Promoter

Hall's willingness to advance Gilman's efforts to ensure smooth relations between town and gown extended even to his inaugural address as a professor. Titled "The New Psychology," the formal public lecture did not really go very far toward explaining what these innovative approaches to the study of the mind consisted in nor what discoveries and insights they had brought forth. It was, instead, aimed primarily at integrating psychology into a conventional narrative of the history of philosophy. It sought more to reassure than enlighten. After brief sketches of some of the key figures of the new psychology—e.g., Weber, Wundt, and Darwin—Hall immediately noted that:

> The needs of the average student, however, are no doubt best served, not by comparative, or even experimental, but by *historical* psychology.... Historical psychology seeks to go back of all finished systems to their roots, and explores many sources to discover the fresh, primary thoughts and sensations and feelings of mankind.[83]

In part, this included, for Hall, the anthropological study of "habits, beliefs, rites, taboos, oaths, maxims, ideals of life, views of death, family and social organizations,"[84] but his primary concern was to bring into the discussion the many European philosophers with whom his audience would be familiar and, to at least some degree, comfortable: Plato, Aristotle, Roger Bacon, Francis Bacon, Descartes, Spinoza, Kant, etc. He then turned approvingly to the traditional course in philosophy—syllogistic logic, ethics, etc.—but included the small plea that "every young man needs a little psychology. He must know the current facts and terms in this literature about the senses, the will, feelings, attention, memory, association, apperception, etc." Then he carefully added the promise that even this would be couched in "copious historical allusions, and especially with their innumerable and very practical applications to mental and physical hygiene but without much of what is called physiological psychology."[85] Hall concluded with what must have been the supreme reassurance that "The new psychology ... is I believe Christian to its root and centre.... The Bible is being slowly re-revealed as man's great textbook in psychology"[86] As if to add emphasis to the point, he published the address in the eminently respectable theological journal *Andover Review*, which bore the paradoxical motto: "thoroughly progressive orthodoxy."[87] There is hardly a phrase that better captures what Hall seems to have been attempting, not only with his inaugural lecture but with much of his early career.

In 1885, a physics building was constructed a block north of the rest of the campus, at Monument St. and Garden St. (now Linden St.). Hall's laboratory soon followed, where it enjoyed larger quarters than it had in the biology building. Hall spent most of his time teaching psychology, but he also taught history of philosophy, as well as pedagogy classes on Saturdays. These last were open to Baltimore's teachers (another part of Gilman's plan to maintain good relations with the city, a tactic that Hall would later adopt himself). Hall also shared in overseeing the Bayview Hospital for the Insane for a time.[88]

As we have seen, the list of students who came under Hall's tutelage at Johns Hopkins was quite extraordinary. Edward Cowles, the superintendent of the McLean Asylum near Boston came to study with Hall for one year. The two formed a lifelong friendship. Even the young future president of the United States, Woodrow Wilson, was a student in some of Hall's classes, taking a minor in psychology. In part, this acquisition of high talent was made possible by Gilman's innovation of offering graduate students fellowships of $400.[89] Harvard's President Eliot disparaged such gestures as "paying students to come," but the success that fellowships found in drawing outstanding students to the school spoke for itself.[90] Gilman also brought in eminent speakers from around America and even Europe. These included, during Hall's time, philosopher Herbert Spencer, evolutionists Thomas Huxley and Alfred Russel Wallace, physicist Lord Kelvin, and poets Matthew Arnold and James Russell Lowell, among others.[91]

Hall published regularly, but not extensively, during his time at Hopkins. In addition to the study on movement with Hartwell, mentioned above, he did work on dermal sensation with Henry Donaldson and with a student from Japan named Yuzero Motora, who would go on to found one of Japan's first psychology laboratories.[92] Hall also published research on rhythm with Joseph Jastrow. Some of Hall's writings appeared in semi-popular periodicals, as was still common at the time. Part of the difficulty lay in the fact that there were, at that time, rather few scientific journals that catered to the kind of work Hall was doing. However, Johns Hopkins' eminent professoriate was the wellspring from which a number of the new American academic journals emerged. There being no American journal dedicated to the new experimental psychology as yet, Hall decided to join in with his colleagues by launching a journal of his own and, in the process, make himself the primary "gatekeeper" of the American form of psychology.

The way Hall told the story in his autobiography, a man named "J. Pearsall Smith of Philadelphia, an entire stranger to me," visited Hall one Sunday and "suggested that I found a journal and then and there gave me a check for five hundred dollars."[93] Historians have since discovered a rather different sequence of events.[94] Psychical research and spiritualism were popular topics in the 1880s, not only in the US but across Europe as well. Interest in these arcane matters was not limited to the "lay" public, but also included many serious academics. Some were advocates of the psychic, but others critically investigated the legitimacy of the numerous mediums who, for a price, would put their alleged abilities at the service of the general public. In 1882, Cambridge's professor of moral philosophy Henry Sidgwick led the founding of the Society for Psychical Research (SPR) in Britain. Sidgwick enlisted several other recognized intellectuals in this endeavor, giving the field a new and heightened respectability. Among these people was Sidgwick's American friend, William James.

It is easy, with hindsight, to dismiss the whole affair as having been naïve or even foolish. But perhaps it is understandable, when viewd in historical context. The "natural historian" of ghosts, Roger Clarke, has opined that "belief in the paranormal (today) has become a form of decayed religion in secular times: Ghosts are the ghosts of religion itself."[95] If that is true today, where it has become commonplace to witness the displacement by naturalistic explanation of whole domains of knowledge that traditionally fell under religious authority, one can only imagine how much more powerful this dynamic would have been in the late 19th century, when not only the understanding of the origin of humans was being revolutionized by Darwin and his associates, but the functioning of the human body—even the mind itself—were besieged by the findings of experimental physiology and its younger cousin, experimental psychology. Spiritualism, telepathy, and the like struck many—credulous and sophisticated alike—as, perhaps, the last remaining refuge of a venerable and deeply felt understanding of the self against the relentless onslaught of naturalism and science.

Put somewhat more delicately, one might view the rising wave of interest in the psychic and the spiritual not simply as a bulwark against the encroachments of naturalism but, rather, as an endeavor in which the very limits of "Nature" were being explored, tested, and possibly revised. Innovative scientific methods were appearing in brisk succession. Probability theory, for instance, once merely a playground for gamblers, had gained new attention and respect as a scientific tool. Darwin's successful use of the previously disdained "method of hypothesis" had served to reformulate the criteria for which investigations might count as "scientific." Whole new realms of knowledge were successfully being opened to scientific endeavor—the elementary chemical constituents of all substances, the physiology of living things, the history of life itself, the age of the earth, and the size of the cosmos. How far these lines of inquiry might go and what secrets they might reveal were anyone's guess. Just as the underlying principles of life had seemed an impenetrable mystery just a few decades before, perhaps seemingly occult powers and spiritual phenomena would turn out to be manifestations of a "Nature" even more magnificent and encompassing than had previously been suspected. Although individual case studies broadly outnumbered controlled experiments in the field of psychical research, the aspiration, at least, was to investigate such phenomena according to the scientific scruples of the day. That said, there were, as today, many who had made up their minds prior to embarking upon their investigations, and were mainly intent on adding a veneer of scientific legitimacy to what they were already certain to be the case, not truly to subject their beliefs to possible refutation.

In 1884, two years after the founding of the SPR in Britain, William James launched a counterpart organization on the western side of the Atlantic: the American Society for Psychical Research (ASPR).[96] Simon Newcomb, Peirce's old nemesis, served as its first president. Peirce's older brother, James Mills Peirce, a Harvard mathematics professor, was on the early ASPR Council as well. G. Stanley Hall agreed to become one of several Vice Presidents, as did his old physiology mentor, Henry Bowditch.[97] Another member of the original ASPR Council of 1885 was Robert Pearsall Smith, author of the 1870 book, *Holiness Through Faith*, which had served as the founding document of the "Holiness Movement" in the US, a popular evangelical offshoot of Methodism. In addition, Smith was a very wealthy man, having built a glassworks in his native Philadelphia. It was Robert (not "J," as Hall reported) Pearsall Smith who contributed $500 to Hall's journalistic venture, and it seems inconceivable that Hall and Smith did not already know each other at the time: they had both served on the ASPR executive for two years. It also seems unlikely that it was Smith rather than Hall himself, who originated the idea of founding a journal dedicated to psychology. Johns Hopkins was at the center of the burgeoning academic journal business in America, being the birthplace of at least five other scholarly periodicals in the first decade of its existence. By launching a psychology journal, Hall was, at least in part, just trying to keep up with his senior, more-celebrated Hopkins colleagues.

The key question with respect to the content of the nascent *American Journal of Psychology* is what Hall's patron, Smith, expected of the journal in return for his investment, and the degree to which Hall may have misled Smith on this matter. It seems probable that Smith expected a periodical dedicated, at least in part, to the serious exploration of psychical and spiritualist matters. The SPR had founded a research journal in England and its American counterpart required no less. What Hall produced instead was a journal dedicated explicitly to "scientific" psychology.

What Hall meant by "scientific" is difficult to fathom precisely. In the inaugural editorial of his new *American Journal of Psychology*, which appeared in October of 1887, he listed several types of research he thought appropriate:

> experimental investigations on the functions of the senses and brain, physiological time, psycho-physic law, images and their association, volition, innervation. etc.; and partly of inductive studies of instinct in animals, psychogenesis in children, and the large fields of morbid and anthropological psychology, not excluding hypnotism, methods of research which will receive special attention; and lastly, the finer anatomy of the sense-organs and the central nervous system, including the latest technical methods, and embryological, comparative and experimental studies of both neurological structure and function.[98]

Hall explicitly rejected "speculative" psychology, by which he meant the old moral and mental philosophy.[99] No mention was made in the editorial of either psychical or spiritual research. However, Hall notably quit the ASPR not long before the new journal launched. Buried in a review of the proceedings of the (English) Society for Psychical Research, Hall declared, to what must have been Smith's chagrin, not only that telepathy had repeatedly failed to pass empirical test, but that "spiritualism, in its more vulgar form, is the sewerage of all the superstitions of the past."[100]

Despite its grand title, the *American Journal of Psychology* carried mainly Hall's own work, and that of his closest colleagues and students. Whatever his initial scientific aspirations might have been, Hall was soon scrambling to fill pages for his subscribers. There were unexplained gaps in the publication schedule. The first two volumes began in November, of 1887 and 1888, respectively. The first issue of Volume 3, however, was dated January of 1890, and the last issue of the volume did not appear until February of the following year, leaving the start of volume 4 to April 1891, nearly half a year late. The contents themselves were eclectic. Much of it was exactly what we today would expect from that time: experiments on vision and touch, psychophysical studies, expositions of what was known about memory, descriptions of new laboratory apparatus, position papers on the relationship between the "new psychology" and bordering disciplines such as neurology and education. But Hall had a wide view of the field. There were studies of applied psychology, such as one on the legibility of small letters. There were articles on psychiatric issues, such as "fixed ideas" and paranoia. There were original neurological studies, including an examination of the brain of the famed "blind deaf-mute," Laura Bridgman about whom Hall had first written in the 1870s. There was an investigation of the roosting patterns of crows, an article on the "folk-lore of the Bahama negroes," another on dreams, a monograph on the ancient Greek philosopher Heraclitus, a study of logic, surveys of children's memories and of their lies, a description of arithmetical prodigies, and a consideration of the psychology of time.

The academic boundaries of "psychology" in the early *American Journal* were porous, to be sure. But it is often forgotten exactly how enormous Hall's challenge was. In essence, it was nothing less than to weave an intellectually disparate set of scientists and philosophers together into a community that shared enough common ground that they could collectively constitute a distinctive and autonomous discipline where one had not really existed before. It had to be large and stable enough that it was capable of sustaining a journal of its own in the coming years and decades. In no small measure, Hall accomplished this by calling upon his colleagues and students in the institutional communities around Johns Hopkins and, later, Clark University. That is, whatever their intellectual differences might have been, they had *Hall* in common with each other. In the journal's early issues Hall attempted to nurture the nascent community's intellectual integration by writing extensive "Notes"—summaries and reviews of the current psychological literature, wherever it happened to be published, in whatever language. The "Notes" were there, it appears, to serve as a shared knowledge base for the new discipline—a common core that any member of the community could draw upon and refer to in the knowledge that other readers would have access to it as well. Around the "Notes," a set of research specialties arrayed themselves: in the early years there were general experimental psychology, vision, mental and moral philosophy, psychiatry, and neurology. As the community developed, experimental psychology differentiated into subspecialties such as cognition and auditory perception, and new specialties in developmental psychology and comparative psychology appeared.[101]

It has sometimes been complained that Hall's insistence on publishing very nearly an "in house" journal led to unnecessary friction with psychological colleagues who were not within Hall's immediate circle but were anxious to publicize their own work. Those on whom Hall called to assist him in his venture, though, were people of known qualities and loyalties. They enabled the journal to take flight without Hall's having to risk depending on people outside of his (remarkably wide) circle. Getting the journal onto sound intellectual and financial footing—i.e., developing a community of dedicated contributors and subscribers—was Hall's first order of business. Extending a hand to the wider world, once the journal had attained a measure of success, seems to have been of secondary importance to Hall.

Still, it is surprising for Hall not to have seen that by being more magnanimous he could have both improved the quality of the work in the journal (earning the journal more scholarly respect) and made other psychologists beholden to him as the editor who had advanced their careers by first distributing their work, rather than resenting him as a parochial editor who ran a closed shop.

Although Hall worked tirelessly to legitimize psychology in the eyes of his university colleagues and those of the wider population, he worked just as tirelessly to secure his own personal position within the discipline and within the university, going so far as to undermine the claims of others, even bright students of his own, whom he thought might pose a threat to his own standing.[102] For instance, as mentioned above, James McKeen Cattell had held the department's only fellowship when Hall first took up the professorship in 1883, but Hall maneuvered behind the scenes to have it stripped from him and reassigned to John Dewey, leading to Cattell's angry departure from the university. The following year Hall refused Dewey a renewal of the fellowship. Dewey finished his degree, but soon left with Morris to Michigan. In 1885, President Gilman suggested to Hall that Morris might be lured back to fill some of the rapidly growing teaching requirements in philosophy. Hall torpedoed the proposal, claiming that his old Union Seminary hero now represented "just what ought not to be."[103] Finally, in 1887, the expanding department still in need of instructors, Gilman suggested that Dewey might be called back, or that another rising young star of the discipline, James Mark Baldwin, a recent graduate of Princeton, might be induced to come. Hall declared both to be not competent.[104]

In 1887, the B&O stock willed by Hopkins ceased to pay any dividends at all.[105] According to the school's early official historian, this state of affairs "hamper[ed] very seriously the work that was already being carried on."[106] In addition, Hall, despite having eliminated all challengers, was still feeling uncertain about his status at the school. His laboratory, although now in university buildings, did not receive the recognition and funding that other laboratories did. His journal did not receive the subsidy that other journals there did. It may have been, as Hall feared, that psychology was not respected as an equal of the better-established sciences. It is certain, however, that Hopkins was entering a period of extreme financial difficulty, and the elevation of upstart psychology was not the issue foremost in the minds of a Board of Trustees that was now unable to open the hospital and medical school that had been envisioned in their benefactor's will.

In addition to the university's financial problems, renewed labor unrest and the fear of mob violence began to descend upon the city of Baltimore, and upon the cities of the United States more generally. Strikes were growing more common again. Worker resentment of poor wages and conditions was growing. In March of 1886, there was a vast strike against Jay Gould's railroad companies in Arkansas, Illinois, Kansas, Missouri, and Texas. It is said to have involved as many as 200,000 workers and, although the strike failed, it led immediately to the formation of the massive American Federation of Labor, the better to coordinate workers' demands and actions across the nation. On May 1, 15 protesters were shot and killed by state militiamen in Milwaukee, Wisconsin when about 2000 Polish workers marched against the ten-hour workday. On May 4 a bomb was thrown during a strike rally at the Haymarket in Chicago that killed seven police officers. An unknown number of strikers were killed and injured in the ensuing melee. The following year, in November 1887, 35 African American sugar cane workers in Louisiana who were demanding $1 a day in wages were shot by the local militia, and two of their leaders were lynched.

Newspapers and politicians across the country spread the rumor that a secret, foreign conspiracy was afoot to overthrow the American system of government and replace it with a socialist tyranny, or perhaps just with anarchist chaos. Paranoia—fear especially of German immigrant labor—spread across the country. It was America's first "red scare." Baltimore, home of the 1877 rail strike that had spread violence and mayhem to many cities, and home of one of the largest populations of German workers in the country, was more jittery than most cities that "the masses" were going to rise up again to fight industry, destroy property, and kill people. Many feared again that all out, between labor and capital, might be close at hand.

For Hall, however, all of these factors—the sense that psychology was being passed over in favor of more established sciences, the visible deepening of Johns Hopkins' financial troubles, and Baltimore's descent into paranoia about the intentions of its working class—must have nudged Hall into looking for "greener pastures."

He reported in his autobiography that it came as a great shock when he was invited to a meeting in Washington, DC with Senator George Frisbie Hoar, from Hall's home state of Massachusetts. When Hall arrived, Hoar asked him to consider becoming president of a wholly new university in Worcester—a smaller city, somewhat sheltered from the worst of America's rising urban violence—that was about to be founded by one of that city's wealthiest entrepreneurs, Jonas Clark. In addition to being a senator, Hoar was the most prominent member on Clark's small Board of Trustees.

Moving away from the increasingly turbulent situation in Baltimore, and away from budgetary shortfalls over which he had no control, back to his home state to take command not just of a department but of a wholly new university that he could mold to his own vision, where psychology could be promoted even above other sciences, where from the presidential pulpit he could outshine even William James—there can be little doubt about why Hall left Johns Hopkins with all haste to take up the new and exalted role for which he been chosen.

6. President Hall of Clark University

Jonas Gilman Clark was born in 1815 outside of Worcester. After becoming a carriage-maker and running a shop in town, he had left the area around 1850 to find his fortune in California. Like so many others who ultimately succeeded there, his aim was not to dig gold out of the ground, but to supply '49ers with the supplies they required. In Clark's case, the main product was chairs. For a decade he steadily built his fortune, then he left the furniture business to invest in real estate. Among Clark's friends on the west coast was the rising industrial and political colossus Leland Stanford—rail baron, governor, senator—who would, of course, soon build a university of his own on the farm he owned south of San Francisco.

Clark moved back east in 1868, setting up in New York City, where he began to accumulate the trappings of the enormous wealth he had acquired—art, rare books, extended European excursions. He is said to have developed a deep interest in European universities, though his own education had extended only through the common school in his rural hometown. As he approached his seventies, he began to consider the possibility of establishing his own legacy by founding a college in the small industrial city near his birthplace—Worcester. Because he had not lived in the Worcester area for so long, he was not well known there, having left more than 30 years before as nothing more than a small tradesman and shopkeeper. It is difficult to know just what Clark personally understood of higher education. Clark was impressed by the grand European universities he visited on his travels, but distinctions such as undergraduate and graduate education, teaching and research, may not have been entirely clear in him. His initial vision was to found a college for poor young men of the area, as he had once been.[107] Some of the local businessmen, lawyers, and politicians he appointed to his original Board of Trustees advised him to look to modern schools such as Johns Hopkins as a model. He eventually conceded that a graduate school might be built after the undergraduate college had opened in order to offer advanced education to those members of the first graduating class who might desire to go on with such studies. Whatever caution Clark's dearth of knowledge might have prompted in those around him, this feeling was more than made up for by the sheer riches he proposed to pour into the project: one million dollars, the largest sum ever contributed by a single individual to an institution of higher learning in New England.[108]

Worcester was Massachusetts' second-largest city, with a population of 63,000 in 1885.[109] The area had first been permanently settled by Europeans in the 1710s.[110] During the Revolution it was home to Isaiah Thomas' famed rebellious newspaper, *The Massachusetts Spy*. It was an early center for New England's Industrial Revolution. It was especially well known, from the 1830s, for the production of steel wire and, from the 1850s, for its textile looms. This early industrial base made it, perhaps, somewhat more cosmopolitan than other secondary cities of the day, but also more familiar with the labor strife and struggles to integrate immigrants that often attended such developments. A Catholic college, Holy Cross, opened in Worcester as early as 1843, but it was unable to obtain a state charter until 1865 due to religious opposition.

The selection of Hall as the new institution's founding president was, in some ways, a curious one. In 1888, Hall was just 44 years of age. His career as a university professor, including his stints at Antioch and Williams, did not total even a decade. He had earned something of a public profile, especially in education, but was not considered a senior figure, even among the faculty at Johns Hopkins. Still, he impressed people with his "modesty, earnestness, and good sense."[111] Perhaps most important of all, Hall was a native of Massachusetts and, therefore, perhaps more likely to stay in a position at Worcester over the long term than, say, an equally ambitious New Yorker, Marylander, or Virginian. In this calculation, at least, Clark and his Board showed remarkable acuity. Hall would stay at Clark for the rest of his career.

Hall was not satisfied, however, to open an undergraduate college for local boys with the vague promise of a graduate school to come.[112] He persuaded Clark (or at least persuaded himself that he had persuaded Clark) to open a graduate school to rival Johns Hopkins from the outset, and then let the undergraduate school emerge from "beneath" in the years to come. Indeed, Hall was convinced that Gilman had developed the secret to successful modern higher education, and aimed to replicate his example to the best of his ability. Apparently thinking that he had come to an understanding about this with his new benefactor, Hall left Johns Hopkins in April 1888 and began to select his Clark faculty: From Johns Hopkins he took his former students Edmund C. Sanford in psychology, Herbert H. Donaldson in physiology, and William H. Burnham in education. From the Johns Hopkins faculty he poached two former students of the Leipzig titan Carl Ludwig: Warren P. Lombard who would come to be best known for his work on the physiology of nerves and muscles, topics that had also occupied Hall early in his career, and Franklin P. Mall, later credited with having revived anatomy as a vibrant scientific discipline in the US.[113] Also from Johns Hopkins, Hall brought mathematician William Story, then renowned for his work on advanced geometry, and two of his assistants, Oskar Bolza and Henry Taber. In chemistry, Hall recruited Arthur Michael of Tufts and John Ulric Nef of Purdue, each of whom discovered reactions that bear their names to this day. From the staff of *Science* magazine he enlisted the young German-Jewish anthropologist Franz Boas who would go on to revolutionize the discipline as it was then practiced. In physics he engaged from Case Institute in Cleveland Albert A. Michelson, fresh from his famous and puzzling 1887 experiment on the nature of light with Edward Morely. In zoology he won the director of the Woods Hole laboratory, Charles O. Whitman, best known for his work in comparative anatomy and for his seminal role in early ethology. In part, Hall's success at obtaining such a great array of talent came from his promise that people would have extremely low teaching obligations, and that they would be free to pursue whatever research they might desire. Some actually took cuts to their salary in order to work as such an institution.

While in the midst of these negotiations, Hall convinced Clark to delay the new school's opening until 1889 so that Hall could travel to Europe to examine the latest practices there, as well as further build his network of international connections, now armed with his prestigious title of University President. Clark agreed but, when he got word that Hall was negotiating to bring over a German professor of history, Hermann von Holst, Clark balked. Humanities had not been among the disciplines that they had agreed would be covered at Clark in the first years. Here Hall got the first inkling that Clark was not going to give him a completely free hand to run the school exactly as he hoped.[114]

Nevertheless, as the American scholarly community began to get wind of the truly impressive character of the new university in Massachusetts, other academics began to inquire whether there might be a place for them at what seemed likely to become the best new school America had seen since the opening of Johns Hopkins. Among these petitioners was none other than Charles Sanders Peirce—William James' longtime friend and Stanley Hall's one-time colleague at Johns Hopkins. Peirce had been out of the academy since his effective dismissal by Gilman, and he was beginning to see that the money he had inherited from his father almost a decade before was not going to last, especially given the younger Peirce's rather extravagant lifestyle. Nevertheless, Hall refused him, disingenuously pleading the poverty of the institution. He may not have wanted to risk the trouble that Peirce brought wherever he went. He may also have not wanted to engage a man five years his senior who was so obviously talented in so many different fields and who might well have upstaged him even on his home turf of psychology.

In the fall of 1889, Clark University opened to its first cohort of students. It was a small school—18 faculty and 34 graduate students—but by all accounts it was everything that had been promised. Donaldson called his time at Clark "splendid," and said that Hall "was the most suggestive and stimulating person with whom I ever came in contact." At least, this was true for the first year. But almost as soon as it had been woven together, the whole glorious dream began to unravel. In the spring of 1890 Hall contracted diphtheria. Incapacitated by the severe illness, he returned to his hometown of Ashfield to recuperate. While he was away, a gas leak in his Worcester home killed his wife, Cornelia, and their young daughter, Julia. His nine-year-old son, Bob, who had been sleeping in a different room at the time, survived, but Hall's personal world was irrevocably shattered.

Still recovering from his illness and emotionally suffering form his catastrophic loss, Hall traveled west to California to consider his options. He considered resigning the presidency of his beloved Clark. Although he had become a strong critic of spiritualists by this point,[115] Hall found himself drawn to a medium in a desperate effort to make sense of the sudden tragedy that had befallen him. Although he did not, could not believe in the events of the séance room, he kept the written record of what transpired there tucked into a scrapbook for the rest of his life.[116] At summer's end, Hall decided to stay on as head of the formidable institution he had just built but, upon his return, he discovered that the interest and commitment of the school's patron and namesake was already starting to fade.

Jonas Clark had hoped to become a hero to Worcester because of the great gift he had given them. But the people of Worcester did not see things that way. To many, he was a cantankerous stranger who had imposed an alien institution upon their landscape. Unlike the familiar Worcester Technical Institute, founded 25 years before by two local industrialists, Clark University employed strange and even foreign men who did not mingle easily with the townsfolk and did not even seem to offer their services as mentors to Worcester's sons. Jonas had expected an outpouring of monetary support from the local gentry, but the school received virtually none. Indeed, one of the town's newspapers, *The Telegram*, embarked on a concerted effort to criticize and antagonize the school for the lurid and possibly dangerous activities that were rumored to be conducted within.[117] The adulation that the school had earned from America's academic community notwithstanding, Jonas Clark seemed to regard his grandest venture as a failure because it, and he, did not win the admiration of the people of Worcester.

The school's problems were compounded by the personal inadequacies of the principals involved. Jonas Clark and his Board seemed unable or unwilling to make direct appeals for donations, either to Worcester's gentry or to other constituencies. They simply waited for voluntary contributions that never came. Hall was unable to persuade Clark that the new university's appeal to the scholarly and scientific world was the true measure, or even an important measure, of its astonishing success. The first year Clark personally made up the difference between the income from his initial $600,000 endowment and the actual operating costs with a check for $65,000. He offered $50,000 for the second year. He later fulfilled his original endowment pledge, bringing it up to $1,000,000, and he offered and additional $30,000 for the third year. This was reduced to $18,000 in the fourth year, and there were no further contributions after that.[118]

The Board considered options that might earn the approbation of the surrounding population—converting to an undergraduate college (the current faculty would leave), adding an undergraduate college (would require a great deal more money)—but they were as enthralled by Hall's ecstatic vision of a scientific research university as Hall was himself was. They could neither compromise on that vision, nor could they sell that vision to the people they needed to win over to succeed.

Hall attempted to appeal to the local populace by launching a summer school on pedagogy, the topic for which he was still best known outside of university circles. At first, he opened it only to principals and superintendents, unable to temper his elitist tendencies. That only exacerbated Clark's image problem with the Worcester public, however, so he soon corrected course and opened the summer school to regular teachers as well. The Worcester Normal School had opened in 1874, just 15 years before Clark, and building relations with this teacher-training institute might also help to ease tensions with the general community. In addition, access to many ordinary classroom teachers, and to their students, would support the extensive questionnaire research about the lives of children that Hall expected to conduct over the succeeding years and decades.[119] Although the summer school may have thawed feelings in town somewhat by making Clark seem less remote and foreboding, it did not change the basic relationship, and the university was forced to carry on without the financial support of its neighbors.

Making matters worse, Hall would not come clean with his faculty about the school's increasingly precarious financial state. He made promises that he later had to break without providing credible explanations. Unable to scrimp on faculty salaries without risking the possibility of losing them to better offers elsewhere, he started to press the assistants and fellows, fining them for being late or for missing days, even when they were ill. He sometimes reduced their compensation arbitrarily, or so it seemed. This, of course, irritated the professors who supervised the assistants, some of whom even threatened resignation.

Late in 1891, a powerful outsider from Chicago, seeing the difficulties with which Hall was beset, though also sharing many of Hall's academic goals, began making inquiries and offers to the most talented members of Clark's increasingly disgruntled faculty. Ultimately, the unwanted visitor would drastically change the face not only of Worcester's troubled university, but also of American higher education more broadly. His name was William Rainey Harper, and he brought with him the incalculable wealth of John D. Rockefeller's industrial empire. A new city and a new university were about to play their part in the construction of the discipline of psychology in the United States.

Notes

1 George Calvert, First Lord Baltimore had died between receiving the patent and establishing the colony.
2 Sherry H. Olson, *Baltimore: The Building of an American City*, revised and expanded bicentennial edition (Baltimore, MD: Johns Hopkins University Press, 1997), 94–98.
3 Ibid., 100–1.
4 Ibid., 103.
5 Ibid., 108–9.
6 It is little recalled that, although Stephen Douglas finished second to Lincoln in the popular vote, in the all-important electoral college he won only Missouri and part of New Jersey, finishing fourth behind Lincoln, Breckenridge, and the Constitutional Union candidate, John Bell (who won Virginia, Kentucky, and Tennessee).
7 Olson, *Baltimore*, 179.
8 The burgeoning horse-drawn street car business was largely controlled by the Irish Catholic immigrant population in Baltimore.
9 Ranking of US cities by population in 1870: 1–New York, 2–Philadelphia, 3–Brooklyn, 4–St. Louis, 5–Chicago, 6–Baltimore, 7–Boston.
10 Olson, *Baltimore*, 156.
11 *Sun,* January 30, 1872. I have taken some slight liberties here. The full passage is:

> If New York is to become another London, as her citizens fondly believe, in magnitude, in commerce, and in population, there is ample room for appreciation in city

real estate. And it will also be observed that when Baltimore shall become another New York—a consummation which may be accomplished before the end of the century—the concurrent advance in the highest present values of city property will be nearly in proportion to the increase in population.

Cited in Olson, *Baltimore*, 172

12 Although, the Peabody Conservatory of Music was founded in Baltimore in 1857, the product of a gift from the prominent Baltimore Quaker and businessman George Peabody. Peabody's extensive program of philanthropy, no doubt, encouraged his friend and fellow Quaker, Johns Hopkins, to do the same, as it did many American barons of the "Gilded Age."

13 See, e.g., Hugh Hawkins, *Pioneer: A History of the Johns Hopkins University, 1874–1889* (Ithaca, NY: Cornell University Press, 1960).

14 Joseph Brent, *Charles Sanders Peirce: A Life*, revised and enlarged ed. (Bloomington and Indianapolis, IN: Indiana University Press, 1998), 127.

15 Charles S. Peirce, "The Class of 1859 of Harvard." MS 1635, Charles S. Peirce Papers, Houghton Library, Harvard University. Cited in Louis Menand, *The Metaphysical Club: A Story of Ideas in America* (New York, NY: Farrar, Straus and Giroux, 2001), 159.

16 See Brent, *Charles Sanders Peirce*, 128.

17 Robert J Richards, *Darwin and the Emergence of Evolutionary Theories of Mind and Behavior* (Chicago, IL: University of Chicago Press, 1987), 431–32.

18 Thomas Henry Huxley, "On the Hypothesis That Animals Are Automata, and Its History," *Fortnightly Review* n.s. 16 (1874): 555–80.

19 William James, *The Principles of Psychology* (New York, NY: Henry Holt, 1890), vol. 1, 141.

20 This claim foreshadowed a position that would later be proposed by psychologist James Mark Baldwin, which is now known in evolutionary circles simply as the "Baldwin effect." For the 1878 lecture notes, see William James's "Johns Hopkins lectures on 'The senses and the brain and their relation to thought'" and "Lowell lectures on 'The brain and the mind'" in Frederick H Burkhardt, ed., *The Works of William James: Manuscript Lectures* (Cambridge, MA: Harvard University Press, 1988), 3–43 especially Lecture 6. For a trenchant interpretation of these sketchy notes, see Richards, *Darwin and the Emergence*, 431–32.

21 James William, "Are We Automata?," *Mind* 4 (1879): 1–22. See also chapter 5 of James, *Principles*.

22 Thomas Cogwell Upham's *Mental Philosophy*, first published in 1831, was used in several eastern colleges. See Alfred H. Fuchs, "Contributions of American Mental Philosophers to Psychology in the United States," *History of Psychology* 3 (2000): 1–19; Alfred H. Fuchs, "The Psychology of Thomas Upham," in *Portraits of Pioneers of Psychology*, ed. Gregory A. Kimble and Michael Wertheimer, vol. 4 (Washington, DC: American Psychological Association and Mahwah, NJ: Lawrence Erlbaum, 2000), 1–14. Noah Porter was president of Yale University. His *The Human Intellect* (New York, NY: Charles Scribner, 1868) was a popular account of conventional Scottish common sense philosophy of mind, combined with a touch of Kantian doctrine, a mixture that had been popularized in William Hamilton of the University of Edinburgh in the 1840s.

23 Porter, *The Human Intellect*, 35.

24 Robert Mark Wenley, *The Life and Work of George Sylvester Morris: A Chapter in the History of American Thought in the Nineteenth Century* (New York, NY: Palgrave Macmillan, 1917), 127.

25 Friedrich Ueberweg, *History of Philosophy*, trans. George Sylvester Morris, 2 vols. (New York, NY: C. Scribner, 1871–1873).

26 Michael M. Sokal, ed., *An Education in Psychology: James McKeen Cattell's Journal and Letters from Germany and England, 1880–1888* (Cambridge, MA: MIT Press, 1981), 48.

27 Thomas C. Cadwallader, "Charles S. Peirce (1839–1914). The First American Experimental Psychologist," *Journal of the History of the Behavioral Sciences* 10 (1974): 291–98. The article in question was Charles Sanders Peirce, "Note on the Sensation of Color," *American Journal of Science and Arts* 3rd series 13 (1877): 247–51.

28 Max H. Fisch and Jackson I. Cope, "Peirce at the Johns Hopkins University," in *Studies in the Philosophy of Charles Sanders Peirce*, ed. Philip P. Weiner and Frederic H. Young (Cambridge, MA: Harvard University Press, 1952), 282.

29 Brent, *Charles Sanders Peirce*, 121–22. Sylvester was a brilliant mathematician. Because of his Jewish heritage, however, he had difficulty obtaining a professorship in his home country. He taught briefly at the University of Virginia in 1841 but resigned after a violent confrontation with a student. He moved to New York, where his brother lived, and applied for a post at Columbia. The college refused him, probably on account of his religion, and he returned to England in 1843. In 1855 he was hired by the Royal Military Academy, Woolwich, where he worked for 14 years until forced into retirement at the age of 55, in 1869. Gilman persuaded him to become Hopkins' first professor of mathematics in 1877, and Sylvester launched the *American Journal of Mathematics* the following year, which is today the oldest continuously-published mathematics journal in the US. In 1883, at the age of 69, Sylvester was offered a professorship at Oxford, which he took up and held until his death in 1897. Since 1901, the Royal Society has awarded a medal for mathematical research named after Sylvester.

30 Wilhelm Wundt, "Philosophy in Germany," *Mind* 2 (1877): 493–518.

31 G. Stanley Hall, "Philosophy in the United States," *Mind* 4 (1879): 89–105. It appeared in the very same issue of *Mind* as James' response to Huxley. A few years before, Hall had written a short letter to the editor of *The Nation* (again, Charles Eliot Norton) sketching similar views (G. Stanley Hall, "College Instruction in Philosophy," *The Nation* 23 (1876): 180). One historian has noted that Hall devoted a surprising amount of space in the 1879 article to sketching Peirce's earliest pragmatic views, and that they may have been an important, if tacit, influence on much of Hall's work. See David E. Leary, "Between Peirce (1878) and James (1898)" G. Stanley Hall, the Origins of Pragmatism, and the History of Psychology," *Journal of the History of the Behavioral Sciences* 45 (2009): 5–20; David E. Leary, "G. Stanley Hall, a Man of Many Words: The Role of Reading, Speaking, and Writing in His Psychological Work," *History of Psychology* 9 (2006): 198–223.

32 Dorothy Ross, *G. Stanley Hall: The Psychologist as Prophet* (Chicago, IL: University of Chicago Press, 1972), 105.

33 G. Stanley Hall, *Life and Confessions of a Psychologist* (New York, NY: Appleton, 1923), 223.

34 Ross, *G. Stanley Hall*, 107–8. Hall does not even mention having taught Williams courses in his autobiography.

35 Letter from William James to Daniel Coit Gilman, July 18, 1880. In Ignas K. Skrupskelis and Elizabeth M. Berkeley, eds., *The Correspondence of William James* (Charlottesville, VA and London, UK: University of Virginia Press, 1992), vol. 5, 125.

36 G. Stanley Hall, *Aspects of German Culture* (Boston, MA: J. R. Osgood, 1881).

37 G. Stanley Hall, "Recent Researches on Hypnotism," *Mind* 6 (1881): 98–104.

38 Opposition to corporal punishment did not spread quickly. For instance, more than a decade later, in 1848, one can find a list published by the Master of the school in Stokes County, North Carolina specifying the number of lashes that each of 46 different offenses would garner—everything from 1 lash for missing a word in one's lesson "without excuse" and 2 lashes for "Not Making a Bow when you come in or go out," ranging up to 10 lashes for things like playing cards, playing bandy (a relative of ice hockey), and "Misbehaving to Girls." Reprinted in "Lists of Note," February 23, 2012. www.listsofnote.com/2012/02/school-punishments-1848.html. Accessed April 26, 2012.

39 John Dewey, *The School and Society* (Chicago, IL: University of Chicago Press, 1900), 35. Lawrence Cremin, *The Transformation of the School* (New York, NY: Knopf, 1961), 104 (cited in Ross, *G. Stanley Hall*, 124).

40 Ross, *G. Stanley Hall*, 113.

41 Hall claimed that 300 tickets were sold for the first lecture, and that attendance increased over the course of the twelve lectures (Hall, *Life and Confessions*, 217).

42 Hall, *Life and Confessions*, 217.

43 Peabody was probably the first to set up an *English-language* kindergarten, but not the first in the US per se. Margarete Meyer Schurz opened the first US kindergarten in Wisconsin in 1856, but it was by and for the German community (Sheldon H. White, "Developmental Psychology in a World of Designed Institutions," in *Beyond the Century of the Child: Cultural History and Developmental Psychology*, ed. Willem Koops and Michael Zuckerman (Philadelphia, PA: University of Pennsylvania Press, 2003), 208). Friedrich Fröbel had founded the very first kindergartens, in the city of Bad Blankenburg in the 1830s. It was a successful movement for a time, spreading to other German states but, in the aftermath of the German uprisings of 1848, an edgy Prussian government banned kindergartens as possible incubators of socialism. Many German refugees, fleeing the wave of political repression after the turmoil, set up new kindergartens once they were settled in their new homelands, including the US. William Torrey Harris, the St. Louis Hegelian, is often said to have founded the first kindergarten as well, though it seems more likely that he was their first widespread popularizer. Like most historical "firsts," much depends on definitions. Harris had moved from the Midwest to Concord, MA in 1880 but, interestingly, there is no mention of his having attended Hall's lectures even though the two were well acquainted. Nether does Francis Parker seem to have been there.

44 G. Stanley Hall, "Moral and Religious Training of Children," *Princeton Review* 9 (1882): 26–48; G. Stanley Hall, "The Education of the Will," *Princeton Review* 9 (1882): 306–25. The *Princeton Review* went by many different names between its founding in 1825 as *Biblical Repertory* and its final incarnation as *Princeton Theological Review* from 1903–1929. For most of the period between 1880 and 1888 (including the time of Hall's articles), it actually ran as two parallel periodicals: *The Presbyterian Review* (1880–1889) and *The Princeton Review* (1878–1884)/*New Princeton Review* (1886–1888). In 1890, they rejoined under the title *Presbyterian and Reformed Review* (see http://scdc.library. ptsem.edu/mets/ mets.aspx?src=prmasterindex.txt, accessed July 23, 2014). Although there was no opening editorial to explain the rationale for the split, a cursory look at the contents shows that the former was directed mainly at ministers (with articles on topics such as sacramental wine and Presbyterial care) whereas the latter highlighted somewhat more general, though still mainly religious and moral, topics (e.g., articles on the Concord School of philosophy and the place of evolution in education, the latter written by a lingering anti-evolutionist naturalist). The question of why Hall chose this vehicle in which to publish his progressive educational views is an interesting one to ponder. He had no particular connection with Princeton, though he had published his article on Dorner's theology in the same journal a decade before ("Outlines of Dr. J. A. Dorner's System of Theology," *Presbyterian Quarterly and Princeton Review* n.s. 1 (1872): 720–47; n.s. 2 (1873): 60–93, 261–73). He was also linked to a liberal branch of the Presbyterian church via his education at Union Seminary. He may well have felt that the *Princeton Review* lent his ideas the weight of traditional authority, rather than their being seen as merely "popular" or "radical."

45 Hall, "Moral and Religious," 32. Although Hall's view is often attributed directly to Ernst Haeckel, ideas of this sort were circulating before Haeckel, especially among Romantic philosophers of pedagogy, especially followers of Herbart. In this particular case, Hall attributed it to the influential German literary and dramatic theorist, Gotthold Ephraim Lessing (Ibid., 39).

46 Ross, *G. Stanley Hall*, 124.

47 Emily S. Davidson and Ludy T. Benjamin, "A History of the Child Study Movement in America," in *Historical Foundations of Educational Psychology*, ed. John A. Glover and Royce R. Ronning (New York, NY: Plenum Press, 1987), 41–59.

48 G. Stanley Hall, "The Contents of Children's Minds," *Princeton Review* 11 (1883): 249–72.

49 Ross, *G. Stanley Hall*, 126.

50 Ibid., 127.

51 Hall, "Children's Minds," 255.

52 Ibid., 255–56.

53 Henry P. Bowditch and G. Stanley Hall, "Optical Illusions of Motion," *Journal of Physiology* 3 (1882): 297–307.

54 Brent, *Charles Sanders Peirce*, 127.

55 Some of the material in this section previously appeared in Christopher D. Green, "Johns Hopkins's First Professorship in Philosophy: A Critical Pivot Point in the History of American Psychology," *The American Journal of Psychology* 120 (2007): 303–23.

56 Hawkins, *History of Johns Hopkins*, 131–34.

57 As mentioned before, Peirce was a key innovator in the practice of "pendulum swinging," which was how 19th-century scientists determined the exact shape of the Earth. He was making and recording observations up and down the east coast, from Montréal to Florida. In addition, a rare transit of Venus was coming in December 1882, and Peirce oversaw the creation of an observation station in Florida (see Max H. Fisch, "Introduction," in *Writings of Charles S. Peirce, 1879–1884*, ed. Christian J. W. Kloesel, vol. 4 (Bloomington IN: : Indiana University Press, 1986), xxxii–xxxiii).

58 Letter from C. S. Peirce to D. C. Gilman, December 18, 1880, Daniel Coit Gilman Papers, MS 1, Series 1, Box 37, Folder 3, John Hopkins University.

59 Brent, *Charles Sanders Peirce*, 133.

60 See Peter J. Behrens, "The Metaphysical Club at Johns Hopkins (1879–1885)," *History of Psychology* 8 (2005): 331–46.

61 Wenley, *The Life and Work of George Sylvester Morris*, 141.

62 Ladd married Johns Hopkins mathematics instructor Fabian Franklin in 1882, just after finishing her studies there. Although it is customary to call her "Ladd-Franklin" today, after her marriage she often published under the name C. L. Franklin. She had originally come to Hopkins under the sponsorship of the mathematics professor, James Sylvester, who was already familiar with some work she had published on the topic, extraordinarily, while she had been an undergraduate. Although Franklin's work as a graduate student was, by all accounts, exceptional, she was not permitted by university rules to be awarded a PhD, and she did not receive one from Hopkins until 1926, 44 years after what would have been her graduation.

63 Fisch and Cope, "Peirce at the Johns Hopkins University," 371–74.

64 Hall told Cattell that the decision had been Gilman's, but Gilman showed Cattell Hall's letter, in which he recommended Dewey and ranked Cattell a lowly fourth. See Sokal, *Cattell's Journal and Letters*, 78.

65 Cattell was furious at the time (see Sokal, *Cattell's Journal and Letters*) but he later admitted that the fellowship "for a thesis on Lotze... [had originally been awarded to him] by a professor of Latin, who knew even less about philosophy than I did, or the fellowship would have been given to John Dewey" (James McKeen Cattell, "Early Psychological Laboratories," *Science* 67 (1928): 547).

66 Charles Sanders Peirce, ed., *Studies in Logic by Members of the Johns Hopkins University* (Boston, MA: Little, Brown, 1883).

67 Brent, *Charles Sanders Peirce*, 128.

68 John Venn, "Review of Studies in Logic," *Mind* 8 (1883): 594.

69 Charles Sanders Peirce and Joseph Jastrow, "On Small Differences in Sensation," *Memoirs of the National Academy of Sciences* 3 (1884): 73–83.

70 J. M. Cattell, cited in Sokal, *Cattell's Journal and Letters*, 64.

71 Ross, *G. Stanley Hall*, 154.

72 G. Stanley Hall and Edward M. Hartwell, "Bilateral Asymmetry of Function," *Mind* 9 (1884): 93–109. Hartwell was a leading advocate of physical education in the United States. See Roberta J. Park, "Edward M. Hartwell and Physical Training at the Johns Hopkins University 1879–1890," *Journal of Sport History* 14 (1987): 108–19.

73 Joseph Jastrow, "Autobiography," in *History of Psychology in Autobiography*, ed. Carl A. Murchison, vol. 1 (Worcester, MA: Clark University Press, 1930), 135–62.

74 Henry H. Donaldson, "On the Temperature Sense," *Mind* 10 (1885): 399–416.

75 John C. French, *A History of the University Founded by Johns Hopkins* (Baltimore, MD: Johns Hopkins University Press, 1946), esp. pp. 57–63. The first several buildings were on the site of what is now Howard Park.

76 Fay is often described as having been an early feminist. She was the founder of the "cooperative housekeeping" movement of the late 1860s and early 1870s, which aimed to enable groups of women to pool their domestic chores in order to open up time for more elevated intellectual pursuits. Her ideas were drawn, in part, from the writings of Charles Fourier who, it will be recalled, was a favorite of Henry James, Sr.

77 Thomas was a Baltimore physician who was known to be a stickler on matters of religious propriety. He is reported to have once "interviewed and cross-examined" the prominent British philosopher James Ward for Hopkins' professorship. At the end of the discussion Thomas declared Ward to be "not orthodox enough," adding by way of explanation "at Baltimore, we are church-going people" (Letter from J. Ward to J. M. Baldwin dated September 15, 1903, published in James Mark Baldwin, *Between Two Wars, 1861–1921* (Boston, MA: Stratford, 1926), vols. 1, 118–19). Newcomb reported, in a letter to his wife, that he had thought Thomas already knew about Pierce's situation, and that he had unintentionally "let several cats out of the bag" (cited in Nathan Houser, "Introduction," in *Writings of Charles S. Peirce*, ed. Cornelius De Waal, vol. 8 (Bloomington, IN: University of Indiana Press, 1986), lxiv–lxv). This was not the only time Newcomb acted in a way that sabotaged Peirce's career, however, and some have argued that he acted out of malice (see, e.g., Brent, *Charles Sanders Peirce*).

78 Hall, *Life and Confessions*, 231. This may seem surprising, given that Johns Hopkins, the man, had been a native Marylander, but his family had been Quaker and they had emancipated their slaves as early as 1817. They had opposed slavery thereafter.

79 Hall, *Life and Confessions*, 245. Lorine Pruette also notes that Hall's first wife, Cornelia, was "intensely religious and . . . endeavored to keep him within the organized church" Lorine Pruette, *G. Stanley Hall: A Biography of a Mind* (Freeport, NY: Books for Libraries, 1926/1970), 90.

80 Nathan Houser, "Peirce as a Sign to Himself," in *Semiotics 2008*, ed. John Deely and Leonard G. Sbrocci (Ottawa, ON: Legas, 2009), 389.

81 Ladd-Franklin's assessment was reported in a letter from the mathematician Edwin Bidwell Wilson to philosopher Paul Weiss, dated November 22, 1946. The quoted passages have been cited many places, including Brent, *Charles Sanders Peirce*, 214 and Houser, "Peirce as a Sign to Himself," (though it is misattributed in the latter to the author E. B. White instead of to the mathematician E. B. Wilson). It is also in Houser, "Introduction," xcvi. It has been argued, however, that Peirce was drawing upon a psychophysiologically monist research tradition that focused on unicellular organisms, led by figures such as Max Verworn, Alfred Binet, and Herbert Spencer Jennings; see Judy Johns Schloegel and Henning Schmidgen, "General Physiology, Experimental Psychology, and Evolutionism. Unicellular Organisms as Objects of Psychophysiological Research, 1877–1918," *Isis* 93, no. 4 (December 2002): 614–45.

82 Interview of Dr. Edwin Wilson by R. Bruce Lindsay and W. J. King in June, 1963, Niels Bohr Library & Archives, American Institute of Physics, College Park, MD USA, www.aip.org/history/ohilist/5065.html. Accessed January 30, 2015.

83 G. Stanley Hall, "The New Psychology," *Andover Review* 3 (1885): 120–35, 239–48, this passage from 128–29.

84 Ibid., 130.

85 Ibid., 245.

86 Ibid., 242–43.

87 Interestingly, the young John Dewey, just graduated from Johns Hopkins, had published an article with the very same title in the very same journal just the year before: John Dewey, "The New Psychology," *Andover Review* 2 (1884): 278–89.

88 Hall, *Life and Confessions*, 232.

89 Hall had stupendous respect for Gilman as an administrator, dubbing him "the most creative mind in the field of higher education that this country has yet produced" (Ibid., 248).

90 Hall, *Life and Confessions*, 230.

91 Hall, *Life and Confessions*, 242.

92 Donaldson, "On the Temperature Sense"; G. Stanley Hall and Yuzero Motora, "Dermal Sensitiveness to Gradual Pressure Changes," *American Journal of Psychology* 1 (1887): 72–98. For more on Motora's time at Hopkins, see T. Sato, T. Nakatsuma, and N. Matsubara, "Influence of G. Stanley Hall on Yuzero Motora, the First Psychology Professor in Japan: How the Kymograph Powered Motora's Career in Psychology," *American Journal of Psychology* 125 (2012): 395–407.

93 Hall, *Life and Confessions*, 227.

94 See, e.g., Ross, *G. Stanley Hall*, 169–70.

95 Roger Clarke, *Ghosts, A Natural History: 500 Years of Searching for Proof* (New York, NY: St. Martin's Press, 2014), 94–98.

96 William was not the only member of the James family interested in mental powers and spirits. One of his brother Henry's most popular novels was *The Turn of the Screw*, published in 1898, which recast the 18th-century story of the haunting of the Tudor manor house, Hinton Ampner, in Hampshire, England (Clarke, *Ghosts, A Natural History*).

97 "Officers for the Year 1884–85," *Proceedings of the American Society for Psychical Research* 1, no. 1 (July 1885): 1; "Council of the Society," *Proceedings of the American Society for Psychical Research* 1, no. 1 (July 1885): 4. http://tinyurl.com/bwyl5ml. Accessed July 25, 2012.

98 G. Stanley Hall, "Editorial Note," *American Journal of Psychology* 1 (1887): 3–4.

99 Ross, *G. Stanley Hall*, 171 claims that introspective psychology was excluded by Hall's prohibition on "speculation." It seems unlikely that Hall would have prohibited *systematic* introspection, given Hall's later alliance with America's pre-eminent advocate of the method, E. B. Titchener. Titchener, however, would not arrive on the scene for another few years. Wundt's laboratory work, in which Hall had personally participated, can be described as having being "introspective," but there has been a great deal of confusion about this due to the term "introspection" having been used as the English rendering of two different German terms—*Selbstbeobachtung* (self-observation) and *innere Wahrnehmung* (inner perception). The first of these Wundt opposed as resulting in unreliable reports. The second, however, he favored, given certain experimental controls, as producing useful scientific data (see Kurt Danziger, "The History of Introspection Reconsidered," *Journal of the History of the Behavioral Sciences* 16 (1980): 241–62, esp. 245). Hall was ambivalent about the rigor of Wundt's laboratory practices, as we have seen above, but it does not appear that he was prepared to ban them from his new journal, and he certainly would not have dismissed them as being merely "speculative." On the other hand, he did not explicitly *include* introspection in his list of example methods in the journal's opening editorial, and such studies did not appear in the opening numbers of the journal (most of it having been authored by his immediate colleagues and students).

100 G. Stanley Hall, "Psychological Literature," *American Journal of Psychology* 1 (1887): 145–46.

101 To trace the evolution of Hall's psychological community in more detail, see Christopher D. Green and Ingo Feinerer, "The Evolution of the American Journal of Psychology, 1887–1903: A Network Investigation," *American Journal of Psychology* 128 (2015): 387–401, https://doi.org/10.1037/a0038406.

102 This insight is properly assigned to Michael M. Sokal, whom I thank for his many discussions with me about both Hall and Cattell, their aims and their characters.

103 Letter from G. S. Hall to D. C. Gilman dated August 28, 1885. In the Daniel Coit Gilman papers, MS 1, Series 1, Box 20, Folder 11, Johns Hopkins University.

104 Ross, *G. Stanley Hall*, 144–46.

105 John C. French, "Johns Hopkins University," in *Baltimore: Its History and Its People*, ed. Clayton Coleman Hall (New York, NY: Lewis Historical Publishing, 1912), 601.

106 Ibid., 603.

107 Hall says he "was much influenced by Leland Stanford's example," (Hall, *Life and Confessions*, 262), but Stanford University wasn't founded until 1891.

108 The monetary figure comes from Amy Tanner, *History of Clark University Through the Interpretation of the Will of the Founder* (Worcester, MA: Clark University Press, 1908), which is cited in Ross, *G. Stanley Hall*, 186. Although it represented a tremendous amount of money at the time—the equivalent of more than 25 million dollars today—it was still dwarfed by the endowments of Harvard and Cornell. Hall's plan to challenge these schools head-to-head was not realistic, at least in financial terms.

109 Elias Nason and George J. Varney, *A Gazetteer of the State of Massachusetts* (Boston, MA: B.B. Russell, 1890), 712–20, retrieved on 4 July 2013 from www.capecodhistory.us/Mass1890/Worcester1890.htm.

110 Earlier efforts to settle, dating back to the 1670s, had ended violently during King Philip's War (1675) and Queen Anne's War (1702).

111 The words come from a report that Senator Hoar sent to Jonas Clark after his first meeting with Hall. They are quoted in Amy Tanner, "History of Clark University through the Interpretation of the Will of Its Founder" (May, 1908), Clark University Papers, Clark University Archives, p. 37; also cited in Ross, *G. Stanley Hall*, 192.

112 See Pruette, *G. Stanley Hall*, 92.

113 Florence R. Sabin, "Biographical Memoir of Franklin Paine Mall, 1862–1917," *National Academy of Sciences Biographical Memoirs* 16 (1934): 3rd memoir.

114 This episode is reported in Ross, *G. Stanley Hall*, 199.

115 As a means of undermining spiritualists' credibility with the public, Hall had even taken to learning and performing conjuring tricks that were commonly used in séances, simply to prove that there was nothing of "the beyond" about them.

116 The report is reproduced in full in Pruette, *G. Stanley Hall*, 97–98.

117 In one case, the paper (falsely) speculated that local pets were being snatched for vivisection experiments, ginning up fear and outrage to the point that owners of lost cats and dogs were showing up at Hall's home demanding to examine the collection of experimental animals they kept. Hall often acceded to these baseless demands in order to clear the air, but his efforts did not do much to alter attitudes. See Pruette, *G. Stanley Hall*, 94–95.

118 The monetary figures are drawn from Ross, *G. Stanley Hall*, 211–13.

119 See, e.g., Jacy L. Young, "A Brief History of Self-Report in American Psychology," in *Self-Observation in the Social Sciences*, ed. Joshua W. Clegg (New Brunswick, NJ: Transaction Publishers, 2012), 45–65.

PLATE 1   Portrait of William James by John LaFarge. c. 1859. Oil on cardboard. National Portrait Gallery, Smithsonian Institution; gift of William James IV.

Credit: National Portrait Gallery, Smithsonian Institution; gift of William James IV.

PLATE 2   Portrait of Henry James Jr., about age 18, by John LaFarge, ca. 1862.

Credit: The Century Association, New York, NY.

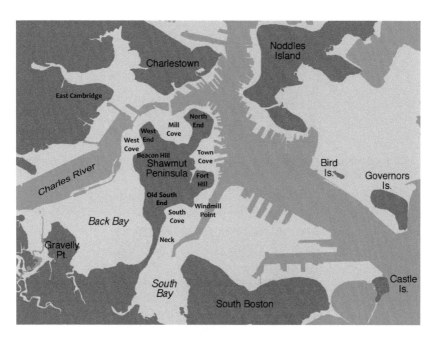

PLATE 3 The dark green areas are the original land of Boston. The light areas show the present land of Boston that was originally water or marsh. The blue shows present areas of water. Some place names added. Reprinted in black & white in Nancy S. Seasholes' magnificent Gaining Ground: A History of Landmaking in Boston. Cambridge, MA: MIT Press, 2003, facing p. 1.

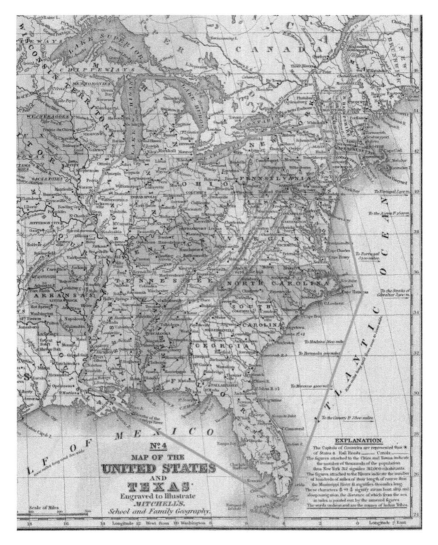

PLATE 4   Blue line (inserted) represents the course of circumnavigation made possible by the Erie Canal and Illinois & Michigan Canal.

Credit: Original image excerpted from the "Map of the United States and Texas" in *Mitchell's School Atlas*. Philadelphia: Thomas, Cowperthwait & Company, 1844. (Retrieved from www.lib.utexas.edu/maps/historical/us_texas-1839-atlas-mitchell-school-04.jpg, August 14, 2013)

PLATE 5 Union Stockyards in the 1870s.

Credit: Image retrieved from http://upload.wikimedia.org/wikipedia/commons/1/16/Union_stock_
yards_chicago_1870s_loc.jpg, August 14, 2013.

PLATE 6 Map of Chicago in the 1870s. Lake Michigan is to the right. Chicago River enters the city about halfway down the map, then splits into North and South Branches near the map's center. Pink area is the zone destroyed by the Great Fire of 1871. Union Stockyards were 20 blocks south of the lower edge of the map at 40th St. The new University and Exposition were southeast of that, in the streets numbered in the 50s and 60s.

PLATE 7 "Bowery at Night," 1895.

Credit: "Bowery at night," 1895. William Louis Sonntag, Jr. (1869–1898)/Museum of the City of New York. 32.275.2.

6
CHICAGO

1. From Wilderness Trading Post to Linchpin of the Continent

Unlike New York, Boston, and Baltimore, Chicago was never a colonial city. It did not even declare itself a town until 1833, at which point it boasted only 150 residents.[1] Before that, it had been known as Fort Dearborn, home only to soldiers and traders. As recently as 1795, the area had been held by the Western Indian Confederacy, who ceded it to the US government in the Treaty of Greenville, which ended the Northwest Indian War.[2] The main purpose of the war had been to establish the new American republic's claim to the Ohio River Valley.

Before that there had been really only a single reason that anyone would take notice of the swampy patch of land on which Chicago would be built: It was positioned where the Chicago River flowed into Lake Michigan. The river itself was not impressive—it was once described as "a sluggish, slimy stream, too lazy to clean itself."[3] But just a mile inland, the river splits into north and south branches, and just a few miles down the South Branch lies an overland passage of less than 10 miles to the Des Plaines River. The Des Plaines runs southwest into the Illinois River which, in turn, flows into the mighty Mississippi. That is to say, the narrow and unprepossessing strip of marsh between the Chicago and Des Planes Rivers serves the critical geographical function of dividing the massive Great Lakes watershed from the equally vast Mississippi River system.[4] Thus, the short *portage* across it (and often it was flooded deeply enough to be navigable by canoe) offered a potential solution America's most pressing transportation and trade challenge: how to move people and goods from the interior of the continent to the Mississippi system, up into the Great Lakes, and thence out to the Atlantic Ocean.

For the US, however, there had been another part to the problem: the only passage from Lake Ontario to the Ocean, the St. Lawrence River, was held by the British in "the Canadas"—Upper (later Ontario) and Lower (Québec). Indeed the powerful British Navy still patrolled Lake Ontario, so even the northern coast of New York State was not safe passage. This pressing question of how to safely transport goods and people from the Great Lakes to the great coastal cities of Boston, New York, Baltimore, and Philadelphia was, as we saw in the first chapter, resoundingly answered by the opening of the Erie Canal in 1825. Only then did the further question of a passage from Lake Michigan to the Mississippi system become urgent enough to focus the attention of politicians, investors, and engineers. It had been suggested as early as the 1670s by some of the area's earliest French explorers, Louis Jolliet and Jacques Marquette, that one could excavate a canal from the South Branch of the Chicago River across the marsh to the Des Plaines. This would effectively convert the entire eastern portion of the US, from New York to New Orleans into a circumnavigable "island." (See Plate 4 in the color plate section.)

Soon after the opening of the Erie Canal, though, a truly bewildering era of land speculation seized the muddy encampment named "Chicago" (after an indigenous term for a stinky wild leek that grew in the boggy flats there). Ambitious real estate dealers from the east took the tiny town by storm, buying and selling parcels of land that had been declared to line the still-fictional streets of a city that was still mostly a figment of their fevered commercial imaginations. "Lots that sold for $33 in 1829 were going for $100,000 by 1836."[5] The English social and political activist Harriet Martineau, who happened to be visiting America at the time, observed that it seemed as though "some prevalent mania infected the whole people."[6] The fictitiousness of the "city," parcels of which were then being furiously bought and sold, had no bearing on the reality of the canal that was giving rise to the madness. Starting in the 1830s, Irish immigrant laborers— some of them the very men who had dug the Erie Canal—began to excavate, by hand, the 100-mile Illinois and Michigan canal connecting the Great Lakes to the Mississippi.

With that the canal built, Chicago became the principal way station for the raw goods of the West traveling to the clamoring markets of the east coast, and to Europe beyond. For instance, the vast grain harvests of the Great Plains were shipped first to Chicago, then distributed to the east. The trade went both ways, of course—from Chicago to the prairies as well as the reverse. An important early exemplar was a pair of brothers from Virginia, Leander and Cyrus McCormick. In the 1840s they had a machine, invented by their father, that enabled farmers to harvest wheat orders of magnitude faster than it could be done by hand: the "mechanical reaper." Replacing the traditional sickles and scythes with the mechanical reaper would allow much larger farms to be efficiently cultivated, making grain not only much less expensive but also much more plentiful. However, the McCormicks and their reaper were in Virginia while the great tracts of wheat-growing land were in what was then considered the "far west."

So, in 1848, the brothers moved their small farm equipment manufacturing business to Chicago where they dubbed it the McCormick Harvesting Machine Company. It was the first major factory in Chicago and it made a great impact, employing 120 people in the first year alone, many of them skilled blacksmiths who hammered out the blades by hand (remember this; it becomes a critical issue in 1887). Selling their innovative harvesting equipment to western farmers, the McCormicks became one of the wealthiest families in the US within just 20 years.[7]

The story that is typically told of the rise of Chicago is the tale of savvy, ambitious entrepreneurs like the McCormicks who had an idea about how to revolutionize an industry (often through a new technology they had developed), saw the opportunity to make a quick fortune, and then did exactly that. Another such opportunist was William Butler Ogden, a land-speculator who had arrived in Chicago in 1835. He made a killing and, in 1837, was elected the (still small) city's very first mayor.[8] In a remarkable coincidence, the very year that the McCormicks arrived in Chicago (1848), Ogden was in the process of launching the city's first rail line westward into the Great Plains. It not only brought prairie farmers' wheat into the city faster, cheaper, and in much greater quantity than the traditional horse-and-wagon could; it could also be used to transport McCormick's machines out to the farmers so that they could, in turn, produce even more wheat to be sent, on more trains, back to Chicago. The expansion was so rapid and so great, that the existing infrastructure could not handle the load. It became necessary to invent specialized grain cars for the trains and a new, massive kind of tower called the "grain elevator." All of this, of course, made the traditional sack of grain on a horse-drawn wagon utterly obsolete: whereas before it might have taken a large crew of men days to load a train with grain, carrying individual sacks from wagons into traditional box cars, the new system could load thousands of bushels in just a few hours, the whole process carried out by just a few men. This chain of innovations was stupendously profitable for investors, but utterly disastrous for the (now former) workmen who used to carry the sacks and drive the wagons, most of whom lost their jobs. It is also a microcosm of the wider story of Chicago's economic miracles and catastrophes throughout the 19th century.

The owner of Chicago's rail line west, Ogden, went on to become president of the massive Union Pacific Railroad. Other men of similar ambition soon followed his lead and, before even a decade had passed, Chicago had more rail lines reaching into it than any other city in America, including New York. The array of new technologies that was, in Chicago, brought to bear on the problem of growing, harvesting, and transporting agricultural goods enabled the American Midwest, in just a few short years, to surpass Ukraine as the greatest grain-producing region in the entire world.[9] Having seen how a chain of innovative technologies could be used to revolutionize the grain trade, Chicago then implemented the very same sort of strategy in the lumber industry, becoming the world's largest lumber market in less than a decade.

And so it went for early Chicago in industry after industry: Pigs started to be brought down from the north, Wisconsin mainly, by train, and the city quickly became the world's largest pork market. Starting in 1867, when the train line was first extended as far west as Abilene, Kansas, cattle were driven up the legendary Chisholm Trail from as far away as Texas, then loaded on to trains bound for Chicago. This massive influx of animals to be slaughtered and processed into meat required a specialized solution of its own: in 1865, a consortium of nine different rail companies decided to consolidate their private livestock yards, then scattered all over the city, into a single massive "factory" to maximize efficiency and lower costs for everyone. The resulting Union Stockyards was situated on 320 acres of swampland just south of the city. Within just five years, the Union Stockyards were processing two million animals a year.[10] It was so successful that it operated continuously for more than a century, closing in 1971. (See Plate 5 in the color plate section.)

One hundred miles to the north, in Milwaukee, a man named Philip Armour owned a burgeoning meat-processing business. Always keen to drive down costs, on hearing of the benefits afforded by the Union Stockyards, Armour pulled up stakes and moved his operation to Chicago. To save even more, Armour developed a unique method of processing livestock by which an animal could be slaughtered and turned into roasts, chops, and steaks in as little as 15 minutes, passing by dozens of workers in the process, each of whom had one specific task to perform on the carcass. Armour dubbed his procedure the "disassembly line" and it soon became the standard in the industry.[11] As with wheat and lumber and trains before, Chicago soon became the world's largest meat packer as well.[12]

By technologically disrupting and reorganizing industry and after industry in this way, the still-young western city swiftly became a commercial "empire," a term that was frequently used to characterize its relationship to its "tributary" rural western states.[13] More than any other American city, Chicago made possible the agricultural development of the West, from the Great Lakes to the Rockies, from the Canadian border to the Mexican frontier. Had there not been a city like Chicago, Western resources and products would have remained locked inside the continent by the expense of transporting them. Chicago's great Midwestern rival, St. Louis, had direct access to the Mississippi, but not to the Great Lakes (except through Chicago), and the difference was felt as St. Louis' population fell behind that of the "Windy City" as early as the 1870s.

Chicago, by contrast, grew explosively: from 4500 in 1840 (92nd in the US); it ballooned to 30,000 by 1850 (24th), 110,000 by 1860 (9th), and then to 300,000 by 1870 (5th)—a 67-fold increase in a mere 30 years. From a soggy trading post in the 1830s, Chicago's population surpassed those of both Boston and Baltimore before 1870. By then it was looking up only at St. Louis; Brooklyn (still then separate from New York City); Philadelphia, which would be overtaken by Chicago during the 1880s; and New York.

Chicago's sky-rocketing population required a vast array of equally expansive municipal services—police, fire, schools, etc. In Chicago's brash youth, though, the bare-knuckle style of both its business and its politics blinkered it to the lessons that its older eastern cousins had learned over centuries of dealing with massive and continuous immigration, voracious capitalism, and the rising demands of the laboring classes who yearned to be simply fed, clothed, and sheltered, with a modicum of education and leisure. In short, workers understandably demanded a reasonable chance to realize the aspirations that had brought them to a city like Chicago in the first place. Immigrants poured into the place: Irish, Germans, Poles, Italians, Bohemians, each group settling into its own separate, mostly miserable ethnic enclave.

A public school system was nominally established in 1857 and it was mandated to be free for all children over five years of age in 1863, but the extreme poverty of the working classes and the lack of effective child labor laws meant that many youngsters went to work in factories and slaughterhouses to help support their wretched families. The schools were only brought under control of the mayor and a municipal Board of Education in 1872. Even then, public education remained far from truly universal.

Moreover, for all of its commercial success, Chicago was notoriously ugly and filthy. The novelist (and University of Chicago English professor) Robert Herrick once described the city as "a stupendous piece of blasphemy against nature."[14] There was no public garbage collection; no proper sewage system; no safe public water system; no restraints on pollution; nothing that might impede in the slightest the industrialists' endless acquisition of ever greater wealth. All these were matters that, decades before, New York and Boston had learned must be attended to, even if they did so imperfectly. Chicago's massive, smoky, noisy, dangerous train yards were near the center of the city, unlike New York where trains line ended far north of the downtown, at 42nd Street, to reduce smoke and noise in the city proper, as well as the danger of explosion. The stockyards were not far south of town, beginning at 40th St., with their revolting smells and sounds. Many of the Stockyard workers lived close by, in the notoriously awful district known as "Packingtown." In addition, belching, clanging factories lined the south branch of the Chicago River, cheek by jowl with much of the city's massive Irish population. Sewage flowed through open ditches into the river and ultimately into the lake that also served as the city's drinking water.[15] The city had been built on a swamp, so infectious disease was rampant and epidemics were a constant threat. Hundreds were killed by a cholera outbreak in 1849.

Finally, however, Chicago's vaunted ingenuity was brought to bear on the sewage problem in the same sort of innovative, technological way that the problem of shipping grain through the city had been. In the 1850s, a system was developed for dredging the river and using the resulting soil to raise the very ground of the city by as much as 10 feet. That gradually brought the streets up out of the swamp and allowed for proper sewers to be dug. However, it left the pre-existing buildings well below the new street level. First floors were now basements. A New York carpenter named George Pullman, who had worked on similar problem along the Erie Canal, was engaged to literally jack the buildings up to the new grade, foundations and all. The entire city center—including major stores, hotels, office-buildings, and other businesses—was steadily lifted out of the muck on Pullman's jacks. And, this incredible feat was pulled off, it was said, without their having to close for even a single business day. Nothing whatsoever was permitted to inter-fere with commerce in Chicago.

Fixing the sewage situation was critical, to be sure. But still, there were virtually no public amenities in the city—no municipal library, no sizeable art gallery, no large concert hall. Chicago was all about private wealth, and not very much at all about civic pride, or even basic civic responsibility. The city was mostly regarded as a mere "machine" for the generation of wealth, not as a good in its own right. That said, the late 1850s saw some rudimentary efforts at founding institutions of higher education, though these were mainly aimed at enhancing the local prestige of various Protestant denominations.[16] Just north of the city, in a new town called Evanston, a Methodist university dubbed "Northwestern" opened to students in 1855.[17] The year 1857 saw, in the city itself, the opening of a small Baptist insti-tution grandly named the University of Chicago. It was built on land that had been donated by Abraham Lincoln's fierce political rival, Stephen Douglas, but it struggled financially for its entire 30-year existence until finally being forced to shut its doors in 1886.[18] Soon, the Presbyterians got into the act as well, opening Lind University in 1860.[19] That school stalled during the Civil War and was not able to re-open to students until 1876, by which time it had adopted a new name: Lake Forest College.

Apart from the beginnings of higher education, the primary social amenity of mid-19th-century Chicago was invented by an Albany dry goods store owner named Potter Palmer. Having arrived in Chicago from New York in 1852, Palmer conceived a plan to encourage the wealthier women of the city to spend their plentiful riches in a new kind of store that carried a startlingly wide array of exclusive merchandise, including the latest European fashions in clothing. The selection of goods was so bountiful, in fact, that it had to be arranged into differ-ent "departments" to keep it organized. The "department store" was born.[20]

Palmer's store was itself an object of beauty—a pleasant place to pass one's leisure hours—and it was staffed with unusually polite and attentive salespeople. Palmer also pioneered advertising in local newspapers. He periodically lowered prices on desirable items for short periods of time in order to encourage poten-tial customers by come by the store: "sales," as we call them today. He made the extraordinary offer of refunding the purchase price for any item the customer found to be unsatisfactory. In essence, Palmer designed the modern diversion that we call "shopping."

Palmer eventually brought investment partners into his lucrative retail busi-ness, including a prized employee named Marshall Field, who would soon take over day-to-day management of the store while Palmer spent the bulk of his time making a (second) killing in the real estate market. He began to purchase

FIGURE 6.1 Potter Palmer's "Marble Palace" on State Street.

Credit: Photograph that ran in the *Chicago Tribune*, October 12, 1868. Image from the Chicago History Museum, ICHi-001584.

properties along the undervalued State Street. No one took much notice until 1868, when he erected there an ornate marble-fronted "palace" as his store. He then rented the building to Marshall Field who put the store under his own name but continued Palmer's profitable formula of having high-quality merchandise sold by smartly dressed and courteous staff in an elegant environment.

Of all the elite Chicago businessmen of the era, Field was perhaps the most vocal and doctrinaire in matters related to the separation of ethnic groups and economic classes. He actively discouraged immigrants from shopping at his store, and immigrants were never hired to staff Field's store. He preferred to take naïve White "country girls" and train them to his urbane needs, rather than deal with the city's European communities and what he viewed as their distasteful inferiority.

While Field minded the store, Palmer continued his reinvention of State Street as the city's high-end commercial district. In 1870, he built the elegant Palmer House Hotel which, at eight stories and 225 rooms, may have been the largest and most luxurious hotel in America at the time. Soon, as Palmer had hoped, other businesses that were hoping to cater to an upscale clientele began clamoring to move to the increasingly fashionable commercial strip. Palmer already owned most of State Street's lots by this time, which he was happy to sell or rent at exorbitant prices.

Just as these developments had begun to alleviate Chicago's reputation as an unremittingly filthy and pestilent engine of exchange, catastrophe struck. On the night of October 8, 1871, a fire broke out in the Irish quarter, in the southwestern part town.[21] It quickly spread to the factories of the South Branch, jumped across to the river's eastern bank, and then moved northward into downtown. Accelerated by the city's wooden sidewalks, the fire destroyed Marshall Field's department store, the Palmer House hotel, the city courthouse, and the Board of Trade, among other Chicago landmarks. Then it leapt across the main branch of the Chicago River to the north side of the city, where it destroyed the German quarter, the McCormick harvester factory, Cyrus McCormick's personal mansion, and William Ogden's lumber and railroad yards. About 300 were killed in Chicago's Great Fire, as it came to be called. In all, some 17,000 buildings were destroyed, and one-third of the city's population—100,000 people—were made homeless. (See Plate 6 in the color plate section.)

The destruction of the city center was nearly complete, and many in the eastern US assumed that it would permanently end what had seemed to be Chicago's preposterous existence (to those who did not understand how its very location had ordained that it be the commercial pivot point of the continent). But Chicagoans were nothing if not extraordinarily resourceful. The rubble was cleared and much of it dumped directly into Lake Michigan (to create even more valuable downtown real estate, of course). Marshall Field built an even more beautiful and enormous store. Palmer built a larger, more elaborate hotel. A new courthouse and Board of Trade were constructed as well. The McCormicks and Ogden started over as well, as did the Irish and German immigrant workers. Astonishingly, the city was mostly rebuilt within about two years' time.

As we have seen, a great deal of Chicago's early wealth was a result of new technologies enabling old occupations to be conducted on previously unimaginable scales—the mechanical reaper, the train, the grain elevator, etc. Nearly always, these new technologies displaced skilled workers, who were then forced to go find other work—often work that required less skill and therefore paid a lower wage. In addition to new *mechanical* technologies, industrialists sometimes implemented new *social* technologies in which a complicated task that required expensive skilled workers was divided into a series of simple tasks that could be executed by unskilled workers. Armour's disassembly line was a classic example of this principle of the division of labor put into splendidly profitable action.

But there were terrible social side effects. Many of the people they employed were forced to live in filthy, crowded, appalling conditions. It is often noted by historians that Herbert Spencer's "social Darwinism" was becoming increasingly popular among America's industrialists at this time, but it is easy to see that, to

FIGURE 6.2 The ruins after the Great Fire in a photo that ran in the *New York Times*.

Credit: Retrieved from http://upload.wikimedia.org/wikipedia/commons/d/d3/Chicago_in_Ruins_ after_the_Fire_of_1871,_New_York_Times.JPG, August 14, 2013

the extent this was true, it was little more than a rationalization for changes that industrialists were intent upon pursuing in any case. Social philosophy was not their *métier*. Business was, and most of these men simply had no conception of, let alone interest in, ameliorating the social problems that their commerical successes might have created. Their sole focus was on relentlessly driving down costs in order to increase returns, regardless of the implications for anyone else. They had mostly risen from modest backgrounds themselves, and they expected everyone else who was capable to do the same. Those who were not capable—and most of them assumed that the immigrant "hordes" were not—got exactly what they were worth, so far as most industrialists were concerned.

Some people were less sanguine in their estimation of the city and its effects on its people. Charles Dudley Warner, co-author with Mark Twain of the satirical 1871 novel *The Gilded Age*, lamented, with respect to Chicago's notorious south side in 1889, that,

> the manufactories vomit dense clouds of bituminous coal smoke, which settle in a black mass in this part of town so that one can scarcely see across the streets in a damp day, and the huge buildings loom up in the black sky in ghostly dimness.[22]

One recent historian of the city phrased the matter rather more starkly, "Chicago wore its cloud like a black halo."[23]

Of course, the impoverished immigrants who lived under these conditions hadn't come from nowhere. They came from other places that had their own histories of social hierarchy, and their own battles to redress the imbalances created by entrenched social and economic privilege. By the 1870s, many immigrants were arriving from central and eastern Europe, where socialist political movements were well known and where violent revolutions had been attempted. As wages in Chicago were ruthlessly cut—whether in the wake of an economic crash or as fallout from the introduction of new industrial technologies—poverty spread farther and the horrors of the tenement slums grew greater, intensifying the workers' sense of desperation, alienation, and, ultimately, rage. Mass protests and strikes started to become frequent in Chicago. The police (and private security guards hired by factory owners) often responded with gunfire and other forms of deadly force. Although the industrialists could be implacable with their own workers, they could be quite generous when it came to purchasing weapons to be turned upon their employees. Marshall Field, for instance, bought four canons and a Gatling gun for the Chicago police to use on strikers and anarchist protesters.

As the rhetoric of the radical pamphleteers, speakers, and protest marchers became more furious, the uneasy feeling spread that the country was verging on a second civil war, this one a contest between capital and labor. In 1877, as recounted in the last chapter, massive violent strikes had erupted throughout the eastern part of the country, including Chicago, after railroad barons had conspired to drive down workers' wages.

One of Chicago's wealthiest entrepreneurs saw that the status quo was likely, sooner or later, to destroy them all—owner and worker alike—so he offered up a novel solution. It was George Pullman, the man from New York who had been hired to jack Chicago's buildings up out of the muck two decades earlier. Like many who had come to Chicago for a temporary job, he had stayed on for the lucrative opportunities that were available. Pullman had decided that there was money to be made in reinventing passenger train travel, to make it more comfortable—even luxurious—for the average traveler. So, instead of hard benches and dirty wooden floors, he built what he called "palace cars" appointed with carpeting, curtains, upholstered seats, and cozy sleeping berths. Food was freshly prepared and served on china dishes by waiters at tables. Many had scoffed at the idea, but Pullman made a fortune leasing his cars to all of America's major railroads.

Pullman may have been personal friends with Field, but he did not share Field's blanket disdain for working people. Although revolutionary for his time, Pullman believed that putting people into beautiful surroundings, no matter their personal histories, had the power to elevate their behavior. The obvious extension of this was that, in order to improve the conduct of his employees, and to deter the disruptions of strikes and riots borne of desperation, he had to move his workers and their families out of the slums, away from the saloons, and provide them with decent, comfortable housing in a safe, attractive neighborhood that featured interesting, wholesome diversions. Provide for them all of these things, he maintained, and they will raise themselves up socially and culturally. That is, Pullman would try to solve the growing conflicts of the age not with laws and guns, but with a kind of social engineering. And, of course, he would make an enormous amount of money at the same time.

The concrete extension of Pullman's philosophy was that, in 1880, he built a complete model town a few miles south of Chicago proper. He named it after himself: Pullman, Illinois. It was full of clean, spacious homes designed with diverse attractive layouts, all set upon charming tree-lined streets, complete with shops, schools, churches, parks, facilities for social clubs, and even a hotel. But no saloons.[24] Next to his town—but not so close that it wrecked the town's serene character—Pullman built his train car factory so that his workers could easily walk to their jobs and back home every day. He employed as many as 12,000 workers at a time. All of the workers were required to live in his town and to adhere to a code of conduct devised by himself.

For a time, it seemed to work remarkably well. Paternalistic though it was, workers found themselves living under far better conditions in the company town than they had been in the dreadful slums of "Packingtown" behind the Union Stockyards, or near the belching factories along the South Branch. Pullman's novel labor scheme turned out to be so beneficial to his industrial enterprise that he also built, as his company headquarters, an almost incomprehensibly huge ten-story "sky-scraper" in downtown Chicago.

Impressive as the Pullman headquarters was, however, it was hardly the only building rising to new heights over Chicago. The recent invention of the Bessemer furnace was making inexpensive steel available for all kinds of previously unimaginable uses. It is hardly an exaggeration to credit the Bessemer process with making the mid-century train revolution possible.[25] Soon, however, architects and engineers in Chicago, New York, and other cities were developing revolutionary designs for buildings based on steel skeletons, which could, in principle, rise to almost any height imaginable. The skeleton would then be covered with

FIGURE 6.3   Photo of a typical street in Pullman today.

comparatively lightweight "curtain walls" of brick or stone rather than having every stone in the building bear the load of the rest of the building above it.

Young architects in Chicago, most notably Louis Henry Sullivan who had arrived in Chicago in 1873 as a 17-year-old, employed the new technology to develop a wholly new style for such buildings: he stripped them of much of their traditional ornamentation above street level, enabling the awe-inspiring height itself to serve as a key aesthetic element. At first, curtain walls were made to imitate traditional ideas of what a building should look like—stone or brick. But since the walls no longer served a load-bearing function, Sullivan soon realized that they could be made from almost anything. "Form," Sullivan famously declared, "follows function." He started replacing large sections of wall with enormous plates of glass. No one had ever seen anything like it. Plate glass windows allowed a tremendous amount of exterior light into the building in an era when interior illumination remained an ages-old challenge, and when electric lighting was still in its dim and unreliable infancy. But plate glass also had a side effect: it allowed people on the outside to see right into the building. Merchandisers started using the massive windows to display their wares and entice into their stores people who just happened to be walking by on the street outside. "Window dressing" suddenly became a pressing issue for retailers, and "window shopping" came into existence as a new leisure activity.

Windows served more than these concrete functions, however. They became part of the "brand" of modern architecture. Sullivan, for instance, often arranged his windows in sets of threes: a large central square pane flanked by two narrower rectangular panes of the same height. It became the signature of the "Chicago Style."

As the population of the city increased and the downtown buildings grew taller and filled with greater numbers of workers, public transportation became an increasing challenge. Horse drawn carts and cable cars, run by myriad private companies, clogged streets everywhere. In 1881, a dodgy Philadelphia financier named Charles Tyson Yerkes arrived to declare that he could resolve the mess. Yerkes first consolidated the various private transit companies. Then he replaced the horse cars with cable cars, and later with electric trollies. Finally, to get the trains out of the increasingly clogged streets, in 1892 he elevated the tracks above the road into approximately the configuration one sees there today, creating the original "L Train." Although he brought a momentous transformation to Chicago and to the lives of its residents, he was also among the most corrupt of men in a city already infamous for its corruption. He seems to have been disliked and distrusted by nearly everyone. Eventually, he was hounded out of town by attacks, legal and otherwise, but only after having made $15 million for himself. Afterwards, he went to London, England, where he was a central figure in the building of that city's famous underground train system, the "Tube."

FIGURE 6.4 Photograph of a building with Chicago style windows.

By the mid-1880s, the tensions between capital and labor were as strained as ever. The German immigrant community had taken the lead among workers,[26] and many of them had left the ranks of socialists for the even more radical anarchists. The anarchists openly advocated violent overthrow of the system. Some wrote elegies to dynamite for the cheap, instant power it delivered into the hands of the underclass. Throughout the 1880s, there were increasingly large and threatening protest marches and strikes. By 1886, the key issue had become the eight-hour workday. This demand was supported even by Chicago's Democratic mayor, Carter Harrison, who had built a hugely successful political career acting as a bridge of moderation between the two seemingly implacable sides. After a long and terrible battle, the large Chicago meat-packing houses finally agreed to the limit the normal workday to eight hours, without cutting wages.

Flushed with success, the protesters then turned their attention on a long-running strike at the McCormick harvester factory. The founder, Cyrus, was now two years dead, and his son was busy replacing skilled metal workers with new machines that could stamp out blades automatically. "Scabs" had kept the factory operating for months during the strike but, on May 3, at the end of their shift, the scabs were attacked by the factory's regular workers. Police were called in and they fired on the strikers, killing at least two of them. A protest rally was called for the next day at Haymarket Square. Many of the socialist and anarchist leaders addressed the massive crowd, issuing their noisy calls for overthrow, but the rally remained peaceful. Legions of police monitored events, though they permitted the rally to proceed. Mayor Harrison attended for a time as well, but left in the evening, recommending to the police that they do nothing. As the last speaker of the day was reaching his climax, the police inexplicably decided to move in and break up the event. Someone—no one knows who to this day—threw a bomb. In the explosion and the panic that followed, seven policemen were killed (some, it appears, were hit by the wild gunfire of their own colleagues rather than by the blast). An unknown number of protesters were killed as well. Days of rioting and running battles with police ensued. The rumor spread that the anarchists were about to declare war on industry, government, and perhaps on law itself.

News of the chaos in Chicago spread across the country instantly, and similar fears of imminent revolution gripped many cities across the nation. The ensuing "crack-down" was like nothing the US had seen since the Civil War. In Chicago, martial law was declared. For weeks afterward, police arbitrarily raided and destroyed union and left-wing political offices, arresting hundreds of people associated with the labor movement, most with only the most tenuous ties to the events at Haymarket. Eight of these were charged with the bombing, although it seemed clear from the outset that none of them had a hand in the act itself. What was put on trial was anarchism itself, as one of the prosecutors declared in court.[27] After what was regarded by many as little more than a show trial, all eight of the defendants were convicted and seven of them were sentenced to death by hanging. Two of the condemned later had their sentences commuted to life in prison. Another committed suicide in jail. The remaining four were hanged in November of 1887.[28]

Just two months after the executions, in January of 1888, a new work of fiction appeared in bookshops that aimed to chart a course away from civil war and self-destruction, away from competition and confrontation, and toward cooperation and reconciliation. It told the story of a wealthy Bostonian gentleman, Julian West, who, after having been put to sleep by a Mesmerist, awoke to find himself in the year 2000. He soon found that the world around him had been utterly transformed, technologically and economically. There was no more labor strife because there was no more poverty. There were no slums, nor were there dirty and dangerous mines and factories. The corporations had gradually, peacefully—not by means of violent overthrow—been absorbed into the state and integrated into a vast public enterprise in which everyone had an equal stake. Each person was drafted into the labor force at the age of 21 and retired at the age of 45.[29] Hours were adjusted according to the arduousness of the labor required. In many cases, new technologies had alleviated the need for human labor entirely. Salaries—equal for all—were delivered by means of a card, much like today's debit cards, rather than by cash. The card could be used to purchase goods at well-stocked public storehouses that remarkably foreshadowed today's "big box" stores.

The novel was titled *Looking Backward* and its author, Edward Bellamy, was a Massachusetts-born journalist and the son of a Baptist minister.[30] Bellamy's book was the sensation of the era—perhaps the second most read book of the 19th century behind only *Uncle Tom's Cabin*.[31] It sold 200,000 copies in its first year.

Although Bellamy's prophecy was decried by some as totalitarian, his vision was intoxicating to the many who were looking for a peaceful escape from what seemed to be a looming and inevitable conflagration. The book inspired the appearance of over 160 Nationalist Clubs: political organizations that advocated the peaceful nationalization of major industries.[32] In the wake of the social movement to which *Looking Backward* gave rise, Bellamy launched a magazine, *The New Nation*.[33] He was also influential in the creation of the *People's Party*—the "Populists"—which, in the early 1890s, scored a series of electoral wins in Western farm states with a radical platform of abolishing the national banks and nationalizing the railroads and telegraphs. In 1897, Bellamy published a sequel to *Looking Backward* titled *Equality*. He died the following year at the age of just 48.

John Dewey, then still a junior instructor at the University of Michigan, was one of those deeply impressed by Bellamy and his vision. Dewey would later laud him as having been a "Great American Prophet."[34] Many credit Bellamy with being the first to sketch the vision that motivated the Progressive Era of the early 20th century.

2. The (New) University of Chicago

The richest man in America at the time, John D. Rockefeller, took in these portentous events. His sprawling commercial empire, Standard Oil, dominated the still relatively young petroleum industry. Standard's headquarters was in Cleveland, where it had begun, until 1885, when Rockefeller moved the business to New York

City. When considering the Rockefeller commercial empire, it is worth recalling that there were no automobiles in America yet and, although oil was about to come into use in some locomotives, the vast majority of trains were still fuelled by coal. It is often forgotten that Rockefeller made most of his money merchandising kerosene for commercial and personal household use.[35] Kerosene had become stupendously important for basic lighting and heating. It was far cheaper than whale oil, the main alternative for lamps, and much cleaner for heating than coal.[36]

Rockefeller was not only fabulously wealthy; he was also devoutly Baptist. When the old Baptist University of Chicago closed in 1886, Lake Forest College, a Presbyterian institution, started to muse about incorporating the word "Chicago" into its name to benefit from the city's growing prestige. The Baptists were horrified at the prospect and appealed to Rockefeller to help them found a new University of Chicago that would keep the name attached to their denomination. He agreed and, using the Baptist minister Frederick Taylor Gates as his intermediary, Rockefeller made combined donations of over $80 million during the school's first few years.[37] The land on which the school sat, in south Chicago, was donated by Marshall Field. The school's first president was William Rainey Harper, an academic prodigy (he earned his Bachelor's degree at the age of 13 and a PhD at 18) who had become a leading ancient languages professor at Yale by the age of 30. It was at this time that he became acquainted with Rockefeller, who personally selected him to be the founding president of the new university.

Harper began touring the country, offering extraordinarily high salaries to recruit some of the best academic talent the nation had to offer. It was at Stanley Hall's Clark University that he found his most fertile hunting grounds. Harper's and Hall's visions of the modern university were uncannily aligned: emphasis on research and graduate education, less focus on classroom teaching.[38] As a result, Clark already had exactly the kind of faculty that Harper was looking for. Fortunately for him, they were becoming disenchanted with Hall's arbitrary and sometimes duplicitous leadership and, so, were open to Harper's entreaties. In the end, two-thirds of Clark's faculty left in 1892. Half of those went with Harper to Chicago, including the anatomists Whitman and Mall, Donaldson in biology, Nef in chemistry, and Michelson in physics.[39] The other half scattered to other places: the physiologist Lombard went to Michigan, the anthropologist Boas to Columbia. Hall was furious with Harper and accused him of running a "Standard Oil institution."[40] Harper's response was to offer Hall himself a professorship in psychology. Hall refused but there was nothing he could do to prevent Harper's "raid" which, in the end, was not all that different, if wider in scope, from what Hall had done to Gilman and Johns Hopkins a few years before. Hall was forced to raise assistants into faculty positions to keep Clark's biology and physics departments open. Chemistry closed for a time. Math retained William Story. The only department to remain essentially intact was psychology, including its pedagogical sub-department. The Clark dream was shattered or, rather, much of it packed up and moved to Chicago.

Where Harper faced a dilemma, however—much as Gilman had 15 years before at Hopkins—was in the department of philosophy and its associated area of psychology. In 1892, he hired Charles Augustus Strong at the rank of associate professor. Strong had a good academic pedigree: he was the son of the head of the (Baptist) Rochester Theological Seminary. He had studied philosophy and psychology at Harvard with William James. He became lifelong friends there with another student, George Santayana, who would later become a renowned Harvard philosophy professor in his own right. A year after graduation, Strong and Santayana went off to Berlin together to further their studies, Strong with Carl Stumpf and Friedrich Paulsen in Berlin.[41] On his return to America, Strong became a docent in psychology under Stanley Hall at Clark, and then he taught part-time at Cornell. Strong had another "qualification," however, that doubtless trumped all others: in 1889, he married John D. Rockefeller's oldest child, Bessie. The two families had known each other as far back as 1865 when Strong's father had served for a time as pastor at the Rockefellers' Baptist church in Cleveland. The Strongs had moved to Rochester in 1872, but they remained close to the Rockefellers and, eventually, became in-laws to them.

The obvious advantages of his Rockefeller connection aside, because Strong had not completed a doctorate, Harper felt he could not give him a full professorship at Chicago. Either he would have to earn one, or someone else would be hired as professor. In the meantime, Strong set up Chicago's first experimental psychology laboratory.

In addition to Strong, Harper hired to the philosophy department a former Yale student of his own, James Hayden Tufts. Tufts was then working as an instructor at the University of Michigan, where he had established that school's first experimental psychology laboratory. Tufts was originally from Massachusetts, descended of old and highly educated New England stock: his father had attended Yale and his paternal grandfather had gone to Rhode Island College (later Brown University). On his mother's side, his grandfather had graduated from Dartmouth in medicine. Tufts himself had gone to Yale where he had taken classes not only from Harper, but also from the philosopher-psychologist George Ladd.[42] He then completed a doctorate in Freiburg under the neo-Kantian philosopher, Alois Riehl. Afterwards, Tufts was called to Michigan as an instructor by John Dewey, who was just starting out as the new professor of philosophy.

3. Dewey at Michigan

Moving backward in time, for a moment, Dewey had followed his mentor, George Sylvester Morris, from Johns Hopkins to Michigan in 1884, induced by the promise of an instructorship. Dewey had another connection to Michigan, however: back in the town where he had been born and raised—Burlington, Vermont—his parents had been friends with the president of the university there, one James Burrill Angell. The Dewey boys had been good friends with Angell's children.[43]

Angell had left Vermont in 1871, when John Dewey was only 12, to take up the presidency of the University of Michigan, a position he would hold for the next 38 years. So, when Dewey arrived at Michigan as an instructor in 1884, he brought greetings to his new boss from the president's old friends, Dewey's parents. The academic world of 1880s America was an intimate one.

Dewey was born in 1859 and raised in a strictly Congregationalist household that was nominally headed by his father, a well-read but untutored grocer named Archibald Dewey. For most purposes, however, the family was *led* by his evangelical mother, Lucina Rich.[44] Although neither she nor her husband had attended college, Lucina's brothers had, and she was determined that her boys would get higher educations as well.[45] When Dewey enrolled at the University of Vermont, the entire faculty complement consisted of eight professors, and his graduating class amounted to just eighteen students. It was there, however, that Dewey first encountered evolutionary theory, particularly that of Thomas Henry Huxley, whose textbook was used in the physiology course. Science was interesting to him, but Dewey fell under the sway of the professor of philosophy, Henry Augustus Pearson ("HAP") Torrey. Torrey was eclectic in his viewpoint, but much impressed by the work of Immanuel Kant (at least as re-interpreted by the English Romantic philosopher Samuel Taylor Coleridge in the 1825 book, *Aids to Reflection*).[46] His inclination toward Idealism rubbed off on the young Dewey and prepared him for the Hegelian turn he would later experience. After graduating from college, Dewey was offered a high school teaching job by a cousin who was a principal in the northwestern Pennsylvania boomtown of Oil City.[47] While teaching classics, science, and algebra, Dewey read philosophy on the side. After two years there, he returned to Burlington, where he wrote an essay on the metaphysics of materialism, which he sent to the editor of the *Journal of Speculative Philosophy*, William T. Harris, then still based in St. Louis. Harris decided to include the paper in the *Journal* and it became Dewey's very first publication.[48] He soon published two additional papers in *JSP*, and it was through these articles that Dewey became known to George Sylvester Morris (also a native of Vermont) under whose supervision he would complete his graduate studies at Johns Hopkins.

Later, as professor of philosophy at Michigan, Morris continued on in the "Christian Hegelian" mode that had made him seem to President Gilman of Hopkins a poor fit to Hopkins' scientific ethos and even a little "dangerous" in the context of Baltimore's guardians of religious orthodoxy. Dewey was, of course, sympathetic to Morris' line of thinking, but he was also intrigued by the more empirical approaches that he had observed in both Peirce and Hall.

One of Dewey's primary aims at this time was to update the Hegelian account of science in light of the recent discoveries in physics by European figures such as Hermann Helmholtz, Michael Faraday, and James Clerk Maxwell. Rather than seeing these developments as challenges to the Hegelian view of science, Dewey cast Maxwell's new "field theory" as a validation of Hegel in which the opposition between forces of attraction and repulsion found in Newton's mechanics had been tangibly brought into synthesis.[49] Further, Dewey believed that he could use this development as a model for solving the question of human consciousness by realizing a similar synthesis of the opposition between neural excitation and inhibition.[50] Indeed, Dewey's faith in the necessity of Hegelian syntheses to authentic scientific progress led him to reject, from the outset, any theory of mind that relied on mechanistic or causal processes. Instead, he perpetually sought out concealed "identities," "balances," and "coordinations"—all alternative labels for Hegelian "synthesis."

At this time, Dewey was still not well known outside of his immediate circle. Two 1886 articles in the British journal *Mind*, however, brought him to the attention of a wider philosophical audience.[51] Soon after, Dewey published a textbook on psychology in which he attempted to integrate the empirical and idealistic approaches to the subject.[52] The result was an unfortunately convoluted mix of experimental fact and grand metaphysical system. For instance, he defined psychology as,

> the science of the reproduction of some universal content or existence, whether of knowledge of or action, in the form of individual, unsharable consciousness. This individual consciousness, considered by itself, without relation to its content, always exists in the form of a *feeling*; and hence it may be said that the reproduction always occurs in the medium of feeling. Our study of the self will, therefore, fall under the three heads of Knowledge, Will, and Feeling.[53]

Individual minds were, as in Hegel, said to be reflections of some grand universal Mind but, unlike in a pure philosophical system, one could not simply dismiss the many seemingly contingent departures from the Ideal—misperceiving, forgetting, bungled reasoning—as mere flaws in the metaphysical "mirror." They had to be integrated into the overall scheme, even if the process became somewhat Procrustean along the way.

Stanley Hall, perhaps then at the height of his insistence that psychology be "scientific" (in some firm, but not terribly well specified sense) bristled at Dewey's attempt to weave the extravagantly metaphysical and the firmly empirical together into a single fabric. (This was, perhaps, ironic given its similarity to some of Hall's early efforts.) In the very first issue of his new *American Journal of Psychology*, Hall published a scathing review of Dewey's book, excoriating it as tendentious and error-ridden:

> That the absolute idealism of Hegel could be so cleverly adapted to be "read into" such a range of [psychological] facts, new and old, is indeed a surprise as great as when geology and zoology are ingeniously subjected to the rubrics of the six days of creation. . . . [T]he author is more intent on

the mutual interpretation and coherence of his network of definitions than he is than on their relation to facts.[54]

William James, by temperament somewhat gentler than Hall, expressed his disappointment, in a private letter to George Croom Robertson, the editor of the journal *Mind*. He observed that Dewey had failed to "mediate between the bare miraculous Self and the concrete particulars of individual mental lives."[55]

Robertson complained in a published review that "the author . . . has a way at times of resorting to a kind of kaleidoscopic play of antitheses, which tend to pass over into one another in a manner more dazzling than edifying."[56] Even Dewey's own pupils made known their consternation with their professor's abstract, sometimes convoluted ideas. An 1888 issue of an undergraduate magazine at Michigan called *The Oracle* satirically "reported" that students were "vending the only authorized translation of Dewey's *Psychology* at fabulous prices."[57]

Whatever the feelings of the advocates of the "new psychology" might have been, the book was well-enough received by the more conventional philosophical community that, in 1888, Dewey was offered a professorship at the University of Minnesota. He might have spent his career there except that, before his first school year there was out, Dewey's longtime mentor, Morris, died suddenly of a pneumonia he had contracted during a winter fishing trip. Dewey was hastily called back from the far northwest to take over as professor of the Michigan philosophy department.

By this time, the course of Dewey's own thought had begun to depart from that of Morris.[58] Partly his intellectual movement was attributable to his naturally strong faculties developing in an environment finally independent of the trammels of his mentor. Dewey was of a different generation than Morris, and he was maturing in a world that was evolving more rapidly—socially, economically, politically, intellectually—than it had ever before. Another part of the change, however, was prompted by one specific person—a woman whom Dewey had met in a boarding house when he had first arrived in Ann Arbor. She was a Michigan native named Alice Chipman. She later became a student in some of his courses. She came from a family of social activists. The grandfather who raised her, Frederick Riggs, had been a vocal defender of the Chippewa Indians with whom he traded furs amidst the increasing incursions of the US Government. Alice's overriding interests were in the social and political challenges that faced America at the time—the injustices that she saw all around. This was fascinating to Dewey, a man who had spent all of his early life in a conventional Christian household in largely rural Vermont. Although Alice thought Dewey was brilliant, she also found his mind to be hamstrung by the abstractions of his philosophical system; he needed to get more firmly grounded in the real world, she thought, especially in the radical social reforms that seemed to be hurtling toward most American cities. Whatever intellectual differences the two may have had, they must have found compensating compatibilities as well, because they became husband and wife in 1886.

FIGURE 6.5   Photo of young John Dewey.

Credit: John Dewey papers, Special Collections Research Center, Southern Illinois University Carbondale.

As the head of the Michigan philosophy department, Dewey began to gather around him a circle of unusual instructors and students who increasingly came to focus on the question of how naturalism, especially evolution, might be made foundational to the explanation of both the psychological and social worlds. These new men included James Tufts, discussed above, whom Dewey hired as an instructor in 1889. Tufts resigned the position in 1891 to take up the assistant professorship offered by Chicago, but the two remained close. Dewey filled the hole left by Tufts' departure with George Herbert Mead, who had taken a bachelor's degree under James at Harvard. Although Mead would gain fame as a social philosopher, in his early career at Michigan, he mostly taught the experimental psychology courses.[59] In 1891, Dewey also hired another Harvard graduate, Alfred Henry Lloyd, as an instructor of philosophy. Lloyd had been a student of Josiah Royce's and, thus, continued to work within the Idealist metaphysical tradition more than the other Michigan philosophers.[60] Another member of Dewey's inner circle was the university president's young son, James Rowland Angell, born in Burlington, Vermont, like Dewey, while his father had been president of the university there. The younger Angell had completed his undergraduate degree at Michigan and was working on a master's degree in 1890. The following year he would go to Harvard to earn a second master's under James;[61] then he would leave for Europe to pursue doctoral studies.

All of these men were "progressive" in temperament, although that word had not quite yet crystalized into the mass movement it would become in a few years' time. They offered an innovative curriculum, including laboratory psychology. Extraordinarily, for the time, they sometimes graded on the basis of quizzes or even journals, rather than on formal examinations. They experimented with interdisciplinary courses. Dewey began to secularize his course offerings—even the ethics course he had inherited from Morris. Still, he maintained his own Congregational church membership—partly out of respect for his still-living, still-devout mother—until he left Michigan for Chicago.[62]

The year 1890 was a crucial turning point in the history of Dewey's thought and for that of American psychology more broadly. It was the year that William James' long-awaited textbook, *The Principles of Psychology*, appeared on bookstore shelves. It was a massive work, over 1400 pages spread across two stout volumes. In the twelve years since the New York publisher Henry Holt had commissioned the book, James had published a number of articles that hinted at the sort of discipline he envisioned, but the full picture was not in public view until the publication of the *Principles*. Laboratory physiology informed James' thought—two chapters on the brain opened the book—but it was evolutionary theory that gave it life. A chapter on habit—"the enormous fly-wheel of society,"[63] James called it—immediately followed those on the brain. This was an unusually prominent position for the topic. Wundt, for instance, had virtually nothing to say on the topic of habit. The topics that had traditionally dominated psychology were all found much later in the book—consciousness in chapters 9 and 10; attention in chapter 11; association in chapter 14; memory in chapter 16; sensation and perception in chapters 17 and 19; reason in chapter 22; emotion in chapter 25; and will—perhaps the *sine qua non* of Medieval philosophy of mind—was pushed all the way back to the third-to-last chapter, 26.

Habit, however, gave James a critical "specimen" that he could use to alter the discipline's course in an evolutionary direction: habits, unlike sensations, are obviously not inherent in the as-yet-untouched mental apparatus of the infant.[64] In precise contrast, habits are acquired by the organism in the course of its life—through active, hard, dirty, sometimes dangerous interaction with the environment. And the story does not end with the simple learning of habits. Even after they are initially won, they continue to be tested, challenged, and modified in a never-ending cycle of attempts, failures, efforts, set-backs, risks, dumb luck, and (occasionally) success. James' psychology was not about the structure of an ethereal spirit or soul, like it was for the Idealists; it was corporeal through and through. It was about living in the hurly burly of the real world: eating, fighting, reproducing, defending, searching, sleeping. It was about being fit not only to survive but to thrive. The primary evolutionary advantage that having a mind gave to the organism, according to James, was the ability to foresee, if still imperfectly, the contingencies that might be met on one's journey through the world, and to select the actions that might help one best navigate that "landscape." This, according to James, was the only reason that natural selection had saved so exotic a thing as consciousness from the scrapheap of, perhaps, a hundred million years of evolutionary history.[65] This emphasis on the relationship of the organism to the environment also had the advantage of offering an obvious framework on which to hang an applied psychology, a project that had been wholly absent from the abstractions of German physiological psychology.

Unlike both the philosophers who had preceded him and the German experimentalists who were his contemporaries, for James the organism and its environment thoroughly infused each other. There were no truly "pure" sensations, no "pure" thought, no "pure" action for the psychologist to study. One (such as Wundt) might endeavor to construct conditions so far removed from everyday life that they appeared to reveal such entities in their solitary glory but, in James' view, these "pure" objects were essentially artifacts of the laboratory and, thus, of little use to the proper work of the psychologist. In reality, James contended, consciousness is a like a stream, continuously flowing through our lives. It is only by artificially segmenting it into mental "objects" for the purposes of analysis that we come to think of it as a "chain" or "train" of thought. This metaphor of the "stream" is widely attributed to James today, but James himself borrowed it from Alexander Bain,[66] the British Empiricist philosopher whose work had been the focus of many discussions in the Metaphysical Club in the early 1870s.

The revolutionary heft of James' masterwork was evident in the first couple of pages of the first volume, in which James explained in terms so clear that every reader—from casual amateur browser to wizened university professor—could see why the old metaphysical approaches to psychology, such as the one that Dewey had attempted to salvage in his 1887 textbook, were permanently doomed to failure.

> Any particular cognition, for example, or recollection, is accounted for on the soul-theory by being referred to the spiritual faculties of Cognition or of Memory. These faculties themselves are thought of as absolute properties of the soul; that is, to take the case of memory, no reason is given why we should remember a fact as it happened, except that so to remember it constitutes the essence of our Recollective Power.... [But] why should this absolute god-given Faculty retain so much better the events of yesterday than those of last year, and, best of all, those of an hour ago? Why, again, in old age should its grasp of childhood's events seem firmest? Why should illness and exhaustion enfeeble it? Why should repeating an experience

strengthen our recollection of it? Why should drugs, fevers, asphyxia, and excitement resuscitate things long since forgotten? . . . . Such peculiarities seem quite fantastic; and might, for aught we can see *a priori*, be the precise opposites of what they are. Evidently, then, *the faculty does not exist absolutely, but works under conditions; and the quest of the conditions* becomes the psychologist's most interesting task.[67]

Dewey and his Michigan cadre were bowled over by the appearance of James' *Principles*. Dewey started to use it in class in preference to his own textbook. Soon it was widely used in psychology courses across America, and it would remain so for many years.

Influenced by James, Dewey attempted to abandon the Hegelian cant that had marked his academic prose to that point and tried his hand at communication with a wider public. In 1892, urged onward by his wife and by Edward Bellamy's calls for social reform, Dewey and a friend attempted to launch a unique form of newspaper called the *Thought News*. It was conceived of as a unique kind of periodical,

which shall not go beyond the fact; which shall report thought rather than dress it up in the garments of the past; . . . which shall not discuss philosophic ideas *per se* but use them as tools in interpreting the movements of thought; which shall treat questions of science, letters, state, school and church as parts of the one moving life of man and hence of common interest, and not relegate them to separate documents of merely technical interest.[68]

The project failed before having published even a single issue. However naïve it may appear to us today, it is interesting how many of the themes that would motivate the work for which Dewey later became famous can be found here in this early flier: stripping away ideological encrustations, using ideas as tools for understanding, dissolving artificial verbal distinctions, viewing all of experience as a seamless whole. The project was at once trivial and prophetic.

4. The Chicago to Which Dewey Moved

When Dewey's Michigan subordinate, James Hayden Tufts, was called to an assistant professorship at Chicago, it soon became clear to Tufts that his immediate superior, Charles Strong, despite his close connection to the Rockefeller family, was not going to make his career there. Strong's wife, Bessie Rockefeller, could not stand the winters, she said,[69] and would be more comfortable back in New York. Strong readily complied, landing a lectureship in psychology at Columbia in 1895.[70]

Both Strong and Tufts recommended to Harper that he recruit Dewey to fill the empty professorship in philosophy, but Harper was not impressed by the

Michigan man at first. He went in search of someone who was more established, someone who would be more of a "draw." He called upon William James, but James had no interest in leaving Harvard, to which he had grown much attached. James recommended, instead, his old friend Peirce (who had, by that point, been out of the academy for nearly a decade). Harper then inquired with another prominent Harvard figure, the professor of natural religion and moral philosophy, George Herbert Palmer. Along with James, Palmer was one of the senior pillars of what would come to be known as the "Great Department."[71] In addition, Palmer's wife, Alice Freeman, was the president of Wellesley College, the first woman president of that school or, indeed, of any college in the United States. Harper offered positions to both of them, but nothing came of his invitation. Palmer caught wind of James' recommendation, however, and felt compelled to volunteer his opinion that that Peirce should be avoided. Although Palmer conceded that he had "no personal acquaintance with Peirce," he still found it necessary to repeat rumors he had heard of Peirce's having a "broken and dissolute character."[72] Peirce, as it turns out, was then working with a Chicago acquaintance of his, Paul Carus—the founding editor of the journals *Open Court* and *The Monist*—to win an opportunity at the new University and prove himself to the academic world once again. Harper heeded Palmer's warning, however, and Peirce was never given a hearing.

Peirce's loss was Dewey's gain. Having struck out with a number of established eastern figures, in 1894 Harper finally decided to call upon the still-young philosopher to leave Ann Arbor for Chicago. It wasn't much of a challenge to reel him in. At Michigan Dewey was stuck under a $2200 ceiling imposed on all faculty members' salaries. In response to the threat that Chicago, with its Rockefeller money, posed to all the colleges in America, Michigan hastily raised its ceiling to $2700, but even that was not a remotely competitive amount. Chicago's opening bid to Dewey was $4000. Dewey deliberated for a bit, then bargained Harper up to $5000.[73] Michigan had nothing to respond with. As Dewey departed for Chicago, he took Mead with him.[74] Needing someone to direct the psychology laboratory, Dewey also brought along his former student, James Rowland Angell who, after his European educational sojourn,[75] had taken the same Minnesota position that Dewey had once briefly held.

Chicago was unlike any place Dewey had ever lived. With over 1.1 million people in 1890 (nearly 120% growth in just the previous decade), it had just passed Philadelphia to become the second-largest city in the US. Although the crackdown immediately after the Haymarket Riot had forced a temporary chill in overt labor strife, the repression had solved none of the challenges that had eventuated the outbreaks of violence in the first place. So the suffering continued, and the tensions inevitably returned.

In 1889, two women from northwestern Illinois—Jane Addams and Ellen Gates Starr—opened a public building in the near west side[76] of Chicago that provided the impoverished residents of the area, first and foremost, with a beautiful place to find rest and recreation. Addams and Starr appointed the interior of their building with reproductions of famous European artworks.[77] It was their belief that beauty, in the form of art, would have an uplifting and "civilizing" influence on those who had so much hardship and ugliness in their daily lives. Second, the house would serve as a place of education and information for both the adults and children of the city. The two women offered lectures on a wide array of topics, from the basics of the English language to "high" literature, from science to politics. Some of these talks they presented themselves, others were given by various guest speakers who shared in their vision of how Chicago's poorest residents could best be helped.

Addams and Starr had encountered and adopted these "progressive" ideas during a tour of Europe that they had made together in 1887–1888. They were especially impressed by their visit to a new kind of institution in the east end of London called a "settlement house." Named Toynbee Hall (in memory of the Oxford historian, Arnold Toynbee), the settlement house served not only the needs of London's poorest residents, but also enabled the Oxbridge students who worked there as volunteers to acquire first-hand understanding of the experience of urban poverty in what was then the world's largest city (approximately 5 million).[78] The two women were immediately taken with the idea of opening a settlement house along the same lines in Chicago.

Such a venture required money, of course, but Addams was a wealthy woman, having inherited about $50,000[79] upon her father's death less than a decade before, at the age of just 21. The two women were also able to successfully solicit donations, mostly from other wealthy women of Chicago, which enabled them to rent and renovate a dilapidated mansion that had been built just over 30 years before by Charles Hull, one of Chicago's early real estate magnates. They named their settlement "Hull House," in honor of the building's owner. Before long, they were expanding their offerings: in addition to the art and the lectures, they soon discovered that their clients required an array of far more concrete social services. They created a nursery and a kindergarten, a library, a night school, and a café. They offered basic health care, a gym, and bathing facilities, as well as music, drama, painting, and various social clubs. They advocated politically for their neighborhood, fighting City Hall for basic sanitation in the streets. Hull House offered Chicago's immigrants and their impoverished working-class descendants access to services that were not offered to them anywhere else in the city. Addams and Starr decided to live in the house, keeping them in close touch with the neighborhood, along with several other volunteers. At its peak, Hull House was visited by 2,000 clients per week. For her work with and on behalf of Chicago's poor, Jane Addams would be awarded the Nobel Peace Prize in 1931.

Despite its continuing urban conflicts, at the start of the 1890s, Chicago felt ready to open its doors to the world and show off what it had been able to accomplish in the 20-odd years since the Great Fire. In 1893, the city hosted the World's Columbian Exposition, a celebration of the 400th anniversary of Columbus' "discovery" of the New World (though a year late). The event was an enormous

FIGURE 6.6 Entrance to Hull House in 2012.

international fair of arts, culture, science, and industry held on the shores of Lake Michigan, well south of the still mostly-hideous downtown, though not far from the newly-opened university. The fairgrounds were still incomplete on opening day—the Exposition was by no means exempt from Chicago's perennial labor disruptions—but the fair's chief architects, Daniel Burnham[80] and Frederick Law Olmstead,[81] had designed and built a fabulous, wholly new "White City"—a kind of life-size maquette of a futuristic vision they called the "City Beautiful." Erected on 600 acres of waterfront property, it was composed of dozens of stunning

Beaux-Arts buildings (most of them temporary and intended for demolition as soon as the fair ended). The elegant structures were connected together by both footpaths and an intricate network of waterways that allowed visitors (for a price, of course) to ride gondolas through the canals and lagoons of the fairgrounds, as though they were in the New World's answer to Venice.[82]

As if the fairgrounds themselves were not a stunning enough contradiction to everything that most visitors thought they knew of the ugly, violent, relentlessly mercantile Great Western Metropolis, at night the entire park was illuminated by electric lights, still a rare sight at that time and never before used for the kind of massive coverage that was seen in the White City. Well over 100,000 incandescent bulbs cast a kind of magical aura over the vast park.[83] Indeed, the power of electricity not just to provide nighttime lighting, but to transform urban life itself became a theme of the fair as a whole. Searchlights that could be seen from as far as 60 miles away guided people to the fair. The first-ever nighttime football game was played under artificial lights. One of the most popular displays was the "electric kitchen," which included the first automatic dishwasher. New York State even exhibited a prototype of a fascinating and horrifying new device that they were now using for executions: the electric chair.

Like most electrical devices of the time, the electric chair provided yet another opportunity for the fierce rivalry between the two top inventors of the

FIGURE 6.7 The "White City" of the 1893 Worlds' Columbian Exposition.

Credit: Retrieved from http://bit.ly/2pDwaWh, May 4, 2017.

FIGURE 6.8   The "White City" at night under electric light.

Credit: Brooklyn Museum. Goodyear Archival Collection:Visual materials [6.1.016]:World's Colum-bian Exposition lantern slides (1893).

time—Thomas Edison and Nicola Tesla—to play itself out in public. The chair had first been proposed by Alfred P. Southwick, a Buffalo dentist and member of a New York State committee that was assigned the task of finding a more humane means of execution than hanging. Edison's team then built the first chair and, in order to evince his bogus but long-running claim that Tesla's alternating current (AC) was more lethal than his own direct current (DC), Edison uncharacteristically used AC for this one project. The chair was first used for an actual execution in 1890, in New York. The event, which was obsessively covered by the press, turned out to be so botched and bloody a mess that Tesla's chief patron, George Westinghouse, quipped that an axe would have done a better job.[84]

Nikola Tesla demonstrated a wide array of novel electrical devices at the fair. He spectacularly refuted Edison's claims that AC was more dangerous than DC by running electricity through his own body to produce what, to all appearances, seemed to be miniature bolts of lightning leaping from his hands. His audiences were, of course, amazed and delighted. The fair is said to have used three times as much power as the entire city of Chicago.[85] Much of this energy was generated by twelve engines of one thousand horsepower each, all producing AC, a coup which probably sealed AC's ultimate victory over DC in the long-running battle over which kind of electricity would power the country as a whole.[86]

Despite having lost the battle over which kind of current would be used at the fair, Edison could not afford to stay away. He displayed a variety of remarkable inventions to astonished crowds, including his new Kinetoscope, a device that allowed a single individual to view a moving image through a peep hole. The motion picture projector had not yet been developed, but the Kinetoscope was the immediate forerunner of the movie theater.

In addition to the electrical spectacle, a wide array of new consumer products were launched at the fair. Many would become icons of American commerce: Quaker Oats, Shredded Wheat cereal, Aunt Jemima pancake mix, Cracker Jack, Juicy Fruit gum, and Pabst Blue Ribbon beer. The state of Wisconsin displayed an 11-ton cheese. Someone else exhibited a replica of the Venus de Milo carved from 1500 pounds of chocolate. There was entertainment too. Buffalo Bill leased 15 acres of land adjacent to the fairgrounds to mount a show that (in keeping with the international theme of the fair) he cleverly dubbed the "Congress of Rough Riders of the World."[87]

Finally, the greatest marvel of them all climbed high into the sky above the fairgrounds: George Washington Gale Ferris' great observation wheel. To many people of the day, the "Ferris Wheel," as it came to be known, seemed impossibly delicate with its slim supports and cables. Surely it would tear itself apart in a catastrophic collapse. But it was built of a kind of structural steel that had only recently come into widespread use and so, defying what seemed like common sense to most, it carried up to 2,000 people at a time 264 feet into the air for an aerial view of the fairgrounds and of the massive city to the north that few had ever before seen. Some declared it a Wonder of the Modern World.

––––––––––––

Psychology had only a tenuous relation to these marvels but, desperate to find its niche among the modern sciences, the discipline was not about to be left out of the greatest spectacle the world had ever seen. The problem was that, in 1893, there wasn't yet anyone in Chicago capable of mounting an impressive display of psychology's "wares" at the fair. Both Strong and Tufts had set up small demonstration laboratories in the region, but nothing on the scale that the senior eastern psychologists thought would be able seize the public's attention and favor. About 150 miles northwest of Chicago, however, was the University of Wisconsin in the town of Madison. One of Peirce's and Hall's former students at Johns Hopkins, Joseph Jastrow, had taken a position in that comparatively remote location in 1888 after two years of post-graduate unemployment (due, at least in part, to the anti-semitism that was then common in many walks of American life). Wisconsin was small and distant, but it was a full-time position where Jastrow could conduct his research. Matters there almost immediately took a downturn, however, when the man who, as president of Cornell, had refused to consider Jastrow's application in 1886, Charles Kendall Adams, became president of Wisconsin just four years after Jastrow had arrived there himself.[88] The two were nearly immediately in conflict.

Jastrow volunteered to mount and run a psychology exhibit at the Chicago Exposition, and a modest space was secured in the Anthropology Building at the southern periphery of the fairgrounds. But President Adams refused to give Jastrow any time away from his normal teaching duties in order to tend to the exhibit. As a result, Jastrow was forced to make the train trip from Madison to

FIGURE 6.9   Joseph Jastrow.

Credit: Joseph Jastrow Papers, David M. Rubenstein Rare Book and Manuscript Library, Duke University.

Chicago and back every week for six months, which took a serous toll on both his physical and mental health. The following year, Jastrow took a medical leave of absence from the university.[89]

Jastrow's psychology exhibit at the Chicago Exposition consisted of two small rooms. In the first were instruments that he had brought down from his own laboratory in Madison, as well as pieces and photographs that he had borrowed from the laboratories at Brown, Harvard, Pennsylvania, and Toronto. There was an apparatus for the generation of various colors and sounds. There was an ergograph for measuring the control of muscular contractions and a dynamometer for measuring strength. There were various timing and recording devices, such as metronomes and kymographs, as well as an array of clocks and chronoscopes. All of this was pretty standard stuff for the psychology laboratories of the day, but exotic-looking high technology for the public.

In the second room, for a small fee, Jastrow offered visitors a comprehensive psychological "examination." Modeled on a data-collection scheme that Francis Galton had pioneered at the 1884 International Health Exhibition in London, and a "mental test" that James McKeen Cattell had developed at Penn (more about which in the next chapter), Jastrow performed a number of tests of sensory and motor skills on his "customers." There were also tests of verbal, numerical, and spatial memory as well as assessments of word association. In addition, there were tests of reaction time, both simple (one stimulus) and complicated (multiple stimuli each requiring a different response).[90] Modest as they might have been, Jastrow's two rooms at the Chicago fair were, in effect, American psychology's "coming out" party.

Stanley Hall, always the self-promoter, could not let so grand an opportunity as the Exposition slip by, so he organized an International Congress of Education to take place in Chicago at the same time.[91] Hall's Congress consisted of two distinct conferences: The first, organized by the recently-retired president of Princeton, James McCosh, was titled "Rational Psychology in Education." Its speakers included leading lights such as Cornell's president, Jacob Gould Schurman and its new psychology professor, Edward Titchener; Harvard's Josiah Royce, and Queen's University's[92] John Watson, probably the two most influential Idealist philosophers on the continent at the time; and William Torrey Harris, the founding editor of the *Journal of Speculative Philosophy*, recently raised to the impressive post of US Commissioner of Education.[93]

This lineup was highly prestigious, to be sure, but Hall regarded most of them as a little stuffy and conservative in their views. He saved the more progressive speakers for the second conference, which he titled "Experimental Psychology and Education." The main topic of discussion was Hall's Child Study movement. He even used the event to launch a new National Association for the Study of Children. It seems that Hall intentionally wanted to operate outside of the auspices of the NEA, over which the stodgy Harris had a great deal of influence. The founding members of Hall's National Association included Professors

THE PSYCHOLOGICAL LABORATORY.

FIGURE 6.10 The two rooms of the Psychology Exhibit in the Anthropology Building of the World's Columbian Exposition.

William Lowe Bryan and George T. W. Patrick of the Universities of Indiana and Iowa, respectively, as well as two rising women researchers: Lillie Williams of the Trenton (NJ) Normal School and Millicent Shinn of California.[94] Hall's National Association was a short-lived affair, collapsing after just a few years, but it did prompt the National Education Association to launch a Child Study Department in 1894, and to place Hall in charge of it.

Two days before the great fair was to end, Chicago was gearing up to celebrate the successful conclusion to what had been, perhaps, the greatest public event in American history.[95] On that day, October 28, 1893, a man named Patrick Prendergast called on the recently re-elected mayor, Carter Harrison, at his home. It was already evening and Prendergast did not have appointment but Harrison's domestic staff informed the mayor that the man was in the foyer to asking to see him. Harrison did not know Prendergast but, despite the odd circumstances, chose to receive him anyway. Prendergast met the mayor with a gun in his hand and shot him dead.

The city was shocked. Harrison had long been the city's critical "linchpin": neither capital nor labor wholly trusted him (because he typically gave each side only part of what they demanded) but he had succeeded in preventing the new "civil war" that so many feared was imminent. Suddenly, he was gone. The populace was not only shocked by the assassination but also by the killer and his motive: Prendergast was not a communist agitator or a wild anarchist bent on destruction of the system. Neither was he an agent of the city's industrial tycoons, hoping to remove the man they saw as the main impediment to their complete domination of municipal affairs. No, instead Prendergast was an ordinary, if mentally unstable man; a Democrat who had supported Harrison's campaign to regain the office he had held from 1879 to 1887.[96] After the election of 1893, Prendergast had begun to write to various figures in the new administration about the municipal position that he presumed he was owed by virtue of his work on behalf of the mayor's campaign. When no one responded, he became disgruntled, then resentful. He ultimately decided that the mayor must die for his ingratitude, a determination that led him to Harrison's house that night. In short, Harrison was killed by the corruption—the unquestioned expectation of favoritism—that had engulfed and infused the city's entire political culture virtually from its beginnings.

What was to have been the Exposition's official closing ceremony, two days after the assassination, was transformed into a massive public memorial for Harrison. Hundreds of thousands of people attended. Not content to be robbed of their choice by an inconsequential madman, four years later the people of Chicago elected the martyred leader's son, Carter Harrison, Jr., to the first of five terms as mayor.

The assassination of Harrison was not the only tragedy to befall Chicago in 1893. Starting back in the spring, just as the Exposition opened, banks in Chicago and other parts of the country had begun to fail, one after another like falling dominoes, until, by the autumn, six hundred had closed. The negative effects roared through the economy. Unemployment among the unskilled shot up to perhaps 25%.[97] The Great Crash of 1893 was underway, though, for a short time, its impact on Chicago was submerged beneath the excitement and the influx of the money generated by the fair.

The Crash put George Pullman's experiment in paternalistic capitalism to its first important test: could he continue to provide his workers their comfortable environs in the face of falling corporate revenues? Pullman had unknowingly created an irresolvable problem for himself. Before the Crash was in view, he had *guaranteed* his investors an 8% return. In the face of the unexpected and massive economic downturn, the only way he was going to be able to make good on his promise was to squeeze his workers very hard. He cut their salaries by 25%, but he kept their rents and other prices in his company town exactly as they had been before. Workers could not move to cheaper housing because they had to live in Pullman's town in order to work in Pullman's factory. And they could not find other work because the country was in the middle of its worst economic downturn since the 1870s. It was difficult for them even to shop at less expensive stores because of their relative isolation from Chicago proper.

Pullman's workers were stuck. In May of 1894, faced with the prospect of not putting food on their families' tables, they went on strike—the very thing that Pullman's vision had been designed to prevent.[98] Pullman saw the workers as ungrateful. They saw him as unreasonable. The two sides were at an impasse. The workers needed outside support if they were to prevail so, at the end of June, the American Railway Union, led by a man named Eugene Debs, called upon railroad workers across the country to boycott any train pulling Pullman cars.[99] What had started as a local labor dispute was rapidly expanding into a nationwide transportation calamity. Nevertheless, George Pullman held firm and let events spin out of control.

5. Dewey Moves to Chicago

The very week that the national Pullman boycott began, John Dewey was making his move from Ann Arbor to Chicago—240 miles by train. His two older children were with his wife, Alice, in Europe. On the evening of June 30 he wrote to them that he expected to be in Chicago the next day. At 2:00 am on July 1, his train was stopped by boycotters in Battle Creek, Michigan. After waiting at the station until 9:00 in the morning, he decided to pay an impromptu visit on some acquaintances there. Later that day he took a Michigan Central train, which pulled the cars of Pullman's main competitor—Wagner.[100] By the time he finally reached Chicago, Dewey was already caught up in the conflict. Talking to a striking worker, he said, made his "nerves more thrilled than they had been in years. I felt as if I had better resign my job teaching & follow him round till I got into life."[101] He didn't, of course, and the events that followed as the strike spread and the two sides became increasingly entrenched must have made him better aware of the dispute's deadly serious nature.

Although Tufts was younger than Dewey, he had been living in Chicago longer and understood the implications better. In his unpublished autobiography, he wrote:

> This Pullman strike made a grim and deep impression. We saw the United States soldiers camped on the lake front. We saw the trains leaving the city, each with a machine gun mounted upon a freight car in front of the locomotive. We saw the smoke of the thousand burning freight cars. It was too nearly like civil war. What proved to be a harmless crowd gave a very real scare to the little suburb in which I was living. . . . It was just at the time when mobs were reported to be threatening railroad properties. One evening some of our neighbors heard what sounded like the distant roar of a crowd. It seemed to be coming nearer. Our little group of houses, we thought, might excite the angry wrath of embittered, homeless and hungry men. One of our neighbors was a retired army officer. . . . He had a considerable stock of rifles and shotguns which he brought out and distributed to the men of the group. Finally, as the noise seem to be passing by us at three or four blocks away two of our number scouted and returned with the report that it was not the roar of an angry mob but the hilarious singing and shouting of a crowd returning, apparently from a celebration at which a grand time had been had by all. We could smile at our mistake, but the conditions in the city were such that we could not think our alarm groundless.[102]

Within weeks of Dewey's arrival in Chicago, Grover Cleveland, the Democratic President of the United States, decided to intervene in the Pullman dispute, using the disruption it caused of the US mail as a pretext for government action. He obtained a court injunction against the strike and then ordered 12,000 federal army troops into Chicago to end it by force. The violence worsened for a time—30 people were killed and there was an estimated $80 million in property damage—but the union finally buckled and the strike ended. The union leader, Eugene Debs, was thrown into prison for six months for having violated the injunction, but his long political career had just begun: he would run for President of the United States on the Socialist ticket five times between 1900 and 1920.[103]

George Pullman had come out the nominal winner of the raucous dispute, but the Illinois Supreme Court soon ruled that his near-total control over his workers' private lives in his "utopian" company town was unconstitutional. The Court forced him to divest his company from the town and, more important, to end the model of labor relations that he had created. Far from ending the state of near-war between capital and labor, his approach had provoked the worst battle the nation had yet seen. The town of Pullman was soon absorbed into the city of Chicago. Pullman himself died just three years later. He was so reviled by the working people of Chicago that his tomb was sheathed in tons of concrete to thwart any would-be vandals.

FIGURE 6.11 James Hayden Tufts.

Credit: University of Chicago Library, Special Collections Research Center. Image identifier: apf1–08382.

Although the giddy excitement that Dewey had felt talking to that striking worker on his first day in Chicago might have been tempered by the calamitous outcome of the Pullman conflict, it was not extinguished. It was a feeling that would infuse much of the rest of his working life. Soon he became involved with Jane Addams' Hull House and the settlement movement, as did Tufts and other members of Dewey's department. Dewey also saw, though, that simply trying to help the poor was only a temporary stopgap. What was really needed was a revolution in the ways in which different groups saw each other: rich and poor, White and Black, Anglo and Irish, German and Pole, Christian and Jew. Tufts sketched the implications of this line of thought for philosophy:

> [In] texts in ethics available at the time . . . Kantian theory was set over against hedonism, but neither seemed to come near to the actual problems

FIGURE 6.12 Photo of the soldiers surrounding the Pullman factory to block strikers.

of life as it presents itself to young people. Little if any attention was given to the economic problems which the nineties were disclosing. And although one might not then foresee how swiftly the religious background and horizon was to change, I felt the necessity of a method of viewing the moral life that would show its deep routes in human nature and social situations.[104]

But ideas of inherent differences between people—prejudices and bigotries—can take root early in the growing person's mind, especially if the child is surrounded by a homogeneous circle of family, friends, and acquaintances who mostly hold and mouth the same set of stereotypes of those they view as alien.

There was emerging in the late 19th century, however, a new opportunity to intervene in this persistent cycle of mistrust and animosity. Children of various ethnic backgrounds were increasingly going to public schools together. Universal primary school had already been mandated in many places. Schools provided an opportunity for children of different ethnicities and classes to learn about each other on their own, outside of the home. Thus, in addition to the work Dewey did at Hull House, he also began to conceive of a wholly new model of childhood education that would be geared not so much toward delivering a fixed set of intellectual contents to students as it would be aimed at undermining, from the early in children's lives, the formation of the kinds of conflicts and misunderstandings that he felt were driving the US to the precipice of a great labor war from which it might never recover.[105]

Dewey's idea was not so crude as to propose a curriculum explicitly about cultural differences and similarities. It is unlikely that such an approach would have been effective; almost certainly it would have been denounced by various camps of "combatants" as mere propaganda. Instead, he set up a school that was open to children from a wide array of different backgrounds. Then he developed, in consultation with the children, a set of questions that *they* wished to investigate. Just as important as the content of the questions, however, was the kind of work in which they would engage to find the answers they sought: collaboration and cooperation. By working together—whether on planting vegetables, building a bird house, cooking an egg, conducting an experiment, or producing a newspaper—they also learned more about each other, learned how to get along with each other, learned to move past the ignorance and mistrust that leads to prejudice.

The aim, said Dewey, was,

> to make each one of our schools an embryonic community life, active with the types of occupations that reflect the life of the larger society and permeated through with the spirit of art, history, and science. When the school introduces and trains each child of society into membership within such a little community, saturating him with the spirit of service, and providing

FIGURE 6.13   Children working at various tasks at his Laboratory School in Chicago.

FIGURE 6.13 (Continued)

him with the instruments of effective self-direction, we shall have the deepest and best guaranty [sic] of a larger society which is worthy, lovely, and
harmonious.[106]

It was an idyllic vision, to be sure, but it seemed to Dewey and his colleagues
to be more engaged with "real life," more likely to bear some sort of practical fruit
than what university faculty members of the era typically did. Unlike when they
were in Ann Arbor, the pressing problems of urban American life were no longer
distant and abstract events to be read about in newspapers. The group was now
living at the very heart of the conflict—possibly at "ground zero" of the new civil
war, if it came. But, their new ideas about education were utterly untested. How
were they to go about developing a curriculum and a set of teaching methods that
would be effective in achieving their aims?

Borrowing a chapter from Hall's "Child Study" program, they saw the issue
as an empirical one. Not just observational, though, as Hall had advocated, but
experimental. One had to try things out, make careful observations, compare the
outcomes with what had been expected, and then revise the program accordingly.
In short, they needed a school that was also a pedagogical laboratory—a "laboratory school," as it came to be known. As Tufts put it:

> To study and test what could be done to adjust our education to the revo-
> lutionary change in our whole method of life, particularly in urban life, a
> laboratory was necessary. Such a laboratory could be only a school in which
> principles could be worked out and tested, and in which[,] as in other sci-
> entific laboratories[,] ideas as to both ends and methods would grow out of
> efforts to face conditions anew.[107]

The style of education that resulted from these radical ideas was simply incomprehensible to many adults of the day who observed it. Gone were the classical
texts and the Bible passages. Gone was the emphasis on rote learning and memorization. Gone were the neat exercise books of age-old mathematical problems.
Gone were the perfect rows of desks bolted to the floor. Gone, even, was the
teacher at the front of room lecturing precisely to quiet, attentive students (often
under the threat of corporal punishment). In its place was something that looked
much more like a workshop than a traditional classroom. As Tufts remembered it:

> Parents who in some cases recalled their own early facility and enjoyment
> in reading, or who shrank with horror from the sight of a mis-spelled word,
> or who had been taught that mathematics was the indispensable, if not the
> sole path of mental discipline, were worried when John and Jane seemed to
> be learning to spin, weave, cook, use carpenters' tools, but be less advanced
> in the three R's. It was also a shock to some to go into a school room and
> see children moving about freely and talking about what they were doing

instead of sitting in silence with "no whispering" rigorously enforced. They were not prepared to grasp at once the change from a competitive to a cooperative atmosphere which was one of the ends sought.[108]

Because of the manual tasks in which children often engaged at Dewey's school, it was not uncommon for some to misunderstand his intention as the setting up of a trade school, and then praise or criticize that putative aim according to the commentator's own personal predilections. Nothing could be further from the truth, however. According to Dewey,

> This kind of work gives the point of departure from which the child can trace and follow the progress of mankind in history, getting an insight also into the materials used and the mechanical principles involved. In connection with occupations the historical development of man is recapitulated.[109]

Although universally characterized as being "progressive," there was, as well, a note of nostalgia in Dewey's vision—a fear of losing something precious from the past. As he put it much later in an autobiography (writing about himself in the third person):

> That his boyhood surroundings played a large part in forming John Dewey's educational theories is clear. As a boy and young man he saw almost all his associates assuming a share in household activities and responsibilities. Young people were brought into intimate contact with a whole round of simple industrial and agricultural occupations.[110]

The curriculum was not set out fully by Dewey and his colleagues ahead of time. There was to be what Dewey called a "shifting of the center of gravity" toward the desires of the child rather than the demands of the teacher.

> It is to be a change, a revolution, not unlike that introduced by Copernicus when the astronomical center shifted from the earth to the sun. In this case, the child becomes the sun about which the appliances of education revolve; he is the center about which they are organized.[111]

The child may have been the center, but still just an instrument in Dewey's greater plan—to cure the ills besetting the urban, industrial society that was rapidly coming to dominate American life.[112] "The school," Dewey said,

> may be connected with life so that the experience gained by the child in a familiar, commonplace way is carried over and made use of there, is carried back and applied in everyday life, making the school an organic whole, instead of a composite of isolated parts.[113]

Dewey and his team were not the only ones in Chicago working to implement progressive school reform. The man who had founded the "Quincy Method" for elementary education in Massachusetts, Francis Wayland Parker, had moved there from Boston more than a decade earlier to become Principal of the Cook County Normal School, the main teacher training institute for the region in and around Chicago. He was producing the teachers who would reform public education there along the lines he had pioneered in Massachusetts. Although the two men—Dewey and Parker—shared many educational ideals, they also had outsized, sometimes conflicting ambitions, as we shall see.

6. Conclusion

We have now sketched of the histories of four major American cities—New York, Boston, Baltimore, and Chicago—and we have begun to explore the impacts that events in those metropolises had on the development of American psychology in the closing decades of the 19th century. Some profound differences were noted in the events that led up to those cities' origins and in their subsequent developments. The Massachusetts and Maryland Colonies were both founded on religious grounds, though the similarity ends there. The former was exclusively Protestant, its residents not able even to accept the presence of Quakers in their midst. The latter was established as a haven for Catholics, though it was modeled on the then-radical idea of religious tolerance. New York and Chicago, by contrast, were founded essentially as centers of commerce, both heavily influenced by natural and man-made transportation corridors. However, because New York was founded 300 years earlier than Chicago, the characters of their respective civic "personalities" differed markedly as the 19th century drew to a close. The old Dutch colony had, over the centuries, repeatedly experienced, and gradually learned to better manage, the major issues that faced cities on the eastern seaboard almost since their inception. It was never easy but, by the 1890s, New York could generally handle challenges more pragmatically, without explosions of mass violence. Chicago, on the other hand, had still not yet matured as a civil society and its domination by a variety of uncompromising, sometimes ferocious political and economic factions meant that violence was not uncommon and the threat of aggression was virtually constant.

Nevertheless, the issues that most challenged all four cities as the turn of the century approached were roughly the same: (1) Massive immigration and the ever-mounting need to find ways to integrate enormous crowds of new residents. What is more, immigration constantly and rapidly increased the array of different ethnic groups that had to be accommodated. Whether it was the Irish and German Catholics in the 1840s and 1850s, or African Americans moving north after the Civil War in the 1860s and 1870s, or the Italians and Eastern Europeans in the 1880s and 1890s, the challenges faced were never quite the same as before, and new adaptations had to be discovered, implemented, and, most important of all, accepted by the longer-established ethnic communities (including the English, Scottish, and Irish Protestants). Perhaps ironically, given that it was the dawn of the Darwinian era, the situation for longtime residents of American cities was not unlike the evolutionary challenge faced by a species when its ecological niche is in constant flux: no one adaptation is sufficient; adaptability itself is the only adequate response.

(2) With the continuous influx of newcomers came continuously increasing demands for paid work. However, at virtually the same time a wave of revolutionary technological innovations was rolling in that could quickly render a suite of traditional skills obsolete, throwing hundreds or even thousands of people out of work with no recourse and no means of acquiring new skills. This persistent conflict between the needs of capital to innovate and the needs of workers for economic stability led to eruptions of disorder and violence on such a regular basis that they caused many to fear for the very possibility of urban peace in the foreseeable future.

(3) The first two challenges—massive and increasingly diverse population growth and revolutionary technological innovation—combined to make the development of a vast and efficient educational system to which all children had ready access a virtual necessity. Without it, businesses would not be able to find workers with the skills that were needed in the new economy they were creating and, concomitantly, future workers could not learn the skills needed to win and hold the new jobs that were available. Beyond the pure economic case, a universal public school system provided a unique and previously unappreciated opening to forge a new kind of civic unity out of the growing diversity of the cities' always-changing citizenry. Psychologists and educators who were faced with these urban challenges on a daily basis—those who lived in the cities themselves—were the ones to first see both the threats and the opportunities.

The chapters of this book thus far have focused on three main figures: William James, Stanley Hall, and John Dewey. In the subsequent chapters we will see the constellation of American psychologists grow exponentially, and we shall also trace an interesting phenomenon—those whose lives and careers were embedded in the major American cities around the turn of the century were also the ones whose approaches to the discipline developed in ways that most directly addressed the problems that the cities faced, even though they may not themselves have seen their work in that way. Those psychologists, however, who worked in more rural settings, however—not feeling so keenly, perhaps, the urgent press of urban events—developed a different style of psychological investigation that was focused more on abstract, "pure," and theoretical aspects of the still-developing field.

Notes

1 Much of the information on the early general history of Chicago was drawn from Donald L. Miller, *City of the Century: The Epic of Chicago and the Making of America* (New York, NY: Simon & Schuster, 1996).

2　See Ann Durkin Keating, *Rising up from Indian Country: The Battle of Fort Dearborn and the Birth of Chicago* (Chicago, IL: University of Chicago Press, 2012).

3　Quoted passage cited in William Cronon, *Nature's Metropolis: Chicago and the Great West* (New York, NY: Norton, 1991); John Lewis Peyton, *Over the Alleghanies [sic] and Across the Prairies* (London, UK: Simpkin, Marshall, 1848/1870), 325.

4　William Cronon explains that the low ridge (just 15 feet above the level of Lake Michigan) that splits the two massive water systems is the point where the great Ice Age glaciers ended their advance over the continent 10,000 years ago. It was there they "deposit[ed] immense loads of soil and gravel" that they had scraped off the northern landscape. Thus, he continues, "Illinois and Iowa, southern Wisconsin and Minnesota, and Chicago itself were all blessed with these Ice Age gifts from the north." Cronon, *Nature's Metropolis*, Loc 761 of Kindle edition.

5　Ibid. Loc 774 of Kindle edition, based on information given in Alfred T. Andreas, *History of Chicago from the Earliest Period to the Present Time*, vol. 1 (Chicago, IL: A. T. Andreas, 1884), 137.

6　Harriet Martineau, *Society in America*, vol. 1 (London, UK: Sauders & Otley, 1837), 180.

7　In 1902, the company was merged with others to form the agricultural behemoth, International Harvester.

8　Ogden had previously served a year as a state assemblyman in his native New York.

9　It was no coincidence that the British Corn Laws had been repealed just two years before, in 1846, opening one of the largest grain markets in the world to imports for the first time in over three decades.

10　Joseph G. Knapp, "A Review of Chicago Stock Yards History," *University Journal of Business* 2 (1924): 331–46.

11　Austin Hoyt, *Chicago: City of the Century*, Video documentary, American Experience, 2003 Disc 1, 47:40. The young Henry Ford, mightily impressed by the efficiency of Armour's operation, was inspired by it to create the fabled "assembly line" in his early car factories.

12　For a comprehensive account of the intricate web of relations that provided Chicago industrialists their competitive advantage, see especially Robert Lewis, *Chicago Made: Factory Networks in the Industrial Metropolis* (Chicago, IL: University of Chicago Press, 2008).

13　See Cronon, *Nature's Metropolis*, Loc. 1050 of Kindle edition.

14　Robert Herrick, *The Gospel of Freedom* (New York, NY: Palgrave Macmillan, 1898), 101.

15　Ultimately, in 1868, this problem was addressed, in the technologically grandiose fashion of Chicago, by literally *reversing the flow* of the Chicago River. Thus, instead of taking the city's sewage out to the lake, the waste was swept inland to the canal, thence to the Illinois River and, ultimately, to the Mississippi. This "solution" was, of course, much to the chagrin of everyone living downstream, but there was no legal recourse to be pursued in that era.

16　Recall, by comparison, that Harvard was opened by Puritans just 16 years after the landing of the Mayflower, and they had considerably less wealth at their disposal at that time than the early tycoons of Chicago possessed in the 1850s.

17　Evanston was named after John Evans, a physician and hospital administrator who had gotten rich on Chicago land speculation. Evans was a major donor to the university and the first president of its Board. A founding member of the Illinois Republican Party, Evans was later appointed governor of the Colorado Territory by his personal friend, Abraham Lincoln. There, he helped to found the college that eventually became the University of Denver.

18　Interestingly, Douglas was not Baptist, nor even particularly religious. He had offered the land to the Presbyterians first, but they had not been able to raise the matching funds he demanded in order to close the deal. Critics charged that Douglas' main aim was actually to raise the value of the surrounding land, which he also owned. The school was unable to draw many major patrons during the few decades of its existence, and this ultimately led to its demise. Douglas was politically unpopular in Chicago because of his support for slavery and, specifically, his authorship of the Kansas-Nebraska Act. Thus, his connection to the new university may have actually served to undermine its fund-raising efforts in the region.

19 Named after Sylvester Lind, a Chicago businessman and antislavery activist. It is said that his house was a stop on the Underground Railroad. He pledged $100,000 to build the new school, but was unable to make good on the promise after the Panic of 1857.

20 Historical "firsts" are notoriously tricky to establish, mainly because human institutions rarely arise fully formed, but nearly always develop from similar precursors. Thus, the process of demarcating between a "precursor" and the first "authentic" instance is often fraught with arbitrary decisions about which features are necessary and which are incidental. That said, New York's Macy's is often claimed to have been the first department store. R. H. Macy's first New York store did not open until 1858 (although he had a series of earlier dry goods stores in other places, dating back to 1843, including one called "R. H. Macy & Co." in Haverhill, Massachusetts in 1851). When either Macy's or Palmer's stores had enough "departments" to be regarded as a "department store" is anyone's call.

21 The old popular tale of the fire having being started when Mrs. (Catherine) O'Leary's cow kicked over a lantern in the barn has long since been exploded by historians.

22 Charles Dudley Warner, *Studies in the South and West With Comments on Canada* (New York, NY: Harper, 1889), 185.

23 Cronon, *Nature's Metropolis,* Loc 449 of Kindle edition.

24 There was a small bar in the hotel, but Pullman employees were not allowed there.

25 Trains had run on cheaper iron tracks early on, rather than expensive steel ones but, as the sizes of locomotives and lengths of trains rapidly grew, iron proved to be too soft for the job; it was easily deformed by the massive new engines hurtling along at unheard of speeds, leading to terrible accidents. Steel was the solution but, until Bessemer, was prohibitively expensive to produce in the massive amount needed.

26 The Irish had gained a foothold in the municipal political system, incredibly corrupt though it was, and they seemed, on the whole, to prefer that form of redress for the many problems that beset them to marching in the streets, which made them vulnerable to violent attack by police.

27 Miller, *City of the Century.*

28 Six years later, in 1893, the Progressive Democratic Governor of Illinois, Peter Altgeld— a native of Germany himself—pardoned and released the three remaining Haymarket convicts.

29 In interpreting this number, it should be remembered that life expectancy for US Whites had plummeted from about 45 years to only about 40 between 1870 and 1880 (the figures for Blacks were far worse). Infant mortality had also spiked from 175 per thousand live births to 215 per thousand, a jump of nearly 25% Those stark figures neatly distill what industrialization and urbanization meant for the masses in the late 19th century: It was killing them and they were literally fighting for their lives. The first, most basic victories on municipal and labor fronts allowed life expectancies to climb back up into the mid-40s by 1890. It should also be noted that things looked somewhat less bleak once one had survived childhood: a White 20-year old in 1880 could expect to live to about 60 years of age.

30 Edward Bellamy's younger New Yorker cousin, Francis Bellamy, was a Baptist minister who co-founded the Society of Christian Socialists, and who wrote the original version of the American "Pledge of Allegiance."

31 Although many sources cite this ranking, John W. Baer reports that *Ben Hur* (1880) also sold also more copies than *Looking Backward* (*The Pledge of Allegiance: A Revised History and Analysis* (Annapolis, MD: Free State Press, 2007)).

32 Arthur E. Morgan, *Edward Bellamy* (New York, NY: Columbia University Press, 1944).

33 The magazine was not a success, in the end, only publishing in the years 1891 to 1894.

34 John Dewey, "A Great American Prophet," *Common Sense* 3, no. 4 (April 1934): 6–7.

35 Charles R. Morris, *The Tycoons: How Andrew Carnegie, John D. Rockefeller, Jay Gould, and J. P. Morgan Invented the American Supereconomy* (New York, NY: Times Books).

36 It is odd to consider, but Rockefeller probably did more to save the whales of the world than any other single individual in history because the introduction of kerosene rendered the massive whaling industry very nearly obsolete in a short period of time.

37 Gates was from New York State, but had moved to Minneapolis in 1880 to become pastor of the Central Baptist Church there. He left the ministry in 1888 to become secretary of the American Baptist Education Society and only met Rockefeller in 1889, in the course of establishing an endowment for the new University. Gates would go on to serve as Rockefeller's representative on the University's Board, and became his primary philanthropic advisor and administrator for many years thereafter.

38 Harper, however, would include an undergraduate college alongside of his graduate school, and Harper's humanities division was to be just as elite as his science division. Of course, Harper did not have to operate within the financial constraints that Jonas Clark had placed on Hall, and so did not have to make the hard decisions to which Hall had been forced. For all the wealth that Jonas Clark possessed, Rockefeller was orders of magnitude wealthier.

39 In his unpublished autobiography, philosopher James Hayden Tufts said that it had not been Harper's original plan to have the natural sciences so well represented at the outset, but the opportunity that presented itself at Clark was irresistible, so additional funds were solicited from various donors to make laboratories, etc. available in the first year. University of Chicago Archives, James Hayden Tufts Collection, Box 3, folder 14, p. B21.

40 See also the account of these events given in Ross, *G. Stanley Hall*, 226–27.

41 Stumpf is well known to historians of psychology for his work on perception—especially sound and music—and for being one of the intellectual "grandfathers" of *Gestalt* psychology (Max Wertheimer, Wolfgang Köhler, and Kurt Koffka all studied with Stumpf at various times). Paulsen, though less well known, was among the most successful students of the "father" of psychophysics, Gustav Fechner. Paulsen developed Fechner's mystical doctrine of panpsychism into an elaborate philosophical position, and Paulsen's theory of mind emphasized the action of the will. He trained a number of early American psychologists, including James Mark Baldwin.

42 Of Ladd, Tufts remarked in his autobiography that

> he was not, like his contemporary James, a brilliant originator of new lines of thinking. Nor like his contemporary Royce an expositor of a system which so lent itself to imaginative charm as romantic idealism. He was essentially a wide reader, careful reviewer and critic who seeks his conclusions rather from reflection upon the systems of others than from the daring development of a central idea. . . . Nevertheless he was far from being a mere compiler. . . . He was not an eminently stimulating lecturer. . . . [H]is method was intended primarily to encourage active study and criticism by members of the class.
>
> University of Chicago Archives, James Hayden Tufts Collection,
> Box 3, folder 11 "Grad Study," 8

43 John Dewey, "Biography of John Dewey" (edited by Jane M. Dewey), in *The Philosophy of John Dewey*, ed. by Paul Arthur Schilpp (New York, NY: Tudor, 1939), 3–45. The Angell children included, of course, James Rowland Angell, who would later become Dewey's student at Michigan and colleague at Chicago. However, since James Angell was just two years old when his family left for Michigan, he was not among Dewey's early playmates.

44 Lucina was born into a Universalist family, but converted to the more intensely evangelical Congregationalism in early adulthood. Lucina's heritage was politically rich. Her grandfather, Charles Rich, had been a member of the US Congress in the 1810s and 1820s (see Dewey's "Biography of John Dewey", 3–45). In addition, a cousin of

Lucina's, John Tyler Rich (son of John W. Rich, who was, in turn, a son of Charles) became active in Michigan politics, winning elections to the US congress from that state and, eventually, the governorship.

45 John Dewey's older brother, Davis, would go on to become a professor of economics and statistics at MIT and editor of *American Economic Review*. His younger brother, Charles Miner Dewey went into business and moved to the west coast.

46 Coleridge introduced (a simplified form of) Kantian thinking to the normally empiricist British in the early 19th century. It caught on with the Scottish philosopher, William Hamilton, who inspired, along with Hegel's thought, the flowering of British Idealism that marked the second half of the century (e.g., Thomas Hill Green, John and Edward Caird, F. H. Bradely, Bernard Bosanquet).

47 See Dewey's "Biography of John Dewey," 3–45. See also, Robert Bruce Williams, "John Dewey and Oil City," *Peabody Journal of Education* 46 (1969): 223–26.

48 John Dewey, "The Metaphysical Assumptions of Materialism. "*Journal of Speculative Philosophy* 16 (1882): 208–13. Dewey returned to private tutelage under Torrey in the year between his sojourn to Oil City and his arrival at Johns Hopkins, and wrote other articles for *JSP* in a similar vein. See, e.g., Raymond D. Boisvert, "Dewey, Subjective Idealism, and Metaphysics," *Transactions of the Charles S. Peirce Society* 18 (1982): 241; Lewis S. Feuer, "H. A. P. Torrey and John Dewey: Teacher and Pupil," *American Quarterly* 10 (1958): 34–54.

49 Although Hegel's philosophy was far too elaborate to outline justly here, it was conveniently, if somewhat problematically, summarized by Johann Gottlieb Fichte as viewing the historical development of thought through a series of conflicts between pairs of incompatible ideas: a "thesis" and an "antithesis." Because each side of the opposition contains some undeniable aspect of reality, neither can ever succeed in wholly negating the other, but the two are ultimately brought into balance through a process of "synthesis," which integrates the necessary aspects of each into a "higher unity." This new "synthesis," however, may go on to become the "thesis" in the next such conflict. For Hegel, the Spirit of the Universe gradually brings itself fully into existence through a dialectical (or "logical") historical process of this sort. Dewey aimed to bring Hegel's dialectical style of reasoning to the historical development of mental science.

50 John Dewey, "Soul and Body," *Bibliotheca Sacra* 43 (1886): 239–63. See also Thomas C. Dalton, *Becoming John Dewey* (Bloomington, IN: Indiana University Press, 2002), 54–59.

51 John Dewey, "The Psychological Standpoint," *Mind* 11 (1886): 1–19; and "Psychology as Philosophic Method," *Mind* 11 (1886): 153–73.

52 John Dewey, *Psychology* (New York, NY: Harper, 1887). Andrew Feffer reported that despite of the official publication date, the book actually appeared in 1886. *The Chicago Pragmatists and American Progressivism* (Ithaca, NY: Cornell University Press, 1993), 58, n. 19.

53 Dewey, *Psychology*, 6.

54 G. Stanley Hall, "Review of books by J. McCosh, B. P. Browne, & J. Dewey," *American Journal of Psychology* 1 (1887): 146–59. The portion on Dewey's *Psychology* begins on p. 154. The quoted passages are on pp. 156 and 157.

55 Letter from William James to George Croom Robertson dated December 27, 1886, in *The Correspondence of William James*, eds. Ignas K. Skrupskelis and Elizabeth M. Berkeley, vol. 6 (Charlottesville, VA and London, UK: University of Virginia Press, 1992), 187. Also cited in George Dykhuizen, *The Life and Mind of John Dewey* (Carbondale, IL: Southern Illinois University Press, 1973), 55; and in Ralph Barton Perry, *Thought and Character of William James*, vol. 1 (Boston, MA: Little, Brown, 1935), 51.

56 George Croom Robertson, "Review of Dewey's *Psychology*," *Mind* 12 (1887): 439–43 (this quotation p. 440).

57 Linda Robinson Walker, "John Dewey at Michigan," [part 1] *Michigan Today* 29, no. 2 (1997). http://michigantoday.umich.edu/97/Sum97/mta1j97.html. Accessed July 17, 2013.

58 For interesting accounts of how Hegel continued to influence Dewey's thought, even years after he had renounced it, see Andrew Backe, "Dewey and the Reflex Arc: The

Limits of James' Influence," *Transactions of the Charles S. Peirce Society* 35 (1999): 312–26; and "John Dewey and Early Chicago Functionalism," *History of Psychology* 4 (2001): 323–40. For a more sympathetic view of Dewey's efforts to synthesize Hegelianism and naturalism, see Trevor Pearce's "The Dialectical Biologist, circa 1890: John Dewey and the Oxford Hegelians," *Journal of the History of Philosophy* 52 (2014): 747–78. See also Richard Rorty, "Dewey Between Hegel and Darwin," in *Modernist Impulses in the Human Sciences, 1870–1930,* ed. by Dorothy Ross (Baltimore, MD: Johns Hopkins University Press, 1994), 54–68.

59 Walter B. Pillsbury, "History of the University of Michigan Department of Psychology." No date (A page of the *University of Michigan 1817–2017* bicentennial celebration website.) http://um2017.org/2017_Website/History_of_Psychology.html. Accessed July 18, 2013.

60 DeWitt B. Parker and Charles B. Vibbert, "History of the University of Michigan Department of Philosophy," No date (A page of the *University of Michigan 1817–2017* bicentennial celebration website.) http://um2017.org/2017_Website/History_of_Philosophy.html. Accessed July 18, 2013.

61 Angell's father, the president of Michigan, warned him against permitting William James' work on psychical phenomena to undermine his Christian faith. Letter of October 30, 1891 in J. R. Angell's "Personal Papers" (Group 2, Series II, Box 3, folder 15), Yale University Archives.

62 Linda Robinson Walker, "John Dewey at Michigan," [part 2] *Michigan Today* 29, no. 3 (1997). http://michigantoday.umich.edu/97/Fal97/mt13f97.html. Accessed July 17, 2013.

63 James, *Principles*, vol. 1, p. 121.

64 Instincts, of course, provide an interesting counterpoint to this generalization, but they do not undermine the main point being made here. In any case, James had a late chapter (24) on instincts as well.

65 Prior to the discovery of radiation, 100 million years was the outer estimate for the age of the Earth accepted by most geologists. Some physicists, such as Lord Kelvin, had estimated much shorter times, such as 20 million years, which called into question whether the Earth had even existed long enough for Darwin's process of natural selection to unfold.

66 The stream of consciousness is a series of ebullitions rather than a calm or steady flow. The calmness that we actually experience belongs to a low or moderate excitement; let there be any considerable intensity of feeling, and the ebullition character will start out convincingly prominent Alexander Bain, *Mind and Body: The Theories of Their Relation* (London, UK: Henry S. King, 1872), 50. For context around the relationship between Bain's and James' ideas in this domain, see Katherine Harper, "Psychoanalysis as an Interdisciplinary Science: From 19th Century Neuropsychology to Modern Neuropsychoanalysis" (Doctoral dissertation, York University, 2017).

67 William James, *Principles of Psychology*, vol. 1 (New York, NY: Holt), 2–3. It is interesting to contemplate why James chose to use a lower-case "g" in "god-given" in an era when, even if one's intent was to call into question the existence of the divine (and there is no indication that this was James' intent here), the Christian capital-G God would have been the only possibility seriously contemplated. A search of "god, God" on Google Ngrams confirms that "God" was found in the English books nearly 20 times as often as "god."

68 Printed advertisement, J. R. Angell Collection, Personal Papers, Groups 2, Series II, Box 16, folder 147, Yale University Archives. See also Willinda Savage, "John Dewey and 'Thought News' at the University of Michigan," *Michigan Alumnus Quarterly Review* 56 (1950): 204–9.

69 Reported in Tufts' autobiography. University of Chicago Archives, J. H. Tufts Papers, Box B, Folder 15, Chicago III, p. 2.

70 Strong was promoted to professor of psychology in 1903 but his wife's failing health led them to move in Paris that same year. After her death in 1906, Strong moved to Italy

where he wrote most of his books on the philosophy of mind. "Biographical Sketch" at the website for the Charles A. Strong Papers, Rockefeller Archive Center, www. rockarch.org/collections/individuals/family/strongbio.php. Accessed July 17, 2013.

71 See Bruce Kuklick, *The Rise of American Philosophy: Cambridge, Massachusetts, 1860– 1930* (New Haven, CT: Yale University Press, 1971).

72 Cited in Nathan Houser, "Introduction," *Writings of Charles S. Peirce: A Chronological Edition*, vol. 8: 1890–1892 (Bloomington, IN: University of Indiana Press, 2010), lxxxi–lxxxii.

73 Linda Robinson Walker, "John Dewey at Michigan," [part 2] *Michigan Today* 29, no. 3 (1997). http://michigantoday.umich.edu/97/Fal97/mt13f97.html. Accessed July 17, 2013.

74 Michigan President James B. Angell was sorry to lose Dewey, but he was privately pleased to be rid of Mead, whom he regarded as having "not succeeded" as a teacher at Michigan, and as being "obscure." He had similar feelings about Alfred Lloyd but would soon be forced by a dearth of alternatives to make him new head of Michigan's philosophy department (from a letter dated June 3, 1894 to his son James R. Angell in the latter's "Personal Papers" (Group 2, Series II, Box 3, folder 18), Yale University Archives). Lloyd would spend his career at Michigan, ultimately serving as Dean of the Graduate Program starting in 1915, and as Acting President of the university in 1925.

75 After stops in Leipzig and Berlin, Angell completed his doctoral dissertation at Halle under Hans Vaihinger and Benno Erdmann. It was accepted in principle but denied final approval because the quality of German in which it was written was deemed inadequate. Having already been hired by Minnesota, Angell never got around to cleaning up the language and, so, never received a doctorate (see Donald A. Dewsbury, "James Rowland Angell: Born Administrator," in *Portraits of Pioneers in Psychology*, ed. by G. A. Kimble and Michael Wertheimer, vol. 5 (Washington, DC: American Psychological Association and Mahwah, NJ: Lawrence Erlbaum, 2003), 57–72.

76 On Halstead Street, just west of the south branch of the Chicago River, in the city's traditional Irish slum.

77 See Jane Addams, *Twenty Years at Hull House* (New York, NY: Palgrave Macmillan, 1912). See also Mary Lynn McCree Bryan and Allen Freeman Davis, *100 Years at Hull House* (Bloomington, IN: University of Indiana Press, 1990); and Peggy Glowacki and Julia Hendry, *Hull House* (Mount Pleasant, SC: Arcadia, 2004).

78 Among the elite students who became interested in unemployment and poverty while working at Toynbee was William Beveridge, who later became the chief architect of the British National Health Service and the rest of its modern welfare state.

79 The equivalent of over a million dollars in today's currency.

80 Designer of the Rand-McNally building in Chicago, the very first all-steel framed "skyscraper" (at 10 stories), among many other famous buildings.

81 Designer of New York's Central Park, over 30 years before, among many other iconic landscapes.

82 Most people were enchanted by the "White City," but those who yearned for a more democratic, more natively American vision of the future (such as Chicago architect Louis Sullivan) complained that the fair clung too slavishly to classical European models, rather than showcasing to visitors from overseas (and from the rest of America, for that matter) the city's newly emerging modern architectural aesthetic.

83 Estimates of the number of light bulbs used vary widely. Robert I. Goler reports 120,000 in "Visions of a Better Chicago," in *A City Comes of Age: Chicago in the 1890s*, ed. by Susan E. Hirsch & Robert I. Goler (Chicago, IL: Chicago Historical Society, 1990), 90–153. Erik Larson says nearly 200,000 (*The Devil in the White City* (New York, NY: Vintage, 2003), 251).

84 Cited in Tom McNichol, *AC/DC: The Savage Tale of the First Standards War* (New York, NY: Wiley, 2006).

85 Larson, *Devil*, 254.

86 The rivalry between Tesla and Edison became so heated and the stakes so high that, a decade later, Edison would distribute a film of the electrocution of a live elephant named Topsy, using AC, in a bogus effort to convince the public that Tesla's AC was more dangerous than his own DC. Of course, DC would have killed the huge animal just as certainly, but public ignorance of the nature of electricity was still profound at this time.

87 Larson, *Devil*, 222.

88 To add to the irony, the president of Wisconsin who had hired Jastrow, and with whom he had gotten along well, Thomas Chrowder Chamberlin, left to take up a new position offered him by Harper at the University of Chicago.

89 Arthur L. Blumenthal, "The Intrepid Joseph Jastrow," in *Portraits of Pioneers of Psychology*), ed. by G. A. Kimble, M. Wertheimer, and C. L. White, vol 1 (Washington, DC: American Psychological Association and Hillsdale, NJ: Lawrence Erlbaum, 1991), 74–87, 82.

90 The sensory battery included comparative judgments of length, weight, two-point touch, roughness of surfaces, as well as test of visual acuity and pain. The motor battery included tests of finger-tapping speed (electrically counted, of course, in line with the fair's theme), dividing a strip of paper into equal segments by muscle sensation alone (i.e., without benefit of sight). The memory tests included reproducing lengths that had been shown and then hidden, aiming at a once-seen but now-hidden target, and reproducing irregular geometrical shapes from memory. See Joseph Jastrow, "The Section of Psychology," in *Official Catalogue—World's Columbian Exposition*, ed. by M. P. Hardy, Part vii (Chicago, IL: W. B. Conkey, 1893), 50–60; and M. Henry De Varigny, "Le laboratoire de psychologie expérimentale de l'Université de Madison," *Revue Scientifique* 1, tome 1 (1894): 624–29.

91 For more information on the Congress, see Dorothy Ross, *G. Stanley Hall: The Psychologist as Prophet* (Chicago, IL: University of Chicago Press, 1972), 281–84, Marlene Shore, "Psychology and Memory in the Midst of Social Change: The Social Concerns of Late-19th-Century American Psychologists," in *The Transformation of Psychology: Influences of 19th-Century Philosophy, Technology, and Natural Science*, ed. Christopher D. Green, Marlene Shore, and Thomas Teo (Washington, DC: American Psychological Association, 2001), esp. 78–81, and Jacy L. Young, "When Psychologists Were Naturalists: Questionnaires and Collecting Practices in Early American Psychology, 1880–1932" (Doctoral dissertation, York University, 2014), 115–16.

92 Queen's University is in Kingston, Ontario, Canada.

93 *JSP* had ceased publication that very year, 1893, after a run of more than a quarter-century.

94 Shinn had graduated from the University of California more than a decade before and, by 1893, was conducting independent research on child development. She would later return to the Berkeley school to earn a PhD. On Shinn's unconventional educational trajectory, see Elissa Rodkey, "Profile of Millicent Shinn," in *Psychology's Feminist Voices Multimedia Internet Archive*, ed. A. Rutherford (2010). www.feministvoices.com/milicent-shinn/.

95 Over 27 million people had attended. In 1890, the population of the entire US was just 63 million. It is estimated that about half of the Fair's visitors had come from outside of the US.

96 Harrison left the mayoralty in 1887, perhaps disillusioned with the city's apparent drift in the wake of the Haymarket affair, and traveled to the West with his daughter. He wrote a book about the experience, then purchased the *Chicago Times* newspaper in 1891. He returned to the mayoralty in 1893 mainly so that he could be the city's principal representative during the Exposition.

97 Robert H. Wiebe, *The Search for Order, 1877–1920* (New York, NY: Farrar, Straus and Giroux, 1967), 91.

98 One must at least mention here that a great strike had taken place at the Carnegie steel plant in Homestead, PA (near Pittsburgh) in July of 1892. Carnegie Steel's chairman,

Henry Clay Frick, called in Pinkerton militiamen to clear the strikers, leading to a violent confrontation that left nine workers dead as well as three Pinkertons. Its remoteness from matters at hand leads me to write no more, but its relevance to the growing sense in America that a great conflagration over labor was in the offing prevents me from skipping it altogether. Although the cause of unionization was set back by the defeat at Homestead, the public revulsion at Frick's ruthless tactics was so intense that he was forced to move permanently from his hometown of Pittsburgh to New York City, where he lived out the remaining 27 years of his life. Carnegie and Frick had also set a horrific precedent that markedly raised the intensity of the Pullman conflict. Workers knew from the outset that it might come to mass shootings, and so this time they armed themselves accordingly.

99 Pullman was a leading manufacturer of freight cars in addition to his "palace" cars.

100 Letter from John Dewey to Alice Dewey, June 30/July 2, 1894 #00145 (Source: ICarbS, Collection: JDP 2/5, Document: ALS). In *The Correspondence of John Dewey 1871–1952* (3rd ed.) [CD-ROM] ed. by Larry A. Hickman Barbara Levine, Anne Sharpe, and Harriet Furst Simon (Carbondale, IL: Center for Dewey Studies, Southern Illinois University, 2005).

101 Letter John Dewey to Alice Dewey. July 2, 1894 #00152 (Source: ICarbS, Collection: JDP 2/6, Document: AL). In *The Correspondence of John Dewey 1871–1952* (3rd ed.) [CD-ROM] ed. by Larry A. Hickman Barbara Levine, Anne Sharpe, and Harriet Furst Simon (Carbondale, IL: Center for Dewey Studies, Southern Illinois University, 2005).

102 Tufts' unpublished autobiography. Chapter titled "Zeublin" ms pp. 2–3. James Hayden Tufts Papers. Box 3, folder 15. University of Chicago Archives.

103 Although little remembered today, Debs had actually served as a member of the Indiana State Senate from 1885 to 1889, prior to his taking over the leadership of the American Railway Union.

104 Tufts' unpublished autobiography. Chapter titled "Chicago III" ms pp. 4–5. James Hayden Tufts Papers. Box 3, folder 16. University of Chicago Archives.

105 It is worth noting that it was precisely on the issue of the role of the family in relation to schooling that Harvard's German-born psychology professor, Hugo Münsterberg, would most severely criticize America's Progressive education movement. Where Dewey saw the home as the primary source of racial prejudice and class conflict, which he sought to counteract through his educational philosophy, Münsterberg saw the family of as the only possible inculcator of proper moral values. As one of Münsterberg's biographers put the matter, "Where progressives attempted to use formal schooling, at least in theory, as a lever to unseat the traditional sources of socialization in society (especially the family), Münsterberg employed it to reinforce them." (Matthew Hale, *Human Science and Social Order: Hugo Münsterberg and the Origins of Applied Psychology* (Philadelphia, PA: Temple University Press, 1980), 60.)

106 John Dewey, *The School and Society* (Chicago, IL: University of Chicago Press, 1900), 27–28.

107 Tufts' unpublished autobiography. Chapter titled "Chicago III" ms pp. 6–7. James Hayden Tufts Papers. Box 3, folder 16. University of Chicago Archives.

108 Tufts' unpublished autobiography. Chapter titled "Chicago III" ms p. 7. James Hayden Tufts Papers. Box 3, folder 16. University of Chicago Archives.

109 Dewey, *School and Society*, 20.

110 Dewey, "Biography of John Dewey," 3–45, 9.

111 Dewey, *School and Society*, 34.

112 By 1890, 35% of American lived in urban settings. By 1920 it would be half. www.theusaonline.com/people/urbanization.htm. Accessed July 25, 2013.

113 Dewey, *School and Society*, 91.

7

THE FORMATION OF PSYCHOLOGY'S "SCHOOLS"

1. A Constellation of American Psychologists Takes Shape

At the start of 1887, there were exactly two experimental psychology laboratories in all of North America—Harvard and Johns Hopkins. Just eight years later, at the end of 1894, the year that Dewey arrived in Chicago, there were 28.[1] This extraordinary explosion in the number of psychology laboratories was the product of some talented and ambitious individuals, to be sure, but also of a radical change in the way Americans began to view colleges—from a small exclusive clubs to mass public institutions.

After Harvard and Hopkins, the third laboratory was founded at the University of Pennsylvania in 1887. It was set up by James McKeen Cattell, the one-time student of Hall at Hopkins and of Wundt in Leipzig (PhD 1886). Cattell was just then embarking on his invention of "mental tests." The fourth American psychology laboratory was established at Indiana University in 1888 by William Bryan.[2] Bryan had studied with the famed memory researcher Hermann Ebbinghaus in Berlin, but he earned his PhD under Hall at Clark. He later became president of his university. The fifth was Jastrow's laboratory at Wisconsin in 1888, and the sixth was Edmund C. Sanford's at Clark in 1889. The seventh psychology laboratory in North America was not in a university at all, but at the McLean Asylum outside of Boston, set up by William Noyes, a Harvard-trained physician who had undertaken some post-graduate research training with Hall. The eighth, ninth, and tenth were, respectively, at the University of Nebraska, founded by a former student of Wundt named Harry Kirke Wolfe (1889); at the University of Michigan, set up by Dewey's junior colleague, James Hayden Tufts (1890); and at the University of Iowa (1890), established by George T. W. Patrick who had been a student of Hall's at Hopkins.[3]

After the first ten laboratories were in place, new ones came in bunches: Columbia (Cattell) and Toronto (Baldwin) in 1890; Cornell (Frank Angell) and Wellesley (M. W. Calkins) in 1891; Brown (E. B. Delabarre), Illinois (W. O. Krohn), Kansas (O. Templin), Catholic University (E. A. Pace), New Jersey State Normal School in Trenton (L. A. Williams), Yale (E. W. Scripture) and Chicago (C. A. Strong), all in 1892; then Princeton (J. M. Baldwin), Minnesota (J. R. Angell), and Stanford (F. Angell) in 1893.

There are many interesting stories buried within this list: (1) Cattell moved to Columbia in 1890, opening the first psychology lab in New York City. (2) James Mark Baldwin moved north, to Toronto, to found the first permanent psychology laboratory not only in Canada, but in the British Empire as a whole.[4] (3) There were three individuals who opened labs in two different places (Cattell, Baldwin, and Frank Angell). (4) There are two women on this list—Mary Whiton Calkins at Wellesley, who would go on to serve as president of both the American Psychological Association (1905) and the American Philosophical Association (1918–1919), and Lillie A. Williams at New Jersey State Normal, who served as one of Hall's most inveterate collectors of questionnaire data.[5] (5) William O. Krohn of Illinois had been commissioned in 1891 to write a report on the state of university psychology laboratories in America by the US Commissioner of Education.[6] The Commissioner at that time was a person whom we have encountered already: William T. Harris, convener of the "St. Louis Hegelians," founder of the *Journal of Speculative Psychology*, sometime associate of the Concord Transcendentalists, and prominent leader of the National Education Association. And finally, (6) it is interesting to note that the "new psychology" (as it was sometimes called) made its way into Catholic higher education (which was still mostly separate from Protestant and public schools), by way of E. A. Pace in Washington, DC.

Perhaps the story with the broadest implications is not about any individual but rather about how, around 1890, experimental psychology started making its way beyond the major eastern cities and into the vast American interior—Indiana, Wisconsin, Nebraska, Iowa, Illinois, Kansas, Minnesota—and even to California. The West was becoming populated with colleges and universities by the dozen. The story behind the spread of higher education to the rural countryside is unique to the US.

In the midst of the Civil War, in 1862, Congress passed and Abraham Lincoln signed into law the Morrill Land Grant Act. The Act was named after Justin Smith Morrill, the visionary Republican Congressman (1855–1867) and later Senator (1867–1898) from Vermont (the boyhood homes, recall, of both John Dewey and James Rowland Angell). The law that he sponsored granted federal land to states at no cost if they used it to establish colleges and universities.[7] Iowa was the first state to found a college under the Morrill Act, an agricultural school that would evolve into Iowa State University in Ames.[8]

The University of Wisconsin, where Jastrow would establish the fifth psychological laboratory in 1888, was a land grant school as well. So was the University of Nebraska where Harry Kirke Wolfe founded the eighth psychology laboratory in 1889.[9] Other land grant schools that were home to early psychology laboratories included Illinois (1892, by Krohn), Minnesota (1893 by James Angell), Pennsylvania State (1895, Erwin W. Runkle, a Yale-educated philosopher), California (1896, George M. Stratton, a Wundt graduate), and Ohio State (1897, Clark Wissler, a student of Cattell's who would go on to renown as an anthropologist).[10]

Perhaps the most interesting of these, for present purposes, was the founding in 1865 of Cornell University, in the town of Ithaca, nestled among the hills and river chasms of rural central New York. Cornell got its start at a meeting between a career-academic named Andrew Dickson White who briefly (1864–1867) held a New York State senate seat, and a fellow state senator (and telegraph magnate) named Ezra Cornell. White was a native of central New York but had gone to Yale in the early 1850s. After a short stint as a professor at Michigan, White returned home to central New York in 1863, in the midst of the Civil War. He was soon elected to the state senate, where he was appointed to the chairmanship of the Education Committee. Ezra Cornell, by contrast, was a carpenter from the Bronx, who had chosen to live in Ithaca. In the 1840s he had met Samuel Morse and convinced him that hanging telegraph wires from poles was superior to burying them in the damp ground.[11] Cornell's telegraph companies were major components in the merger that created the gigantic Western Union in the 1850s. Needless to say, he made a fortune.

While they both held political office in the 1860s, White and Cornell worked on a plan to use the newly-passed Morrill act to fund a new university in central New York. The working assumption had been that the land granted by the federal government would serve as the campus for the school, but that assumption was not actually written into the law. So, White and Cornell arranged for their university to be granted timberland in Wisconsin, the profits from which would be used to fund the building of the school and for its early operational costs. Ezra Cornell donated a plot of land in Ithaca from his sizeable fortune to serve as the campus and, thus, became the school's namesake. White became the university's first president, serving from 1865, three years before the school opened its doors to students, until his retirement in 1885.[12]

White was succeeded by his protégé, Charles Kendall Adams. Among Adams' early projects was to find a man to found a psychology laboratory at Cornell. Joseph Jastrow, who had just graduated from Johns Hopkins, was probably better suited to the job than anyone in America who did not already have a professorship (but for Charles Peirce, of course). For two years after his graduation, in 1886, Jastrow remained in Baltimore, publishing regularly in a wide variety of journals: *Mind, Science, American Journal of Psychology*, and *Popular Science Monthly*, among others. His areas of expertise were original and diverse: psychophysics, population statistics, the perception of rhythm, the perception of space, star magnitudes, science education, logic, genius, and the techniques of deception used by stage magicians and spirit mediums, among others. Despite this prodigious output, however, Jastrow was unable to find an academic position suited to his education.

Even though Cornell was looking to hire someone with precisely Jastrow's qualifications, President Adams refused Jastrow's application. It is said that he was so adamant in his opposition to Jastrow that he preferred to defer the establishment of a laboratory to hiring the Hopkins graduate.[13] The reason for Adams' animosity toward Jastrow is not clear. Personal anti-Semitism has been assumed in some accounts, and it may have well been in play. Adams was not a worldly figure, by any means. Unrelated to the famous Adamses of Quincy, Massachusetts, he had been raised in rural Vermont before leaving, at the rather advanced age of 21, to attend the University of Michigan. There, he was "discovered" by White and became his protégé. A prominent member of the Cornell faculty described Adams as having "a certain heaviness of style coupled with apparent slowness of wit, and considerable uncouthness of manner."[14] The issue with Jastrow, however, may not have been entirely Adams' doing. It was also the case that the psychology position was attached to a department that had been endowed by lumber baron and trustee Henry W. Sage explicitly to advance Christian Ethics and Mental Philosophy.[15] The public outcry that might have been unleashed by the appointment of Jastrow, a secular Jew, to such a post is easy to imagine.

As matters unfolded, it took until 1891 before Adams discovered the "right" man to found Cornell's psychology laboratory. He was Frank Angell, a newly-minted graduate of Wundt's Leipzig laboratory. He hailed from a family with a grand academic tradition: He was a nephew of Michigan president James Burrill Angell (and, thus, the older cousin of James Rowland Angell). The Angell family had a history in Providence, Rhode Island dating back to Colonial days. Even today, there is an Angell Street running alongside of the Brown University campus.

Frank Angell left Cornell, however, after only a single year for a professorship at the newly-launched Stanford University, in northern California. The reasons behind Angell's abrupt departure from Cornell remain somewhat mysterious. The official story was that he left because his health could not endure the harsh winters.[16] A private letter by his illustrious uncle, James Burrill Angell, however, hints that Henry W. Sage, the patron of Cornell's new school of philosophy, demanded that a conventional Christian line be upheld among the faculty, and there was something unorthodox about Frank's "attitude" that made him ill-suited for such a position, though no details were revealed.[17]

Making matters curiouser still, the person who succeeded Angell (and who had been recommended by him) was Edward Bradford Titchener. Titchener—like Angell, a graduate of Leipzig—was no devout Christian. He was agnostic, at best: in an 1899 letter to William James, he would complain that no young instructor could espouse "agnosticism" in the manner of Thomas Henry Huxley (who had invented the term in 1869) "without suffering for it."[18] Nevertheless, the Board of Trustees appointed Titchener assistant professor of psychology on July 26, 1892.[19] Titchener arrived in the US at precisely the time that department chairmanships were starting to grow into positions "of great importance at most of the larger universities." It is also said that Titchener "ruled psychology with a hand of iron."[20] Nevertheless, he ultimately built the Cornell laboratory into one of the most prestigious, if somewhat idiosyncratic, psychology programs in the entire US.

2. The Founding of the American Psychological Association

Following the tragic deaths of his wife and daughter in 1890, and the loss of most of his prized faculty in 1892, one might have expected Stanley Hall to retreat somewhat from the psychological scene. At the very least, one would think that he needed time to rebuild both his school and his personal life. But that was not Hall's way. He barreled forward, intent as ever on seizing and retaining the national leadership of psychology in America.

Probably in the spring of 1892, Hall wrote to a number of colleagues, inquiring about the possibility of forming a national organization of psychologists that would hold an annual conference.[21] It is not known exactly how many people he invited but, given the response, it was probably on the order of three or four dozen. He proposed to hold a preliminary meeting in Worcester in July. We know that 26 people either attended the meeting or sent a letter of approval, but we do not know exactly how many traveled to Clark for the meeting. Perhaps having learned from the resentment generated by his restrictive editorial policies at the *American Journal*, the geographical spread of Hall's "call" was enormous: in addition to the "usual suspects" from the east, he included John Dewey then at Michigan, Mark Baldwin at Toronto, William Bryan at Indiana, George Patrick at Iowa, Harry Wolfe at Nebraska, Joseph Jastrow at Wisconsin, and Frank Angell who had just gone to Stanford. At the meeting itself, five additional members were elected, including Edward Titchener who had just arrived at Cornell, Hugo Münsterberg who had just arrived from Freiburg to enlarge and modernize William James' laboratory at Harvard, Edward Pace who had just opened his laboratory at Catholic University in Washington, DC, and Thomas Wesley Mills of McGill University in Montréal. The group showed remarkable breadth for the era—there was a Catholic member (Pace), a Jewish member (Jastrow),[22] two Canadians (James G. Hume of Toronto and T. Wesley Mills of McGill),[23] an Englishman (Titchener), and a German (Münsterberg). There were, however, no women in the new Association and no people of color.

The preliminary meeting seems to have been a one-day affair. Six papers were read, and a steering committee was selected. The committee consisted, first, of the discipline's three "old men": Hall, who was elected president of the new organization; William James, who was in Europe and did not attend the meeting;[24] and George Trumbull Ladd of Yale.[25] In addition, the committee included Jastrow, who was starting work on what would be his World's Fair exhibit; Cattell and Baldwin, who were about to clash mightily with Hall over his editorship of *American Journal of Psychology*, ultimately resulting in their creation of a rival journal, *Psychological Review*; and George Stuart Fullerton of the University of Pennsylvania, who offered to host the first official meeting of the new American Psychological Association (APA) in December of that year.[26]

The "first annual" meeting of the APA that took place in Philadelphia was attended by just 18 of the 31 members.[27] It featured twelve talks, including a presidential address by Hall, now lost, titled, "History and Prospects of Experimental Psychology in America."[28] The other talks were mostly experimental in character—a paper on theoretical psychophysics by Cattell, one on the perception of thickness by Pace, talks on aesthetics and on reaction-time research by Lightner Witmer (a former student of Fullerton's and Cattell's at Penn, who had just completed his PhD under Wundt at Leipzig), a presentation on the psychology laboratory at the upcoming Exposition in Chicago by Joseph Jastrow, a talk on illusions by Herbert Nichols, talks by William Bryan on a problem in the reaction-time literature and on psychological testing, a report of experimental studies at Clark by Edmund Sanford—but also a theoretical assessment of the state of experimental psychology by Hugo Münsterberg. There weren't only experimentalists in the early APA. A number of individuals who identified primarily as speculative philosophers were also members. Because there was no philosophical association at the time (and wouldn't be until after the turn of the 20th century) the new organization did a kind of double-duty, much to the consternation of a few of the stricter experimentalists, who attempted to sequester the philosophers and their disagreeable metaphysical talk into a separate "section" of the organization.[29]

Eleven new members were accepted into the fold at the first annual meeting. This brought the membership to 42. The additions included Nicholas Murray Butler of Columbia, who would become president of that university in less than a decade's time; George Herbert Mead, still then at Michigan with Dewey; Charles Sanders Peirce, who listed his affiliation merely as Milford, Pennsylvania; Charles Strong, still the senior philosopher at Chicago; Jacob Gould Schurman, who had just acceded to the presidency of Cornell University; James Rowland Angell, then at Minnesota; and the McGill philosopher John C. Murray (whose first name was mistakenly printed in the official *Proceedings* as "James"). George Trumbull Ladd was elected to succeed Hall as the president of the organization. He would be followed the next year by William James. Only then would the younger members take their turns as president: Cattell, Fullerton, and Baldwin. In 1898 Hugo Münsterberg would become the first APA president who had not been on the original steering committee of 1892. The first women to join the APA were Mary Whiton Calkins of Wellesley College and Christine Ladd-Franklin,[30] whose names were accepted onto the membership rolls at the second annual meeting, held in 1893 in New York City.[31]

3. Edward Bradford Titchener, a Psychologist *Not* of the City

Titchener was among the most conspicuous of the newcomers to the American psychological scene in the early 1890s. There was no doubt that he regarded himself as intellectually superior to nearly all Americans in the discipline at the time. He was paradoxically defiant in his loyalty to the orthodox Wundtian model of scientific psychology (as he understood it, at least). Despite being an outwardly stiff character, rigidly holding to views of the mind that did not find much resonance in the US, he was nevertheless tremendously respected for his experimental acumen. His *Manuals of Laboratory Practice*, first published a decade after his arrival in the US, became the standard to which many psychologists adhered.

Born in Chichester, near the south coast of England, in 1867, Titchener took his bachelor's degree at Oxford in 1889. He became interested in psychology after reading George Trumbull Ladd's textbook, published that same year, but he sought a more naturalistic account of the field.[32] English universities of the day did not offer experimental psychology, so Titchener returned to Oxford for a year of physiological training, mainly to acquire a measure of laboratory skill, and then entered Wilhelm Wundt's psychology laboratory at Leipzig. He completed his PhD there in 1892. Because English universities were slow to take up experimental psychology, there were no openings for Titchener in his home country. Instead, he accepted the position at Cornell that was just being vacated by Frank Angell, who also had been a student of Wundt's.

Titchener well knew that many of his new American colleagues had trained, like him, under Wundt, so it came as something of a shock to him that psychologists in the US were engaged in such a wide array of activities that, in his opinion, would never have been permitted in the Leipzig laboratory.[33] This was partly a result of the influence of William James, whose *Principles* had appeared just two years before Titchener's arrival. However, a more pressing factor than James' influence was probably the fact that universities created under the Morrill Act were mandated by law to disseminate knowledge of a "practical" character, which is why so many of them included words like "agricultural," "technical," "mechanical," or "normal" (educational) in their very names. Boards and administrators wanted assurances before paying for something so exotic as a psychology laboratory that *practical* knowledge, in some recognizable sense of the term, would be the final product. It was all well and fine to have a psychophysics laboratory for instructing students on the foundations of the field, but psychology's success in America was more likely to rise or fall on the direct benefits that it produced in the public school, the factory, the sales floor, the court of law, and the like.

Interestingly, Wundt's challenge in promoting experimental psychology in German Universities had been almost exactly the opposite. He was determined that psychology would reside in the best universities and, to achieve and maintain that status, it had to present itself to administrators and government officials as a "pure" academic discipline. Any hint that it was an applied art would result in its relegation to the less prestigious technical schools. Many traditional philosophy professors in the Germanic states were not pleased with the arrival of laboratories in "their" departments. They fought against acceptance of Wundt's approach to psychology, once going so far as to present to the German education ministry a petition signed by dozens of professors who opposed the appointment of psychologists to philosophy professorships. Wundt ultimately won the day (and psychology eventually came to occupy its own departments, rather than being forced to share philosophy departments with ethicists and metaphysicians), but Wundt's victory depended on his consistently rejecting just those "practical" potentialities of psychology that, by contrast, would win psychologists a solid spot in many American universities.[34]

Titchener, however, adopted Wundt's vision of a "pure" psychology as being the One True Way to pursue the field, rather than as having been a strategic decision relevant mainly to the context of the late 19th-century German university system.[35] Upon seeing what he regarded as the "muddle" of psychology in the US, he immediately cast himself as the one wholly orthodox disciple of the Wundtian program in America. He declared that "experimental" psychology was largely a matter of carrying out a particularly rigorous form of introspection, during which the psychologist would "objectively" record all the elementary sensations, images, and feelings out of which each distinct kind of complex mental experience was putatively composed. He regarded it as critically important that the "experimenter" not confuse this technical analysis of fundamental mental phenomena with the common understandings of the physical stimuli being contemplated. For instance, one must never speak of rose-like properties when introspecting upon the perception of a rose: its color had a certain hue, brightness, and saturation; its smell had a certain intensity, sweetness, etc. But it would never do to say flatly that one was experiencing a rose. That would be to commit the highest Titchenerian sin: the "stimulus error." One's mental attitude must remain entirely detached and "objective"—no everyday meanings or significances of the object were allowed to taint the "purity" of the analysis. This was *science*, after all.

Titchener even preached a certain regimen of abstinence on the part of the scientist himself in everyday life; one did not want to damage or bias the "equipment" of his all-important introspective capacities through extreme or intemperate activities.[36] The practitioner of scientific introspection was a kind of machine, and his "mechanism," like any piece of scientific apparatus, must be maintained in pristine condition if it was to be depended on to detect to tiniest fluctuations in the elements that were believed to underpin mental experience.

Titchener would often rail against what he viewed as the perversions of science committed by American psychologists, even some of those who had studied with Wundt. "Pure" science was the only appropriate course for Titchener and, although he conceded that there might be a need to produce "technology" (as he called applied work), based on scientific findings, he did not think it proper for the university professor to sully himself with such pursuits.

The Leipzig program in which Titchener had trained sought out the features of the "generalized" human mind. There was presumed to be only one, just as there is only one kind of gold or any other "natural kind." Any variation discovered among subjects, according to the Wundtian paradigm, revealed only experimental error, or an inability on the part of the subject to carry out the task of the experiment correctly (due to insufficient prior training or a dearth of the required native capacities). If the experiment were done correctly, so the theory went, all subjects would produce one and the same result. Of course, this is not what actually occurred, even in the Leipzig lab; it was an ideal to be pursued. Wundt and his colleagues were, after all, working at the very edges of science, using highly temperamental advanced equipment, such as the Hipp chronoscope.[37] A certain amount of unsteadiness was to be expected in the early steps of any such endeavor. Nevertheless, abandoning the ideal of the generalized mind in favor of explicitly conducting research on "sub-optimal" subjects—insufficiently-educated men, women,[38] children, the mad, non-Europeans, animals—would lead not to knowledge but only to uninterpretable chaos.

Many American psychologists disagreed with Titchener's assessment, however. Following the model of (English) evolutionary theory rather than that of (German) experimental physiology, they reasoned that the variability Leipzigers spurned was, in fact, the true natural state of things and that, in combination with an understanding of the kinds of environments in which humans typically subsist, it might be able to explain how human mental function had come to be the way it was. The debate might have come to nothing had the Wundtian research program not encountered a set of research results that threatened to undermine the entire project, forcing its members to rethink their assumptions and develop a new understanding to explain away the contentious data.

4. Leipzig's Problem With Reaction Time

Wundt theorized that a reaction to a stimulus consisted of five distinct stages: sensation (action of the peripheral sense organs), perception (conscious awareness of the stimulus), apperception, an act of will (to respond), and the actual motor response. Apperception—a term which had first arisen in German philosophy a century earlier—meant (to Wundt) to have the object in focal consciousness; something could be merely *perceived* peripherally—e.g., a distraction to the main matter in mind—but to be *apperceived* an object had to receive full conscious attention. Wundt and his students studied all the various stages. The central task was to fractionate the process from stimulation to reaction into its five constituent parts, measuring the length of time each one took. The study of apperception, however, was accorded special status in Wundt's overall experimental program.[39]

The Leipzigers' results were dogged, however, by certain inconsistencies. Some people were consistently faster responders than others, and there was no explanation for this fact under the idealizing assumption they made about the generalized human mind. The anomaly was only sharpened when James McKeen Cattell, then still a student, discovered a flaw in the mechanism of the much-vaunted Hipp chronoscope that was artificially lengthening the reaction times that were at the core of Wundt's experimental psychology.[40] He developed technical innovations to improve the instrument's accuracy, but also made more stark the inexplicable discrepancy in reaction times, bringing the research program to a crisis point.

Soon after Cattell graduated, in 1886,[41] a theoretical innovation by the second of Wundt's Laboratory Assistants, Ludwig Lange, promised to salvage the program by explaining away the problematic discrepancies: Lange suggested that there might be two distinct types of simple reaction to a stimulus that were being mistakenly conflated in the experiments—a completely "sensorial" reaction in which the attention of the subject (*Reagent* in German) was focused on the stimulus to be presented, and a quicker "muscular" reaction in which the attention of the subject was focused on the motor response he was to make. Lange hypothesized that the faster muscular reaction was possible because it somehow skipped over the stage of true apperception—that it was a "brain-reflex," by analogy with reflexive motor movements in which, for the sake of speed, incoming sensory signals are "reflected" into outgoing motor ones within the spinal cord, and do not require time-consuming processing in higher brain centers. The longer sensorial reaction, however, was said to include all of the stages specified in Wundt's theory, including apperception, making them longer. Indeed, Lange found that the reaction times of subjects who were *instructed* to focus their attention on their motor reaction rather than on the stimulus were consistently shorter than those of subjects who were instructed to focus on the stimulus.[42] Wundt himself adopted this explanation in the third edition of his *Grundzüge der physiologischen Psychologie* (*Principles of Physiological Psychology*, published in 1887): the longer reaction time in the "sensorial" condition was the result of it including a full apperceptive stage, whereas apperception was absent in the faster "muscular" case.

Cattell, for his part, wrote home disparagingly of Wundt's much-vaunted laboratory. He had doubts that people could reliably make the kinds of distinctions among their own conscious states that Wundt's experiments demanded, such as that between when a stimulus is merely "perceived" and when it is fully "apperceived" and, although he did not yet say so publicly, he privately harbored doubts that Lange's reinterpretation of the data actually rescued Wundt from his dilemma.[43] First, he traveled to England, where he was able to indulge a longtime interest in evolutionary theory that had not found expression in the Leipzig lab. For a year he worked intermittently with Charles Darwin's cousin, Francis Galton. Since the publication of *Origin of Species*, Galton had been fascinated with the implications of natural selection for the human species, even arguing that evolutionary "progress" could be helped along by a conscious program of what he dubbed "eugenics." He reasoned that natural selection must still be working on small variations among humans, and he sought to discover precisely the range of those variations by collecting data on a large number of people's basic physical attributes and capacities. He called this research topic "anthropometry"—literally the "measurement of humans." For three pence, in the mid-1880s, one could be measured in about two dozen different ways in Galton's laboratory at the South Kensington museum in London—everything from height and weight, to the length and breadth of one's head, to the strength of one's squeeze to the keen-ness of one's eyesight and hearing, to one's reaction time to visual and auditory stimuli. Over the years, Galton carried out such measurements on thousands of members of the public. Cattell was captivated by this search for the range of indi-vidual differences—the very stuff on which natural selection operated—but he wanted to focus the study more squarely on the realm of the mental than Galton had, studying *psychological* differences between people and the degree to which evolution might work upon them.

As we have seen, in 1887, Cattell won a professorship at the University of Pennsylvania and returned home to America. He set up a laboratory there and worked to develop what he called a "mental test," using Galton's anthropometrical work as his model.[44] Cattell's tests, however, included more psychological items such as tactile sensitivity, the ability to discriminate between slightly different weights, the amount of pressure required to cause pain, the time needed to name the color of a stimulus, the ability to correctly bisect a line freehand, memory for spoken letter strings, the estimation of various lengths of time, and, of course, reaction time. By 1891, Cattell had been offered a more lucrative position at Columbia University in New York City. Once established there, he founded a new experimental laboratory and began developing a plan to conduct his mental tests on hundreds of college students.

In 1892, he started publishing data that seemed to undercut the theoretical maneuver that had enabled Lange to apparently salvage Wundt's research program. He was able to show that the "sensorial" and "muscular" reaction times did not differ from each other in either an experienced or a naïve subject (i.e., himself and his wife). Another subject was reported to have displayed substantially *shorter* sen-sorial reaction times, contrary to the findings of Lange and others. In short, there was no single "normal" pattern to the reactions. Different individuals reacted dif-ferently from one another. Rather than publishing in an English-language journal, Cattell sent his findings to Wundt himself who, to his credit, published them in his influential journal, *Philosophische Studien* (*Philosophical Studies*).[45]

Now, however, the battle over the correct interpretation of the results was joined in earnest. In response to Cattell's article, Titchener reviewed some ten different studies of the reaction-time phenomenon Cattell had questioned.[46] Even though he found just six in favor of Lange's interpretation and four opposed, he proceeded to exclude most of the contrary findings on the grounds that the subjects were not experienced in the task and, therefore, did not have what Titchener regarded as the proper *Anlage* or "mental disposition" to execute it correctly. The question at issue shifted to whether experience with the reaction-time procedure winnowed away unwanted "noise" to reveal the "true" underlying phenomenon or whether it served only to enforce a false, preconceived consensus on the data. For those interested in psychology's evolutionary aspect, differences between people were the essential raw material on which natural selection operates. For those committed to the older Wundtian paradigm, such differences were mere clutter that obscured the truth.

James Mark Baldwin, another up and coming American experimental psychologist, responded to Titchener's gerrymandered critique of Cattell's findings in scathing and dismissive terms. Baldwin had been born and raised in the capital city of South Carolina, Columbia.[47] He did not follow his family's tradition of attending Yale, going instead to the College of New Jersey (later Princeton University). He spent some time pursuing graduate studies in Europe—he even attended some of Wundt's lectures and served as a subject in a few Leipzig students' experiments—but he returned to New Jersey to earn his PhD under the Scottish philosopher James McCosh. After graduating, Baldwin briefly worked at Lake Forest College outside of Chicago (1887–1889) and at the University of Toronto (1889–1893), where, as mentioned, he founded the first permanent experimental psychology laboratory in the British Empire.[48] Then he was called to a professorship at his *alma mater* of Princeton.

By that time, he had written a two-volume textbook,[49] the first part of which had come out a year prior to William James' *Principles*, and he had developed some startlingly original ideas about mental evolution.[50] He and Cattell, now both rising stars of the new discipline, grew increasingly unhappy with Stanley Hall's editorial policies at the *American Journal of Psychology* (who virtually restricted access to his own former students and colleagues who were close to his laboratories at Johns Hopkins and Clark). So, in 1894, they launched a new journal together, *Psychological Review*, to capture the rest of the growing American market in academic psychological research.

Titchener's blast against Baldwin's partner, Cattell, gave Baldwin an opportunity to enter the fray. Interestingly, Baldwin chose to publish his retort to Titchener not in *Mind*, where the original article had appeared, but in his own *Psychological Review*.[51] Baldwin argued that Titchener and the Leipzigers were engaged in a circular self-justification, excluding those who did not conform to their theoretical position—those said not to have the correct "disposition"—for no reason other than that they did not confirm the theory. Baldwin presented new data showing not only that different individuals react differently depending on whether they focus on the stimulus or on the response, but also that they react differently depending on whether they can watch their hand responding (motor-visual) or they are forced to only feel it by being blindfolded (motor kinaesthetic). Baldwin proposed the theory—contrary to everything the Leipzigers presumed—that there are inherently different "types" of reactors in the human population: sensory types and motor types, the motor types dividing into visual and kinaesthetic subtypes. He also hinted that there might be visual and auditory sensory types, reacting differently to various kinds of stimuli.

Baldwin claimed to have borrowed the idea of different mental "types" from the literature on aphasia—some brain-injured people are unable to speak language but can understand it well (Broca), others cannot understand language but still speak it fluently (Wernicke). It seems, however, that another factor at work here was Baldwin's interest in evolutionary theory. At the very time that Baldwin was debating Titchener, he was also writing a series of articles on how acquired behaviors—cultural activities—might come to be inherited by offspring from parents *without* having to resort to a Lamarckian explanation of the phenomenon; that is, without having to assert that the extensive use and exercise of a particular function by an animal (e.g., a giraffe stretching its neck to eat leaves that are high up in trees) will lead to the strengthened function being passed directly on to that animal's future offspring (e.g., being born with a longer neck than it otherwise would have been).[52]

Returning to Baldwin's theory that the inconsistent reaction times found in the laboratories of Wundt and others were due to there being "natural" variations in people's mental constitutions—the sensory type, the motor type, etc.—one can see the connection between his psychology and his speculative evolutionary biology. Just as heritable physical variations or "types" are needed for natural selection to do its work on the body, so are heritable *mental* variations needed among individuals for natural selection to work effectively on psychological characteristics. Baldwin's reaction "types" were just the kind of variations he required to ground scientific psychology in a natural selectionist framework.

In response, Titchener (back in the journal *Mind*) expressed no interest in Baldwin's evolutionary innovations.[53] He contended, instead, that Baldwin had simply misconstrued the Leipzig position on the puzzling reaction-time data. Quoting the words of Wundt's former assistant, Ludwig Lange, he wrote,

> our experience shows that there are certain persons who are incapable . . . of reacting consistently. . . . It would, of course, be useless for the normal psychologist to make experiments upon subjects in so obviously pathological a condition.[54]

Titchener then questioned the reliability of Baldwin's new data and the very coherence of a type-theory of reaction. He once again attempted to dismiss, on various grounds, each of the contrary cases Baldwin had brought forth. "The evidence for the [type theory] at present," he concluded, "is so slight that it is hardly more than a conjecture."[55]

Rejoinders followed, and the debate rapidly descended into a war of words:

Baldwin: "I cannot help thinking that Professor Titchener sometimes allows the dust of his machinery to obscure his vision."[56]

Titchener: "Professor Baldwin objects to bringing facts together: he distributes them sparsely in a matrix of theory,—like the infrequent plums in school plum-cake."[57]

Baldwin: "If I were [being] criticized by one whose standing I did not know, I should say [it] showed incompetency or playing to the galleries."[58]

Titchener: "I . . . have no wish to emulate Professor Baldwin in the matter of name-calling."[59]

This public exchange of increasingly empty invective did little to enhance the reputations either of the two young scientists involved or of the new science that they represented.

5. The First "Schools" of American Psychology

While Titchener and Baldwin were sparring rhetorically in the journals, over in Chicago James Rowland Angell and an assistant named Addison W. Moore were conducting the most extensive set of reaction-time experiments yet. Responses were made by hand, foot, and lips, to visual and auditory stimuli, in both the "sensory" and "motor" modes. The auditory series, both hand and foot, were split into sets staged in regular lighting and in the dark. Like Baldwin, they found that *initially* different people displayed different patterns of reaction. As the subjects became more practiced, however, the differences between the "sensory" and "motor" reactions narrowed to the point of being nearly indistinguishable.[60]

To explain the shifting reaction patterns that were produced by simple practice, Angell and Moore offered what they called a "dynamo-genetic" interpretation,[61] in place of the "static" explanations given by both Titchener and Baldwin: they rejected the idea that a straight reflex was at work, contending instead, under the influence of their mentor, Dewey, that "the whole act to be performed is not the mere response of the hand to the ear, but the act of attention in coördinating the incoming stimuli from both the hand and the ear." This dense clause requires some unpacking, to be sure, but Angell and Moore provided it themselves:

> What holds the ear to its work? Why does the reagent [i.e., participant] maintain his listening attitude? It may be replied that it is "because he is told to." But he is not told to listen any more than he is told to move his hand. If the telling suffices in one case it should in the other [i.e., "he is told to" does not explain why the muscular version is faster, initially, than the sensory version]. Moreover, he is not merely to listen, or even to listen just for the click, but to listen for the click as a pressure signal [i.e., a signal to press the response key]. It is this character of the click as a signal for pressure that keeps the interest in it and the attention to it. . . . [The hand and the ear are] both stimulus and response to the other [i.e., pressing in response to the last click stimulates the ear to return to its active listening phase]. The distinction of stimulus and response is therefore not one of *content*, the stimulus being identified with the ear, the response with the hand, but one of *function*, and both offices belong equally to each organ.[62]

With this theoretical framework in place, Angell and Moore went on to argue that the sensory form of the reaction typically takes longer not because it involves "apperception," as Wundt believed, but rather because, in most unpracticed subjects, it involves a shift of focal attention from the ear to the hand. Since, Angell and Moore claimed, listening with the ear is, for most people coming into the experiment, already more under the control of habit than pressing a button with the hand, the attention that is initially focused on the ear or eye in the "sensory form" is "unnecessary work" which takes additional time. With practice, however, the connection between the hearing and the pressing becomes better coordinated, "more and more reflex," as Angell and Moore put it.[63] The sensory and motor forms of the task gradually become nearly equivalent though, because the "ear adjustment affords less material for the continued exercise of attention than that presented by the hand," the motor form continues to be slightly shorter even in most well-practiced subjects.

> We should, then, expect that act to be faster in which the focus of attention is upon the less stable phase of the hand element of the coördination rather than when it is "artificially" occupied in breaking up the more completely established ear adjustment.[64]

Just a few weeks later, Dewey published a full account of the theoretical position that had been tacitly employed by Angell and Moore to explain the reaction-time problem in an article titled "The Reflex Arc Concept in Psychology."[65] This article came to be regarded as the founding document of the Functionalist school of psychology (though the name did not yet exist in 1896). Nearly fifty years later, in a survey of academic psychologists, it would be declared to be the most influential article in the entire history of *Psychological Review*.[66]

Dewey, invoking one of his favorite philosophical themes, argued that the idea of the stimulus-response reflex arc, then coming into vogue as a possible "basic element" for all of psychology, simply recapitulated the dualisms of psychologies past: sensation versus idea, subject versus object, body versus soul. As such, it did not result in

> a comprehensive or organic unity, but a patchwork of disjointed parts, a mechanical conjunction of unallied processes. . . . What is wanted, is that the sensory stimulus, central connections and motor responses shall be viewed not as separate and complete entities in themselves, but as divisions of labor, *function factors*, within the single concrete whole, now designated the reflex arc.[67]

To explain this, he borrowed an example from the opening pages of William James' *Principles of Psychology*—that of the child reaching for the flame of a candle:

> We find that we begin not with a sensory stimulus, but with a sensori-motor coördination, the optical-ocular, and that in a certain sense it is the movement which is primary, and the sensation which is secondary, the movement of the body, head and eye muscles determining the quality of

what is experienced. In other words, the real beginning is with the act of seeing; it is looking, and not a sensation of light.[68]

Dewey started by establishing a framework in which the organism is an active explorer of its environment, not merely a passive sense organ that is impinged upon by an external stimulus; the animal co-creates its experience with the environment. For instance, if the animal does not turn its head toward the flame, or does not consciously attend to the objects in its visual field when it does so, then there is no perception of light. To the extent that this is true, sensation is not strictly the "first" event in the reflex arc. Things are more complicated, more nuanced, than is implied by that crude but common characterization. Dewey continued:

> Now if this *act of seeing* stimulates another act, the reaching, it is because both of these acts fall within a larger coördination; because seeing and grasping have been so often bound together to reinforce each other, to help each other out, that each may be considered practically a subordinate member of a bigger coördination. . . . The reaching, in turn, must both stimulate and control the seeing. The eye must be kept upon the candle if the arm is to do it work. . . . [W]e now have an enlarged and transformed coördination; the act of seeing no less than before, but it is now seeing-for-reaching-purposes.[69]

For Dewey, the experience cannot be correctly understood if it is torn from its context. The animal's life history—its past experience with coordinating its

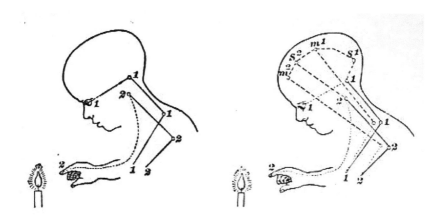

FIGURE 7.1 William James' diagram, in chapter 2 of *The Principles of Psychology*, of a child reaching for a flame, and the various mental associations that arise from the experience.

sensory and motor organs (e.g., looking, seeing, then reaching for what is seen)—participates in the interpretation and understanding of the animal's behavior.

> Now take the affair at its next stage, that in which the child gets burned. . . . Only because the heat-pain quale [feeling] enters into the same circuit of experience with the optical-ocular and muscular quales [sic], does the child learn from the experience and get the ability to avoid the experience in the future.[70]

Dewey then attempted to build a general theory of the reflex out of his reinterpretation of James' example. It is instructive to quote Dewey at some length here in order to see the style of language that he employed, which provoked equal shares of enlightenment and bewilderment on the part of his audience.

> [T]he so-called response is not merely *to* the stimulus; it is *into* it. The burn is the original seeing, the original optical-ocular experiences enlarged and transformed in its value. It is no longer mere seeing; it is seeing-of-a-light-that-means-pain-when-contact-occurs.[71]
>
> The reflex arc idea. . . . in its failure to see that the arc of which it talks is virtually a circuit, a continual reconstitution, it breaks continuity and leaves us with nothing but a series of jerks, the origin of each jerk to be sought outside the process of experience itself.[72]
>
> [S]timulus and response are not distinctions of existence but teleological distinctions, that is, distinctions of function, or part played, with reference to reaching or maintaining an end.[73]
>
> Neither mere sensation, nor mere movement, can ever be either stimulus or response; only an act can be that; the sensation as stimulus means the lack of and search for such an objective stimulus, or orderly placing of an act; just as mere movement as response means the lack of and search for the right act to complete a given coördination.[74]

As can be seen here, Dewey's aim was to profoundly change the rules of "scientific" psychology. According to him, the objects of the world are responded to by psychological beings not simply on the basis of their physical qualities but also on the basis of their practical significance for the organism—whether dangerous, nutritive, pleasurable, etc. Whereas Titchener preached a doctrine of decomposing the perceptions of objects into their presumably constituent sensations, images, and feelings, Dewey looked primarily to the object's import, to its meaning, to how it *functioned* in the organism's mental and behavioral "ecology." However, unlike earlier metaphysical psychologists (including his own earlier self), Dewey did this in a way that was scientifically respectable. Indeed, his younger colleagues, Angell and Moore, had already conducted laboratory experiments based on this position which had, to all appearances, resolved a bitter scientific debate. What more could one ask of a scientific theory?

Titchener did not respond immediately to these events in Chicago. His textbook, *An Outline of Psychology*, appeared in 1896, soon followed by his co-translation of Oswald Külpe's *Introduction to Philosophy*.[75] Then came a revision of the *Outline*, and some articles about other matters in *Nature, Science, Mind*, and the *American Journal of Psychology*. Late in December of 1897, at an APA held on Titchener's home campus at Cornell, William Caldwell, a former Cornell colleague but now a professor of philosophy at Northwestern (near Chicago), sketched a critique of the theory of the "self" that Titchener had presented in his *Outline*.[76] Caldwell attempted primarily to bring the tools of traditional philosophy of mind to bear on the new scientific psychology. Nevertheless, his comment provided Titchener an opening to respond to Dewey and Angell without having to openly concede that they were the ultimate cause of his concern.[77] Notably, Titchener chose to respond to Caldwell not in the journal in which his critique had appeared, *Psychological Review*, in all likelihood because it was co-edited by Titchener's opponents, Baldwin and Cattell. Instead, he turned to *Philosophical Review*, the journal that had recently been founded by the president of his own university, Jacob Gould Schurman.[78] This was, perhaps, a little ironic coming from a man who was at pains to distinguish and separate scientific psychology from its philosophical precursor, but it provided him a conduit to his desired audience without risking obstruction by an unfriendly editor.

Titchener first attempted to draw an illustrative parallel between psychology and biology. He noted that biology is composed of, on the one hand, morphology, the study of the physical structure of organisms, and, on the other hand, physiology, the study of the functions of those structures. One, however, cannot study the functions, he warned, until one is certain of the structures. Similarly in psychology, he continued, there is, on the one hand, the study of mental structures—the attempt to "isolate the constituents in the given conscious formation."[79] This was how he characterized his own approach to the discipline, and he dubbed it "structural psychology." On the other hand, there may be a study of mental function as well, encompassing topics such as memory, imagination, attention, and volition—a "functional psychology," he called it. But this latter form, he went on, cannot proceed successfully until the basic structures of the mind have first been worked out." Finally, taking direct aim at his critics, Titchner wrote,

> it cannot be said that this functional psychology, despite what we may call its greater obviousness to investigation, has been worked out either with as much patient enthusiasm or with as much scientific accuracy as has the psychology of mind structure.[80]

Far from having resolved the debate with his analogy, however, Titchener had succeeded only it making more plain the intellectual distance that existed between himself and many of his American colleagues. Caldwell replied, again in *Psychological Review*, labeling Titchener's article a "manifesto."[81] Titchener once again attempted to explain himself, again in *Philosophical Review*, but his title alone said more about what the work of Angell and Moore and Dewey had crystalized within American psychology: "Structural and Functional Psychology."[82] From this point forward, Titchener, though he remained well respected, would reside at some intellectual distance from the discipline's center of gravity in the US. Or, perhaps better, he formed his own subordinate center of gravity, carrying on an alternative form of the discipline, complete with its own set of issues and debates, and eventually even a separate professional association. Occasionally someone would attempt to bridge between the two parallel realms, but one could also carry on in one of the two, more or less ignoring the other. Although in the coming decades Functionalism would grow in many different directions, sometimes even turning against itself, it was now the "mainstream" in American psychology. The portion of Wundt's program that had been brought across the Atlantic and nurtured by Titchener not even a decade before would, from this point in time, begin to recede into an historical moment in scientific psychology's development.

Although Titchener longed to move from Ithaca to a larger, more cosmopolitan locale, it may well have been, ironically, that being so removed from the hurly burly of modern urban life was what made it possible for him to so single-mindedly pursue so restricted and idealized a research program. Out in the wilds of central New York State, there were fewer racial tensions, little labor unrest, no sprawling immigrant slums teeming with the desperate and destitute, and no massive public school system struggling to manage the ever-expanding variety of students. By contrast with the continuous clashes and upheavals of New York, Boston, Baltimore, and especially Chicago—with their constant questioning of assumptions and renegotiation of practices—in Ithaca one could still believe that the world was a relatively well-ordered, settled, and peaceable place; a place where the ideal of a single, "generalized" human mind might still seem plausible.

The large cities of the US, however, afforded no such illusions. By contrast with Titchener's ideal, many American psychologists began to revel in research with animals, children, and the mad, driven in no small part by their daily observations of difference and diversity, of chaos and conflict. The modern world was not a well-ordered place. It was a place where competition was fierce and where, for many, survival itself was at stake. Of course, the psychologists themselves—mostly men of means who enjoyed relatively cozy existences—were rarely at the pointed end of these events. They mostly watched from the sidelines, seated at various distances from the "action." Nevertheless, the imperatives of competition and survival in the urban jungle[83] were impressed upon them on a nearly daily basis. More excited by new Darwinian evolutionary theory than by old German physiology, and looking for a way to break out of the scientific cul-de-sac that many sensed lay at the end of Wundt's experimental program, they hypothesized that the study of mental variations, far from being merely a source of error, might well be the pathway to scientific success. By examining the full range of variation, one could discover how change—whether physiological, mental, or behavioral—actually comes about.

There was so much more to psychology than pursuing the elusive Wundtian wraith of pure apperception. There were thoughts and emotions, images and desires, all of which were, in some mysterious way, not just "pure" consciousness but were somehow able to refer to objects and events outside of the mind. How can a thought be *about* another thing—e.g., about your father, about your house, about another country? No other object in the natural world—a tree, for instance—is *about* another thing in this way.[84] What is more, thoughts can refer to things that do not even exist: an empire long since collapsed, a child not yet born, a wholly mythical unicorn. By what mechanism do mental acts come by this unique and mysterious power?

Then there was behavior—the very nexus between the organism and its environment. Actions are undertaken in pursuit of the particular interests and goals of the organism. Success at a particular act might help one survive; failure might lead to extinction. Action of this sort seemed to many to be the very engine of evolution. More strangely still, there were behavioral habits: actions that were once carried out in a conscious and laborious manner that had somehow become more or less "automatic" after many repetitions. Despite their seemingly humble nature, perhaps habits were the most important actions of all. They enabled the organism to carry out an action without conscious attention, freeing up the mind to simultaneously deliberate on another possible action (e.g., walking to work while planning what one will do when one gets there). As mentioned in the previous chapter, James had dubbed habit the "the enormous fly-wheel of society."[85]

Moreover, if one could understand how habits worked, perhaps one could *use* psychology—*apply* it—to better educate children, to more effectively train laborers, to more agreeably manage workforces, to entice more customers, and to alleviate the suffering of the insane. Nothing could be further from Titchener's demand that experimental psychology be pursued as a pure science, the proper output of which is "useless," abstract knowledge of how the generalized mind operates. While Titchener may have been admired for his principled rigor, he did not succeed in producing a cadre of loyal disciples. Whereas "functional" and applied psychology increasingly came to be the leading topics of interest everywhere in the US, especially in the cities, Titchener's "school" of psychology—Structural psychology—was pretty much confined to his actual school, Cornell. It was also taught in some of the training laboratories that were springing up in colleges and universities around the country, but mainly as a preliminary background to the original research in which psychologists were engaged. Even most of Titchener's personal students did not pursue it vigorously once they had earned their degrees and started their own professorships elsewhere.

6. Adolf Meyer and the Rise of Psychiatry

The most prominent domain in which psychological knowledge was being applied in the "real" world was education, as we have seen with both Hall and Dewey. However, the universal public school classroom was only one arena for early applied psychology. In 1892, a young Swiss comparative neurologist named Adolf Meyer arrived in Chicago to begin his research career.[86] Meyer had earned his MD in Zurich, under the tutelage of August Forel, an early advocate of the idea that the brain is not a continuous network but is composed of distinct neural cells,[87] and of Constantin von Monakow, perhaps best known for his theory of how the brain recovers after traumatic injury. Despite the opportunities promised by this illustrious intellectual heritage, Meyer was determined to leave the German-speaking world, which he found philosophically hidebound, for a more open intellectual climate. He ultimately took up a very modest offer of laboratory space but no salary from Henry Donaldson in America's newest and most vibrant city, if all too often its most chaotic: Chicago. After just a few months as a docent at the university, he was offered a full-time position as pathologist at the Eastern Hospital for the Insane, 60 miles south of the city in Kankakee.

Meyer's arrival came at a particular low point for the country's patchwork system of mental asylums. The optimism of the early 19th century that the new "moral treatment" would lead the mad to rapidly regain their mental balance and resume productive lives had waned. By the late 19th century, many asylums had become stagnant state bureaucracies, encrusted with political patronage and starved by legislators who found little potential gain in tending to society's least politically valuable citizens. Predictably, conditions inside these institutions deteriorated as the means and motivation to find effective treatments evaporated. Although most asylums employed an attending physician (often overseeing thousands of inmates), general medical science progressed more rapidly, leaving the asylums far behind.[88]

In 1888, a 24-year-old reporter who wrote under the pen name "Nellie Bly,"[89] was working for Joseph Pulitzer's *New York World* newspaper. By faking madness while living in a New York City rooming house, she connived to be committed to the Women's Lunatic Asylum on Blackwell's Island in the East River (since renamed Roosevelt Island). She was brought before a judge, who suspected that she had been drugged, but several physicians—"insanity experts"—declared her to be mad, so the judge sent her to Blackwell's. She spent more than a week in the asylum, where she experienced and witnessed a plethora of bad conditions and harsh treatments: inmates were forced to sit silently on hard benches for up to fourteen hours a day. They were fed rotten food and dirty water in rooms that were strewn with garbage and that they shared with rats. They were given little protection from the cold weather and were subjected to icy baths, all overseen by a rude and abusive nursing staff. "What, excepting torture," Bly asked rhetorically, "would produce insanity quicker than this treatment?" After ten days, Pulitzer had her sprung from the asylum to write her story, first in the *World* and later as a book titled *Ten Days in a Mad-House*.[90] The public outcry was immediate. New York City promised an additional $850,000 for its Department of Public Charities and Corrections. Although the much-needed funds solved New York politicians' immediate political problem, there was little doubt that conditions in asylums around the country were similar to those Bly had experienced. In addition, the nation's supposed experts on madness—the physicians and nurses who ran the asylums—had been exposed as charlatans, fools, or worse.

In the wake of the scandal, the wider medical profession quickly moved to distance itself from both the asylums and the physicians who ran them. As one of the country's leading neurologists, Silas Weir Mitchell, said bluntly in 1894, "Your hospitals are not our hospitals; your ways are not our ways." His vision of asylum conditions was nearly as dark of Bly's: "[T]he insane, who have lost even the memory of hope, sit in rows, too dull to know despair, watched by attendants." Then, turning to the quality of physicians who typically managed asylums, he continued,

> It is a grave injustice to insist that you shall conduct [the business affairs of] a huge boarding house—what has been called a monastery of the mad—and keep yourselves honestly able to move with the growth of medicine, and to study your cases, or add anything of value to our store of knowledge. . . . [Y]ou are cursed by that slow atrophy of the energizing faculties that is the very malaria of asylum life.[91]

The condition of the patients that Adolf Meyer encountered when he arrived at Kankakee was somewhat better than those described by Bly and Mitchell, but efforts to understand the course and causes of their insanity were unsystematic, at best. Meyer aimed to change the situation by dint of his superior European medical and neurological training. His initial efforts to establish, by means of autopsy, correlations between types of insanity and brain lesions were frustrated by the lack of detailed records on the patients. So, he instituted a regimen—commonplace in most of medicine, but new to the asylums—of carefully recording the mental and physical history of each patient on what he dubbed a "life chart." He then followed with a standardized case record of changes in the patient's condition while at the institution.[92] The practice gradually caught on throughout American "psychiatry" (a new German term which gradually replaced the older "alienism," and which connoted a slowly rising scientific *esprit* in asylums).[93]

Soon after Meyer's arrival in the US, Dewey and his circle began to assemble in Chicago. The Swiss doctor—who had admired William James' early psychological writings even from Europe—became involved both with their research and with their social causes. Meyer was taken with Dewey's image of the interdependence of the stimulus and response in a learned reflex.[94] The importance that the early Functionalists accorded to an organism's ability to adapt to its environment, the role that learned habit plays in people's lives, and the significance of social context to one's sense of meaning soon began to influence Meyer's psychiatric ideas too.

The extensive patient records that he was having his staff compile at Kankakee could do more than inform post-mortem examinations. As Meyer would eventually see, they could help the psychiatrist to better appreciate the quite "rugged" adaptive landscapes that patients had often been forced to navigate prior to their arrival at the asylum. He could, thus, understand more fully how their mental problems might have resulted from perversely successful adaptations to their deformed personal circumstances, even if those adaptations seemed maladaptive in the broader "normal" world. Meyer eventually adapted Baldwin's language of "reaction types" to explain why only some people respond to the challenges of life by developing neuroses such as hysteria, hypochondriasis, and neurasthenia, or, more severely, psychoses such as manic-depression, paranoia, and dementia praecox (later renamed schizophrenia).

Although Meyer came to call his position "psychobiology"—a name that may suggest today an effort to find organic underpinnings for psychological phenomena—the trend of Meyer's thought was away from the entrenched idea of his time that insanity is normally the result of an untreatable brain disorder. Instead, he was inclined toward the newer, evolutionary proposal that insanity is often the

FIGURE 7.2 Adolf Meyer, photographed by Doris Ulmann.

Credit: Published in Doris Ulmann, *A Book of Portraits of the Medical Faculty of the Johns Hopkins University* (Baltimore: Johns Hopkins University Press, 1922). The Alan Mason Chesney Medical Archives of The Johns Hopkins Medical Institutions.

result of a poor "fit" between learned habits and the environment's demands. By adjusting the maladaptive habits, Meyer suggested, a better integration with the world can be achieved and, thus, a person's mental suffering can be alleviated.

It took years, for these ideas to mature in Meyer's thought, however. In 1895, just three years after first arriving in Illinois, Meyer moved to a position at the Worcester State Hospital for the Insane, where he became personally acquainted with Stanley Hall and William James. His novel approaches to insanity were so refreshing—stimulating renewed hope that the insane might be "cured" after all— that, in 1902, he was offered the directorship of the New York State Pathological Institute in Manhattan. Meyer immediately had it renamed the *Psychiatric* Institute to reflect his commitment to modern, "scientific" modes of treatment. From his lofty perch in New York City, Meyer was able to broadly influence the course of psychiatry across the nation. His ideas about the relationship between insanity and maladaptive habits offered an optimistic vision of full recovery from insanity, a view that became widely popular in the increasingly Progressive ethos of the early 20th century. In 1904 he was granted a courtesy professorship in psychiatry at Cornell.

Four years later, in 1908, Meyer accepted a professorship at Johns Hopkins, and the directorship of a fledgling psychiatric clinic there. As we have seen many times before—with Johns Hopkins, Jonas Clark, John D. Rockefeller, Ezra Cornell, Henry Sage, and Leland Stanford, among others—the clinic was endowed by (and thus named after) a captain of American industry, a "robber baron" who had taken to redistributing the vast wealth he had accumulated during the "Gilded Age" just past. In this case, the benefactor was a Philadelphia-based steel magnate named Henry Phipps.[95] Meyer, who had been nearly constantly on the move since his arrival in the US sixteen years earlier, would move to Hopkins and stay there for the next thirty years. The following year, 1909, Meyer helped to found the National Committee for Mental Hygiene with Clifford Beers, a former mental patient who had recounted the abuse he had encountered in traditional asylums in the popular book *A Mind that Found Itself*. At Hopkins, Meyer would become, in the words of one significant pair of historians, "the most prominent and influential American psychiatrist of the first half of the twentieth century."[96] In 1927, Meyer was elected president of the professional and scientific society that would later become the American Psychiatric Association.[97] He died in 1950. Beginning in 1957, the APA began granting an annual award in Meyer's name to honor outstanding investigators of mental illness.[98]

Titchener battled with Meyer over the Swiss physician's misappropriation, as the Cornell professor saw it, of the term "psychology." In a fascinating exchange of letters between the two men in September and October of 1909,[99] Titchener essentially accused Meyer of being out of his depth:

> Who is to make and to define the pure science? The men who are interested to apply?—That is not the lesson of history. The makers of science

have been the men to whom the useful was uninteresting. The appliers of science have been the men to whom theory made very scant appeal. You can hardly conceive of a civil engineer propounding a definition of physics, or of a medical practitioner seriously concerning himself to define the limits of physiology. Why then should the psychiatrist offer a novel definition of psychology? What claim has he, that should empower him to do this? How can he expect to do it adequately when psychology has its own technique, attitude, procedure,—things that must be gained by special study extending over many years? How, to put it bluntly, can the psychiatrist expect that his definition of psychology can be anything more than an amateur's?[100]

Rather than taking offense, as he might well have, Meyer responded with civility, attempting to stake out a broader, more holistic, more *functionalist* psychology. Titchener's style of research was an important element of this great psychology, to be sure, but there was no need, Meyer thought, to establish firm, uncrossable boundaries *in advance* between psychology and biology, psychology and psychopathology, psychology and psychoanalysis, or even between pure and applied science more broadly. "Who shall say what is pure? And what is useful?" he inquired.[101] "As scientists, we *must quit* starting from a priori divisions," he declared.[102] To Meyer, Titchener's insistence that analysis was the sine qua non of science seemed parochial. The "study of conditions of synthesis," he offered, is equally important to understanding nature.[103]

Titchener was flummoxed, bemoaning "the hopelessness of argument without any common standing-ground."[104] The exchange continued on, nevertheless, through several more letters over the course of the next month. Meyer concluded that they had been unable "to single out any specific issue that might have caught some light from the one or the other."[105] Perhaps surprisingly, nine years later, in 1918, the two men went at it again, composing a several more detailed letters on their deepest convictions about the nature of psychology but, still, they were still unable to find the common ground Titchener had declared did not exist back in his second letter of the exchange.

Whether or not Titchener was able to fight Meyer to a draw, one on one, his overall plan for psychology in America remained a losing battle. Psychiatry was only one of a panoply of realms in which "functional" ideas in psychology were being applied, apparently successfully, in the "outside" world.

Notes

1 The following dates, places, and people were drawn from C. R. Garvey's "List of American Psychology Laboratories," *Psychological Bulletin* 26 (1929): 652–60. Garvey obtained his information by surveying department heads in the 1920s, but there are known to be some errors (or, more often, local nuances that are not reflected) in Garvey's list. See also Ludy T. Benjamin Jr., "The Psychology Laboratory at the Turn of the 20th Century," *American Psychologist* 55 (2000): 318–21.

2 He is now commonly known as William Lowe Bryan, but he added the middle name—his wife's maiden name—only after he married in 1889. http://psychology.wikia.com/wiki/William_L._Bryan.

3 The University of Iowa's departmental history disagrees slightly with Garvey, saying that "The Psychology Laboratory of the University of Iowa was started in 1887 and dedicated in 1890." http://www2.psychology.uiowa.edu/general_info/history. Accessed August 23, 2013. For a short account of Patrick's career, see Ernest R. Hilgard's "Psychology at Iowa Before McGeoch and Spence" and Leonard D. Goodstein's "The Iowa Department of Psychology and the American Psychological Association: A Historical Analysis," both in *Psychology at Iowa: Centennial Essays*, ed. by Joan H. Cantor (Hillsdale, NJ: Lawrence Erlbaum, 1991), 37–50, 51–60. Being so far west, Patrick was not active in the American Psychological Association, but he was a founding member of the Western Philosophical Association, serving as its third president in 1903–1904. The WPA eventually became the Western (and later Central) Division of the American Philosophical Association.

4 Cattell had set up a temporary laboratory at Cambridge soon after his graduation from Leipzig.

5 For more about Williams, see Roger Chaffin and Kevin E. Gruenfeld's "Leslie (Lillie) A. Williams: Founder of an Early Psychology Laboratory for Teaching," *Psychology of Women* 24, no. 2 (Spring 1997): 19, 30.

6 W. O. Krohn, "Facilities in Experimental Psychology in the Colleges of the United States," in The *Report of the Commissioner of Education for the Year 1890-'91*, vol. 2 (Washington, DC: Government Printing Office, 1894), 1139–51.

7 In 1887, a follow-up bill sponsored by Missouri congressman William H. Hatch offered federal funds to land grant schools to found agricultural research stations. In 1890, a third bill, sponsored by Morrill, required states accepting federal land for colleges show that race was not a factor in admission, or to provide equal facilities for people of all races.

8 The University of Iowa, in Iowa City, where G. T. W. Patrick founded the tenth psychology lab in the US, was founded in 1847, long before the Morrill Act and just over eight weeks after Iowa had been granted statehood. Iowa State did not open a psychology lab until 1912, 71st on the continent according to Garvey (1929), under the direction of a Methodist minister and professor of history and psychology named Orange Howard Cessna. www.add.lib.iastate.edu/spcl/arch/rgrp/13-22-10.html. Accessed August 23, 2013.

9 For a detailed account of Wolfe's tragic career, see Ludy T. Benjamin, Jr. *Harry Kirke Wolfe: Pioneer in Psychology* (Lincoln, NB: University of Nebraska Press).

10 To be entirely fair, there were also western American schools that had not depended on the Morrill Act and also founded early psychology laboratories: In addition to Iowa (mentioned previously), Indiana University was not a land grant school, nor was Michigan. Obviously, the University of Toronto was not under the jurisdiction of the Morrill Act, but had come into being (under the name King's College) by way of a distinctively British form of government support in 1827.

11 Cornell is also credited with having invented the glass insulator that one can find on telephone poles to this very day.

12 The circle of American university presidents was tightly knit. While White was an undergraduate at Yale, he met and befriended classmate Daniel Coit Gilman, the future president of Johns Hopkins. The two had traveled Europe together after graduation. In 1891, long after White's retirement from Cornell, Leland and Jane Stanford asked him to become president of their new university just south of San Francisco. He refused, but recommended his former student, David Starr Jordan, who was then president of Indiana University. Jordan would be replaced at Indiana by philosopher-psychologist William Lowe Bryan, mentioned above. White was also the founding president of the

American Historical Association (1884–1885), and he served as US Ambassador to Germany (1879–1881, 1897–1902) and to Russia (1892–1894).

13 See Blumenthal, Jastrow, *op. cit.* p. 81.

14 Professor of Greek and Comparative Philology Benjamin Ide Wheeler, later president of the University of California, 1899–1919, quoted in Charles Forster Smith, *Charles Kendall Adams: A Life-Sketch* (Madison, WI: University of Wisconsin Press, 1924), 31. The seminal historian of the American university, Laurence R. Veysey, said of Adams that "he always remained a plodder; yet in some mysterious fashion he moved steadily upward" (*The Emergence of the American University* (Chicago, IL: University of Chicago Press, 1965), 102).

15 Henry W. Sage (1819–1897) made a fortune buying trees that were being cleared for new farmland in Ontario and shipping them by train to New York State to sell as lumber. From 1857, when he relocated to Brooklyn, he became a congregant of Henry Ward Beecher's church, and ultimately sponsored a Lectureship on preaching at Yale that was named after Henry's firebrand pastor of a father, Lyman Beecher, encountered in an earlier chapter. (Henry was also brother to Harriet Beecher Stowe, the author of *Uncle Tom's Cabin*.) After the death of Sage's wife in a carriage accident in 1885, he decided to memorialize her by endowing the Susan Linn Sage School of Philosophy at Cornell, where he had long been one of the most productive members of the Board of Trustees.

16 According to one early history of Cornell,

> Unfortunately Professor Angell's health broke down soon after the opening of the laboratory in the second half of the year, so that his programme of work could not be carried out with anything like completeness; and he was himself compelled in 1892 to resign his professorship and take up new work in a milder climate.
>
> (Waterman Thomas Hewett, *Cornell University, A History*, vol. 2 (New York, NY: University Publishing Society, 1905), 84–85).

17 Letter from James Burrill Angell to James Rowland Angell, January 19, 1892. In James Rowland Angell Collection, "Personal Papers" Group 2, Series II, Box 3, folder 16. Yale University Archives. Frank Angell went on to found a laboratory at Stanford as well, teaching philosophy and psychology courses there for many years. He is best remembered there, however, for having been the athletic director. Stanford's primary running track there is named after Angell to this day.

18 Titchener to James, May 28, 1899. In *Correspondence of William James*, vol. 8, ed. by I. K. Skrupskellis and E. M. Berkeley (Charlottesville, VA: University Press of Virginia, 1899), 535–37. Thanks to Rand Evans for alerting me to this passage, and to Michael Pettit for his discussions on this matter.

19 Minutes of the Executive Committee of the Cornell Board of Trustees for July 26, 1892, Cornell University Archives. This was just over two months after Adams had resigned the presidency, replaced by a man who would be exquisitely sensitive to questions of religious orthodoxy if they, indeed, existed: Cornell's Professor of Christian Ethics and Mental Philosophy, Jacob Gould Schurman. Schurman was a Canadian, originally from Nova Scotia, and had earlier that year launched the *Philosophical Review*, one of the earliest scholarly journals of general philosophy in America (see next). As fellow "British subjects," he and Titchener formed a special bond. Schurman turned out to be a man of astonishing talents: in addition to his academic achievements, he went on to serve as US Ambassador to Greece (1912–1913), China (1921–1925), and Germany (1925–1929).

Early competitors with *Philosophical Review* included *Journal of Speculative Philosophy*, founded by William T. Harris' back in 1867. One can quibble about whether the earlier periodical was either "general" or even "scholarly," given that its core mission was to spread the Hegelian gospel far and wide. By the early 1890s, though, it was sputtering to its dénouement. In October of 1890, the *International Journal of Ethics* appeared. It was certainly scholarly, but dedicated to ethics rather than to general philosophy. A few years before, in February 1887, a zinc magnate named Edward Hegeler and his theologian son-in-law, Paul Carus (both German immigrants to the Chicago area) launched a liberal theological journal titled *Open Court*. It was not devoted to general philosophy, of course, but in October 1890, they began a second journal called *The Monist*. It was definitely scholarly and general, and it published the writings of a wide array of international intellectual "stars." One might reasonably regard it as being a slightly earlier entrant into the same category of journals as *Philosophical Review*.

20 Veysey, *The Emergence of the American University*, 322.

21 Much the information here on the early APA meetings derives from the Macmillan reprint of the proceedings that was found in the archives of James McKeen Cattell by Michael M. Sokal of Worcester Polytechnic Institute (MA). For further information and analysis see: Michael M. Sokal, "Origins and Early Years of the American Psychological Association, 1890–1906," *American Psychologist* 47 (1992): 111–21.

22 Münsterberg was born to a Jewish family that had converted to Lutheranism along with his brothers soon after their father's death in 1880. See Matthew Hale, *Human Science and Social Order: Hugo Munsterberg and the Origins of Applied Psychology* (Philadelphia, PA: Temple University Press, 1980), 19–20. This conflicts with Andrew Heinze's claim that Münsterberg remained a secular Jew throughout his life. (*Jews and the American Soul: Human Nature in the Twentieth Century* (Princeton, NJ: Princeton University Press, 2004), 105–10). A. A. Roback, ever devoted to promoting Jewish identity in American psychology, repeatedly described Münsterberg as having been Jewish, even over the objections of Münsterberg's widow (who was also from a Jewish family that had converted to Christianity) (1927 Letter from A. A. Roback to Selma Münsterberg in the A. A. Roback Collection, Series I "Correspondence," folder 778 "Münsterberg, Hugo, 1863–1916," Houghton Library, Harvard University). Not all who mentioned Münsterberg's Jewish background did so with the aim of extolling it, however. Nicholas Murray Butler, president of Columbia University, once described Münsterberg as a "very offensive German Jew" (cited in Harold S. Wechsler, *The Qualified Student: A History of Selective College Admission in America* (New York, NY: John Wiley, 1977), 179). See also Andrew S. Winston, "'The Defects of His Race': E.G. Boring and Antisemitism in American Psychology," *History of Psychology* 1 (1998): 27–51; Andrew S. Winston, "'As His Name Indicates': R. S. Woodworth's Letters of Reference and Employment for Jewish Psychologists in the 1930s," *Journal of the History of the Behavioral Sciences* 32 (1996): 30–43. Thanks to Nicole Barenbaum, Jeremy Blatter, Andrew Winston, and Alexandra Rutherford for helping me sort out this matter.

23 Baldwin was at Toronto, for the moment, but was American.

24 Eugene Taylor argued that Hall intentionally called his meeting at a time when James would be unable to attend, in order to not have his vision for psychology be disrupted by his longtime academic rival. In "An Epistemological Critique of Experientalism in Psychology; or, Why G. Stanley Hall Waited Until William James Was out of Town to Found the American Psychological Association," in *Aspects of the History of Psychology in America, 1892–1992*, ed. Helmut E. Adler and Robert W. Rieber (New York, NY and Washington, DC: New York Academy of Sciences and American Psychological Association, 1994), 37–61.

25 In July of 1892, James and Ladd were both 50 years old; Hall was 48.

26 Fullerton was an interesting and tragic character. Born in India in 1859 to American missionaries, he studied at the University of Pennsylvania and at Yale Divinity School, before taking an instructorship in philosophy at Penn. In addition to hosting the first annual APA meeting, he also served as the fifth president of the Association, in 1896. He rose through the ranks at Penn to the level of Vice-Provost before taking up a position at Columbia in 1904. On a scholarly exchange trip in Vienna at the outbreak of World War I, he was imprisoned for most of the conflict, an experience that

permanently damaged his health, and rendered him an invalid for the rest of his life. In 1925, he committed suicide.

27 See Christopher D. Green, "Introduction to Section II: The Founding of the Journals," in *Institutions of Early Experimental Psychology: Laboratories, Courses, Journals, and Associations*, ed. Christopher D. Green, 2001. http://psychclassics.yorku.ca/Special/Institu tions/journalsintro.htm. Accessed August 30, 2013.

28 According to the very brief summary in the proceedings of the meeting (see previous footnote 21), Hall's address "consisted of an abstract of an extensive History of Psychology in this country beginning with [the 18th-century Puritan theologian] Jonathan Edwards." A slightly enlarged account that appeared in the journal *Science* reported a more modest paper:

> President Hall presented a brief outline of the history and prospects of experimental psychology in America, tracing the beginnings of this study from the first American laboratory founded at Johns Hopkins University some eight years ago, up to the present time

(Anonymous, "The American Psychological Association," *Science* 21 (1893): 34–35). Robert S. Woodworth believed that the text of Hall's presidential address "doubtless closely paralleled" an article that he published in 1894. The article was G. Stanley Hall, "On the History of American College Text-Books and Teaching Logic, Ethics, Psychology and Allied Subjects," *Proceedings of the American Antiquarian Society* 9 (1894): 137–74; Woodworth's claim appeared in "The Adolescence of American Psychology," *Psychological Review* 50 (1943): 17.

29 See, e.g., E. C. Sanford, "Report of the Secretary and Treasurer for 1895," *Psychological Review* 3 (1896): 121–23; Anonymous, "The American Psychological Association," *American Journal of Psychology* 7 (1896): 448–49, which Michael Sokal says was "almost surely written by Titchener"; Michael M. Sokal, "Origins and Early Years of the American Psychological Association, 1890–1906," *American Psychologist* 47 (1992): 119.

30 No hyphen was included between her maiden and married names in the "Proceedings," a practice she did not seem to adopt until later in her life. She gave her affiliation as simply "Baltimore, MD."

31 It is not known with certainty who the first African American member of the APA was. It may well have been Francis Cecil Sumner, who earned his PhD under Hall at Clark in 1920 and joined the APA as an Associate Member in 1930. The category of "Associate Membership" was approved at the 1924 APA meeting and implemented in 1926 for individuals who had earned PhDs but had not published research after completing their dissertations. Ingrid G. Farreras, "Before Boulder: Professionalizing Clinical Psychology, 1896–1949" (Doctoral dissertation, University of New Hampshire, 2001), esp. pp. 83–90. Charles Henry Turner took his PhD under Charles Herrick at the University of Chicago in 1907 and, although some of his research was behavioral in character, he seems to have identified as a physiologist rather than a psychologist and, thus, was never a member of the APA.

32 Ladd, like Dewey and Morris, was deeply influenced by Hegelian philosophy and Christian theology and these lines of thought were woven through his psychological work.

33 For more on Titchener's background and scientific outlook, see, e.g., Rand B. Evans, "The Scientific and Psychological Positions of E. B. Titchener," in *Defining American Psychology: The Correspondence Between Adolf Meyer and Edward Bradford Titchener*, ed. Ruth Leys and Rand B. Evans (Baltimore, MD: Johns Hopkins University Press, 1990), 1–38; and Rand B. Evans, "E. B. Titchener on Scientific Psychology and Technology," in *Portraits of Pioneers in Psychology*, ed. Gregory A. Kimble, Michael Wertheimer, and Charlotte L. White (Washington, DC and Hillsdale, NJ: American Psychological Association and Lawrence Erlbaum, 1990), 89–104. See also Christopher D. Green, "Scientific Objectivity and E. B. Titchener's Experimental Psychology," *Isis* 101 (2010):

697–721; and Saulo de Freitas Araujo and Cintia Fernandes Marcellos, "From Classicism and Idealism to Scientific Naturalism:Titchener's Oxford Years and Their Impact Upon His Early Intellectual Development," *History of Psychology* 20 (2017): 148–71.

34 A very interesting discussion of the German situation can be found in the opening chapters of Mitchell Ash's *Gestalt Psychology in German Culture, 1890–1967: Holism and the Quest for Objectivity* (Cambridge, UK: Cambridge University Press, 1998).

35 To be entirely fair, Titchener was not opposed to the existence of applied psychology so long as it was clearly acknowledged to be a "technology" of inferior epistemic status to the "pure science" of "experimental psychology."

36 See Francesca Bordogna, "Scientific Personae in American Psychology: Three Case Studies," *Studies in History and Philosophy of Biological and Biomedical Sciences* 36 (2005): 95–134; Deborah J. Coon, "Standardizing the Subject: Experimental Psychologists, Introspection, and the Quest for a Technoscientific Ideal," *Technology and Culture* 34 (1993): 757–83.

37 See, e.g., Henning Schmidgen, "Of Frogs and Men:The Origins of Psychophysiological Time Experiments, 1850–1865," *Endeavour* 26 (2002): 142–48; Henning Schmidgen, "Physics, Ballistics, and Psychology:A History of the Chronoscope In/As Context, 1845–1890," *History of Psychology* 8 (2005): 46–78.

38 Women were a rarity in the early psychology laboratories, but not entirely absent. We have seen the difficulties that Christine Ladd encountered. Mary Whiton Calkins learned her laboratory skills from E. C. Sanford, and completed a thesis under William James' supervision, but she was never awarded a doctorate by Harvard. She was offered a doctorate from Radcliffe—Harvard's women's college—many years later, but refused it saying that she had never attended Radcliffe. Titchener's first graduate student was a woman, Margaret Floy Washburn. Hugo Münsterberg allowed Resa Schirnhoffer to work in his Freiburg laboratory, but she never completed a degree there (see, e.g., Carol Diethe's *Nietzsche's Women: Beyond the Whip* (Berlin: de Gruyter, 1996)). Throughout most of Wundt's career, there were no women students in the Leipzig lab. However, near the end of his career, Wundt did allow one woman, Anna Berliner, to complete a PhD in his laboratory. Rachel Uffelman, "Anna Berliner, 1888–1977," *The Feminist Psychologist* 29, no. 2 (2002). www.apadivisions.org/division-35/about/heritage/ anna-berliner-biography.aspx (electronic only). See also Anna Berliner's own "Reminiscences of Wundt and Leipzig," from January 1959 (Berliner Papers, M50, Archives of the History of American Psychology, University of Akron, Akron, OH).

39 For an excellent account of the crisis in the Wundt research program, David K. Robinson, "Reaction Time Experiments in Wundt's Institute and Beyond," in *Wilhelm Wundt in History: The Making of a Scientific Psychology*, ed. Robert W. Rieber and David K. Robinson (New York, NY: Kluwer, 2001), 161–97, esp. pp. 169–75.

40 Cattell served as Wundt's first official "Laboratory Assistant," an important role in the German laboratory. However, he was not Wundt's first American student. That honor went to James Thomas Bixby who wrote a dissertation on Spencer's ethics in 1885. Hall, of course, had been there post-doctorally (so not formally as a student) even earlier. Michael M Sokal, ed., *An Education in Psychology: James McKeen Cattell's Journal and Letters from Germany and England, 1880–1888* (Cambridge, MA: MIT Press, 1981), 11.

41 For English versions of Cattell's dissertation work see James McKeen Cattell, "The Time It Takes to See and Name Objects," *Mind* 11 (1886): 63–65; "The Time Taken up by Cerebral Operations," *Mind* 11 (1886): 20–242, 377–92, 524–38. For Cattell's account of working in Wundt's lab see his "The Psychological Laboratory at Leipsic," *Mind* 13 (1888): 37–51.

42 Ludwig Lange, Neue Experimente über den Vorgang der einfachen Reaction auf Sinneseindrücke.) *Philosophische Studien* 4 (1888): 479–510. An English translation by of this article by David D. Lee from 2009 is available at http://psychclassics.yorku.ca/LangeL/ NewExperiments.pdf. Lange was a talented laboratory scientist, but was pursued by

inner demons. He eventually had a complete mental breakdown from which he never fully recovered. He is probably the chief reason that a rumor began to circulate in Germany that the level of mental strain brought about by the scientific study of psychology could drive an otherwise healthy and intelligent young man mad.

43 On the possibility that Cattell was personally incapable of engaging the kind of introspection that Wundt's research demanded, see Michael Sokal, "Scientific Biography, Cognitive Deficits, and Laboratory Practice: James McKeen Cattell and Early American Experimental Psychology, 1880–1904," *Isis* 101 (2010): 531–54.

44 James McKeen Cattell, "Mental Tests and Measurements," *Mind* 15 (1890): 373–81. See especially the appended remarks on the project by Galton.

45 James McKeen Cattell, "Aufmerksamkeit Und Reaction [Attention and Reaction]," *Philosophische Studien* 8 (1893): 403–6; translated as "Attention and Reaction," in *James McKeen Cattell: Man of Science*, ed. Robert S. Woodworth, vol. 1: Psychological Research (Lancaster, PA: Science Press, 1947), 252–55.

46 Edward Bradford Titchener, "Simple Reactions," *Mind* N.S. 4 (1895): 74–81.

47 Baldwin was the son of an abolitionist in the South. The Baldwin family had moved north during the final stages of the Civil War to avoid retribution from slavery-supporting neighbors. After the war, however, they returned and Baldwin's father was appointed mayor of Columbia during the military occupation.

48 See James Mark Baldwin, "Autobiography of James Mark Baldwin," in *History of Psychology in Autobiography*, ed. Carl A. Murchison, vol. 1 (Worcester, MA: Clark University Press, 1930), 1–30.

49 James Mark Baldwin, *Handbook of Psychology*, vol. 1. Senses and ntellect (New York, NY: Henry Holt, 1889); vol. 2. Feelings and Will (New York, NY: Henry Holt, 1891).

50 The locus classicus is James Mark Baldwin, "A New Factor in Evolution," *American Naturalist* 30 (1896): 441–51, 536–53. However, that article is quite patchy and difficult to understand. The full theory comes out much more clearly in his "Darwinism and Psychology," in *Darwin and the Humanities* (Baltimore, MD: Review Publishing, 1909).

51 James Mark Baldwin, "Types of Reaction," *Psychological Review* 2 (1895): 259–73.

52 This is the way in which this matter is commonly discussed today, under the label the "Baldwin Effect." It turns out, however, to be a drastic oversimplification of what Baldwin was actually attempting to accomplish. For a more detailed analysis of what Baldwin was trying to achieve, see Christopher D. Green, "James Mark Baldwin, Organic Selection, the 'Baldwin Effect,' and the American 'Immigrant Crisis' at the Turn of the Twentieth Century," in *Entangled Life: Organism and Environment in the Biological and Social Sciences*, ed. Gillian Barker, Eric Desjardins, and Trevor Pearce (New York, NY: Springer, 2013), 33–49.

53 Edward Bradford Titchener, "The Type-Theory of Simple Reaction," *Mind* N.S. 4 (1895): 506–14.

54 Titchener, Type-theory, 1895, 506.

55 Titchener, Type-theory, 1895, 514.

56 J. M. Baldwin, "The 'type-theory' of reaction," *Mind, N.S.* 5 (1896): 81–90, 81.

57 E. B. Titchener, "The 'type-theory' of simple reaction," *Mind, N.S.* 5 (1896): 236–41, 240.

58 Baldwin, "Type-theory," 85.

59 Titchener, "Type-theory," 241.

60 James Rowland Angell and Addison W. Moore, "Studies From the Psychological Laboratory of the University of Chicago: 1. Reaction-Time: A Study in Attention and Habit," *Psychological Review* 3 (1896): 245–58.

61 It is critical to recall that the term "genetic," in this era referred to growth or development, not, like it does today, to fixed heritable traits. Thus, the cumbersome term "dynamo-genetic" means something like "moving development"; i.e., the basic idea is that, as newly acquired skills are practiced and perfected, they can change, even with

respect to each other. In this case, two response profiles that were originally quite different become nearly identical with practice.

62 Angell and Moore, "Reaction-Time," 253 italics added. Short glosses by the present author have been inserted in square brackets.

63 Ibid., 256.

64 Ibid., 258.

65 John Dewey, "The Reflex Arc Concept in Psychology," *Psychological Review* 3 (1896): 357–70.

66 Herbert S. Langfeld, "Fifty Volumes of the Psychological Review," *Psychological Review* 50 (1943): 143–55. The full results of the survey were somewhat complicated. In an initial vote by 52 psychologists (out of 70 invited to participate) of the 25 most important articles to have appeared in the *Review*, Dewey's "Reflex Arc" article ranked third behind J. B. Watson's 1913 "Psychology as the Behaviorist Views It," and an 1897 study of the acquisition of telegraphy by William L. Bryan and Noble Harter. When the participants were asked to rank the top five articles, however, Dewey's piece surpassed Watson (2nd) and Bryan and Harter (4th). E. L. Thorndike and R. S. Woodworth's 1901 "The Influence of Improvement in One Mental Function Upon the Efficiency of Other Functions" ranked third.

67 Dewey, "Reflex Arc," 358 italics added.

68 Ibid., 358–59.

69 Ibid., 359.

70 Ibid., 359. Usually "qualia," rather than "quales," is used as the plural of "quale."

71 Ibid., 359–60.

72 Ibid., 360.

73 Ibid., 365.

74 Ibid., 367.

75 Edward Bradford Titchener, *Outline of Psychology* (New York, NY: Palgrave Macmillan, 1896); Oswald Külpe, *Introduction to Philosophy*, trans. Walter B. Pillsbury and Edward Bradford Titchener (London, UK: Sonnenschein, 1897).

76 William Caldwell, "Professor Titchener's View of the Self," *Psychological Review* 5 (1898): 401–8. In 1903, Caldwell would move to McGill University in Montréal where he would succeed John C Murray in the philosophical professorship there.

77 Personal communication, Rand Evans, February 17, 2005.

78 Edward Bradford Titchener, "The Postulates of a Structural Psychology, 1898," *Philosophical Review* 7 (1898): 449–65.

79 Ibid., 450.

80 Ibid., 452.

81 William Caldwell, "The Postulates of a Structural Psychology," *Psychological Review* 6 (1899): 187–91.

82 Edward Bradford Titchener, "Structural and Functional Psychology," *Philosophical Review* 8 (1899): 290–99, doi:10.2307/2176244.

83 It would not be long before Upton Sinclair first popularized that now hackneyed metaphor in *The Jungle* (New York, NY: Doubleday, Jabber & Co., 1906), a novel about the harshness of urban life as a poor immigrant in America.

84 Philosophers call this aspect of thought "intentionality," in the sense that thoughts are "intended" at objects like an arrow may be intended or aimed at a target. One of Wundt's chief philosophical rivals, Franz Brentano at the University of Vienna, promoted intentionality, rather than pure consciousness, as the "mark of the mental." His students included Carl Stumpf and Christian von Ehrenfels, both of whom influenced the *Gestalt* movement in psychology. Titchener, in his final, uncompleted book, vigorously strove to defend Wundt against the challenge posed by Brentano. Although Brentano's name is not well known among psychologists today, the aim of late-20th-century

cognitive science to elucidate the nature of the mental representation was a descendant of Brentano's work on the intentionality of mind.

85 William James, *The Principles of Psychology*, vol. 1 (New York, NY: Henry Holt, 1890), 121.

86 The only book-length biography of Meyer is Susan D. Lamb, *Pathologist of the Mind: Adolf Meyer and the Origins of American Psychiatry* (Baltimore, MD: Johns Hopkins University Press, 2014). I wish to acknowledged Dr. Lamb's kind assistance in commenting on earlier versions of this passage about Meyer.

87 This view foreshadowed the modern neuron doctrine, for which Santiago Ramón y Cajal would win the Nobel prize in 1906. In addition to his neurological work, Forel was also the world leading expert on the social life of ants.

88 The treatment of patients in expensive private facilities, such as the McLean Asylum near Boston, could be better, but the state of therapeutic knowledge was essentially the same.

89 Her birth name was Elizabeth Jane Cochran, of suburban Pittsburgh.

90 Nellie Bly, *Ten Days in a Mad-House* (New York, NY: Ian L. Munro, 1888). Extensively illustrated with drawings, Bly's exposé had a profound effect on Jacob Riis who, in 1890, would take his camera and the newly-invented *Blitzlicht*—the first widely used flash powder—into the tenements of New York's Five Points slum to reveal to an astonished and soon-outraged public the extent of the filth and suffering there.

91 Astonishingly, Mitchell said all this directly to the asylum physicians themselves in his "Address Before the Fiftieth Annual Meeting of the American Medico-Psychological Association," in *Proceedings of American Medico-Psychological Association at the Fiftieth Annual Meeting in Philadelphia, May 15–18, 1894* (Utica, NY: Utica Hospital Press, 1895), 101–21. For a fuller exploration of the context, see Andrew Scull, "Contending Professions: Sciences of the Brain and Mind in the United States, 1850–2013," *Science in Context* 28 (2015): 131–61.

92 For a detailed description of the use of the life chart, see Ruth Leys, "Types of One: Adolf Meyer's Life Chart and the Representation of Individuality," *Representations*, no. 34 (1991): 1–28.

93 See especially, Lamb, *Pathologist of the Mind*, chapter 1.

94 Dewey, "Reflex Arc."

95 Phipps had previously endowed a tuberculosis clinic at Hopkins. Legend has it that while Phipps was visiting Baltimore to check up on "his" clinic, he asked Hopkins' Dean of Medicine, William Welch, if there were other projects that needed funding. After Welch showed him Clifford Beers' new book, *A Mind That Found Itself* (New York, NY: Longman, Green, 1908) and described how Meyer's new "psychobiology" was revolutionizing the way the insane were being treated, Phipps agreed to endow a new psychiatric clinic to the tune of $1.5 million (the equivalent of about $38 million today). Welch, of course, immediately recruited Meyer to run it. The Phipps Clinic formally opened in 1913. See Neil Grauer, "Origin of the Phipps Psychiatric Clinic," n.d., www.hopkinsmedicine.org/psychiatry/about/anniversary/origin_Phipps.html.

96 Andrew Scull and Jay Shulkin, "Psychobiology, Psychiatry, and Psychoanalysis: The Intersecting Careers of Adolf Meyer, Phyllis Greenacre, and Curt Richter," *Medical History* 53 (2009): 5–36.

97 The organization did not adopt that name for itself until 1921, marking the final victory of the term "psychiatry" over its earlier rivals, but it dated back to the old Association of Medical Superintendents of American Institutions for the Insane, founded in 1844.

98 Meyer published no books in his lifetime, but his most influential articles have been reprinted in Adolf Meyer, *The Collected Papers of Adolf Meyer*, ed. Eunice E. Winters, 4 vols. (Baltimore, MD: Johns Hopkins University Press, 1950–1952).

99 The correspondence began in the wake of Sigmund Freud's 1909 trip, at Stanley Hall's invitation, to Clark University—The Viennese doctor's only venture across to America. Freud presented the lectures that, in translation, formed the basis of "The Origin and Development of Psychoanalysis," (first published in the *American Journal of Psychology* 21 (1910): 181–218; later republished in book form). Titchener's and Meyer's ensuing letters are reproduced in Ruth Leys and Rand B. Evans, eds., *Defining American Psychology: The Correspondence Between Adolf Meyer and Edward Bradford Titchener* (Baltimore, MD: Johns Hopkins University Press, 1990).

100 Letter from Titchener to Meyer, September 20, 1909, reprinted in Leys and Evans, *Defining American Psychology*, 121.

101 Letter from Meyer to Titchener, September 23, 1909, reproduced in Ibid., 129.

102 Letter from Meyer to Titchener, September 23, 1909, reproduced in Ibid., 133.

103 Letter from Meyer to Titchener, September 23, 1909, reproduced in Ibid., 129.

104 Letter from Titchener to Meyer, September 25, 1909, reproduced in Ibid., 137.

105 Letter from Meyer to Titchener, October 30, 1909, reproduced in Ibid., 178.

8

PSYCHOLOGY IN NEW YORK AND BOSTON IN THE 1890S

1. The World's Metropolis

By the 1890s, New York was a very different city from the one the James family had abandoned in 1855. As the population exploded—from 520,000 in 1850 to 810,000 just ten years later—the city rapidly pushed its way up Manhattan Island. The daily transportation of hundreds of thousands of people through the growing city—to work, to play, and back home again—became a pressing urban challenge.

The burgeoning metropolis grew so large, in fact, that many of its residents started to have difficulty ever leaving it for a respite from the noise and bustle of urban life. The need for a common green space within the city became urgent. In 1858, the English landscape designer, Calvert Vaux, and his American partner, Frederick Law Olmstead, won a competition to design a space that had been newly designated by the city as "Central Park." The upheavals of the Civil War intervened but, after more than a decade of work, the park was finally completed in 1873. New York's population had just topped one million. Vaux and Olmstead's creation featured diverse landscapes across the massive 778-acre recreational space: broad lawns, manicured gardens, "wild" wooded areas, rugged rocky regions, ornate terraces, ponds, etc. The park rapidly became a focal point for the city's mammoth population, and some of New York's greatest public institutions gathered around its edges—the Metropolitan Museum of Art and the American Museum of Natural History, among many others.

With so many people and so many attractions now "uptown," getting around became increasingly difficult. To ease the burden, a system of elevated trains, drawn mostly by steam engines, started to become a part of the New York cityscape over the course of the 1870s. (See Plate 7 in the color plate section.) Commuter trains were hardly the only technological innovation to both bless and curse the city. Electrical wires and telephone lines were hung higgledy piggledy everywhere,

FIGURE 8.1   Electric wires in New York City, 1887.

Credit: Accessed May 13, 2017 from http://gizmodo.com/19th-century-new-york-was-covered-in-an-insane-web-of-t-5987564

making it seem, in some places, as though the metropolis lay beneath a vast and chaotic spider web.

Also by the 1870s, the masses of Irish and German Catholic immigrants who had arrived in the 1840s and 1850s (and their immediate descendants) gradually began to integrate into city life—familiar to, if not wholly accepted by, the descendants of earlier immigrants to New York. In 1880, New York elected its first Irish-descent Catholic mayor, William Grace, who, perhaps ironically, ran his campaign *against* Tammany Hall which, for all its corruption, had been the one institution in the city that had strenuously worked to assist immigrants as they arrived. (The first Irish mayor of Boston would pursue an analogous political strategy. See below.)

Still, New York continued to be a magnet for Europeans fleeing poverty and oppression in their homelands; a second great migration was getting under-way in the 1880s. This time the arrivals were largely from southern and eastern Europe: Italians, Greeks, Russians, and Poles, including many Jewish refugees of the pogroms. Throngs of newcomers crowded into the same Five Points tenement slum that the Irish had occupied earlier. Just as when the Irish had first come, longtime residents of the city now fretted over the impact the exotic foreigners would have on the city's physical and moral well-being. Again, there was a great wringing of hands over whether the city could cope, or if its final descent into chaos was nigh. In 1890, Jacob Riis' famous photographic exposé, *How the Other Half Lives*, focused the city's attention like never before on this second wave of impoverished and miserable, but also hopeful and industrious, people.

The Brooklyn Bridge, started in 1870, was finally completed in 1883. Until then, Manhattan and the most metropolitan of its neighboring municipalities had been separated by the fast-flowing East River, making simple travel between them an expensive inconvenience. The bridge was so popular with New York residents that, just a week after it opened, a pedestrian stampede led to the trampling deaths

FIGURE 8.2 A photograph by Jacob Riis of an immigrant family in their tenement home.

FIGURE 8.3   Brooklyn Bridge, ca. 1900.

Credit: Accessed 12 May 2015 from http://historicbridges.org/newyork/brooklyn/loc07.jpg

of 12 people. The physical link of a bridge changed relations between the two cities forever. It bound them together so intimately that, just over a decade later (1894), with Manhattan's population passing the two million mark, a charter to consolidate them into a greater New York City was approved in a general referendum.[1] After New York's usual array of political horse-trading, the unification took effect on the first day of 1898, increasing New York's population by more than a million at a stroke. Now only London was larger among the cities of the world.

With open land becoming increasingly scarce in Manhattan, companies began building the tallest buildings that anyone had ever seen; they were called "skyscrapers." Newspaper companies took the early lead, building a series of monumental towers on Park Row, near City Hall. By the late 1890s, New York had more skyscrapers than any city in the world. With the increased commercial density the skyscrapers generated, pressure on the already-grim transportation situation was further intensified.

2. James McKeen Cattell Moves to New York

It was into this massive, roiling metropolis that James McKeen Cattell, then just 30 years old, arrived in 1890. After completing his PhD in Leipzig in 1886, Cattell had gone to Cambridge to begin studies in medicine. He returned to the US to take up a lectureship at the University of Pennsylvania in the winter of 1888 but, the following spring, returned to Cambridge, where he briefly set up an experimental psychology laboratory.[2] For the rest of the year, he hobnobbed with a number of prominent British intellectuals, including Francis Galton. He learned about Galton's "anthropometric" tests, and decided to pursue a similar course of research himself. However, he wanted to steer it in a more psychological direction—to make it into a specifically "mental test," as he dubbed it.[3]

In January of 1889, Cattell returned to Penn, now as the head of a new Department of Psychology, and created a permanent laboratory there.[4] He collaborated on psychophysical research with the philosopher George Stuart Fullerton, but his main aim was to develop and deploy his new mental test. Cattell's test was truly something new in psychology. James, Royce, Hall, and some others had used questionnaires as a way of gathering information from the general public. In Royce's and James' cases, the aim had been to survey people on their "extraordinary" experiences for the American Society for Psychical Research. Hall had been an early member of the ASPR as well, but he used questionnaires to find out about the nature of children's minds as part of his Child Study research. These questionnaires were quite informal, by modern standards, asking open-ended questions to which the person being questioned (or the person administering the questionnaire) might write anything from a single word to a short essay. With no standardization, combining these widely divergent responses into a formal research result—something that might provide a general answer to the question asked—posed a problem that was nearly insoluble for those engaged in this novel form of research.[5]

Cattell's test, by contrast, mostly asked rather narrow questions that called for very specific, often quantified responses. In addition, his questions usually called for arcane measurements to be taken at the time of testing that could only be obtained by means of specialized laboratory equipment. One might call into question the depth of understanding that such procedures made possible, but there was no debate over the ease of manipulating them into a formal result. In addition, these kinds of data could be easily combined using a suite of basic statistical tools that were just then coming into use in psychology: averages, ranges of variation, etc.

Although Cattell rarely expressed himself in broad theoretical terms, the primary theoretical appeal of mental tests was that they could survey the full range of human variation in the mental functions they assessed. This variation—if the mental traits were heritable, as they were often presumed to be—could serve as the basis for human mental evolution. This had been Galton's explicit aim, and Cattell had "inherited" it, so to speak, from the older investigator.[6]

Data of the sort generated by Cattell's tests, whatever its ultimate contribution to knowledge might have been, fundamentally changed the character of the debate over the nature of the human mind. For instance, although questions about the equality of different "races" had long been a topic of heated debate in America (and elsewhere), the terms of the debate had been carried on primarily in a

FIGURE 8.4 James McKeen Cattell.

Credit: University Archives, Rare Book & Manuscript Library, Columbia University in the City of New York.

qualitative mode. There were, of course, some measurements of putative physical "indicators" of mental variation (such as the volumes and shapes of skulls) but, until this time, no one had attempted to measure the powers of the mind directly.

Cattell's test transformed the character of such disputes by casting them in quantitative terms. It is one thing to claim merely that in one's own experience (even if that experience is considerable), a certain group of people has shown themselves to be intellectually inferior to another. It is quite another, again, to hold up a sheaf of numerical data to support the claim that, on average, people of that group score measurably less well on a "scientific" test of their faculties of perception, memory, and reasoning.[7] The earlier style of argument could be plausibly challenged simply on the basis of one's contrasting personal and qualitative judgment (followed by a usually-irresolvable debate about which disputant's experience was more representative and whose judgment more trustworthy). The more modern quantitative approach, by contrast, required countervailing research of an equally exacting character. In short, Cattell's mental tests—flawed as they turned out to be—generated a kind of "intellectual arms race" over the importance of race, ethnicity, and even gender to mental "strength" in turn-of-the-century America. Even if they did not accomplish what he had hoped they would scientifically, they made it clear to everyone just how sophisticated one's tools would have to be if one hoped to participate respectably in such a debate in the future.

In 1890, Cattell left Penn for a more lucrative position at Columbia University in New York City.[8] Columbia had opened its doors as King's College, more or less under Anglican control, in 1754. This was more than a century after Harvard had started, and a half-century after Yale, but it was nearly simultaneous with the founding of Princeton (then known as the College of New Jersey) and of Rutgers (then called Queen's College). King's was originally located in downtown New York, at the corner of Murray and Church Streets (just a few blocks from the modern site of the World Trade Center). About a century later, in 1857, looking to expand its campus, the college moved uptown to Madison Avenue and 49th Street, which is where it was located when Cattell arrived. The school would soon be on the move again, however, shifting further north and west to the Morningside Heights site at 120th Street, on the Hudson River, where it sits today.[9]

Cattell was not much impressed by either location. For a man who was employed by universities in two large and venerable cities—Philadelphia and New York—and whose research into mental testing had such obvious import for the problems facing the American metropolis, Cattell spurned cities as being "neither physically, mentally nor morally healthy."[10] While at Penn, he had lived 65 miles to the west, in Mount Nebo. When he shifted operations to Columbia, he built a mansion on a hill 40 miles north of the city in the small town of Garrison. It was virtually across the Hudson River from West Point, home of the US Military Academy.[11] He adopted the name of "Fort Defiance" for his imposing new abode after discovering the moniker on a Revolutionary-era map of the site.

Cattell spent his first couple of years at Columbia focused on founding a new psychological laboratory and getting its research operations up to speed. In the spring of 1892, Stanley Hall convened his preliminary meeting of the American Psychological Association at Clark. By the end of the meeting, a steering committee had been formed that was anchored by the discipline's three senior scholars—Hall, Ladd, and James—but also included four younger men—Cattell, Joseph Jastrow, James Mark Baldwin (then at Toronto) and George Stuart Fullerton (Cattell's psychophysical research partner at Penn). It will be recalled that the first annual meeting of the APA was held at Penn in December of that same year, presided over by Hall who served as the new society's first president. Cattell presented a paper at that meeting (a methodological talk on the problem of observational error), and he offered to host the second annual meeting at Columbia, in December of 1893.

Although Cattell was rapidly becoming a major player in the growing field, all was not well between him and Hall. Hall was still running his *American Journal of Psychology* more or less as an in-house organ for his students and colleagues at Johns Hopkins and Clark. American psychologists who were not in Hall's immediate circle needed a publication vehicle for their research as well, and some of them were feeling put out by Hall's exclusionary editorial tendencies. Cattell and Baldwin (who had, in 1893, returned to his alma mater of Princeton after four years in Canada) attempted to persuade Hall to open up the journal to other American scholars. Hall dithered on the question for some time, stringing Cattell and Baldwin along, but he ultimately refused. This led Cattell and Baldwin to launch a competing journal in 1894—*The Psychological Review*.[12] Paradoxically, the existence of a second journal forced Hall to adopt a number of the reforms Cattell and Baldwin had suggested: In 1895, Hall appointed his closest colleague, E. C. Sanford, and Cornell's E. B. Titchener as co-editors. He also established an editorial board of international standing, including Henri Beaunis of France, Joseph Delboeuf of Belgium, Victor Henri of France (but then in Leipzig), August Kirschmann of Germany (but then in Toronto), Oswald Külpe of Germany, and Augustus Waller of England, among several others.

After a busy few years at Columbia—setting up the lab, helping to organize the APA, founding and running a new journal—Cattell finally returned to the program of mental testing program he had begun at Penn. He obtained permission from Columbia's administration to test every incoming student over a number of years. He worked closely with a young physician and Columbia colleague named Livingston Farrand.[13] The two men produced a sizeable report on the mental testing project late in 1896, which Cattell published in his own journal.[14]

The work attracted widespread attention, not least because Cattell made a point of presenting it at a variety of professional conferences—such as the New York Schoolmasters' Association—as well as scholarly ones—such as the American Association for the Advancement of Science.[15] In short order, others were taking up various forms of testing as well: As described in an earlier chapter, Jastrow conducted mental tests on visitors to the Chicago Exposition. Another early mental tester was Harry Kirk Wolfe, the founder of the psychology laboratory at Nebraska who had been just the second American to earn a PhD under Wundt at Leipzig (after Cattell). A third participant was Edward Scripture, also a product of the Leipzig laboratory, who had briefly worked at Clark until the chaos produced by Harper's "raid" had facilitated a move to Yale, where he founded that school's psychology laboratory.

Not everyone was on board with mental testing, however. There was much early criticism. When Cattell was president of the APA in 1895, he struck a committee to "draw up a series of physical and mental tests" for college students.[16] He packed the committee with allies like Jastrow, Scripture, and Witmer, as well as his co-editor at *Psychological Review*, Baldwin. When the committee reported back in 1897, most of them predictably extolled the potential of Cattell's form of mental testing, but Baldwin separated himself from the pack, questioning the emphasis on sensorimotor measurements and calling for more direct assessments of "higher" mental functions, such as memory.[17] Work of this kind was, in fact, being developed in France by Alfred Binet and Victor Henri, and it was known to some Americans, such as Cattell and Baldwin. Cattell, however, thought that the accurate measurement of higher functions would be too difficult and unreliable, especially if the easier-to-quantify sensorimotor tests turned out to be successful as proxies for them.[18] Baldwin remained unsure, though, and he was not entirely alone.

One of Titchener's doctoral students, Stella Emily Sharp, employed some of Binet's "higher" mental tasks in tests of her fellow students—perhaps the first person to do so in the American context. She had people remember whole sentences, or verbally recall complex pictures, rather than simply memorize strings of random letters or reproduce arbitrary line lengths. Her results showed not only that these rankings did not agree well with the results of the sensorimotor tasks—undermining the working assumption that simpler tasks could act as reliable proxies for more complex ones, but she also found that the results of the complex tasks did not agree well with one another. That is, there seemed to be more than one undifferentiated kind of mental power at work. Some people could be good at task A and poor at task B while others would show the reverse pattern.[19]

As troubling as these findings may have been, the lethal blow against Cattell's mental testing program came from his own laboratory. In 1895 in England, a former student of Galton's named Karl Pearson published a new statistic that precisely measured the degree of correlation between any two sets of paired numbers (such as fathers' and sons' heights).[20] Galton had produced measurements along these lines for decades, but Pearson's new "product-moment correlation coefficient" had the advantage of always falling into the same range (-1.0 to $+1.0$) regardless of the scale of the original numbers. This made it easy to compare correlations between numbers that displayed quite different ranges (e.g., is the correlation between fathers' and sons' heights weaker or stronger than the correlation between their weights?).

Cattell himself did not have much mathematical facility, but one of his best graduate students at Columbia, Clark Wissler, was mathematically proficient and volunteered to compute the new Pearson coefficient on the relationship between students' scores on Cattell's test and their course grades at Columbia. It was hoped that this would show, once and for all, that Cattell's tests captured something important about mental ability. Cattell was mightily disappointed by the outcome, however. Wissler found that none of the tasks correlated strongly with students' grades; that is, they were not a good proxy for more complex mental functions. Worse still, most of the tasks on Cattell's test did not even correlate well with each other; they were not measuring a singular underlying mental "power." Even tasks that seemed conceptually similar—e.g., simple reaction-times versus the speed of locating every instance of a particular letter in a matrix of random letters—often did not correlate well with each other.[21]

Wissler's dissertation sounded the death knell not only for Cattell's mental testing program, but it also marked the end of Cattell's career as a research psychologist. His time in the laboratory and even the testing room was effectively over.

Another occupation had seized Cattell's fancy by that time, however. It would ultimately confer upon him higher status and much more wealth than psychology: owning and editing scientific journals. In addition to the *Psychological Review* (which was co-owned and edited with Baldwin until 1904), Cattell started or acquired *Popular Science Monthly* (purchased 1900); *Journal of Philosophy, Psychology, and Scientific Methods* (founded 1905); *Archives of Psychology* (founded 1906); *American Naturalist* (purchased 1908); and *School and Society* (founded 1915), among others.

His most important acquisition, however, was the journal *Science*. Today considered among the most prestigious in America, *Science* was first launched back in 1880 under the editorship of a New York journalist named John Michaels. The venture had been financed by luminaries such as Thomas Edison and, later, Alexander Graham Bell, but Michaels was unable to make a go of it. The journal collapsed in less than three years. In 1883, it was purchased by a Boston entomologist named Samuel H. Scudder[22] who assigned the editorship to Nathaniel D. C. Hodges in 1885. Scudder and Hodges started the practice of reserving some pages of the journal for coverage of the meetings of scientific organizations such as the American Association for the Advancement of Science (AAAS). Still, the periodical did not attract enough subscribers to keep it afloat so, within a decade, Scudder was forced to look for a buyer.

Cattell purchased *Science* in 1894 and soon began working with the AAAS to make it the organization's official organ. Once the deal was complete, in 1900, Cattell was able to exert a steadily increasing degree of control over the AAAS, even though he did not hold a high-level office in the organization, apart from his editorship of the journal. He would eventually be elected to the AAAS presidency in 1924. Cattell enhanced his status by holding presidencies in several other scientific organizations: the American Society of Naturalists (1902), the New York Academy of Science (1902), and the Eugenics Research Association (1914), among others.[23]

In 1903, Cattell surveyed psychologists about who they thought were the most eminent members of their discipline, from which he was able to generate a ranked list of over 50 individual psychologists.[24] The results, not published until 1933, placed William James in first place, followed by (2) Cattell himself, (3) Hugo Münsterberg (much about whom follows), (4) G. Stanley Hall, and (5) James Mark Baldwin. Rounding out the top ten were: (6) E. B. Titchener, (7) Josiah Royce, (8) G. T. Ladd, (9) John Dewey, and (10) Joseph Jastrow. The top women on the list were (12) Mary Whiton Calkins, (19) Christine Ladd-Franklin, and (42) Margaret Floy Washburn. Cattell's work in this line was not limited to psychologists. Indeed, it became a major preoccupation of his: In 1906, following directly from Galton's *English Men of Science*,[25] Cattell launched a periodical titled *Biographical Dictionary of American Men of Science*. In each volume, which came out every few years, each individual listed was ranked according to the results of a survey Cattell had conducted among his or her peers.

It is often said that, after the collapse of his testing program, Cattell turned solely to editing and administration, but this is not completely true. He continued to pursue research questions doggedly, but not within the laboratory traditions of psychology, or even according to his own mental tests. Instead, he invented (or at least greatly expanded, from Galton's example), the field that is today known as "scientometrics": the measurement of the status and eminence of scientists and the institutions in which they work.

3. Robert S. Woodworth and Edward L. Thorndike

A pair of Cattell's students from the 1890s came to stand among the most significant psychologists of the 20th century. Robert Sessions Woodworth and Edward Lee Thorndike were born five years apart (1869 and 1874, respectively) in western Massachusetts towns that were just 20 miles apart (Belchertown and Williamsburg, respectively).[26] This was the same area that had produced Stanley Hall a quarter-century earlier. Unlike Hall, though, both men had itinerant upbringings, each being the son of a Protestant minister (Woodworth Congregationalist and Thorndike Methodist). Woodworth spent his early childhood in Iowa, his middle childhood in Connecticut, and his teenage years near Boston. For his bachelors degree (completed in 1891), he went Amherst College, close to his birthplace. After graduation, Woodworth taught high school for two years, then took a mathematics professorship at Washburn College in Kansas. Thorndike's family also moved frequently during his childhood, though only within the state of Massachusetts. For basic schooling he was sent to the venerable Roxbury Latin School (founded 1645). Then, for college, he traveled to Connecticut for a Bachelors of Science at Wesleyan (completed in 1895).

Both men enrolled at Harvard in 1895, which is where they met. Although Woodworth already had his Wesleyan degree, he took a second undergraduate degree at Harvard, shifting from math to philosophy and psychology. Thorndike, by contrast, began his graduate studies immediately. Both studied with William James and Josiah Royce, among others. Woodworth was awarded a Master's degree in 1897, then served as an assistant in the psychology department. Thorndike started conducting research on the problem of how children learn, but found the topic too complicated, so he switched to the simpler problem of learning in chickens. He was convinced that "evolutionary continuity" assured that his results would extend to the more complex human case as well. Soon he was working with a number of different animal species. He finished his Master's degree in 1897, then left for Columbia to embark on a PhD in animal learning under Cattell's guidance. The following year, Woodworth arrived at Columbia as well, also to begin doctoral work with Cattell. Both men completed their degrees in 1899. Woodworth wrote a creditable dissertation on the accuracy of voluntary hand movements under various environmental and mental conditions. Thorndike, however, wrote one of the most influential studies of the coming century: *Animal Intelligence*.[27] He examined

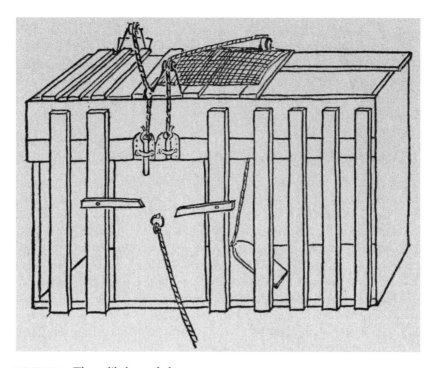

FIGURE 8.5 Thorndike's puzzle box.

Credit: From Thorndike, E. L. (1911). *Animal Intelligence.* New York, NY: Macmillan.

a wide array of species, testing the learning abilities of each with purpose-built apparatus that presented his animal-subjects with problems to be solved.

The most famous of these was the "puzzle box" for cats—a crude wooden cage with a latched door that could be opened by a mechanism inside of the enclosure, if only the animal knew how to trip it. To motivate the cat to try to escape (rather than just curl up and go to sleep), Thorndike placed a piece of food just outside of the cage—within sight and smell but out of reach. Eventually, some arbitrary movement made by the cat would accidentally trip the latch and open the door, releasing the animal from the box. Some animals might hit the mechanism with their paw, others with their head, still others with their behind. It didn't matter, so long as it resulted in opening the door. After escaping the cage and getting its food reward, the cat would be returned to the box and the door latched again. On this new trial, Thorndike discovered that the animal was likely to engage in the very same movement, whatever it had been, that had immediately preceded its previous escape. As the number of trials mounted, the escapes became gradually quicker. After many repetitions, the cats could trip the mechanism immediately upon being returned to the box, typically re-using whatever action had opened it by chance in the early stages of the experiment.

For Thorndike, there was no need to posit some sort of "insight" on the cat's part into the mechanism that released the latch. There was simply the gradual forging of a "connection" between a certain kind of movement and the subsequent escape from the box. As a result, his theory of learning became known as "connectionism." By the time he published his studies in book form,[28] he had elevated his simple but powerful conclusion to the status of a scientific law—The Law of Effect:

> Of several responses made to the same situation, those which are accompanied or closely followed by satisfaction to the animal will, other things being equal, be more firmly connected with the situation, so that, when it recurs, they will be more likely to recur; those which are accompanied or closely followed by discomfort to the animal will, other things being equal, have their connections with that situation weakened, so that, when it recurs, they will be less likely to occur. The greater the satisfaction or discomfort, the greater the strengthening or weakening of the bond.[29]

Although Thorndike is often assimilated to the later behaviorists because his methodology was similar to what theirs would be, it is important to note that there was no denial or even "bracketing" of the animal's inner mental states in the Law of Effect: the driving force of the learning was its "satisfaction" or "discomfort," terms that would not have been found in the strict behaviorist's vocabulary (unless suitably re-defined in behavioral terms).

Thorndike was attracted to the conclusion that what was true for animals in general must be true for the human animal as well. Learning, for him, was a gradual process of building up increasingly complex connections through trial and error, reward and punishment. Traditional beliefs to the contrary, that humans have some special capacity to learn in more sophisticated ways was, in Thorndike's view, just the cultural residue of earlier Romantic speculation, not supported by the available scientific evidence.

Almost immediately, there was a great deal of criticism of Thorndike's method, especially from animal researchers who followed a more "naturalistic" approach. Thomas Wesley Mills, an irascible physiologist and physician at McGill University in Montréal, argued that one could no more draw valid conclusions about cat learning from what they did cooped up in a cage than one could "enclose a living man in a coffin, lower him, against his will, into the earth, and attempt to deduce normal psychology from his conduct."[30] Thorndike's response was that traditional naturalistic observations of animal behavior led to vague, impressionistic descriptions that were of little use in comparing one species to another or one set of conditions to another. By contrast, he argued, with experimental methods one could answer specific research questions with quantified data (e.g., How many seconds did it take for the cat to escape the box?). Indeed, Thorndike was enthusiastic about bringing to psychology many analytic techniques that were, by then, regularly found in other sciences. He had, for instance, been among the first psychologists to use line graphs to demonstrate learning by his animals.[31] At Clark University, Edmund Sanford and two graduate students—Linus Kline and Willard Small—attempted to resolve the dispute by designing more "natural" environments in which controlled experimental studies like Thorndike's could be conducted. In the process, they were the first to use mazes to study rat learning.[32]

After graduation, Thorndike took a job in far-away Cleveland, where he taught at the Women's College of the Western Reserve University. After only a single year, though, he was called back to Columbia University Teachers College, where he would remain for the balance of his long career. Much like Cattell, Thorndike shunned the city, buying land in Montrose, NY, almost as far up the Hudson River as Cattell had gone. He encouraged other scholars and scientists to buy property in the area to form a small informal academic colony. However, also like Cattell, despite his refusal to personally live in New York City, Thorndike's research was closely connected to a pressing problem of modern urban life: education.

Thorndike's research interests soon turned back toward human learning. In 1901, he and his old Harvard chum, Robert S. Woodworth, teamed up on an extensive project to test the entrenched pedagogical truism that "formal disciplines," such as math and Latin, remain important school topics despite their abstract and even antiquarian aspects because they train the mind in uniquely rigorous ways that facilitate the future learning of other difficult subjects. The two men published an extensive three-part research report in *Psychological Review* in which they concluded that there was little evidence of "transfer of training" from one topic to another. The result thereby undermined the primary rationale of the educational traditionalists of the era. Through research of this sort, Thorndike became one of the leading educational psychologists in America. He became a staunch advocate of the use of objective scientific data in making educational decisions, and he became a supporter of standardized tests, as they became available. Thorndike would also become a strong promoter of eugenics.

Woodworth, after completing his PhD in 1899, taught physiology at various New York City locations for a few years, then spent the 1902–1903 school year doing advanced research under the eminent English physiologist Charles Sherrington in Liverpool. He returned to Columbia in 1903 to take up an instructorship in psychology that Cattell offered him. He was promoted to professor in 1909 and remained at Columbia for the rest of his career. Like Thorndike, Woodworth became a leading exponent of the scientific approach to psychology, though he was notable for remaining "eclectic" in his outlook, rather than committing himself to a particular "school."[33]

Woodworth worked comfortably on both sides of the sometimes-acrimonious divide between "pure" and "applied" psychology. He was wary of the popular eugenics movement, with its statistically-facile comparisons of different "races." He stressed the complexity of the relations between hereditary and environmental factors, calling into question the common practice of treating them as simply additive (e.g., "intelligence is 75% heredity and 25% environment"). His best-known textbook—*Experimental Psychology*, nicknamed the "Columbia Bible"—was widely used for decades.[34] Woodworth would be awarded the American Psychological Association's very first Gold Medal for "unequaled contributions to shaping the destiny of scientific psychology" in 1956.

Thorndike, Woodworth, and their common supervisor, Cattell, collectively comprised what is sometimes called the "Columbia School" of Functionalism. They did not use this description for themselves, but there were several general similarities with their contemporaries at Chicago: (1) a broad sense that evolutionary "logic" was a more powerful tool in the construction of psychological theory than physiology had been, (2) an abandonment of Wundt's insistence on experimental "purity" coupled with (3) a willingness to delve into the "application" of psychology to real world problems (e.g., education), and (4) a rejection of the strict boundaries that Titchener placed on "proper" introspective research, replaced by (5) an eclectic willingness to develop and employ novel research methods and use novel research subjects in order to get at answers to the scientific questions that interested them.

4. Boston at the Close of the 19th Century

Like most the other major American cities, toward the end of the 19th century Boston was growing and changing rapidly. The "Back Bay" landfill project was essentially completed by 1882, opening up huge vast new tracts of real estate to urban development. A new crossing of the Charles River—the Harvard Bridge—was opened in 1891, connecting the Back Bay directly to the Massachusetts Institute of Technology (founded 1861) and, up the road a few miles, to Harvard itself.

Beginning in the early 1880s, the ethnic balance of the long-impoverished North End of the city began to swing from the Irish Catholics, who had moved there in the wake of the Great Famine, to southern Italians, who were escaping the devastating economic fallout of Italian unification, and Eastern European Jews, who were fleeing a wave of pogroms in Kiev, Odessa, Warsaw, and other cities of the Russian Empire.

The traditional wealthy Brahmin families who had dominated Boston politics for generations had gradually come to believe that the Irish, rustic and raucous as they might have been at first, would, through a combination of public education and various other public acculturation projects, eventually be assimilated to "civilized" American ways. In the 1880s and 1890s, however, the Brahmins were faced with a new wave of destitute, mostly illiterate, and even more "alien" immigrants who were pouring, seemingly unabated, into the city. In open panic that they would ultimately lose "their" city to what, in their eyes, was a horde of miserable rabble, the Brahmin response was to found the Immigration Restriction League of Boston, in 1894. Their most prominent spokesperson was Massachusetts's newest US Senator, Henry Cabot Lodge.[35] During his six years as a Congressman (prior to his 1893 appointment to the Senate), Lodge had campaigned for a literacy test to block "inferior races" from entering the US. In 1896, the US Congress passed a bill requiring a literacy test of all immigrants but it was vetoed by President Grover Cleveland.[36]

Although the Irish of New York and Chicago had discovered, early on, ways in which they could exert some political influence over their cities, the Irish of Boston had not broken through into the political mainstream as effectively. This was quite possibly because no small, exclusive, entrenched group of wealthy families in New York or Chicago had been able to so effectively implement a paternalistic, even proprietary, view of their city as the Brahmins had been able to exert over Boston. As a new generation of Boston-born children of immigrants emerged into adulthood in the 1880s, wealthier and more confident than their parents had been, the old assumptions began to crumble. In 1884, Irish-born Hugh O'Brien was elected to the first of four one-year terms as mayor of the city. Although he was Boston's first Irish Catholic mayor—an immigrant from the 1830s, well before the time of the Great Famine—the key to O'Brien's success was to suppress most traces of his background. According to one historian of Boston, "his preoccupation with holding down the tax rate, improving and widening the streets, and expanding the powers of the mayor, made him almost indistinguishable from the procession of Yankee mayors who had preceded him."[37] Democrats like O'Brien could get elected in Boston, but not if they offended the Brahmin powerbrokers. After O'Brien, it was more than a decade of alternating "Yankee" Republicans and Democrats before another Irish immigrant, Patrick Collins, was elected mayor in 1902. Although Collins died in office in 1905, he seemed to finally break the Brahmin's Republican grip for good. Collins was succeeded by John "Honey Fitz" Fitzgerald.[38] From the time Collins assumed office until the present day, every mayor of Boston but two has been a Democrat.

5. William James: Becoming America's Intellectual

Although William James's professional successes were multiplying in the 1880s, it was a terribly difficult decade for him personally. In 1882, both of his parents died—Mary in January and Henry Sr. in December. The following year, his younger brother, Wilky long hampered by the terrible wounds he had suffered in the Civil War, died at just 38 years of age, leaving behind a widow and daughter. In the summer of 1884, William's troubled brother, Bob, returned to the Boston area from Milwaukee, where he had been unable to make a go of it as the curator of a small museum. Bob's marriage had fallen apart—destroyed by his alcoholism, infidelity, and vocational failure—and he now threw himself upon the mercy of his oldest brother. That same year, William's sometimes brilliant but often erratic sister, Alice, impulsively traveled to England with her longtime companion, Katherine Loring, and then, just as unexpectedly, decided to take up residence there permanently. (Fortunately, brother Henry was already living there to monitor the situation for the family and lend assistance when needed.) Disease also paid frequent visits on the James family during these years. Near the end of 1884 William's oldest son, Harry, contracted diphtheria, but managed to survive. The following spring William's wife, Alice, came down with scarlet fever and also recovered, though only after a long, often solitary convalescence. A few months later, in July of 1885, the Jameses' youngest son, Hermann, died of whooping cough at the tender age of just 17 months.

It was soon after this wrenching family tragedy that the Jameses started to attend the séances of the Boston spiritualist, Leonora Piper. Piper had been recommended to William by his mother-in-law, Eliza Gibbens. Although he had attended some spiritualist meetings the year before, and declared them to be "nauseous,"[39] he was convinced of Piper's authenticity when, during an early session, she came up with the name of their recently lost child, "Hermann," apparently out of the blue.[40] William came to regard Mrs. Piper, as she was known, as the "white crow": the one instance that disproved the belief common among his peers that all spiritualists were frauds. His association with Mrs. Piper would be long and complicated.[41]

Although many tried strenuously to prove mediums to be fraudulent—Stanley Hall, Joseph Jastrow, and Hugo Münsterberg, among others—James' old friend Charles Peirce regarded the whole matter as being fundamentally unserious. In 1887, he impishly wondered why,

> these spirits and apparitions are so painfully solemn. . . . I fancy that, were I suddenly to find myself liberated from all the trials and responsibilities of this life, . . . I should regard the situation as a stupendous frolic, should be at the summit of gayety, and should only be too glad to leave the vale of tears behind. Instead of that, these starveling souls come mooning back to their former haunts, to cry over spilled milk.[42]

Within two years of Hermann's death, in 1887, the Jameses had their only daughter, Margaret (or Peggy). In 1890 they also had another son, Alexander. Personal tragedy struck again, however, in July of 1891 when sister Alice, still living in England, wrote the family that she was suffering from breast cancer and did not have long to live. That September, James rushed across the ocean for just 10 days to see her a final time. On March 5, 1892, she had Henry wire William wishing him farewell. The next day she was gone.

Through the many peaks and valleys of his personal life, James had done his level best to produce the psychology textbook that he had promised Henry Holt back in 1878. The project seemed to resist at every turn, almost as though it were one of James' conscious organisms with interests of its own to fight for. The scope of the work kept expanding, growing to proportions that overwhelmed even its author. Holt tried to urge James along as competing textbooks hit the shelves authored by both James' equals in seniority, like George Trumbull Ladd, and by youngsters, such as fresh-out-of-Princeton James Mark Baldwin.[43]

It was not until the middle of 1890 that James finally completed the massive manuscript. That fall, it appeared in two stout tomes, totaling over 1,300 pages: *The Principles of Psychology*. James infamously spat out his assessment of what was, by far, his most substantial work: It was "a loathsome, distended, tumefied, bloated, dropsical mass, testifying to nothing but two facts: 1st, that there is no such thing as a science of psychology, and 2nd, that W. J. is an incapable."[44] The public response to the textbook, however, was not in accord with James' acerbic self-assessment. It was a great hit across America and received positive notice in Europe as well. James was now emerging as one of America's most famous and popular scholars. As we saw, John Dewey, then still at Michigan, replaced his own textbook with James' in his psychology course.

James' reputation as a teacher was growing as well, and his Harvard affiliation brought him into contact with some of the most promising young students the US had to offer. In 1888, a young W. E. B. Du Bois arrived from Fisk College and took James' ethics course in his first year. "He was my friend and guide to clear thinking," Du Bois later recalled.[45] A few years later, in 1893, Gertrude Stein arrived. She conducted experiments on the phenomenon of "automatic writing" under James' and Delabarre's guidance.[46] Of James, she later said simply, "He was my big influence when I was at college."[47]

Successful as he was as a writer and teacher, though, by 1890 the laboratory enterprise that he had started at Harvard back in the mid-1870s was starting to fall well behind developments at competing universities. By the end of 1892, there were laboratories at 11 other schools in North America, most of them better equipped than Harvard's. The truth was that James' own interest in laboratory work had long since flagged. In his textbook he had quipped (alluding to the intellectual predilections of Germans like Weber, Fechner, and Wundt) that laboratory psychology "could hardly have arisen in a country whose natives could be *bored*."[48] So, he was now faced with the choice of either ceding the experimental discipline he had once championed to the leadership of other, younger men whose enthusiasm for the brass and glass still burned bright, or he would have recruit to Harvard a talented and energetic psychologist who would be prepared to upgrade and expand the Harvard lab (while still accepting James' seniority in the department and in the discipline, of course).

In 1890, a member of Harvard's Board of Overseers, John Fiske, secured a massive contribution of $3,000 from a "W. A. Slater of Norwich," for the purpose of expanding the laboratory from the demonstration rooms that James had set up 15 years before into a modern facility that could support original scientific research.[49] James was able to raise another $1,500, mainly from his own circle of friends.[50] The following year, one of Hall's graduates, Herbert Nichols, was recruited from Clark to equip and design the expanded Harvard laboratory. Notably, the laboratory was also moved at this time from the Lawrence Scientific School, where James the physiologist had gotten his start, to Dane Hall, which was then the main philosophy building at Harvard, symbolically establishing which discipline would foster the still-young science.

James's relationship to the discipline of psychology was ever-complicated and ever-changing. He had the odd ability to simultaneously seem peripheral and central, *passé* and *avant-garde*. It is often claimed that James more or less abandoned psychology for philosophy during the early 1890s. Although James remained willing to dive into theoretical debates about scientific psychology, particularly if the matter touched on one of his earlier positions, [51] his chief writings in this period started to take on an increasingly philosophical cast. [52] The matter is complicated further by the question of how to regard James' increasing and enthusiastic contributions to psychical research at this time. [53] In the past, it has been common practice to minimize the significance of these writings, regarding them, at best, as one of James' idiosyncratic "hobbies." It is clear, however, that James took psychical matters very seriously and wrote about them not only for popular publications or for those of a specifically psychical character, but also for mainstream psychological and broader scientific journals. [54] James was even willing to enter into vituperative public disputes with leading colleagues, such as Cattell and Titchener, over the reality of psychical phenomena. [55]

The late historian of psychology Eugene Taylor argued that James did not abandon psychology at all but, instead, tried to carve out a broader psychology than was then being erected by the "laboratory men." Taylor maintained that, in this quest, James became the founder of a somewhat hazy third stream of psychology, neither "scientific" nor "applied"; one that was comfortable with discussions of "anomalous" mental phenomena that made most experimental psychologists cringe at the ridicule such debates were likely to bring down upon the discipline they were working so diligently to present as a legitimate, rigorous science. [56] James, however, was pointedly uninterested in his colleagues' careful "boundary work"—i.e., laboratories in, spiritualists out—and he was undeterred by the fact that some of the very spiritualists whose powers he had publicly declared "authentic" were later shown to have been frauds, often by the very men who had followed him into "scientific" psychology. [57] His longtime friend, Oliver Wendell Holmes, once said of him, "his reason made him sceptical and his wishes led him to turn down the lights so as to give miracle a chance." [58]

Here we see, perhaps better than anywhere else, the intimate but complicated relationship between William James' philosophical vision and that of his father. William had acquired more formal training in both philosophy and science than Henry Sr. had, and William's modes of attacking the project were distinctly more "modern" in character (although still idiosyncratic). But the actual content of the project—the central issue that occupied him and impelled him forward—centered on the nature of the relation between the spiritual and scientific realms. How were these two great domains of thought—one ancient, the other more recent but patently powerful—to be coordinated and reconciled? This is the question that had driven Henry Sr., first, to visit Faraday in England and, later, to embrace Swedenborg. The scientific investigation of the spiritual world offered William as promising a path to the answer as he, now in his 50s, was likely to find in his lifetime. Although James is often put forward as the first "modern" philosopher (where "modern" is glossed roughly as taking science seriously as well as taking problems that were closer to people's everyday experience more seriously than the Idealists had), one can see that he was truly a transitional character, one foot firmly in each camp—employing incipient forms of the methods that would come to dominate the century to come as a means of addressing the problems that had preoccupied the century just then closing.

Thus, as disinterested in the hands-on practice of laboratory psychology as James had become, he still recognized the need to have a modern laboratory and a top laboratory man to run it, if Harvard were to remain among the leading institutions of American psychology. The new recruit from Clark, Herbert Nichols, talented and energetic as he might have been, was not destined to be that man. He was to be handed, instead, the role of trusty assistant. Someone with more "star power" would be needed to play the lead.

6. Hugo Münsterberg: "Man of Genius"

In 1890, one of James' recent graduate students, Edmund Burke Delabarre (soon to be the psychology professor at Brown University in Providence, Rhode Island), decided to travel to the German city of Freiburg to hone his laboratory skills and earn a PhD from the founder of the new laboratory there.[59] The psychologist in Freiburg, Hugo Münsterberg, had graduated from Wundt's laboratory in Leipzig during the mid-1880s (the same time as Cattell, coincidentally). He was no clone of Wundt, though. Young as he was, he had written critically of Wundt's theory of the will, and had engaged his old mentor in a public debate on the topic. James appreciated Münsterberg's view of the will, one that emphasized actual motor action over abstract conscious intent and, so, paralleled James' controversial view of emotion.[60] James had also personally met Münsterberg briefly in 1889 at the International Congress of Psychology in Paris—a meeting that Wundt's lab had refused to attend because it included psychopathology on the program—but he did not know the Freiburg man well. The following year, James received a highly appreciative first-hand account of Münsterberg from his former student, Charles Strong, who was then studying under Münsterberg and others at Freiburg.[61] With the addition of Delabarre's new and favorable reports, James began to form in his mind a plan that would permanently alter the trajectory of Harvard psychology.

Münsterberg was born in 1863 in the city of Danzig (modern Gdansk, Poland) in the state then known as West Prussia. He had two older half-brothers, and

FIGURE 8.6   Hugo Munsterberg.

Credit: Accessed May 12, 2015 from www.biografiasyvidas.com/biografia/m/fotos/munsterberg.jpg

a younger "full" brother. His mother—his father's second wife—died when he was not yet 12 years old. His father, a prosperous lumber merchant, had great aspirations for the boys, which they mostly succeeded in fulfilling: the two older brothers became successful businessmen and politicians while Hugo and his younger brother became prominent scholars.[62] Although Hugo and his brothers were raised in a highly assimilated bourgeois Jewish family, the three younger boys converted to Lutheranism soon after their father's death in 1880 in order to improve their future prospects.[63] In what may have been the first indication that Münsterberg possessed a strong *Wanderlust*, when it came time to select a university to attend, he decided to travel nearly 1,700 km southwest, to Geneva, Switzerland for a summer of literary study. Then he moved 1,000 km back northeast to attend Leipzig, where he began a medical degree. During the first year, he took a course from Wilhelm Wundt on the new psychology. He decided to include this topic in his future studies. He was interested in the study of the will. Wundt was an avowed voluntarist—he believed in freedom of the will—but Carl Ludwig, from whom Münsterberg took physiology, was one of those, along with Hermann Helmholtz and Emil Du Bois-Reymond (both one-time mentors of Wundt), who had pioneered a wholly mechanist approach to physiology. Perhaps wanting to avoid a clash of wills (ironically), Wundt disallowed the topic and Münsterberg wrote a critique of evolution for his dissertation, earning his PhD in 1885.[64] He returned to his medical studies, but moved again, this time 500 km southwest to Heidelberg, to complete his MD in 1887. He wrote his dissertation on the visual perception of space. That same year, he married Selma Oppler, also a Lutheran convert from a Jewish family, and he secured an unpaid *Privatdocent* position (this time just 200 km away) at Freiburg. This sort of position required one to submit an original piece of research (*Habilitation*) as a kind of application. Münsterberg submitted an essay on the subject of the will, the very topic that Wundt had forbidden. Münsterberg rejected Wundt's voluntarist position, siding with mechanists like Ludwig. This earned him the negative of attention not only of Wundt but also of Göttingen's psychologist George Elias Müller, founder of the other major laboratory in Germany at the time. In the long run, the dispute with Wundt and Müller may not have been a bad thing, for it drew Münsterberg into public debate with major figures in the field, bringing attention both to him and to his relatively small university.

Münsterberg built a new psychology laboratory in Freiburg—still one of the first few in Germany[65]—but, as a mere *Docent*, he had to locate it in his home, and to purchase the equipment himself. Fortunately, his family's money was more than equal to the expense, and the laboratory quickly became the main rival to Wundt's and Müller's laboratories. Münsterberg's productivity and his ability to successfully engage with the "giants" of the field impressed his colleagues and superiors sufficiently that he was offered an "extraordinary" professorship just five years after arriving. [66]

His laboratory attracted an interesting range of students, a number of whom are shown in the photograph above.[67] In addition to Delabarre and an array of young German gentlemen, there was also, for a time, a woman named Resa von Schirnhofer.[68] She was a young Austrian of independent means and mind. She had traveled the 700 km from her home in Krems (near Vienna) to Zurich, where she earned a PhD in philosophy under the famed positivist Richard Avenarius, writing her dissertation on Schelling and Spinoza.[69] Through friends from her Zurich years, she became part of a circle of unconventional women who were drawn to the radical classicist and philosopher, Friedrich Nietzsche. Schirnhofer visited him in Nice in the spring and summer of 1884, even living at the same boarding house as he did. The precise nature of Nietzsche's relationship with these women is a little mysterious, though it is notable that when he invited her to travel alone

FIGURE 8.7   An 1890 photograph of Münsterberg's Freiburg laboratory. The image
was taken at the photographer's studio, not at Münsterberg's home (where
his lab was located). The people in the photo, from left to right, are: Donald McKay, Edmund B. Delabarre, James G. Hume, Samuel Alexander,
Resa von Schirnhofer, A. Jankovich, Hugo Münsterberg, Waldemar Lewy,
Johannes Hoops, Hermann Stahr, Abraham Slatopolsky, and Karl Siebert.

Credit: From Margaret Münsterberg, *Hugo Münsterberg, His Life and Work* (New York, NY: D. Appleton,
1922), 26.

with him to Corsica, she declined the offer (though she also attempted to locate a
chaperone to enable her to go).[70] How she came to be in Münsterberg's Freiburg
laboratory a few years later is not known, but her presence there poses intriguing
questions about the young professor's views of higher education during the liberalization that took place in Imperial Germany in the years immediately following
the death of Kaiser Wilhelm, in 1888.

In addition to Schirnhofer, for a short time the Australian-Jewish philosopher
Samuel Alexander worked in Münsterberg's laboratory as well. Alexander had
traveled halfway around the world to England as a teen, where he had secured a
scholarship at Oxford. There, he came under the philosophical influence of the
British Idealist, T. H. Green. After graduating in 1881, he became the first Jewish person to be accepted as a Fellow by Oxford (or Cambridge). By the time
he came to Freiburg, nearly a decade later, in the winter of 1890–1891, he had
already published what would prove to be his most influential book, *Moral Order
and Progress*.[71] Although increasingly respected for his philosophical work, Alexander experienced great difficulty obtaining a professorship at an English university,

undoubtedly due to ambivalence in the British academy about the "proper" boundaries of religious tolerance.[72] He was finally hired at the not-so-prestigious University of Manchester in 1893, where he remained until his death in 1938.

Also in Münsterberg's laboratory in 1890 were two young Canadians, Donald McKay and James Gibson Hume, both from Toronto. McKay and Hume were the first representatives of their country to study experimental psychology in Europe.[73] McKay had been a senior undergraduate student at the University of Toronto when the longtime philosophy professor there, George Paxton Young, had suffered a fatal stroke in February of 1889. McKay was well-enough regarded by the faculty to be asked to teach the balance of Young's courses that term. After graduation, he went on to Freiburg, where he completed his PhD under Münsterberg, but the experience was said to have left him with "shattered nerves and a broken-down constitution." Instead of recovering at his family home near Toronto, he moved to Colorado to recuperate. While there, he entered the ministry. When James Mark Baldwin, who had been hired to replace Young at Toronto in 1889, left for Princeton in 1893, McKay was locally considered a favorite to fill the position, but before he could even apply, he was "seized with paralysis" (perhaps suffered a stroke?) and died a few months later, in February of 1894, at the age of only 34.[74]

Hume had been a slightly earlier student of Young's at Toronto, and had gone on to graduate work with Stanley Hall at Johns Hopkins and (after Hall packed up for Clark) with James, Royce, and especially George Herbert Palmer at Harvard. He completed a master's degree and, when news of Young's death came, he applied for the position, claiming that the late professor had privately promised it to him if he were to acquire laboratory training. Despite Hume's lack of doctorate, a swell of public support for the local boy led to his being hired, in 1889, to a philosophy position alongside of the much better qualified James Mark Baldwin. Hume was immediately given two years' leave to earn a PhD. He decided to go to Freiburg, where he studied mainly with the philosopher Alois Riehl, though he spent some time working in Münsterberg's laboratory. Not long after Hume's return to Toronto, Baldwin left for Princeton, leaving Hume in full charge of the philosophy department, a position he would retain until 1926.

Also in the photograph of Münsterberg's laboratory is Johannes Hoops, who earned his Freiburg PhD in philology and history under Hermann Eduard von Holst (who would soon after take the professorship of History at the new University of Chicago). Hoops went on to become a professor of English at Heidelberg and a leading German expert on the great Anglo-Saxon epic poem, *Beowulf*. Hoops traveled to the US for lectures several times in the 1920s and 1930s. Hoops' son, Reinald, would come to be known for his work on psychoanalysis and literature.[75] This diverse array of interesting characters must have made quite an impression on Delabarre, the young, parochial New Englander with the French surname. He wrote about his experiences in the Freiburg laboratory to his American mentor, William James.

In February of 1892, James wrote a letter to Münsterberg announcing that actions toward "regenerating our philosophical department" were required, but that a "man of genius" would be needed to reach the goal. He proposed a three-year "experiment" in which Münsterberg, then not yet 30 years old, would come to Harvard as a professor to modernize and expand the laboratory. From the very start, James' plan was quite specific about things such as his title and salary. Münsterberg was more than intrigued by the offer—his *Wanderlust* was triggered again—but he was concerned that his English was not adequate to the task of college lecturing.[76]

Negotiations proceeded back and forth by mail and, in May, an agreement was reached. Münsterberg was granted a leave of absence by Freiburg.[77] The Jameses traveled to Europe to meet with the Münsterbergs. As things turned out, the Jameses would remain in Europe the whole of the first year that the Münsterbergs were at Harvard. Still, the Münsterbergs set sail for America in August of 1892. They arrived in New York, where they spent a few days taking in the sights of the largest, most chaotic city in which they had ever set foot. Then they traveled to Cambridge, MA, where they were greeted and befriended by Josiah Royce, Herbert Nichols, George Herbert Palmer, and other members of the Harvard community.

FIGURE 8.8 A drawing of Münsterberg's laboratory, from Herbert Nichols' 1893 article in *McClure's Magazine*, "The Psychological Laboratory at Harvard" (vol. 1 (1893): 399–409).

Münsterberg soon set to work. Nichols, who had already completed much of the labor of moving and refurbishing the laboratory, was given the job of being Münsterberg's assistant.[78] The German professor was exempted from lecturing during the first year, while he improved his English, so Nichols took over the teaching of James' undergraduate psychology course for the year.[79]

One of the more notable graduate students who Münsterberg encountered on his arrival was Mary Whiton Calkins. Calkins was already an instructor of Greek at nearby Wellesley College. She was a native of Connecticut, and her undergraduate degree, at Smith College in central Massachusetts, had been in philosophy and classics. In the late 1880s, Wellesley wanted to expand its philosophical offerings to include the "new" psychology, so they offered Calkins, who was known to take an interest in such matters, a more permanent position if she would agree to change departments and take a year of advanced training in the topic.[80] She accepted the offer and contacted Harvard, among several other schools. The ancient Crimson College did not allow women into its regular courses in that era, but it did run an

FIGURE 8.9 Mary Whiton Calkins, 1889.

Credit: Mary Whiton Calkins Papers, Wellesley College Archives (ref. WCA_2017_05_25_002).

"Annex" for women that would soon be rechristened Radcliffe College. Calkins enrolled in a course taught by Josiah Royce, but there was no experimental psychology taught in the Annex. Royce and James attempted to convince President Eliot that Calkins should be admitted, but he adamantly refused. Only when additional persuasion was brought by Calkins' father, Wolcott Calkins (a Presbyterian Minister) and by the president of Wellesley College, Helen Shafer, did Eliot agree to allow her to attend lectures at the college proper, but he still refused to enroll her as a regular student.[81]

She started her psychological studies in 1890 in a private "seminar" with James (the other students who were supposed to have been in the course dropped out early in the year) in which he held forth on his brand new textbook, *Principles of Psychology*. To learn experimental technique, Calkins went to Clark (about the same distance west of Wellesley that Harvard was east of it), where Edmund Sanford taught her the methods of that school's more advanced laboratory.

When Münsterberg arrived at Harvard in the fall of 1892, he welcomed Calkins into his laboratory as one of his first students. He had, of course, allowed women students in his laboratory at Freiburg long before, so the situation was not as unnerving to him as it was to Harvard. Apparently Münsterberg's attitude won the day, for Calkins later recalled her "gratitude for the friendly, comradely, and refreshingly matter-of-fact welcome which I received from the men working in the Laboratory as assistants and students, by whom the unprecedented incursion of a woman might well have been resented."[82] Calkins' work was both innovative and superior. She developed new methods for studying memory, and published in both *Philosophical Review* and *Psychological Review*. James and Münsterberg thought they might be able to persuade Harvard to grant Calkins a doctorate if they put her through the ordeal of a standard dissertation defense. Both professors passed her oral performance and praised her research highly. Eliot still refused to grant her a degree, though, on the grounds that she had never been formally registered at the school.[83]

Calkins graciously wrote of her experience that: "My natural regret at the action of the Corporation has never clouded my gratitude for the incomparably greater boon which they granted me—that of working in the seminaries and the laboratory of the great Harvard teachers."[84] She returned to Wellesley and, with the assistance of Sanford, set up a laboratory there—just the 14th in the country and the first at a women's college. Calkins became a full participant in the American psychological scene. She published many experiments, and she and her students engaged in a spirited defense of women's mental powers in a literature debate with Joseph Jastrow in 1895–96.[85] In 1898, Calkins turned the operation of the Wellesley laboratory over to Eleanor Gamble, an alumna of the school who had also completed a PhD under Titchener's supervision at Cornell. Calkins' own work turned to the psychology of the self.[86] She became not only the first woman to serve as president of the American Psychological Association (1905), but also the first woman to be president of the American Philosophical Association (1918).

Just a few months after Münsterberg had arrived in the US and begun revitalizing the Harvard laboratory, he attended the first annual meeting of the American Psychological Association in Philadelphia (Hall had added him to the membership roll the previous July, before he had even arrived in the country). Münsterberg and his wife, Selma, were eager to see the vast country in which they were now living, so they visited one of its greatest natural wonders, Niagara Falls, during the winter of 1893.[87] Things were going as well as could be expected for Münsterberg until the spring of 1893, when he was struck down with diphtheria. Selma suddenly found herself left to contend with a seriously ill husband, in a foreign country where she did not know the language well, with no family and few friends. Even after the worst of the crisis was past, Hugo needed weeks of bed rest to regain his strength. Perhaps paradoxically, the protracted illness brought the Münsterbergs and their new Harvard neighbors even closer together. A German-speaking physician was located—Walter Wesselhoeft of the Massachusetts Homeopathic Hospital—and Harvard community members frequently inquired about his progress and offered their best wishes for his complete recovery. Selma grew close to Louis Agassiz's widow, Elizabeth Cabot Cary, who, 20 years after the great zoologist's death, still lived nearby and had just become the first president of Radcliffe College. By summer, Hugo's recovery had progressed far enough that he and Selma could travel to the World's Columbian Exposition in Chicago.

At the start of their second year in Cambridge, the Münsterbergs moved to a house on Qunicy Street, where many Harvard professors lived. From this more gracious base, Münsterberg was able to host German visitors to Cambridge, Hermann Helmholtz among them, and to "present" them to the Harvard community. However, beyond his European connections, Münsterberg was a highly cultured individual. The exclusive education that he had received at *Gymnasium*—that highly specialized form of secondary school that traditionally produced the German ruling class—had infused him with that prized attribute which the Germans term *Bildung*: In addition to his broad scientific learning, he was also knowledgeable about literature and painting. He wrote and even published poems and stories. He was a proficient musician and a formidable chess player. This elevated degree of cultivation instantly made him a respected member and desirable companion within of the Cambridge community.

Before the start of Münsterberg's second year at Harvard, the Jameses returned from Europe to belatedly welcome him to Harvard. Münsterberg's English, by this time, had improved to the point that it was possible for him to lecture to classes. He gave his first lecture at the new women's college, Radcliffe, in February of 1894. He co-taught the introductory psychology course with James as well. Quickly gaining confidence in his new linguistic skill, Münsterberg became a regular speaker not only in classrooms, but in broader public settings also. He even debated Stanley Hall on the place of psychology in education at the Boston Schoolmaster's Club.[88]

During the summer of 1894 he attended, with several of his colleagues, a kind of rugged philosophy "camp" in the Adirondack Mountains that was organized by an independent scholar well known to the Harvard community named Thomas Davidson.[89] The men slept in tents. The ladies slept together "under the one wooden roof."[90] Although the Americans seemed to appreciate this return to what, in their imaginations, must have seemed to be philosophy's natural state, the Münsterbergs were underwhelmed by the rustic digs, to say the least. Hugo sent his wife and child to a nearby hotel.

After the rigors of Davidson's camp, the Münsterbergs enjoyed a less arduous summer vacation in the resort town of Swampscott, in northeastern Massachusetts. It was here that Hugo first became closely acquainted with James Mark Baldwin, then at Princeton.[91] Baldwin and Münsterberg had an important theoretical agenda in common: they were both wary of the heavy emphasis that Wundt and his followers lay on consciousness—especially "apperception"—and they were trying to work out, each in his own way, a "motor interpretation of many of the mental functions." Münsterberg once described the two of them as being "the 'motor men' on the psychological car."[92]

Having shared the psychology course with James in the winter of 1894, in the fall of that year Münsterberg taught the course on his own for the first time. Enrollment increased substantially from the previous go-round. Whether this was due to the reputation he had earned as an interesting lecturer, or simply from the students' realization that the eminent German visitor might soon be gone is anyone's guess. For his part, Münsterberg complained that he felt slightly "humiliated," having to lecture to mere undergraduates, just one of many differences between the German and American university systems to which he would have to adapt. [93] Not just status, but the visibility of one's place in the hierarchy was an ongoing concern for the man.

In the winter of 1895, the Münsterbergs decided to take in the vast western part of the country before the time came for their return home. They traveled out to the Great Plains, where they stayed for a time before striking out for the west coast, visiting both the nascent Stanford University, where Frank Angell had recently opened a new psychology laboratory, and the more venerable University of California, which did not yet have a laboratory of its own.[94]

As the 1894–95 school year drew to a close, James and Eliot attempted to persuade Münsterberg to stay on at Harvard permanently. A patriotic German to the core, Münsterberg firmly refused. It was his duty, he told James, to return to his country.[95] Eliot was able to frame Münsterberg's departure as a leave of absence, though, so that at the end of two years Münsterberg would be forced to "choose" one more time whether or not to stay in Germany.

Münsterberg returned to Germany with three "reminders" of his connection to Harvard right behind him. Harvard students Edwin Bissel Holt, Robert Mearns Yerkes, and Ethel Puffer followed him back to Freiburg in order to study with him.[96] In addition, his earlier American student, Edmund Delabarre, now a professor at Brown University, was hired by Harvard to take over the directorship of Münsterberg's laboratory during his absence. In short, Harvard made a point of not letting him forget about them.

For all of the intensity of his desire to find success in his homeland, Münsterberg's position at Freiburg was still that of *Extraordinarius*, roughly the equivalent of an American associate professor. If he were to finally and forever decline Harvard's entreaties, he would have to find an *Ordinariat*, a full professorship, at a reputable German university. Freiburg seemed unwilling to promote him. The senior physiologist, Johannes Von Kries, seems to have opposed Münsterberg's promotion for reasons that are unknown. Like many physiologists of the day, he may have regarded the research topics of the new psychology as overlapping with the proper domain of physiology—a turf war in which experimental psychologists were often involved at that time. Münsterberg believed that lingering anti-Semitism was at work; there was talk that the local clergy wanted a Catholic philosopher in the professorship. His suspicion, however, is hard to square with the fact that Münsterberg's successors at Freiburg, Jonas Cohn and Edmund Husserl, were both Jewish.[97]

The following year, 1896, the faculty of the University of Zurich selected Münsterberg for their philosophy professorship on the strength of a recommendation by none other than Wundt (for a position that Wundt had once held, no less).[98] It looked like Münsterberg's prayers were at last answered, but things immediately started to go wrong. The regional Ministry of Education had the final say over the position and, instead of approving the faculty report, it inexplicably decided to lower the position's rank to *Extraordinarius*. Münsterberg was rightly insulted and refused to make what would have been a lateral move (which the Ministry must have expected). The reason for the change was never presented, and the position was eventually taken by another of Wundt's former students, Ernst Meumann.

Harvard asked, once again, whether Münsterberg would be returning for the fall of 1897. He attempted to extract a third year of leave, but Harvard's patience had finally run out. Eliot had given Münsterberg as much leeway as he would get. The decision had to be made. James urged Münsterberg to return.[99] Baldwin begged him to do so.[100] Münsterberg's former Freiburg colleague, Hermann Eduard von Holst, who had left for Chicago back in 1892, recommended that Münsterberg throw his lot in with America.

Finally, reluctantly, fearing that prejudice would prevent him from ever winning a full professorship in Germany, Münsterberg agreed to return to Harvard in 1897.[101] James welcomed him back by having his own title changed to Professor of Philosophy, partly in order to open up the primary position in Psychology for his young German colleague. Nevertheless, where the first trip to America had been a kind of fascinating adventure to a strange and distant realm, the return carried a darker tone. Münsterberg felt rejected by his homeland, and that he was being forced to "settle" for a secondary post in the scholarly "boonies" of America.

7. Münsterberg's Return to Harvard

His sense of superiority—of his being better than this—was palpable. Within the high German *Kultur* to which Münsterberg was devoted, it was given that American society was inferior because of its crass materialism and corruption. Ironically, though, it was Münsterberg who started to quarrel with Eliot over the grubby matter of salary. It was almost as though Münsterberg was determined to extract from America in crude dollars the equivalent of the respect and status that his Fatherland had denied him. He may have been coming to America, but he had no intention of becoming American. Despite living in the US for nearly a quarter-century before his death in 1916, Münsterberg remained as determinedly German as possible. The Stanford psychologist Frank Angell wrote a few years after Münsterberg's death that "twenty-two years of residence over here . . . wrought no fundamental change in the Germanism of his nature."[102] His clothing, his mustache, his bearing, and most of all his attitudes spoke to everyone around him of a loyal German subject cast into an alien land.

Münsterberg viewed America as a benighted country that, for all of its legendary wealth, was chaotic, unformed, and without proper direction. He made it his personal mission to inject a dose of proper German values into what he saw as a morally and intellectually flabby American society. Through proper social discipline, he thought, it might attain the potential afforded it by its vast resources and riches and take its place among the leading countries in the world.[103] Naturally, this stance had the tendency rub many Americans the wrong way, and Münsterberg's social position steadily deteriorated, even as his academic status rose, during his years in the US.

Münsterberg began by positioning himself in America as an emphatically "pure" scientist.[104] Relatively untutored in the historical American situation with respect to higher education (the Morrill Act, the focus on "practical" knowledge, etc.), his attitude about the purpose of institutes of higher learning was derived from the very different aims of the German educational system. He was, of course, intimately familiar with the reasons behind Wundt's efforts to establish a place for the new psychology within the prestigious university system, rather than allow it to be relegated to the technical schools. This meant that the singular goal of psychology had to be the accumulation of abstract knowledge and understanding, not the development of mere "tools" for practical use elsewhere in society. One can find precisely the same fervently-held perspective from the "other" most prominent non-American Wundt graduate then working in the US: Edward Bradford Titchener. Whatever disagreements Münsterberg and Titchener may have had in terms of psychological theory, and there were many, they were agreed, in the 1890s, that experimental psychology must be pursued as a wholly pure science, and not be contaminated by considerations of its possible applications to problems in the "real world."

Münsterberg was not in the least shy about criticizing his new American colleagues, especially those not at Harvard. In 1898 he published—not in an obscure academic journal, but in the widely-read magazine *Atlantic Monthly*—an excoriating review of *The New Psychology* by Yale psychologist Edward Wheeler Scripture.[105] He called the book a "climax of blunders," and declared "dangerous" Scripture's view, then common among experimental psychologists, that "psychical facts" are "measured" in modern laboratories. He professed it absurd to believe that true measurement could be brought to bear on the mental; "pseudo-measurements," he called them. [106] His explanation of this provocative claim, though, strayed into Arthur Schopenhauer's philosophy of the will which, even if it were known to some American academics, would not have been familiar, or even comprehensible, to most readers of the *Atlantic*.[107] We are, Münsterberg argued, neither physical nor psychical beings but, rather, "subjects of will"—a will that separates the things of the world into those that, by virtue of their permanence, can be objects for all subjects (the physical) and those things that are objects not just for one subject, but for a single subjective act, and then vanish, never to be renewed thereafter.[108] He also used the occasion to take a swipe at Stanley Hall's "child study" ("where the dangers are not less threatening") and to dissuade any educator tempted to read laboratory studies with an eye toward applying their findings in the classroom from attempting such a venture. "In the hands of the teacher," he wrote, "those results are odd bits and ends which never form a whole and which have no meaning for real life."

One of the strongest responses against Münsterberg's harsh critique came from an unexpected quarter—Charles Bliss, a newly hired psychologist at the NYU School of Pedagogy. Not only was Bliss training aspiring teachers in the methods and results of psychology in his small laboratory, he was also a recent graduate of the chief target of Münsterberg's attack: Yale's Edward Scripture.[109] Perhaps flush with the combativeness of youth, Bliss's reply openly parodied the melodrama of Münsterberg's dark warnings: "A strange discord breaks upon our ears over the fair New England Hills,—words out of harmony with the whole educational spirit of our times . . ."[110] And later, "The teachers of our land must be treading on the very verge of the bottomless pit, into which they are about to plunge, drawing after them the youth of our land."[111] Bliss went on to reject Münsterberg's central claims about the book: Scripture had titled sections of the text after Space, Time, and Energy, in a suggestive analogy with key categories of physics. This conceit launched Münsterberg into some of his most extravagant critical digressions. Bliss deflatingly opined that Münsterberg had mistaken a mere pedagogical framing device for a full-blooded ontology of mind. He also pointed out that Münsterberg himself had secretly published educational materials based on psychological discoveries—his "Pseudoptics," a set of optical illusions and color-mixing toys for use in the classroom—which he had been published pseudonymously under the name of the famous games manufacturer, "Milton Bradley." Bliss also took issue with Münsterberg's rejection of the very possibility of "measuring a psychic fact": "If mental measurements are not being made in the Harvard Laboratory, pray, forsooth, what is being done? What mean those long columns of figures that appear so regularly?"[112] Even Münsterberg's devotion to "pure" science was mocked: "There is no practical value, even from the standpoint of pure science, in counting the grains of sand upon the seashore, no matter how regularly, patiently, and carefully it is done."[113] So far as Bliss was concerned, Harvard's new German genius had stumbled badly out of the gate: "Prof. Münsterberg has not realized the inspiration of the hour. He misses the whole spirit of modern science and American science teaching. He betrays a low ideal of what teaching should be and an almost intentional ignorance of schoolroom work."[114] In the end, Bliss chalked the whole incident up to another tiresome episode in the long-running Harvard–Yale rivalry.[115]

A second response came from New York City. Although Münsterberg had not mentioned Cattell's mental tests directly, the Columbia professor could not help but see the writing on the wall: surely his tests were intended to measure something important about the mind, even if it was not, at the moment, wholly clear what mental element they measured. Cattell leapt to defend all three—Scripture, his claim of psychological measurement, and the educational value of psychology—in a short riposte published in his own journal, *Psychological Review*.[116]

Münsterberg was undeterred, returning to the question of Stanley Hall's "child study" in an article published in *Educational Review* later that year.[117] He mercilessly criticized the method Hall had chosen—having teachers fill out questionnaires about what their students know and do—as being tantamount to pursuing botany by seeing what flowers happen to grow in one particular garden, then another garden, and so forth. It is a haphazard collection that does not have the control required to result in systematic conclusions. He also denounced teachers who try to use what they have read about the structure of the brain to inform their classroom practice:

> if the teacher, in the hope of understanding the inner life of children better, studies the ganglion cells under the microscope, he could substitute just as well the reading of Egyptian hieroglyphs. All talk about the brain is, from the standpoint of the teacher, merely cant.[118]

Similarly, he declared the "elements" of the psyche (e.g., sensations, feelings, volitions) that are isolated and studied in experimental psychology laboratories to be useless to the teacher as well. Instead, he offered the vision of specialized "psycho-educational" laboratories, directed by a new breed of educational scientists, who would study problems pitched specifically at the level of analysis most useful to teachers. Some of the names of these problems might look familiar to psychologists—attention, memory, imagination—but in the new educational laboratories, the experiments on them would be designed in ways that, as we might say today, are "ecologically valid" for the classroom, not arranged to suit the needs of the pure scientist. Cattell's former student, Lightner Witmer, had already opened a "clinic" at Penn with some slight similarities to what Münsterberg had in mind, though it was focused more on the identification and correction of learning disabilities (as we would now call them) than on general research about learning. Interestingly, Münsterberg did not address Dewey's call for a "laboratory school"—perhaps it was too new for him to have fully digested in 1898, whereas Hall's child study dated back to the early 1880s—but it seems clear enough that Dewey's idea was not what Münsterberg had in mind as an educational laboratory.

Indeed, the "Progressive" movement in education promoted by Dewey and others horrified Münsterberg. To his mind, it was ridiculous to ask children to pick the topics of their own education. This would only create lazy and self-indulgent adults, he said, who were useless to society. School, for Münsterberg, should be about inculcating conventional morality and respect for established authority, as well as developing self-discipline. Given his belief that American society was being held back by too much of its twin indulgences—freedom and equality—Progressive education was bound to only exacerbate the problem.[119]

And it was not just the public school system that came in for Münsterberg's wrath. The American college system he felt was a shambles as well, focusing far too much on teaching and not enough on original research. But, of course, even the few research schools that existed were gummed up by the poor quality of American graduate students—coddled with scholarships rather than being forced to struggle and battle to make their way, weeding out the weak, allowing only the best to succeed and move on. Then there was his critique of the disorder of the American family, and especially of the self-centeredness of American women. . . . It went on and on.[120]

Although Münsterberg appreciated the American values of hard work and personal initiative, he disapproved of many other central aspects of American society, and he was not reluctant to prescribe German ways of doing things as the logical remedy. In this way, he was a bit reminiscent of Titchener, another European national who yearned for things to be as they had been in the "old country," tucked away in a college town and blissfully separated from real tumult of the large metropolises where what it meant to be American was being revised nearly every day. Unlike Titchener, however, Münsterberg was willing to enter into public debates of broad social import, though he did so like the anthropologists of old, speculating from first principles and second-hand reports, safely ensconced in his armchair, rarely venturing into the schools, the workplaces, or the homes of the people against whom he made his reactionary pronouncements. There was no going down to the local Settlement House for him, as there was for Dewey, to teach science to downtrodden immigrant workers. There was no designing and administering a real school at which a diverse cross-section of urban kids could receive their lessons together. In reality, Münsterberg had little understanding of the American sociopolitical situation, and his German background gave him no experience whatever of coaxing and cajoling a wildly heterogeneous population of continuously changing ethnic makeup to join together into a common, if never-quite-defined, national project. For a man who sometimes wielded his

Kultur like a cudgel, Münsterberg never seemed to quite grasp the degree to which culture matters, nor that the solutions accepted and effective in one society may fail or, indeed, act as provocations, in other cultural contexts. Like the strict, authoritarian father that he took to be ideal, he seemed to believe that he could simply lecture, then hector, into obedience the inferior society with which he had been saddled.

However grating Münsterberg's continuous public commentary was to his American colleagues—and, to be entirely fair, there were some prominent traditionalists who agreed with him[121]—it did not seem to slow his professional progress, at least in the early years of his American sojourn. Just months after his arrival on a permanent basis, he was elected president of American Psychological Association for the year 1898. In 1900 he became head of the philosophy division at Harvard. He was a prominent organizer of psychological events at the St. Louis World's Fair of 1904. In 1908 he would become president of the American Philosophical Association.[122] Interestingly, as the first decade of the 20th century progressed, his attitude toward the possible application of psychological knowledge to everyday problems would evolve significantly.

Notes

1 Most of Queens County, Richmond (Staten Island), and the eastern Bronx were included as "boroughs" of the expanded city as well. (The western portion of the Bronx had been annexed by Manhattan two decades before, in 1874.) Much controversy attended the referendum. The Brooklyn poll was extremely close—less than 300 votes difference among nearly 130,000 ballots cast—provoking widespread claims of election fraud.

2 Michael M. Sokal, "Cattell and Mental Anthropometry," in *Psychological Testing and American Society, 1890–1930*, ed. Michael M. Sokal (New Brunswick, NJ: Rutgers University Press, 1987), 21–45.

3 See, e.g., Annette Mülberger, "Mental Associaton: Testing Individual Differences before Binet," *Journal of the History of the Behavioral Sciences* 53 (2017): 176–98, doi:10.1002/jhbs.21850.

4 Charles R. Garvey ("List of American Psychology Laboratories," *Psychological Bulletin* 26 (1929): 652–60) reported that the Penn lab was founded by Cattell in 1887 and, thus, that it was just the third in the country, behind just Harvard and Hopkins. Cattell only arrived for his lectureship at Penn in December of that year, however, and what he founded must have been extremely spare. Even Garvey notes that the laboratory was not "adequate" until 1889, when Cattell returned to head the department. That would have made it fifth in the US, behind Indiana and Wisconsin, but just before Clark, whose laboratory was founded by Hall and Sanford later that year.

5 Jacy L. Young, "When Psychologists Were Naturalists: Questionnaires and Collecting Practices in Early American Psychology, 1880–1932" (Doctoral dissertation, York University, 2014).

6 For Cattell's account of those very early years of his testing work, see his "Mental Tests and Measurements," *Mind* 15 (1890): 373–81.

7 For an early version of this argument, see also the discussion of the "comparative worth of races" in *Hereditary Genius*, ed. Francis Galton (London, UK: Palgrave Macmillan, 1869).

8 He actually held both positions for a year, commuting from Philadelphia to New York as needed. He finally severed ties with Penn in 1891 and moved permanently to the New York vicinity.

9 See, e.g., David C. Humphrey, *From King's College to Columbia, 1746–1800* (New York, NY: Columbia University Press, 1976).

10 Letter from Cattell to his parents, 8 January 1885. Box 50 of the J. M. Cattell Collection, Library of Congress, Washington, DC.

11 A little ironically, Garrison is just 17 miles south of the town of Newburgh, the site that had been proposed for King's College by Cadwallader Colden, one of the leading critics, back in the late 1740s, of the plan to locate the new college amidst the "Bad Company and Examples" of New York City (cited in Humphrey, *From King's*, 6).

12 Michael M. Sokal, "Baldwin, Cattell and the Psychological Review: A Collaboration and Its Discontents," *History of the Human Sciences* 10, no. 1 (1997): 57–89.

13 Farrand would soon shift interests, traveling with noted anthropologist Franz Boas, who was also a professor at Columbia, and becoming a professor of anthropology himself in 1903. In 1914 he became president of the University of Colorado and, in 1921, president of Cornell University. He was also the brother of Stanford and Yale history professor Max Farrand.

14 James McKeen Cattell and Livingston Farrand, "Physical and Mental Measurements of Students of Columbia University," *Psychological Review* 3 (1896): 618–48.

15 Sokal, "Cattell and Mental Anthropometry," 32.

16 Quotation from Edmund C. Sanford, "Meeting of the American Psychological Association," *Science* 3 (1896): 618–48.

17 The report was first presented at the December 1897 meeting of the APA, but was published in 1898 as: James Mark Baldwin, James McKeen Cattell, and Joseph Jastrow, "Physical and Mental Tests," *Psychological Review* 5 (1898): 172–79.

18 Alfred Binet and Victor Henri, "La Psychologie Individuelle" [Individual Psychology], *L'Année Psychologique* 2 (1895): 411–15.

19 Stella Emily Sharp, "Individual Psychology: A Study in Psychological Method," *American Journal of Psychology* 10 (1898): 329–91.

20 Karl Pearson, "Notes on Regression and Inheritance in the Case of Two Parents," *Proceedings of the Royal Society of London* 58 (1895): 240–42.

21 Clark Wissler, "The Correlation of Mental and Physical Tests," *Psychological Review Monograph Supplements* 3, no. 16 (1901): 1–62. Wissler went on to become a prominent anthropologist. After graduating from Columbia in 1901, he served as an assistant to Franz Boas at the American Museum of Natural History in New York. He rose to replace Boas as Curator of Ethnology and, later, of Anthropology (when the Ethnology and Archaeology Departments were combined under that name). He conducted extensive fieldwork on the cultures of the Dakota, Gros Ventre, and Blackfoot Native American tribes, writing several books on these topics. Although he had trained with Boas, he did not adopt Boas' liberal sociopolitical views. Wissler firmly believed in the superiority of the European "races" to those of Africa, Asia, and North America. He also became a vocal advocate of eugenics in the early 20th century. From 1924, he taught at Yale University in both psychology and anthropology until his retirement in 1942. He died in 1947 just before turning 77.

22 Perhaps showing just how small a circle the American scientific community was at this time, Scudder had been a student under Mark Hopkins at Williams College, like G. Stanley Hall, and had done his advanced naturalist training under Louis Agassiz, like William James.

23 Walter B. Pillsbury, "Biographical Memoir of James McKeen Cattell, 1860–1944, 25, First Memoir.," *Biographical Memoirs of the National Academy of Sciences* 25, first memoir (1949).

24 James McKeen Cattell, "Statistics of American Psychologists," *American Journal of Psychology* 14 (1903): 574–92; *American Men of Science* (New York, NY: Science Press, 1933).

25 Francis Galton, *English Men of Science* (London, UK: Palgrave Macmillan, 1874).

26 Information on Woodworth's life is somewhat sparse. There is no book-length biography. In addition to obituaries, there is his own autobiographical chapter: Robert S. Woodworth, "Robert S. Woodworth," in *A History of Psychology in Autobiography*, ed. Carl A. Murchison, vol. 2 (Worcester, MA: Clark University Press, 1930), 359–80. The best third-person source is Andrew S. Winston, "Robert S. Woodworth and the Creation of an Eclectic Psychology," in *Portraits of Pioneers in Psychology*, ed. Donald A. Dewsbury, Michael Wertheimer, and Ludy T. Benjamin Jr., vol. 6 (Washington, DC and Mahwah, NJ: American Psychological Association and Lawrence Erlbaum, 2006). For Thorndike, the standard, though now dated account of his life is G. Jonçich, *The Sane Positivist: A Biography of Edward L. Thorndike* (Middletown, CT: Wesleyan University Press, 1968). There is also his autobiographical chapter: Edward L. Thorndike, "Edward Lee Thorndike," in *A History of Psychology in Autobiography*, ed. Carl A. Murchison, vol. 3 (Worcester, MA: Clark University Press, 1936), 263–70. Somewhat more recently, there is a biographical chapter written by his grandson, Robert L. Thorndike, "Edward L. Thorndike: A Professional and Personal Appreciation," in *Portraits of Pioneers in Psychology*, ed. Gregory A. Kimble, Michael Wertheimer, and Charlotte L. White, vol. 1 (Washington, DC and Hillsdale, NJ: American Psychological Association and Lawrence Erlbaum Associates Publishers, 1991), 138–51.

27 Edward L. Thorndike, "Animal Intelligence: An Experimental Study of the Associative Processes in Animals," *Psychological Monographs* 2, no. 4 (whole no. 8) (1898).

28 Edward L. Thorndike, *Animal Intelligence: Experimental Studies* (New York, NY: Palgrave Macmillan, 1911) which also included a second "monograph" article—Edward L. Thorndike, "The Mental Life of Monkeys," *Psychological Monographs* 3, no. 5 (whole no. 15) (1901)—and a great deal of novel theoretical elaboration.

29 Thorndike, *Animal Intelligence: Experimental Studies*, 244.

30 Thomas Wesley Mills, "The Nature of Animal Intelligence and the Methods of Investigating It," *Psychological Review* 6 (1899): 266. On Mills's life and career, see Faith Wallis, "Mills, Thomas Wesley," *Dictionary of Canadian Biography* (Toronto, ON and Québec, QC: University of Toronto/Université Laval, 2003). www.biographi.ca/en/bio/mills_thomas_wesley_14E.html.

31 See also William Lowe Bryan and Noble Harter, "Studies on the Telegraphic Language: The Acquisition of a Hierarchy of Habits," *Psychological Review* 6 (1899): 345–75.

32 Linus W. Kline, "Suggestions Toward a Laboratory Course in Comparative Psychology," *American Journal of Psychology* 10 (1899): 399–430; Willard S. Small, "Notes on the Psychic Development of the Young White Rat," *American Journal of Psychology* 11 (1899): 80–100; Willard S. Small, "Experimental Study of the Mental Processes of the Rat—II," *American Journal of Psychology* 12 (1901): 206–39.

33 See esp. Winston, "Woodworth." Perhaps paradoxically, Woodworth's 1918 book, *Dynamic Psychology* (New York, NY: Columbia University Press, 1918) came to be characterized as the basis of a psychological system or school by Edna Heidbredder in her *Seven Psychologies* (New York, NY: Century, 1933). See also Woodworth's last book, *Dynamics of Behavior* (New York, NY: Holt, 1958).

34 Robert S. Woodworth, *Experimental Psychology* (New York, NY: Holt, 1938; 2nd ed. with H. Scholsberg, 1954). On the history of this influential book, see Andrew S. Winston, "Robert Sessions Woodworth and the 'Columbia Bible': How the Psychological Experiment Was Redefined," *American Journal of Psychology* 103 (1990): 391–401. Although the fact is not well remembered today, *Experimental Psychology* was not Woodworth's first general textbook. His first, *Psychology: A Science of Mental Life* (New York, NY: Holt, 1921) went through five editions, including two (1940, 1947) *after* the first edition of *Experimental Psychology* had appeared. Woodworth's *Psychology* is sometimes regarded as having been the first "modern" textbook in the field (in contrast to earlier books that tended to outline the author's particular "system"). Even earlier still,

in 1911, Woodworth revised and updated the venerable George Trumbull Ladd's *Elements of Physiological Psychology* (New York, NY: Scribner's, 1915), which had originally been published in 1887.

35 The Boston chapter was part of a wider national Immigration Restriction League, led by Madison Grant in New York City. Lodge would remain a senator for more than 30 years, and is probably best remembered today for leading the campaign to block the US from entering Woodrow Wilson's League of Nations after World War I.

36 Similar bills would be passed by congress and vetoed by William Howard Taft in 1913 and by Woodrow Wilson in 1916. Congress was able to override the Wilson's veto, however, and include the restriction in the 1917 Immigration Act. The original Boston chapter of the League disbanded after the death of its key founder, Prescott Hall, in 1921. The New York chapter, however, led by Madison Grant, continued to press for even greater restrictions, which came with the Immigration Act of 1924.

37 Thomas H. O'Connor, *Bibles, Brahmins, and Bosses: A Short History of Boston*, 3rd ed. (Boston, MA: Boston Public Library, 1991), 174.

38 John Fitzgerald was the father of Rose Fitzgerald who, in turn, was the mother of US President John F. Kennedy. Daniel A. Whelton served as acting mayor for just over 100 days after Collins' death, so technically, Fitzgerald did not directly succeed Collins.

39 The quoted word comes from a letter William James wrote to his wife Alice, dated August 29, 1884. It was published in *The Correspondence of William James*, ed. I. K. Skrupskelis and E. M. Berkeley, vol. 5 (Cambridge, MA: Harvard University Press, 1997).

40 The story is relayed in Robert D. Richardson, *William James: In the Maelstrom of Modernity* (Boston, MA: Houghton-Mifflin, 2006), 258. It turns out, however, that Piper's maid and one of the Jameses' servants were friends, and this was probably the source of Piper's "spiritual" knowledge (Massimo Polidoro, *Final Séance: The Strange Friendship Between Houdini and Conan Doyle* (New York, NY: Prometheus Books, 2001), 36). Evidence that Piper was a fraud was uncovered several times. Stanley Hall once invented a "dead" niece for Piper to contact, and she readily channeled the fictitious "spirit." For James, though, there was somehow never enough evidence for one to draw a firm conclusion. Episodes such as this have led some to argue that James' legendary "openness" was too often indistinguishable from simple chronic indecisiveness (e.g., Louis Menand, *The Metaphysical Club: A Story of Ideas in America* (New York, NY: Farrar, Straus and Giroux, 2001)). On the other hand, James' one-time student, Gertrude Stein, said in an interview many decades later that he had told her as a college student, "Never reject anything. Nothing has been proved. If you reject anything, that is the beginning of the end as an intellectual" (Robert B. Haas, *A Primer for the Gradual Understanding of Gertrude Stein* (Los Angeles, CA: Black Sparrow, 1971), 34).

41 Opinions of Piper's sincerity vary widely to this day. See, e.g., Gardner Murphy and Robert O. Ballou, *William James on Psychical Research* (New York, NY: Viking Press, 1960); Martin Gardner, "How Mrs. Piper Bamboozled William James," in *Are Universes Thicker than Blackberries?* (New York, NY: W. W. Norton, 2003); Francesca Bordogna, *William James at the Boundaries: Philosophy, Science, and the Geography of Knowledge* (Chicago, IL: University of Chicago Press, 2008).

42 Charles Sanders Peirce, "Chapter XX," in *Science and Immortality: The Christian Register Symposium*, ed. Samuel J. Barrows, revised and enlarged (Boston, MA: George H. Ellis, 1887), 71.

43 George Trumbull Ladd, *Elements of Physiological Psychology* (New York, NY: Charles Scribner, 1887); James Mark Baldwin, *Handbook of Psychology*, vol. 1. Senses and Intellect (New York, NY: Henry Holt, 1889).

44 Letter from William James to Henry Holt dated May 9, 1890. Published in *The Correspondence of William James*, ed. I. K. Skrupskelis and E. M. Berkeley, vol. 7 (Cambridge, MA: Harvard University Press, 1999), 23–24.

45 W. E. B. Du Bois, *Dusk of Dawn: An Essay Toward an Autobiography of a Race Concept* (Oxford, UK: Oxford University Press, 1940), 19.

46 Leon M. Solomons and Gertrude Stein, "Normal Motor Automatism," *Psychological Review* 3 (1896): 492–512; Gertrude Stein, "Cultivated Motor Automatism; A Study of Character in Its Relations to Attention," *Psychological Review* 5 (1898): 295–306.

47 Quoted in a "transatlantic interview" that Robert B. Haas conducted with Stein, January 5–6, 1946. Published in Haas, *A Primer for the Gradual Understanding of Gertrude Stein*, 34.

48 William James, *The Principles of Psychology*, vol. 1 (New York, NY: Henry Holt, 1890), 192.

49 John Fiske (1844–1901), who was chair of the Overseers' committee responsible for the philosophy department, mentioned Slater's donation to the laboratory fund in a letter to his mother dated July 4, 1890 (Huntington Library, Papers of John Fiske, Box 11). Fiske was a longtime friend of James; he had been a member of Chauncey Wright's Metaphysical Club back in the early 1870s when he was studying law, and he had lectured at Harvard on both philosophy and history. After graduating, Fiske spent most of his time speaking and writing on American history, a subject in which he had a part-time professorship at Washington University in St. Louis. He was best known to the public, however, for his publications on evolution. Although an admirer of Darwin, he was a fervent advocate of Herbert Spencer's approach to the topic. Information on Fiske's generous donor, Slater, is sparse but it was probably William Albert Slater (1857–1919), the son of a fabulously wealthy textile mill owner, John Fox Slater, who had been based in Norwich, CT. In 1882, the elder Slater had contributed the fantastic sum of one million dollars for the purpose of educating southern former slaves. Why the younger Slater, who directed the disbursement of his late father's estate to various philanthropic causes, agreed to contribute to the psychology laboratory remains something of a mystery; he does not seem to have had a particular interest in the topic, nor does he seem to have known James: although Slater was a Harvard alumnus, James referred to him formally as "Mr. Slater" and conceded (in a joking aside) that he did not even know Slater's physical size (see letter from James to George Bucknam Dorr dated Aug 12 1890, published in *The Correspondence of William James*, vol. 7). Fiske referred to Slater as a friend, so one obvious speculation is that Fiske, assisting James's effort to fundraise for the lab, called in a favor from a rich old chum for whom $3,000 would be a trivial amount. (I would like to acknowledge Trevor Pearce of University of North Carolina, Charlotte for alerting me to Fiske's letter.)

50 See letter from James to George Bucknam Dorr, Aug 12, 1890, *Correspondence of William James*, vol. 7. In an 1895 letter published in *Science*, James claimed that *he* had "raised several thousand dollars" for the laboratory expansion ("Experimental Psychology in America," *Science* n.s. 2, no. 45 (1895): 626), but the bulk of the fund seems to have come from Fiske's efforts.

51 E.g., William James, "A Plea for Psychology as a 'Natural Science,'" *Philosophical Review* 1 (1892): 146–53, doi:10.2307/2175743; "Professor Wundt and Feelings of Innervation," *Psychological Review* 1 (1894): 70–73; "The Physical Basis of Emotion," *Psychological Review* 1 (1894): 516–29.

52 E.g., William James, "The Moral Philosopher and the Moral Life," *International Journal of Ethics* 1 (1891): 330–54; "Is Life Worth Living?," *International Journal of Ethics* 6 (1895): 1–25; "The Will to Believe," *The New World* 5 (1896): 327–47, later reprinted in *The Will to Believe and Other Essays in Popular Philosophy* (New York, NY: Longmans Green, 1897).

53 E.g., William James, "What Psychical Research Has Accomplished," *Forum* 13 (1892): 727–42; "A Case of Psychic Automatism, Including 'Speaking With Tongues,'" *Proceedings of the Society for Psychical Research* 12 (1896): 277–79.

54 E.g., William James, "Psychical Research," *Psychological Review* 3 (1896): 649–52.

55 In particular, there was a debate with Cattell over Leonora Piper: James McKeen Cattell, "Mrs. Piper, the Medium," *Science* n.s. 7 (1898): 534–35; William James, "Mrs. Piper,

'the Medium,'" *Science* n.s. 7, no. 175 (1898): 640–41; James McKeen Cattell, "Untitled Letter," *Science* n.s. 7, no. 75 (1898): 641–42. There was another debate with Titchener over a Danish disproof of "thought-transference" (or telepathy): William James, "Messrs. Lehmann and Hansen on Telepathy," *Science* n.s. 9 (1899): 654–55; Edward Bradford Titchener, "Professor James on Telepathy," *Science* n.s. 9 (1899): 686–87; William James, "Telepathy Once More," *Science* n.s. 9 (1899): 752–53; Edward Bradford Titchener, "The Telepathic Question," *Science* n.s. 9 (1899): 787. See also Hugo Münsterberg, "Psychology and Mysticism," *Atlantic Monthly* 83 (1899): 67–85. It is interesting to note that Cattell was willing to publish James' remarks on telepathy in *Science*, which he owned and edited at the time, but rebuked James for undermining psychology's credibility by publicly holding forth on such matters. Earlier than either of these public debates, Joseph Jastrow had engaged with the redoubtable Mark Twain on the issue. Twain had begun writing on the topic in 1878, but decided not to publish for fear of ridicule, he said. When the Society for Psychical Research was launched in London, he eagerly became an early member (see S. L. Clemens, "Mark Twain on Thought-Transference," *Journal of Society for Psychical Research* 9 (1884): 166–67). He finally published his long-delayed article in 1891 (Mark Twain, "Mental Telegraphy, A Manuscript with a History," *Harper's*, December 1891, 95–104), and a short companion piece in 1895 ("Mental Telegraphy Again," *Harper's*, September 1895, 521–24). Jastrow fired off a response in another popular magazine, dismissing Twain, whose astonishment, he condescended, was the product of a naïveté about the probabilities of simple coincidences (Joseph Jastrow, "The Logic of Mental Telegraphy," *Scribner's*, November 1895, 571–77). Deborah Blum, *The Ghost Hunters: William James and the Search for Scientific Proof of Life after Death* (New York, NY: Penguin, 2006).

56 Eugene Taylor, *William James on Consciousness beyond the Margin* (Princeton, NJ: Princeton University Press, 1996); Eugene Taylor, *Shadow Culture: Psychology and Spirituality in America* (Washington, DC: Counterpoint, 1999). For more on the tangled relationship between early psychology and psychical phenomena, see Peter Lamont, *Extraordinary Beliefs: A Historical Approach to a Psychological Problem* (Cambridge, UK: Cambridge University Press, 2013); Andreas Sommer, *Psychical Research and the Formation of Modern Psychology* (Stanford, CA: Stanford University Press, in press).

57 See, e.g., Deborah J. Coon, "Testing the Limits of Sense and Science: American Experimental Psychologists Combat Spiritualism, 1880–1920," *American Psychologist* 47 (1992): 143–51.

58 Letter from Oliver Wendell Holmes, Jr. to Frederick Pollock dated 1 September 1910. Published in Mark de Wolfe Howe, ed., *Holmes-Pollock Letters: The Correspondence of Mr. Justice Holmes and Sir Frederick Pollock, 1874–1932*, vol. 1 (Cambridge, UK: Cambridge University Press, 1941), 167.

59 See the letter from James to Münsterberg dated July 2, 1890. Published in *The Correspondence of William James*, ed. by I. K. Skrupskelis and E. M. Berkeley, vol. 7 (Cambridge, MA: Harvard University Press, 1999), 49–50.

60 James had argued that emotions are just the conscious feelings of the physical effects that emotion-causing stimuli have on the body: e.g., my feeling of fear at the sight of a bear is nothing more than the sensations produced by my racing heart, my shallow breathing, my trembling legs, etc. (William James, "What Is an Emotion?," *Mind* 9 (1884): 188–205). Dewey would soon pointedly note that James' theory could not explain why the sight of a bear would produce the physical responses associated with fear in the first place unless we already thought of bears as "fearful object[s]" (John Dewey, "The Theory of Emotion. (2) The Significance of Emotions," *Psychological Review* 2 (1895): 13–32). Not all psychologists were as impressed with Münsterberg's theory of the will as James was, however. Edward Titchener, then still a doctoral student at Leipzig, sneered that "Dr. Münsterberg has the fatal gift of writing easily— fatal especially in science, and most of all in a young science, where accuracy is the one thing needful" (Edward Bradford Titchener, "Dr. Münsterberg and Experimental

Psychology," *Mind* 16 (1891): 521–34, quotation from p. 534; the final word is often misquoted as "most needed"). Titchener's open derision, published in the only British journal on the topic, served to notify the English-language psychological community of Wundt's disapproval of his erstwhile student in Freiburg. Wundt's displeasure only made Münsterberg that much more attractive to James.

61 Strong described Münsterberg as being "a universal devourer and producer" (of scholarly work), working "till three or four in the morning," "writing from fourteen to sixteen printed pages at a sitting." Strong evaluated him as being "deeper, more trenchant" than Jacob Gould Schurman of Cornell, and "superior" to Max Dessoir (then only 23) as a "reasoner." Letter from Charles Augustus Strong to William James dated May 13, 1890. Published in *The Correspondence of William James*, ed. by I. K. Skrupskelis and E. M. Berkeley, vol. 7 (Cambridge, MA: Harvard University Press, 1999), 24–31).

62 The major biography of Münsterberg is Matthew Hale, Jr., *Human Science and Social Order: Hugo Münsterberg and the Origins of Applied Psychology* (Philadelphia, PA: Temple University Press, 1980). See also Jeremy Todd Blatter's doctoral dissertation, "The Psychotechnics of Everyday Life: Hugo Münsterberg and the Politics of Applied Psychology, 1887–1917" (Harvard University, 2014). Not long after Münsterberg's death, his daughter, Margaret Münsterberg, wrote *Hugo Münsterberg, His Life and Work* (New York, NY: D. Appleton, 1922). Although quite engaging in its style, some of the accounts in this work have been found to contain errors in detail and self-protective interpretations of events, as is understandable when a child attempts to reconstruct the life of a beloved. Another useful account is Merle J. Moskowitz, "Hugo Münsterberg: A Study in the History of Applied Psychology," *American Psychologist* 32 (1977): 824–42.

63 See Hale, *Human Science*, 19.

64 Ibid., 22.

65 Jutta and Lothar Spillman ("The Rise and Fall of Hugo Münsterberg," *Journal of the History of the Behavioral Sciences* 29 (1993): 322–38) asserted that the only earlier German laboratories were Wundt's in Leipzig in 1879, G. E. Müller's in Göttingen in 1887, and another in Breslau (now Wrocław, Poland) in 1888. Other sources, however, say that Hermann Ebbinghaus opened the first psychology laboratory in Berlin in 1886, and give 1894 as the date that the first laboratory was established in Breslau (by Hermann Ebbinghaus, after he lost the philosophy professorship in Berlin to Carl Stumpf). Either way, Münsterberg's Freiburg laboratory was the fourth in Germany.

66 Hale, *Human Science*, 25. This position was not as prestigious as the full or "ordinary" professorship, which was usually reserved for senior scholars, but it still made one a paid and permanent member of the faculty with the opportunity to rise to "ordinary" professor in the future.

67 Henning Schmidgen has argued that the arrangement of people and equipment in the photograph is a play upon formal aspects of Leonardo Da Vinci's "Last Supper." It is notable that one student, Waldemar Lewy, is shown holding a pistol key to his professor's ear. See Henning Schmidgen, "Münsterberg's Photoplays: Instruments and Models in his Laboratories at Freiburg and Harvard (1891–1893)," *The Virtual Laboratory* (ISSN 1866–4784), 2008, http://vlp.mpiwg-berlin.mpg.de/essays/data/art71.

68 Wundt, for instance, did not admit a woman to his laboratory until the arrival of Anna Meyer Berliner in the early 1910s. The fact that she was married to the physicist, Sigfrid Beliner, who held a position at Leipzig, may have smoothed her path. It is interesting to note, also, that she was Jewish. After Germany's defeat in World War I, Wundt (and many Germans) adopted strongly antisemitic views. By contrast with Berliner and Wundt, Schirnhofer did not earn a degree under Münsterberg (she already had a PhD), but the fact that she appears in this photograph would seem to indicate that she was a regular in the laboratory.

69 Most sources mentioning Schirnhofer report no specific degree. Others give Leipzig as the place she earned her PhD. This is incorrect. According to Norbert Miller and Renate Muller-Buck, eds., *Friedrich Nietzsche Briefwechsel—Kritische Gesamtausgabe (Correspondence, Critical Edition)*, vol. 3 7/3, 1 (Berlin, Germany: Walter de Gruyter,

2004), 123: "Resa von Schirnhofer promovierte im Januar 1889 an der Universität Zürich mit der Arbeit Vergleich über die Lehren Schellings und Spinozas (Druck von Rürcher und Furrer, Zürich 1889)." [Resa von Schirnhofer completed a PhD in January 1889 at the University of Zürich with work comparing the teachings of Schelling and Spinoza (published by Rürcher and Furrer, Zürich 1889)]. There is a minor typographical error here: the publisher was, in fact, *Zürcher* and Furrer.

70 Carol Diethe, *Nietzsche's Women: Beyond the Whip* (New York, NY: Walter de Gruyter, 1996), 91.

71 Samuel Alexander, *Moral Order and Progress: An Analysis of Ethical Conceptions* (London, UK: Trübner, 1889).

72 Recall that the Jewish mathematician James Joseph Sylvester had been unable to find work in England appropriate to his talents, and had finally immigrated to America to take up a professorship at Johns Hopkins.

73 Wundt did not have a Canadian student until quite late in his career, John M. Mac-Eachran, an Ontarian who had already earned a PhD in philosophy at Queen's University (Kingston, ON), under the supervision of the prominent Idealist, John Watson (not to be confused with the future behaviorist, John B. Watson). MacEachran arrived in Leipzig in 1907, completing a thesis on pragmatism in 1909. While in Europe, he also studied with Carl Stumpf, Emile Durkheim, Alfred Binet, and Henri Bergson. He was invited to become head of the philosophy and psychology department at the newly formed University of Alberta in 1909, a position he would hold until 1945. More darkly, he became president of Alberta's Eugenics Board where, between 1928 and 1965, he oversaw the sterilization of about 2,000 individuals, mostly for reasons of alleged low IQ or mental illness.

74 The quotations and the general outline of this account was drawn from Sketch XIV of W. A. McKay, *Zorra Boys at Home and Abroad Or, How to Succeed* (Toronto, ON: William Briggs, 1900).

75 See his entry in the *Deutsche Biographie*. www.deutsche-biographie.de/sfz33727.html. See also the article titled "An Editorial Diary" in the *Glasgow Herald*, December 9, 1937, p. 10. http://bit.ly/1mOYScK. The best-known work of Johannes' son, Reinald, was probably Reinald Hoops, *Der Einfluss Der Psychoanalyse Auf Die Englische Literatur (The Influence of Psychoanalysis on English Literature)* (Heidelberg, Germany: C. Winter, 1934).

76 Many of these letters were reproduced in chapter 4 of Margaret Münsterberg's biography of her father, *Hugo Münsterberg, His Life and Work*.

77 William James, apparently always ready to demean Irish Catholic immigrants to America, felt compelled to inform Münsterberg in the midst of these discussions that our servants are the weakest spot of our civilization—mostly Irish, ill-trained, very independent, and able to ask enormous wages. Five dollars a week is as little as one can now get a decent cook for. . . . If you have two decent servants, bring them <u>mit</u>! (William James to Hugo Münsterberg, letter of April 19, 1892, Hugo Münsterberg Papers, 1890–1916, Box 10, Folder 1834B: James, William, 1842–1910, Item 6). Although one would obviously expect a professor to make much more than a domestic cook, by comparison, James had offered Münsterberg $3000 per annum, or about $60 per week.

78 See Herbert Nichols, "The Psychology Laboratory at Harvard," *McClure's Magazine* 1 (1893): 399–409.

79 William James, "Experimental Psychology in America," *Science*, n.s. 2, no. 45 (1895): 626–28. This "article," briefly mentioned in an earlier footnote, consisted of four letters, the other three being from George T. Ladd, J. Mark Baldwin, and James M. Cattell (who had just become the owner-editor of *Science* in 1894). Its aim was to contest the claim, made by G. Stanley Hall in *American Journal of Psychology* the year prior, that he was the true founder of the "new psychology" in America, a claim in which each of the four respondents had a stake and strove to refute.

80 Virginia Onderdonk, "The Curriculum," in *Wellesley College 1875–1975: A Century of Women*, ed. Jean Glasscock (Wellesley, MA: Wellesley College, 1975), 122–63.

81 The letters from Rev. Calkins and President Shafer can be found in the Records of the President of Harvard University, Charles W. Eliot, 1869–1930, (UAI 5.150, Box 135, Folder 1890).

82 Mary Whiton Calkins, "Autobiography of Mary Whiton Calkins," in *History of Psychology in Autobiography*, ed. Carl A. Murchison, vol. 1 (Worcester, MA: Clark University Press, 1930), 31–61, quotation from pp. 33–34.

83 Indeed, this appears to be the justification Harvard still employs today when campaigns are mounted, as they periodically are, to grant Calkins a posthumous PhD.

84 Calkins, "Autobiography," 35.

85 Cordelia C. Nevers and Mary W. Calkins, "Dr. Jastrow on Community of Ideas of Men and Women," *Psychological Review* 2 (1895): 363–67; Joseph Jastrow, "Community of Ideas of Men and Women," *Psychological Review* 3 (1896): 68–71; Mary Whiton Calkins, "Community of Ideas of Men and Women," *Psychological Review* 3 (1896): 426–30.

86 Mary Whiton Calkins, "Psychology as Science of Selves," *Philosophical Review* 9 (1900): 490–501; "Psychology as Science of Self. I: Is the Self Body or Has It Body?," *Journal of Philosophy, Psychology and Scientific Methods* 5 (1908): 12–20; "Psychology as Science of Self. II: The Nature of the Self," *Journal of Philosophy, Psychology and Scientific Methods* 5 (1908): 64–68; "Psychology as Science of Self: III. The Description of Consciousness," *Journal of Philosophy, Psychology, and Scientific Methods* 5 (1908): 113–22; "The Self in Scientific Psychology," *American Journal of Psychology* 26 (1915): 495–524.

87 Münsterberg, *Hugo Münsterberg, His Life and Work*, 50.

88 Ibid., 49.

89 Thomas Davidson (1840–1900) is a difficult character to describe. Born and raised in Scotland, he was a teacher and master at several British schools before moving to North America, where he lived near London (Ontario), St. Louis, and finally Boston. Proficient in a wide array of languages, he traveled often and studied relentlessly, spending long stints in Greece and Italy working on Classical topics and on the history of the Catholic Church. He lectured and published widely. He developed an eccentric panpsychist philosophy (derived from Leibniz), and he could speak with apparent authority on exotic topics that were not widely known about in the English-speaking world at the time, such as Confucianism. James adored his eclecticism.

90 Münsterberg, *Hugo Münsterberg, His Life and Work*, 49.

91 Münsterberg and Baldwin had almost certainly met nearly two years before at the first full meeting of the APA in December of 1892.

92 Both quotations are from James Mark Baldwin, "Autobiography of James Mark Baldwin," in *History of Psychology in Autobiography*, ed. Carl A. Murchison, vol. 1 (Worcester, MA: Clark University Press, 1930), 1–30. The Baldwin quotation appears on p. 3. Münsterberg's characterization is related in footnote 4.

93 Hale, *Human Science*, 50.

94 The philosopher at Berkeley, George Howison, was an Idealist without much interest in the new psychology. He recognized the need for a psychology laboratory in a modern department, however, and hired a native of the San Francisco bay area, George M. Stratton, who had earned a PhD under Wundt at Leipzig. Stratton would found the Berkeley laboratory in 1896, the year after the Münsterbergs visited. Except for a few years he spent directing the Johns Hopkins laboratory for Baldwin, Stratton would remain at "Cal" for the rest of his career.

95 Hale, Jr., *Human Science*, 52.

96 Spillman and Spillman, "Rise and Fall," 325.

97 Ibid.

98 There has been some debate over Wundt's role in the ensuing debacle. A. A. Roback (*History of American Psychology* (New York, NY: Library Publishers, 1952)) claimed that Wundt, G. E. Müller, and Paul Natorp ganged up to write negative letters about Münsterberg to undercut his position. Wolfgang G. Bringmann and Walter Balance, "Wundt vs. Münsterberg: Roback's Version Challenged," *American Psychologist* 28 (1973): 849–50

published a full translation of Wundt's letter, which praised Münsterberg as the best candidate for the position, but also lamented that his work had not risen to Wundt's original expectations for him. No relevant letters from either Müller or Natorp were found in the Freiburg archives.

99 Another hint of James' politics comes through in one of these letters, dated September 2, 1896. He writes of the upcoming presidential election "Of course the Silver Party must be beaten, but they have much that is ideal on their side" (cited in M. Münsterberg, *Hugo Münsterberg, His Life and Work*, 55). The "Silver Party" was the coalition of Populists, Democrats, and a faction of the Republican Party that rallied around the candidacy of William Jennings Bryan, the young (just 36) firebrand congressman out of Nebraska who, in the midst of the worst economic slump the US had ever seen, advocated using silver as well as the traditional gold for the US monetary standard. Everyone agreed that this "bimetalism" would be inflationary but, in the deflationary economic context of the mid-1890s, it was argued by some that inflation would actually stabilize the economy and bring more money to farmers, whose crop prices had fallen dramatically. The policy was favored mainly by wheat and corn farmers of the Midwest, cotton farmers of the South, and silver miners of the West (especially Nevada). It was strongly opposed by Northeast industrialists and bankers, however, who stood to lose much in a risky inflationary economy. Bryan ran for president three times (1896, 1900, 1908). He was eventually appointed Secretary of State by Woodrow Wilson (after his 1912 election), but resigned in 1915 in protest of Wilson's demands of Germany after the sinking of the *Lusitania*. Bryan later supported Prohibition and, most (in)famously, became involved in the Scopes "Monkey Trial" on the side against the teaching evolution (which, in his understanding, implied the acceptance of Social Darwinism, anathema to any populist).

100 Interestingly, James, Royce, and Baldwin seemed to have struck a secret deal that, should Münsterberg decide against Harvard, Baldwin would be brought in from Princeton in his place. Such a move—Münsterberg never coming to America permanently and Baldwin moving, presumably permanently, to Cambridge in 1897 instead of to Baltimore in 1903 (where he would meet his academic demise)—would have changed the history of American psychology in important ways. See the letters from James to Baldwin dated March 9, 1896 and February 27, 1897, published in *The Correspondence of William James*, ed. by I. K. Skrupskelis and E. M Berkeley, vol. 8 (Cambridge, MA: Harvard University Press, 2000), 139–236. Thanks to Robert H. Wozniak for pointing out to me this little-known aspect of the episode.

101 Münsterberg sold the instruments in his Freiburg laboratory to University College London, where they formed the nucleus of James Sully's new laboratory there. Some of them remain on display to this day. See Elizabeth R. Valentine, "The Founding of the Psychological Laboratory, University College London: 'Dear Galton . . . Yours Truly, J. Sully,'" *History of Psychology* 2 (1999): 204–18.

102 Frank Angell, "(Review of) *Hugo Münsterberg: His Life and Work*, by Margaret Münsterberg," *American Journal of Psychology* 34 (1923): 123–25.

103 Although Münsterberg took his role as informal ambassador of German *Kultur* quite seriously, he may not have been so visible and important to the effort as some historians of psychology have implied in the past. For instance, he rated only two brief mentions in Clifton J. Child's book on the topic, *The German-Americans in Politics* (New York, NY: Arno Press and The New York Times, 1970).

104 Ludy T. Benjamin Jr., "Hugo Münsterberg's Attack on the Application of Scientific Psychology," *Journal of Applied Psychology* 91 (2006): 414–25. See also Ludy T. Benjamin Jr., "Hugo Münsterberg: Portrait of an Applied Psychologist," in *Portraits of Pioneers in Psychology*, ed. Gregory A. Kimble and Michael Wertheimer, vol. 4 (Washington, DC: American Psychological Association, 2000), 119–35.

105 Hugo Münsterberg, "The Danger from Experimental Psychology," *Atlantic Monthly* 81 (February 1898): 159–66.

106 Ibid., 165.

107 For some contemporary discussion of Münsterberg's relation to Schopenhauer, see Richard Burdon Haldane, "Prof. Münsterberg as Critic of Categories," *Mind* n.s. 9 (1900): 205–17. Haldane studied in Göttingen, and was one of the earliest translators of Schopenhauer into English (in the 1880s). He was brother to the prominent physiologist John Scott Haldane and uncle to the polymath J. B. S. Haldane. He was also a politician, holding the posts of Secretary of State for War (1905–1912, under Prime Ministers Henry Campbell-Bannerman and H. H. Asquith) and Lord Chancellor under Asquith (1912–1915). He was knighted 1st Viscount Haldane in 1913. Because of his German education, at the outbreak of World War I he was accused of being sympathetic to the German cause and forced to resign from cabinet. In 1923, long after the War was over, he left the Liberal Party for Labour and served briefly as Lord Chancellor again, under Ramsay MacDonald (1924).

108 Münsterberg, "Danger," 163–64.

109 Charles B. Bliss, "Professor Munsterberg's Attack on Experimental Psychology," *Forum* 25 (1898): 214–23.

110 Ibid., 214.

111 Ibid., 216–17.

112 Ibid., 219.

113 Ibid., 222.

114 Ibid., 214.

115 Ibid., 218.

116 James McKeen Cattell, "Professor Münsterberg on 'The Danger from Experimental Psychology,'" *Psychological Review* 5 (1898): 411–13.

117 Hugo Münsterberg, "Psychology and Education," *Educational Review* 16 (1898): 105–32, reprinted in Hugo Münsterberg, *Psychology and Life* (Boston, MA: Houghton-Mifflin, 1899).

118 Münsterberg, "Psychology and Education," 124 (p. 130 of the 1899 reprint).

119 Hugo Münsterberg, "School Reform," *Atlantic Monthly* 85 (1900): 656–69, reprinted in *American Traits from the Point of View of a German* (Boston, MA: Houghton-Mifflin, 1901).

120 And yet when the ancient and venerable University of Oxford established a new Readership in Psychology in 1898 and offered it to Münsterberg, he turned it down, claiming that America was more hospitable than England to Continental modes of thought (Münsterberg, *Hugo Münsterberg, His Life and Work*, 65).

121 For instance, the Hegelian journal editor and educator, William Torrey Harris, as well as the founder of Teachers College and, from 1901, president of Columbia University, Nicholas Murray Butler.

122 He was elected to the post after Royce, Ladd, Dewey, and James had all taken their "turns," but well before Tufts, Mead, and Calkins. In those days, the American Philosophical Association was really just the philosophical association of the eastern US. The Western Philosophical Association was actually slightly older than its eastern counterpart. The junior association attempted various ploys aimed at luring the Western one into a merger. Eventually the two groups did achieve a merger of sorts, as the Eastern and Western Divisions of a larger American Philosophical Association (though the two retained separate presidents and conferences; a presidency for the whole Association did not come into being until 1970). Eventually a Pacific Division was added, and the Western Division renamed itself "Central." To this day, however, the three divisions continue to hold their conferences at separate times and places. No accommodation could ever be found to persuade a fourth group, the Southern Society for Philosophy and Psychology (founded at about the same time as the Eastern and Western Associations) to formally affiliate with the national association.

9

THE DAWN OF THE 20TH CENTURY

1. America's Rush Into a New Era

The crowd that gathered to see President McKinley—to personally greet him, if they could—was large but not unruly that September afternoon in 1901. The site was the Temple of Music, the main auditorium at the Pan-American Exposition in Buffalo. The day before, McKinley had given a speech to a crowd of 50,000 at The Esplanade, a large outdoor area on the fairgrounds. The man had, during his first term in office, presided over the return of American prosperity after the crash of 1893, preached an end to isolationism, and called for increased foreign trade.

Today, however there were to be no more speeches. McKinley arrived at the Temple of Music, which had been cleared of chairs to accommodate the large body of onlookers that was expected to be on hand. Along one wall of the vast room, a wide pathway was created, leading up to the President, where visitors could momentarily shake his hand. Despite the great expectant throng that arrived, the reception was scheduled to last only ten minutes. The president's secretary had tried to cancel the event, but McKinley insisted on keeping it. Mingling with the public was one of his favorite aspects of politicking.

Seven minutes after the event began, a man stepped up to McKinley whose right hand was wrapped in cloth. Perhaps thinking the hand was injured, McKinley reached for the man's left hand instead. As he did, two shots rang out from the pistol concealed in the man's right hand. McKinley was hit and fell backwards into the arms of the attendants around him. The shooter was tackled by nearby security men and others. The wounded president was taken to a small hospital on the Exposition grounds. A doctor was soon summoned, but he was not a surgeon and could offer only the most basic treatment. When a surgeon finally arrived, he was unable to locate the bullet that had pierced McKinley's abdomen and decided to stich the wounds without removing it. For the next few days, McKinley appeared to recover, but on the seventh day after the attack, gangrene began to take hold. McKinley died the next day, September 14, 1901—almost precisely 20 years after the last presidential assassination, that of James Garfield.[1]

The assassin turned out to be an unemployed factory worker named Leon Czolgosz. He was a Polish Catholic immigrant's son from the midwest and had lost his job during the Panic of 1893. In his despair, he had turned to anarchist politics, becoming obsessed with Emma Goldman after seeing her speak.[2] In short, he was the very specter of what Americans feared most when they imagined hordes of untutored, undemocratic, desperate alien newcomers and the chaos they might unleash on America if not kept strictly in check. Czolgosz's trial began just nine days after the President's death. The defense called no witnesses, and Czolgosz was convicted and condemned to death within days. Just a month afterwards, on October 29, 1901, he was executed by electric chair.

McKinley was immediately succeeded by his youthful, new vice president, Theodore Roosevelt. It was a transition that probably changed the course of US history as decisively as any event since the Civil War. Although McKinley and Roosevelt were both Republicans, the two men saw eye-to-eye on very little. Indeed, Roosevelt had been chosen for the vice presidency by the Republican Party brass, first, to use his personal popularity to help get McKinley re-elected and, second, to bury him in a powerless job where his Progressive views were unlikely to see the light of day. To fully understand the significance of Roosevelt's rise to power, one must go back to the most significant event of McKinley's first term—the Spanish–American War.

In February of 1898, a US Navy ship, the *Maine*, had exploded and sunk in the harbor of Havana, Cuba, killing 266 American sailors. The disaster occurred just weeks before Cuba was to start a new period of autonomy from its historical colonial master, Spain, after decades of violent revolts. Rumors were rife that the American ship had been sunk by Spanish loyalists in retaliation against alleged US support for the Cuban *independentistas*.

Political pressure quickly built on McKinley, who had been president for less than a year, to respond to the putative provocation with military force. The actual cause of the explosion was far from clear, however—it may have come from within the ship itself—and McKinley was eager to the resolve matter diplomatically in order to preserve American commercial interests on the massive Caribbean island. Indeed, the *Maine* had been docked at Havana for the very purpose of protecting US assets in the wake of riots that had rocked the Cuban capital in the weeks leading up to autonomy. War with Spain would not only put those assets at risk, but might undermine the whole process leading to Cuban self-rule. With the deaths of hundreds of American sailors to avenge, though, it became increasingly difficult for McKinley to resist the demands of the "war party" without seeming irresolute.

In late April, more than two months after the sinking, McKinley finally yielded to the politics of the situation and ordered the US Navy to blockade Cuba. Days later, predictably, Spain declared war on the US. Cuba, however, was not the only problem in Spain's aging and rickety empire. The US immediately took advantage of its adversary's widespread troubles: In the Philippines, a revolution that had broken out two years earlier had settled into an uneasy ceasefire. In an effort to stretch Spanish military resources to the breaking point, McKinley ordered a fleet of seven gunships to sail for Manila.[3] When they arrived on May 1, they quickly destroyed the 12 Spanish ships protecting the capital and blockaded Manila Bay. Later that same month, the US attacked Puerto Rico and, in June, took control of Guam as well. Over the summer of 1898, the two countries fought in multiple theaters but, by August, Spain was exhausted and sued for peace. The US annexed the Philippines, Puerto Rico, and Guam, but granted Cuba its independence.

Over the short course of the Spanish–American war, a new and valiant personage had emerged on to the American scene: Theodore Roosevelt. He had been McKinley's assistant secretary of the Navy but at the outbreak of war he abruptly resigned his office to form a volunteer cavalry regiment. Roosevelt came from a wealthy New York family that traced its lineage all the way back to Dutch rule. Back in the 1880s, when he had been in his 20s, he had served three terms in the New York State legislature. However, shattered by the sudden death of his young wife in 1884, he had quit politics and moved to Dakota Territory where he had become a rancher. He first came to national prominence during that time, through a multivolume book he wrote about the American conquest of the West.[4]

When he finally returned east, Roosevelt was appointed to the US Civil Service Commission by then-president Benjamin Harrison. He later became commissioner of the New York City police, where he rooted out corruption and helped Jacob Riis clean up the notorious Five Points district (as we saw earlier). When McKinley was elected president in 1896, Roosevelt lobbied him intensively for a post in the Naval Department. He got the posiiton he wanted but, when the opportunity arose to personally fight in a war—especially one to evict an old power from the New World—it was more than he could resist. He quit his government job and assembled his regiment: "The Rough Riders."

Through a series of well-publicized exploits in the Cuban theater—especially at San Juan Hill—Roosevelt rose from a mere author and politician to a national war hero. He returned home and was able to exploit his new renown to win the Republican gubernatorial nomination in New York. He beat his Democratic opponent in the general election,[5] but he made "machine" Republicans nervous and unhappy with his advocacy of Progressive policies that were seen as unfriendly to big business, the traditional ally of the Republican Party. His personal popularity, though, enabled him to accomplish things no other governor could have. During his single term in office, he regulated business to ensure more fairness and honesty, he imposed a business tax, and he pushed through legislation limiting the length of the workday for women and children.

Progressives across the country were drawn to him, but New York's Republican leadership was aghast. Scrambling for a way to dissuade Roosevelt from running for re-election (which he surely would have won), the top officials of his own party turned to President McKinley during the run up to his 1900 re-election campaign, pleading with him to nominate Roosevelt for the vice presidency.[6] McKinley was no fan of Roosevelt's Progressivism, but he thought that the dashing and vigorous New Yorker might appeal to voters as the president competed for a second time against the more youthful and charismatic Democrat, William Jennings Bryan. After the election was won, it was thought, Roosevelt would be safely neutralized by the impotency of his new office, and his "radical" views would have no impact on government policy.

Roosevelt privately resisted the nomination. At just 41 years of age, he had presidential aspirations of his own, and no vice president had subsequently been elected to the presidency since the 1830s. McKinley's wishes prevailed, of course, and Roosevelt reluctantly accepted the call. In March of 1901, he was sworn in as vice president.[7] But just over six months later, McKinley was dead and the popular champion of Progressivism, Theodore Roosevelt, was unexpectedly thrust into the presidency of the United States. He was the youngest chief executive in the nation's history and the future of the republic suddenly afforded possibilities that had seemed hardly imaginable a week prior.

Still, although the head of government had changed, the raucous labor situation that Roosevelt faced was more or less the same one the country had been grappling with for decades, except that the conflicts were now more intense and fraught with even greater danger. Unions had technically been legal in the US since 1842, but a variety of legal restrictions had prevented them from being terribly effective. Increasing frustrations on the parts of both labor and capital brought about violent confrontations between them on a regular basis. A large union called The Knights of Labor had been the most prominent defenders of the working class, boasting as many as 800,000 members in the mid-1880s. After the Haymarket explosion in 1886, however, the Knights were beleaguered by accusations of being in cahoots with violent anarchists. Many workers left the organization, turning instead to the newer and more moderate American Federation of Labor. The AFL was not a union, per se, but an association of independent unions that were each dedicated to a specific "craft": railway workers, miners, textile works, etc.

The first crisis of Roosevelt's administration, in May of 1902, was a strike by more than 100,000 coal miners in Pennsylvania. Not atypically, the miners demanded a 20% wage increase, a reduction in the workday from ten hours to eight, and recognition by mine owners of the United Mine Workers of America (UMWA) as their collective bargaining agent. Owners, for their part, refused to negotiate with the union at all, seeing the setting of wages and hours as their own God-given prerogative.[8] The strike dragged on through the summer. It was not totally peaceful but neither did it break into the open warfare that some earlier coal strikes in the West had. By October, Roosevelt could foresee that a winter without Pennsylvania's anthracite coal, which was used to heat tens of millions of urban homes, would quickly lead to a national crisis. So, working through the pre-eminent financier, J. P. Morgan, Roosevelt created a commission to study the situation and make recommendations. The strike was suspended during the commission's three months of fact finding and hearings, thereby enabling Roosevelt and the country to dodge a winter disaster. In the end, the commission recommended a resolution that could have been proposed at the outset, splitting the difference between the two sides: a 10% pay hike and a nine-hour workday. The workers dropped their demand for union recognition and agreed to the compromise. Mine owners resisted, but finally capitulated when Roosevelt privately threatened to nationalize the entire American coal industry. There would not be another major coal strike in the US for a generation.

Roosevelt was a "hero" once again. The "Square Deal" that he promised the American public did not end there. He went on to break up large corporate monopolies, he capped often-erratic rail rates, and he coaxed Congress to pass laws that ensured the purity of commercially processed of food and drugs.[9] Government intervention aimed at moderating the excesses of unbridled capitalism without capitulating to the revolutionary demands of communists and anarchists had, in a few short years, become the new American reality.

2. William James and the Psychology of Religion

In 1901, William James was entering his sixtieth year. Nearing the peak of his philosophical powers, he was invited to give a series of twenty lectures on the topic of "natural theology" at the University of Edinburgh. The annual event was supported by the estate of a wealthy lawyer, Adam Lord Gifford, whose 1887 will had provided for lecture programs at each of Scotland's four universities—St. Andrews, Glasgow, Aberdeen, and Edinburgh. James' junior Harvard colleague, Josiah Royce, had given the Aberdeen Gifford Lectures back in 1899, where he had presented the lectures that would be published as *The World and the Individual*.[10] The subject of James' lectures was nearly as expansive: *The Varieties of Religious Experience*. The published version of these lectures became, perhaps, James' most popular book, read to this day by students of religion, philosophy, and psychology. It ranged far and wide, discussing such diverse topics as neurology, religious conversion, saintliness, and mysticism. James also introduced an influential distinction between two religious motivations—the "healthy mind" and the "sick soul." In the midst of his discussion of the latter, he revealed the details of his own mental crisis, more than thirty years before, but disguised them as coming from a letter sent to him by an anonymous French correspondent.[11]

Toward the end of the lecture series, however, James framed his assessment of theology, as traditionally practiced, in terms of a philosophical position that was probably unfamiliar to his listeners. Invoking the name of his longtime friend, Charles Sanders Peirce, whom he described as "an American philosopher of eminent originality," James introduced what he called the "principle of pragmatism."[12]

The only motivation for thought, he began, is to arrive at a settled belief. Only once belief is set, he continued, can action "firmly and safely begin." Thus, he concluded, "the whole function of thinking is but one step in the production of active habits."[13] This is not exactly how Peirce had put the matter in the article published 24 years before which James cited as his source, "How to Make Our Ideas Clear."[14] It was close enough, however, for his intended purposes.

James went on to use this form of pragmatism to argue that philosophical theology, as it was then practiced, was religiously sterile and could never be sufficient, with its logical gymnastics, to bring nonbelievers to faith. As James bluntly put it, "to prove God's goodness by the scholastic argument that there is no non-being in his essence would sound to such a witness [a skeptic] simply silly."[15] Only personal experience of the divine, James said, can compel faith. Theology only follows along in a secondary role, organizing and elaborating on faith that was initially attained through entirely other means. Then, after quoting a long passage from the great religious philosopher John Caird, James commented,

> You will readily admit that no description of the phenomena of the religious consciousness could be better than these words of your lamented preacher and philosopher [Caird had died just three years before]. They reproduce the very rapture of those crises of conversion of which we have been hearing. . . . But when all is said and done, has Principal Caird—and I only use him as an example of that whole mode of thinking—transcended the sphere of feeling and of the direct experience of the individual, and laid the foundations of religion in impartial reason? Has he made religion universal by coercive reasoning, transformed it from a private faith into a public certainty? . . .
>
> I believe that he has done nothing of the kind, but that he has simply reaffirmed the individual's experiences in a more generalized vocabulary.[16]

Because no philosophy of religion could ever live up to the task of creating compelling foundations for religious belief, according to James, he called for its replacement by a "Science of Religions"—a discipline that could take the various definitions of the divine that it finds in the world and, "by comparison eliminate the local and the accidental from these definitions. . . . Sifting out in this way unworthy formulations, she [science] can leave a residuum of conceptions that at least are possible." Gathering steam, he even went on to suggest that he did not see why,

> a critical Science of Religions of this sort might not eventually command as general a public adhesion as is commanded by a physical science. Even the personally non-religious might accept its conclusions on trust, much as blind persons now accept the facts of optics—it might appear as foolish to refuse them.[17]

The connections to James' long effort—empirical and otherwise—to bring scientific credibility to spiritualism here are obvious. While it may be easy to smile at his enthusiastic optimism about the potential of a Science of Religions to "command general public adhesion," it is important to note that he was speaking to a critical and growing divide in Euro-American religious life. Challenges continued to press in from every side against the simple Calvinist faith that had long served as America's moral bedrock. From "above," there was the importation of the German "Higher Criticism," which called into question the historical accuracy of the familiar Biblical account of Christianity's origins and meaning. From the "sides," every day brought new scientific revolutions that clashed with common sense ideas about nature. Darwin's Natural Selection had only been the start. Mendel's genetic principles, first published in the 1860s, were rediscovered and popularized around 1900. Max Planck's Quantum Hypothesis also appeared in 1900; Einstein's Special Relativity would come in 1905. In addition, there was a flood of challenging and seductive new technologies: personal cameras, cylinder phonographs, moving pictures, telephones, electric light, affordable automobiles, and even powered flight.

As if philosophical questioning from above and scientific disruption on all sides weren't challenging enough, from "below" came the press of new (to America) religious denominations—Catholicism, Eastern Orthodox Christianity, Judaism, and even Buddhism were brought to the nation's shores by wave after wave of desperate immigrants. From within the US itself, new and unorthodox religious beliefs were on the rise. In some cases whole new denominations were coming into existence and attracting huge followings. The Mormons of New York State—not even regarded as Christians by many—had migrated to Utah in the 1840s, where they had been granted statehood in 1896. From New England, Mary Baker Eddy had captured the country's attention with her doctrine that disease is illusory and can be cured by the power of prayer alone.[18] Her Church of Christ, Scientist, chartered in 1879, built a monumental edifice in the middle of Boston in the 1890s. Christian Science was the fastest growing religion in the US in the early years of the 20th century.[19] There was also the Watchtower Society (later renamed Jehovah's Witnesses), the Seventh Day Adventists, and many other sects not as well known, each declaring new and absolute "Truths" that deviated from those of conventional Christianity.

Older Christian denominations were changing too, growing increasingly liberal in their stances toward sin and salvation—especially the Universalists and the Unitarians who now dominated Harvard. It was a perplexing, confounding time for conventional Protestants and it would not be long before religious traditionalists began to fight back. Starting in 1910, a Baptist pastor named Amzi Clarence Dixon and a Congregationalist minister named Reuben Archer Torrey began issuing a 12-volume book series titled *The Fundamentals*.[20] The 90 essays therein, written by 64 different authors, were aimed at defining exactly the boundaries of conventional Protestant piety and, in doing so, creating the basis of modern

Christian Fundamentalism in America. *The Fundamentals*, however, was not the product of a "grassroots" movement generated by disgruntled, ordinary religious traditionalists. It was top-down project from the start, anonymously funded by a California oil tycoon named Lyman Stewart. He invested $300,000 in the project, so that the full sets of *The Fundamentals* could be given away to ministers, missionaries, and other Christian workers, enabling them to fight the "modernism" that he feared was undermining traditional American faith.

3. A Science of Pastoral Care? Psychotherapy Is Born

In Boston, one church in particular was exactly the kind that most alarmed conventional old-line Christians like Lyman Stewart. Perhaps surprisingly, its denomination was neither new nor radical. It was, in fact, Episcopal—the highest rung on the social ladder of American Protestant denominations. It was called the Emmanuel Church and, since 1860, it had stood on Newbury Street, in the fashionable Back Bay neighborhood that William James had seen come into existence over the course of his 40 years in the Boston area.

In the early 20th century, the Emmanuel Church was led by a priest, Elwood Worcester, whose academic qualifications included a doctorate from Leipzig, where none other than Wilhelm Wundt had served as the secondary professor (*Zweitgutachter*) on his thesis. Worcester had been born in Ohio in 1862, but he was raised in Rochester, New York where he had become close with a noted Episcopal priest and Social Gospel advocate Algernon Crapsey.[21] During the 1880s, as a college student, Worcester earned a BA at Columbia and a divinity degree at the General Theological Seminary (for Episcopalians), also in New York. Then, like so many others, he went to Germany to learn the new psychology. Although Worcester wrote that, "it was [Wundt] who had brought me to Leipzig," he also recollected with particular fondness the time he spent in Gustav Fechner's final lecture course.[22] "His soul entered so deeply into my soul," Worcester recalled, "his thought has so accompanied me through life, that I can no longer distinguish the transcendent quality of his mind from the man of flesh and blood—what I have read from what I have heard."[23] It was not Fechner's pioneering work on psychophysics that most affected Worcester but the "haunting, unforgettable beauty" of his lesser-known and eccentric spiritual writings: *Zend Avesta*; *Nana, the Soul-Life of Plants* (*Nanna oder über das Seelenleben der Pflanzen*); *The Question as to Souls* (*Über die Seelenfrage*); and *The Three Motives and Grounds of Faith* (*Die drei Motive und Gründe des Glaubens*).[24] Although it is sometimes reported that Worcester took his doctorate in experimental psychology under Wundt, his thesis, completed in 1889, was actually on the religious opinions of John Locke, supervised by the historian and philosopher Max Heinze.[25] After graduating, Worcester took an academic appointment at Lehigh University and, after a few years, added parish work in Philadelphia (where he became friends with the noted neurologist and neurasthenia researcher, Silas Weir Mitchell).

FIGURE 9.1   Portrait of Elwood Worcester by Pollak-Ottendorff, 1917.

Credit: Elwood Worcester, *Life's Adventure: The Story of a Varied Career* (New York, NY: Scribner's, 1932)

In 1904, Worcester was appointed rector at the Emmanuel Church. In Boston, he found a community of like-minded intellectuals who were experimenting with a variety of unorthodox means of alleviating various kinds of mental distress that, although sometimes deeply troubling to the individual, did not often rise to a level of severity that required confinement in the local asylum.[26] This community included a number people we have already encountered—William James,[27] Stanley Hall, Josiah Royce, Adolf Meyer. In addition, there was Harvard's professor of nervous diseases, James Jackson Putnam. There were also a Tufts College neurologist named Morton Prince and a brilliant physician and psychopathologist who had emigrated from Ukraine named Boris Sidis.[28]

In 1905, Worcester persuaded an Irish Presbyterian minister who especially impressed him, Samuel McComb, to convert to Episcopalianism and become his new Associate Rector. Worcester also set out to earn the trust of three prominent local physicians: two Massachusetts General Hospital doctors named Richard C. Cabot and Joseph Pratt, as well as a Tufts College neurologist named Isador Coriat (a one-time student of Adolf Meyer).[29] Worcester assisted them in the treatment of local tuberculosis patients—primarily by helping them to better comply with medical recommendations about physical activity, nutrition, and fresh air. He also taught a class for these patients on "morale and obedience."

Worcester then brought this elite group together for a new project: to address the "spiritual maladies of mankind" by "forming a class . . . for the moral and psychological treatment of nervous and psychic disorders."[30] In the fall of 1906, over the course of four successive Sunday evenings, Putnam, Cabot, McComb, and Worcester presented lectures to interested members of the Emmanuel congregation on mind and brain, on the effects of alcohol and drugs on consciousness and the body, and on "Jesus' healing ministry." When the series concluded, they announced they would be opening a "clinic" to assist any parishioners who were troubled by mental distress. The response was as immediate as it was astonishing. The very next morning, Worcester found 198 people lined up for help. Thereafter, his clinic, held twice per week, drew hundreds more.[31]

The Emmanuel's therapeutic sessions included hymns and prayers, as one might expect at a church event, but they also featured examinations and consultations with the physicians. They seem to have also used a variety of hypnotic techniques that, despite their strenuous claims to be entirely distinct from the past "mind cure" movement, were drawn from sources such as Phineas Quimby's early-19th-century "New Thought" teachings.[32] There were also private consultations with ministers (called "moral clinics"), sessions of what we would now call "group therapy," and even private house calls.

The response to the success of Worcester's clinic was nothing short of a nationwide sensation. Newspaper and magazine articles about the psychological practices being pioneered at the Emmanuel Church multiplied rapidly, many of them more sensational than informative. Ministers came from other churches in Boston to learn the techniques (and to win some popular attention) for themselves. Worcester and McComb toured other cities to spread word of their experiences. Soon, New York and Chicago both had their own Emmanuel-like centers providing the same kinds of services to their own flocks.

One of the things that made the original Boston group different from other "mind cure" movements was that it was eager to establish and sustain the scientific credibility of its practices. For this reason, they chose the ugly neologism "psychotherapy" to describe their activities, in order set them apart.[33] As Cabot once put the matter:

> psychotherapy is a most terrifying word, but we are forced to use it because there is no other which serves to distinguish us from Christian Scientists, the New Thought people, the faith healers, and the thousand and one other

schools which have in common the disregard for medical science and the accumulated knowledge of the past.[34]

To bolster their claims to scientific respectability, Cabot kept and published statistical tallies of their results: of 178 men examined, 82 were neurasthenic, 24 were "insane," 22 were alcoholic, 18 had "fears or fixed ideas," 10 had sexual neuroses, 5 were hysterics, and so forth. Of 123 outcomes, he reported, there were "seventy-five cases in which undoubted benefit has resulted . . . and nothing to offset it."[35]

The actions of a few men at the Emmanuel Church had unexpectedly exploded into a national "Emmanuel Movement," many offshoots of which were well beyond the control of the careful little group that had started the uproar. Unable to keep up with the demand for their guidance in person, in 1908, Worcester, McComb, and Coriat combined efforts to author a book on the Emmanuel program.[36] Nevertheless, many unscrupulous imitators who had no connection with the Emmanuel Church, but who were eager to exploit the situation for their own gain, began to ply their own trades under the Emmanuel name. This caused the nascent institution of uncertain intellectual standing to quickly topple into disrepute.

Cabot's careful quantitative reassurances notwithstanding, the response from the medical and broader scientific community was quick and, for the most part, negative. The judgment of many was that Emmanuel was nothing more than doctors and ministers of unusual naïveté who had been duped by Christian Scientists. Emmanuel's connection to Boston, which was also the headquarters for Mary Baker Eddy's church, did nothing to help matters. Boston was "the land of witchcraft and transcendentalism" sneered Johns Hopkins psychiatrist Clarence B. Farrar in his effort to tar Emmanuel with the same brush. The physicians involved, he thundered, are "sell[ing] their birthright and surrender[ing] a part of their legitimate province, . . . hand[ing] over impotently to the clergy for treatment . . . manifestations of disease or trauma."[37]

Many traditional clergy objected to the Emmanuel movement as well, fearing that their grand vision of the divine was being crudely reduced to a mere spa. Some demanded to know by what authority Worcester and McComb had taken these actions in the name of the church, as though matters of heresy might be at stake. The Emmanuel ministers typically responded to such accusations with Biblical allusions about Jesus healing the sick and comforting the afflicted.[38]

Psychologists were split on the matter. Some, such as James Rowland Angell of Chicago (a one-time student of James), were favorable. Others, such as Lightner Witmer (who had founded a "psychological clinic" to assess and treat learning problems in school children at the University of Pennsylvania) condemned it as unsound and unscientific. [39] Still others staked out an intermediate position. Hugo Münsterberg, whose own book *Psychotherapy* came out in 1909, was critical of Christian Science and its like for "cheapen[ing] religion by putting the accent in the meaning of life on personal comfort and absence of pain" but, contrary to many clergymen, he argued that "the originators of the Emmanuel Movement stand well above such error." Nevertheless, he thought that many of the followers in "their national congregation" had taken a hedonistic misstep.[40] In the end, although he believed Emmanuel to represent a case of "actual cooperation of physician and minister" (unlike Christian Science, which he felt simply abused the latter term), he expected Worcester's movement to serve only as a transitional stage for psychotherapy in its journey from the realm of religion to that of science.[41]

The physicians associated with Emmanuel soon withdrew from the group under pressure from their professional communities. Within just a few short years, the Emmanuel "flash" had mostly burnt itself out. Worcester and McComb scaled back their operation to a small clinic running solely out of their own church, increasingly focused on the problem of alcoholism, but they continued on for twenty years more, until Worcester retired in 1931.

4. The American Debut of Psychoanalysis

The year 1909 was Clark University's 20th anniversary and Stanley Hall planned to have a memorable celebration at which some of the world's most important scholars and scientists would present lectures and be awarded honorary degrees.[42] The celebration was to be a multifaceted affair: Hall mounted conferences on a number of different subjects—mathematics, physics, chemistry, and biology—but the conference on psychology was, of course, closest to his heart. He began planning in December of 1908, inviting Wundt and Freud each to give a series of lectures and to receive honorary degrees. Wundt was, of course, a towering figure in the field internationally, and Hall had been the first American to study under him at Leipzig. Freud, on the other hand, was less known, but Hall had read and appreciated his work since the start of the decade. It was a bold opening gambit to invite the two of them, but both men turned Hall down. Wundt pleaded old age; he would be 77 in 1909. Freud was young enough, just 53, but he averred that in July—the proposed time—it would be impossible for him to undertake such a voyage. Hall then invited Alfred Binet, whose new test of mental ability was starting to be used in the US, but the Sorbonne professor declined as well.

It was not a promising start. Hall was finally able to entice Hermann Ebbinghaus, the notable memory researcher, and Ernst Meumann, an innovative educational psychologist. Meumann had taken up the Zürich professorship that Münsterberg had refused back in the 1890s, but he had since moved on to Königsberg, Münster, and Halle. Hall's bad luck continued, however, when Ebbinghaus died suddenly in February 1909, and then Meumann changed his mind about coming.

Undoubtedly frustrated with his lack of progress, Hall finally managed to engage William Stern (who would later develop the idea of the intelligence quotient or IQ) for the "experimental psychology" slot that had first been offered to Wundt and then to Ebbinghaus. Carl Jung was eventually landed for the "pedagogy" slot that had been refused by both Binet and Meumann. It was an odd fit, though: Jung's best-known work at the time—a word-association test for psychopathology—had little to do with pedagogy. Interestingly, Jung may have been better known to American psychologists than Freud was because the younger man had studied and worked at the Berghölzi Clinic in Zürich, where Adolf Meyer had studied as well. They had even shared some of the same teachers.[43] In addition, Jung's 1903 dissertation, *On the Psychology and Pathology of So-Called Occult Phenomena*, had attracted the attention of William James, among others.

Hall then circled back to invite Freud once again, raising his honorarium and changing the time of the conference to September to suit Freud's schedule. This time Freud agreed to attend. Hall also gathered some well-known professors working in America: Cornell experimentalist Edward Titchener, psychiatrist Adolf Meyer (who was just then moving from New York to Johns Hopkins), Columbia anthropologist Franz Boas (who had once been a professor at Clark), and Johns Hopkins biologist Herbert Spencer Jennings. Although it is often presumed that Freud had "first billing" at Hall's conference, it was Jennings' lectures that actually received the bulk of the press coverage.[44]

Freud and Jung stayed with Hall at his home. William James visited the day before the conference was to begin, spending an evening with them. Although he is said to have been impressed with Freud's theories, he was not captivated by the man himself. By contrast, his connection with Jung was nearly immediate. James had arrived brandishing a reprint of his latest report on the spiritualist, Leonora Piper, and he discussed it with Jung animatedly.[45] It is unclear what James knew, at that point, of the far less favorable conclusions that Hall's assistant at Clark, Amy Tanner, was about to publish on Piper's putative psychic abilities.[46]

Freud gave his five lectures over the course of the second week of September 1909. First, he spoke about the famous case of Anna O., an "hysteric" who had been treated by Freud's older colleague, Joseph Breuer. Freud related how the case had led him to the conclusion that hysterical symptoms are the products of traumatic events that the patient cannot consciously recall. When the memories were coaxed back into consciousness—under hypnosis, for instance—the symptoms would sometimes vanish.[47] In the second lecture, Freud elaborated a general theory of how traumatic memories could be "repressed" into unconsciousness, how the memories re-emerged symbolically in the form of neurotic symptoms, and how the patient's "resistance" to recalling them consciously could be overcome by the analyst. In the third lecture, he argued that symbolic expressions of repressed memories might emerge in less obvious forms, such as slips of the tongue and dreams. Correspondingly, he advocated techniques such as free association and the analysis of dreams to help draw them back into consciousness. In the fourth lecture, he shifted to his stage-wise theory of infant sexuality and its importance for healthy psychological development. In the final lecture, Freud elaborated his belief that some of the greatest products of civilization are, in fact, the result of people struggling with their own repressions and frustrations, through an unconscious process that he dubbed "sublimation."

The lectures were well received in the press although, because they had been in German, scholars such as Hall himself facilitated (or even wrote) a fair bit of the coverage. Titchener, of course, was opposed to nearly everything Freud stood for. The completion of pure experimental psychology was going to have to come before a truly valuable application of its principles would be possible. In any case, he scoffed that Freud's exotic conclusions were based on little more than a primitive associationism. Titchener and Meyer entered into their fascinating and contentious correspondence on the topic in the weeks following the conference. Their debate illustrated as well as anything how far the "pure" and "applied" portions of the field had already diverged from each other during the discipline's short history.[48] Hall seems to have provoked an active debate between Titchener and Freud at the conference. Titchener was never shy about extolling his brand of psychology above all others, but there was a little extra at stake for him at this event due to confidential discussions that he was having with Hall at the time about the possibility of taking over as Clark's professor of psychology when Hall's protégé, Edmund Sanford, was promoted into the principalship of the newly created undergraduate college at Clark.[49]

Jung's three lectures were interspersed among Freud's five, as well as those of some other speakers. He presented the results of a test that purported to ferret out emotional "complexes" (psychopathologies) simply by asking people to say whatever first came to mind in response to a list of seemingly ordinary words, and measuring their reaction times. The longer it took to reply, Jung theorized, the more likely an unconscious complex lay there, interfering with the normal process of mental association. Jung's talks left a marked impression on the American psychological scene. In the years immediately following the conference, many articles testing and debating Jung's "association method" appeared in Hall's *American Journal of Psychology*.[50]

Both Jung's and Freud's lectures were translated and published in the *American Journal* in 1910. The Clark conference would be Freud's only trip to the US. After the gathering, he toured some sights of the eastern US and spent a good deal of private time at the country house of James Jackson Putnam, in whom he found a significant convert to the psychoanalytic cause. After the visit, Freud returned home to Europe forever, but remained a regular correspondent of Putnam's for years afterwards.[51]

For Jung, by contrast, the Clark conference would be only the first of many visits to America. He returned the following spring, visiting New York, Chicago, and Boston (where he met with James for a second time). He was, by then, held in such high repute by Americans that he was asked to consult on the cases of Fanny Bowditch (daughter of the Harvard physiologist Henry Bowditch, who had given James his original laboratory training) and of Stanley McCormick (son of the Chicago farm equipment magnate, Cyrus McCormick, who we met in

Chapter 6). Jung made additional visits to the US in 1912 and 1913, holding seminars at prominent American universities and hospitals.[52]

Putnam, still smarting from the Emmanuel fiasco, became an active advocate of psychoanalysis after Freud's visit. He served as the first president of both the American Psychoanalytic Association in 1911 and the Boston Society for Psychoanalysis in 1914. It may have been that Freud afforded Putnam a "scientific" mode in which to talk about the aspects of the human psyche that most fascinated him—dreams, emotions, sex, instincts, neuroses, psychoses, and other "irrationalities"—without becoming entangled in the religious complexities of the Emmanuel movement.

According to the historian of psychology Eugene Taylor, however, the version of psychoanalysis that grew up in the US after Freud's appearance at Clark was more "transcendental" in character than Freud's original. In the minds of many Americans who adopted the label "psychoanalysis," like Putnam, the unconscious was not merely a repository of repressed impulses and traumatic memories. It was, instead, the site of a "greater" mind, a "deeper" mind than the thin layer available to consciousness. It contained not just the tawdry secrets of one's own life, but also profound secrets of life itself. Thus, the psychoanalytic unconscious of New England mingled the views of Viennese psychiatry with those of Concord philosophy; it was a blending of Freud and Emerson. Because of the tendency toward the metaphysical, even mystical, this American reading of psychoanalysis had a closer affinity with Jung's construal of the subject, even as it went by Freud's name.

This "transcendental" understanding of psychoanalysis remained common in America until the 1930s, when the major American psychoanalytic institutes were established in New York and Chicago. By that time, a significant number of Freud-trained European psychoanalysts had come to the US, fleeing the Nazi storm that was starting to engulf central Europe. It was under their orthodox influence that the New England flavoring began to fade, and a more authentic Freudian tone was restored to American psychoanalysis.[53]

Even so, psychoanalysis remained a minority position in American psychiatry. Adolf Meyer was the dominant figure in the field. His and Clifford Beers' National Committee for Mental Hygiene (mentioned in Chapter 7) took the lead. It would not be until World War II that (yet another flavor of) psychoanalysis rose to prominence in American psychiatry. That shift was driven primarily by the US military's confidence in the abilities of William and Karl Menninger— enterprising brothers who ran a psychiatric clinic in Topeka, Kansas—to train the hundreds of professionals required to handle the psychiatric fallout from the vast European and Asian conflicts then underway.[54] It was for similar reasons that, at about this time, the US government urged the American Psychological Association, then still primarily a scientific organization, to merge with the American Association for Applied Psychology and, together, organize and assist universities in training clinical psychologists. This would produce hundreds more mental health professionals to conduct much-needed psychotherapy for veterans who had been mentally injured by their wartime experiences. It was this intervention by the government that spurred the development, led by David Shakow, of the "Boulder Model" of clinical training, with its emphasis on producing not mere clinicians (like training of physicians did) but "scientist-practitioners" who, it was hoped, would heal the long-standing rift between "pure" and "applied" psychology by working both as primary researchers and as front-line practitioners. It is the model that governs much of the clinical PhD curriculum in America to this very day.[55]

5. Public Schools and the Invention of the Psychological Clinic

As important as the appearance of the Emmanuel movement and the arrival of psychoanalysis were, mental disorder was hardly the only pressing issue of the early 20th century that called out for an application of psychological knowledge. The challenges posed by the ever-expanding system of universal schooling created another arena in which psychologists could readily apply their skills. Among the most difficult of these challenges was dealing with children who had trouble with the standardized curriculum that any public school system had to employ. When children failed to learn as expected, it was often not immediately clear why, especially in an environment as tumultuous as a large, turn-of-the 20th-century American city. Are the children able to see and hear clearly? Do they understand the language of instruction? Are they well cared for at home? Is some sort of domestic crisis distracting them? And finally, do they have the general mental ability required to cope with the material of their grade level?

Having to deal with hundreds of thousands of students at a time, urban public school systems often did not have the capacity to sort through these various alternatives. What was needed was a new institution dedicated to sorting these problems out, staffed with professionals who could assess pupils and make recommendations. Often enough, this new institution would be expected to then carry out the treatment, whatever it might be, as well. As mentioned in passing earlier, Lightner Witmer was the person who had first attacked this challenge in an organized, systematic way. Working out of the University of Pennsylvania, where he had been professor since 1893, Witmer opened what he called a "psychological clinic," in 1896. He gradually gathered together a number of different professionals—physicians, social workers, educators, and, of course, psychologists—to serve the needs of Philadelphia's public schools. Although he is often billed as the "father of clinical psychology," his work was, in fact, more closely akin to what we, today, would call "school psychology."

Witmer had been born in 1867 to a Pennsylvania "Dutch" family of long standing in Lancaster County.[56] His father had been a pharmacist who founded and operated a successful wholesale drug company.[57] Although business was the main source of their wealth, education seems to have been the family's main aspiration: Witmer and all three of his siblings attained higher degrees. He attended the prestigious Episcopal Academy in Philadelphia from the age of 13. In 1884 he enrolled at the University of Pennsylvania in Arts. The main development on campus at that time was the opening of the graduate school which, in short order, came under the direction of the philosopher George Stuart Fullerton. Witmer's main interest during the last two years of his undergraduate degree were finance and political economy, but it seems likely that he was also exposed to Hermann Lotze's *Outlines of Psychology* in Fullerton's course on "Logic and Psychology."[58] After graduating in 1888, Witmer taught English and history at a local private school and, then, in 1889, he began graduate work back at Penn in politics, though in the Philosophy Department. It just so happened that, at about this time, James McKeen Cattell arrived to become Penn's first instructor in psychology in the same department.

Cattell began to equip his new laboratory, and Witmer took an interest in the novel field. He became Cattell's paid laboratory assistant for the 1890–91 school year. Before the year was out, though, Cattell had accepted Columbia's lucrative offer to move there. Not wanting to give up on its new graduate program in experimental psychology—no doubt encouraged by Fullerton and Cattell—the university agreed to support Witmer while he completed his PhD in Leipzig, under Wundt, on the condition that he return to be the university's lecturer in psychology for at least three years afterwards.[59] Witmer agreed to the promising deal. Interestingly, foreshadowing his future direction, Witmer took a number of courses in pedagogy while in Leipzig. His dissertation project, suggested by Wundt, was a series of experiments on the aesthetic value of the Golden Section.[60] This was a continuation of work that had been started in Leipzig by Gustav Fechner, the founder of both psychophysics and of experimental aesthetics.[61] Fechner had died just four years prior to Witmer's arrival in Leipzig, and he actually called upon the late scientist's widow for materials that were related to his study.[62] Witmer completed his doctorate in 1892 and, in the fall of that year, took up the promised lectureship at Penn.[63] Later that winter, he presented two research papers at the first annual meeting of the APA, hosted at Penn by his departmental chair, Fullerton. In 1893, Witmer graduated his first PhD, Caspar Wistar Miller, whose dissertation was also on experimental aesthetics. In 1894 Witmer was promoted to assistant professor and, that same year, he taught a course on child psychology for the first time. In 1895, the APA meeting returned to Penn, this time with his old mentors, Cattell and Fullerton, as president and president-elect, respectively.

Although 1896 is conventionally given as the year Witmer "founded" his psychological clinic, there was no formal event as such. As he told the story,[64] he offered a seminar on psychology for teachers in 1895–96. In March of 1896, one of the students in that course, Margaret T. McGuire, brought up in class the case of a 14-year-old student she was teaching who was unable to spell, though he seemed to have normal mental abilities otherwise. Witmer proposed to have the student, whom he codenamed "Charles Gilman," brought to his laboratory with the hope of uncovering the precise nature of his difficulty. Witmer noted that Charles' disability was not limited to spelling; he actually had a profound inability to read or write. One of the more telling symptoms was that he often mistook similar-looking words for each other (e.g., "was" for "saw"). Witmer decided to have the boy's vision checked by a physician. Charles did have a mild vision problem, but correcting it did not solve his word-identification problem. Witmer decided to embark on a course of intensive training on word-recognition for Charles. By the following spring, there was great improvement—he was able to read some from the newspaper, though he still suffered from occasional word confusions and, when writing, letter transpositions (e.g., "htat" for "that"). Witmer continued to follow Charles for years afterwards, reporting steady improvement, to the point that Charles could read "great" novelists such as Alexandre Dumas and Honoré de Balzac (presumably in translation) by the age of 21. Charles graduated from school at 17 and then entered a trade school, where a talent for drawing served him well. Unfortunately, he contracted tuberculosis as a young man and died in 1907 at the age of just 24.

Witmer diagnosed Charles' condition as "verbal visual amnesia"—an inability to recall the images of words. Though we may quibble with this assessment today, what he had accomplished was of landmark importance: he showed that an apparent spelling problem was, instead, a defect in visual and cognitive processing apparently related exclusively to the verbal domain. The defect could be improved, but only by a person, like Witmer, who had specialized knowledge of psychological assessment and treatment. Obvious as this may seem for us, it came as something of a revelation in the 1890s: psychologists could profitably run "clinics" in which their expertise could solve "real world" problems experienced by members of the public.

As word of Witmer's accomplishment spread, educators around the city began bringing other cases to Witmer's attention. He consulted on something like two dozen different cases that first year, 1896. Additional assistance was hired to help Witmer manage with the load. One of his favorite aides was a woman named Mary E. Marvin. She was a Philadelphia teacher who had independently developed a specialty working with deaf and otherwise disabled children. How she became aware of Witmer is not known—she may have been a student in one of his earliest courses—but she actively participated in Witmer's program for many years. During the summer, he ran a short laboratory course on child psychology under the university's "extension" program, intended for the city's teachers. Over the course of that same year he published an article on his clinical work in an education journal, as well as two others in a medical journal.[65] At the APA meeting in Boston that December, he called on his colleagues to take up the challenge of applying their knowledge to the workaday challenges facing their fellow citizens.

The power struggle between "pure" and "applied" psychology was underway.[66] The most immediate response to Witmer was Hugo Münsterberg's APA presidential address the following year, denouncing applied psychology of all kinds as being premature.[67] (As we shall see, he would soon reverse his position, becoming one of the most successful, if not always the most perspicacious, appliers of psychological knowledge in America.) The APA resisted the inclusion of applied psychology in its mandate for another half-century.[68]

While Witmer was plumping for the acceptance of his practical psychology, he was also busy attempting to exclude philosophers from the APA. He formally proposed that philosophers be ejected from the organization and that a separate philosophical society be formed. Not able to achieve that end immediately, he proposed that experimentalists leave the APA for a new association. Witmer asked Titchener, who had left the APA already, to take the lead. Titchener demurred at the time but, in 1904, would start a private, invitation-only group that he pointedly called "The Experimentalists" (today, the Society for Experimental Psychology).[69]

In 1897, Witmer hired his younger brother, Ferree, then a Penn graduate student in physiology, and a former undergraduate student of Witmer's named Albert L. Lewis, to assist with the teaching of courses. The added help enabled Witmer to expand his clinical practice even further. He saw at least 15 new cases that year. He also offered, for the first time, a summer course in which he specifically taught his "clinical method" to students. One measure of the impact that Witmer's work had on the surrounding scholarly community was that, in the fall of 1897, he was elected to membership in the prestigious American Philosophical Society, a Philadelphia scientific institution dating back to the time of Benjamin Franklin.

With the outbreak of the Spanish–American War in 1898, Witmer volunteered for army duty with the First Troop, Philadelphia City Cavalry. He was stationed in Puerto Rico, but saw no action. He was able to return to his university position before the year was out. Nevertheless, his time in this legendary corps raised his stature within Philadelphia society probably as much as his membership in the Philosophical Society had.

In 1899, Witmer's clinic picked up where it had been left before the war. Initially he saw clients only once per week. After a time, he ran a daily clinic for a number of weeks at a time, presumably to handle busy periods or to clear backlogs. Decades later, his one-time student, Samuel Fernberger, would relate that Witmer saw most of the clients himself during the first decade of the clinic's existence, building his own clinical expertise, often seeing about three clients per day.[70] As Witmer's reputation grew, he started to be regularly invited to speak to various groups in the Philadelphia area about children and their education. As the most prominent psychological scientist in the city, he was sometimes asked to comment publicly on general issues of the day. In February of 1900, for instance, he was asked about the authenticity of the spiritualist Leonora Piper, who was then being promoted not only by William James, but also by Columbia University philosopher James Hyslop. Witmer deftly poked holes in Hyslop's account and, more broadly, poured doubt on Piper's claims of contact with the hereafter.[71]

FIGURE 9.2   Lightner Witmer as a young professor at Penn.

Credit: From the Collections of the University of Pennsylvania Archives.

In 1902, Witmer published his first book, *Analytical Psychology*, which contained instructions on how to conduct a collection of simple experiments. The book's aim was to facilitate the teaching of scientific psychology in the absence of specialized equipment and laboratories. The text was revised in 1907, and it stayed in print until the 1930s. In 1903, Witmer was promoted to full professor.

In 1904, Witmer was invited by Titchener to become a founding member of his new group, The Experimentalists. When asked who else should be invited, Witmer advised Titchener to exclude Cattell, Baldwin, and Münsterberg for fear that they would be "running the society in the course of a year." He also agreed with Titchener that women should be excluded from the new organization lest they be offended by the "smoke filled and coatless atmosphere" of a "vigorous association where we can speak out our minds in perfect freedom . . . owing to the personal attitude which they take even in scientific discussions."[72] Women were indeed excluded from the new group, despite the persistent protestations of Christine Ladd-Franklin.[73] It was not until 1911 that Titchener would permit two of his female students to even sit outside the door of the meeting room to secretly hear the goings-on. Women would not be permitted into the meeting proper until after Titchener's death in 1927.[74] Titchener's and Witmer's attitudes are somewhat difficult to fathom, considering how many successful female graduate students and assistants both men supervised.

Despite Titchener's misgivings about "applied" psychology, he invited Witmer to speak about his work on "backward children" at the Experimentalists' first meeting in 1904. That same year, Witmer married a staffer at the library of the American Philosophical Society, Emma Repplier. He was 37 years old at the time. In 1905, he began a three-year term on the APA Council. Mary Whiton Calkins became the first woman president of APA at the same time.

By the end of 1906, Witmer had seen nearly 100 distinct clinical cases, and he was ready to raise his operation to the next level. First, he forged formal affiliations with "training schools" for (using the terms of the day) "feeble-minded" and "mentally-deficient" children in the Philadelphia region. Next, he toured major Western cities—Chicago, St. Paul, and Denver—addressing Penn alumni groups on behalf of the university (raising his own public profile with potential donors in the process). Finally, he befriended Mary L. Corzer who, with her husband, J. Lewis Crozer, were wealthy benefactors of hospitals, colleges, and libraries in eastern Pennsylvania. In the winter of 1907, Witmer wrote his new friend a letter asking outright for the staggering sum of $10,000 to support his clinic. She initially balked, but soon agreed to make the entire donation that Witmer had requested.

This enormous boon sent Witmer into a frenzy of activity. He immediately founded a journal, *The Psychological Clinic*, through which he could to promote his work. The title of his inaugural article, "Clinical Psychology," may well have been the first time the phrase was used in print.[75] In that piece, he described his clientele as,

> children [who] had made themselves conspicuous because of an inability to progress in school work as rapidly as other children, or because of moral defect that had rendered them difficult to manage under ordinary discipline. When brought to the clinic such children are given a physical and mental examination. . . . The result of this conjoint medical and psychological examination is a diagnosis of the child's mental and physical condition and the recommendation of appropriate medical and pedagogical treatment.[76]

Witmer then described the path that had led him to found his clinic, the kinds of phenomena it typically dealt with, and his own views on the relationships of his new practice to medicine, to pedagogy, and to sociology. In addition to his introductory article, the first volume of the new journal contained 18 other articles (five authored by Witmer himself, including the full account of his first case, "Charles Gilman"). One of these articles was by the Isador Coriat, the Tufts neurologist who was already involved with the Emmanuel Movement that Witmer would excoriate in print just two years later. There were also reviews, news, and commentary.

In addition to the launch of the journal, Witmer massively expanded his core operation: the clinic took on 75 new cases in 1907, rather than the customary 15 or so. Obviously, Witmer could not handle all of these cases personally; he began hiring staff in order to remake his little clinic into a sizeable institution. In 1908, he set up a residential school as a private venture just outside of the city, in Rose Valley, to enable him to give intensive treatment to his most severe cases. This school (and its successor in Devon, PA) became the main focus of Witmer's efforts for the rest of his career. This larger operation drew ever-widening notice from educators. Requests for assistance began coming to Witmer from across the country. Imitators, inspired by his model, began setting up similar institutions in other cities. In 1909, the university recognized Witmer's tremendous success by contributing more space for Witmer's original campus-based clinic. Witmer was himself becoming a kind of national institution.

The expansion and elevation of Witmer's operation, however, seems to have led to a corresponding swelling of his ego. He began making public pronouncements on the worthiness of others' efforts to advance the field. For instance, he not only sharply criticized the Emmanuel Movement in print, as we saw above, but he ignited a heated dispute with Münsterberg (who was then developing his own system of psychotherapy), terminating what had, until then, been friendly relations between them.[77] He also rebuked William James, essentially dismissing him as a relic of the past and notoriously describing him as the "spoiled child of psychology."[78] Many in the discipline were unhappy with James' advocacy of spiritualism and psychical research, thinking that it brought disrepute to psychology, but none went so far as Witmer in also calling his very real contributions to the discipline into question. Completing a kind of "Harvard trifecta," Witmer decided to denigrate Josiah Royce's philosophical work as well. The state of his personal relations with other psychologists notwithstanding, Witmer's career was a great success. Many school children were helped and many important psychologists of the future were first trained in his laboratory, his clinic, and his school.

6. Hall and the "Discovery" of Adolescence

Although Witmer was the first to found a formal clinic for school children, he was far from the only American psychologist working on the psychology of childhood. Hall's "child study" continued apace, filling volume after volume of *Pedagogical Seminary*, an educational journal he had launched in 1891. Chicago's "raid" of his Clark faculty back in 1892 had left the school damaged, but not broken. It carried on, staffed by Hall's closest loyalists, though now dominated by its schools of psychology and pedagogy. As it did for many American psychologists, evolutionary theory played a key role in Hall's thinking about childhood and the process of maturation. Unlike nearly every other psychologist, however, it was the theory of one German naturalist in particular that drew Hall's allegiance. That theory, advanced by Ernst Haeckel of Jena, held that the embryological development of each individual organism repeats, in condensed form, the entire evolutionary history of the species as a whole.[79] Haeckel sought to establish this extraordinary claim with exquisitely detailed drawings of the *in utero* growth of diverse animals—a fish, a chicken, a pig, a human. The aim was to show that, at their earliest stages, vertebrate embryos are nearly identical—just as all animals, under Darwinian theory, evolved from a single common ancestor. However, as they develop into fetuses, they begin to diverge from each other, just as their ancient ancestors did (see Figure 9.3). Haeckel coined terms—novel at the time but now in common usage—that would allow him to summarize his theory in a single sentence: "ontogeny recapitulates phylogeny"; the development of the organism follows the same path as did the evolution of its species.

Hall adapted Haeckel's controversial claim to the theory of mental development: the thought processes and favored activities of (European) children, he claimed, recapitulate those of mature humans earlier in evolutionary history. Indeed, Hall went on, the profound cognitive and cultural differences that he believed to exist between "civilized" peoples and "savage" ones was the result of the (putative) fact that "savages" were still at this earlier stage of development, while "civilized" ones had moved on to a more "advanced" stage.[80] Stated this bluntly, the very idea makes Hall seem quite extreme in his racism. While obviously most people today would not countenance his stark distinction between "civilized" and "savage," Hall's view of "primitives," was more charitable and protective (if rather condescending) than condemnatory or vicious:

> What we call low races are not weeds in the human garden, but are essentially children and adolescents in soul, with the same good and bad qualities and needing the same kind of study and adjustment. The best of them need no less our lavish care. They have the same right to linger in the paradise of childhood. To war upon them is to war upon children, and without them our earthly home would be left desolate indeed. To commercialize and overwork them is child labor on a large scale. If unspoiled by contact with the advanced wave of civilization, which is too often its refuse and in which their best is too often unequally matched against our worst, they are mostly virtuous, simple, confiding, affectionate, and peaceful among themselves, curious, amazingly healthful, with bodies in nearly every function superior to ours and frequently models for the artist.[81]

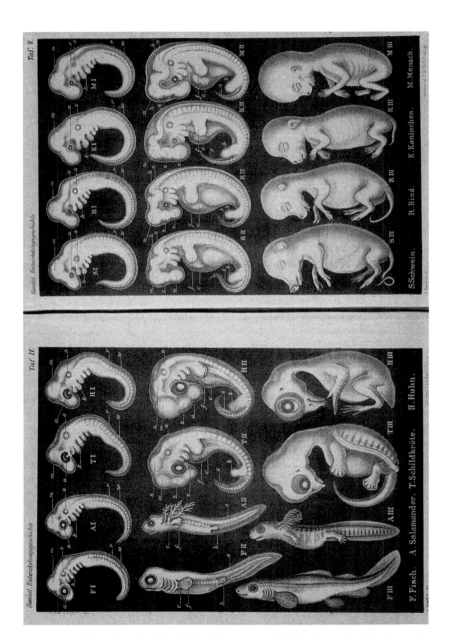

FIGURE 9.3 Plate from E. Haeckel's *Anthropogenie* (1874), illustrating his claim that ontogeny recapitulates phylogeny.

Hall's acceptance and psychological extension of Haeckel's view dated back to the start of his career,[82] but it became more pronounced as his ideas became more elaborately articulated in the early 20th century. It may have reached its pinnacle in 1904, when he published the most important book of his long career, *Adolescence*.[83] The term is common enough today, but it was the impact of Hall and his book that raised it from an obscure bit of technical jargon into a word that everyone now recognizes and understands.

There can be little doubt that the popularity of Hall's book was the product of two growing national trends: the popular campaign against child labor and the high school movement. After decades of agitation against child labor by workers' unions, in 1892 the national Democratic Party called for a ban on all labor by children under the age of 15. By the end of the 1890s, John Dewey and Jane Addams had both become outspoken advocates for children's rights. In 1903, the legendary labor leader Mary Harris "Mother" Jones—the "most dangerous woman in America," as she was dubbed by West Virginia's US District Attorney Reese Blizzard—organized the "Children's Crusade," a mass march against child labor from Philadelphia to Roosevelt's home on Long Island (NY). The following year, 1904, saw the founding of the National Child Labor Committee (NCLC), which called for the abolition of all child labor. The NCLC included in its early membership such luminaries as former US president Grover Cleveland and long-time Harvard president, Charles Eliot.

As with Jacob Riis' work on the New York slums more than decade earlier, the topic of child labor gained widespread popular attention when a photographer, Lewis Hine, visually documented for all to see the dreadful conditions in which many American children were forced to work. Hine was well-educated: he had taken sociology degrees at Chicago and Columbia before becoming a New York City school teacher. He soon quit that job, though, to become a full-time photographer of some of America's most pervasive, but well-hidden, social challenges. Starting in 1904, he began photographing the thousands of immigrants who arrived daily at Ellis Island, the massive immigration-reception center just off Manhattan. Then, in 1908, he took a position as photographer for the NCLC, which is how he came to record the plight of working children, especially in the Carolina Piedmont, a region stretching from New Jersey in the north, through eastern Pennsylvania, Maryland, Virginia, the Carolinas, and into Georgia and Alabama. It was this work, more than anything else, that made child labor a national issue.

The second trend that drew national attention to the special needs of teenagers was a mass movement to make high school education universal.[84] Although teenagers had, up to the turn of the 20th century, been widely seen as little more than young adults who should be put to work as soon as possible (but for the few who had the advantages conferred by a privileged background), a slowly growing practice of keeping children in school until the age of 17 or so made evident the special psychological challenges posed by the teenage years. The start of the "high

FIGURE 9.4 "Midnight at the Glassworks," a photograph by Lewis Hine of children working in Indiana, 1908.

school movement," usually dated to 1910, arrived a little after Hall's book was published. But, when adolescence was recognized as a special concern beyond the boundaries of the discipline of psychology, Hall's monumental work was already there for the movement to draw upon. The book was fortuitously positioned to take advantage of these two swelling political tides.

In two stout volumes, totaling over 1,300 pages, Hall put forth everything that he had learned about mental growth between roughly the ages of 12 and 20. Haeckel's grip on Hall's thought was displayed on the very first page, where Hall stated with admirable directness, "Individual growth recapitulates the history of the race."[85] Studying adolescence was particularly important for Hall not just because of what it told us about individual development, but also because of what (he thought) it told us about human evolutionary history. He speculated that:

> The child from nine to twelve is well adjusted to his environment and proportionately developed; he represents probably an old and relatively perfect stage of race-maturity. . . . [A] terminal stage of development at some post-simian point. At dawning of adolescence, this old unity and harmony with nature is broken up; the child is driven from his paradise and must enter upon a long viaticum of ascent, must conquer a higher kingdom of man for himself, break out a new sphere, and evolve a more modern story to his psycho-physical nature."[86]

So important was evolution in Hall's general cast of mind that, nearly 20 years later, he exulted that "there was a kind of mystic prelusion by which Darwin, Huxley, Spencer, Haeckel, and even Tyndall were, it seemed to me, prepared for in my philosophic history."[87] He even included a photograph of Haeckel his autobiography.

Although Hall's work was so speculative in places as to make it seem a relic of an earlier era, other younger psychologists were eager to bring modern science to bear on the questions of childhood and education. The same year as Hall published, *Adolescence*, Thorndike, then at Columbia's Teachers College, published *Theory of Mental and Social Measurements*, an early statistics textbook. Although he had made his name in the arena of animal learning, Thorndike changed course once he joined Teacher's College, becoming a champion of quantification and objective measurement in the field of education.[88] His oft-quoted motto was, "Whatever exists at all, exists in some amount," and the measurement of that "amount" was one of his primary goals.[89]

He conducted some of the earliest studies on the inheritance of intellectual ability using twins.[90] Although he did not distinguish between identical and fraternal twins (the genetic significance of the difference not being understood at the time), he found that twins were more similar in ability on average than non-twin siblings.[91] He would go on to become an early leader in intelligence and standardized achievement testing.[92] Thorndike also wrote a number of school textbooks, particularly in arithmetic, as well as children's dictionaries, redesigning them to be more relevant to younger students' needs.

7. Psychology at the St. Louis Congress of Arts and Sciences

The year 1904 also saw one of the greatest academic conferences in North American history, and psychologists more than played their part. The main event was the Louisiana Purchase Exposition, a world's fair held in St. Louis just 11 years after the Columbian Exposition in Chicago had brought the world to St. Louis' longtime rival. Perhaps ironically, it was the University of Chicago's president, William Rainey Harper, who suggested that an International Congress of Arts and Sciences should be held in conjunction with the St. Louis Fair. Plans began two years before, in 1902, with an advisory Board that consisted of Harper, the president of Columbia University (and early APA member) Nicholas Murray Butler, as well as an American diplomat of German birth named Frederick Holls. Simon Newcomb was appointed president of the congress, but the main responsibility for planning the event and inviting European speakers soon fell to none other than Hugo Münsterberg (who was already well acquainted with Holls). Münsterberg, Newcomb, and Chicago sociologist Albion Small drew up a list of some 300 potential speakers, including more than 100 Europeans. Many of the Europeans refused (including Wundt), while others initially agreed to attend, but later withdrew. There was also bitter contention between Germany and France over which of the two rival nations received more invitations. In the end, over a hundred European scholars and scientists came to present their views, including such luminaries as mathematician Henri Poincaré, physicist Ernest Rutherford, and sociologist Max Weber.[93]

Of all the various disciplinary sections of the Congress, the one closest to Münsterberg's heart was, of course, the one devoted to psychology. The speakers included Münsterberg himself, naturally, and many figures we have already encountered: Hall, Ladd, Titchener, Cattell, Baldwin, Meyer, Royce, Sanford, and Calkins, along with a promising young lecturer from Chicago named John B. Watson (among others). The impressive European contingent included C. Lloyd Morgan of Bristol, Pierre Janet of the Collège de France, James Ward of Cambridge, Harold Høffding of Copenhagen, and Max Dessoir of Berlin.[94]

Münsterberg had attempted to organize the presentations according to rather abstract "logical" principles (normative, historical, physical, and mental) that were supposed to demonstrate the essential unity of all knowledge. This scheme was opposed by Münsterberg's fellow committee member, Small, who proposed an arrangement that reflected more humane categories (health, wealth, religion, and harmony in human relationships).[95] Münsterberg's plan ultimately held sway, but the matter rankled the pragmatic Americans so greatly that it became a topic of debate in its own right. John Dewey, for instance, criticized the decision in print before even a single talk had been delivered.[96] James Rowland Angell noted in a summary of the proceedings after the fact that, "the unification of knowledge which this congress was to glorify is, in this department [psychology] at least, is for the most part a figment of the imagination, an ideal toward which progress may ultimately bear us, but from which at the present moment we are conspicuously remote."[97]

Most of the talks, Angell lamented, opted to take stock of the discipline's past, "cater[ing] to a retrospective and somewhat obituary attitude of mind."[98] The sole exception for Angell was the "delightful persiflage of parts of Mr. Cattell's paper."[99] Cattell's "brilliant and racy,"[100] talk, openly repudiated Münsterberg's effort to formally define the boundaries and categories of science. "Sciences are not immutable species, but developing organisms," he declared.[101] Every person, indeed every day, creates its own science and, from among these, "there arises by a kind of natural selection a *quasi* objective science of psychology."[102] Like science more broadly, psychology has no set definition either; the psychologist is free to study whatever he likes with whatever methods seem likely to bear fruit. Cattell even dismissed the self-evidence of the distinction between mind and matter, declaring it an empirical matter yet to be worked out, rather than an axiom that the psychologist must accept. "Matter and consciousness may not be two entities set over against each other. . . . I am not convinced that psychology should be limited to the study of consciousness as such, in so far as this can be set off from the physical world."[103]

Perhaps the most interesting part of Cattell's thought here was the nonchalance with which he dismantled the austere vision of pure psychology that had been so assiduously assembled by Titchener over the previous decade:

> The rather widespread notion that there is no psychology apart from intro-spection is refuted by the brute argument of accomplished fact.
>
> It seems to me that most of the research work that has been done by me or in my laboratory is nearly as independent of introspection as work in physics or in zoology. The time of mental processes, the accuracy of percep-tion and movement, the range of consciousness, fatigue and practise, the motor accompaniments of thought, memory, the association of ideas, the perception of space, color-vision, preferences, judgments, individual differ-ences, the behavior of animals and of children, these and other topics I have investigated without requiring the slightest introspection on the part of the subject or undertaking such on my own part during the course of the experiments. It is usually no more necessary for the subject to be a psy-chologist than it is for the vivisected frog to be a physiologist.[104]

Not only did Cattell here demolish Titchener's methodological imperative that introspection is the One True Method of experimental psychology, he also flat-tened Titchener's carefully erected barrier between pure and applied psychology: "It may also be true that pure science should precede the applications of science. But of this I am not sure; it appears to me that the conditions are most health-ful when science and its applications proceed hand in hand, as is now the case in engineering, electricity, chemistry, medicine, etc."[105] It is sometimes suggested that Cattell's comments in St. Louis foreshadowed the coming behaviorist "revo-lution." That probably goes too far, however.[106] He was really just stating with admirable succinctness what Titchener's Functionalist opponents had been saying all along. The difference was that few had said it in quite so blunt a fashion, nor in quite so public a forum. The days of circumspection about Titchener's Structural-ist position were quickly coming to an end.

8. Psychology's "Discovery" of Women

One of the most obvious human "variations" that had not received much atten-tion in the psychology laboratory was whether women systematically differ from men in their psychological makeup. From the start, psychology had been some-what more hospitable to women than most sciences.[107] That did not mean, of course, that they had anything approaching real equality. As we saw in earlier chapters, both Christine Ladd-Franklin and Mary Whiton Calkins were denied PhDs by Johns Hopkins and Harvard, respectively, despite having completed the degree requirements. There were no women students in Wundt's laboratory until Anna Berliner arrived in 1914. Titchener would not allow women into his

"Experimentalists" group, despite the fact that four of the six PhD students he graduated at Cornell in the 1890s had been women.[108] Still, women were accepted into most activities of the discipline, such as the APA. Calkins even became the first woman president of the APA in 1905. Washburn would serve as the second, though not until 1921.

Arguments against higher education for women were as many and varied as there were men who did not want women in college classrooms. Some felt that women were simply incapable of higher thought. Others felt that higher education might be positively hazardous to women physically, mentally, and socially (i.e., it would damage their marriage prospects). As a result of the general refusal to accept women in the colleges that already existed, a number of separate women's colleges were set up in America during the mid-19th century. The first was Mt. Holyoke, founded in 1837. A full bachelor's degree was not offered to women, however, until the opening of Vassar College in 1865 (where Christine Ladd studied, starting in 1866).

One of the most common beliefs about the psychological differences between women and men in the late 19th century was that men simply had larger brains than women did and, therefore, greater mental ability. There was also a widespread assumption that women's mental powers tended more toward the instinctual and emotional rather than to the intellectual. As anatomical studies of the brain began to show that, proportionally to their body size, women's brains were not smaller than men's (and may even have been proportionally larger), a more refined argument was required.[109]

One of the more ingenious was that men were not mentally superior to women overall, but that men displayed greater *variation* in their mental abilities than women did. This idea, known as the "Variability Hypothesis," served a couple of distinct rhetorical purposes. First, it explained both why men seemed to rise to greater intellectual heights than women as well as why men also seemed to sink to greater depths of depravity and criminality. Second, it did all this while being able to politely maintain that, *on average*, women and men are mental equals. It is just that, in practice, women do not rise as far because the *range* of their abilities is not as great.

In 1891, Joseph Jastrow decided to test this popular hypothesis by asking the students in his one of his classes to write down 100 different words as quickly as they could.[110] He found that, collectively, the men chose a somewhat wider range of words than women (1,376 versus 1,123, a difference of about 20%). He took this result as evidence in favor of the variability hypothesis. In 1895, Mary Whiton Calkins and one of her Wellesley students, Cordelia Nevers, decided to attempt a replication of Jastrow's experiment.[111] They found that the women students of Wellesley performed much more similarly to Jastrow's Wisconsin men than to his Wisconsin women. Various explanations for the discrepancy were exchanged,[112] and no firm conclusion was reached, but male psychologists were put on notice that female psychologists were prepared to respond—with data—to any claims in this area that they felt were not adequately judicious.

In 1900, a student of Angell's at Chicago, Helen Bradford Thompson, completed a doctoral dissertation on sex differences. Published in 1903, Thompson made careful tests of motor ability (e.g., reaction time), sensation (in all five traditional modalities), intellect, and affect. Her conclusions were: (1) Men, perhaps not surprisingly, had the advantage in strength, speed, and physical endurance. (2) The results with sensation were mixed, though they favored women slightly. (3) In intellect, women had "decidedly" better memories while men had an advantage in "ingenuity." (4) There was little measurable difference in the realm of feeling. More important than the brute differences though, were their probable sources. Thompson concluded that what differences there were did not result from inherent disparities in capacity or disposition but, rather, from "differences in the social influence brought to bear on the developing individual from early infancy to adult years."[113]

Some older psychologists, like Stanley Hall, dismissed Thompson's findings in favor of their old prejudices.[114] Some younger psychologists, however, such as Edward Thorndike, welcomed Thompson's conclusions as authentic contributions to science.[115] Kate Gordon, a 1903 doctoral graduate of Chicago, scoffed at the image of women put forward by Hall as positively medieval. In response to the claim that co-education would masculinize women (and possibly effeminize men), Gordon pointed out that, if men and women can marry and live together without harm, then surely they can be in school together for a few hours a day without danger.[116] Like many other academic women, Gordon's career trajectory would not be straightforward. She passed through a number of different short-term teaching jobs over the course of two decades before UCLA finally offered her an associate professorship in 1923, at the age of 45. She was promoted to full professor in 1934.

Indeed, it was not uncommon that, even once women received a graduate education, they were unable to obtain a permanent academic post, except in the women's colleges. Christine Ladd-Franklin, who had been working since the 1890s with a group called the Association of Collegiate Alumnae to create scholarships for women, was never offered any position better than an unpaid lectureship at Columbia, despite her recognized status in the fields of both logic and color vision. Lillien Jane Martin, a Vassar graduate who attended Göttingen for advanced research, won a permanent position at Stanford in 1899. She was promoted to the rank of professor in 1911, but hers was a very rare case.[117]

Often, marriage was the critical determinant. Ethel Puffer, for instance, had completed the requirements for a PhD under the supervision of Münsterberg at Harvard in 1898 but, as with Calkins a few years before, the degree had gone unawarded. In 1902 Harvard offered both women a PhD from Radcliffe, Harvard's extension college for women. Puffer accepted, but Calkins refused, pointing out that she had never attended Radcliffe. Even though Puffer had a PhD, once she married, in 1908, even Columbia's women's college, Barnard, refused to hire her.

One of the breakthrough cases was that of Leta Stetter Hollingworth.[118] She had become engaged to her University of Nebraska classmate, Harry Hollingworth. When Harry moved to New York to do his PhD at Columbia under Cattell, Leta stayed behind in the Cornhusker State for a time teaching high school. When she finally joined him in New York and the two were wed, she discovered that married women were not allowed to teach in the city's public schools. With few job prospects, she decided to get a master's degree in education at Columbia, which she completed in 1913. She then became the first "psychologist," so titled, in the New York Civil Service, administering intelligence tests to the children who were then termed "mental defectives." She soon returned to Columbia for a PhD under Thorndike. Her dissertation focused on whether, as was widely believed, women suffered a periodic mental decline during menstruation. She was able to find no evidence of such a phenomenon, and was awarded her degree in 1916.[119] Although she was offered a professorship in education at Teacher's College, her career truly flourished outside of the academy. She became best known for her work with "gifted" children, a term that she coined. She was also instrumental in the organization of the American Association of Clinical Psychologists, a group that came together in 1917 in response to the APA's refusal, at that time, to admit professional, nonacademic psychologists as members.

9. Münsterberg's Emergence as "America's Most Famous Psychologist"

As we saw in the last chapter, during the final years of the 19th century, Harvard's Hugo Münsterberg was adamantly, even vitriolically, opposed to the application of psychological knowledge to everyday realms such as education.[120] As the century turned, though, he reversed his opinion and declared that scientific psychology had now progressed far enough to be effectively applied, after all. It is easy to suggest that Münsterberg's exposure to attitudes in the US, and perhaps a desire to fit in to his new home, explained his profound change of heart. However, there is little indication that Münsterberg's guiding presumption that American "culture" was inherent inferior to German *Kultur* had changed. Instead, the trigger for his about-face was more probably the recent appearance of prominent psychologists *in Germany* who had begun to pursue practical psychology in a diverse array of fields.

Wundt had long frowned upon applied psychology and the related study of individual differences. His fear had been that, in the German educational context of the time, emphasizing practical knowledge would undermine experimental psychology's claim to be a natural science and, as such, a university discipline. Such a diminishment of its status would, under the Prussian system, have consigned the topic to the technical schools, a fate that Wundt would never have accepted for himself.

By the start of the 20th century, however, the climate had changed somewhat, and William Stern—a professor at Breslau (present-day Wrocław, Poland) who had once been a student of the memory research pioneer Hermann Ebbinghaus in Berlin—published a book titled *Uber Psychologie der individuellen Differenzen* (*The Psychology of Individual Differences*) in 1900 without any notable harm to his academic reputation.[121] Stern, who would later invent the idea of the intelligence quotient (IQ), followed his book on individual differences with a 1903 article called "Angewandte Psychologie" (Applied Psychology).[122] Soon after, he would establish an entire journal, *Zeitschrift für angewandte Psychologie* (*Journal of Applied Psychology*) and, in 1906, he would co-found an Institute in Berlin devoted to the topic.

Other Germans soon followed Stern's lead. Ernst Meumann, for instance, was a former student of Wundt's who had taken his old professor's position at Zurich in 1896. He did not hold to the Leipzig model of a purely experimental psychology, however. He pointedly founded a journal for "the whole of psychology" (*Archiv für die gesamte Psychologie*) in 1903 to succeed Wundt's *Philosophische Studien*. In 1911 he co-founded a journal dedicated to the explicitly applied topic of educational psychology (*Zeitschrift für Pädagogische Psychologie und Experimentelle Pädagogik*).

With this newfound Imperial German approval, applied psychology could now be regarded as a legitimate pursuit for even so upright and eminent a professor as Münsterberg. The Harvard man quickly scrambled to become the leader of the field he had, for so long, dismissed as worthless. The approval of his fellow Germans may not have been the only reason that Münsterberg suddenly embraced the applied form of the discipline so enthusiastically. In March of 1905, he was finally offered what he had always most sought: a German professorship. The call came from Königsberg, a provincial university in far northeastern Prussia, but the chair had once been held by Immanuel Kant, and the location was not far from his childhood home. Also, once ensconced back in Germany, it was possible that he would be called to more prestigious positions in due course. Münsterberg vacillated. German colleagues told him it was time for him to come home to finally claim his due. American colleagues, however—including some who, like him, had emigrated from Germany—advised him to stay in America where the social and intellectual strictures were less confining than in his homeland. At first, he tentatively accepted the job, pending permission to stay at Harvard for one more year; he had been the driving force behind the construction of a new building for philosophy and psychology at Harvard, Emerson Hall, and he wished to see the project through to its completion.[123] After further consideration, though, he withdrew his acceptance of the Königsberg chair, telling both his prospective employer and himself that his talents would go to better use in America than they would in Germany. Having decided to permanently throw his lot in with America, applied psychology, crudely technical as it might have seemed before, now appeared as the most opportune path to (ever greater) professional status and public prominence in his adopted home.

The following year, 1906, there was a sensational murder case in Chicago. A man, possibly of limited intellectual capacity, had confessed to the murder of a young woman, under the sway of police interrogation. The accused, Richard Ivins, was sentenced to death for the crime. Ivins' defense attorney claimed that the confession was false and had been the result of hypnotic suggestion. He called upon various "experts" to publicly comment on the case. James and Münsterberg both published opinions. James called for more investigation. Münsterberg, by contrast, proclaimed his certainty, on the basis of the written record alone, that Ivins was innocent and that "dissociation and auto suggestion" had been at play in the confession.[124]

The Harvard professors' interventions were ignored by the courts of Illinois, and Ivins was executed as scheduled. Nevertheless, with this declaration of special expertise, Münsterberg began to publicly develop a theory that the American justice system was hidebound by ancient assumptions about the value of "common sense." The time had finally come, he thought, to favor the testimony of specialists who were better equipped than ordinary witnesses to protect their perceptions and conclusions from bias and distortion.[125] Some psychologists agreed, but the legal community, by and large, strenuously opposed the German professor's view.[126]

In 1907, Münsterberg continued this new line of work, becoming involved in another high-profile murder case, this time in Idaho. "Big Bill" Haywood was a national labor leader who had just, in 1905, founded the Industrial Workers of the World, an organization that was widely seen as being more "radical" than traditional unions (mainly because its sheer size threatened the possibility of a general strike that could bring industries across the country to a halt). Haywood was accused of having ordered the murder of a former governor of Idaho named Frank Steunenberg. The accusation came, interestingly enough, from the actual assassin, a man named Harry Orchard. Orchard had originally denied involvement, but had been interrogated by none other than James McParland, the Pinkerton investigator who had putatively "broken" the notorious Molly McGuires case thirty years earlier.[127] McParland promised Orchard leniency if he fingered those who had put him up to the crime. Orchard named those who McParland and Idaho government officials most wanted to implicate—a group of Western labor leaders that included Haywood. There was no physical evidence connecting Haywood to the Steunenberg case, and only tenuous connections between Haywood and Orchard, but McParland arranged to have Haywood arrested in Denver and secretly spirited out of Colorado to Idaho before the courts could intervene.

The case became a national sensation, and the popular magazine *McClure's* commissioned Münsterberg to set forth his views on the case. Münsterberg traveled to Idaho with a box full of laboratory equipment. After ingratiating himself to local officials there, he was permitted to visit Orchard in jail. Once inside, Münsterberg proceeded to test the truth of Orchard's accusations. Even as a laboratory psychologist of long experience, there were no standard methods for Münsterberg

FIGURE 9.5   "Science vs. the 3rd Degree, Or Will Psychology Unmask Crime," anonymous cover article in *Washington Times* (Magazine Section), Oct 20, 1907.

to call upon to assess "truth." He was, however, deeply impressed by the potential of the timed word-association test that Carl Jung had recently developed to assess psychopathology.[128] The idea was that it normally takes a certain amount of time, when presented with a word, for a person to generate another word that is associated with it (e.g., dog-cat, hot-cold). However, if there is a mental conflict associated with the word presented, the time it takes to produce an associate interval might be lengthened or otherwise distorted. For instance, if the tester says "blood" and the subject delays even a fraction of a second longer than he normally would in coming up with a related word, the subject's normal mental processes may have been disrupted by a disturbing event that he associates with blood—for instance, a murder that he committed.

After testing Orchard in this and various other ways, Münsterberg became convinced that his accusations were true, that Haywood was guilty of ordering the murder. In the article he wrote for *McClure's*, however, he was more circumspect about his findings.[129] This turned out to be a wise choice, for Haywood had something better going for him than Münsterberg's chronoscope. He had the famous lawyer Clarence Darrow leading his defense team. Darrow eviscerated Orchard on the stand, forcing him to confess not only to other bombings before he had ever even met Haywood, but also to having accepted cash from the Pinkerton Agency for his incriminating confession. With Orchard's credibility destroyed, Haywood was acquitted.

Even if Münsterberg has been wrong about Orchard, he had simultaneously managed to create the field of forensic psychology, virtually out of thin air. He quickly collected together various magazine articles he had written on the topic and produced a book: *On the Witness Stand: Essays on Psychology and Crime.*[130] The book's most explosive contention was that a longtime mainstay of American jurisprudence—the assumption that the eyewitness is a nearly infallible source of evidence—was deeply flawed. He described a plethora of ways, known primarily only to laboratory psychologists, whereby people can be fooled by tricks of perception and cognition, into being certain they have witnessed things that did not really happen (at least, not as they remember them). In undermining the credibility of eyewitnesses, he simultaneously put forward the corollary that psychologists are uniquely qualified by their scientific training to tell which witnesses are correct and which are deluded.

The idea that truth could be "scientifically" distinguished from falsehood quickly caught on with the press and with the public. Münsterberg continued to develop his popular new craft. He experimented with muscular twitches of the hand, as well as changes in breathing rate and vascular pulse as signs of possible deception. One of Münsterberg's students, William Moulton Marston (BA 1915, PhD 1921) would later develop the idea that changes in blood pressure were an even better means of lie detection.[131] Marston's discovery would soon be included in the "polygraph" developed by John Larson, a Canadian psychologist hired by the Berkeley police who is often identified as the inventor of the "lie detector." Marston would go on to a fascinatingly unorthodox life and career developing, among other things, the cartoon character Wonder Woman who, notably, could compel confessions from criminals with her Golden Lasso of Truth.[132]

Münsterberg's work in this line became so well known that his persona served as the basis of a series of popular short stories written by two *Chicago Tribune* writers (and brothers-in-law) Edwin Balmer and William MacHarg. Their main character, Luther Trant, was an advanced psychology student who used the equipment and techniques of the experimental psychology laboratory to crack crimes that had stumped the police. The stories were originally published serially in *Hampton's Magazine*, in 1909 and 1910, and were later collected together in book form.[133] Interestingly, Balmer also authored a slim volume titled *The Science of Advertising*, a topic to which Münsterberg would also make important contributions.[134] Balmer probably achieved his greatest fame later, in 1933 when he co-authored with Philip Wylie the science fiction novel *When Worlds in Collide* (and its 1934 sequel, *After Worlds Collide*). He would also edit the popular women's magazine *Redbook* from 1927 to 1949.

Although forensics was where Münsterberg made his first splash in applied psychology, it was far from the only practical area into which he enthusiastically threw himself. As we saw earlier, he was involved in the debate over the Emmanuel Movement, writing a book of his own on psychotherapy in which he claimed to have successfully treated hundreds of patients.[135] The book came out at a time when no less an authority than Adolf Meyer complained that, "psychotherapy is in the air and wildly exploited in the book-market and in magazines."[136] In short, it was precisely the kind of topic that would enable Münsterberg to have more public impact. He could not choose between the tugs of two different audiences—the professional and the popular—so he wrote *Psychotherapy* with the hope of appealing to both audiences. In the first part, he set forth an array of abstract foundations that even the author admitted would probably bore or baffle the novice reader, but interest the expert. It was followed by a section in which he described various mental conditions and their treatments. He thought might would be more interesting (and perhaps more entertaining) to a lay audience. Reviewing the book, Meyer concluded that Münsterberg had failed, though sometimes in interesting ways, to achieve his goal of satisfactorily addressing the two diverse audiences simultaneously; that it would have been better if he had simply written two books.

Münsterberg's primary biographer, Mathew Hale, characterized his approach to psychotherapy as "functional," though the Harvard professor did not openly align himself with the Functionalist psychologists of his day, even though the influence of that school of thought was then at its high point.[137] Indeed, Münsterberg explicitly distanced himself from Adolf Meyer, saying that psychotherapy was "sharply to be separated" from psychiatry.[138] Psychiatry was to be reserved for serious "mental disease," while the psychotherapy was for "the mild abnormalities of mind, and especially the nervous disturbances which exist outside the field of insanity."[139] More philosophically, or perhaps just enigmatically, he also claimed that psychotherapy was "the last word of the passing naturalistic movement, and yet in another way tries to be the first word in the coming idealistic movement."[140]

Jousting with psychiatry was not his primary object, though. He aimed, rather at demarcating the boundary between psychiatry's "turf" and his own. The faction he most vehemently opposed was, instead, psychoanalysis, which was just beginning to receive a hearing in the psychiatric world. He felt that Freud's emphasis on unconscious motivation was utterly misguided. "The story of the subconscious mind," he bluntly proclaimed, "can be told in three words: there is none."[141] So complete was his contempt for the rising Viennese star that, nearly alone among prominent eastern-US psychologists, Münsterberg did not attend Freud's and Jung's appearances at Clark in 1909, preferring to vacation in Canada instead.

Rather than delving into the subconscious, Münsterberg's approach to therapy was to adjust outward conduct so that it better suited societal demands. He was promiscuous when it came to method. Sometimes he used hypnosis, sometimes direct instruction, sometimes drugs. Even an appeal to religious ideas, though fraught with dangers in Münsterberg's opinion, could sometimes be put to effective use.[142] In his mind, all of these techniques drew their legitimacy from being tied back to the findings of "scientific" psychology. He did not consider the speculations of Freud and others, even if based upon individual cases, to be an adequate basis for valid theorizing.

Beyond forensics and psychotherapy, Münsterberg also made sizeable contributions to the burgeoning fields of vocational guidance and testing. He became involved with the Boston Vocation Bureau, an enterprise pioneered by a lawyer and social reformer named Frank Parsons. As with his forays into law and therapy, Münsterberg again argued that scientific training imbues the psychologist with an ability to discern a person's best vocational path, even when the subjects themselves may be unable to see it.[143] He eventually wrote two textbooks on the topic.[144] He also contributed to the early psychological study of business and industry, as we shall see next chapter.

It seems that Münsterberg felt that nary a topic was beyond the possibility of his beneficent intervention. As popular sentiment began to grow in favor of the prohibition of alcohol, for instance, the eminent professor weighed in publicly to argue that prohibition would likely bring with it a number of negative social and psychological side effects that would ultimately outweigh the evil it had been intended to correct.[145] The alcohol question had, of course, for decades been a source of tension between "old stock" Protestant Americans on the one hand, and newer immigrant groups from Germany, Ireland, and elsewhere. Münsterberg's article, measured and reasonable though it seemed, led to scandal when it was revealed that he had received funds for a number of his Harvard research projects from one of the leading brewers of beer in the US, Adolphus Busch (a fellow German emigrant). There is no evidence that Münsterberg was paid in advance to promote the cause; his positions were his own.[146] However, the appearance of collusion was difficult to erase, and Münsterberg's perhaps overly-broad denials led to a growing public suspicion of his motives that soon threatened to topple both the popular and academic statures that he had worked so assiduously to attain.

Although Münsterberg's Harvard colleague, William James, is widely and correctly praised for the humaneness of his thought, it is interesting to contrast

Münsterberg's growing interest, during the first decade of the 20th century, in problems that beset urban America—crime, labor strife, vocation, business, alcoholism—with James' general aloofness from them. However humane James might have been, his chief interests seemed to grow ever more esoteric and abstract.

Relations between James and Münsterberg had become increasingly strained over the years—the Emerson Hall dispute was mentioned above—but the matter that finally led to a permanent break between them was, of all things, the authenticity (or not) of a popular Italian spiritualist named Eusapia Palladino. Palladino was one of the most celebrated mediums in the world at the time. The strange thing was that she had already been caught using fraudulent methods, but her supporters were mostly undeterred, dismissing these embarrassments as mere attempts to enhance the impact of her true abilities. William James was among her apologists. The manager of her American sojourn was a British-born magazine editor named Hereward Carrington. Carrington was also an assistant to a prominent psychical researcher and Columbia University philosopher-psychologist named James Hyslop.

Carrington invited several American scientists, including Münsterberg, to observe Palladino's séances and evaluate her abilities. At first they agreed, on the condition that they would be able to conduct controlled experiments, but they soon got word that they would only be passive observers and, worse still, that Carrington was using their agreement to participate as an advertising gimmick. Almost all of them withdrew.[147] Münsterberg, however, prodded by James, agreed to attend a séance despite his skepticism of the entire event. It took place a week before Christmas in 1909. Many of the standard spiritualist phenomena were manifested—strange raps and knocks, inexplicable gusts of wind, unexplained bulging of curtains, etc. Münsterberg noted, however, that they all occurred no more that three feet from the medium, never in a more distant part of the room. Then, in the midst of the session, one of Münsterberg's assistants, while checking for wires under the furniture, caught Palladino's flesh-and-bone foot in the act of attempting to "levitate" a table.[148]

Münsterberg, now more convinced than ever that Palladino was a fraud, wrote an article exposing her trickery and published it in the February, 1910 issue of *Metropolitan Magazine*.[149] James was beside himself with fury. He tried to excuse what even he described as her "detestable" performance as just another instance of her gilding the lily of her authentic powers. In a letter to the British physicist and fellow spiritualism-enthusiast Oliver Lodge, he called Münsterberg's piece a "buffoon article."[150] To Palladino's American manager he called it "disgraceful."[151] To the French psychologist Théodore Flournoy, he described it as "infamous."[152] But even this storm of defensiveness could not change the facts. A few weeks later, Wisconsin psychologist Joseph Jastrow snuck two hidden observers under the table of a Palladino séance where she did not know she was being tested and caught her rigging the game even more flagrantly than Münsterberg had. The jig was up; Palladino was revealed to be a fraud.

10. James' Final Philosophy

William James did not often make public appearances at overtly political events, but in October of 1904 he took the stage at the Universal Peace Conference, which was held in Boston.[153] The conference was but one manifestation of a popular peace movement that had arisen in the US in the aftermath of the Spanish–American War, and in opposition to the bellicose pronouncements of the new president, Teddy Roosevelt. The war had, at a stroke, transformed the US from a nation that viewed itself as largely neutral and isolationist into a burgeoning imperial power, with colonies not only in the nearby Gulf of Mexico, but also in the far flung South Pacific.

The imposition of American rule in the Pacific had not occurred peacefully. Philippine Revolutionaries, who had already been fighting Spanish colonial rule when the Americans arrived, simply redirected their fight against American forces once it became clear that the US would not be granting independence to the islands. A brutal three-year conflict ensued, causing tens of thousands of Filipino casualties. Reports of terrible atrocities by American forces gradually made their way into the US press despite strenuous efforts by the Army to suppress them. Many Americans simply could not understand how their nation had so swiftly changed from apparent defender of the oppressed into being just the latest in a long line of cruel colonial oppressors.

William James' exact political leanings have been notoriously difficult to pinpoint. He has been cast by various authors as a social democrat, a radical participatory democrat, a communitarian, a populist, a crypto-capitalist, even an anarchist.[154] In 1884 he had identified with a group of upper-class New Englanders and New Yorkers who could not abide the corruption that clung the Republican candidate for president, James G. Blaine, and so bolted to the Democratic candidate, Grover Cleveland. They were led by Boston "Brahmin" Adams brothers, Henry and Charles Jr., and they came to be called the Mugwumps. James' university president, Charles Eliot, counted himself among their number as well. Even here, James was an uncomfortable fit. The Mugwumps mostly abandoned the Democratic Party when it nominated populist William Jennings Bryan for the first time in 1896, but James had some positive things to say about Bryan, though he did not actively support him. On the other hand, Mugwumps were at the forefront of the Anti-Imperialist League when it launched in 1898, the political movement to which James devoted himself most publicly.

True to his natural cast of mind, James began to theorize about why war had such a strong psychological appeal that it seemingly could not be suppressed by even the most "advanced" civilizations. His speech at the Universal Peace Conference of 1904 began a line of thought on this matter that led to a famous 1906 lecture at Stanford titled "The Moral Equivalent of War" which, in 1910, would become James' very last work published in his lifetime.[155] Whereas most other speakers at the conference aimed to cast war as primitive throwback to an earlier time in human history that held no proper place in "advanced" society, James argued, by contrast, that the adventure and self-sacrifice of war continued to hold an irresistible grip on the human mind. If true, efforts to simply banish it as "beneath" modern civilization would never succeed. Instead, he proposed that we should create new outlets to satisfy these deep psychological needs that did not also result in war's terrible human consequences. Instead of a war against other humans, he declared, we needed a war against nature in its place:

> To coal and iron mines, to freight trains, to fishing fleets in December, to dishwashing, clotheswashing, and windowwashing, to road-building and tunnel-making, to foundries and stoke-holes, and to the frames of skyscrapers, would our gilded youths be drafted off, according to their choice, to get the childishness knocked out of them, and to come back into society with healthier sympathies and soberer ideas.[156]

Although the idea that nature is an enemy that we must, or even can, perennially fight against now seems foolish, James' "moral equivalent" argument is often seen as the starting point for later national and international service projects, such as the Works Progress Administration developed by Franklin Roosevelt during the Great Depression of the 1930s, and the Peace Corps, founded by the US government in the 1960s.

Direct interventions in public affairs like this were unusual for James. His efforts were more commonly directed at his philosophical projects. The same year as his speech at the Universal Peace Conference, James also published two articles that exploded what was widely taken to be the central concept of psychology: consciousness. The articles appeared in the latest of James McKeen Cattell's many publishing ventures—*The Journal of Philosophy, Psychology, and Scientific Methods*—and they immediately established the new periodical's scholarly reputation. Titled "Does 'Consciousness' Exist?" and "A World of Pure Experience," the two essays crystalized themes that had run through James' thought for decades into the explicit foundations for a position that he dubbed "radical empiricism."[157] This revolutionary stance would constitute the final stop on James' lifelong philosophical journey. It also baffled many of his most admiring disciples, as well as most his determined critics.

It is a position that is difficult to describe plausibly because it runs contrary to assumptions about the fundamental nature of psychological phenomena that are so deeply-ingrained in our understanding of the mind that they date back to at least Descartes. In 1900, it was common to think of the mind, essentially, as an organ of consciousness; as a thing with a general capacity to receive perceptions and entertain thoughts. Of course, there had been various proposals about unconscious mentality, such as Freud's, but most agreed on the leading role played by conscious thought. It was the common paradigm against which exotic proposals about unconscious thought and motivation were set. The content of conscious perceptions and thoughts was presumed to arrive in the mind from elsewhere, from "the world" broadly speaking. I see a dog because a dog-in-the-world produces the image of a dog in my sensorium, to a first approximation. I remember my mother because I have a memory of her that I retrieve from some sort of storage and place it before my "mind's eye." So basic were assumptions of this sort that they had come to be regarded by many as the fundamental facts of the situation to be explained by psychology, rather than as assumptions. It can be difficult to see how such a thing as "psychology" could even arise if these assumptions were somehow undermined.

This model of mental activity, however, immediately leads to a number of intractable problems. What are we to say about mental contents that do not seem to come from the world of sensation? How do I arrive at general ideas (e.g., of the species "dog," but not any particular dog)? What of abstract ideas such as numbers and logical relations and morality and truth? Might there be whole separate realms of general and abstract ideas to which my consciousness has some sort of access, though not through my eyes and ears? How could that possibly work? Perhaps most perplexing of all, how is it that these various kinds of mental content could come from the world and connect with a thing as ethereal as consciousness?

It is all well and fine to *assume*, as many people have, that consciousness is somehow produced by brain activity, but that does not explain how it actually happens. Indeed, it is so difficult to account for that many have presumed exactly the opposite—that the mind is non-physical in some way (e.g., spiritual or Ideal) and that it only interacts with objects of its own kind. Then the question becomes how real dogs become ideal dogs, or vice versa, such that the mind is able take them up. Of course, this second approach is equally founded on assumption.

James sought to break through this centuries-old conundrum by rejecting the dualism—mind versus world—that underpins it. There is no "empty" consciousness that is waiting to be activated by content. There is, instead, just "experience," a unified thing in which the knower and the known are not distinct parts, except in as much as we decide to abstract them from each other for our own purposes. What is more, experience is not built up of parts like sensations and images and feelings. Those, too, are abstractions that we have created in our effort to understand experience but, in doing so, we have created for ourselves a whole raft of artificial pseudo-problems on which we futilely expend our philosophical and scientific efforts.

Experience for James was not only unified but continuous: it flows smoothly through time from moment to moment. The transitions from one mental "state" to the next are every bit as much a part of experience as the parts we call "states." But, too often, in our analyses, we eliminate these transitional experiences at the outset in order to simplify the situation, only to later wonder what has happened to them as our theoretical project begins to expand. Think, for instance, of the 18th-century Scottish philosopher David Hume, who declared that our experience of an apple is really just a "bundle" of the sensations of redness, roundness, crispness, sweetness, etc.[158] How the bundle comes to be integrated by our mind into a unified idea—the apple—then became a philosophical problem of some import. So another philosopher such as Immanuel Kant then comes along to declare that the very things Hume had called into question are, in fact, "transcendental concepts of the understanding" that form a priori conditions for any sort of understanding: unity, substance, reality, existence, etc.[159] And so the centuries-old dispute between empiricism and Idealism heads off into yet another round of abstruse claim and counterclaim.

According to James, however, this was all based on a false premise, a problem that we had created ourselves by artificially decomposing our naturally unified experience of the apple into its supposedly "elementary" components. "This is the strategic point," James declared, "the position through which, if a hole be made, all the corruptions of dialectics and all the metaphysical fictions pour into philosophy."[160] And it was James' principal aim at the end of his career to salvage philosophy from the elaborate constructions that philosophers from Plato to Aquinas to Descartes to Kant to Hegel had, for centuries, erected to remedy problems that were, in reality, not of the world's making but of our own.

Although James had a number of prominent figures on his side (with certain variations in the details)—Dewey, most notably, along with James' own former students Edwin B. Holt and Ralph B. Perry—there were large numbers of equally accomplished thinkers who simply found it to be puzzling and incomprehensible.[161] James' explication of "experience" did not come with an instruction manual for how psychology was to proceed if, indeed, he succeeded in obliterating its core concept of consciousness. While James' ideas about the unity and continuity of experience were picked up by some thinkers in the decades to come, the discipline of psychology was left with the urgent matter of finding or assembling a new conceptual foundation, lest it be reabsorbed as a special topic of physiology, on the one hand, and philosophy on the other.

As things turned out, James' demolition of consciousness was far more persuasive than his proposal to replace it with experience. Experience was not a thing that could easily be subjected to experiment. Instead, he had thrown psychology into a period of turmoil and had unintentionally set the stage for the rise of a new kind of psychology—one that would replace the problematically "subjective" idea of consciousness with the seemingly more "objective" one of behavior.[162]

11. Upheavals in the Disciplinary Landscape

The 1900s were not only a time for profound change in psychology intellectually, but also institutionally.[163] During the first few years of the existence of the American Psychological Association, the debates continued about what kinds of talks should be allowed at meetings and what kinds of people should be granted membership. Most of the original APA members had been trained in philosophy departments, and many of them did their research in areas that had not yet succumbed to the experimental imperatives of the age. Should these people be forced out into the academic wilderness—there were no philosophical associations at the time—or should the APA be as inclusive as possible in an effort to recruit as many academic allies as possible?

In 1900, a group of 46 philosophers and psychologists formed a new scholarly society called the Western Philosophical Association (WPA). They elected Missouri philosopher Frank Thilly as their president and held their first meeting at the University of Nebraska in January of 1901. Despite the various efforts to evict or segregate the philosophers in the APA, these pressures were not the main reason the western philosophers banded together to form a separate organization. This can be seen from an examination of the two groups' memberships. In 1900, only 10 of the 125 members of the APA lived west of the Mississippi, and only six of those joined the WPA. Of those six, four were laboratory psychologists: George Patrick and Carl Seashore of Iowa, Harry Wolfe of Nebraska, and Max Meyer of Missouri. Thus, the main reason for the formation of the WPA appears to have been geographical rather than intellectual. The westerners felt remote from the APA, which had always met at an eastern school, and they felt the need for something closer to home. Apparently, geographical concerns of this sort had already arisen within the APA: Wisconsin's Joseph Jastrow proposed at the 1899 meeting that the 1901 meeting be held in Chicago, which the association agreed to. What is more, at the APA meeting of 1900, a motion was approved to empower members to "organize themselves into a local section for the holding of meetings." A "Western Branch" of the APA was immediately formed, holding its first meeting in Chicago in 1902.[164]

The WPA was not to be the only philosophical association in America. Just a year after it formed, in 1902, an American Philosophical Association—a new APA—came together around the leadership of James Creighton, a philosopher at Cornell. The new group's founding membership was a robust 98. Of those, 62 were already members of the American Psychological Association. Three decades later, the psychologist Samuel Fernberger reported that, with the creation of a philosophical association in the east, "the number of philosophical papers [presented at the psychological association meetings] dropped to almost zero."[165] Still, there was no mass exodus from the old APA to the new one. The psychological association actually added eight members the following year. It appears that the philosophers merely added a membership in the new APA to their prior affiliation with the older one. What is more, a number of prominent psychologists joined the new philosophical association, including Hall, Ladd, Baldwin, Cattell, Dewey, Münsterberg, Calkins, Washburn, Thorndike, and Woodworth.

The real surprise is that William James did not join. "I don't foresee much good from a philosophical society," he groused. "Philosophical discussion proper only succeeds between intimates who have learned how to converse by months of weary trial and failure. The philosopher is a lone beast dwelling in his individual burrow," he declared. "Count me out!"[166] His early griping aside, James did eventually join the American Philosophical Association, in 1904, perhaps at the behest of his longtime Harvard colleague and friend, Josiah Royce, who served as president that same year. Ladd was president after Royce, then Dewey. James eventually capitulated entirely, becoming president of the new APA in 1906–1907. He was immediately followed by Münsterberg. So, all the grumbling in the 1890s about philosophy being on the psychological association's program notwithstanding, the memberships of the two associations were intricately interwoven through first decade of the 20th century.

In 1905, a fourth group was added to the first three, the Southern Society for Philosophy and Psychology (SSPP).[167] The South presented a particular challenge. The region's colleges had long resisted the modernization that had been seen elsewhere in the country since the end of the Civil War. Indeed, in 1890, one Southern candidate for governor had run, and won, on the campaign promise of shutting down his state's public university.[168] As one Atlanta historian of the time put matters:

> Our educational institutions for the most part have lain dormant, satisfied if the educational fires already lighted could be kept burning. Until very recent years no new departments were organized, no improved educational methods were recognized, no advanced or revolutionary ideas were tolerated.[169]

The new SSPP—led by Edward F. Buchner, then at the University of Alabama,[170] and James Mark Baldwin, who had just moved from Princeton to Johns Hopkins—aimed, in part, to revive a portion of the Southern educational establishment. Unlike the WPA and the two APAs, which separated philosophy and psychology, the SSPP sought to keep them together. It is hard to tell to what degree this was an explicit desideratum, and to what degree is was simply a practical matter of building a large enough membership to keep the group viable—the SSPP began with only 36 members in 1905. Just seven of those 36 were also members of the American Psychological Association.

Even with the arrival of these philosophical organizations, some experimental psychologists remained dissatisfied with the scientific "purity" of the APA. Chief among these was Cornell's Edward Titchener, who had once lamented that "the retirement of the experimentalists,—emphasized further by the proposal to devote a certain amount of the time of each meeting to philosophical enquiries,—cannot but be regretted."[171] As we have already seen, in 1904, Titchener invited a small number of psychology *laboratories*—he left it to the laboratory directors to decide which of their assistants and students to bring along—to join him at Cornell as "The Experimentalists," to speak frankly of their scientific endeavors in a casual "smoke filled and coatless atmosphere."[172]

With the rise of more organizations, each with its own particular mission, there came an increasing specialization of the discipline. The first decade of the

20th century also saw a new generation of psychologists gradually take over the leadership of the field. Dewey was elected president of the APA for 1899. After him, the presidents from 1900 to 1903 were Joseph Jastrow of Wisconsin, Josiah Royce of Harvard, Edmund C. Sanford of Clark, and William Lowe Bryan of Indiana. Then, in 1904, William James became the first person to serve as APA president for a second time. The year 1905 saw Mary Whiton Calkins become the first woman president of any of these four organizations. She would also go on to become the first woman president of the American Philosophical Association, in 1918–1919. The APA presidents of 1906 to 1909 were James Rowland Angell, by then head of the psychology department at Chicago; Henry Rutgers Marshall, a New York architect who was academically unaffiliated at the time, George M. Stratton, then at Johns Hopkins, and Charles Hubbard Judd, the newly appointed director of the Department of Education at Chicago.[173]

Beneath the level of APA executives, a wider, if not quite so obvious, "changing of the guard" was underway in psychology during the 1900s. Probably the most visible individual change was Dewey's departure from Chicago in 1904. This was the result of an unpleasant series of conflicts that were first set in motion by the death in 1902 of Francis Wayland Parker. Parker, it will be recalled, was the man who had first pioneered "progressive education" in Quincy, Massachusetts back in the mid-1870s, then led the Boston school system through a progressive reform starting in 1880. He had come to Chicago in 1883 to launch a similar transformation of the Cook County Normal School where he would train a generation of young teachers in the new approach.[174] Although Parker was able to institute many reforms at the Normal School, being a public institution, there were continual political battles to be fought and compromises to be made. In 1899, an heiress to the enormous riches of the McCormick Harvester empire, Anita Blaine, offered Parker the fantastic sum of one million dollars to set up a private teachers college instead. The offer appealed to Parker because it would free him from entanglements with Illinois' notoriously corrupt politicos. The Chicago Institute, as the new facility came to be called, was originally conceived as an independent professional school, but University of Chicago's president, William Rainey Harper, persuaded Parker and Blaine to affiliate it with the university, to enhance the prestige of both.

This situation posed several problems for Dewey. First, his famed Laboratory School, was in perpetual financial difficulty. It had never been able to balance its books and, apart from an initial start-up grant, Harper had consistently refused Dewey's requests to fund its operation with university money. The Laboratory School was wholly dependent on tuition and on private donations. Parker, however, had found an extraordinarily wealthy patron, and Dewey's school was now going to have to compete, virtually head-to-head, with the elementary school that would be attached to the new, stupendously financed teachers college.

Harper attempted to allay Dewey's concerns by proposing, in 1901, a division of labor between Parker and Dewey, so that their roles would not come into conflict: Dewey would train principals and pedagogical researchers; Parker would train teachers and run the elementary school necessary to do so. Unfortunately Harper's scheme would have left the function of Dewey's Laboratory School on Parker's side of the ledger, an outcome Dewey could not accept. After months of letter campaigns, public meetings, and other upheaval, Harper allowed Dewey's school to remain, but the situation was thrown back into crisis when Parker died the following year. Everyone seemed to agree that Dewey was the best person to take over management of Parker's school, but how that might affect the school's mission was a concern, especially of the teachers who were loyal to Parker's original aims.

There are conflicting accounts of what then ensued, but it seems that Dewey acted, if not actually in bad faith, then at least clumsily in a delicate situation. After first seeming to pledge respect for Parker's mission, he soon attempted to merge the two schools, dismiss (or force out by pay cuts) a number of Parker's teachers, and then place the amalgamated school under the direction of his wife, Alice (which signaled the replacement of Parker's mission with that of the Laboratory School). Although Alice Dewey is remembered today for her firm commitment to the cause of social justice, her very certainty in her convictions also made her a difficult person to work for. There is evidence that her high-handed style had caused at least some of the trouble at the Laboratory School, harming its ability to attract and retain both students and high-quality staff.[175]

Harper had originally accepted Dewey's proposal to merge the two schools; indeed, he had proposed it himself not long before, though under different circumstances. He also approved of Alice Dewey becoming principal. Many teachers at Parker's school, however, regarded the prospect of her becoming their boss with more than a little trepidation. Probably more troubling to Harper was that Anita Blaine, Parker's primary patron, and now chair of his Institute's Board of Trustees, was sympathetic to the teachers' concerns. Dewey was infuriated at what he regarded as interference in his rights as head of the entire Education Department at Chicago. Harper, though, faced with the threat of a teacher revolt and, perhaps more significant, the displeasure of a major financial donor, brokered a compromise in which Alice Dewey was offered a contract as principal but only for one year. During that year, Anita Blaine commissioned a report that described in excruciating detail the many ways in which Alice failed to rise to the difficult situation in which she found herself. Harper asked for Alice Dewey's resignation at the end of the school year, telling both her and John Dewey that the reason was the conflict of interest that arises when a wife works under her husband's supervision. That is, Harper used the then-common rationale of nepotism to shield himself from having what would have been an even more fractious discussion about Alice Dewey's personal and professional inadequacies. It appears than neither of the Deweys learned of the report that was the real cause of her dismissal. Faced with the prospect of being unceremoniously dumped from her position at the end of the contract, Alice Dewey resigned from the school in April 1904

Just days later, John Dewey, who had long distrusted Harper's motives, resigned from all of his university positions in protest. He immediately wrote to close colleagues in the east about possibilities for a new professorship. His old friend from their days as graduate students at Johns Hopkins, James Cattell, soon arranged for a post at Columbia, which housed what was probably the best conventional education school in the country. It is interesting that Dewey never sought to open a new laboratory school at Columbia. Also, his association with psychology faded as the discipline increasingly differentiated itself from both philosophy and pedagogy. He soon became America's leading public intellectual, writing many books on the character that education should assume in a democratic society, as well as on more speculative topics such as ethics, epistemology, art, and the nature of experience itself.

Back in Chicago, Nathaniel Butler, a colleague of Harper's dating back to their days together at the "old" University of Chicago (the Baptist school that had collapsed back in 1886), was appointed Dean of Education in Dewey's stead, a position he would hold until the arrival of Charles Judd from Yale in 1909. It was not only Education that was left in disarray by Dewey's departure. He had also been head of the Department of Philosophy and Psychology, which was filled with people he had hired, some of them dating back to his days at Michigan. Harper took this opportunity to divide the department in two—another sign that psychology was coming into its own as an independent discipline. James Hayden Tufts was put in charge of the new Department of Philosophy. George Herbert Mead went with him. The new Department of Psychology was placed under the leadership of James Rowland Angell. Angell, who, it will be recalled, came from a distinguished family of university professors and administrators, was promoted to Dean in 1908, but also remained as head of psychology. A decade later we would rise to Acting President of the university, apparently only failing to take the position permanently because he was not Baptist, the school's official denomination. In 1921, however, he would be asked to become president Yale—the first non-Yale graduate to hold the position in centuries.

Yale, as it turns out, was another major university at which psychology experienced a significant shakeup. George Trumbull Ladd, it will be recalled, had been one of the earliest expositors of early "physiological psychology" there. Although a beloved teacher and an accomplished philosopher (in addition to being an experienced international ambassador for American-style education), Ladd had never been an experimenter himself. So, in 1892, Yale hired a recent graduate of Wundt's Leipzig laboratory, Edward Wheeler Scripture, to update the university's psychological facilities and course offerings.[176] Scripture was industrious and productive, but also brash and often difficult to get along with. Although professionally respected, it is fair to say that he was not well liked. His *Yale Studies* journal had been the source of James' complaint about psychology having only "College tin trumpets" instead of a truly national journal.[177] His book *Thinking, Feeling, Doing* had been the object of one of Münsterberg's nastiest early reviews.[178] He had come into conflict with Titchener over an accusation of plagiarism against him.

As the century turned, Scripture's research became increasingly focused on language and speech disorders.[179] The Yale administration, now led by its first non-clerical president, Arthur Twining Hadely, still continued the resistance to innovation that had prompted its very founding in the early 1700s.[180] Hadley was unimpressed by Scripture's modern tendency toward original research and was irritated by him personally. He dismissed Scripture outright in 1903.[181] Another man might have been destroyed, but Scripture barely slowed down. He moved to Munich where he earned a medical degree in 1906. He continued his research on speech, now with a new and impressive neurological aspect. In 1915, he took a position at Columbia University for a time. In 1919, he founded a speech clinic—a quite novel venture at the time—in London. Finally, in 1929, he took up a professorship in Vienna.

Back at Yale, however, the purge was not over. Having thrown out Scripture, the administration turned its eye on Ladd, forcing him to retire in 1905. The young Charles Hubbard Judd, then just 32, was left behind to hold the fort but, as we saw previously, he would escape to Chicago in 1909. Yale would not be a significant factor on the American psychological scene until Hadley was succeeded in the presidency by James Rowland Angell more than a decade and a half later.[182]

In 1903, Cattell conducted a survey of American psychologists, asking them who the most important members of the discipline were. He tried to ensure absolute honesty by promising not to publish the results until "ten or twenty years hence."[183] True to his word (and quite a bit more), the results were presented in the 1933 volume of his *American Men of Science*.[184] Topping his list, perhaps not surprisingly, was William James. Cattell himself ranked second. Münsterberg was third. Hall, no doubt much to what would have been his consternation, was relegated to fourth. In fifth place, though, was a figure who has not gained so prominent a place in the standard histories of the discipline: James Mark Baldwin.

Baldwin, it may be remembered, had earned his PhD at Princeton, taught for a short time at Lake Forest, then moved to Toronto for four years, where he founded a laboratory. In 1893 he had returned to Princeton as a professor, where he founded a second laboratory and wrote most of his important work on evolutionary and developmental theory.[185] In addition, he (co-)founded and (co-)edited *Psychological Review*, *Psychological Monographs*, and *Psychological Index*. After buying Cattell's half of the *Review*,[186] he split the journal into two parts, creating *Psychological Bulletin*. As well, he edited (and wrote much of) the landmark *Dictionary of Philosophy and Psychology*.[187] By any measure, he was a major player in the field.

In 1903, however, he became entangled in a dispute with an intransigent and high-handed university president who just happened to be named Woodrow Wilson. More than a little intransigent himself, Baldwin could no longer tolerate what he viewed as Wilson's arrogance and his haughty dismissal of the significance of science.[188] Although history usually thinks of Wilson, because of his later American presidency, as an architect of the modern age of international relations, to Baldwin, Wilson at Princeton was a fusty old relic of a bygone era in American colleges. Not prepared to refight a battle that had already been fought and won elsewhere, Baldwin sought out a position at a prestigious school that had once been the very beacon of the new American university and of the new psychology: Johns Hopkins. Hopkins offered him what every professor desires: less teaching, more pay, and less paternalistic interference in his academic affairs. He jumped at the opportunity and moved to Baltimore. He hired George Stratton of Berkeley to be his laboratory director. He surrounded himself with several other promising assistants and instructors as well. Everything seemed aligned for Baldwin to go from being one highly significant figure of his time to becoming one of the truly exceptional figures in the history of the field.

Then, one day in June of 1908, when his wife and children were probably out of town, Baldwin was approached on the street near his home by a young African American woman, likely a teenager (or, at least, that was his account of the event). We do not know what was said, but she persuaded him to follow her to a nearby "social house"—a combined bar, gambling parlor, jazz club, and brothel. Baldwin entered, sat down, and may have just had time to order a drink. Then, without warning, the police burst in and arrested everyone. Baldwin had been lured into a police trap.[189] He was hauled off to the local stationhouse for questioning. He lied about his name. He denied knowing that prostitution was the main business of the place.[190] Several hours passed before the police figured out who he really was. When they did, to what must have been Baldwin's great relief, they decided to release him without charge. He had dodged a bullet, one that could easily have ended his career, perhaps even his marriage. Or so it seemed.

The story had not yet played out completely. In March of the following year, 1909, the mayor of Baltimore nominated Baldwin for a position on the municipal school board. Only then was the mayor made aware of the arrest more than nine months before. Baldwin was called to the mayor's office, questioned about the event, and asked to decline the position he had just been offered. He did, but it was already too late. The story appeared in the newspapers, which put Baldwin on a collision course with the Johns Hopkins administration, always nervous about questions of morality because of its non-denominational status.[191]

The ultimate conclusion was practically foregone. Baldwin was forced to resign his professorship. Probably because his Laboratory Director, Stratton was returning to Berkeley, Baldwin decided to hand not only his departmental chair-manship, but also the editorial control of his journals, over to a young professor he had, just months before, hired out of the University of Chicago: John B. Wat-son.[192] Watson would go on to use the journals, especially *Psychological Review*, to great effect in spawning his behaviorist "revolution" during the following decade. By contrast, Baldwin's professional downfall was catastrophic.[193] After the scandal became public, he was unable to find academic work anywhere in the US. He consulted on the expansion of the National University of Mexico for a short time, but soon moved himself and his family to Paris, where he would reside for the remaining 24 years of his life. There, he was able to acquire a minor appointment at the *École des hautes etudes sociales*, but he was never again a university professor. He became close friends with the foremost French psychiatrist of the day, Pierre Janet. Janet would later mentor the young Jean Piaget, and it has long been speculated that the striking similarities between Baldwin's and Piaget's approaches to child development may have been mediated by Janet's long discussions with both. As a result of the scandal and the sudden extinction of his career when he was just 48 years of age, Baldwin was virtually written out of the standard histories of the topic.

Finally, we turn to William James. As the decade of the 1900s drew to a close, James was increasingly ill. An injury to his heart, dating back to a particularly arduous mountain climb in 1898, began to take a serious toll on his health.[194] He was invited to Stanford by the school's owner, Jane Lathrop Stanford. She was much more interested in his psychical research than in pragmatism or radical empiricism, but it would give him an opportunity to spread his messages to a new region of the country. Mrs. Stanford died unexpectedly in February of 1905, before James had arrived, but he decided to go anyway, teaching there in the winter of 1906. Early on the morning of April 18th, he was awoken when his "bed beg[a]n to waggle." He sat up, kneeling in his bed, but, as he later reported:

> I was thrown down on my face as it went *fortior* shaking the room exactly as a terrier shakes a rat. Then everything that was on anything else slid off to the floor, over went bureau and chiffonier with a crash, as the *fortissimo* was reached, plaster cracked, an awful roaring noise seemed to fill the outer air, and in an instant all was still again, save the soft babble of human voices from far and near that soon began to make itself heard, as the inhabitants in costumes *negligés* in various degrees sought the greater safety of the street and yielded to the passionate desire for sympathetic communication.[195]

What James had experienced was the Great San Francisco Earthquake of 1906, which damaged portions of the nearby Stanford campus.

The rest of the semester was canceled, and James left for home soon thereafter. He later confessed to Harvard President Eliot, though, that he now found mere lecturing so exhausting that, if his time on the west coast had not been cut short by the disaster, he didn't think he would have made it through to the end of term. He returned to teaching at Harvard for the fall, but soon realized that he was rapidly becoming physically incapacitated. He hastily arranged for his retirement, to begin in late January of 1907.

Despite his ill health, James was able to write and deliver a series of eight lectures in December at Lowell Institute in Boston. The topic was pragmatism, the theory of truth that he had first publicly adopted in 1898, and that he had popularized in *Varieties of Religious Experience* in 1902. The published edition of these lectures—*Pragmatism: A New Name for Some Old Ways of Thinking*—would immediately become one of James' most important and enduring contributions to philosophy.[196] The book provoked such vociferous debate even in its own time that James was impelled to write a second book on the topic, *The Meaning of Truth*.[197] As though retirement itself had spurred him on to new creative heights despite his growing illness, in 1908 James traveled to Manchester to deliver a series of lectures titled *A Pluralistic Universe* which were also published the following year.[198]

By the time James met Freud in September of 1909, he was unable to endure even the relatively mild rigors of the full conference. His chest pains and short-ness of breath had become nearly constant companions. His energies were severely curtailed. Nevertheless, James' legendary openness to new experience was as evident as ever in his search for a cure, or at least some relief. He consulted orthodox physicians and he went to homeopaths. He tried bed rest and he tried exercise regimens. He took the baths at exotic spas and he tolerated injections of arcane "animal extracts." He ingested vile purgatives and he sought out Christian Science faith healers. Early in 1910, he rushed, once last time, to Europe where he endured some exotic new electrical therapy. Nothing helped. Finally, he sub-mitted to the astonishing new technology of x-ray—a photograph of the inside of his body. The plate showed that he was suffering from an enlarged aorta. There was little more that could be done.[199]

With a definite cause finally determined, James visited a few friends and col-leagues around Paris—James Mark Baldwin and philosopher Henri Bergson, among them. He visited with his brother Henry, living in London. Then, in August, he returned home, not to Harvard, but to his beloved country home in Chocorua, New Hampshire. He lasted only a week longer, passing away on August 26 at the age of just 68. An era in American psychology seemed to pass away with him.

Notes

1 For an extensive account of McKinley's assassination, see Scott Miller, *The President and the Assassin* (New York, NY: Random House, 2011).

2 According to Richard L. McElroy, Czolgosz was so persistent in his efforts to see Gold-man that she had become apprehensive of him (*William McKinley and Our America: A Pictorial History* (Canton, Ohio: Stark County Historical Society, 1996)).

3 The commander of the fleet, George Dewey, was not related to John Dewey. He was also a Vermonter, but from Montpelier rather than Burlington.

4 Theodore Roosevelt, *The Winning of the West*, 4 vols. (New York, NY: G. P. Putnam, 1889–1896).

5 Although Roosevelt attained the governorship, he won it by less that two percentage points over his Democratic rival, whereas the Republican nominee two years before him had won by twelve points.

6 The vice president of McKinley's first term, Garret Hobart, had died of a heart attack in November of 1899, a full year before the election of 1900, and had not been replaced.

7 In the election of 1900, McKinley won several western states that he had lost to Bryan in 1896. These included South Dakota, where Roosevelt had ranched in the 1880s. It is hard to tell whether Roosevelt's presence on the ticket swung these states into

McKinley's column, or whether McKinley's status as the presidential incumbent in 1900 drew voters to him who had opposed him in 1896, when he was merely a former governor of Ohio.

8 The claim of divine right was often explicit: George Baer, President of the Philadelphia and Reading Railroad, declared in the midst of the dispute that the "rights and interests of the laboring man will be protected and cared for—not by the labor agitators, but by the Christian men to whom God in His infinite wisdom has given the control of the property interests of the country" (cited in Henry William Brands, *T.R. The Last Romantic* (New York, NY: Basic Books, 1997), 457).

9 A later revision of this very law would enable the US government to win the legendary 1917 judgment againt Clark Stanley for transporting his infamous Snake Oil across state lines.

10 Josiah Royce, *The World and the Individual*, 2 vols. (New York, NY: Palgrave Macmillan, 1899). Royce (1855–1916) was born to English immigrants to California in the wake of the gold rush. His undergraduate degree was from the state university there, and then, after some study in Germany, he traveled to the newly-opened Johns Hopkins University, where he earned one of that school's first PhDs in philosophy, in 1878. He returned to a lectureship at Berkeley but was soon called to Harvard to replace James during the latter's 1882 sabbatical. Although Royce's philosophical orientation— Objective Idealism—was more conventional than James', his innovative integration of Idealism with fallibilism made him more interesting to James than most Idealists, and Royce was made permanent at Harvard in 1884. He came to be regarded as the leading spokesman for Idealism in North America. He served as president of the American Psychological Association in 1901, and of the American Philosophical Association in 1903–1904.

11 This was also discussed briefly back in Chapter 3, n. 83. The passage appears on p. 160 of the original edition of William James, *The Varieties of Religious Experience* (New York, NY: Longmans, Green, 1902).

12 This was not the first time James had used the term "pragmatism" in print. In a lecture given at the University of California in August 1898, James reported that Peirce had coined it back in the early 1870s ("Philosophical Conceptions and Practical Results," *University of California] Chronicle* 1 (1898): 287–310). Strangely, though, Peirce does not seem to have used the term in his own published works during the intervening quarter-century. So James' Berkeley lecture, published in September 1898, may well have been the first time "pragmatism" appeared in print.

13 Returning, it is worth noting, to an important theme in his *Principles of Psychology*. All passages quoted in this paragraph are from James, *Varieties*, 444.

14 Charles Sanders Peirce, "How to Make Our Ideas Clear," *Popular Science Monthly* 12 (1878): 286–302.

15 James, *Varieties*, 448.

16 Ibid., 453.

17 Ibid., 455–56.

18 Mary Baker Glover [Eddy], *Science and Health with Key to the Scriptures* (Boston, MA: Christian Scientist Publishing, 1875).

19 Rodney Stark, "The Rise and Fall of Christian Science," *Journal of Contemporary Religion* 13 (1998): 190–91.

20 Amzi Clarence Dixon and Reuben Archer Torrey, eds., *The Fundamentals: A Testimony to Truth*, 12 vols. (Chicago, IL: Testimony Publishing, 1910–1915).

21 The Social Gospel was a liberal wing of Christianity that focused on social reform, such as alleviating poverty, alcoholism, crime, and supporting labor fairness, education, and peace. Crapsey's unorthodox views on Jesus' humanity would lead, in 1906, to his conviction for heresy, for which he was defrocked.

22 Fechner would die the very year that Worcester arrived in Leipzig, 1887.

23 Elwood Worcester, *Life's Adventure: The Story of a Varied Career* (New York, NY: Scribner's, 1932), 90–91.

24 Concerning the last of these, upon reading William James' *Pragmatism* years later, Worcester wrote to the Harvard professor his surprise that James had not credited Fechner with first making the pragmatist argument for faith. At first James was doubtful but, after rereading *Three Motives*, came to agree with Worcester's understanding of the relation between the two (ibid., 92–93).

25 Worcester wrote that "My first thought was to major with Wundt in psychology," but he did not have the full year to devote to laboratory work that Wundt demanded, so he opted for the philosophical thesis with Heinze, which took only half the time. Worcester wrote that he "attended every [lecture] course he [Wundt] gave, as well as his seminar" but there is no mention of any work in the famed laboratory (ibid., 89). Ludy Benjamin could find evidence that Worcester took only two courses with Wundt, however, and that Wundt served on his thesis committee ("Wundt's American Doctoral Students," *American Psychologist* 47 (1992): 123–31).

26 For more information on these events, see Eugene Taylor, *William James on Consciousness Beyond the Margin* (Princeton, NJ: Princeton University Press, 1996); *Shadow Culture: Psychology and Spirituality in America* (Washington, DC: Counterpoint, 1999); "Psychotherapeutics and the Problematic Origins of Clinical Psychology in America," *American Psychologist* 55 (2000): 1029–33; Eric Caplan, *Mind Games: American Culture and the Birth of Psychotherapy* (Berkeley, CA: University of California Press, 1998); Sanford Gifford, *The Emmanuel Movement: The Origins of Group Treatment and the Assault on Lay Psychotherapy* (Cambridge, MA: Harvard University Press, 1998).

27 See James' prior work on the nature and significance of unusual conscious states in Eugene Taylor, ed., *William James on Exceptional Mental States: The 1896 Lowell Lectures Reconstructed* (New York, NY: Scribner's, 1983).

28 James Jackson Putnam (1846–1918) was a native Bostonian who studied in Europe with luminaries such as Theodor Meynert and John Hughlings Jackson. He founded the Department of Neurology at Harvard Medical School and served as president of the American Neurological Association in 1888. Just prior to the events described here, he had published *Studies in Neurological Diagnosis* (Boston, MA: G. H. Ellis, 1902). Morton Prince (1854–1929) was a wealthy Bostonian who, after a Harvard medical degree, had studied with Jean-Martin Charcot at the Salpêtrière in Paris. He specialized in neurology and became an expert in dissociative personality (Morton Prince, *Dissociation of a Personality: A Biographical Study in Abnormal Psychology* (New York, NY: Longmans, Green, 1906)). Prince was also the founding editor of the *Journal of Abnormal Psychology*, launched in 1906. Boris Sidis (1867–1923) had been jailed for as long as two years simply for being Jewish under the religious repression of Czarist Russia in the 1880s (the "May Laws"). He immigrated to America from Ukraine in 1887, where he earned a PhD and a MD, both at Harvard. He became a leading psychopathologist and an intriguing, if rather idiosyncratic, theoretical psychologist. See, e.g., Boris Sidis, *The Psychology of Suggestion: A Research Into the Subconscious Nature of Man and Society* (New York, NY: D. Appleton, 1898); *Psychopathological Researches: Studies in Mental Dissociation* (London, UK: Stechert, 1902); Boris Sidis and Simon P. Goodhart, *Multiple Personality: An Experimental Investigation Into Human Individuality* (New York, NY: D. Appleton, 1904).

29 Eugene Taylor found that this group was already treating "hundreds of patients . . . each year in the outpatient clinics of local hospitals with psychotherapeutic methods of suggestion, persuasion, light hypnosis, dream analysis, and with regimes such as social milieu therapy" (*Shadow Culture*, 176).

30 Worcester, *Life's Adventure*, 285.

31 Ibid., 287.

32 There was a family of trance-inducing methods that have a long history, often outside of, or even in opposition to, the medical mainstream. In the Western tradition,

they date back to at least Anton Mesmer and almost certainly well before. The "New Thought" of Phineas Quimby (1802–1866) was a peculiarly American incarnation of this tradition, focusing on the curing of illness by "mind power." It fell to a student of Quimby's, Warren Felt Evans, to commit the New Thought teachings to print. Evans also integrated them with ideas of Emmanuel Swedenborg, which may have been part of the reason that William James was so fascinated by them. Mary Baker Eddy had been a patient and student of Quimby's in the 1860s, and she later combined his techniques with her own unorthodox religious beliefs to form Christian Science.

33 Before the Emmanuel Movement, "psychotherapy" was not commonly used in English. Daniel Hack Tuke had coined the term "psychotherapeutics" in 1872, specifically linking it to the practice of Mesmerism. But the term did not really come into its own until the prominent Nancy (France) medical professor, Hippolyte Bernheim, mentioned it in passing in an 1886 book, and then put in into the title of his 1891 *Hypnotisme, suggestion, psychothérapie, études nouvelles* (see Sonu Shamdasani, "'Psychotherapy': The Invention of a Word," *History of the Human Sciences* 18 (2005): 1–22 for a more detailed history). It seems plausible that James adopted the term from Bernheim's work, bringing it with him to the Emmanuel Movement. He had also attended an earlier conference in Paris where two former students of Bernheim used the term in their presentation (Albert Willem van Renterghem and Frederik Van Eeden, "Clinique de Psycho-Thérapie Suggestive Fondée à Amsterdam Le 15 Août 1887," in *Prémier Congrès International de L'hypnotisme Expérimental et Thérapeutique*, ed. Edgar Bérillon (Paris, France: Octave Doin, 1889), 57–78).

34 Richard C. Cabot, "The American Type of Psychotherapy," *Psychotherapy: A Course Reading in Sound Psychology, Sound Medicine, and Sound Religion* 1 (1908), cited in Caplan, *Mind Games*, 4.

35 Richard C. Cabot, "New Phases in the Relation of the Church to Health," *Outlook*, February 29, 1908, cited in Caplan, *Mind Games*, 127–28.

36 Elwood Worcester, Samuel McComb, and Isador H. Coriat, *Religion and Medicine: The Moral Control of Nervous Disorders* (New York, NY: Moffat, Yard, 1908).

37 Clarence B. Farrer, "Psychotherapy and the Church," *Journal of Nervous and Mental Disease* 36 (1909): 11–24.

38 Worcester, *Life's Adventure*, 288.

39 Lightner Witmer, "Review and Criticism: Mental Healing and the Emmanuel Movement," *The Psychological Clinic* 2 (1909–1910): 212–24, 239–50, 282–300.

40 Hugo Münsterberg, *Psychotherapy* (New York, NY: Moffat, Yard, 1909), 341. It is uncertain what role, if any, Münsterberg's mindfulness of the involvement of his Harvard colleague, William James, may have played in his careful parsing of the situation.

41 Ibid., 331.

42 Many people have written about the psychological component of this Clark Conference of 1909. In this section I have drawn especially on Rand B. Evans and William A. Koelsch, "Psychoanalysis Arrives in America: The 1909 Psychology Conference at Clark University," *American Psychologist* 40 (1985): 942–48; Saul Rosenzweig, *Freud, Jung, and Hall the King-Maker* (St. Louis, MO: Rana House, 1992); and Taylor, *Shadow Culture*.

43 Indeed, Meyer and Eugen Bleuler (Jung's supervisor, and the man who coined the terms "schizophrenia" and "autism") had both studied there under August Forel. See Taylor, *Shadow Culture*, 212 for a discussion of the network of connections.

44 Taylor, *Shadow Culture*, 211. Of course, it was not inconsequential that Freud's lectures were delivered in German, making them difficult for most journalists even to understand, much less report on extensively, while Jennings' were given in English.

45 William James, "Report on Mrs. Piper's Hodgson Control," *Proceedings of the American Society for Psychical Research* 23 (1909): 470–589. See Rosenzweig, *Freud, Jung, and Hall the King-Maker*, 80 ff. for a detailed description of the scene.

46 Amy E. Tanner, *Studies in Spiritism* (New York, NY: Appleton, 1910). Tanner had earned a PhD in psychology at Chicago in 1898. Then she had taken a teaching position at Wilson College in Chambersburg, PA before moving to Clark in 1907 as an Honorary University Fellow. Although she became Director of Experimental Pedagogy at Clark's Child Institute in 1909, she was unable to obtain a permanent position and left in 1918 (Jacy L. Young, "Amy Tanner," ed. Alexandra Rutherford, *Psychology's Feminist Voices*, 2010, www.feministvoices.com/amy-tanner/; see also Michael Pettit, "The New Woman as 'Tied-Up Dog': Amy E. Tanner's Situated Knowledges," *History of Psychology* 11 (2008): 145–63).

47 Anna O. was a pseudonym for Bertha Pappenheim, who went on to become an important feminist activist in Austria; she founded the League of Jewish Women (*Jüdischer Frauenbund*). The full story of Anna O.'s treatment and recovery departed considerably from Freud's publish account. See Henri F. Ellenberger, "The Story of 'Anna O.': A Critical Review With New Data," *Journal of the History of the Behavioral Sciences* 8 (1972): 267–79.

48 These letters are reproduced in Ruth Leys and Rand B. Evans, eds., *Defining American Psychology: The Correspondence Between Adolf Meyer and Edward Bradford Titchener* (Baltimore, MD: Johns Hopkins University Press, 1990).

49 Titchener had long desired to move of moving out of the backwoods of New York state to a major city (if he could not return to his beloved Oxford). The negotiations ultimately came to nothing, however, because Cornell would not release Titchener until he completed his multiyear contract. Hall and Sanford could not wait. See Evans and Koelsch, "Psychoanalysis Arrives in America."

50 See Christopher D. Green and Ingo Feinerer, "The Evolution of the *American Journal of Psychology*, 1904–1918: A Network Investigation," *American Journal of Psychology* 129 (2016): 185–96.

51 Nathan G. Hale, ed., *James Jackson Putnam and Psychoanalysis: Letters Between Putnam and Sigmund Freud, Ernest Jones, William James, Sandor Ferenczi, and Morton Prince, 1877–1917* (Cambridge, MA: Harvard University Press, 1971).

52 Taylor, *Shadow Culture*, 222–23.

53 Ibid., esp. pp. 227–31.

54 Andrew Scull, "Contending Professions: Sciences of the Brain and Mind in the United States, 1850–2013," *Science in Context* 28 (2015): 131–61.

55 David B. Baker and Ludy T. Benjamin Jr., "The Affirmation of the Scientist-Practitioner: A Look Back at Boulder," *American Psychologist* 55, no. 2 (2000): 241–47. I specify PhDs here because, since the 1970s, there has been a second form of clinical psychology doctorate, the PsyD, which lays a greater emphasis on "practitioner" and far less on "scientist" than the PhD.

56 The "Dutch" of Pennsylvania were actually *Deutsch* or German, rather than originating in the Netherlands.

57 Most of the background here derives from Paul McReynolds, *Lightner Witmer: His Life and Times* (Washington, DC: American Psychological Association, 1997). See also Robert A. Brotemarkle, ed., *Clinical Psychology: Essays in Honor of Lightner Witmer* (Philadelphia, PA: University of Pennsylvania Press, 1931); Lightner Witmer, "Clinical Psychology," *The Psychological Clinic* 1 (1907): 1–9.

58 The full story is somewhat complicated. See McReynolds, *Witmer*, 21 for details.

59 Interestingly, Witmer's financial aid came from an enormous fund ($60,000) that had been bequeathed to Penn by the prominent and wealthy chemist and mineralogist, Henry Seybert for the purposes of studying the claims of spiritualism (McReynolds, *Witmer*, 45–46, 58).

60 A mathematical curiosity know at least as far back as Euclid's time, the Golden Section is a proportion in which a line is unequally divided such that the ratio of the smaller part to the larger part is equal to the ratio of the larger part to the whole line. It is

an irrational number equal to approximately 1.618. During the Renaissance, it was claimed that the Golden Section had profound aesthetic properties when incorporated into artworks. In mid-19th-century Germany, these claims were revived and greatly elaborated, which led Fechner to take them up experimentally. See, e.g., Christopher D. Green, "All That Glitters: A Review of Psychological Research on the Aesthetics of the Golden Section.," *Perception* 24 (1995): 937–68.

61 Gustav Theodor Fechner, *Elemente Der Psychophysik* (Leipzig, Germany: Druck und Verlag Von Breitkopf and Härtel, 1860); Gustav Theodor Fechner, *Vorschule Der Aestheiik* (Leipzig, Germany: Druck und Verlag Von Breitkopf and Härtel, 1876).

62 Cited in McReynolds, *Witmer*, 42.

63 His doctorate was not formally conferred until 1893.

64 McReynolds, *Witmer*; Lightner Witmer, "A Case of Chornic Bad Spelling—Amnesia Visualis Verbalis due to Arrest of Post-Natal Development," *The Psychological Clinic* 1 (1907): 53–68.

65 Lightner Witmer, "The Teaching of Psychology to Teachers," *The Citizen* 2 (1896): 158–62; Lightner Witmer, "The Common Interests of Child Psychology and Pediatrics," *Pediatrics* 2 (1896): 390–95; Lightner Witmer, "Practical Work in Psychology," *Pediatrics* 2 (1896): 462–71.

66 Lightner Witmer, "The Organization of Practical Work in Psychology [Abstract]," *Psychological Review* 4 (1897): 116–17.

67 Hugo Münsterberg, "The Danger from Experimental Psychology," *Atlantic Monthly* 81 (February 1898): 159–66.

68 The APA reluctantly created a Clinical Section in 1919 in order to quell competition from J. E. Wallace Wallin and Leta Hollingworth's fledgling American Association of Clinical Psychologists. The Clinical Section failed after less than a decade (See Donald K. Routh, "Clinical Psychology Training: A History of Ideas and Practices Prior to 1946," *American Psychologist* 55 (2000): 236–41; Franz Samelson, "The APA Between the World Wars: 1918–1941," in *100 Years: The American Psychological Association. A Historical Perspective*, ed. Rand B. Evans, Virginia Staudt Sexton, and Thomas C. Cadwallader (Washington, DC: American Psychological Association, 1992), 119–47).

69 Titchener had resigned his membership in 1895 in protest over the APA inaction on what he believed to be a case of plagiarism by Yale's Edward Wheeler Scripture. See C. James Goodwin, "On the Origins of Titchener's Experimentalists," *Journal of the History of the Behavioral Sciences* 21 (1985): 383–89.

70 Samuel W. Fernberger, "The History of the Psychological Clinic," in *Clinical Psychology: Essays in Honor of Lightner Witmer*, ed. Robert A. Brotemarkle (Philadelphia, PA: University of Pennsylvania Press, 1931), 10–36.

71 "Hyslop's Spirit Talk Is Viewed Skeptically," *Philadelphia Inquirer*, February 16, 1900, 5.

72 Letter from Witmer to Titchener, January 25, 1904, cited in McReynolds, *Witmer*, 109–10.

73 Laurel Furumoto, "Shared Knowledge: The Experimentalists, 1904–1929," in *The Rise of Experimentation in American Psychology*, ed. Jill G. Morawski (New Haven, CT: Yale University Press, 1988), 94–113.

74 Edwin G. Boring, "Titchener's Experimentalists," *Journal of the History of the Behavioral Sciences* 3 (1967): 315–25; see also Alexandra Rutherford, Kelli Vaughn-Johnson, and Elissa Rodkey, "Does Psychology Have a Gender?," *The Psychologist* 28 (2015): 508–11.

75 At least in English. There had been a minor French journal titled, *Revue de Psychologie Clinique et Thérapeutique* from 1897 to 1901.

76 Witmer, "Clinical Psychology," 1.

77 Actually, Witmer had insulted the highly sensitive Münsterberg a few years before by criticizing the Harvard department for being purely scientific, admitting no practical aspect to their psychology. Indeed, Münsterberg himself had once insisted on just this state, but, by the early 1900s, he had reversed himself completely and was beginning to

work in a number of different applied areas, though few people knew it at the time. By 1909, Witmer knew full well of Munsterberg's efforts, and he sharply disparaged the value of the German man's applied work. Münsterberg was, of course, predictably furious over the slight, and he called on the APA to sanction Witmer for his harsh words. The APA demurred, but Witmer did not attend that year's association meeting, which just happened to be hosted at Harvard by Münsterberg.

78 Witmer, "Emmanuel Movement."

79 As noted in chapter 4 (n. 104), Herbert Spencer and some in the Herbartian school—proposed similar ideas earlier, but Haeckel drew the attention with his elegant illustrations. Ernst Haeckel, *Anthropogenie Oder Entwickelungsgeschichte Des Menschen [Anthpogeny, or the Developmental History of Man]* (Leipzig, Germany: Wilhelm Engelmann, 1874).

80 On the issue specifically of Hall's recapitulationism, see Sheldon H. White, "Developmental Psychology in a World of Designed Institutions," ed. Willem Koops and Michael Zuckerman, vol. Beyond the century of the child: Cultural history and developmental psychology (Philadelphia, PA: University of Pennsylvania Press, 2003); Charles E. Strickland and Charles Burgess, "G. Stanley Hall: Prophet of Naturalism," in *Health, Growth, and Heredity: G. Stanley Hall on Natural Education*, ed. Charles E. Strickland and Charles Burgess (New York, NY: Teachers College Press, 1965); Robert E. Grinder, "The Concept of Adolescence in the Genetic Psychology of G. Stanley Hall," *Child Development* 40 (1969): 355–69; Robert E. Grinder, *A History of Genetic Psychology* (New York, NY: Wiley, 1967); Christopher D. Green, "Hall's Developmental Theory and Haeckel's Recapitulationism," *European Journal of Developmental Psychology* 12 (2015): 656–65.

81 G. Stanley Hall, "Civilization and Savagery," *Proceedings of the Massachusetts Historical Society* n.s. 17 (1903): 11.

82 G. Stanley Hall, "The Contents of Children's Minds," *Princeton Review* 11 (1883): 249–72; G. Stanley Hall, "New Psychology as a Basis of Education," *Forum* 17 (1894): 710–20.

83 G. Stanley Hall, *Adolescence: Its Psychology and Its Relations to Physiology, Anthropology, Sociology, Sex, Crime, Religion, and Education*, 2 vols. (New York, NY: Appleton, 1904).

84 Although only 19% of American 15–18 year olds were in high school in 1910, by 1940 the rate would grow dramatically to 73%; see Claudia Goldin, *The Race Between Education and Technology* (Cambridge, MA: Harvard University Press, 2008).

85 Hall, *Adolescence*, vol. 1, 1.

86 Ibid., vol. 1, 71.

87 G. Stanley Hall, *Life and Confessions of a Psychologist* (New York, NY: Appleton, 1923), plate opposite p. 216.

88 For more on Thorndike's life and career, see especially G. Joncich, *The Sane Positivist: A Biography of Edward L. Thorndike* (Middletown, CT: Wesleyan University Press, 1968) and the tribute of his son, Robert L. Thorndike, "Edward L. Thorndike: A Professional and Personal Appreciation," in *Portraits of Pioneers of Psychology*, ed. Gregory A Kimble, Michael Wertheimer, and Charlotte L. White, vol. 1 (Washington, DC and Hillsdale, NJ: American Psychological Association and Lawrence Erlbaum Associates Publishers, 1991), 138–51.

89 Edward L. Thorndike, "The Nature, Purposes and General Methods of Measurements of Educational Products," ed. G. M. Whipple, *The Measurement of Educational Products. National Society for the Study of Education Yearbook* 17, no. Part 2 (1918): 16–24.

90 Edward L. Thorndike, "Measurements of Twins," *Columbia University Contributions to Philosophy and Psychology* 13 (1905): 1–64.

91 Probably because the identical twins in his twins sample raised the average similarity in that group, even though the fraternal twins should have been no more similar to each other than non-twin siblings.

92 After work in World War I personnel selection, he developed the *IER Intelligence Examination for High School Graduates* (a forerunner of the Scholastic Achievement Test, or SAT) and the Intelligence Scale CAVD, which was long used as an entrance screening test at a number of elite universities, including his own Columbia.

93 For more complete descriptions of these events and Münsterberg's role in them, see Matthew Hale, Jr., *Human Science and Social Order: Hugo Münsterberg and the Origins of Applied Psychology* (Philadelphia, PA: Temple University Press, 1980), 93–97; Margaret Münsterberg, *Hugo Münsterberg, His Life and Work* (New York, NY: D. Appleton, 1922), 95–117.

94 Ludy T. Benjamin Jr., "Meet Me at the Fair: A Centennial Retrospective of Psychology at the 1904 St. Louis World's Fair," *APS Observer* 17 (2004), www.psychologicalscience.org/index.php/uncategorized/meet-me-at-the-fair.html.

95 Hugo Münsterberg, "The St. Louis Congress of Arts and Sciences," *Atlantic Monthly* 91 (1903): 671–84.

96 John Dewey, "The St. Louis Congress of the Arts and Sciences," *Science* n.s. 18 (August 28, 1903): 275–78.

97 James Rowland Angell, "Psychology at the St. Louis Congress," *Journal of Philosophy, Psychology and Scientific Method* 2 (1905): 533. It is worth noting that both of these critics—Dewey and Angell—were colleagues of Small at the University of Chicago.

98 Ibid., 534.

99 Ibid., 535.

100 Ibid.

101 James McKeen Cattell, "The Conceptions and Methods of Psychology," *Popular Science Monthly* 66 (1904): 176.

102 Ibid.

103 Ibid., 179.

104 Ibid., 179–80.

105 Ibid., 185.

106 Even if Cattell really did have a constitutional inability to introspect, as has been suggested by Michael Sokal in "Scientific Biography, Cognitive Deficits, and Laboratory Practice: James McKeen Cattell and Early American Experimental Psychology, 1880–1904," *Isis* 101 (2010): 531–54.

107 The *locus classicus* for women in early psychology is Elizabeth Scarborough and Laurel Furumoto, *Untold Lives: The First Generation of American Women Psychologists* (New York, NY: Columbia University Press, 1987). Also see Katherine Milar, "The First Generation of Women Psychologists and the Psychology of Women," *American Psychologist* 55 (2000): 616–19 and Elizabeth Johnston and Ann Johnson, "Searching for the Second Generation of American Women Psychologists," *History of Psychology* 11 (2008): 40–72. The advantages of the internet, however, have enabled Alexandra Rutherford to supersede these resources with her stupendous website, "Psychology's Feminist Voices," 2008, www.feministvoices.com.

108 Margaret Floy Washburn, Alice Julia Hamlin (Hinman), Eleanor A. M. Gamble, and Stella Emily Sharp. See Robert W. Proctor and Rand B. Evans, "E. B. Titchener, Women Psychologists, and the Experimentalists," *American Journal of Psychology* 127 (2014): 501–26.

109 A classic discussion of this matter can be found in Stephanie Shields, "Functionalism, Darwinism, and the Psychology of Women," *American Psychologist* 30 (1975): 739–54.

110 Joseph Jastrow, "A Study of Mental Statistics," *New Review* 5 (1891): 559–68. To make the groups equal in size, Jastrow used the responses of all 25 women and those of the first 25 men to finish the task. What impact this arbitrary form of sampling had on the results is difficult to say.

111 Cordelia C. Nevers and Mary W. Calkins, "Dr. Jastrow on Community of Ideas of Men and Women," *Psychological Review* 2 (1895): 363–67.

112 Joseph Jastrow, "Community of Ideas of Men and Women," *Psychological Review* 3 (1896): 68–71; Calkins, Mary Whiton, "Community of Ideas of Men and Women," *Psychological Review* 3 (1896): 426–30.

113 Helen Bradford Thompson, *The Mental Traits of Sex: An Experimental Investigation of the Normal Mind in Men and Women* (Chicago, IL: University of Chicago Press, 1903), 182.

114 Perhaps ironically, Hall used the dissertation of Millicent Shinn (University of California, 1895) to buttress his claim that educated women tended not to marry. Conversely, though, Shinn had shown that the very large discrepancy that some cited was actually caused by the fact that most educated women of that time were still rather young and, thus, were not *yet* married. Among educated women over the age of 50, more than 50% had married. This was about 2/3 the rate of women who had not gone to college, but hardly the reproductive disaster that some men foresaw.

115 Edward L. Thorndike, *Educational Psychology*, vol. III: Mental work and fatigue and individual differences and their causes (New York, NY: Teachers College, Columbia University Press, 1914).

116 Kate Gordon, "Wherein Should the Education of a Woman Differ From that of a Man?," *School Review* 13 (1905): 789–94.

117 Martin's education is often misdescribed. She went to Göttingen to study under G. E. Müller. She was there for four years (1894–1898) and, by all accounts, did excellent psychophysical research, but she left before completing her PhD It is not the case, as is often reported, that Göttingen refused her a degree that she had earned. The story seems to have been confused with a related one—that Martin applied to Bonn in 1895 and was refused entry because she was a woman, but she was later granted an honorary doctorate by Bonn in 1913.

118 For a complete account of her life, see, Harry L. Hollingworth, *Leta Stettler Hollingworth, a Biography* (Bolton, MA: Anker, 1990) (originally published in 1943).

119 Leta Stetter Hollingworth, "Functional Periodicity: An Experimental Study of the Mental and Motor Abilities of Women During Menstruation" (Teacher's College, Columbia University, 1914).

120 Ludy T. Benjamin Jr., "Hugo Münsterberg's Attack on the Application of Scientific Psychology," *Journal of Applied Psychology* 91 (2006): 414–25, doi:10.1037/0021–9010.91.2.414.

121 William Stern, *Uber Psychologie Der Individuellen Differenzen* (Leipzig, Germany: Johann Ambrosius Barth, 1900).

122 William Stern, "Angewandte Psychologie," *Beiträge Zur Psychologie Aussage* 1 (1904 1903): 11–12, 19–23.

123 Although tensions between Münsterberg and James had been growing gradually since his arrival, it was a dispute over the ceremonies around the opening of Emerson Hall, of all things, that finally drove the two men into open conflict. Münsterberg, as Division Chairman, believed that he was the proper chief official for the occasion. James resented what he saw as Münsterberg's continuous status-seeking and expressed his openly nationalistic view that a German should not play so prominent a role at an American institution. President Eliot was forced to intervene between the men, reminding James that it was he who had recommended they hire this particular German in the first place. See, e.g., Hale, Jr., *Human Science*, 102–3.

124 "Ivins Innocent, Is Belief of Two Note Alienists," *Chicago Tribune*, June 13, 1906, 5, http://archives.chicagotribune.com/1906/06/13/page/5/article/stork-backs-8-hour-day. Also cited in Hale, Jr., *Human Science*, 111.

125 "Untrue Confessions" (*Times Magazine*, January 1907) was just the first of several popular articles that Münsterberg published on the topic. Other outlets included *Reader's Magazine, McClure's,* and *Cosmopolitan*. See M. Münsterberg, *Hugo Münsterberg, His Life and Work*, 368–69, for a complete list.

126 A particularly tart satire was penned by the famed jurist, John H. Wigmore, "Professor Munsterberg and the Psychology of Testimony: Being a Report of the Case of Cokestone v. Munsterberg," *Illinois Law Review* 3 (1909): 399–445.

127 See chapter 4 on the Molly McGuires. McParland was born in Northern Ireland to the name McParlan. Hale renders it in the original form in *Human Science and Social Order*, 116, but once in America, the (in)famous Pinkerton used McParland.

128 This test, described above, was still mostly unknown to Americans at this time. Jung would not present his findings to an American audience until his first trip to the USA, at Clark University in 1909, four years after these events. Münsterberg, however, kept close track of developments in the German journals of the day. Interestingly, the German psychologist Max Wertheimer (who would soon to co-found the *Gestalt* school of psychology) independently developed as similar test at about the same time, but he never received the same recognition for it as Jung did.

129 Hale, Jr., *Human Science*, 117–18.

130 Hugo Münsterberg, *On the Witness Stand: Essays on Psychology and Crime* (New York, NY: Doubleday Page, 1908). (Note, there is some confusion about the date because it was copyrighted in 1908, but not published until 1909.)

131 Marston also sometimes went by the pen name Charles Moulton.

132 For more on Marston's life, see Geoffrey C. Bunn, "The Lie Detector, Wonder Woman and Liberty: The Life and Work of William Moulton Marston," *History of the Human Sciences* 10 (1997): 91–119; Jill LePore, "The Last Amazon: Wonder Woman Returns," *The New Yorker*, September 22, 2014, www.newyorker.com/magazine/2014/09/22/last-amazon. Interestingly, it appears that Wonder Woman's nemesis, Dr. Psycho, was modeled on none other than Münsterberg.

133 Edwin Balmer and William McHarg, *The Achievements of Luther Trant* (Boston, MA: Small Maynard, 1910). See also Melissa M. Littlefield, *The Lying Brain: Lie Detection in Science and Science Fiction* (Ann Arbor, MI: University of Michigan Press, 2011).

134 Edwin Balmer, *The Science of Advertising* (New York, NY: Wallace Press, 1910).

135 Münsterberg, *Psychotherapy*.

136 Adolf Meyer, "[Review of] Psychotherapy, by H. Münsterberg.," *Science* N.S. 30, no. 761 (1909): 150.

137 Hale, Jr., *Human Science*, 128. James Rowland Angell's textbook, the most complete statement of functionalist thought, had just been published: *Psychology: An Introductory Study of the Structure and Function of Human Consciousness* (New York, NY: Henry Holt, 1904).

138 Münsterberg, *Psychotherapy*, 1.

139 Ibid., 70.

140 Ibid., 3.

141 Ibid., 125.

142 Ibid., 208–11.

143 Hugo Münsterberg, "Finding Life's Work," *McClure's* 34 (1910): 398–403.

144 Hugo Münsterberg, *Vocation and Learning* (St. Louis, MO: People's University, 1912); Hugo Münsterberg, *Business Psychology* (Chicago, IL: La Salle Extension University, 1915).

145 Hugo Münsterberg, "Prohibition and Social Psychology," *McClure's* 31 (1908): 438–44.

146 Hale, Jr., *Human Science*, 119–20.

147 Michael Pettit, *The Science of Deception: Psychology and Commerce in America* (Chicago, IL: University of Chicago Press, 2013). See also Andreas Sommer, "Psychical Research and the Origins of American Psychology: Hugo Münsterberg, William James and Eusapia Palladino," *History of the Human Sciences* 25 (2012): 23–44.

148 His daughter, Margaret Münsterberg, claimed that the assistant was a man named Edgar Scott of Philadelphia (*Hugo Münsterberg, His Life and Work*, 181).

149 Hugo Münsterberg, "My Friends the Spiritualists: Some Theories and Conclusions Concerning Eusapia Palladino," *Metropolitan Magazine* 31 (1910): 559–72.

150 William James to Oliver Lodge, Jan 22, 1910, Ignas K. Skrupskelis and Elizabeth M. Berkeley, eds., *The Correspondence of William James* (Charlottesville, VA and London, UK: University of Virginia Press, 1992–2004), vol. 12, 418.

151 William James to Hereward Carrington, January 24, 1910, Ibid., vol. 12, 420.

152 William James to Théodore Flournoy, April 9, 1910, Ibid., vol. 12, 466.

153 See, e.g., Linda Schott, "Jane Addams and William James on Alternatives to War," *Journal of the History of Ideas* 54 (1993): 241–54.

154 Francesca Bordogna lucidly lays out each of these possibilities in turn in *William James at the Boundaries: Philosophy, Science, and the Geography of Knowledge* (Chicago, IL: University of Chicago Press, 2008), 193–94.

155 William James, "The Moral Equivalent of War," *McClure's* 35 (August 1910): 463–68.

156 Ibid., 467.

157 William James, "A World of Pure Experience," *Journal of Philosophy, Psychology, and Scientific Methods* 1 (1904): 533–43, 561–70; William James, "Does 'Consciousness' Exist?," *Journal of Philosophy, Psychology, and Scientific Methods* 1 (1904): 477–91. See also William James, *Essays in Radical Empiricism*, ed. Ralph Barton Perry (New York, NY: Longmans, Green, 1912), in which his former student collected together many related essays in "an attempt to carry out a plan which William James is known to have formed several years before his death" (from the start of the Preface).

158 David Hume, *A Treatise of Human Nature* (London, UK: John Noon, 1739–1740), Book 1, part 4, sections 3–6.

159 Immanuel Kant, *The Critique of Pure Reason*, trans. Norman Kemp Smith (London, UK: Palgrave Macmillan, 1781/1929), 113.

160 James, "A World of Pure Experience," 536.

161 James' two articles of 1904 and many responses to them were reprinted in Eugene I. Taylor and Robert H. Wozniak, eds., *Pure Experience: The Response to William James* (Bristol, UK: Thoemmes Press, 1996). Charles Peirce was aligned with this group as well, but still very poorly known outside of a narrow circle (see Douglas Anderson, "Another Radical Empiricism: Peirce 1903," in *Conversations on Peirce: Reals and Ideals*, ed. Douglas R. Anderson and Carl R. Hausman (New York, NY: Fordham University Press, 2012)).

162 Interestingly, one of James' principal students, Edwin B. Holt, would go on to develop a behaviorist philosophical psychology, though one expansive enough to include concepts such as plans, purposes, and goals. Although Holt is not well known today, he supervised the dissertation of Edward C. Tolman, who would become the leading advocate of a position called "purposive behaviorism" during the neobehaviorist era of approximately 1930 to 1960. See, e.g., David W. Carroll, *Purpose and Cognition: Edward Tolman and the Transformation of American* Psychology (New York, NY: Cambridge University Press); Eric P. Charles, *A New Look at New Realism: The Psychology and Philosophy of E. B. Holt* (Piscataway, NJ: Transaction Publishers, 2011).

163 For more information on the psychological and philosophical associations, see Christopher D. Green et al., "Bridge Over Troubled Waters? The Most 'Central' Members of Psychology and Philosophy Associations Ca. 1900," *Journal of the History of the Behavioral Sciences* 52 (2016): 279–99.

164 The "Western Branch" did not last long, though. It met intermittently until just 1908. A separate Midwestern Psychological Association formed in the 1920s. (See Samuel W. Fernberger, "The American Psychological Association: A Historical Summary, 1892–1930," *Psychological Bulletin* 29 (1932): 1–89; Ludy T. Benjamin Jr., "The Midwestern Psychological Association: A History of the Organization and Its Antecedents, 1902–1978," *American Psychologist* 43 (1979): 201–13; W. A. Russell, "The Midwestern Psychological Association," in *No Small Part: A History of Regional Organizations in*

American Psychology, ed. James L. Pate and Michael Wertheimer (Washington, DC: American Psychological Association, 1993), 43–67.) A New York regional branch formed in 1900 as well. It eventually evolved into the Eastern Psychological Association, which still exists today, though it is no longer affiliated with the APA.

165 Fernberger, "American Psychological Association," 60.

166 Cited in Harry Norman Gardiner, "The First Twenty-Five Years of the American Philosophical Association," *Philosophical Review* 35 (1926): 148.

167 See James L. Pate, "The Southern Society for Philosophy and Psychology," in *No Small Part: A History of Regional Organizations in American Psychology*, ed. James L. Pate and Michael Wertheimer (Washington, DC: American Psychological Association, 1993), 1–19; James Burt Miner, "The Twenty-Fifth Anniversary of the Southern Society for Philosophy and Psychology," *Psychological Bulletin* 28 (1931): 1–13.

168 "Pitchfork Ben" Tillman, governor of South Carolina from 1890 to 1894, US Senator from 1895 until his death in 1918 (cited in Laurence R. Veysey, *The Emergence of the American University* (Chicago, IL: University of Chicago Press, 1965), 15).

169 Haywood J. Pearce, professor at Emory College and a founding member of SSPP, cited in Miner, "Twenty-Fifth Anniversary," 3–4.

170 Buchner was at Alabama from 1903 to 1908. He would spend the rest of his career as Professor of Education at Johns Hopkins.

171 Although the editorial in which this comment appeared was anonymous "The American Psychological Association," *American Journal of Psychology* 7 (1896): 448), Michael Sokal asserts that it was "almost surely written by Titchener" ("Origins and Early Years of the American Psychological Association, 1890–1906," *American Psychologist* 47 (1992): 119).

172 Boring, "Titchener's Experimentalists"; Goodwin, "On the Origins of Titchener's Experimentalists."

173 Marshall taught aesthetics at Columbia in 1894–1895 and at Princeton in 1915–1916, but his main vocation was as an architect, not a professor (Robert Kugelmann, "Introspective Psychology, Pure and Applied. Henry Rutgers Marshall on Pain and Pleasure," *History of Psychology* 4 (2001): 34–58). Stratton, who had earned his PhD under Wundt, was mostly a vision researcher. A native of the San Francisco area, he spent the bulk of his career at the University of California, but also directed the Johns Hopkins laboratory under James Mark Baldwin between 1904 and 1909 (Edward Chace Tolman, "Biographical Memoir of George M. Stratton (1865–1957)," *National Academy of Sciences of the United States of America, Biographical Memoirs*, 1961, 290–306). Judd, also a Leipzig graduate, taught at Yale from 1902 to 1909, but was then hired to chair Chicago's Department of Education in the wake of Dewey's contentious departure, about which more immediately below (Adrian Brock, "Charles Hubbard Judd: A Wundtian Social Psychologist in the United States," *Psychologie und Geschichte (1992)* 3, no. 3/4 (1992): 17–23).

174 The entire complicated and sorry episode is recounted in great detail by Michael Knoll, "John Dewey as Administrator: The Inglorious End of the Laboratory School in Chicago," *Journal of Curriculum Studies* 47 (2015).

175 See ibid.

176 Published accounts of Scripture's career are somewhat rare. I have relied here on several papers presented by Russell Kosits of Redeemer College (Ancaster, Ontario) at the conferences of Cheiron: The International Society for the History of the Behavioral and Social Sciences in 2008 and 2009, and at the conventions of the American Psychological Association in 2011.

177 Letter from William James to Josiah Royce dated December 18, 1892. Skrupskelis and Berkeley, *Correspondence of William James*, vol. 7, 351.

178 Edward Wheeler Scripture, *Thinking, Feeling, Doing* (New York, NY: Flood and Vincent, 1895).

179 Edward Wheeler Scripture, *The Elements of Experimental Phonetics* (New York, NY: Charles Scribner's Sons, 1902); Edward Wheeler Scripture, "How the Voice Looks," *Century Magazine* 64 (May 1902): 148–53.

180 David Starr Jordan, president of Stanford, reported that, in response to a public lecture Hadley gave in 1904 on the virtues of the 13th-century university, President Eliot of Harvard rose to pointedly opine that "the American University has nothing to learn from Medieval universities, nor yet from those still in the medieval period" (*Days of a Man: Being Memories of a Naturalist, Teacher, and Minor Prophet of Democracy*, vol. 2 (Yonkers-on-Hudson, NY: World Book, 1922), 2). And so the ancient Harvard–Yale rivalry carried on into the new century.

181 Indeed, Yale's historic conservatism put it on the outskirts of the revolution taking place in American universities at the turn of the century with respect to the importance ascribed to the conduct of original research. Although Yale was a charter member of the prestigious Association of American Universities in 1900 (along with 13 other schools), one leading historian of the American university wrote that "by 1910, if a research-oriented observer had been asked to name the leading American universities, he probably would have listed Harvard, Chicago, Columbia, and Johns Hopkins, in that order" (Veysey, *The Emergence of the American University*, 171).

182 It was Angell's hiring of neobehaviorist Clark Hull in 1929 that really marked Yale's return to the top ranks of American psychology.

183 James McKeen Cattell, "Statistics of American Psychologists," *American Journal of Psychology* 14 (1903): 575.

184 James McKeen Cattell, *American Men of Science* (New York, NY: Science Press, 1933).

185 James Mark Baldwin, *Mental Development in the Child and the Race* (New York, NY: Palgrave Macmillan, 1895); James Mark Baldwin, *Social and Ethical Interpretations in Mental Development: A Study in Social Psychology* (New York, NY: Palgrave Macmillan, 1899); James Mark Baldwin, *Development and Evolution* (New York, NY: Palgrave Macmillan, 1902).

186 On Baldwin's and Cattell's chronic inability to get along, and the bizarre auction they ultimately had to decide which would take full control of the 9, see Michael M. Sokal, "Baldwin, Cattell and the Psychological Review: A Collaboration and Its Discontents," *History of the Human Sciences* 10, no. 1 (1997): 57–89.

187 James Mark Baldwin, ed., *Dictionary of Philosophy and Psychology*, 3 vols. (New York, NY and London, UK: Palgrave Macmillan, 1901).

188 James Mark Baldwin, *Between Two Wars, 1861–1921* (Boston, MA: Stratford, 1926).

189 The details of this story, long a mystery, come from the extraordinary research of Robert H. Wozniak and Jorge A. Santiago-Blay, "Trouble at Tyson Alley: James Mark Baldwin's Arrest in a Baltimore Bordello," *History of Psychology* 16 (2013): 227–48.

190 Baldwin's denials seem hardly credible to us today. It is possible, however, that he was there for the other recreations the establishment afforded. In any case, it appears that Baldwin was a victim of rival factions of police who were trying to show each other to be lax in their duties, and possibly corrupt (Ibid.).

191 It may be recalled from the scandal that had forced Charles Sanders Peirce out of the same school 25 years earlier, that Hopkins a non-denominational school continually having to demonstrate its moral rectitude to Baltimore's various religious communities.

192 To be precise, Baldwin sold the journals to his former student and then Princeton professor, Howard C. Warren. Warren and Watson split the editorships between them. The lurking irony in Watson's takeover of Baldwin's professional positions here is that Watson had been refusing overtures from Baldwin for years, and had only finally agreed to the move when it became apparent that Chicago was about to fire him over an extra-marital affair that he had indulged in there (Kerry W. Buckley, *Mechanical Man: John B. Watson and the Beginnings of Behaviorism* (New York, NY: Guilford, 1989)).

193 Robert H. Wozniak, "James Mark Baldwin, Professional Disaster, and the European Connection," *Rassegna Di Psicologia* 26 (2009): 111–28.

194 Daniel W. Bjork, *William James: The Center of His Vision* (Washington, DC: American Psychological Association, 1997), 230.

195 William James, "On Some Mental Effects of the Earthquake," *Youth's Companion*, June 7, 1906.

196 William James, *Pragmatism: A New Name for Some Old Ways of Thinking* (New York, NY: Longmans, Green, 1907).

197 William James, *The Meaning of Truth: A Sequel to "Pragmatism"* (New York, NY: Longmans, Green, 1909).

198 William James, *A Pluralistic Universe* (New York, NY: Longmans, Green, 1909).

199 Bjork, *William James*, 257–61.

10

PSYCHOLOGY ON THE PUBLIC STAGE

1. Cities in the 1910s

At the time this story began, the early 1840s, New York was a city of 313,000 people with no reliable source of drinking water. There was no electricity, of course. Dim gaslights had only recently been installed on its main streets. There were few buildings taller than four stories. Church steeples dominated the low skyline. There was no professional police force and no formal educational system. The top three-quarters of Manhattan was still rural countryside. Trains came in only as far as 27th Street, not into the city proper. There were no cars, of course. Transport within the city was by horse or by foot. There were no bridges or tunnels to the mainland or to Long Island. Brooklyn was a separate city, reachable only by ferry boat. Photography was just beginning to appear—the word itself had only been coined by John Herschel in 1839—but there were no movies, no recorded music, and no telephones. The first telegraph lines were just coming into existence, and there wouldn't be a line from New York to Washington, DC until 1846. Commerce and trade had begun to concentrate in the city after the opening of the Erie Canal in 1825, but New York was still a relatively minor city by international standards. Immigration into the city was a bare trickle compared to the torrent it would soon become.

In 1910—about one lifetime later—the city would have been unrecognizable to the resident of 1840. Trains not only ran into the city, but above the city and beneath the city as well. The streets were clogged with traffic as people, horses, wagons, carriages, streetcars, bicycles, and now, private automobiles pushed their way on to the roadways. The urban landscape extended as far north as the Harlem River, and beyond that into the Bronx. Electric lights lined many streets and filled many buildings. Electric elevators whisked people up and down the tallest towers the world had ever seen.

Instant communication—both near and far—was becoming common: not only were there telegraph lines to every part of the country but, starting in 1858, service across the Atlantic Ocean had become available. In addition, telephones now allowed for direct voice communication not only within the city but, starting in 1892, between New York and far-away Chicago. Publishing was transformed as well. Liberated from the arduous work of manual typesetting by the invention of the Linotype machine in 1886, the New York news industry had grown from just a few daily papers in the 1840s to dozens of them in 1910, catering to every possible class and taste. In addition to the newspapers, publishers now offered hundreds of magazines and thousands of "dime novels" in inexpensive paperback form.

Recorded music at home and moving pictures in theaters were becoming ubiquitous. Public radio broadcasts were just beginning. The impact on the news industry would be profound. Between home radio and public movie houses (which started showing newsreels about 1910), the news industry would undergo its greatest transformation since the emergence of the penny press in the 1830s.

Despite all these groundbreaking technological advances, peace did not come to the massive metropolis. As it had so often been in the past, New York remained the front line for a series of contentious battles between the city's government and its gigantic, often distrustful, sometimes raucous, population. The city's seemingly endless explosion of residents made even so basic a function as transportation—especially onto and off of Manhattan Island—a never-ending challenge. The system of elevated trains, the earliest segments of which were only 30 years old in 1910, was already inadequate at the start of the new century. Not only was it dirty and noisy, making further expansion of the system politically problematic, but it occupied a large swath of increasingly valuable land. A wholly new mode of public transit was needed. London had used underground trains as early as the late 1860s. Paris was in the process of building a similar system. *Even Boston*—ever New York's rival—had opened a small "subway," as the underground train systems were coming to be called, in 1897. The road ahead for New York was clear enough, if not easy: in 1900, ground was broken for a system of electric trains to run beneath the streets—even under the East River—connecting Manhattan to Brooklyn by tunnel. The first New York subway opened in 1904.

Nothing could keep up with the surge of demand for fast, cheap transit, though. Capacity remained such a pressing issue that even the new subway would not start to actually displace the old elevated train lines until the 1930s. Above ground, despite the opening of the greatest bridge the world had ever seen not 20 years before, it became necessary to start building an additional link to Brooklyn in 1901. The new Manhattan Bridge—a modern steel structure, contrasting sharply with the heavy masonry of the Brooklyn Bridge—opened in 1909.

The communication and transportation revolutions affected every corner of society, and psychology was no exception. Although putatively national journals

FIGURE 10.1 Manhattan Bridge.

and a national association had existed for nearly two decades, the day-to-day *communities* of psychologists had existed mostly on a local basis: New York psychologists could talk, on a daily basis, mostly with other New York psychologists. Indeed, before the 20th century, psychologists were more likely to be in daily touch with physicians, neurologists, educators, anthropologists, and other scholars from their own university and city than they were to converse with fellow psychologists from elsewhere. Trains and telephones began to change all of this. As with the wider country, psychology began to develop a deeper, more intricately interconnected national culture that was no longer hamstrung by the constraints of the postal service, the quarterly journal, and the once-per-year meeting of the national association.

As always, wider cultural developments conditioned what psychologists saw as their most productive courses of action. The labor question continued to be contentious. In 1905, after many workers had won often-violent battles to legislatively limit the length of the workday, a Supreme Court decision in the case of *Lochner v. New York* ruled that regulations on work hours violated a clause of the 14th Amendment holding that states shall not "deprive any person of life, liberty, or property, without due process of law." It is ironic that this amendment, originally passed in 1868 to secure the rights of former slaves, was used here to restrict the rights of paid laborers, not a few of whom had been those very slaves, or were the children of former slaves. The *Lochner* ruling would be used to strike down many labor regulations over the next generation-and-a-half, until it was quashed in 1937.[1]

Rulings like *Lochner* made it seem to many in the labor movement as though the legislative "game" was rigged against them. This led many to consider more radical solutions to the challenges—often matters of life and death—that they faced. "Big Bill" Haywood, who we met in in connection with Münsterberg's excursion into the psychology of law, founded the Industrial Workers of the World (IWW) the very same year as the *Lochner* ruling was issued. The IWW organized many industries that had been ignored by the older unions, especially where the workforces were dominated by immigrants and by women. The ultimate aim of the IWW was to create a single union for all workers nationwide, rather than having individual unions according to each "craft," which could too easily be divided from one another and thereby conquered by business interests. One of the IWW's most visible battles was the 1912 Textile Strike in Lawrence, Massachusetts, in which the working conditions revealed were so terrible that Congress saw fit to hold hearings on the matter. The owners quickly settled rather than risk further government intervention.

Government acted erratically in these matters, and so it was not trusted by either side. In 1916, the federal government passed the Adamson Act, which established an eight-hour day for interstate railroad employees, plus additional pay for overtime work. It was the first federal law to regulate the work hours of private companies. Surprisingly for the *Lochner* era, the Supreme Court upheld Adamson's constitutionality, citing the Interstate Commerce Clause of the Constitution.[2] By contrast, so threatening did the federal government find the power of the IWW that just two years later, in 1918, Woodrow Wilson used the extraordinary measures he had enacted during World War I to have Haywood and 100 other IWW leaders convicted of "espionage." Haywood was sentenced to 20 years in prison, but he fled to the nascent Soviet Union where he would die in 1928.

Labor strife was hardly limited to the courts. On March 25, 1911, a fire at the Triangle Shirtwaist Factory—situated along a street that William James had lived as a child (Washington Place)—led to the deaths of 146 garment workers, mostly young immigrant women between the ages of 16 and 23. Because the factory owners had locked the doors to the stairwells to prevent their employees from leaving the work floor, many of the women were forced to leap eight floors or more to their deaths on the street below rather than be consumed by the rapidly advancing flames. The enormity of the tragedy caused a national outcry and was key in shifting public opinion in favor of labor's demands. Factory safety legislation soon followed, as did increased membership in the International Ladies' Garment Workers Union.

2. Psychology Sells Itself to Business and Industry

Many psychologists saw business and industry as potentially lucrative arenas in which to ply their own trades. Very often, however, they allied themselves with capital against labor. Frederick Winslow Taylor was not a psychologist but, rather, a mechanical engineer who spent over a decade as a management consultant with several industries. His general aim was to help companies solve production problems that were costing them money. From about 1890 forward, Taylor consulted for a number of companies, most famously Bethlehem Steel, which brought him to the general conclusion that workers often fail to deliver maximum effort and, as a result, saddle their employers with unnecessary labor costs. If only workers could be induced to work as efficiently as possible *mechanically* (he was a mechanical engineer, after all), labor costs could be substantially reduced. He attacked the perceived problem by closely scrutinizing workers' actions—timing them with a stopwatch and sometimes photographing them as well, while they did their jobs—a process that came to be known as the "time study." Then, he would design a precise sequence of actions that, he argued, maximized the worker's efficiency. In order to enforce the execution of his detailed action scheme, he recommended that workers be paid according to their ability to generate the level of production that he had determined should result from employing his mechanically "ideal" sequence exactly.

In 1911, after more than two decades of this kind work, Taylor published his general outlook in a controversial book titled, *Principles of Scientific Management*.[3] The choice of the term "scientific" was rhetorically shrewd. Almost paradoxically, it simultaneously conveyed an air of both "objectivity" and "normativity"; these schemes are how things *are* made maximally efficient, therefore one *should* act in accordance with them. Interestingly, this verbal shrewdness had not been Taylor's originally. The phrase "scientific management" was coined not by Taylor but by the future Supreme Court Justice, Louis D. Brandeis. In a case before the Interstate Commerce Commission, Brandeis argued against an application by the Eastern Rail Road Company to raise its freight rates. Brandeis contended that Eastern's financial problems were caused by poor oversight, not by insufficient revenue, and that the public should not have to bear the cost of Eastern's inefficiency. If only its management took a more "scientific" (i.e., Taylorist) approach, Brandeis continued, the company could easily reduce its operating costs. In the wake of Brandeis' claim, Taylor was called to testify before the Commission, which brought him and his system enormous publicity. Soon after, Taylor adopted Brandeis' phrase, "scientific management."

Taylor's book became a sensation among the American managerial class, not only because it promised to save them money, but also because it effectively placed blame for inefficiency on the putative ignorance and laziness of workers. Although Taylor claimed to be reconciling management and labor through "science," there could be little doubt about where his sympathies lay: he once sneered that anyone who is "physically able to handle pig-iron and is sufficiently phlegmatic and stupid to choose this for his occupation is rarely able to comprehend the science of handling pig-iron."[4] Not surprisingly, Taylor and his paternalistic condescension were despised by labor organizations who not only found his interventions degrading to workers but also indifferent to the pace of action that human bodies were actually capable of sustaining over the course of a long workday. "Scientific management" was denounced by the American Federation of Labor and became the primary point of contention in a variety of strikes. Taylorism rapidly became so controversial a political issue that, in 1912, Congress held hearings on the matter. Although Taylor was considered a prophet in the business world, things did not go so well for him in the arena of politics. In 1914, the US government banned Taylorist practices in all government operations, including in the military.[5] Taylor died the following year, but his ideas were taken up and developed by others.[6]

A Massachusetts building contractor named Frank Gilbreth was developing ideas about work efficiency that were superficially similar to Taylor's. His focus, however, was not so much on increasing the pace of work as it was on eliminating unnecessary movements and redesigning equipment so that work would induce less fatigue (e.g., physically raising the brick supply to the current height of brick-laying work with a multilevel bench, so that workers were not constantly stooping to pick up the next brick to be laid). This attention to the worker's experience tempered the hostility that Taylor had generated. Gilbreth was also more techni-cally sophisticated than Taylor. Rather than using a stopwatch alongside of photo-graphic stills, Gilbreth exploited the new technology of motion pictures to record the complete sequence of the worker's actions, often with a clock in the frame to exactly track the passage of time. The films were then taken back to Gilbreth's offices to be studied, frame by frame, in order to design better work systems. These were called "motion studies," in contrast to Taylor's more rudimentary "time stud-ies," and they may constitute the first time that film was used in a behavioral study of any kind. Starting in 1911, Gilbreth began publishing books on his general approach to work efficiency.[7] The growing popularity of his approach led to con-siderable friction with Taylor and his disciples.[8] Gilbreth, however, was talented at drawing favorable publicity. Late in May 1913, for instance, he hauled his motion picture setup out to the Polo Grounds in northern Manhattan and filmed motion studies of a couple of pitchers in front of 20,000 fans who had come to watch the New York Giants play.[9] The *New York Tribune* had organized the event and was there, of course, to spread word of these curious goings-on to its tens of thousands of readers.[10]

In 1904, Gilbreth married a woman from California named Lillian Moller. She had a Master's Degree in English from the University of California, but she had also taken some psychology courses with Edward Thorndike at Columbia. Lillian immediately became Frank's collaborator in the motion studies. She returned to California to pursue a PhD in psychology. The dissertation that she completed in 1911 would eventually be published as *The Psychology of Management* in 1914.[11] Because she did not meet the University of California's residency requirements while writing her dissertation—working at Frank's consulting business, and rais-ing the first few of their eventual twelve children—the university would not grant her the degree she had earned. Lillian returned to school once again, this time at Brown University, where she completed another PhD, awarded this time, in 1915. Here she began to extend her and Frank's findings to realms beyond the industrial: her Brown dissertation was titled, *Some Aspects of Eliminating Waste in Teaching*.[12] Her formal education in psychology enabled her to incorporate more effectively

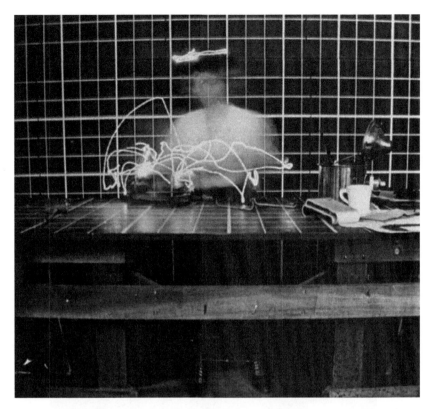

FIGURE 10.2 A time-motion photograph by Frank Gilbreth, ca. 1914. The paths of light record all hand motions, which can be exactly measured by reference to the grid on the wall behind the worker.

Credit: National Museum of American History, Smithsonian Institution Washington, DC.

into management studies the mental aspects of workers' lives, such as the impacts of interest and boredom on the quality of their work.

Frank and Lillian's collaboration in the new industrial psychology continued apace for another decade, until Frank died suddenly at the age of just 59, in 1924.[13] By that time, he had begun lecturing on management at Purdue University. After his death, Purdue asked Lillian to lecture in his place. This continued for another decade until, in 1935, her appointment was converted to a visiting professorship. In 1940, Purdue promoted her to full professor, and she stayed there for another eight years until she retired. Lillian's work on efficiency in the decades after Frank's death expanded from the workplace and the school right into the home itself. She designed an "ideally" efficient kitchen to help alleviate the burden of labor for housewives. Her best-known invention from this period is probably the foot-pedal trashcan, which continues to be widely used to this day.[14]

FIGURE 10.3 Frank and Lillian Gilbreth.

Credit: Frank and Lillian Gilbreth Collection, Courtesy of Purdue University Libraries, Karnes Archives & Special Collections.

Not all of psychologists' forays into business and industry were quite so focused on the shop floor as the Gilbreths' was. A psychologist at Northwestern University named Walter Dill Scott, for instance, built a consulting practice around assisting businesses to identify the best types of people for particular roles they needed to fill. For example, salespeople are most successful when they have certain personal qualities. Those qualities are different from the ones that make for a successful accountant or executive. Businesses need a variety of different types—people with different personal makeups—in order to thrive. Scott tailored evaluation schemes—questionnaires and interview strategies—to help businesses identify the best candidates for their positions. In contrast to the mental tests of the past, and the intelligence tests just then coming into view (more about which to follow), Scott's focus was on the specific *constellation* of qualities that is needed for a particular job—e.g., intelligence *as well as* honesty, persuasiveness, attractive appearance, etc.—rather than studying "general intelligence" and abstract "personality traits," as we would now call them. This more pragmatic approach to the question would later bring him into conflict with other prominent psychologists of his day but, in the end, it would also lead to the highest accolade of his life.

Scott was effectively inventing a new kind of psychology, and it was not at all the kind for which he had been trained. Like so many others young Americans of his day, he had gone to Leipzig to earn a doctorate, where, like many of Wundt's

FIGURE 10.4 Walter Dill Scott.

Credit: Courtesy Northwestern University Archives.

students, he had been enlisted in the effort to fractionate simple mental activities into their component processes. Although this prestigious education, which he successfully completed in 1900, won him his professorship at Northwestern, his undergraduate alma mater, it bore only a modest relation to the applied sort of psychology he would help to invent. He admired the work of Frederick Winslow Taylor, but he also wanted to get below the level of explicit rational motivations to which Taylor limited himself (e.g., monetary incentives), down into emotionally driven impulses. And not just for the worker but also for the consumer as well.[15]

At first, Scott focused on advertising, developing the theory that suggestibility is the key to consumer behavior. By playing on consumers' emotions—rather than simply presenting the facts about a given product—advertisements could become more persuasive. He wrote a short popular book on the topic in 1903, which was written up in the *New York Times*.[16] The publicity won him a national audience, so he wrote a longer book, published in 1908, which established him as the leading authority on a topic—the psychology of advertising—that had hardly existed before he took it up.[17] Always the entrepreneur, Scott was able to parlay that prominence into a lucrative consulting business.

Another psychologist who contributed significantly to the psychology of advertising was Harry Hollingworth. Having graduated from Columbia in 1909, he was just an impoverished instructor at Barnard College when Coca-Cola came calling in 1911. The company was under indictment by the US Government for including in its popular drink an allegedly toxic and addictive substance: caffeine. For the upcoming trial, they needed scientific evidence that caffeine was, in fact, harmless. They had, at first, sought out the prominent James McKeen Cattell, but he had declined, recommending his recent graduate, Hollingworth, instead. Hollingworth agreed to take up the project and did the necessary experiments in just a few weeks' time. He testified in court that caffeine was a mild stimulant, but that it caused no detectable negative effects.[18] Although the event was momentous for the credibility of psychology in courts of law, the charges against Coca-Cola were dismissed by the judge the week after Hollingworth's testimony, and no decision was ever rendered on the legal value of his experimental conclusions. Nevertheless, the incident made Hollingworth a kind of accidental celebrity in the world of advertising. Two years later, he published a book on the topic.[19] Much later, Hollingworth would also conduct landmark research of the effects of chewing gum for the Beech-Nut company.[20]

As the controversy over Taylorism heated up during the second decade of the 20th century began, a number of psychologists started taking advantage of the sensation by publicly weighing in on the controversy. Walter Dill Scott Scott, for instance, issued his own book on the fraught question of industrial efficiency in 1911.[21] Similarly, Hugo Münsterberg, of course, could not allow such an opportunity for self-promotion to slip by unmolested. Just a year after Scott's major book on advertising had come out, Harvard's unofficial German "ambassador" published an article on the same topic in the popular *McClure's Magazine*. Although he did not mention Scott by name, he deployed his signature tactic of calling for "special laboratories for applied psychology [that] could examine the market demands with careful study of all the principles involved."[22] This strategy enabled him to imply that earlier efforts had been little more than unreliable speculation, and that only he was being truly "scientific" about the matter. In 1913, following the path of publicity again, Münsterberg published his thoughts on industrial efficiency in book form.[23] Because of his body of work in the field, it is not uncommon to see Münsterberg declared the "Father of Industrial Psychology," and that seems to be exactly how he hoped it would play out. His outsized public stature brought into public view ideas which were not yet widely known. On closer examination, however, one can see that, although he made some significant contributions, he was often more of a quick and canny follower than a true originator.[24]

One of those who was first made aware of industrial psychology by Münsterberg's 1913 book was the president of the Carnegie Institute for Technology in Pittsburgh, Arthur Hamerschlag. His interest piqued, he decided to attend the meeting of the American Psychological Association, which was in Philadelphia that year. There he met a young Dartmouth psychologist who was working on the questions of business, Walter Van Dyke Bingham. Thinking that it might be interesting to add industrial psychology to the Carnegie Institute curriculum, which was only a decade old at the time, Hamerschlag asked Bingham to write a report about how a psychology department might benefit the school. What Bingham proposed was entirely new on the American academic scene: he outlined a vision for a department devoted solely to applied psychology. The development and application of personnel testing, and other forms of evaluation, would play a large role in its activities. Not only would it align elegantly with Carnegie's educational mission. It would also be able to attract funding from corporations, both local and national, who would commission the department to conduct research that had real economic consequences for them.

Bingham recommended that Hamerschlag hire an applied psychologist then working at the University of Illinois, Guy Montrose Whipple. Hamershlag decided instead to poach Bingham himself.[25] Faced with the prospect of chairing an entire Division of Applied Psychology—the first academic unit of its kind in the US—located in America's industrial heartland, rather than teaching seven courses[26] at a small, if elite, New England college, Bingham jumped at the offer. He immediately hired James Burt Miner, then a Minnesota professor who had earned his PhD under Cattell at Columbia,[27] and Louis L. Thurstone, just then completing his PhD at Chicago. Miner would later write an influential book on the relationship between intelligence and criminality,[28] and he pioneered the assessment of vocational interest in ways that were eventually molded by Edward K. Strong into the widely used *Strong Vocational Interest Blank*.[29] Thurstone, by contrast, would become a legendary psychometrician, developing, among other things, factor analytic techniques that were said to reveal the existence of multiple "primary mental abilities" rather than a singular "general intelligence" as Charles Spearman had claimed.[30] It was an extraordinarily good start for a new program.

In 1916, Bingham added to his Carnegie roster Walter Dill Scott, who agreed to relocate from Northwestern, bringing with him his experience in developing business-oriented tests tailored for particular clients. Scott oversaw the "Bureau of Salesmanship Research" within Bingham's Division of Applied Psychology. Relationships were forged with several of America's greatest companies, including Carnegie Steel, and dozens of doctoral students were trained, many of whom went on to bring industrial research to psychology departments across the country.

The Carnegie program represented a high point for academic industrial psychology, but it was not to last for long. Less than a decade after it had begun, a new president at Carnegie shifted priorities elsewhere. Miner left for Kentucky, where he remained for the next two decades. Thurstone returned to Chicago, where he worked for nearly 30 years, founding the Psychometric Society in 1936, along with its journal *Psychometrika*. Scott was elected president of the APA in 1919, and then president of Northwestern University, a post he would hold for nearly 20 years.

3. Psychology Educates the Masses

Business and industry were, of course, not the only domains in which psychologists attempted to apply their specialized knowledge and skills. The ongoing expansion of universal public education created ever more possibilities for the development and use of new psychological practices. As the historian of psychology Kurt Danziger observed, educational psychology underwent a transformation at this time from a topic that had originally been aimed at assisting teachers in the classroom to one increasingly directed at facilitating the administration of an enormous and ever-growing institution.[31]

Education continued to be a bone of public contention as well. Culture clashes often became most intense when the issue was children, and the kinds of adults they should be molded into. As urban infrastructures groaned under the weight of vast and rapid population growth, the strains on school systems, in particular, became nearly unsustainable. Budgets never seemed sufficient and some new method was needed to coordinate the ever increasing numbers of students around the often inadequate school buildings and equipment. It was probably inevitable that aspects of the efficiency movement, then sweeping the industrial realm, would be brought into discussions of public education as well, but these ideas were even more controversial when it came to schools than they had been in factories and construction sites.

In 1907, the superintendent of schools in Gary, Indiana, a man named William A. Wirt, hatched a new plan for public schools that would not only use resources more efficiently, but also bring more students into greater contact with the specialized facilities that urban schools were beginning to design. Instead of having secondary students sit in the same room all day while teachers brought different topics to them, Wirt conceived the idea of moving the students in and out of different rooms, each customized for particular purposes: listening to lectures (classrooms), working on projects (workshops, art studios, auditoriums), and being physically active (gymnasiums, sports fields).

To us, in the 21st century, accustomed as we are to the high school system that grew from Wirt's "Gary Plan," moving about during the school day seems completely natural. To many people of the early 20th century, though, who were mainly familiar with the old one-room school house, the Gary Plan seemed like an abomination. To immigrants, especially, often uncomfortably crowded in unpleasant urban ghettos, Wirt's plan seemed to threaten all the sacrifices they had made so that their children's lives could be better than theirs had been. The parents may have had to endure the degrading ritual of efficiency "experts" coming to their workplaces and telling them how to "properly" do jobs they had been doing for years, but their children, they fervently hoped, would have educations full of arts and literature and sciences, so that they could go on to become doctors and lawyers and professors. The Gary Plan seemed to many of them to consign their children in advance to dank, dangerous factories and dirty, exhausting construction sites. Its controlling clocks and scheduled shufflings from place to place would turn them into the robotic mechanisms that Taylor and his followers wanted manual laborers to be.

In fact, Wirt was no Taylorist. He was an unabashed "progressive." He was a disciple of John Dewey. Indeed, the Gary Plan had been publicly praised by Dewey himself.[32] But the distrust was often too great, and the implementation of the Plan too often corrupted by politicians who were sympathetic to the business interests that wanted precisely that children be molded by schools into efficient and compliant workers.[33]

The Gary Plan was controversial in many places across America, but nowhere did it spur as fervent an opposition as in New York City. On New Year's Day 1914, a new reformist mayor took office in New York City, John Purroy Mitchel. At just 34 years of age, the second youngest mayor New York ever had, Mitchel had beaten back the deeply entrenched power and corruption of Tammany Hall, and he was determined to take the city in a new, modern direction. His first initiative was to clean up the police force, a project he attacked with both vigor and a good measure of success. In April, Mitchel survived an assassination attempt by one Michael Mahoney, who the *New York Times* described as "a shabbily dressed man of 71 years, who fancied he had a series of grievances against the Mayor for his mode of administering the City Government."[34] Mitchel was not hit by the shots fired at him.

In 1911–1912, Mitchel had been in charge of a massive survey of New York's public schools that had found deficiencies and failures in nearly every aspect of the system. Thus, his next order of business as mayor was to overhaul how the city delivered education to its children. At the time, New York employed some 20,000 teachers, who oversaw some 800,000 children. More than two-thirds of the students were foreign born, so language was a serious issue. Half of the students left school after the sixth grade; only one in ten completed high school. The education budget was large—$44 million—but, still, buildings were badly overcrowded and many people questioned the quality of the education provided.[35]

Mitchel believed that shifting New York Schools to the Gary Plan would provide a better educational experience by using the space the school system had more efficiently (thereby reducing overcrowding) and by modernizing the curriculum. For many, however, "modernizing" was a dog whistle for replacing traditional academic topics with ones that were of more immediate vocational value—job training. The two issues, though distinct in principal, were intricately intertwined in the minds of many New Yorkers of the era. After touring Gary's schools with an entourage of New York's educational leaders, Mitchel hired Wirt to consult on the conversion of the city's schools to the new plan.

The New York City School Board was then presided over by a Tammany politician, Thomas Churchill. Churchill was, at first, willing to entertain a changeover to the Gary plan, but he wanted to ensure that he and his Board retained control of the process. The Progressives of Mitchel's administration, however, believed that such matters were better handled by experts and, in any case, they did not trust the motivations of old Tammany loyalists like Churchill. During 1914 and early 1915, Mitchel had a few schools changed over as a pilot project. In the fall of 1915, he pre-emptively declared that all schools would be converted to the Gary Plan as soon as possible.

Churchill objected that the mayor was illegitimately meddling in school affairs. He claimed that the mayor's motivations, far from being a concern for student welfare, were primarily budgetary in character. Making matters worse for Mitchel, in 1916, Churchill was replaced as president of the School Board by William Willcox, a man who adamantly opposed the Gary Plan, and who was ready to publicly campaign against it.

The changeover progressed slowly. At the start of 1917, only 30 of New York's 680 schools had been converted, but the plan was rapidly becoming a public controversy that Tammany and other opposition groups were starting to milk for partisan gain. Some argued that children require the surrogate mother of a single teacher all day long. Others claimed that moving from room to room would displace a large amount of precious learning time from the school day. It was even suggested that the periodic movement from room to room would make children ill.

The opposition campaign worked. By the fall of 1917, large segments of the public were up in arms—particularly the Jewish and Italian communities. On Oct 17, a raucous crowd of several hundred students demonstrated at a school in the Upper East Side of Manhattan, throwing stones at the school. Police had to be called out to disperse the mob and protect the building. The next morning, though, over 1,000 protesters turned out, and this time they were faced by a throng of counter-demonstrators. The ensuing mêlée could not be quelled, and it started spreading to other schools in the area. As the protests grew in size to thousands of people—still mostly students at this point—the police started arresting people. At first they focused mainly on the adults, who were thought to be leading the protests, but eventually children were taken into custody as well, raising an the outcry from parents the city over. Within a couple of days, the protests had spread to the Bronx, where police had to set up guards at every school in the borough. Mayor Mitchel tried to shift blame for the disorder on to Tammany *agents provocateurs*, but the accusation only seemed to enflame things further.

Next, hundreds of mothers became actively involved in the protests. The *New York World* reported that many "non-English speaking Yiddish mothers" believed that the Gary system would turn their children into "slaves" of John D. Rockefeller.[36] From the Upper East Side and the Bronx, the protests spread to Brooklyn and, finally, to the Lower East Side. What had started as an unruly neighborhood demonstration was rapidly turning into a violent, city-wide riot. The crowds began to turn against the police, throwing bricks, stones, and bottles. The number of arrests multiplied rapidly. Activist students started being expelled, suspended, and fined. Mitchel's plan to improve the city's schools had blown up in his face.

Of course, how New York organized its schools was hardly the only pressing issue of the day. Wholly unexpected by Mitchel or anyone else, back when the Gary Plan process had started to take shape in early 1914, was that it would become weirdly entangled with the most horrific war the world had ever seen. As is well known, when, in June 1914, the heir to the Austro-Hungarian throne was assassinated by a Serb nationalist, the political fallout rapidly spun out of control, culminating in war among the great European powers. Although many expected the conflict to last only a few months, at first, the conflict soon descended into a bloody stalemate in which hundreds of thousands were killed, month over month, by the most destructive, most technologically sophisticated, most "modern" weapons ever produced.

No military anywhere really understood how to attack successfully under such conditions and, as a result, the battlefield itself became a kind of giant laboratory of war. A whole generation of young men were thrown into a fight that has often been likened to a meatgrinder. In the US, President Woodrow Wilson insisted that America would remain neutral, even when the nation was provoked by the deaths of American passengers on ships that were torpedoed by the German navy. Wilson even premised his 1916 re-election campaign on keeping America out of the increasingly catastrophic conflagration. However, when evidence emerged in January of 1917 that Germany was secretly urging Mexico to attack the US, Wilson swiftly changed course: Congress declared war on Germany in April. The US implemented mandatory military conscription in May. Then, in June, it passed an Espionage Act, making it a crime to "obstruct" military recruitment (meaning the draft), among other things. Although the country would not be on a full war footing for several months yet, national anxiety at the prospect of sending American boys across the ocean to lay down their lives in a European quarrel grew over the course of the year.

These events, momentous as they were, might be expected not to have had much impact on the local issue of how New York's schools organized their time and space but, because Mayor Mitchel actively supported both US entry into the war and Wilson's controversial military draft, the two issues became closely connected in the public's mind. At the very height of the disorder over the city's public schools, James McKeen Cattell was dismissed by Columbia University, ostensibly for having written a letter to a US Congressman opposing conscription.[37] Cattell's firing launched an uproar over his freedom of speech, and he, in turn, used his moment in the public spotlight to declare that the Gary Plan would bring mandatory military training to the city's schools, so that the government could more efficiently deliver New York boys into Europe's "meatgrinder." What made Cattell's pronouncement particularly effective at that instant was that it was not merely the opinion of a lone, if notable, intellectual. It was, in fact, the political platform on which the socialist, Jewish lawyer, Morris Hillquit, was running to displace Mitchel as mayor.[38] The Gary Plan and the violence that it generated became the major issue of the New York City election of 1917. Mitchel stood by his proposal, but it led to his demise, both political and personal: He was routed by the Tammany candidate for mayor, John F. Hylan, by a 2-to-1 margin. After the humiliating defeat, Mitchel joined the US Air Service and was killed in a flying accident the following year.[39]

4. Psychology's Starring Role: Intelligence Testing

One of the greatest challenges for those facing the gargantuan task of designing a school system that could accommodate hundreds of thousands of children of all ages, language groups, races, and socioeconomic backgrounds was figuring out exactly at what intellectual level to pitch the curriculum such that it could be learned by the vast majority of those in each particular grade. No one wanted children to be left out, but there seemed no getting around the fact that, no matter what one did, some children were going to need extra individualized attention in order to succeed than could be provided by a massive, bureaucratic, institution such as public school.

Rather than waiting for children to fail, then trying to pick them up again, many school systems sought out ways of identifying children who were likely to have trouble in advance, so that the proper educational supports could be brought to bear ahead of time, rather than after the fall. It wasn't only American schools facing this problem. In Paris, the Ministry of Public Instruction called upon a psychologist at the Sorbonne who had just published a book on the question of intelligence, Alfred Binet.[40] In response, Binet developed a series of tests, to be administered by a single tester to a single child, designed to distinguish children who were of normal mental ability from those who were likely to have significantly more trouble learning standardized school material than the bulk of children. Working with a physician named Théodore Simon, Binet's first test, published in 1905, simply distinguished between those who were "normal" and those who would require special attention. Quickly revising the test in 1908, Binet and Simon developed the idea of an "intellectual level" (*niveau intellectuel*), and they normed their test on each age in a range from 3 years old to 13 ("mental age" was a term later used by Americans, though it was not a phrase that Binet and Simon used). Children whose intellectual level lagged too far behind their chronological age would either be assigned to a regular class that was more appropriate to their intellectual level, or they would attend special classes for children with similar ability. In 1911, Binet added some adult level items to the test, taking the age range up to 16 years.[41]

The items that Binet employed in his test were different from those used in the anthropometric tests that had been pioneered by Galton and Cattell earlier. Binet included some of their sensory and motor tasks in his most preliminary tests, but his test also asked children to solve more complex cognitive problems: Name common things shown in pictures. Repeat a list of words. Answer questions about a picture from memory. Draw geometric figures from memory. Create sentences that include particular words. Distinguish the meanings of two closely related words. Binet and Simon normed each problem carefully, determining the age at which most children could solve it, and sometimes the time typically needed to solve it as well.

Educators in the US faced similar challenges and were in need of a similar tool to assess the intellectual levels of school children. One American psychologist in particular, Henry Herbert Goddard, did more than any other to bring the new French intelligence tests to American shores. Back in 1896, Goddard had been the headmaster of a private Quaker academy in Maine when he saw Stanley Hall give one of his famous lectures on educational reform.[42] Goddard was so inspired by Hall's vision that he left his comfortable position to attend Clark and earn a PhD under Hall's guidance. His dissertation was on the power of mental suggestion in both the "miracle cures" of religious figures and those spontaneous remissions occasionally observed by conventional physicians. In the style of his mentor, Hall, Goddard loosely connected the power of suggestion to the process of evolution. Also like Hall, he was determinedly scientific without wholly abandoning his respect for religion. Indeed, Goddard revered Hall, once writing to him, "I know that mine [my life] is incomparably larger, higher and broader than it would have been had I not come under your instruction and inspiration."[43]

For several years after graduation, Goddard taught at the West Chester Normal School, just outside of Philadelphia, where he trained future school teachers. Almost as soon as he arrived, though, he joined a discussion group on the training of the "feeble-minded" (the accepted term of the era). The group was led by one Edward R. Johnstone, the new superintendent of a training school for feeble-minded children that was situated amidst the farm fields of Vineland, New Jersey,

FIGURE 10.5 Henry Herbert Goddard.

Credit: H. H. Goddard Collection. Archives of the History of American Psychology, The Drs. Nicholas and Dorothy Cummings Center for the History of Psychology, The University of Akron.

about 40 miles south of Philadelphia. Johnstone—born in Ontario but raised in Cincinnati—did not have a college degree, but he had become a devotee of Hall's "child study" nevertheless. Thus, the arrival in the Philadelphia area of a graduate of Hall's program, such as Goddard, was immediately interesting to Johnstone. He could see, though, that the kinds of children in his charge would not benefit much from Hall's efforts to uncover general laws of child development. Specialized research, tailored to the specific challenges that Johnstone faced, would be needed if Vineland were going to avoid sliding into being a merely custodial facility, as did so many "schools" for the feeble-minded in that era. In Goddard, Johnstone found a man who was not only interested in the question of intellectual disability, but who also had the research skills to perhaps do something about it. In 1906, Johnstone created a new position at Vineland, Director of Research, and persuaded Goddard to take it.

Once Goddard was face-to-face with the reality of over 300 children of every age and ability, he realized as never before that feeble-mindedness was, in reality, a grab-bag category that took on a bewildering array of specific forms. Unless he could find a way to elicit or impose some sort of order on the wide range of disabilities before him, any truly productive research program would remain elusive. "Feeble-mindedness" was, at the time, distinct from the category of "retardation" that Lightner Witmer was then working on at his clinic at Penn. The retarded, it was thought, could be treated for the particular learning problem they presented and, once it was corrected, they could be returned to the regular classroom. The feeble-minded, by contrast, were cases in which mental development seemed to have completely stopped at some point. There was little hope of returning these children to regular schools. They needed "special education," as the fashionable pedagogical phrase of the day had it. Indeed, some of Goddard's "children" at Vineland were not really children at all, but young adults in their 20s whose intellectual abilities still were those of a child many years younger.

The medical establishment of the US, in whom the power to formally diagnose was typically vested, had not been able to develop a useful taxonomy of these "mental defectives" (another technical term of the age). It was apparent to Goddard, however, that the problem facing him was not really medical but, rather, *psychological* in character. Of course, there was probably some physiological cause underlying each child's disability, but Goddard, as the children's *educator*, did not really need to categorize them in those terms so much as he needed to know what each was ultimately capable of learning and how each would best learn. Knowledge of that sort would enable Goddard to construct a curriculum appropriate to the abilities of each child. In 1908, Goddard took a summer research excursion to Europe to see how scholars and scientists there were handling the matter.[44] It was during this trip that Goddard was more or less accidentally introduced to the Binet-Simon intelligence test.[45] Binet's work was not unknown in America at the time. The problem was, rather, that its significance could only really be fully appreciated by someone in Goddard's unique position. As his biographer wrote,

> two years of frustrating institutional experience had prepared him to see what Janet, Cattell, and even Hall, the most prescient of contemporary psychological entrepreneurs, had missed. Contained within Binet's articles . . . was an entirely new psychological approach toward diagnosing and classifying feeble minds.[46]

Goddard seized upon the Binet-Simon test, translating it into English as soon as he returned home, and publishing it in a local journal before the year was out.[47] Goddard also began administering the test to his many charges at Vineland. He quickly found that he was able to sort them into the three categories of intellectual disability that Binet and Simon had distinguished: *idiot, imbécile,* and *débile.* The first two of these terms, representing the two greatest degrees of disability, were easily rendered in English as idiot and imbecile. The third one, however, Goddard decided to render not as "debilitated" but as "moron," a term derived from the Greek term for "dull."[48] "Morons" were people whose intellectual development had stopped at between 8 and 12 years of age. Unlike "idiots" and "imbeciles," however, "morons" typically looked and acted very much like "normals," even though they were subtly inferior, intellectually. This made them particularly problematic, in Goddard's eyes, perhaps even dangerous. Indeed, it was this third category, the "moron," that would soon become the focus of one of America's great moral panics.

Goddard immediately became an evangelist for the Binet–Simon test in America. In 1910, he persuaded a New Jersey public school superintendent who was also a member of Johnstone's "Feeble-Minded Club" to allow him to test all of the children in his district. Within a year, Goddard and his assistants tested two thousand children. He found that 78% of the children scored within one year of their grade level, but that 15% scored two or three years behind. He assumed these latter children were "retarded" or "backward" and that they would benefit from remedial training of the kind that Witmer's clinic was providing. A further 3%, though, were more than three years behind their grade level. Goddard concluded that these were "feeble-minded"; their intellectual development was arrested.[49] Goddard published his findings in Hall's *Pedagogical Seminary*.[50] More than anything else, it was this article that first launched the Binet–Simon test in America, as well as an American mania for intelligence testing that would endure into the 1970s. Not everyone embraced either the test or Goddard's conclusions, but the debate was intense and included several recognized leaders in the field. In that way, it put both the Binet–Simon test and Goddard "on the map" of American educational psychology.

In 1911, Goddard was invited to join the massive survey of New York City public schools that was being headed by future mayor and Gary Plan advocate, John Purroy Mitchel. Using the Binet–Simon test, Goddard discovered both that New York's special education classes contained many essentially normal students who had been misassigned by teachers, and that there were many undiagnosed "defectives" in the regular classes.[51] New York City school officials, of course, took great umbrage at his findings, encouraging even the powerful Witmer to take a public stand against the new test, but the controversy only increased Goddard's stature among psychologists and educators.

Goddard in particular, and America in general, did not interpret the test and its scores in the way that Binet had intended when he had created it, in the French context just a few years before.[52] Binet saw the test merely as a practical tool—a quick way of distinguishing children for whom the standard school curriculum might not be well-suited. The scores, far from being a measure of anything particularly important scientifically, were seen as reflecting an admixture of basic mental ability and whatever knowledge had been acquired by the child, either inside or outside of the classroom, all filtered through difficult-to-isolate issues with respect specific linguistic ability (as distinct from general intellectual ability).[53] Goddard and many other Americans, however, saw the tests as having the power to distill a pure form of innate intelligence out of the welter of knowledge, experience, and expectation that every child brought into the testing situation. What is more, it was widely believed that this innate intelligence, whether high or low, was largely hereditary, passing from generation to generation and, to some substantial degree, determining in advance the level of achievement that a person would be able to attain during his or her lifetime. Thus, in America, the results of intelligence tests rapidly took on moral overtones that interacted with a widespread (though by no mean universal) fear of the impact that race, ethnicity, and immigration might be having on the strength and purity of what was regarded by many as the true American character.

The apprehended danger was illustrated most forcefully in a book that Goddard published in 1912 called *The Kallikak Family*.[54] Goddard claimed to have traced the lineage of a feeble-minded woman at Vineland back more than a hundred years to a dalliance that a "normal" 18th-century soldier had indulged in with a feeble-minded woman during the Revolutionary War. The soldier, it was said, had eventually "straightened up" and married a "normal" woman of good morals, and from that "legitimate" side of the family had come nothing but "normal" children. But, from the relationship with the feeble-minded woman, Goddard claimed, hundreds of feeble-minded offspring, grand-offspring, great grand-offspring, etc. had arisen. This was true even though some of them had paired with "normal" spouses along the way; the feeble-mindedness seemed to be "dominant" in a Mendelian sense that was just then coming into scientific fashion. Goddard luridly illustrated the book with photographs that his assistants had been able to take of some descendants of the "Kakos" side of the family.[55]

Goddard's dark message was clear: the feeble-minded lurking in society must be somehow discouraged from reproducing even, perhaps especially, with people of "normal" intelligence, otherwise their inferior genetic material would gradually spread throughout the population, eventually bringing it down to their sad level. Of course, Goddard's methods and conclusions seem hopelessly simplistic and inadequate to us now (e.g., there could be no Binet-testing of long-dead ancestors, so how exactly was their feeble-mindedness determined?). The book was a sensation nevertheless.

Goddard was hardly the first to sound the call for eugenics in America. He initially favored institutionalization to keep the feeble-minded out of the gene pool. He also believed the feeble-minded should not be entitled to vote. Many others proposed more radical "solutions." As far back as 1897, a bill calling for the compulsory sterilization of feeble-minded persons had been proposed in Michigan. In 1905, a similar bill was passed by the Pennsylvania legislature, only to be vetoed by the governor. Indiana was the first to successfully enact a compulsory sterilization law, in 1907. California and Washington soon followed suit, in 1909. Ultimately, forced sterilizations were performed in two-thirds of US states, mostly on women.[56] Two years prior to Goddard's book on the Kallikaks, in 1910, the Carnegie Institution of Washington began to fund an organization called the Eugenics Records Office (ERO) in Cold Spring Harbor, New York. The ERO was founded by a biologist named Charles Davenport, and its purpose was to conduct research and propose policy that would prevent the feared deterioration of the American genetic pool.[57] The ERO was a major proponent of sterilization

FIGURE 10.6 Children of Guss Saunders, with their grandmother. From the "feeble-minded" side of the Kallikak family.

Credit: From Goddard, H. H. (1912). *The Kallikak Family: A Study in the Heredity of Feeble-Mindedness.* New York, NY: Macmillan.

legislation. In addition to Goddard, several important psychologists were involved with its work, including Adolf Meyer, Edward Thorndike, and Robert Yerkes. Goddard continued to be a leader in the call for eugenic control, as well, publishing more popular books on feeble-mindedness and criminality over the next few years.[58]

Eugenic considerations were also often used as justification for restricting immigration to the US Popular books of the day, such as sociologist E. A. Ross' *The Old World in the New* and zoologist Madison Grant's *The Passing of the Great Race*, warned of the collapse of Western civilization if northern and western Europeans, and their descendants, did not act to protect themselves not only from African and Asians, but also from eastern and southern Europeans.[59] Grant, who walked the streets of New York every day—from his home in midtown to his office on Wall Street—seemed to take the matter quite personally:

> The man of the old stock [himself, presumably] is being crowded out of many country districts by these foreigners just as he is to-day being literally driven off the streets of New York City by the swarms of Polish Jews.[60]

Although Goddard had mostly refrained from discussing race or immigration in his studies of feeble-mindedness to this point, there were many who saw his work as a valuable tool in advancing the case that the borders should be closed.[61]

In 1910 Goddard and Johnstone were invited to consult on the screening of would-be immigrants at the famous Ellis Island facility, just off Manhattan. Congress had passed a law in 1907 specifically barring the "feeble-minded," but the physicians at Ellis Island were uncertain of how to enforce this new requirement. Goddard's initial report was that there was little reason to expect that immigrants were feeble-minded in any greater numbers than native-born Americans. In 1912, though, Goddard returned to Ellis Island with the Binet test in hand and an experiment in mind. He had his experienced assistants pick people out of line who appeared to them to be mentally deficient. Then, to check the accuracy of their professional judgment, each of those selected was tested. Goddard found that his assistants were much better—ten times better, he claimed—at spotting feeble-minded individuals than the physicians were. Of course, the physicians were scanning for a number of other prohibited medical conditions at the same time, but Goddard's experiment suggested that the Immigration Commission should hire experts in feeble-mindedness alongside of the physicians. The proposal was not taken up, but the Ellis Island physicians themselves started adopting portions of the Binet test, along with nonverbal performance tests of their own design, such as simple puzzles, to help them make their determinations.

In 1913, Goddard started his most elaborate study yet, focusing on Jewish, Hungarian, Russian, and Italian immigrants. These groups had drawn the most attention from anti-immigration political movements. It was often claimed that people of these "races" did not have the mental qualities needed to become successful American citizens. Although Goddard partially recognized the problems of giving a largely verbal test to people who often spoke no English, he felt that the physicians' nonverbal tests were too dependent on merely sensory factors to reveal the mental trait that he was truly after—intelligence. He induced physicians who spoke (at least some of) the needed languages to act as translators for him.

Shockingly, Goddard found that 80% or more of each group tested below the criterion for feeble-mindedness. This was true even after he had lowered the threshold from a mental age of 12 to one of just 10. Although these results disturbingly confirmed the worst fears of the anti-immigration lobby, Goddard could not bring himself to wholly believe them. He began to examine the questions closely. Questions that demanded literary facility in any measure (e.g., create a sentence containing certain words), he dropped. He removed the demand that "mature" word definitions go beyond indicating a basic function (e.g., "What is a table?" "For eating on."). He dropped questions that depended on understanding conventional divisions of time (e.g., What month is it?). There were other deletions, as well. Nevertheless, even after all of his clarifications and simplifications, still about 40% scored as feeble-minded.

Finally, deciding that the best test of an immigrant's suitability for American life was to see how they actually fared in American society, he decided to track down some of the immigrants who had appeared to be feeble-minded when they first arrived. What had actually become of them on the tough streets of New York? He sent out some of his best assistants to find them, but they were able to find almost no one. Partly, they were met with suspicion when they arrived, as government representatives, in immigrant tenements. Partly people moved frequently and often did not form strong bonds with their neighbors. Taking another tack, Goddard had one assistant visit the institutions where they would have been likely to end up had they failed at "being American": missions and other charities for the destitute. He did not find any of them there either.[62]

It appeared that either they had succeeded, at least minimally, or, if they had failed, they were being cared for within their own ethnic communities. At this point, it occurred to Goddard—a lifelong academic and researcher—that there was, in fact, an enormous amount of menial work to do in American society and that, perhaps, even someone who was "feeble-minded," by the lights of American psychologists, might be able to earn enough sweeping sidewalks or digging ditches or collecting garbage to live a simple but "successful" life in which they could sustain themselves and perhaps their families. It also occurred to him that, perhaps, all the instances of feeble-mindedness that he had happened upon were not, in fact, hereditary in origin, but had been the product of early deprivation in their home countries. If this were true, then the American public had little to worry about with respect to the gene pool being "thinned" by these immigrants' presence. Such people might well raise better, smarter children in the more enriched American environment, just as they had hoped when they left their places of origin to seek out better lives across the ocean.[63]

The ambiguities and uncertainties of Goddard's research notwithstanding, in 1913 Congress passed an immigration bill requiring all potential newcomers to pass a literacy test. The outgoing president, William Howard Taft, recognized that this would effectively shut the borders to those who were then immigrating in the greatest numbers, so he vetoed it. In 1916, Congress passed an even more restrictive immigration bill which excluded from entry into the US:

> All idiots, imbeciles, feeble-minded persons, epileptics, insane persons; persons who have had one or more attacks of insanity at any time previously; persons of constitutional psychopathic inferiority; persons with chronic alcoholism; paupers; professional beggars; vagrants; persons afflicted with tuberculosis in any form or with a loathsome or dangerous contagious disease; persons. . . [with a] physical defect being of a nature which may affect the ability of such alien to earn a living; persons who have been convicted of or admit having committed a felony or other crime or misdemeanor involving moral turpitude; polygamists, or persons who practice polygamy or believe in or advocate the practice of polygamy; anarchists[64]

The list was very long indeed. It also barred most Asians. Further, like the 1913 bill, it required all newcomers to pass literacy test. The new president, Woodrow Wilson, vetoed the new bill as promptly as Taft had vetoed the 1913 version. This time, however, in February of 1917, Congress was able to gather the votes needed to override Wilson's veto, and the bill became the Immigration Act of 1917. As a result, immigration to the US began a rapid decline (see Figure 10.7). After an even more restrictive law was passed in 1924, immigration to the US was choked off almost completely until laws were relaxed somewhat after World War II.

Immigration was by no means the only realm in which the Binet test seemed valuable. Indeed, school teachers took up the test with such enthusiasm that a strong backlash developed among psychologists who felt that only they, as mental health "professionals," should be permitted to give the tests and interpret its results (much as physicians jealously protected their exclusive right to diagnose medical conditions and prescribe treatments).[65] On the far-away west coast, a young psychologist was already working on a revision and extension of the Binet test, this one especially designed to reveal as much about the upper end of the intelligence spectrum as its predecessors already had about the lower end. That psychologist's name was Lewis Madison Terman.[66]

Terman was an Indiana farm boy who went teacher's college in his home state. Ultimately, he made his way to Clark University, where, like Goddard, he became a product of Hall's vaunted graduate program in psychology and pedagogy. Hall suggested that Terman might study childhood "precocity." The suggestion turned into a thesis on mental testing but, because Hall was skeptical of the "quasi-exactness of quantitative methods," Edmund Sanford became his graduate advisor instead.[67]

After graduation, suffering chronic ill health, Terman declined job offers in Florida and Texas to go to southern California, where he soon caught on at the Los Angeles State Normal School (the precursor to today's University of California, Los Angeles). It was in 1910 that an old graduate school friend of his, Edmund Huey, told Terman of the Binet test and of Goddard's increasingly influential work

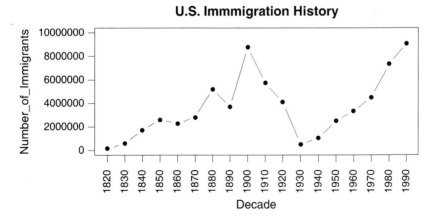

FIGURE 10.7 Number of immigrants to the US, 1820–1990. Based on data from the US Census Bureau.

with it. Terman was hired by Stanford University later that year, and began to work seriously with the Binet test immediately upon his arrival there.[68]

His first publication on the test appeared the following year.[69] His first "tentative" revision of the test appeared as a series of journal articles in 1912.[70] It was not until 1916 that he published his complete revision of the test, in book form.[71] It was quickly dubbed the Stanford–Binet test and became, far and away, the most widely used intelligence test in American schools for several decades afterward. Many of the individual items in the test were taken directly from Binet's original, but Terman provided an extended justification for intelligence testing as well as a detailed manual for the correct administration, scoring, and interpretation of the scores.

Whereas most psychologists and educators, up to this time, had been interested primarily in testing for feeble-mindedness, Terman's research focused on highly intelligent people instead. In truth, he had published on this question from the days of his graduate work.[72] After World War I he received a major research grant from the Commonwealth Fund, which enabled him to begin an extensive, longitudinal study of hundreds of "geniuses," the project for which he may be best known today.[73]

5. Psychology's Intellectual Core in Transition

At the start of the 20th century, Functionalism was the ascendant American "school" of psychology. One measure of this is the string of APA presidents who were affiliated with the school in one way or another: Dewey in 1899, Jastrow in 1900, Sanford in 1902, James (for the second time) in 1904, Angell in 1906. Angell's presidential address was even titled "The Province of Functional Psychology." This had followed his 1904 textbook, which was the most extensive and detailed statement of functionalism to date.[74]

Functionalists were an eclectic bunch, to be sure, but they rarely doubted that the core concept of psychology, in all of its multifarious forms, was consciousness. As we saw at the end of the last chapter, though, as early as 1904, James had called into question the scientific character—even the real existence—of individual conscious states. Not many psychologists followed James on his late philosophical excursion into the realm of "pure experience" but many agreed with him that consciousness had become too problematic an entity to ground a discipline that aspired to be scientific.[75]

The problem was especially acute in the realm of animal psychology. Without language to verbalize their conscious mental states, animal researchers often found themselves in the position of having to impute particular conscious states to their mute subjects. Such guesswork was, of necessity, based on the experience of being a human, and there was no compelling reason to believe that the experience of being a dog or a cat or a rat, much less a fish or an insect, paralleled that of being a human very closely at all.

The English animal researcher, C. Lloyd Morgan, who was squarely in the intellectual tradition of Darwin, had stated the problem all too clearly when he adapted the Medieval principle known as Occam's Razor to the specific circumstances of the investigator of animal mentality: "In no case may we interpret an action as the outcome of the exercise of a higher mental faculty, if it can be interpreted as the exercise of one which stands lower in the psychological scale."[76] The sentence became widely known as "Morgan's Canon."

In the US, a number of psychological researchers were already working with animals. There had, of course, been Edward Thorndike's dissertation in 1898 (though it was not published in book form until 1911).[77] Immediately after Thorndike's dissertation, as we saw in Chapter 8, Linus Kline and Willard Small of Clark University attempted to conduct more "naturalistic" studies of rat behavior, inventing maze learning as they went.[78] In 1903, John B. Watson completed a doctoral dissertation at Chicago, under the supervision of Angell, titled *Animal Education*.[79] He even made an appeal for "Studying the Minds of Animals," in a popular magazine in 1907.[80] That same year, Robert M. Yerkes published a book of his studies under the evocative title, *The Dancing Mouse*, in 1907.[81] Propelled by this research was the landmark article that outlined the famous Yerkes-Dodson Law: Rising physiological arousal can improve behavioral performance up to a certain level, but overarousal beyond the optimal point will increasingly interfere with performance again.[82] Yerkes produced a great deal of groundbreaking research on animal behavior during the decade following *The Dancing Mouse* but, at the time, the topic was regarded as being more or less peripheral to "mainstream" psychology.[83] Thus, Yerkes was refused a permanent position at Harvard because his extensive, original work on animals was not regarded by the university's leaders as being sufficiently valuable. Nevertheless, there were enough animal researchers on the edges of American psychology that, in 1908, Margaret Floy Washburn—a one-time student of the staunch opponent of animal psychology, E. B. Titchener—gathered together enough material to publish a textbook on the topic.[84]

By the 1910s, another more radical trend began to take hold. A growing cadre of scientists were coming to believe that Morgan's Canon did not go far enough; that *all* animal action should be interpreted as being the outcome of a "lower faculty"—a mere association between what the animal perceived and what the animal did in response. This was effectively how Thorndike had interpreted his puzzle box studies of the 1890s, though he had referred to the animal's "satisfaction" and "discomfort," which seem to imply the existence of internal mental states. Yerkes had raised new questions about the criteria required to determine consciousness in animals as early as 1905.[85] This shift began to gather momentum as word spread among American psychologists of a new research program that was being pursued by the Nobel Prize-winning Russian physiologist, Ivan Pavlov.[86] Pavlov was able to "condition" the involuntary motor responses of dogs to new stimuli with which they had not been previously associated. However, being a physiologist, he never spoke of the animal's putative conscious states. He simply postulated a kind of speculative neurology by which stimuli and responses that had not previously been associated could become connected if the new stimulus was repeatedly presented in conjunction with a stimulus that "naturally" elicited the desired response. Thus, salivation could become a dog's response to a certain sound if the sound had previously been frequently paired with something that naturally caused salivation, such as food.

Pavlov's work gave animal researchers something they desperately needed: a language in which they could describe the relationships between stimuli and responses without invoking intervening mental states. They stimulus and response were just connected "functionally," as Dewey had said in his famous reflex arc article.[87] Consciousness was no longer needed for the explanation of behavior. Only the history of the behavior's relationship with various stimuli was required. If this new scheme could be made to work over a wide range of behaviors, the long-problematic, but seemingly-indispensible concept of "consciousness" could finally be dispensed with in animal research. And, so the argument rapidly proceeded, if such a replacement could be done for animals, why could it not also be done for the "highest" of the animals: humans? Of course, the instantaneous retort was that humans engage in behaviors so incredibly complex—going to university, falling in love, appreciating art—that they could never be explained by mere connections of stimuli and responses. But now, in the age of Pavlovian conditioning, that was merely an assertion. It would be up to the new "behaviorists" to find out just how far their new system could take them in explaining complex human behavior.

On February 24, 1913, Watson gave one of the most influential talks in the history of psychology at Columbia University.[88] Titled, "Psychology as the Behaviorist Views It," it called for a revolution in psychology in which introspection was completely abandoned as a method, and conscious states were excluded as an explanatory principle.[89] Instead, psychologists would seek out pure "laws of behavior" no different, in principle, from those that biologists used to explain the movements of amoebas and other "lower" animals. Indeed, Watson chided, if psychologists truly believe in Darwinian evolutionary theory as much as they said, then they would be forced to concede that the behavior of humans is phylogenetically continuous with the behavior of the lowest animals and, thus, that the principles governing one must also govern the other. Watson published the article in his own journal, *Psychological Review*, later the same year.[90]

Watson called his radical position, "behaviorism," the history of the development of which has been discussed and debated in a thousand different ways over the decades since it was proposed. I will not review those arguments here. The goal of this book is only to bring us up to this point in American psychology's history. Watson, of course, would write a great deal more on behaviorism. Interestingly, although behaviorism is now often treated as a kind of abstract psychological metatheory, in Watson's mind, it was not at all separated from the applied aspects of psychology that were discussed previously, but which are often left out of surveys of the discipline's history. Knowing what we know now about the urban contexts in which Watson was working—first Chicago, then Baltimore—we can make a new kind of sense of a seemingly innocent example he put forth in his 1924 book, *Behaviorism*:

> the behaviorist is primarily interested in the behavior of the whole man. From morning to night he watches him perform his daily round of duties. If it is brick-laying, he would like to measure the number of bricks he can lay under different conditions, how long he can go without dropping from fatigue, how long it takes him to learn his trade, whether we can improve his efficiency or get him to do the same amount of work in a less period of time.[91]

In direct opposition to Titchener, who proclaimed that scientific psychology was wholly about the pursuit of "pure" knowledge with no obvious application to any practical realm, Watson's counter was that his version of scientific psychology—behaviorist psychology—was not only going to have immediate practical applications, but it was going to perfect and refine one of the most lucrative forms of applied psychology then in existence.

Watson's behaviorism was, in effect, Taylor's "scientific management," raised to the level of a laboratory science. No longer would university presidents have difficulty justifying the expense of having a Department of Psychology to inquisitive potential donors or skeptical political masters. From now on their reply (or perhaps "response") would be as easy as asking "Do you want your employees to work faster, more efficiently, and less expensively?" It is hardly any wonder that, within a decade or so of Watson's announcement, Behaviorism had spread around the country and was well on its way to becoming the dominant approach to psychology in many different fields.

Watson was elected president of the APA for the year 1915. Yerkes would be president in 1917. The era of behaviorism and animal research had begun.

6. The Stresses and Strains of Professionalization

The explosion in applied psychology—whether in business, education, law, therapy, or what have you—led to a number of new pressures on the discipline, considered as a kind of social institution. Reacting to the uncontrolled spread of testing through the education system, in 1915 the American Psychological Association passed a resolution discouraging mental testing by people who had not received advanced training in psychology. This statement constituted the first official position on applied psychology ever issued by the APA, an organization that had clung firm its identity as a purely "scientific" society. Until then, it had more or less disdained the psychological "profession" that was, in effect, its own sibling. The statement on testing was proposed by two educational psychologists: J. E. Wallace Wallin of the University of Pittsburgh and Guy M. Whipple, then at the University of Illinois. Although they may seem to have been too remote from the centers of APA power to have had so great an influence on the organization, both had earned the PhDs in eastern schools—Yale and Cornell, respectively—so were both well acquainted with the APA's key powerbrokers.

The year after the APA extended its own authority over mental testing, the New York Psychiatrical Society issued its own statement insisting that medical doctors alone should have jurisdiction over the diagnosis and treatment of the ill, including the mentally ill. The new "clinical" psychologists might be useful for carrying out some tests, they sniffed, but it was up to physicians alone to interpret the medical results and recommend subsequent courses of medical action.[92] The clinical psychologists, most of whom were not members of the APA at the time, decided they would have to band together themselves if they were to mount a strong defense against the physicians' assertion of exclusive authority. In 1917, Wallin, along with Leta Hollingworth (who had completed her PhD at Columbia just the year before) and a number of others created a new professional society, the American Association of Clinical Psychologists (AACP). With this new body, clinicians would be able to present a common front for the purposes of persuading the public, the government, and other social institutions of their professional legitimacy. Wallin took up the presidency of the fledgling group and strove to create the kind of licensing and accreditation system that had served medicine so well during the time of its professionalization.[93] Such a regimen would serve the goals of creating explicit standards of professional practice, while also excluding those who diluted the "brand" by claiming psychological expertise in the absence of advanced education and training.

The creation of the AACP posed a dilemma for the APA. On the one hand, the older association was committed to advancing psychology as a science, and it had often been downright dismissive when it came to professional issues. On the other hand, the presence of a rival psychological association might prove unmanageable when it came to defending what might be termed "greater psychology" against quacks and cranks, on the one hand, and against skeptical physicians, natural scientists, and politicians on the other. The psychiatrists' derision of clinical psychology as a mere adjunct to medicine forced the APA to defend the legitimacy and autonomy of the discipline that it claimed to represent. Thus, in 1919, with great trepidation on both sides, a plan was hatched to absorb the AACP into the APA as a special "Section on Clinical Psychology." From the APA's point of view, this would unify the psychological "front," and it might also afford some "scientific" influence over what the clinicians were doing in the name of psychology. From the AACP's perspective, merging with the APA provided clinicians the "cover" of a better-established and avowedly "scientific" organization, while also representing a step toward expanding the APA's traditionally narrow mandate to include professional matters as well.

Within just two years, the Clinical Section persuaded the larger APA to endorse a certification scheme for consulting psychologists. As it turned out, however, very few psychologists actually took up the certification process and, after a few years, the Clinical Section became more or less moribund. In the coming years, clinical and other applied psychologists drifted off on their own to create a series of independent associations. Applied psychology would not re-renter the APA until the creation of its modern divisional structure, after merging with the American Association for Applied Psychology, just after World War II.

Associations were hardly the only manifestations of the developing complexity of psychology in the early 20th century. There was also an explosion of specialized journals each addressing an increasingly narrow range of topics. In the last chapter we saw that Cattell's *Journal of Philosophy, Psychology, and Scientific Methods* (launched 1904) and Lightner Witmer's *Psychological Clinic* (launched 1907) were added to Hall's *American Journal of Psychology* and Baldwin and Cattell's *Psychological Review*. In addition, Morton Prince founded the *Journal of Abnormal Psychology* in 1906. The new decade saw many specialized periodicals come into existence. For instance, 1910 saw the launch of *Journal of Educational Psychology*. It was the product of four co-editors: J. Carleton Bell of the Brooklyn Training School for Teachers; Guy Whipple, then at Cornell; Carl E. Seashore of Iowa, who would become well known for his work on art and music education; and William C. Bagley, then at Illinois.

In 1911, Robert M. Yerkes, then at Harvard, founded the *Journal of Animal Behavior*. In 1917, Knight Dunlap would launch his own, related journal, *Psychobiology*. In 1921, the two would merge into the *Journal of Comparative Psychology* under the editorship of Dunlap.

In 1916, *Journal of Experimental Psychology*, was launched John B. Watson of Johns Hopkins, with the assistance of Howard Warren of Princeton, James Rowland Angell of Chicago, Shepherd Ivory Franz, then at the Government Hospital for the Insane in Washington, DC, and Madison Bentley, then at Illinois. The following year, as though in response to the experimentalists throwing down a gauntlet, a *Journal of Applied Psychology* was created by G. Stanley Hall and two junior colleagues of his—John Wallace Baird, who would become the first Canadian president of the APA in 1918, and Ludwig R. Geissler, who was from Germany.[94] Both had been trained in Titchener's laboratory at Cornell.[95]

The intellectual structure of psychology was no longer a simple, informal matter of the various topics on which individual psychologists chose to write. It was now beginning to be inscribed on the names of the associations to which they belonged and the very titles of the journals that they chose to read. It could now be plainly seen on the shelves of any college library that decided to subscribe to their journals or buy their textbooks, without even having to open a single volume.

7. American Psychologists and World War I

While American psychology was embracing intelligence testing, considering the possibilities of behaviorism, and rearranging its bureaucratic structures, much of Europe was collapsing. Germany's attacks across the Belgian and French borders quickly devolved into a kind entrenched, mechanized conflict for which no country was militarily prepared. The casualty tolls were fantastically high, completely dwarfing those of the last great pan-European conflict, the Napoleonic wars of a century earlier.

Early in the war, the impact upon Americans came mostly on the naval front. On May 7, 1915, a British ocean liner named the *Lusitania*, making its regular run from Liverpool to New York, was torpedoed off the coast of Ireland by a German U-boat. The ship sunk in less than 20 minutes, killing 1,198 and leaving 761 survivors floating on the surface. The number of US citizens among the victims, 138, was fairly small proportionally, but the targeting of a passenger vessel outraged the American public, and it turned what had been a relatively mixed view of the war decisively against the German side. Morton Prince, the Boston neurologist who had founded the *Journal of Abnormal Psychology* a decade earlier, quickly composed a short speculative book in which he declared Kaiser Wilhelm II's aggressive actions to be the result of a "subconscious phobia" of losing power to democrats.[96]

Less than year later, on March 24, 1916, another British passenger vessel—a Channel ferry named the *Sussex*—was torpedoed by the Germans as well. This ship did not sink, but the damage was extensive and more than 50 of 379 passengers and crew were killed. For American psychologists, this incident hit close to home because James Mark Baldwin and his family had been on board at the time. They all survived, though one of his daughters was injured. Baldwin had been exiled from the discipline for several years by that time, but he was still well known to his former colleagues, of course, and he was active in France, writing books that urged the US to enter the war against the Germans. Another survivor of the attack on the *Sussex*, although he was mostly unknown at the time, was Wilder Penfield, then just an American student of the prominent English neurologist, Charles Scott Sherrington, at Oxford. Penfield would go on to a celebrated career as a neurologist at McGill University in Montréal.

Back in the US, Hugo Münsterberg, who had long presented himself a kind of unofficial emissary of German *Kultur*, strove mightily to defend the German case in the war to an increasingly hostile American public. It was to no avail. He rapidly turned himself into one of the most despised public figures in the US His Harvard colleagues abandoned him. There was a rumor that some wealthy magnate had offered Harvard a million dollars to fire him, though the truth of this claim has never been established. There were even death threats. It is hard to know what would have become of him after the US entered the war, but it never came to that because, in December of 1916, he collapsed and died while lecturing at Radcliffe College, the victim of a stroke.

Perhaps a more immediate American concern than the war across the Atlantic, was the Mexican Revolution, which had been raging across the southern border since 1910. Occasionally, hostilities spilled over the border, as in March 1916 when Mexican rebels attacked the town of Columbus, New Mexico. Under pressure from conservatives, Wilson agreed to send several thousand troops into northern Mexico in search of Pancho Villa, who was thought to have been responsible. They located and defeated the group of men who had attacked Columbus, but Villa escaped.

Soon after the end of this military incursion, in January 1917, British intelligence announced that it had intercepted a coded message sent by the newly appointed German Foreign Secretary, Arthur Zimmermann, to the Mexican government, proposing a military alliance in which Mexico would attack the US in order to distract the American army, keeping it out of the European war. Zimmermann also held out the lure of Arizona, New Mexico, and Texas being returned to Mexican sovereignty after the war was successfully concluded. At first, many in the American government thought that the telegram must be a British forgery. The British had good reason to provoke the US in to action. After many months of relative calm, the German navy had resumed the torpedoing of British civilian ships in February of 1917. Britain lost 105 ships that month alone and, after two and a half years of the most intense warfare it had ever seen, the island nation was finally beginning to experience food and equipment shortages. Without American intervention, the Kingdom might soon be forced to sue Germany for peace.

In March, however, Zimmermann himself confirmed that the message was authentic, so it seemed clear that the German government was actively working against US interests.[97] In addition, in March of 1917, the Czar of Russia was deposed by a revolution led by the moderate socialist Alexander Kerensky.[98] Although this development raised the hope of a democratic government being established in Russia, it also meant that the Eastern Front was about to collapse, and the German military would be free to move masses of men and materiel to the Western Front where they might well determine the outcome of the war.

All of these factors led Wilson to have Congress declare war in April of 1917. When he did so, Robert M. Yerkes, then president of the APA, saw an opportunity to advance both the government's and the public's perception of psychology to an entirely new level. As we have seen, up to about 1900, American psychology consisted of a fairly small circle of people. Much energy was put into convincing college administrators and politicians that it was a "real science" with real value to deliver, at least within the academic fold. A great deal of this effort was devoted to distinguishing the "new" psychology from various other more or less established institutions—e.g., philosophy, physiology, religion, medicine, spiritualism. Succeeding at this narrow task enabled psychology to forge an independent reputation based upon its own intellectual accomplishments.

Over the first decade and a half of the 20th century, however, psychology began to venture beyond the boundaries of the college campus and offer services to various individuals and institutions in society at large. Many of these encounters went well, enhancing psychology's reputation, and some of them went abominably off course, resulting in the kind of sideshow antics that many skeptics anticipated. On balance, however, the trend was toward greater and wider acceptance of psychology as a new and legitimate presence on the American cultural scene.

When the US entered World War I, it opened up an entirely new and much larger stage for psychology to perform upon. It was not inevitable that the war would serve psychology in this way. The emergence of psychology into so prominent a position required the actions of particular individuals who happened to have the right set of intellectual and political skills to successfully negotiate the discipline's participation within much larger and more powerful institutions, such as the army. When it was done, though, psychology had fully integrated itself into American civilization.

In 1917, Yerkes was probably best known for his pioneering work on animal behavior, but he had also tried to capitalize on the growing vogue for intelligence testing with an entry of his own, the *Point Scale*, created with a Canadian psychologist, James W. Bridges, and a Boston educator, Rose S. Hardwick.[99] When Yerkes heard, early in 1917, that the US was about to conscript millions of young men into the military, he conceived an audacious plan that would constitute the largest psychological research project ever attempted, as well as announcing psychology's readiness to put its considerable abilities at the service of the wartime nation. He declared that psychology, collectively, should offer to test the intelligence of the millions of recruits so that the military could more efficiently select those most appropriate for officer training and other high-skill positions.

Yerkes called together the APA Council to consider the ways in which psychology might be of use to the military.[100] The Council created 12 different committees. Yerkes himself chaired the Committee on Psychological Examination of Recruits. The Committee quickly recognized that it would need a new kind of test that could be given to masses of men simultaneously—a pencil-and-paper intelligence test that could be administered to whole rooms full of men, rather than the one-on-one tests that had been used thus far. Fortunately, Terman, who had joined the Committee with Yerkes, had a student, Arthur Otis, who was already working on such a test. The project came together amazingly quickly. A draft test was ready by July. In fact, there were two: Test *a* for literates and Test *b* for illiterates. The latter contained pictorial problems of various kinds. What was needed was a body of men on which to pilot and perfect the tests.

Through a network of government connections, Yerkes was able to make his way to the Army's Surgeon General, William Gorgas, who recognized the value that a one-hour test might have for the quick assignment of the millions of men who were already beginning to enter training camps around the country. There were many in the army who were suspicious not only of the practical usefulness of the tests, but also of the psychologists' true motives. Would their test really help the Army, or were they just taking advantage of the mass of drafted men for their own research purposes? In the end, most decided that the test scores would be helpful alongside of other more traditional means of assessment. The US had never before fought a war on this scale, and it could use all the help it could get.

By November, Yerkes' team of 40 psychologists had tested 80,000 men. On the basis of those results, they revised the two initial tests and gave them the names by which they are better known today, the Alpha and Beta. In December, Yerkes received approval for a full-scale testing program of all recruits, and the promise of a military school in which to train the hundreds of testers who would be needed, in Olglethorpe, Georgia.

Two key members of the APA Council had not come on board with Yerkes. They were Walter V. Bingham and Walter Dill Scott of the Carnegie Institute who, as personnel assessors for business, disagreed that intelligence tests were the best means of evaluating potential soldiers. They found their way to the Secretary of War, with whom they concocted a separate testing program which involved much more than mere intelligence. Yerkes was worried about the impact they might have on his much larger program, and ultimately persuaded them to work through his Committee, even if not on his project.[101]

Once Yerkes' Oglethorpe school began producing testers—400 in all—the number of men tested quickly ramped up to 200,000 every month. In the end, more than 1.7 million men were tested. There was ongoing controversy over the value of the tests. Traditionalist officers were rankled by the sense that their judgment and authority were being questioned or even usurped. Other officers, however, liked the fact that the test scores were used to assign to army units a balance of intellectually superior, average, and inferior men.[102]

At the war's end, with a new Army Surgeon General in place who was not as sympathetic to the project as Gorgas had been, Yerkes' testing program was ended and dismantled. This was not what Yerkes had hoped for but, by participating so prominently in the war effort, Yerkes had succeeded in transforming psychological testing from a practice that was surrounded by controversy and suspicion into a respectable and legitimate procedure for use in social institutions of all kinds.

After the war was complete, Yerkes' issued a final report on his Army intelligence testing project.[103] It presented a shocking picture of intelligence in America. For the first time, the intelligence of a broad cross-section of men from all parts of the country—all major ethnic groups and races—had been tested with the best instruments then available. Before the war, the widespread assumption—based on small samples of mostly middle- and upper-class men, using individual tests—had been that the mental age of the "average" (White) man was about 16 years. By contrast, Yerkes, testing hundreds of thousands of ordinary men, found that the average mental age of White men of northern and western European heritage was only 13 years. Given that a mental age of 12 years was the upper limit of Goddard's category of "moron," this finding seemed to imply that the nation as a whole was already teetering on the edge of feeble-mindedness. The figures for other ethnic and racial groups were even more alarming: Russian, Italians, and Poles were said to have an average mental age of about 11 years. For African Americans, the number was reported to be closer to 10 years.

These "findings," of course, confirmed the worst that had been feared by those who opposed continued immigration to the US and those who supported aggressive eugenic policies to keep America's genetic heritage "strong" and "pure." Yerkes' report was placed in evidence at many hearings and debates on the topic in the coming years. The history of American intelligence testing's deep entanglements with eugenics has been told many places, and I do not propose to repeat it here.[104] It is no exaggeration, though, to say that, after the war, businesses, schools, and government agencies flocked to Yerkes and his coworkers for assistance in setting up testing programs of their own. He had succeeded in his aim of raising the image of "scientific" psychology to new heights of authority and prestige.

Notes

1 See in the *West Coast Hotel Co. v. Parrish* Supreme Court ruling of 1937, in which a minimum wage law in Washington state was upheld, finally establishing the power of the legislature to regulate business practices.
2 Wilson v. New, 243 US 332, 1917.
3 Frederick Winslow Taylor, *Principles of Scientific Management* (New York, NY: Harper & Brothers, 1911). Tellingly, he first submitted the book for publication to his home professional association, the American Society of Mechanical Engineers (ASME), of which he had been president in 1906–1907. The book was rejected by the ASME, and Taylor was forced to route it through a commercial publisher instead.
4 US Congress House of Representatives, *Hearings Before the Special Committee of the House of Representatives to Investigate the Taylor and Other Systems of Shop Management* (Washington, DC: Government Printing Office, 1912), 1397; cited in David Montgomery, *The Fall of the House of Labor: The Workplace, the State, and American Labor Activism, 1865–1925* (Cambridge, UK: Cambridge University Press, 1987), 251.
5 Thomas J. Van de Water, "Psychology's Entrepreneurs and the Marketing of Industrial Psychology," *Journal of Applied Psychology* 82 (1997): 486–99.
6 It is often claimed that Taylor was a professor at the Tuck School of Business at Dartmouth College. Laura Schieb of the Rauner Special Collections Library at Dartmouth, however, assures me that there is no record of his ever having been a professor there, though he may have lectured there on occasion.
7 Frank Gilbreth, *Motion Study* (New York, NY: Van Nostrand, 1911); Frank Gilbreth, *Primer of Scientific Management, NY, D. Van Nostrand Co., 1912* (New York, NY: Van Nostrand, 1912).
8 Brian Price, "Frank and Lillian Gilbreth and the Motion Study Controversy, 1907–1930," in *A Mental Revolution: Scientific Management Since Taylor*, ed. Daniel Nelson (Columbus, OH: Ohio State University Press, 1992), 58–76.
9 The pitchers were actually from Brown University, not, as is often reported, from the Giants' own roster.
10 Elspeth H. Brown, *The Corporate Eye: Photography and the Rationalization of American Commercial Culture, 1884–1929* (Baltimore, MD: Johns Hopkins University Press, 2005), 102.
11 Lillian M. Gilbreth, *The Psychology of Management: The Function of the Mind in Determining, Teaching and Installing Methods of Least Waste* (New York, NY: Sturgis and Walton, 1914).
12 Lillian M. Gilbreth, *Some Aspects of Eliminating Waste in Teaching* (Brown University, 1915).

13 e.g., Frank Gilbreth and Lillian M. Gilbreth, *Fatigue Study, NY, Sturgis & Walton Co., 1916* (New York, NY: Sturgis and Walton, 1916); Frank Gilbreth and Lillian M. Gilbreth, *Applied Motion Study* (New York, NY: Sturgis and Walton, 1917).

14 For a more complete account of the Gilbreths' work, see Arlie R. Belliveau, "Micromotion Study: The Role of Visual Culture in Developing a Psychology of Management" (Master's thesis, York University, 2012).

15 See esp. Richard T. von Mayrhauser, "Making Intelligence Functional: Walter Dill Scott and Applied Psychological Testing in World War I," *Journal of the History of the Behavioral Sciences* 25 (1989): 60–72.

16 Walter Dill Scott, *The Theory of Advertising* (Boston, MA: Small Maynard, 1903), much of which had been previously serialized in *Mahin's Magazine*; Anonymous, "Advertising: Walter Dill Scott's Theory of Its Principles on a Psychological Basis," *New York Times*, December 12, 1903.

17 Walter Dill Scott, *The Psychology of Advertising* (Boston, MA: Small Maynard, 1908).

18 Harry L. Hollingworth, *The Influence of Caffeine on Mental and Motor Efficiency*, Archives of Psychology 22, 1912; see also Benjamin, Ludy T., Jr., A. M. Rogers, and A. Rosenbaum, "Coca-Cola, Caffeine, and Mental Deficiency: Harry Hollingworth and the Chattanooga Trial of 1911," *Journal of the History of the Behavioral Sciences* 27 (1991): 42–55.

19 Harry L. Hollingworth, *Advertising and Selling: Principles of Appeal and Response* (New York, NY: D. Appleton, 1913).

20 Harry L. Hollingworth, "The Psycho-Dynamics of Chewing," *Archives of Psychology* 239 (1939).

21 Walter Dill Scott, *Increasing Human Efficiency in Business* (New York, NY: Palgrave Macmillan, 1911).

22 Hugo Münsterberg, "Psychology and the Market," *McClure's* 34 (November 1909): 90.

23 Hugo Münsterberg, *Psychology and Industrial Efficiency* (Boston, MA and New York, NY: Houghton-Mifflin, 1913). This was actually a translation and revision of a 1911 book he had first published in German, *Psychologie und Wirtschaftsleben*, written just after a year-long sabbatical he had enjoyed in Berlin.

24 e.g., Anonymous, "Hugo Munsterberg [sic]," *New World Encyclopedia*, n.d., www.newworldencyclopedia.org/entry/Hugo_Munsterberg.

25 Much of this account follows Ludy T. Benjamin Jr. and David B. Baker, "Walter Van Dyke Bingham: Portrait of an Industrial Psychologist," in *Portraits of Pioneers of Psychology*, ed. Gregory A. Kimble and Michael Wertheimer, vol. 5 (Washington, DC: American Psychological Association, 2003), 141–57; Ludy T. Benjamin Jr. and David B. Baker, *From Séance to Science: A History of the Profession of Psychology in America* (Belmont, CA: Wadsworth, 2004).

26 Van de Water, "Psychology's Entrepreneurs."

27 M. M. White, "James Burt Miner: 1873–1943," *Psychological Review* 50 (1943): 632–34.

28 James Burt Miner, *Deficiency and Delinquency: An Interpretation of Mental Testing* (Baltimore, MD: Warwick & York, 1918).

29 A version of the test is still used today, under the title *The Strong Interest Inventory*.

30 Charles Spearman, "General Intelligence, Objectively Determined and Measured," *American Journal of Psychology* 15 (1904): 201–93.

31 Kurt Danziger, *Constructing the Subject: Historical Origins of Psychological Research* (Cambridge, UK: Cambridge University Press, 1990).

32 John Dewey and Evelyn Dewey, *Schools of To-morrow* (New York, NY: E. P. Dutton, 1915).

33 See, e.g., Raymond E. Callahan, *Education and the Cult of Efficiency* (Chicago, IL: University of Chicago Press, 1962); Lawrence A. Cremin, *American Education: The Metropolitan Experience, 1876–1980* (New York, NY: HarperCollins, 1988).

34 Anonymous, "Identified as Michael P. Mahoney, Man With Many Grievances," *New York Times*, April 18, 1914. Interestingly, Mitchel's predecessor in the mayoralty, William Jay Gaynor, had also been shot by an assassin, on August 9, 1910. He had survived, though with a bullet permanently lodged in his neck. He continued on with his municipal duties, nearly serving out his term before dying from complications due to his wounds some three years later.

35 This account draws on Raymond A. Mohl, "Schools, Politics, and Riots: The Gary Plan in New York City, 1914–1917," *Paedagogica Historica* 15 (1975): 39–72; and Kenneth S. Volk, "The Gary Plan and Technology Education: What Might Have Been?" *Journal of Technology Studies* 31, no. 1 (2005): 39–48.

36 *New York World*, October 18, 1917, cited in Mohl, "Schools, Politics, and Riots," 68.

37 Michael M. Sokal has provided good reason to believe that Columbia's president used Cattell's actions as a pretext for retaliating for years of conflicts between them. See "James McKeen Cattell, Nicholas Murray Butler, and Academic Freedom at Columbia University, 1902–1923," *History of Psychology* 12 (2009): 87–122. In fact, Cattell got off rather easy. Eugene Debs, who we met earlier as the leader of the Pullman Boycott of 1894 and who had run for president against Wilson in 1912, would be convicted of violating the Sedition Act (a harsher successor to the Espionage Act) for giving an anti-war speech in Canton, Ohio 1918. He was sentenced to 10 years in prison. He appealed to the Supreme Court on the ground that the Sedition Act violated the free speech provisions of the First Amendment of the US Constitution. His appeal was rejected, the author of the court's decision being none other William James' old friend, Oliver Wendell Holmes. Even after the war ended, with the health of the 63-year-old Debs deteriorating, Wilson refused to grant him a pardon. It was left to Republican president Warren Harding to do so in 1921. Debs would die in 1926.

38 See Melissa F. Weiner, *Power, Protest, and the Public Schools Jewish and African American Struggles in New York City* (New Brunswick, NJ: Rutgers University Press, 2010). Hilquit, born Moishe Hillkowitz in Latvia, immigrated to the US at the age of 15. He worked his way up from the Jewish tenements and the garment sweatshops of New York, becoming a fixture in the socialist party, where he clashed with radicals like "Big Bill" Haywood of the International Workers of the World.

39 Hillquit, the socialist, finished just 7,000 votes (a single percentage point) behind Mitchel. Cited in Mohl, "Schools, Politics, and Riots," 69.

40 Alfred Binet, *L'étude Expérimentale de L'intelligence* (Paris, France: Schleicher Frères, 1903).

41 Alfred Binet and Théodore Simon, "Méthodes Nouvelles Pour Le Diagnostic Du Niveau Intellectuel Des Anormaux," *Année Psychologique* 11 (1905): 191–244; Alfred Binet and Théodore Simon, "Le Développement de L'intelligence Chez Les Enfants," *Année Psychologique* 14 (1908): 1–94; Alfred Binet, "Nouvelles Recherches Sur La Mesure Du Niveau Intellectuel Des Anormaux," *Année Psychologique* 17 (1911): 145–201.

42 For the full story of Goddard's life and career, see Leila Zenderland, *Measuring Minds: Henry Herbert Goddard and the Origins of American Intelligence Testing* (New York, NY: Cambridge University Press, 1998). For a broader account of the development and use of intelligence tests, see Raymond E. Fancher, *The Intelligence Men: Makers of the IQ Controversy* (New York, NY: W. W. Norton, 1985).

43 Letter from H. H. Goddard to G. S. Hall, dated October 19, 1901. G. S. Hall Papers, Clark University Archives. Cited in Zenderland, *Measuring Minds*, 30.

44 Goddard had been to Europe once before. In 1903, he had taken a sabbatical from West Chester to learn experimental techniques with Ernst Meumann in Zurich.

45 As Goddard told the story, a Belgian physician named Ovide Decroly was recommended to him as a person interested in the same sorts of questions as he was. Decroly

turned out to be aware of work on German children that Goddard had published during his earlier European jaunt five years before. Decroly told Goddard of the Binet-Simon test, even though Goddard's contacts in Paris had either not known of it, or not thought it worth mentioning. Cited in Zenderland, *Measuring Minds*, 92.

46 Ibid., 93.

47 Henry Herebrt Goddard, "The Binet and Simon Tests of Intellectual Capacity," *Training School Bulletin* 5 (1908): 3–9. This journal had been founded by Johnstone in 1904 to bring together the experience and research of those who had, until then, been working on roughly the same set of problems, though in relative isolation.

48 Henry H. Goddard, "Four Hundred Feeble-Minded Children Classified by the Binet Method," *Journal of Genetic Psychology* 17 (1910): 387–97.

49 The remaining 4% were more than a year ahead of their grade level, a group of children that did not attract Goddard's notice, but others, such as Leta Hollignworth and Lewis Terman, would take great interest in them in the years to come.

50 Henry Herbert Goddard, "Two Thousand Normal Children by the Binet Measuring Scale of Intelligence," *Pedagogical Seminary* 18 (1911): 231–58.

51 Henry Herbert Goddard, *School Training of Defective Children* (Yonkers-on-Hudson, NY: World Book, 1914).

52 For a fascinating study of the different interpretations of "intelligence" in the divergent French and American democracies, see John Carson, *The Measure of Merit: Talents, Intelligence, and Inequality in the French and American Republics, 1750–1940* (Princeton, NJ: Princeton University Press, 2006).

53 Binet, "Nouvelles Recherches."

54 Henry Herbert Goddard, *The Kallikak Family: A Study in the Heredity of Feeble-Mindedness* (New York, NY: Palgrave Macmillan, 1912). The name was fictional, combining the Greek words *kallos* (beauty) and *kakos* (bad).

55 The modern evolutionist Stephen J. Gould pointed out that the photographs seem to have been retouched in order to make the eyes and mouths darker and, he suggested, more menacing (*The Mismeasure of Man* (New York, NY: W. W. Norton, 1981)). Historian of psychology Raymond Fancher countered that, because of the weakness of photography at this time, it was common to retouch photographs in order to bring out the features ("Henry Goddard and the Kallikak Family Photographs: 'Conscious Skullduggery' or 'Whig History'?" *American Psychologist* 42 (1987): 585–90). Of course, both observations may well be true: Goddard may have retouched the images to bring out the features, but done so in a way that was unflattering to the subjects and reflective of the point he was attempting to make in the accompanying text.

56 Rebecca M. Kluchin, *Fit to Be Tied: Sterilization and Reproductive Rights in America, 1950–1980* (New Brunswick, NJ: Rutgers University Press, 2009).

57 Davenport had been a close correspondent of Goddard since 1909, when the biologist had written Vineland inquiring about data on the heredity of feeble-mindedness.

58 Henry Herbert Goddard, *Feeble-Mindedness : Its Causes and Consequences* (New York, NY: Palgrave Macmillan, 1914); *The Criminal Imbecile; an Analysis of Three Remarkable Murder Cases* (New York, NY: Palgrave Macmillan, 1915).

59 Edward Alsworth Ross, *The Old World in the New; the Significance of Past and Present Immigration to the American People* (New York, NY: Century, 1914); Madison Grant, *The Passing of the Great Race; Or, the Racial Basis of European History* (New York, NY: Scribner's, 1916).

60 Grant, *The Passing of the Great Race; Or, the Racial Basis of European History*, 91. I thank Andrew Winston for pointing this passage out to me..

61 Zenderland, *Measuring Minds*, 264–65.

62 Henry Herbert Goddard, "Mental Tests and the Immigrant," *Journal of Delinquency* 2 (1917): 243–77.

63 Zenderland, *Measuring Minds*, 279.

64 The full text of the Immigration Act of 1917 can be found at http://library.uwb.edu/static/USimmigration/39%20stat%20874.pdf. See Chap. 29.

65 See, e.g., J. E. Wallace Wallin, "Danger Signals in Clinical and Applied Psychology," *Journal of Educational Psychology* 3 (1912): 224–26.

66 The authoritative account of Terman's life can be found in Henry L. Minton, *Lewis M, Terman: Pioneer in Psychological Testing* (New York, NY: New York University Press, 1988).

67 Lewis M. Terman, "Lewis M. Terman," in *The History of Psychology in Autobiography*, ed. Carl A. Murchison, vol. 2 (Worcester, MA: Clark University Press, 1930), 318.

68 Terman, "Lewis M. Terman."

69 Lewis M. Terman, "The Binet-Simon Scale for Measuring Intelligence: Impressions Gained by Its Application upon Four Hundred Non-Selected Children," *Psychological Clinic* 5 (1911): 199–206.

70 Lewis M. Terman and H. G. Childs, "A Tentative Revision and Extension of the Binet-Simon Measuring Scale of Intelligence," *Journal of Educational Psychology* 3 (1912): 61–74, 133–43, 277–89.

71 Lewis M. Terman, *The Measurement of Intelligence* (Boston, MA: Houghton-Mifflin, 1916).

72 Lewis M. Terman, "A Study in Precocity and Prematuration," *American Journal of Psychology* 16 (1905): 45–83; "Genius and Stupidity: A Study of Some of the Intellectual Processes of Seven 'Bright' and Seven 'Stupid' Boys," *Pedagogical Seminary* 13 (1906): 307–73.

73 Lewis M. Terman, *Mental and Physical Traits of a Thousand Gifted Children*, vol. 1, Genetic Studies of Genius (Stanford, CA: Stanford University Press, 1925).

74 James Rowland Angell, *Psychology: An Introductory Study of the Structure and Function of Human Consciousness* (New York, NY: Henry Holt, 1904); "The Province of Functional Psychology," *Psychological Review* 14 (1907): 61–91.

75 Dewey adopted began to work with the term "experience" instead of "consciousness" as early as 1899, but it was published obscurely, appearing as "Psychology and Philosophic Method" in the *University* [of California] *Chronicle* in August of that year. His linguistic and conceptual shift became better known when he reprinted that article under the title "'Consciousness' and Experience," in *The Influence of Darwin on Philosophy, and Other Essays* (New York, NY: Henry Holt, 1910). "Experience" would become a central concept of Dewey's philosophical outlook: *Experience and Nature* (Chicago, IL: Open Court, 1925); *Art as Experience* (New York, NY: Putnam, 1934); *Experience and Education* (Urbana-Champaign, IL: Kappa Delta Pi, 1938).

76 Conwy Lloyd Morgan, *An Introduction to Comparative Psychology* (London, UK: W. Scott, 1894), 53.

77 Edward L. Thorndike, *Animal Intelligence: Experimental Studies* (New York, NY: Palgrave Macmillan, 1911).

78 Linus W. Kline, "Suggestions Toward a Laboratory Course in Comparative Psychology," *American Journal of Psychology* 10 (1899): 399–430; Willard S. Small, "Notes on the Psychic Development of the Young White Rat," *American Journal of Psychology* 11 (1899): 80–100; "Experimental Study of the Mental Processes of the Rat—II," *American Journal of Psychology* 12 (1901): 206–39.

79 Published as John B. Watson, *Animal Education: An Experimental Study on the Psychical Development of the White Rat, Correlated with the Growth of Its Nervous System* (Chicago, IL: University of Chicago Press, 1903). Although Angell was Watson putative supervisor, he seemed to spend more time with the neurologist (and one-time student of Hall), Henry H. Donaldson.

80 John B. Watson, "Studying the Mind of Animals," *The World Today* 12 (1907): 421–26.

81 Robert M. Yerkes, *The Dancing Mouse: A Study in Animal Behavior* (New York, NY: Palgrave Macmillan, 1907).

82 Robert M. Yerkes and John D. Dodson, "The Relation of Strength of Stimulus to Rapidity of Habit-Formation," *Journal of Comparative Neurology and Psychology* 18 (1908): 459–82.

83 Robert M. Yerkes and John B. Watson, *Methods of Studying Vision in Animals* (Boston, MA: Henry Holt, 1911); Robert M. Yerkes, *The Mental Life of Monkeys and Apes: A Study of Ideational Behavior* (Cambridge, MA: Henry Holt, 1916).

84 Margaret Floy Washburn, *The Animal Mind: A Text-Book of Comparative Psychology* (New York, NY: Palgrave Macmillan, 1908).

85 Robert M. Yerkes, "Animal Psychology and Criteria of the Psychic," *Journal of Philosophy, Psychology, and Scientific Methods* 2 (1905): 141–49.

86 Robert M. Yerkes and Sergius Morgulis, "The Method of Pawlow in Animal Psychology," *Psychological Bulletin* 6 (1909): 257–73.

87 John Dewey, "The Reflex Arc Concept in Psychology," *Psychological Review* 3 (1896): 357–70.

88 The date comes from Robert H. Wozniak, "Theoretical Roots of Early Behaviorism: Functionalism, the Critique of Introspection, and the Nature and Evolution of Consciousness," in *Theoretical Roots of Early Behaviorism: Functionalism, the Critique of Introspection, and the Nature and Evolution of Consciousness*, ed. Robert H. Wozniak (London, UK: Routledge/Thoemmes, 1993), ix–xiii.

89 Watson said that he had first revealed his behaviorist views in a 1908 lecture that he gave at Yale, but that they had been received so poorly that he did not speak publicly of them again for five years. John B. Watson, *Psychology from the Standpoint of a Behaviorist* (Philadelphia, PA: Lippincott, 1919).

90 John B. Watson, "Psychology and the Behaviorist Views It," *Psychological Review* 20 (1913): 158–77.

91 John B. Watson, *Behaviorism* (Chicago, IL: University of Chicago Press, 1924), 15.

92 Cited in Leta Stetter Hollingworth, "Activities of Clinical Psychologists," *Psychological Bulletin* 14 (1917): 224–25; see also Benjamin and Baker, *From Séance to Science*, 53.

93 Leta Stetter Hollingworth, "Tentative Suggestions for the Certification of Practicing Psychologists," *Journal of Applied Psychology* 2 (1918): 280–84. On medicine's professionalization, see esp. Abraham Flexner, *Medical Education in the United States and Canada: A Report to the Carnegie Foundation for the Advancement of Teaching*, Bulletin no. 4 (New York, NY: The Carnegie Foundation for the Advancement of Teaching, 1910).

94 For more on Baird's strange and somewhat tragic career, see Daniel Lahham and Christopher D. Green, "John Wallace Baird: The First Canadian President of the American Psychological Association," *Canadian Psychology* 54 (May 2013): 124–32. On Geissler and the founding of the journal more generally, see Roger K. Thomas, "Ludwig Reinhold Geissler and the Founding of the Journal of Applied Psychology," *American Journal of Psychology* 122 (2009): 395–403.

95 For the definitive listing of periodicals in psychology, see D. V Osier and Robert H Wozniak, *A Century of Serial Publications in Psychology, 1850–1950* (Millwood, NY: Kraus, 1984).

96 Morton Prince, *The Psychology of the Kaiser* (Boston, MA: Richard G. Badger, 1915), 107.

97 US Army historian Thomas Boghardt discovered that, far from being a high-level German government plot, the telegram was actually drafted by a minor functionary in the Foreign Office, Hans Arthur von Kemnitz, and hastily approved by Zimmermann, who did not seek formal government approval, probably because they were all preoccupied at the time with preparations to commence unrestricted submarine warfare on February 1, 1917. See *The Zimmermann Telegram: Intelligence, Diplomacy, and America's Entry Into World War I* (Annapolis, MD: Naval Institute Press, 2014).

98 Because Russia used a different calendar than the West, this is often called the February revolution, but it took place in March according to the Western calendar. The Provisional Government that resulted from this revolution would, of course, be overthrown by Lenin and the Bolsheviks in November of 1917, marking the beginning of the communist Soviet Union.

99 Robert M. Yerkes, James W. Bridges, and Rose S. Hardwick, *A Point Scale for Measuring Mental Ability* (Baltimore, MD: Warwick & York, 1915).

100 For a more detailed account of Yerkes' work with the army, see Daniel J. Kelves, "Testing the Army's Intelligence: Psychologists and the Military in World War I," *Journal of American History* 55 (1968): 565–81; Another popular account can be found in Gould, *The Mismeasure of Man*, but many historians find it to be sensational and one-sided. In all fairness, Gould intended his book as a critique of intelligence testing, not a neutral history. See also Franz Samelson, "Putting Psychology on the Map: Ideology and Intelligence Testing," in *Psychology in Social Context*, ed. Allan R. Buss (New York, NY: Irvington, 1979), 103–68.

101 von Mayrhauser, "Making Intelligence Functional."

102 A fascinating archival film has been posted by the historical YouTube channel called *Critical Past* which shows a room of Army recruits taking the test: www.youtube.com/watch?v=cmaAc6pruqQ.

103 A preliminary report was released immediately after the war: Robert M. Yerkes, "Report of the Psychology Committee of the National Research Council," *Psychological Review* 26 (1919): 83–149. A final report, nearly 900 pages in length, was published two years later: Robert M. Yerkes, ed., "Psychological Examining in the United Sates Army," *Memoirs of the National Academy of Sciences* 15 (1921).

104 See, e.g., Daniel J. Kelves, *In the Name of Eugenics: Genetics and the Uses of Human Heredity* (New York, NY: Alfred A. Knopf, 1985); William H. Tucker, *The Science and Politics of Racial Research* (Champaign, IL: University of Illinois Press, 1994).

EPILOGUE

When this story began in the 1840s, there was, essentially, no discipline or profession answering to the name "psychology." Philosophical systems of "mental philosophy" or "mental science" (occasionally called "psychology") were common enough in colleges, but the idea that one could investigate the mind scientifically, much less apply those findings to the real world of social institutions and personal problems lay somewhere between radical and unheard of in America. Of course there were common truisms about the processes of learning and about techniques of memory that found their origins in the Medieval or even Ancient world. For instance, the assumption that the study of mathematics and Classical languages would discipline the mind, or the idea that the method of loci would facilitate the memorization of long lists—but these were not the conclusions of formal empirical investigation any more than were sayings like "spare the rod, spoil the child."

The 1860s and 1870s saw, in Germany, the emergence of an experimental psychology that took the recent successes of experimental physiology as its model, but this development was noticed and acknowledged as valuable by a very small number of young American scholars at the time: James, Hall, Ladd, and perhaps a few others. This changed quickly, though. By the 1880s and 1890s, dozens of young Americans were racing to Germany to earn their PhDs in the "new psychology" so that they could land professorships back home in a new discipline that, though sometimes a hard sell to college administrators, presented the distinct advantage of not being already ruled by an older generation of professors. In creating new spaces for themselves, though, the new psychologists ran into a cultural conflict—Wundt and the other German psychologists who had mentored them were adamant that psychology must be a "pure" science in order to prevent it from being relegated downward from the prestigious universities to the pedestrian technical schools. Thus, no "practical" psychological questions were permitted.

In America, by contrast, the college system was expanding rapidly as a result of the Morrill Land-Grant Acts, but the emphasis was quite the opposite of that in Germany: "practical" knowledge was paramount. Some psychologists in America continued to insist upon the purity of experimental psychology, such as Titchener, ensconced in his position in central New York State, but those who were more sensitive to the social revolution then underway in America, especially in the country's large and expanding cities, saw intellectual, financial, and political opportunities in virtually every direction. Even some who disdained city life for themselves, like Cattell and Thorndike, enhanced their reputations with work that had great appeal to committed urban reformers (of a variety of political stripes).

In addition, psychology rapidly became so popular a topic for American graduate students that their numbers quickly outpaced the number of available university professorships. This forced many young psychologists—especially those whom colleges were reluctant to employ, such as women—to find or create for themselves psychological vocations that had not existed up to that point. Many carved out new consultancies with social institutions that had both money to spend and a need for psychologists' expertise: business and industry, public education, the courts, immigrant settlement, and mental health, among others. Of course, along with any new "profession" comes new opportunities for grifters and charlatans who see an opportunity to make a quick buck and move on. So the new professional psychologists—not seen as equals by their academic cousins—were soon forced to organize themselves into associations and develop systems of licensure so that their potential clients could distinguish between those with the relevant training and expertise and those without it who simply hoped to benefit from the confusion surrounding a emergence of a new class of paid professional.

The relationship between academic and professional psychologists was never fully settled—indeed, one might argue that it isn't fully settled in the present day—but the two sides were never able to exist completely separately either. The academics depended on the professionals to maintain and enhance the public visibility and appreciation of "psychology," and the professionals depended on the academics to maintain and enhance the discipline's scholarly and scientific status.

Either way, by the 1920s, "psychology" had become a permanent presence in American society at large. It seemed that everyone knew something about it, and many people began to feel that they needed whatever they thought it offered in order to live their lives to the fullest. Dozens of popular new magazines promoted the topic, with titles like *Psychology*, *Popular Psychology*, *Herald of Psychology*, *Super Psychology*, *Mind Power Plus*, *National Brain Power*, and *The Golden Rule*.[1] In 1921, no less a public figure than the legendary baseball player Babe Ruth was put through his psychomotor paces at the Columbia University psychology laboratory to uncover the secrets to his great athleticism. A prominent sports writer of the era, Hugh Fullerton, made sure the public learned of every detail by writing the event up a lavishly illustrated account published in *Popular Science Monthly*.[2] The psychological din soon became so great that the popular humorist Stephen Leacock declared the nation was experiencing an "outbreak of psychology."[3]

AS A TEST WE SEE WHETHER HE CAN PRONOUNCE TH BACKWARD

FIGURE 11.1   One of several cartoons by John Held Jr., that appeared in Stephen Leacock's "A manual for the new mentality."

Credit: Harper's Magazine, vol 148, March 1924, 471–480.

According to Leacock's satirical vision:

> It is generally admitted that the human mind was first discovered about four years ago by a brilliant writer in one of the Sunday journals. His article "Have We a Subconscious Ego?" was immediately followed by a striking discussion under the title "Are We Top Side Up?" This brought forth a whole series of popular articles and books . . . and such special technical studies as *The Mentality of the Hen* and the *Thought Process of the Potato*.
>
> This movement, once started, has spread in every direction. All our best magazines are now full of mind. In every direction one sees references to psychoanalysis, auto-suggestion, hypnosis, hopnoosis, psychiatry, inebriety, and things never thought of a little while ago. Will power is being openly sold by correspondence at about fifty cents a kilowatt. College professors of psychology are wearing overcoats lined with fur, and riding in little coupé [sic] cars like doctors. The poor are studying the psychology of wealth, and the rich are studying the psychology of poverty. Memory has been reduced to a system. A good memory is now sold for fifty cents.
>
> Everybody's mind is now analysed. People who used to be content with the humblest of plain thinking, or with none at all, now resolve themselves

into "reflexes" and "complexes" and "impulses." Some of our brightest people are kleptomaniacs, paranoiacs, agoraphobists, and dolomites. A lot of our best friends turn out to be subnormal and not worth knowing. Some of the biggest business men have failed in the intelligence test and have been ruined. A lot of our criminals turn out not to be criminals at all, but merely to have a reaction for another person's money.[4]

The increasing popularity of psychology in society at large fed back into the academy, rapidly making the discipline an essential part of the modern college rather than an exotic and expensive add-on to philosophy. Autonomous departments of psychology began to appear in many colleges across the country. Illinois had started the process in 1893, long before any other school. It was later followed by its neighbors, Chicago and Northwestern, in the first decade of the 20th century. Johns Hopkins and Cornell created separate psychology departments in the 1910s. Yale, California, and (in Canada) Toronto and McGill followed suit in the 1920s. Before long, it became a foregone conclusion—especially in schools that encouraged research among their faculty—that psychologists and philosophers not only increasingly operated from very different sets of theoretical assumptions, but that they required very different kinds of spaces and resources to do their work properly.

The theoretical scene changed as well. From the 1920s, behaviorism rapidly became popular among the younger generation of psychologists. Under close scrutiny, though, Watson's simple, original behaviorism quickly revealed unsustainable weaknesses. Psychologists of myriad theoretical predilections attempted to shore up the crucial Watsonian imperative that behavior, not consciousness, would be psychology's core concept. As an unintended result of this focused attention, behaviorism rapidly splintered into several competing schools of thought: Jacob Kantor's interbehaviorism, Edwin Guthrie's contiguity theory, Edward C. Tolman's purposive behaviorism, B. F. Skinner's operant behaviorism, Clark L. Hull's drive theory, to name a few of the most influential.[5]

Although behaviorism and learning theory were ascendant in this era, they did not dominate all areas of psychology. During the 1920s and 1930s, a number of new specialties appeared from the general psychology of previous years. Research on sensory perception and its physiological underpinnings continued apace.[6] The psychological study of early child development was revolutionized by Arnold Gesell, a graduate of Clark and an assistant at Goddard's Vineland School.[7] Social psychology entered a new era with the appearance of Floyd Allport's controversial textbook.[8] A new kind of trait-based personality theory began to establish itself as distinct from the older study of "character," also led by an Allport: Gordon.[9] As psychology's boundaries expanded, the principles of scientific method and statistical analysis took on greater importance as well.[10]

Soon, American psychology was being buffeted by novel influences from Europe. As early as the early 1920s, the new *Gestalt* psychology started to arrive in English translation.[11] This holistic movement—led by Max Wertheimer, Wolfgang

Köhler, and Kurt Koffka—posed significant challenges not only to traditional theories of perception—where it was, perhaps, most successful—but also to developmental psychology and to the behaviorists' home turf: learning theory.[12]

Specialization of this kind—learning, perception, development, social, personality, methodology, etc.—started to become a widespread phenomenon in psychology. The days of the "general" psychologist were dwindling rapidly. One psychologist at Illinois even founded an entire laboratory dedicated to the psychology of sport, the first of its kind in North America.[13]

Perhaps the most interesting episode of the 1920s, though, was the sudden and nearly simultaneous appearance of several new textbooks on the history of psychology. These were authored by Edwin Boring, Gardner Murphy, Walter Pillsbury, and, slightly later, Edna Heidbredder.[14] All four of these texts represented a significant break with history texts of a decade or two before in that they markedly reduced coverage of the discipline's deep philosophical antecedents in favor of coverage of the relatively recent emergence of the scientific ethos.[15] Boring even pointedly include the word "experimental" in his title lest the object of his interest be confused with some "other" form of psychology. Details of the titles aside, though, all four of them aimed at recasting psychology as a discipline more strongly allied with natural sciences such as physiology, neurology, evolution, and even physics (thus the oft-repeated story about the British Astronomer Royal Nevil Maskelyne firing his assistant for apparently poor time-keeping of celestial events, thereby unintentionally opening the question of the "personal equation" in psychology). Any connection that psychology might have had with philosophy (apart from, perhaps, the British empiricism of Locke, Hume, and Mill) was rendered distant and tentative. This dramatic shift in tone does not seem to have been the personal decision of a few textbook writers either. Prior to their publication, other scientifically-oriented psychologists had been calling for such a change in perspective, sometimes even in print.[16] Indeed, one of these four texts, Boring's, came to be seen (in America) virtually as *the* history of psychology for the next thirty years.[17]

Frequently in the past, psychologists have attempted to portray themselves as somehow separate from the workaday world, uninterested and uninfluenced by the grimy business of "politics" (in its pejorative sense). But this has never really been the case, of course. To be sure, some researchers have had the luxury of working on abstruse topics that have no immediate relevance to society's major institutions, but virtually from its arrival on America's shores, psychology has built its reputation and its social authority by inserting itself into the business of those very institutions—schools, hospitals, industry, government, etc. And those institutions have been intimately connected with the growth and health of America's large cities. Indeed, with two scholarly societies that now boast a combined membership of over 100,000 (APA and APS), psychology has now carved out a significant societal role for itself with such success that it now *is* a major social institution, exerting own its influences on the others.

Although rarely acknowledged, it is an astonishing coincidence that psychology rose to prominence in the US at precisely the same time as cities became the residences of a majority of the American population. It is hard to imagine that psychology could have grown to the proportions we see today had it not repeatedly claimed for itself an important role in the modern urban scene. Psychology and cities have had a remarkable history together, and they will probably have a remarkable future together as well.

Notes

1 Issues of these titles and many other similar ones are available at the Cummings Center for the History of Psychology at the University of Akron in Ohio. They were collected and donated by Ludy T. Benjamin, Jr. who has also written on the topic: Ludy T. Benjamin Jr. and W. H. M. Bryant, "A History of Popular Psychology Magazines in America," in *A Pictorial History of Psychology*, ed. Wolfgang G. Bringmann et al. (Carol Stream, IL: Quintessence, 1997), 585–93.

2 Hugh S. Fullerton, "Why Babe Ruth Is Greatest Home-Run Hitter" 99, no. 4 (1921): 19–21, 110. For a modern account, see Alfred H. Fuchs, "Psychology and 'The Babe,'" *Journal of the History of the Behavioral Sciences* 34 (1998): 153–65.

3 Stephen Leacock, "A Manual for the New Mentality," *Harper's Magazine* 148 (March 1924): 471–80.

4 Ibid., 471–72.

5 J. R. Kantor, *Principles of Psychology*, 2 vols. (New York, NY: Knopf, 1924); (see also B. D. Midgley and E. K. Morris, eds., *Modern Perspectives on J. R. Kantor and Interbehaviorism* (Reno, NV: Context Press, 2006)); Stevenson Smith and Edwin R. Guthrie, *General Psychology In Terms of Behavior* (New York, NY: D. Appleton, 1921); E. R. Guthrie, *The Psychology of Learning* (New York, NY: Harper & Row, 1935); Edward Chace Tolman, *Purposive Behavior in Animals and Men* (New York, NY: Century, 1932); (see also Laurence D. Smith, "Purpose and Cognition: The Limits of Neorealist Influence on Tolman's Psychology," *Behaviorism* 10 (1982): 151–63; David W. Carroll, *Purpose and Cognition: Edward Tolman and the Transformation of American Psychology* (New York, NY: Cambridge University Press, 2017)); B. F. Skinner, *Behavior of Organisms* (New York, NY: Appleton-Century, 1938); Clark L. Hull, *Principles of Behavior: An Introduction to Behavior Theory* (New York, NY: Appleton-Century-Crofts, 1943); (see also A. Amsel and M. E. Rashotte, eds., *Mechanisms of Adaptive Behavior: Clark L. Hull's Theoretical Papers with Commentary* (New York, NY: Columbia University Press, 1984)).

6 For a review, see the landmark textbook, Robert S. Woodworth, *Experimental Psychology* (New York, NY: Holt, 1938), especially chapters 16–26.

7 Arnold Gesell, *The Mental Growth of the Pre-School Child: A Psychological Outline of Normal Development from Birth to the Sixth Year, Including a System of Development Diagnosis* (New York, NY: Palgrave Macmillan, 1925).

8 Floyd H. Allport, *Social Psychology* (Boston, MA and New York, NY: Houghton-Mifflin, 1924); contrast with the earlier William McDougall, *An Introduction to Social Psychology* (London, UK: Methuen, 1908).

9 Gordon W. Allport, *Personality: A Psychological Interpretation* (New York, NY: Holt, Rinehart, & Winston, 1937).

10 The most prominent early methods and statistics textbooks that were widely used by American psychologists were Ronald A. Fisher, *Statistical Methods for Research Workers* (Edinburgh, UK: Oliver & Boyd, 1925); Ronald A. Fisher, *The Design of Experiments* (Edinburgh, UK: Oliver & Boyd, 1935). Early textbooks by Americans included G. W. Snedecor, *Calculation and Interpretation of the Analysis of Variance and Covariance* (Ames,

IA: Collegiate Press, 1934); G. W. Snedecor, *Statistical Methods* (Ames, IA: Collegiate Press, 1937); and C. B. Davenport and M. P. Ekas, *Statistical Methods in Biology, Medicine, and Psychology* (New York, NY: Wiley, 1936). For reviews of these developments, see Gerd Gigerenzer, "Mindless Statistics," *Journal of Socio-Economics* 33 (2004): 587–606; Anthony J. Rucci and Ryan D. Tweney, "Analysis of Variance and the 'Second Discipline' of Scientific Psychology: A Historical Account," *Psychological Bulletin* 87 (1980): 166–84.

11 Kurt Koffka, "Perception: An Introduction to the *Gestalt-Theorie*," *Psychological Bulletin* 19 (1922): 531–85.

12 Kurt Koffka, *The Growth of the Mind*, trans. R. M. Ogden (London, UK: Routledge and Kegan Paul, 1924 [original German work published 1921]); Wolfgang Köhler, *The Mentality of Apes*, trans. Ella Winter (New York, NY: Harcourt, Brace & World, 1925 [original German work published 1917]). See Tolman, *Purposive Behavior in Animals and Men* for an instance of the direct impact of Gestalt ideas on American learning theory.

13 Coleman R. Griffith, *The Psychology of Coaching: A Study of Coaching Methods from the Point of Psychology* (New York, NY: Scribner's, 1926); Coleman R. Griffith, *Psychology and Athletics: A General Survey for Athletes and Coaches* (New York, NY: Scribner's, 1928). See also Christopher D. Green, "Coleman Roberts Griffith: 'Adopted' father of Sport Psychology," in *Portraits of Pioneers in Psychology*, ed. Donald A. Dewsbury, Ludy T. Benjamin, and Michael Wertheimer, vol. VI (Washington, DC: American Psychological Association and Mahwah, NJ: Lawrence Erlbaum Associates Publishers), 2006), 151–66.

14 Edwin G. Boring, *A History of Experimental Psychology* (New York, NY: Century, 1929); Gardner Murphy, *Historical Introduction to Modern Psychology* (New York, NY: Harcourt, Brace, 1929); Walter B. Pillsbury, *The History of Psychology* (New York, NY: W. W. Norton, 1929); Edna Heidbredder, *Seven Psychologies* (New York, NY: Century, 1933).

15 For instance, compare them with George Sidney Brett, *A History of Psychology*, 3 vols. (London, UK: G. Allen, 1912); James Mark Baldwin, *History of Psychology: A Sketch and an Interpretation*, 2 vols. (New York, NY: G. P. Putnam, 1913) in which philosophical material far outweighs coverage of the more recent scientific developments.

16 Coleman R. Griffith, "Some Neglected Aspects of a History of Psychology," *Psychological Monographs* 30 (1921): 17–29; Coleman R. Griffith, "Contributions to the History of Psychology—1916–1921," *Psychological Bulletin* 19 (1922): 411–28.

17 Edwin G. Boring, *A History of Experimental Psychology*, 2nd ed. (New York, NY: Appleton-Century-Crofts, 1950) It is worth noting that Murphy's textbook went through 2nd and 3rd editions, but Boring's book came closest to seeming "definitive."

INDEX

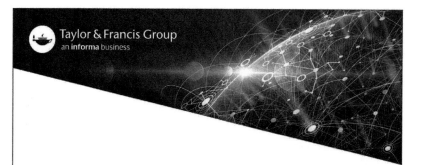